Child Abuse and Neglect
A Clinician's Handbook

For Churchill Livingstone

Publisher: Lucy Gardner
Copy Editor: Ruth Swan
Indexer: Monica Trigg
Production Controller: Mark Sanderson
Sales Promotion Executive: Kathy Crawford

Child Abuse and Neglect
A Clinician's Handbook

Christopher J. Hobbs BSc MB BS MRCP DObstRCOG
Consultant Community Paediatrician, St James's University Hospital, Leeds;
Senior Clinical Lecturer, Leeds University, Leeds, UK

Helga G. I. Hanks BSc MSc DipPsych AFBPsS
Consultant Clinical Psychologist, St James's University Hospital, Leeds;
Honorary Lecturer, Leeds University, Leeds, UK

Jane M. Wynne MB ChB FRCP
Consultant Community Paediatrician, Leeds General Infirmary, Leeds;
Senior Clinical Lecturer, Leeds University, Leeds, UK

CHURCHILL LIVINGSTONE
EDINBURGH LONDON MADRID MELBOURNE NEW YORK AND TOKYO 1993

CHURCHILL LIVINGSTONE
Medical Division of Longman Group UK Limited

Distributed in the United States of America by Churchill
Livingstone Inc., 650 Avenue of the Americas, New York,
N.Y. 10011, and by associated companies, branches and
representatives throughout the world.

First published 1993

ISBN 0-443-04146 6

British Library Cataloguing in Publication Data
A catalogue record for this book is available from the British
Library.

Library of Congress Cataloging in Publication Data
Hobbs, Christopher James.
  Child abuse and neglect: a clinician's handbook/Christopher
James Hobbs, Helga G. I Hanks, Jane M. Wynne.
    p.   cm.
  Includes bibliographical references and index.
  ISBN 0–443–04146–6
  1. Abuse children.   2. Child abuse   I. Hanks, Helga G. I.
II. Wynne, Jane M.   III. Title.
  [DNLM: 1. Child Abuse.   WA 320 H68125c]
RJ375. H6 1993
616.85' 8223--dc20
DNLM/DLC
for Library of Congress   92-48782
                                                                CIP

The
publisher's
policy is to use
**paper manufactured
from sustainable forests**

Produced by Longman Singapore Publishers (Pte) Ltd
Printed in Singapore.

Contents

MAR 26 1996

Preface

The origins of our interest in child maltreatment lie with our good friends and colleagues Dr Michael Buchanan and the late Jill McMurray. For many years Jill was a social worker who developed an understanding and interest in protecting children that was well ahead of her time. Michael Buchanan's interest started around the time that Henry Kempe described 'battered babies' in the 1960s. The authors joined the team later, towards the end of the 1970s, by which time procedures for handling physical abuse and neglect were being established. The idea of working as a team appealed to all of us because we recognised at an early stage in this work the importance of sharing information, concerns and above all our anxieties about the children and families who we were seeing. Being able to talk about a subject which has its own taboos, stigma and secrecy was an important part of getting to grips with the broad issues which surround it and which can make this work so difficult. We also recognised that our training only equipped us in part for dealing with this problem and that we needed to talk to others who held different perspectives if we were to progress. Increasingly the developmental view of child maltreatment is offering the most valuable insights into its pathways and patterns, its prevention and treatment.

This book sets out to be a clinical handbook for clinicians who find themselves confronted by child maltreatment in their work with children and families and wish to read more widely. We recognise that individual cases present some of the most difficult problems encountered in clinical practice with children and that a sound knowledge base is vital.

The book comprises separate chapters on all the various major forms of abuse and neglect which come under the broad umbrella of child maltreatment. Their recognition, assessment, management and treatment are all described. We have also attempted to explain the wider context in which maltreatment occurs in order to give a broader understanding of the nature and origins of maltreatment. However, there remain many unsolved problems and unanswered questions in this field, which has been growing rapidly in recent years.

The high mortality of children at the beginning of this century has now been replaced by an expectation that children will survive. This has focused child care on the quality of children's lives, their rights as human beings and inevitably child maltreatment. As a result child maltreatment is now being recognised as a major morbidity for children and therefore indirectly for society. The scientific, humanistic and compassionate study of the complex relationship between parents and their offspring is fraught with resistances of every kind.

If this book appears to have all the answers, then this is folly on our part as there is much that is not known or understood. Nor is this a book for bedtime reading or casual voyeurism. It is a book about the suffering and sadness of children and the hope and expectation that things may be a little better in the future for the generations to come.

1993
Leeds

C.J.H.
H.G.I.H.
J.M.W.

1. Introduction: a theoretical perspective

The purpose of writing this book is to present the current thinking of a group of individuals who are actively interested and working in the field of child abuse. The book is meant for practitioners and written by practitioners but we hope that in our active and deliberate preoccupation with practice we have nevertheless had time to stand back and reflect more widely on the many issues for everyone which child abuse raises. We hope, therefore, that others with a greater interest in developing a theoretical understanding will study this text because theory should learn from practice just as practice must have a sound theoretical basis.

By avoiding the issue of definition in this introduction, it is hoped that the book itself will serve to fulfil that function. Defining child abuse is notoriously difficult and itself raises other issues relating to the purpose for which the definition is to be used and how narrow or how wide the definition should be made. It should be sufficient to say that there are definitions, many of which are embodied within the legal framework of child protection practice (see Ch. 17), and that these will be referred to in the various chapters on the major kinds of abuse. These definitions are essential as starting points in understanding, and they provide clear statements at an early stage of dealing with a problem which is still emerging in societal consciousness.

This book is written from the perceptions of those in health professions and presents to some extent a medical model for the understanding of abuse. In no way should this diminish any other model or perspective on the subject, a full understanding of which requires that views are shared and that we seek to combine different ideas rather than seeing them as mutually exclusive or as inherently affording more or less insight than other views.

THEORETICAL VIEWPOINTS OF CHILD ABUSE

In the jigsaw puzzle approach to child maltreatment various perspectives from different disciplines and professional viewpoints are combined to provide an overall picture. This can be compared, for example, to the complex process which is involved in individual case diagnosis where information from a variety of individuals and agencies covering many aspects of the child and family is put together to obtain a comprehensive record. The individual pieces in our theoretical jigsaw overlap or fit together but in themselves do not purport to provide 'the answer or solution to our understanding'.

Table 1.1 illustrates 12 areas which have provided valuable understanding, and some of these are described below.

Table 1.1 The jigsaw approach to a theoretical understanding of child abuse

Historical perspective	Medical model	Psychological theory
Sociological theory	Legal standpoint	Education
Societal beliefs and attitudes	Violence and criminality	Children's rights
Power and political theory	The family as a system. Family violence	Biological views of aggression

Historical perspective

This is dealt with in the next chapter. History not only informs us that child abuse has happened in many cultures examined closely over the time of recorded history but also shows how social history has been reflected in the evolution of child-rearing practice. As societies have become more tolerant and respectful of the individuals within them so it seems that children have enjoyed greater protection and better care. Recent experience from Romania has demonstrated the relationship between wider social and political pressures and child maltreatment. In the past widespread practices which would now be termed maltreatment were either condoned or found to be socially acceptable. History suggests that societies have struggled at times with the problem of child abuse, although not always with great success or effect.

The medical model

The adoption of *Non-Accidental Injury* (NAI) as a diagnostic category of disorder by medicine has arguably been the single most important step in catalysing the recent progress in understanding child abuse. Caffey's 'parent–infant stress disorder' (1946) and Kempe's 'battered baby syndrome' (Kempe et al 1962) did much to focus attention onto the problem of child abuse and at the same time implied that, with the adoption of a medical model, a therapeutic approach might be useful.

In the medical world, the disorder lies primarily with the child whose condition requires to be recognised, diagnosed and treated. Fortunately medicine has been less willing to apply loose pathological or psychiatric diagnoses to the parents who have abused their children, recognising the inherent difficulties in that approach. This is not to say that there has been no acknowledgement of the perpetrators' difficulties and need (often denied) for help.

Psychological theories including the stress model

There is no single psychological theory to explain child abuse. Theories have focused on an understanding of the broad area of parent–child behav-iour and incorporate developmental psychological thinking. A recognition that infants born prematurely appeared to be at greater risk of abuse suggested that if attachment or bonding was impaired, e.g. by separation in the special care or neonatal unit, then abuse was more likely (Lynch & Roberts 1977). This coincided with strenuous attempts to promote early attachment in hospital with breastfeeding and the focus shifting onto parents' emotional health after birth (Klaus & Kennell 1976). Other insights from the psychological approach have emphasised that abusers are not recognisable as different within society and do not suffer from psychiatric disorder. They are characterised principally by the fact of their abusing behaviour. It has also been established that abuse is not simply an occurrence in situations where everything is going badly (e.g. unemployment, poverty, bad housing, history of maltreatment as a child, unintelligent, uneducated or depressed parents; or where society condones brutal treatment of children). These formulations do not work out in practice and therefore theoretically form a doubtful basis for our understanding of child abuse. There appears to be more to this problem than the insights afforded to us by the stress model; a predisposed or deviant parent plus an at-risk child plus a stressful situation does not produce child abuse in a predictable way.

Crittenden & Ainsworth (1989) remind us that more sophisticated and comprehensive ecological models such as those of Garbarino (1977) and Belsky (1980) provide us with infinite complexity, but we are still left wondering what it is that determines when abuse will take place. They suggest that it is necessary to focus on the critical causes of maltreatment and propose that anxious or insecure attachment is a critical concept in regard to both the origin of family maltreatment and the rehabilitation of families.

Attachment theory

This is a recent theory which grew out of the work of Bowlby (1969). He proposed that survival of humans, especially infants, was best ensured by proximity to an attachment figure(s). Infants are able to emit signals which lead to responses in the attachment figure; this draws the pair together when the situation requires. The process of attachment develops in phases the early part of life and is closely linked to maternal behaviour and responsiveness. Carers who are inaccessible, unresponsive, or inappropriately responsive to the child's behaviour are likely to produce children who are insecure or anxious in their attachments to them.

In maltreatment it has been postulated (and there is observational work to support this by Ainsworth et al 1978) that the children are anxiously attached and that this can be demonstrated in the testing construct of the 'strange situation'. In this manoeuvre the child is briefly placed with a stranger while his/her mother leaves the room. The child's reactions are then observed under the standardised situation. It appears that it is not the absence of 'a bond' that is important in situations of child abuse but rather the nature of the bond. Children who were neglected also appeared to show similar patterns of anxious attachment, although they tended to be passive rather than either difficult or compulsively compliant (Crittenden 1981). This is discussed further in Chapter 3.

Sociological theory

Sociologists view child abuse as an aspect of much wider social issues. For example they point out that it was only because of the challenges of judicial policy relating to sex crimes and rape against women that the scene was set for the sexual abuse of children to be confronted. Sociologists see the family as a microcosm of society. The power struggles between men and women in the family reflect the wider issues of women's rights in society. Research work on prevalence which is discussed more widely in Chapter 8 suggests that sexual abuse is a far more common occurrence than previously imagined. This in itself raises issues which cannot easily be addressed by reference only to personal or individual factors. Wider forces are at work.

Goodwin (1988) provides another interesting example of the importance of social attitude in this field when she analyses the decision process which occurs when societies, individuals and families consider intervention in childhood sexual abuse. She points out that in doing so they are simultane-

ously taking positions along at least five axes of beliefs and attitudes which are based on society's values and rules:

1. The preference for informal social controls versus the preference for legal controls,
2. Viewing the child as parental (mainly paternal) property versus the view of the child as an autonomous individual,
3. The need for inviolate family privacy versus the need for the community overseeing child-rearing,
4. Viewing the child as a sensual expert versus view of the child as a virginal innocent,
5. Viewing sexuality as dangerous and secret versus viewing sexuality as harmless or natural.

Sociologists would further wish to point out that other issues of social justice are involved in child abuse. Poverty, unemployment, racism and inequality place individuals, including children, at risk of neglect and abuse as individuals within that society.

Legal standpoint

Kempe said that child abuse is what the law says it is. Most countries have developed a legal framework for handling the problem of child abuse. This framework does not in itself prevent child abuse but provides a formal structure for dealing with the problem. Those who argue for the decriminalisation of child abuse are asking for a less punitive and more therapeutic response to the problem. However, even where more radical therapeutic solutions have been introduced, as in Holland's 'confidential doctor' programme, there is also a legal framework to be used as appropriate. In English law it is still permissible for a parent to hit a child but only to use reasonable force. The law reflects societal views — for example the recommended sentence for indecent assault of a male child is greater than that for a female child.

Violence and criminality

There is a great deal of information to link child abuse with other violent and criminal behaviour in the parents. The NSPCC statistics indicate that of cases reported to their system from 1983 to 1987 (Creighton & Noyes 1989), 15% of the mothers and 41% of the fathers had criminal records prior to the abuse being diagnosed. Among the recorded crimes, violent offences are over-represented, particularly in the case of the fathers where crimes of assault against both children and adults outnumbered non-violent criminal records; this contrasts with national data where non-violent crimes heavily outnumber violent crimes. Interestingly, when the recorded abuse was broken down into categories (physical injury, sexual abuse, neglect, failure to thrive, and emotional abuse), the highest rate for criminal records for all offences was encountered amongst both mothers and fathers in the neglect cases. However, the highest number of crimes of violence against adults was recorded for the fathers of physically injured children (18%). Finally, the data also indicate that in cases of physically injured, sexually abused, and neglected children, parents with a criminal record of any kind were significantly more likely to be implicated in the abuse or neglect of their child.

It seems that there is a link between abuse and offending in general, particularly violent offending against adults, although the NSPCC data are undoubtedly biased as they represent cases that have come to professional attention, and this is more likely when the parents have criminal records.

From another standpoint, Lewis et al (1989) believe that a high proportion of violent delinquents have been severely abused. There are several American studies which have found that 80% or more of juvenile offenders had been abused or neglected, often as pre-school children. Other studies (Welsh 1976, Feshback 1979) have linked the severity of corporal punishment received as a child with the degree of aggressiveness shown by delinquents. Similar findings have emerged from the work of the Newsons (Newson & Newson 1968) in Nottingham who found a 'very clear association' between the frequency of physical punishment at age 11 and the child's perceived delinquency.

Similar associations have been claimed for adult violent offenders. In one particularly disturbing study (Feldman et al 1986) of 15 death row inmates awaiting execution for murder, 8 had been victims of potentially filicidal assaults as children. Others had been physically and/or sexually abused by their parents.

Of course, some would pose the question the other way round: perhaps these individuals as children invited and deserved such treatment in view of their inherent badness? However, the view which blames the children grossly misrepresents the situation. The existence of neurological, psychological and behavioural difficulties in these individuals has been reported with greater frequency than in the population as a whole. Whether these have resulted from abusive head injury or other causes remains speculative, although there is some evidence to implicate the former (Oliver & Buchanan 1978).

Family violence

In the USA today it has been said that people are more likely to be killed, physically assaulted, hit, beaten up, slapped or spanked in their own homes by other family members than anywhere else or by anyone else (Gelles & Cornell 1990). Some observers have proposed that violence in the family is more common than love (Strauss et al 1980). These statements apply not only to American families but are also accurate assessments of family life in Britain, Western Europe and many other countries and societies around the globe (Gelles & Cornell 1990).

This view is in conflict with the traditional idealised view of the family as a safe haven to which one can flee from the dangers of the hostile outside world. Much of the violence is denied, ignored and not seen. Traditionally 'domestic' violence was often viewed as outside the province or interest of the law but these attitudes have now been challenged. This is reflected in the reorganisation of the Police and the establishment of Family Violence Units.

Categories of Family Violence

Adult perpetrator
Child abuse
Spouse abuse
Elder abuse
Courtship abuse

Child perpetrator
Sibling abuse
Parent abuse

There has been a tendency for the above categories to be viewed and studied in isolation. However the family functions as a system and it is common to observe more than one type of abuse occurring within the family. Browne (1989) suggests that abuse be categorised into 'active' and 'passive' forms, active involving violent acts in a physical, emotional or sexual context, and passive abuse referring to neglect which can only be considered violent in a metaphorical sense as it does not involve physical force. Neglect can, of course, result in both physical and emotional injury.

Spouse abuse (Bowder 1974, Gayford 1975, London 1978, Walker 1979, Andrews & Brown 1988, Dickstein 1988). This refers to physical and/or psychological violence by a man or woman towards his or her intimate partner (Browne 1989), whether married or unmarried. Clearly there is a spectrum of violence from slaps, pushes, shoves and spanking to punches, kicks, bites, chokings, beatings, shootings and stabbings where the injury clearly may be severe or fatal. Psychological violence is more difficult to define but includes verbal or non-verbal threats against a person or their belongings e.g. threatening suicide, punching walls, destroying pets and throwing things (Gelles & Cornell 1990). Spouse abuse also includes material deprivation, emotional and sexual abuse, marital rape and pornography.

Traditionally spouse abuse is considered to be a male to female directed behaviour but Strauss et al (1980) observed in a US National Incidence Survey of 2143 families that 4.6% of wives had engaged in abusive violence towards their husbands.

The lifetime incidence of marital violence has been estimated to lie between 11 and 28% of all marriages, making this the second most common form of interpersonal violence reported to police in Scotland in one study (Dobash & Dobash 1987). Between 20 and 40% of all homicides in the USA are domestic murders, 9% of women in one study (Hall 1985) in London reported forced sex by spouses and in San Francisco 4% experienced forced sex, 14% were raped and battered and 12% battered but not raped (Russell 1982).

There are also various accounts in the literature of husband abuse (e.g. Steinmetz 1978), refuting the view that women are the only victims of violence in the home. However, men are typically stronger, have more physical and social resources to hand and rarely suffer as much damage as women. Recent changes in the law have acknowledged the crime of marital rape.

Refuges. Erin Pizzey, who established a refuge in Chiswick, wrote in 1974 'Scream quietly or the neighbours will hear'. Refuges are now widespread for women seeking a place of safety from violence for themselves and their children. By the end of the 70s it was estimated that 11 400 women and 20 850 children used 150 refuges in a 12-month period. The women reported physical and mental cruelty, including being kept prisoner, verbally tormented and threatened as well as the batterings. Sadly, those who have worked with battered women report the difficulties that some women have in breaking the bonds of these violent, dangerous and symbiotic relationships (Pizzey & Shapiro 1982). Sometimes it seemed almost as though there was an addiction to the violence although there was very real fear as well as excitement accompanying the violent interactions. However, difficulty for a woman in separating and protecting herself frequently relates to the social, legal and material entrapments of marriage.

Children of course are frequently witnesses to this violence which is often chronic, lasting for years before the woman moves out or away from her husband or partner.

It is also important to acknowledge that family violence, whilst reported more often from lower social classes, also occurs in middle and upper class homes. Levinger (1966), in studying the reasons cited for divorce, found that while 40% of working class applicants named abuse as the reason for the divorce, 23% of middle class applicants mentioned violence as the reason for wanting to end the marriage. It occurs within every culture and refuges have been opened for women and teenage girls from ethnic minorities in Britain. There are also 'safe houses' for children.

It is beyond the scope of this text to discuss in detail the causes of spouse violence. Understandably cultural values and exposure to models of aggression which are sanctioned and unpunished are factors. Social structural explanations emphasise the importance of the existence of asymmetric social relationships within society (as in poverty, unemployment, homelessness) and in the family (authoritarian, wife dominance). Domestic violence is then a means of improving low status and low self-esteem. Finally, psychological explanations have focused on personality characteristics, psychiatric history and alcohol and drug use (for example the explosion of 'crack'-related violent crime in the USA). Many women describe drunkenness as a factor contributing to violence in their husbands. For further details the reader is referred to Browne (1989) and Gelles & Cornell (1990).

Elder abuse. There is increasing information available on this form of abuse; there are obvious parallels with child abuse. Cloke (1983) defined granny battering as the systematic and continuous abuse of an elderly person by the carer — often, although not always, a relative on whom the elderly person is dependent for care. The abuse may involve physical violence, threats of physical violence, sexual abuse including rape and pornography, neglect, abandonment, psychological abuse and exploitation (Eastman 1989). The incidence of elder abuse is difficult to ascertain, but in the USA it is estimated that 7% of the elderly population is abused. With increasing numbers of elderly persons dependent on relatives or institutional care, it is likely that this form of abuse will become more prevalent. It is associated with the stress and frustration of the care-giver faced with the elderly person's increasing age and continual presence. Other factors similar to those described in other aspects of family violence may also apply, e.g. alcohol, personality characteristics.

Courtship violence. Researchers in this country and in North America have drawn attention to this form of interpersonal violence (Browne 1989, Gelles and Cornell 1990). Studies have found that between 10 and 67% of dating relationships involve violence of some kind. The violence ranges from mild (pushing, shoving, slapping) to severe, which is surprisingly common (Gelles & Cornell 1990). Interestingly attitudes frequently included an acceptance of the violence as a protective sign of the romantic illusion of dating. In addition to physical violence, sexual violence in the form of 'date rape' is also described.

Both men and women report being the victims in the situation of courtship violence and there is considerable evidence of the interactive nature of the behaviour. It is not surprising that courtship violence is frequently continued into the marital relationship and that 20% of battered women claim that the first violent assault occurred prior to marriage or cohabitation (Dobash et al 1978).

Human aggression (Storr 1974)

Lorenz (1966) wrote 'what is the significance of all this fighting?'. He had started by looking at coral fish and found that some species, particularly some of the brightly coloured ones, were very fierce and very willing to fight. In the animal kingdom aggression is either inter-specific (between members of different species) or intra-specific (between members of the same species). In a sense inter-specific aggression and fighting seem to make some sense within the Darwinian construct of the struggle for existence, although it is successful competition which determines species survival rather than the results of the more active struggles in which aggression plays a part. Clearly some species prey on others and all animals have some capacity for self defence. The predator–prey relationship is a classic one in the history of evolution, each species changing under the influence of the other's evolution in a process which leads to a balance so that neither party has too much of an upper hand. Predators do not necessarily or usually exhibit aggression in their predation but predators are frequently counter-attacked by their prey and in this situation aggression can be clearly defined. Crows may mob a bird of prey or a cat if they see it in the day when its advantage is less. Aggression is therefore useful and has survival value. Within species, aggression is encountered in fights over territories leading to spacing out of the individuals and in sexual selection of the strongest by rival fights and in defence of the young. In all these situations it is functional and serves to assist in the preservation of the species. It is not surprising therefore that the aggressive drive in animals is a vital and essential part of their make-up and is a major motivation in much behaviour.

Lorenz reasons that in considering human behaviour from a distant position where one could look at the broad patterns such as migration, wars, historical events, one would not gain an impression that such behaviour was dictated by intelligence, still less by moral responsibility. It is difficult to make sense of much human behaviour if one assumes that it is determined by reason and cultural tradition alone. Lorenz suggests it continues to be subject to the laws prevailing in all phylogenetically adapted instinctive behaviour.

Is there any help in understanding child abuse from this perspective? Certainly it helps us to understand the role of aggression in human behaviour and how it can become adapted in destructive ways towards other members of the species. In social animals (of which man is a good example) there are inhibitions controlling aggression to other members of the species but because man is not a predator or carnivore as such, these inhibitions are not as well developed as in species where there is a much greater risk from a single act of aggression. Rapid changes in human ecology and sociology by cultural development may disrupt phylogenetically adapted behaviour mechanisms and lead to dysfunctional patterns.

Child abuse, as described in twentieth-century Britain, is clearly an extreme form of dysfunctional behaviour between members of the human species. There are no clear parallels within the animal kingdom and it is difficult to discern any survival or functional value in such behaviour.

CONCLUSIONS

— It is not possible to provide a single comprehensive and simple theory by which to understand child abuse.
— There are as many viewpoints as there are disciplines and each individual has a personal and differing perspective.

— Child abuse appears to be a uniquely human problem embedded in psychological and social factors in the complex societies in which people live. Attitudes and beliefs are fundamental to an understanding, and politics, morality and religion also seek to be heard in this debate.
— The stakes are high. It is not just the health, wellbeing and happiness of generations of children as they grow up into adults but more than this, the future of the society which the children will construct out of their childhood experiences.
— There is little doubt that aggression is a central part of much abusive behaviour and it seems likely that it is linked in some way to perceived or imagined threats upon the individual who perpetrates the abuse. However, the complex way in which aggression is directed towards an individual's offspring remains incompletely understood.
— The mechanisms in the human for managing and coping with trauma, including psychological as well as physical injury, also begin to suggest the special problems which confront the highly developed human mind. Thus, for example, whilst the immediate effects of emotional dissociation which may follow extremely traumatic situations may provide acute survival value, in the long term these very effects may present challenges of adaptation for the individual. The increased likelihood of abusive behaviour to be 'handed on' from generation to generation suggests that long-term adaptations are playing a part in these processes (Widom 1989).

REFERENCES

Ainsworth M O, Blehar M C, Waters E, Wall S 1978 Patterns of attachment: a psychological study of the strange situation. Erlbaum, Hillsdale NJ
Andrews B, Brown G W 1988 Marital violence in the community: a biographical approach. British Journal of Psychiatry 153: 305–312
Belsky J 1980 Child maltreatment: an ecological integration. American Psychologist 3: 320–335
Bowder B 1974 The wives who ask for it. Community Care 1: 18–19
Bowlby J 1969 Attachment and loss. Vol 1: Attachment. Basic Books, New York
Browne K D 1989 Family violence: spouse and elder abuse.

In: Howells K, Hollin C R (eds) Clinical approaches to violence. J Wiley & Sons, Chichester
Caffey J 1946 Multiple fractures in the long bones of infants suffering from subdural haematoma. American Journal of Roentgenology 56: 163–173
Cloke C 1983 Old age abuse in the domestic setting: a review. Age Concern, England (cited in Eastman 1989)
Creighton S J, Noyes P 1989 Child abuse trends in England and Wales 1983–87. NSPCC
Crittenden P M 1981 Abusing, neglecting, problematic and adequate dyads: differentiating by patterns of interaction. Merrell-Palmer Quarterly 27: 210–218
Crittenden P M, Ainsworth M D S 1989 Child maltreatment

and attachment theory. In: Cicchetti D, Carlson V (eds) Child maltreatment. Cambridge University Press

Dickstein L J 1988 Spouse abuse and other domestic violence. Psychiatric Clinics of North America 11 (4): 611–628

Dobash R E, Dobash R P 1987 Violence towards wives. In: Coping with disorders in the family. Guildford Press, Surrey, pp. 169–193

Dobash R E, Dobash R F, Kavanagh K, Wilson M 1978 Wifebeating: the victims speak. Victimology 2 (3/4): 608–622

Eastman M 1989 Old age abuse. In: Archer J, Browne K (eds) Human aggression: naturalistic approaches. Routledge, London

Feldman M, Mallouh C, Lewis D O 1986 Filicidal abuse in the histories of 15 condemned murderers. Bull A M Acad Psychiat Law 14 (4): 345–352

Feshback N D 1979 The effects of violence in childhood. In: Gil D G (ed) Child abuse and violence. AMS Press, New York

Garbarino J 1977 The human ecology of child maltreatment: a conceptual model for research. Journal of Marriage and the Family 39: 721–727

Gayford J J 1975 Wife battering: a preliminary survey of 100 cases. British Medical Journal i: 194–197

Gelles R J, Cornell C P 1990 Intimate violence in families, 2nd edn. Sage, London

Goodwin J M 1988 Obstacles to policy making about incest. In: Wyatt G E, Powell G J (eds) Lasting effects of child sexual abuse. Sage Books

Hall R 1985 Ask any woman. Falling Wall Press, Bristol

Kempe C H, Silverman F N, Steele B F, Droegmuller W, Silver H K 1962 The battered child syndrome. JAMA 181: 17–24

Klaus M, Kennell J 1976 Maternal-infant bonding. C V Mosby, St Louis

Levinger G 1966 Sources of marital dissatisfaction among applicants for divorce. American Journal of Orthopsychiatry 26: 803–897

Lewis D O, Mallouh C, Webb V 1989 Child abuse, delinquency and violent criminality. In: Cicchetti D, Carlson V (eds) Child maltreatment. Cambridge University Press, p 707

London J 1978 Images of violence against women. Victimology 2: 510–524

Lorenz K 1966 On aggression. Methuen, London

Lynch M, Roberts J 1977 Predicting child abuse: signs of bonding failure in the maternity hospital. British Medical Journal 1: 624–626

Newson J, Newson E 1968 Four years old in an urban community. Allen & Unwin, London

Oliver J E, Buchanan A 1978 Maltreatment of children as a cause of impaired intelligence. In: Smith S M (ed) The maltreatment of children. MTP Press

Pizzey E 1974 Scream quietly or the neighbours will hear. Penguin, Harmondsworth

Pizzey E, Shapiro J 1982 Prone to violence. Hamlyn, London

Russell D 1982 Rape in marriage. Macmillan, New York

Steinmetz S K 1978 The battered husband syndrome. Victimology 2 (3/4): 499–509

Storr A 1974 Human aggression. Penguin, Harmondsworth

Strauss M A 1978 Wife-beating: how common and why? Victimology 2 (3/4): 443–458

Strauss M A, Gelles R J, Steinmetz S K 1980 Behind closed doors: violence in the American family. Anchor Press, New York

Walker L E 1979 The battered woman syndrome study. In: Finkelhor D, Gelles R, Hotaling G, Strauss M (eds) The dark side of families: current family violence research. Sage, London

Welsh R S 1976 Severe parental punishment and delinquency: a developmental theory. J Clin Child Psychology 5: 17–21

Widom O S 1989 The cycle of violence. Science 244: 160–166

2. Child abuse and neglect — a historical perspective

THE LESSONS OF HISTORY

This chapter relies heavily on the now classic contributions on the history of child abuse of Lloyd De Mause (1980), Samuel Radbill (1987) and Margaret Lynch (1985). These authors and others have shown us that there is nothing new about child abuse. Its existence has been recognised for a very long time. What is new is the recent willingness to address its existence and to look for ways of preventing its occurrence.

The historical perspective allows us to stand back from the everyday experience of confronting the battered or neglected child and to reflect on the wider issues of what has been presented to us as a single incident in time. Those who have sought to uncover evidence of child abuse in the past have had to collect their material widely, often reading between the lines and recognising indirect messages of what was happening. There is much to support a view of history that 'the things that really matter are hardly ever committed to paper'. Thus wrote Lloyd De Mause in the Preface of his history of childhood. William Langer, Professor of History at Harvard University, wrote:

The direction of human affairs has never been confided to children, and historians, who have concerned themselves primarily with political and military affairs and at most with the intrigues and rivalries of royal courts, have paid almost no attention to the ordeals of childhood. Even the students of education have, on the whole, devoted themselves to the organisation and curriculum of schools, and with theories of education with only occasional reference to what happened to the pupils at home and in the World at large.

Yet the history of childhood must be of major importance to any study of human society, for if, as it is said, the child is the father of the man, it should be possible, with an understanding of any individual's or any group's past, to form a more intelligent judgement of their performance as adults.

Unhappily, the results of these investigations are most depressing. They tell a long and mournful story of the abuse of children from the earliest times even to the present day. We need not assume that the generalisations here advanced apply to all people at all times. No-one can doubt that there have always been parents who loved and cherished their children and that such mistakes as they may have made in the upbringing were due to ignorance rather than to ill will.

While the true frequency of child abuse today remains unknown, it is clearly altogether a common occurrence, but it must be said that since the 18th century a more humanitarian attitude has gradually emerged (De Mause 1980).

Langer comments that much of the wanton abuse of children related to the fact that humans produced more babies than they could possibly care for, or have room or employment for. Hence the widespread practice of infanticide existed in one form or another, the chief victims usually being the female infants because it was they who would eventually produce yet more souls. From this probably also arose the notion that sexual relations were sinful and that the resultant offspring was, from the moment of birth, evil. How else could one explain the cruel practices designed to exorcise the evil and make children less of a nuisance than they were?

So it is not an exaggeration when de Mause (1980) said that, 'The history of childhood is a nightmare from which we have only recently begun to awaken'. The further back in history one goes, the lower the level of child care and the more likely children were to be killed, abandoned, beaten, terrorised, and sexually abused.

Where the historians usually look to the sandbox battle of yesterday for the causes of those today, we instead ask how each generation of parents and children creates those issues which are later acted out in the arena of public life. These links have been recognised for centuries. St Augustine's cry of 'give me other mothers and I will give you another World' was quoted by De Mause to indicate the importance of parent–child relations in the process of social change. Links between parents and the development of personality of the child were recognised in the 17th century, when it was considered that traits might be transmitted in breast milk from mother to baby. Much attention was therefore given to the choice of a suitable wet nurse to give such to the offspring of the affluent. Such was the advice given by Burton in 1651 to parents: 'that they make choice of a sound woman of good complexion, honest, free from bodily diseases, if it be possible, and all passions and perturbations of the mind, as sorrow, fear, grief, folly, melancholy. For such passions corrupt the milk and alter the temperature of the child which now being moist and pliable clay, is easily seasoned and perverted.' (Fomon 1974)

However it was Freud who more dearly changed our view of childhood. Now at case conferences we are interested to know of the parents' childhoods to understand their present actions. History, in the same way, must turn itself towards childhood if it is to understand some of the upheavals of the societies which it studies.

De Mause's studies draw together various important threads:

1. Parent–child relationships are undergoing a process of constant evolutionary change. Each generation is able to regress to the psychic stage of their children and work through the anxieties of that age so as to manage them better the next time.

2. The history of childhood suggests that there is a general improvement in child care, i.e. the further back, the worse things seemed to be. Therefore, while today in the USA there may be as many as one million abused children, one could imagine a time earlier in history when most children would, by today's standards, be considered abused.

THE PRESENT DAY, SO DIFFERENT?

It would, however, be unwise to distance ourselves too much from the past. Samuel Radbill (1987)

reminds us that in 1895, the NSPCC summarised many of the ways that London children were battered: 'by boots, crockery, pans, shovels, straps, ropes, thongs, pokers, fire and boiling water'. In the Newsons' studies in the 1980s, they found that by the age of 7, 26% of boys and 18% of girls had been hit with an implement and a further 53% (65% boys and 41% girls) threatened with an implement, so perhaps change should be seen as gradual and faltering. Neglected children in 1895 were described as miserable, vermin infested, filthy, shivering, ragged, nigh naked, pale, puny, limp, feeble, faint, dizzy, famished, and dying. One hundred years ago, begging was common but children begging in the streets of London has become a common occurrence in 1991.

It was not assumed that children automatically had a right to live in ancient times. This right was ritually bestowed and if it was withheld the child could be disposed of as a nonentity with little compunction. Usually it was the father who had to acknowledge the child, proclaiming him or her for his own. In some cultures, until nourishment had passed the child's lips, the child was not really of this world.

Radbill comments that the fitness to live could also be tested. The Germans would plunge the child into icy cold water, the Greeks would leave the child on a mountain top, North American Indians threw children into a pool of water to see if they floated. Naming of the child is another important way of recognising the child's existence. The Christian child required to be christened and given a name before his soul could go to heaven. Without christening, he would have to be buried in unhallowed ground along with the dogs and cats. Children born out of wedlock have long been outlawed and especially liable to abuse and infanticide. William Blake expressed this as 'the youthful Harlot's Curse Blasts the new-born Infant's tear'. In 1917, of 4–5000 illegitimates born in Chicago, 1000 disappeared without trace (Radbill 1987).

EXPOSURE AND INFANTICIDE (Hobbs 1991)

These are the time-honoured methods of lethal child abuse. Weak, premature or deformed infants were frequently disposed of in ancient times. However, although infanticide was common in many cultures, the Egyptians would sentence parents who killed their children to hug the corpse continuously for 72 hours. The Greeks actually encouraged the disposal of handicapped children, believing that they would pass on defects to the next generation. It is interesting to note how even today the handicapped are at greater risk of abuse than other groups of children. The existence of the practice of infanticide is reflected in the passing of laws, e.g. the Chinese in 1654 banned the drowning of little girls, but laws have never stopped infanticide, which continues to exist to the present day in our society. While it is clear today that most 'cot deaths' do not arise from abuse, a small proportion — certainly less than 1:10 — arise from infanticide (Emery 1985).

If children are seen as property of parents, or more usually their fathers, then it is not surprising that the owners are given a fairly free hand in how they treat them. In Roman law, patriae potestia was the concept which meant children were property and fathers were in charge.

CHILD LABOUR

Child labour remains another major way in which children have been abused and misused over the centuries. The statute of artificers in 1562 gave the government regulatory controls over apprentices, binding children to their masters by indenture for seven years (Radbill 1987). This produced a situation of enslavement which lasted until 1815. The stories of children being beaten in clothing mills in England in the 1800s are well known, and the child chimney sweeps were described as England's disgrace. 'Little black things among the snow crying "weep", "weep" in notes of woe,' wrote William Blake (quoted by Radbill 1987). The children were intentionally kept small and thin (failure to thrive) so that they could clamber up the soot-clogged flues. The major causes of child labour today in developing countries are poverty and inequality (Naidu 1986). Development is inversely related worldwide to the incidence of child labour. High illiteracy rates, backwardness in economic development, and poor environmental resources encourage child labour. In develop-

ing countries today, child labour remains a major issue.

Estimates of the number of children worldwide in the official workforce vary. A United Nations Report (Bouhdiba 1982) estimated that there were 145 million children, aged between 10 and 14, most of them in developing countries, and younger children may also be involved. Child work is exploitative when it prevents access to education, leaves no time for recreation or is hazardous to health. In addition, the physical and emotional stresses of work can produce psychosocial hazards.

SEXUAL ABUSE

There is little doubt that sexual abuse of children has been recorded as long as human beings have kept records. De Mause (1980) wrote 'the child in antiquity lived his earlier years in an atmosphere of sexual abuse'. Growing up in Greece or Rome often included being used sexually by older men. In Rome, boy brothels were common and there was a rent-a-boy service in Athens. The abuse involved not only boys over 11 or 12, but also much younger children.

Girls were also involved, as well as women. Petronius described the rape of a 7-year-old girl with women clapping in a long line around the bed, suggesting that women were not exempt from playing a role in the process. Aristotle commented that homosexuality often becomes habitual in 'those who are abused from childhood'. The Jews attempted to eradicate adult homosexuality with severe punishments but were more lenient in the case of young boys. The penalty for sodomy, or as we would know it, buggery, with children over 9 years of age was death by stoning. Despite Moses' injunction against corrupting children, copulation with younger children was not, however, considered a sexual act and was punishable only by whipping 'as a matter of public discipline'.

There are remarkable parallels between the patterns of abuse in ancient Greece and what is being witnessed in England in the present day (Hobbs & Wynne 1986). Martial said the favourite sexual use of children was not oral sex but anal intercourse. There has always been an awareness of the harmful effects of sexual abuse of children.

The concept of children's innocence was well accepted, but there were dangers in this because it was suggested that children would not suffer from abuse because they could not be corrupted.

In the Renaissance moralists warned against sexual use of children, but in the 18th century the moral view took an unusual turn. Children were punished for touching their genitals. Prohibitions against masturbation are generally unusual in primitive societies, and this seems to be a late development in the historical sequence of rejecting child abuse. The sinfulness of masturbation was supported by the medical profession, who advised that it could cause insanity, epilepsy, blindness, and death. Mutilation, circumcision, and infibulation were sometimes used as punishments, and casts and cages used to restrain the child.

In the 18th century, sexual abuse was widespread amongst servants and others acting in parent roles. Cardinal Bernis, who was himself sexually abused as a child, warned that 'there is nothing so dangerous for morals and perhaps for health as to leave children too long under the care of chambermaids or even of young ladies brought up in the Chateaux. I will add that the best among them are not always the least dangerous. They dare with a child that which they would be ashamed to risk with a young man'.

Freud said he was seduced by his nurse when he was two.

DISCOVERY AND DENIAL

In more modern times, there have been various attempts to bring the issue of the continued existence of the sexual abuse of children out into the open (Summit 1989). Ambrose Tardieu, the Dean of Forensic Medicine in France, published in 1860 a startling exposé (Tardieu 1860 cited by Masson 1984) entitled: 'a medico-legal study of Cruelty and Brutal Treatment Inflicted on Children'. In his book on rape, reviewing an 11-year period from 1858 to 1869, he cited 11 576 people accused of completed or attempted rape in France. Of these cases, 9125 (or almost 80%) involved child victims, mostly girls aged 4–12 years. Tardieu's work encouraged a transient interest in the publication of a new journal — Archives of Criminal Anthropology and the Penal Science,

— which encouraged studies of Child Sexual Abuse. Soon after Tardieu's death, Fournier in 1880 (quoted in Masson 1984) proclaimed that children were faking sexual abuse and that respectable men were targets of extortion by perfidious children and their lower class parents.

Brouardel, a student of Tardieu, also attacked the treachery of children, asserting that 60–85% of their complaints were unfounded. He used an attractive argument to blame the victims. In his address in the 1880s.

'The causes of error in Expert Opinion with respect to Sexual Assault', he asserted that: The child comforts herself by touching herself, fantasies that she knows are false on every point . . . This child, to whom one ordinarily paid only the most minor attention, finds an audience that is willing to listen to her with a certain solemnity and to take cognisance of the creations of her imagination. She grows in her own esteem, she herself becomes a personage and nothing will ever get her to admit that she deceived her family and the first people who questioned her. (Brouardel, quoted in Masson 1984).

Freud also became aware of child sexual abuse, not only from his work with his adult patients in psychotherapy, but also from visits to the mortuary in Paris where he observed signs of rape in children (Masson 1984). On this latter point, it is interesting to note that Tardieu said that if doctors are called in they should tell the police, and the pathologists should not be surprised at anything they see. Freud made the link between early sexual assault of a child and emotional illness in the victims in later life — particularly from his studies of patients with hysteria. The story of his recantation of the seduction theory in favour of the Oedipus Complex — children are traumatised by projection of their own wishful masturbatory fantasies and not by actual sexual assault — is well known (Masson 1984). Freud found that he was alienated and isolated and in danger of rejection. He had discovered the stuff of our nightmares, a lost world of hidden pain, and society did not wish to join him in his discovery. By diverting his awareness into more acceptable channels he kept face and was accepted back into the fold of his professional colleagues. Only one of his followers, Sandor Ferenczi, continued to accept his original theory.

Ferenczi (1932) wrote of his experience of

abused children: 'The over-powering force and authority of the adult makes them dumb and can rob them of their senses. The same anxiety, however, if it reaches a certain maximum compels them to subordinate themselves like automata to the will of the aggressor to divine each one of his desires and to gratify these; completely oblivious of themselves, they identify with the aggressor'.

Lynch reviews the nineteenth- and twentieth-century literature up to the time of Kempe (1962). The way in which medicine gradually accepted the traumatic nature of the bony lesions in babies is well described.

Tardieu also described battered children, but it was John Caffey (1946), Silverman (1953) and others working in the 1940s and 1950s who identified multiple fractures and subdural haematoma and suggested that they resulted from trauma and were not due to previously unrecognised disease. The papers were largely ignored. In 1961 Henry Kempe presented his paper, 'The Battered Child', and people listened (Kempe et al, 1962). In that paper he estimated that there could be as many as 447 cases of the battered child syndrome in the USA. Krugman, writing in 1986, declared the above figure to be an eight-hour total for in 1983 there were 1 007 658 reported cases and in 1985 1 700 000. A rise in reported cases involving sexual abuse is also included in these figures. In 1984 200 000 new cases were reported to the child protective services in 19 states, with 100 000 cases substantiated — 22% involving a male child, 78% a female child.

We need not, however, look to reported cases for estimates of the size of the present day problem. Over the last 15 years a number of prevalence studies of sexual abuse have examined the lifetime rates for at least one incident having occurred before age 18 years and found a range of 6–62% for females and 3–31% for males in the USA (Peters et al 1986). The wide ranges relate to methodological variations, especially data collection, sampling techniques and differences as to how CSA is defined (see Ch. 8).

Despite all this, society still moves slowly to acknowledge the existence of the problem. In the UK reported rates are rising (Creighton 1988) but the discovery of over 100 children over a few months in 1987 in Cleveland led to widespread disbelief and a formal inquiry took place (Butler-Sloss 1988). Even now there are many who believe that the problem of sexual abuse was grossly overexaggerated despite the clear message of the report. Will the present be historically yet another episode that is buried and passed over, leaving children much as before — unprotected, abused and harmed — or is this the dawning of an era of new social justice for children and society?

EVOLUTION OF SOCIAL AND LEGAL PROTECTION

If within people's minds child abuse remains the unthinkable, then progress cannot be made. Advances in the sociolegal mechanisms have been occurring in the past 150 years in both Britain and America. The story of Mary Ellen (Williams 1980) is worth recounting. Mary Ellen was born in the USA in the 1860s and was found starved and physically abused by her adoptive parents which included being chained to a bed. In 1874 publicity for her plight reached national awareness but there was no child protection agency in existence to handle her case. The founder of the Society for the Protection of Animals, Henry Berg, invoked action when the New York police refused to do anything. This led to the foundation of the Society for the Prevention of Cruelty to Children in 1875. Interestingly, in 1876 a photograph of the abused, neglected, and starved child was displayed alongside specimens of abused members of the animal kingdom as part of the Society for the Prevention of Cruelty to Animals' exhibit at the Philadelphia Centennial Exhibition to mark the nation's centenary. The Society for the Prevention of Cruelty to Children (SPCC) was organised by the leadership of the SPCA and modern American child protection was born. Mary Ellen grew up to be married, and had two children. She died aged 92 years but bore the scars of her injuries for life (Lazoritz 1990).

Societies such as the NSPCC and Speedwell Society, actively promoted children's causes at the turn of the century. There was a gradual shift in child-rearing methods from punitive to more sensitive ones. Radbill (1973) reminds us that child welfare was recorded as long ago as 6000 years in Mesopotamia, where orphans had a patron goddess to care for them. Institutional care has a long history going back to ancient Greece and Rome and then, in Europe, in the 7th century in France.

Unfortunately, the foundling hospitals and homes, who aimed to rescue abandoned and unwanted children, offered minimal care in many cases, and death from exposure and malnutrition was the fate of many children (Chapin 1915). Because of the failings of institutional care, children were readily fostered, although the mortality in London in the 19th century was 80% from abuse or neglect (Radbill 1987). Nurses who were skilled baby killers were called 'angel makers' or 'harpies' and could earn profits from insurance benefits on dead infants. In Germany, giving the baby nothing but a dummy soaked in brandy usually saw it off. A report in 1881 estimated that 31% died in foster-care in Germany (Radbill 1987).

An article in the British Medical Journal (1903) criticised systems of baby farming and urged licences for foster-parents and inspectors. Although fostering has improved in modern times, it should come as no surprise that children are occasionally abused in the system which is designed to protect them.

Child protective laws

There have been many laws which have as their central concern the protection of children. In 1224 overlaying was so prevalent that the Statutes of Winchester penalised women for keeping infants in bed with them. Infanticide is still viewed as a lesser crime than murder, but murder in the first year of life remains 5–10 times higher than at any other age, with a rate of 66 per million population.

Most countries have laws prohibiting incest. Incest became a criminal offence in England in 1908, although it was briefly a criminal offence from 1650 to 1660. Prior to 1909 it was punishable by ecclesiastical courts.

The legal age of consent varies from country to country and between states of the USA. It is 16 years in the UK and theoretically serves to reduce sexual abuse and exploitation. Mrazek (1982) noted that anthropologists have documented that all societies have some kind of incest taboo with or without formal criminal sanctions or punishments. This suggests that all human societies have a tendency to encounter incest.

Much of the present law and new law incorporated in the Children Act (1989) is based on experience accumulated in child care practice in the latter half of this century. A series of inquiries following on from the Inquiry into the death of Maria Colwell (OHSS 1974) have led to changes in practice and legislation.

CONCLUSION

De Mause suggests that parent–child relations have evolved historically through various key modes or stages. His sequence is:

1. Infanticidal mode   Antiquity–4th century AD
2. Abandonment mode   4th–13th AD
3. Ambivalent mode   14th–17th AD
4. Intrusive mode   18th century
5. Socialisation or   19th–mid 20th training mode
6. Helping mode   Mid 20th

In the infanticidal mode, parents routinely resolved their anxieties about caring for their children by killing them. Gradually, as parents accepted the notion of the child possessing a soul, the only way they could escape from the difficulties with their children was through abandonment, either physically to wet nurses or foster families or by severe emotional abandonment at home. Between the 14th and 17th centuries parents allowed children more into their emotional lives and saw themselves as having a task to mould the child who was seen as clay or soft wax to be beaten into shape. Child instruction manuals first appear around this time.

As the 18th century was reached, parents became more intrusive in their child care, punishing the child with threats and guilt but also developing more understanding and empathy with the child.

During the socialisation mode, which is still prevalent today, the child was seen as someone to be trained, guided and taught to conform. This grew with a behaviourist and sociological function. The father started to become more involved in child care for the first time.

The helping mode judges that the child must be supported and helped through his development, which he can explore for himself. There is more tolerance, the child is not struck or scolded, and the process requires great emotional and time commitment from the parents. The reader is referred to De Mause (1980) for further details.

Obviously there are considerable overlaps and ranges of parental behaviour within and between different societies. However, the study of European culture in particular suggests that child-rearing practices have gradually evolved for the better. Recently we have seen six European countries outlaw the hitting of children altogether, and in Great Britain corporal punishment has been prohibited in state schools since 1987.

History gives us a perspective which helps us understand our shortcomings towards children better. Mankind strives to do better by its children and thereby to secure a future for itself and generations to come. This history of childhood is one which should not deter us or depress us too much. The good old days were surely the bad old days but we should not pretend that the lives of children are always so different, even now, and be aware that change is often painfully slow and faltering.

REFERENCES

Bouhdiba A 1982 Exploitation of child labour. United Nations Report, New York

British Medical Journal 1903: 154–155

Butler-Sloss E 1988 Report of the Inquiry into Child Abuse in Cleveland 1987. HMSO

Caffey J 1946 Multiple fractures in the long bones of infants suffering from chronic subdural haematoma. American Journal of Roentgenology 56 (2): 162–173

Chapin H D 1915 Are institutions for infants necessary? Journal of the American Medical Association 64: 1–3

Creighton S J 1988 The incidence of child abuse and neglect. In: Browne K, Davies C, Stratton P (eds) Early prediction and prevention of child abuse. J Wiley & Sons, Chichester, ch 3, pp. 31–41

De Mause L 1980 The history of childhood. Souvenir Press, London DHSS 1974 Report of the Committee of Inquiry into the care and supervision provided in relation to Maria Colwell. HMSO

Emery J L 1985 Infanticide, filicide and cot death. Archives of Disease in Childhood 60: 505–507

Ferenczi S 1932 Confusion of tongues between adults and the child: the language of tenderness and of passion. In: Balint M (ed) & Mosbacher E (trans) Final contributions to the problems and methods of psychoanalysis 1955. Basic Books, New York. See also International Journal of Psychoanalysis 1949 30: 225–230

Fomon S J 1974 Infant nutrition, 2nd edn. Saunders, Philadelphia

Hobbs C J 1991 Infanticide and the battered baby. Current Paediatrics 1: 116–122

Hobbs C J, Wynne J M 1986 Buggery in childhood — a common syndrome of child abuse. Lancet ii: 792–796

Kempe C J, Silverman F N, Steele B F, Droegmueller W, Silver H K 1962 The battered child syndrome. Journal of the American Medical Association 181: 17–24

Krugman R 1986 Child maltreatment and its presentation in industrialised countries. In: Battered children and child abuse. Proceedings of XIXth Council of the International Organisation of Medical Sciences Round Table Conference. CIOMS, Switzerland, pp. 14–21

Lazoritz S 1990 Whatever happened to Mary Ellen? Child Abuse and Neglect 14: 143–149

Lynch M A 1985 Child abuse before Kempe: an historical literature review. Child Abuse and Neglect 9: 7–15

Masson J N 1984 The assault of truth: Freud's suppression of the seduction theory. Farrar, Strauss & Giroux, New York

Mrazek P B 1982 Definition and recognition of sexual child abuse. Historical and cultural perspective in sexually abused children and their families. In: Mrazek P B, Kempe C H (eds). Pergamon, Oxford, pp. 5–16

Naidu U S 1986 Exploitation of working children. Situation analysis and approaches to improving their conditions. In: Battered children and child abuse. Council of the International Organisation of Medical Sciences, Switzerland, pp. 70–80

Newson J, Newson E 1968 Four years old in an urban community. Allen & Unwin, London

Newson J, Newson E The extent of parental physical punishment in the UK. Available from Child Development Research Unit, University of Nottingham, University Park, Nottingham NG7 2RO

Peters S D, Wyatt G E, Finkelhor D 1986 Prevalence. In: Finkelhor D (ed) A sourcebook on child sexual abuse. Sage, London, pp. 15–59

Radbill S X 1973 Mesopotamian paediatricians. Episteme 7: 283

Radbill S X 1978 Children in a world of violence: a history of child abuse. In: Helfer R E, Kempe R S (eds) The battered child, 4th edn. University of Chicago Press, London, pp. 3–22

Silverman F 1953 The roentgen manifestations of unrecognised skeletal trauma. American Journal of Roentgenology 69: 413–426

Summit R C 1989 Hidden victims, hidden pain: societal avoidance of child sexual abuse. In: Wyatt G E, Powell G J (eds) Lasting effects of child sexual abuse. Sage, pp. 39–60

Tardieu A 1860 Etude medico-legale sur les services et mauvais traitments exerces sur des enfants. Ann Hyg Pub Med Leg 13: 361–398

Williams G J 1980 Cruelty and kindness to children: documentary of a century, 1874–1974. In Williams J G, Money J (eds) Traumatic abuse and neglect of children at home. Johns Hopkins University Press, Baltimore, pp. 68–77

3. Failure to thrive

The term failure to thrive ('FTT') refers to children who are growth retarded secondary to malnutrition. The use of 'failure to thrive' rather than 'malnutrition' is preferable not only because it is less emotive but also because it allows us to consider a wider range of pathways and mechanisms in its causation. The subdivision of children who fail to thrive into two broad groups, organic and non-organic, has been criticised because of its oversimplification of a complex area. Clearly there are many patterns of failure to thrive — as many as there are individual cases.

It is useful, however, to differentiate physical from psychosocial factors albeit with the acknowledgement that both can exist in a single child and that physical factors can have profound effects on psychological functioning such that one is bound to feel that these factors are almost primary in causation.

In the USA, paediatricians who have written much about this problem mention that the term failure to thrive was used at the beginning of this century to describe the sad and pathetic state of infants living in institutions or hospitals (Spitz 1945). Radbill (1987) referred to 'children who failed badly under the dismal routine of institutions. They suffered from deprivation and starvation with little consideration for their recreational needs. A visitor to a foundling asylum was dejected by the sight of children sitting all day long bound to potty chairs. Few survived'.

Interestingly, in more recent times, Izuora & Epigbo (1983) found similar reactions amongst adult Africans who were looking after children with severe kwashiorkor in Nigeria in the 1980s. In this study, the effects of such children not only on their parents but also on the staff caring for them was found to be marked. Adults tended to become depressed, apathetic and unresponsive to the needs of the children, thus perpetuating the cycle. Kwashiorkor, a prevalent form of malnutrition in the developing world, has also been described elsewhere, for example in the USA.

The recognition of the importance of institutional factors in the aetiology of failure to thrive was the first time attention had been focused onto this problem and links made between 'depression' (usually termed 'anaclitic' depression), malnutrition and growth failure. With the interest after the Second World War in the wider welfare of the family and children, and the beginning of official acknowledgement of physical abuse, it became recognised that failure to thrive could also occur within the family (Coleman & Provence 1957).

However, non-organic failure to thrive has received little attention until recently. In one British paediatric textbook (Ellis & Mitchell 1965), whilst the battered baby syndrome was beginning to be recognised, marasmus or infantile atrophy received only brief mention, acknowledging that 'whilst it may arise simply from underfeeding, it is more often due to a variety of other causes, e.g. chronic infection of any type, chronic diarrhoea, coeliac disease, mental defect, parasitic infection, metabolic disorder or even prolonged hospitalisation'. There is no discussion of psychosocial factors or what is meant by 'underfeeding'. Similarly, in the chapter on growth, dwarfism is linked to various skeletal, endocrine, metabolic and other problems or referred to as 'simple hereditary' — racial and familial.

However, the proof of any hypothesis must be in its testing and it is with the theoretical basis of failure to thrive. The clinical trials of Whitten et al, published in 1969, confirmed that failure to thrive resulted from a lack of food and could be largely resolved by feeding adequate calories. Supernormal calorie intake was required in order for the underweight children to grow if they were admitted to hospital and simply fed without providing additional stimulation or affection. What Whitten et al's studies showed was that it was basically a deficiency of calories which caused the clinical picture and that if the calories could be replaced then the child would recover. However, not all the children responded by taking extra food and growing. This observation does not detract from the main hypothesis that these children are primarily short of calories. However, it does indicate that the situation is more complex for some of the children than simply food withholding: the child becomes part of the process, i.e. it is interactional, and there are important additional factors in operation in many cases.

In summary, therefore, although failure to thrive in the absence of organic disease was originally regarded as an outcome of emotional deprivation, it is now clearly accepted that it results from inadequate nutrition and nurturing, though the causes of poor feeding practices may well have origins in psychological difficulties of the parents and are ultimately contributed to by the child. This formulation is vitally important. The fact that treatment is possible through improvement in the child's nutritional intake provides strong support to this view.

DEFINITION

Failure to thrive occurs when an infant or child fails to achieve the expected growth as assessed by measurements of weight and height. The child may also fail to achieve full potential in other parameters of development.

In a sense it is best considered a symptom of a wider disorder, in psychosocial terms, usually involving the parents and the family situation. In practice, it is best not to spend too much time debating on the grounds of growth criteria whether the child is failing to thrive or not, but instead to stand back and look at the wider situation surrounding the child. Failure to nourish an infant usually occurs amidst a range of parenting

difficulties and these become apparent as the picture of the family emerges over time.

Failure to thrive is defined as a failure to achieve the normal potential for growth and is related to undernutrition and insufficient calories. This may come about simply by the infant or child not having enough food or being fed on a bizarre diet, including for instance a vegan diet. Adults may do well on a strict vegetarian diet but infants and small children simply do not thrive under such circumstances.

Failure to thrive undoubtedly persists throughout childhood into adolescence, and patterns of poor feeding may be found in adults who have failed to thrive as infants. However, the term is most usually applied to babies and toddlers, although it is quite legitimate to use it with older children.

As the problem of failure to thrive most often comes to notice through deviations of growth from the normal expected pattern, it should be said that the definition of failure to thrive must start with an understanding of the nature of normal and abnormal growth within populations of children. Failure to thrive includes not only failure to grow but also failure to develop intellectually and emotionally. These other aspects are equally important in the whole problem of failure to achieve potential. Figure 3.1 demonstrates the theoretical model of failure to thrive described in this chapter.

CONSEQUENCES OF FAILURE TO THRIVE

Mortality and morbidity

Failure to thrive is linked with an increased risk of death. In developed countries death following failure to thrive may be linked to serious abuse or neglect but there will also be deaths from infectious disease where failure to thrive must be considered an important contributing factor. The major area of concern remains the substantial morbidity that arises from undernutrition at important and critical times in the development of the individual.

Because growth, especially of the brain, is so rapid early on in life, particularly up to the second year, this early period is the most vulnerable part

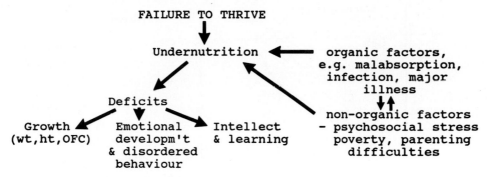

FAILURE TO THRIVE

↓

Undernutrition ← **organic factors,
e.g. malabsorption,
infection, major
illness**

↓↑

Deficits

**non-organic factors
– psychosocial stress
poverty, parenting
difficulties**

**Growth
(wt,ht,OFC)** | **Emotional
developm't
& disordered
behaviour** | **Intellect
& learning**

Fig. 3.1 Pathways in failure to thrive.

of the human life cycle (Fig. 3.2). According to Taylor & Taylor (1976), 'The period between the start of weaning and the fifth birthday is nutritionally the most vulnerable segment of the human life cycle. Rapid growth, loss of passive immunity and as yet undeveloped acquired immunity against infection produce dietary needs more specific and inflexible than at later periods'.

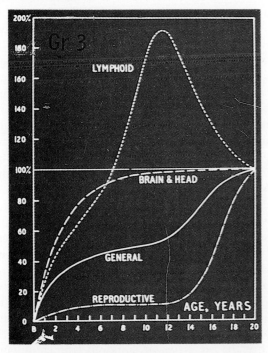

Fig. 3.2 Growth patterns of different parts and tissues of the body, showing the four chief types. All the curves are of size attained and plotted as percentage of total gain from birth to 20 years, so that size at age 20 is 100 vertical scale. (Reproduced with permission from Tanner 1962 Growth at adolescence, 2nd edn. Blackwell Scientific Publications, Oxford.)

Undernutrition at this stage rapidly leads to a curtailment of growth in order to preserve other essential body functions vital to survival. The damage inflicted by this is almost certainly likely to be permanent, related to both the severity of growth retardation, its duration and the age at which it occurs. Illingworth (1983) indicated that '... studies all over the world have shown that severe growth retardation in the first year retards later mental development, and the longer the duration of the growth retardation, the greater is the effect on mental development'.

We now appreciate that 'catch-up' is possible leading to improved growth and development but how far potential can be permanently reduced remains unclear and certainly unquantifiable at present (Fig 3.3).

Continued poor growth

Athough all failure to thrive children have the potential to catch up growth it is a feature of failure to thrive that poor growth continues in many cases once it has begun. However, there are other children who do not catch up satisfactorily or do so only in part. Skuse (1988) studied a cohort of 200 children born in an inner city population and identified FTT in 39 cases. Interestingly the majority (over 70%) of these children had not been referred for a specialist opinion for their failure to thrive. He successfully followed up 34 of the children noting that 15 (44%) remained below the third centile for weight on their 3rd birthday.

Even with hospitalisation and outreach programmes, Sturm & Drotar (1989) found significant

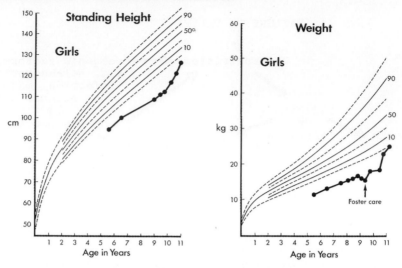

Fig. 3.3   Growth charts (height and weight) of a girl suffering from severe and longstanding social deprivation and failure to thrive. Admission to foster-care at age 9 years resulted in improvement in growth, general wellbeing and emotional development and behaviour but educational attainment remained poor with moderate to severe learning difficulties.

continuing growth problems in 59 3-year-olds hospitalised as infants. When children are followed up for longer, fewer children are likely to remain below the 3rd centile. Oates et al (1985) found that on follow-up of 14 children admitted to hospital 13 years earlier, none were below the 3rd centile for weight and only one was below the 3rd centile for height, although 6 were one or more years below their chronological age for height and also for weight.

Reduced developmental attainment

Whilst it is clear that some improvement in growth can be expected with or without intervention in some children over time (Mitchell et al 1980), it is not so clear how neurodevelopmental attainment progresses in these children. Developmental scores on follow-up of these children have shown a high frequency of being depressed (Elmer et al 1969, Chase & Martin 1970, Hufton & Oates 1977, Skuse 1988). Children who have failed to thrive show reduced scores on tests of language development, reading age, social maturity and verbal intelligence on follow-up in school (Hufton & Oates 1977). Furthermore, Skuse (1988) suggests from his data that late improvement of growth by age 4 for children who have

severely failed to thrive is not correlated with any better neurodevelopmental attainment in comparison to those children who persist in poor growth. It is beyond the scope of this text to discuss in detail the relationship between intellectual development and nutrition. However, there is evidence to show that brain growth is maximal up to the end of the second year of life and that the adult number of neurons is achieved quite early in brain development, perhaps as early as 20 weeks after conception (Frank & Zeisel 1988). A further period of cellular multiplication commences at about 25 weeks and probably ends in the second year of postnatal life. The difficulties of disentangling the direct effect of nutrition from the concomitant effects of poor social environment which are usually also present in families with malnourished children pose a problem for research. However, studies such as that of Evans et al (1980) support the view that improved nutrition in malnourished children early in life may improve verbal intelligence.

For the same reason, children who show poor brain growth (linked to head circumference) should theoretically command our increased concern as potentially they are at greater risk of intellectual retardation. This may necessitate more aggressive and early intervention.

Personality and behaviour problems

Behavioural disturbance is commonly associated with failure to thrive. On follow-up, children who fail to thrive score lower on tests of ego strength and emotional stability. Behavioural difficulties may persist even after recovery in growth. The psychological consequences are discussed throughout the chapter. However two studies substantiate some of the concerns for these children. While Mitchell et al (1980) reported that FTT children in an outpatient sample did not show more behavioural problems when compared with a control group, Oates et al (1985) showed clear differences in their clinical group of children failing to thrive. There was a high prevalence of reported behavioural problems in the children who failed to thrive when they were followed up at 12 years of age. Both Mitchell and Oates in the same studies found that those children who FTT showed long-term intellectual deficits.

CASE HISTORY 1
A mother was informed from the antenatal observations of her doctors that her first infant had congenital heart block. She was very carefully monitored both before and during labour and her baby was taken to the special care unit for management after birth. She remembered vividly when visiting her baby an overwhelming feeling that her infant had died and it was a great shock to find that she was alive. The infant required no initial treatment and had good circulatory function maintained with a bradycardia of around 50–60 beats per minute.

The mother was intelligent but from a poor family, her husband unemployed and their housing in poor condition and damp. She soon became pregnant again and her first child started to fail to thrive. There were difficulties with in-laws who tended to use the couple to sort out their arguments. The mother continued to believe that the child would eventually die and was sure that the obvious malnutrition was directly caused by the congenital heart block although she was strongly advised to the contrary by the doctors. Observations of the mother and child revealed little physical contact and generally negative patterns of interaction. The child was hyperactive, attention seeking and resorted to difficult and 'naughty' behaviour to get her mother's generally 'hostile' attention.

At about two years of age, a pacemaker was inserted because of persisting bradycardia without any signs of cardiac failure. The pacemaker worked well and the mother was able to check for herself that the heart was beating faster. The child started to thrive, her behaviour improved, the second child was born and thrived and the mother spontaneously commented that she felt closer to her first child. An air of optimism surrounded the situation and she had arranged a holiday — the first she had had since the child had been born.

This case illustrates the complexity of the problem of failure to thrive. Clearly the serious anxieties surrounding the child's condition before and after birth had affected the mother–child relationship. The insertion of the pacemaker had changed the situation and the mother had allowed the relationship to become more secure and herself to feel closer to her child.

It is therefore better to understand what is happening in the processes surrounding the child's nutrition than to have an over-inclusive categorisation.

CASE HISTORY 2
The parents had brought baby Emma to the clinic because both the health visitor and the general practitioner had told the parents that they were concerned that Emma was not putting on weight as she should and that her growth was falling behind. The health visitor had paid extra attention to the case and given the mother help and advice. During this time she had noted that the mother found it hard to hold Emma when she was feeding her and was much inclined to prop her up with cushions and resting the bottle in such a way that Emma could feed by herself. Emma was inclined to go to sleep during the feed. If father was around during the feeding he did not attempt to intervene, leaving the child care to his wife. When he was asked whether he would take over feeding Emma at those times he was at home, he said that he felt this would interfere with his wife's routine and that he did not wish to 'meddle' in what she was doing in the home.

It is important to pay particular attention to what contributes to the FTT of the child both from the parental and the child's point of view. The case of the mother and child described above highlights a number of issues relevant to the relationship of mother and child, father and child and mother and father, as well as the fact that the child is not growing. Discussions with the parents can bring in issues to do with the feeding, with mother's difficulties about holding Emma, and what thoughts the couple have on why this might be so. At the next stage it might be feasible to explore what holds father back from feeding his child and — as he put it — 'meddle' in his wife's business. When the health visitor asked what Emma's sleeping pattern was like, she was informed that Emma had previously been a poor sleeper, that she would wake and scream in the night, but that during the last three months this had disappeared and Emma had her last feed at 20:00 to 20:30 and did not make a noise until 7:00 the following day. The sequence of events is often not 'visible' to the parents and a discussion about what has been noted, particularly if it can be undertaken in a neutral and non-blaming way, can frequently have a positive effect.

ASSESSMENT OF GROWTH

Normal infants and children never remain static in their physical and mental characteristics due to the continuing process of growth and development. Understanding the normal patterns of growth and development is essential if the problem of failure to thrive is to be addressed. Data from populations of children relating to growth and development is widely available (for example in Buckler 1979).

Centile distributions

For any given measurement, for example weight or height, the distribution of values within a defined population is conveniently shown on a centile chart. The position on the chart indicates the proportion (or percentage) of the population with values greater or smaller than that of the particular individual measured. Therefore, if the individual lies on the 25th percentile, 25% of individuals will have smaller values and 75% greater values at a given age. Relationships between centiles and standard deviations for a Gaussian distribution are shown in Figure 3.4.

From this, it can be seen that – 2 SD from the mean lies at 2.28% and + 2 SD at 97.72%, i.e. roughly corresponding to 3rd and 97th percentiles.

The relationship of a particular measurement to the concept of normality is complex and various factors need to be considered, best summarised in the following statements:

1. We should be less interested in the terms 'normal', mean, or average and more interested

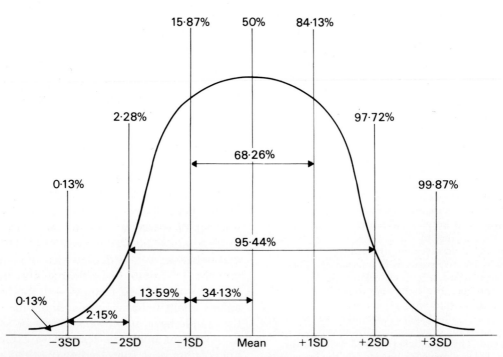

Fig. 3.4 Relationship between centiles and standard deviations for values with a Gaussian distribution. (Reproduced with permission from Buckler J M H 1979 A reference manual of growth and development. Blackwell Scientific, Oxford.)

in optimal measurements. For example, in some western countries, there are large numbers of overweight individuals which has the effect of skewing the distribution. Optimal values relate to those associated with good general health and appropriate development.

2. Whilst it is generally true that the closer one is to the mean value the greater the probability of 'normality' there may be situations — for example when a child has tall parents — where a mean value represents a failure to achieve optimum growth.

3. It is necessary to consider a wide range of information when making judgements about growth data.

Common measurements in failure to thrive

Weight

This should be a nude weight in a baby; an older child should be weighed in underclothes only. Because instrumental variation is possible, the same scales should be used for serial measurements. The baby is laid on a cloth or paper towels whose weight has been adjusted for. Older children stand on scales, not touching anything or anybody. Sometimes if a child is fretful or refuses to be weighed, subtraction weight can be obtained after being held in arms by an adult.

It is reasonable to record weight in kilograms with an accuracy to 0.1 kg or 100 g. There is little to be gained by any greater degree of accuracy as minor fluctuations with state of bowel or bladder occur in normal circumstances from day to day. Growth charts usually only permit charting to 100 g. Stones and pounds are now obsolete in professional practice but parents will want to know the weight in these units so conversion charts should be available.

Assessing changes in weight — frequency of weighing. Regular weighing of babies is valued by parents and acts as a focus of visits to a clinic or doctor's surgery. Mothers vary in the frequency which they choose for this but, in the first months, the more anxious or less experienced mother may visit weekly whilst others may come less often, perhaps 2 or 3 times only in the first year of life (Hall 1989).

Guidelines for weight increases are traditionally taught. The average weight gain in the first three months is 7 oz (196 g) per week, and 5.3 oz (148 g) in the second three months, falling to 1.5 oz (42 g) per week in the second year (Illingworth 1981). According to Illingworth, there is a strong correlation between birth weight and subsequent weight and height in the years up to puberty. If weight gain becomes erratic, static or negative, it will be necessary to follow the child more closely at regular intervals, depending on the situation. It is usually sufficient to weigh the child no more often than weekly and, in many cases, less often, say every 2–4 weeks, in order to check for subsequent growth.

Height and length

Up to the age of 2 years, conventionally length is measured with the infant horizontally extended and firmly held by two persons. Whilst measuring table or infantometer are most accurate, cheaper alternatives, e.g. Pedobaby, are now widely in use. Measurements (metric) up to 0.1 cm accuracy are made with the feet at 90 ° and the legs straight. Infants do not particularly enjoy this manoeuvre and poor cooperation can lead to inaccuracies.

Height is measured using a stadiometer or a microtoise fixed to a wall with the child's feet together, without shoes and with the child standing as straight as possible. The child's head should not be tilted and the lower margin of the eye socket should be on the same horizontal plane as the external auditory meatus. Height is usually about 1 cm less than length. It is not customary to measure length or height routinely in clinics or surgeries but the recent working party on Child Health Surveillance (Hall 1989) recommended a single height measurement at age 3 or sooner if the opportunity occurs. If, however, there is concern about a child's weight, and failure to thrive is being considered, measurement of height/length is essential both at assessment and for serial growth monitoring.

Head circumference

Routine measurement of head circumference is used to detect both excessively large or small heads. In severe failure to thrive, poor growth of the head may also be observed with head circumference measurements falling across the centiles. The measurement should represent the maximum measurement around the head in the horizontal plane. The tape measure should be of a non-stretch material and the child's head may need to be held firmly by an assistant or parent.

Mid upper arm circumference (Burgess & Burgess 1969, Jellife & Jellife 1969a, b, Frisancho 1974, McDowell & King 1982)

This measurement has been widely used for nutritional screening in the developing world but used much less in the UK or USA. There are no readily available centile charts. We have used the measurement most often from the age of 9–12 months as an adjunct to other measurements.

Between the ages of 12 and 60 months, there is only a small increase in the values for the 50th percentile — 15.9 cm at 1 year, 17.0 cm at 5 years for boys and 15.6 cm–16.9 cm respectively for girls, based on Burgess and Burgess 1969. Cut-off points should be derived from clinical assessments including weight and height. Between the ages of 12 and 60 months, the following values have been found to be useful and presented as instructions for primary care professionals.

MUAC less than 14.0 cm — very likely to be a significantly malnourished child and needs skilled paediatric assessment.
MUAC 14.0 – 15.0 cm — may be malnourished (likelihood greater if age nearer 5 than 1 year). Useful to make a more detailed assessment and monitor future growth.
MUAC greater than 15.0 cm — nutrition likely to be reasonable. At school entry (usual age of examinations between 5 and 6 years) add 1.0 cm to each of the above measurements.

In addition to this use of the arm circumference in complementing weight measurements and helping to sort out small normals from small malnourished, serial measurements assist in detecting improvements in nutritional state in failure to thrive. An increase of 0.5–1.0 cm in MUAC as measured by the same examiner usually correlates with a significant improvement in the general appearance and wellbeing of the child.

There are various methods for taking this measurement but the one which is most simply adopted includes the use of a loop of non-stretched tape measure in gentle apposition measuring against the 10 cm mark so as to give two tape 'ends' for the examiner to hold. The child's arm should be straight and, if possible, relaxed (down by the side). It is not necessary to accurately measure the midpoint of the upper arm in clinical work.

PATTERNS OF GROWTH IN FAILURE TO THRIVE

The normal situation

There can be differences of professional opinion regarding what does or does not constitute normality in the growth chart, but it is important that the chart is interpreted in the light of other information relating to the child's circumstances. The closer the child is to the midpoint (50th centile), the more confident one can be of normality, and the more closely the child follows such a centile the more likely he is to be in good health. Most healthy children match height for weight centiles fairly closely — for example if a child is on the 25th centile for weight, it is usual for the height to be fairly close to or on the 25th centile.

Irregularities in the growth chart of a normal healthy child usually reflect the methodologies of measurement. In general, growth is a smooth and continuous process and the longitudinal growth studies of individual children measured regularly under standardised conditions attest to this fact (Tanner 1978).

Abnormal patterns in failure to thrive

1. Falling centiles.
2. Parallel poor centiles.
3. Height and weight centiles markedly discrepant.
4. Family pattern discrepant.
5. Retrospective rise.
6. Saw-tooth — erratic fluctuating pattern (also referred to as dipping) Batchelor & Kerslake (1990).

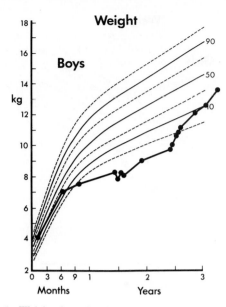

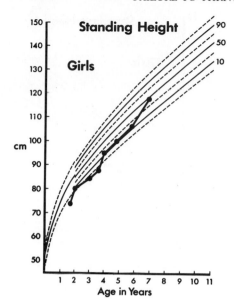

Fig. 3.5 Weight chart showing catch-up growth from age 2½ years when a diagnosis of neglect was made and conveyed to the parents. The child remained at home, showing that his normal growth potential could be reached. Same case as Plate 56.

Fig. 3.6 Height chart demonstrating gradual catch-up of height to 50th centile at age 7 years in an emotionally abused child. Same case as Fig. 3.8.

1. Falling centiles

This is the classic feature of failure to thrive.

Growth may often be maintained along, for example, the 50th centile until 4 or 5 months of age when a drop away commences, ultimately leading to a fall below the 3rd centile unless the situation is remedied. The child may continue to gain weight, although insufficiently to prevent the centile position falling, however, actual loss of weight will strongly hasten the decline in centile position. The 3rd and 97th centiles, below and above which theoretically 3 in every 100 children lie, are the conventional limits of 'normality' and clearly weights for children at the severe end of the failure to thrive spectrum will lie below the 3rd centile.

2. Parallel poor centiles

Many children who fail to thrive appear to go through a situation when their centile position falls and they then take a position of continuing to grow, sometimes rather erratically but overall parallel to the 3rd percentile for both weight and height.

Very often there is a small difference between centile position for height and weight, with the height generally the greater centile. It is now thought that these children adapt to an abnormal situation of poor nutrition and the situation becomes chronic. This is common in medicine where a homeostasis is established in an abnormal situation. These children are undernourished, their growth compromised and there are usually other developmental and educational deficits. Behavioural and feeding patterns also change but the children grow, albeit at a slower rate and the absolute deficit from the 50th centile becomes gradually greater. Only if there is a change in the child's circumstances, for example nutrition, social relationships or environment, will there be a significant change in the growth velocity; sometimes if the child is well adapted to the original environment the change will be slow and gradual. For others, it is more dramatic and allows one to perceive the abnormality of the previous situation. This is the so-called retrospective pattern and is seen when children are taken into care, often for reasons other than growth, and then show a growth spurt in a foster-home.

3. Height and weight centiles markedly discrepant

Other situations where failure to thrive should be suspected include discrepancies in the centile

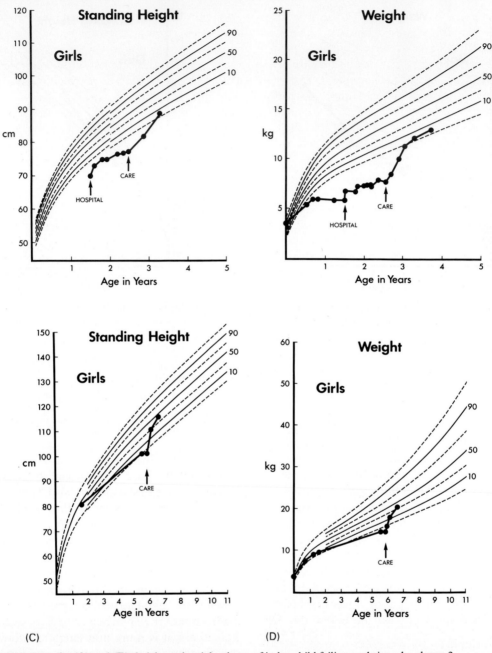

Fig. 3.7a-d (**A**) and (**B**): height and weight charts of index child failing to thrive who shows 2 episodes of catch-up growth. (**C**) and (**D**): height and weight charts of older sibling whose failure to thrive was unrecognised prior to admission to foster care but recognised only retrospectively when she showed accelerated growth.

ranking between height and weight and between the individual child and other family members.

Tanner (1978) states that at most ages a person at the 50th centile for height should be within the limits of the 10th and 90th for weight. A person at the 75th centile for height should be within somewhat higher limits for weight, very roughly estimated by moving all the centile lines in the weight chart upwards so that the 50th lies at the printed 75th and then taking the 10th and 90th in this position. It is possible that smaller differences in centile ranking for height and weight may have significance but Tanner's guidelines are useful. Rate of growth in height in some children appears better preserved than weight, and indeed many of the anthropometric measures of malnutrition depend on assessing the percentage expected weight for height. These deficits are more pronounced of course in children who are not growth retarded but who are malnourished. The relationship between height and weight is complex and its intricacies not within the scope of this text. However, one system found useful in practice is the Cole's slide rule (Cole et al 1981) which enables a weight for height ratio to be calculated, standardising for age. Cole has validated his method and provides a centile ranking for percentage weight for height up to and during puberty. The 3rd centile is at 85% and figures of 80% or below normally indicate wasting. However, not all children who fail to thrive show height and weight discrepancy, particularly those children who appear to be both nutritionally and emotionally abused. Skuse (1989) discusses these children and suggests that growth hormone secretion is probably dysfunctional, leading to a child who is proportionately stunted and has a low linear growth rate. Such children may appear not to be particularly thin and certainly not wasted but their bone age is likely to be significantly retarded. The child may be growing well below the 3rd centile and the body proportions remain infantile. There are other behavioural and developmental associations well described in the literature.

4. Family pattern discrepant

Children who fail to thrive frequently show marked discrepancies from the parent's attained height centiles. Ideally one should measure parents' heights and weights, not just relying on parents' estimates. Certain patterns seem to us to be prominent. Many mothers are thin, underweight and have poor eating habits. These 'failure to thrive' mothers can be seen as representing a generational pattern of failure to thrive. Obviously dismissal of the significance of the child's failure to thrive because the mother (and sometimes father) is also small on the grounds of a genetic predisposition would be unwise if there are other indicators of poor parenting and deprivation in the parent's past. At the other end of the spectrum, some mothers of children who fail to thrive are obese and are frequently trying to diet. This is another manifestation of eating difficulty, and the contrast in these cases between the mother's body build and that of her child is startling.

In some families there is a single child who fails to thrive and stands out from the growth pattern of the siblings and parents; it is always worth measuring and plotting all the children. However, in other families, all the children may show a period of poor growth, sometimes with recovery as they grow older. It is always important, therefore, to look at the whole family in assessing the significance of findings in an individual child.

5. Retrospective rise (Fig 3.7 C & D)

Improvement in a child's centile position may occur if nutrition is improved. Children who fail to thrive have a capacity to demonstrate catch-up growth. This was described by Prader et al in 1963 and occurs following recovery from severe illness or malnutrition. Children showing catch-up growth have supernormal rates of increase of weight and height during recovery. During these periods enormous food intakes have been described and foster-mothers have commented that several sizes of shoes and clothes have been outgrown at relatively short intervals. Occasionally brain growth is so rapid that it outstrips growth of the skull, leading to widening of the sutures and confusion with increased intracranial pressure in infants (Capitanio & Kirkpatrick 1969).

Figures 3.8 and 3.6 show periods of catch-up growth in an emotionally abused and malnourished girl. Between the ages of 1 year and 2 years and between 3 years and 4 years there is rapid growth — up to 3–4 times the normal rate.

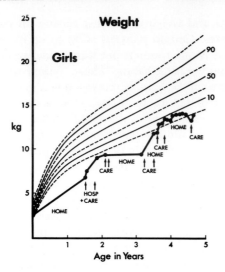

Fig. 3.8 Weight chart demonstrating the use of weights and life events to chart progress in a child with severe emotional abuse and failure to thrive. Prolonged efforts at rehabilitation to parents care have failed whilst the child repeatedly shows catch-up growth in substitute care.

6. Saw-Tooth

This pattern has also been referred to as dipping (Batchelor & Kerslake 1990), where the weight goes up and down, crossing and recrossing centile positions. Dips may be related to episodes of intercurrent illness, usually infection, but commonly reflect family stress around life events, e.g. parents experiencing difficulty in their relationship, mother feeling depressed, difficulty with child care or just having a good week or a bad week. Ups often coincide with support being given e.g. by GP, health visitor, grandparents, dips when help is withdrawn. Sometimes an association can be seen in some children with physical injury or abuse, as is well demonstrated in Figure 3.9.

Dips tend to be associated with incidents of injury and improvements in weight with active intervention. Actual loss of weight over several weeks is a warning sign that acute intervention is required.

Plate 52b shows this point clearly. This girl started to fail to thrive at around 4 months of age when care was transferred from grandmother to aunt but failure to thrive became more severe at about 11 months when she moved to her natural mother's care. She experienced actual weight loss which culminated in injury at 14 months. She

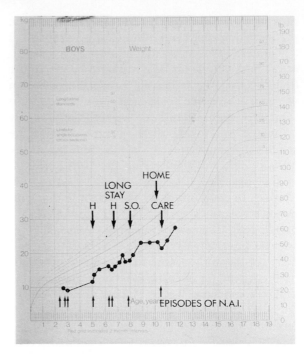

Fig. 3.9 Growth chart of a boy with a long history of failure to thrive and physical abuse demonstrating life events (H = hospital, S.O. = Supervision Order, CARE = foster-care) growth pattern and recorded episodes of physical injury.

demonstrates catch-up growth in foster-care, both in weight and linear growth. The absence of earlier measurements of length is usual in clinical practice in this area and needs further consideration.

CLINICAL APPROACH TO FAILURE TO THRIVE

Primary identification

Recognition that a child is failing to thrive may be parental, professional or both. Sometimes it is a member of the extended family or a friend who comments that the child is small and/or lagging behind in development. Active denial by parents or professionals is common, making intervention difficult. Initially, assessment may involve regular weighing until a growth pattern has been established and it is clear whether there is a problem or not. Many cases have been missed but with the routine use of growth charts for all children from birth, active health visiting and a greater willingness to comment on the kind of abnormal patterns discussed previously, more cases of failure to thrive will come to attention and before patterns of poor nutrition and growth become firmly entrenched.

Batchelor & Kerslake (1990) discovered that there was widespread failure of health professionals to discover failure to thrive even when they had collected the necessary measurements of growth. In two studies in which they focused on the work of health visitors they found a significant non-recognition of children falling below the 3rd centile as children who have failed to thrive. The reasons for non-recognition related to:

1. Social class — a child under the 3rd centile from an owner-occupying, two-parent family was more likely to be considered 'small'.

2. Well cared-for child — a child who shows no signs of being physically neglected in addition to low weight is less likely to be diagnosed as failing to thrive.

3. No reported feeding difficulties — if there are feeding difficulties, it is more likely that a child will be identified as failing to thrive.

4. Under-use of growth charts — the significance of single or unplotted measurements is less likely to be appreciated than where growth charts are routinely plotted.

5. Lack of treatment facilities — where there is little treatment on offer, it is less likely that a child will be recognised and referred.

Paediatric referral and assessment

The paediatrician faced with a child who is failing to thrive must decide how to proceed. Conscious that organic disease can contribute, he is faced with the question of whether to investigate for occult organic pathology or not. Goldbloom (1982) reviewed the literature on this question and concluded that 'with no exceptions, the differentiation between organic and psychosocial causes of failure to gain, grow or develop, can and should be based on positive findings, not on exclusion'. In both instances, the history, physical examination and simple observation of family interaction usually suffice to point to appropriate investigation and management. In expressing this view, he quoted Glaser et al (1968) and Sills (1978), and to these

can be added Berwick et al (1982), Homer & Ludwig (1981) and Rosenn et al (1980).

Sills (1978) found, for example, that many laboratory tests had been performed in 185 children with failure to thrive but that out of 2067 tests only 1.4% were of positive assistance and in every case there was a specific indication from the history and physical examination that there was an organic component to the FTT. It is therefore perfectly reasonable and sound practice not to undertake laboratory or other investigations unless there is an indication from the history and examination.

The subdivision of failure to thrive into organic and non-organic is somewhat arbitrary and artificial. The boundaries are not clear and there are many cases where the aetiology is complex and multifactorial. It is far better to think of the child who fails to thrive as having a nutritional deficiency and then set about trying to understand the existing factors. This will then avoid the kind of compartmentalised thinking that says that all children with cerebral palsy who fail to thrive must have chewing and swallowing difficulties and that the only reason that children from poor families fail to thrive is because there is no food in the house.

The next section will briefly indicate the main points to be considered in checking for organic factors and then proceed to discuss non-organic failure to thrive.

Organic factors in failure to thrive

Group one	
Adequate intake with poor weight gain	Malabsorption, e.g. coeliac disease, cystic fibrosis, occasionally cow's milk intolerance.
Group two	
Inadequate intake due to swallowing difficulties, inability to eat large quantities or vomiting or regurgitation. Conditions interfering with appetite.	Central nervous system disease. Oesophageal or oropharyngeal malformation. Gastro-oesophageal reflux. Severe cardiopulmonary disease. Chronic infections, e.g. tuberculosis. Inflammatory bowel disease, e.g. Crohn's disease. Intestinal obstruction, e.g. pyloric stenosis. Metabolic disease, e.g. methylmalonic acidaemia. Renal failure. Diabetes mellitus and insipidus.

This is not an exhaustive list. Almost any paediatric condition, if severe enough, may interfere with normal growth. Organic factors exist in some children and may be in a small number of cases the principal reason for the FTT. They need to be recognised and treated but details are not included here.

Assessment in non-organic failure to thrive

While the history is being taken there should be an assessment including the following points:

1. Both parents present.	Assess the family as a whole, parents' relationship, father's involvement and position of siblings.
2. Schedule more than one session.	In FTT cases the parents are often reluctant to talk about the difficulties.
3. Observe parents with child.	Valuable information can be obtained by watching patterns of relationships and the way parents and child manage the situation (e.g. who is the child most/least attached to).

History

Feeding history (supplement with diary card, videotaped or direct observation as necessary)	How much, what food, how often? Any difficulties in feeding. Refusal, vomiting, spitting or ruminating. Who feeds and how successfully? Do parents give up or force (find out indirectly).
Pregnancy and birth history	Helps to establish the emotional climate surrounding this child, e.g. was he wanted or planned for? Have there been miscarriages or cot deaths? Is this a replacement child?
What kind of child?	Is s/he the wrong sex, appearance, personality? what is easy or difficult about him? Contrast him with other children in and out of the family.
Child's health	Illnesses — infections, hospital admissions. Immunisation. Physical symptoms, e.g. diarrhoea, vomiting. Behaviour — sleeping, crying, tantrums, irritability. Developmental — history particularly language and social delay. Review of growth chart. Identification of major dips and rises in the growth chart.
Sibling(s)	Failure to thrive? Health, development, growth (measurements if possible). How is the family spaced? Other recognised maltreatment.
Parents' history	Are they married — if so, happily? What is the quality of their relationship? Are there stresses or tensions, anger? What is their psychological wellbeing? Do the parents agree the child is too small? Is the parenting good enough?
Mother's history	Health, eating difficulties, depression, low coping, tired, overworked, frustrated, poor self care. Is mother underweight, overweight, dieting?
Father	Present or absent, supportive or rejecting? Caring or distant? Doing the feeding?
Social history	Evidence of family dysfunction? Arguments, violence. Support systems, relations, friends. Alcohol, drugs. Bereavement, loss. Economic situation — employment, income, debts, expenditure on food. Housing, overcrowding, poverty, stress.
Professionals and others	Their views, advice, attitudes. Names, telephone numbers. Who can help? Nursery or playgroups. Childminders. What is the parent's view of professional advice?

Physical examination of child

Measurements

Weight Height Head circumference Arm circumference Other measurements, e.g. skin-fold thickness, velocity of weight gain or height gain may occasionally be useful.	Calculate weight and height age (i.e. age at which child's actual height or weight reaches 50th centile) and inform parents. Demonstrate and explain growth chart. Assess severity of failure to thrive and pattern: improving, worsening, acute, chronic. Comment on nutritional status.

Associated signs

Skin folds, hair, wasting, prominent bones, musculature e.g. back.	Pinch up abdominal skin between finger and thumb. Hair fine, scruffy, alopecia. Wasted buttocks, thighs. Ribs and spinal musculature may appear prominent and outlined.
Posture (Krieger & Sargent 1967)	Persistent flexed or folded, especially arms. Floppy.
Hands and feet	Cold and red 'deprivation' hands and feet.
Face	Pale, apathetic, lack of expression.
Mouth	Check teeth, dental caries, delayed eruptions, signs of injuries, e.g. traumatic ulcers on palate, torn frenulum.

Abdomen	Protuberant
Signs of neglect	Nappy rash, bald patch on back of head, dirty, ungroomed, poorly dressed.
Signs of abuse	Bruises, scars, other injury.
Behavious	Quiet, sad, withdrawn, pathetic, overfriendly, attention seeking, indiscriminate, overactive, constantly 'on the go', poor communication.
Development	Delay variable. Social and language, if severe, gross and fine motor.
Signs of organic disease	Depends on nature of condition. General effects on nutrition similar regardless of cause.

Behavioural and emotional signs

Certain characteristics may be more apparent in children who fail to thrive than in those who do not. Noting these behaviours over a number of years has produced some interesting results. The checklist (common signs, see below) showed that children in situations like failure to thrive may hold opposing behaviours in their repertoire which can be puzzling as well as informative for the parents, the observer and the child. In some ways this is of course perfectly ordinary; most human beings are fairly complex and can hold opposing thoughts, feelings and behaviours. As will be clear from the lists shown below this is nevertheless sometimes surprising, though for the purpose of establishing how to intervene it is most helpful.

Common signs: behavioural
(establish both the behaviour and date of onset)
attention seeking
in perpetual motion
restless
absence of appropriate play
impaired concentration
clinging or whining
disturbed sleeping patterns
screaming
destructive (self/others)
poor eating patterns
fussy or reluctant eater
ruminating
overactive
lethargic
noisy
going rigid
poor language
withdrawn
crying
over friendly
food fads
vomiting
fast eater
diarrhoea

Common signs: emotional
(establish both the signs and date of onset)
frantically searching
confused
stillness
expressionless
unresponsive
not inquisitive
diminished vocalisation
minimal or no smiling
demanding
sadness
depression
detached
insecure
anxious
angry
frustrated
tearful
rejecting

Observations
(Made either in the clinical setting, the home, or by video recording the child in either situation.)
poor feeding/eating
fear of feeding situation
fear of sitting down
fear of food entering the mouth (too hot, too harsh, etc.)
fear of adults
poor sleeping patterns
note periods without food
poor attachment
poor interaction with child
distant from child
over protective and over intrusive
parents' inability to play with child
child's inability to play with others or self

As already indicated, the material above is included to help to establish a pattern relating to the child who is FTT, not to make a diagnosis of FTT.

Parents of children who fail to thrive

May present as:

- depressed
- mourning, having lost someone close
- in ill health

- stressed
- having eating problems
- neglectful of themselves and children
- having poor maternal attachment to the child
- maternal rejection
- having difficulties in parenting
- having distorted and unrealistic expectations of the child
- lacking in education/knowledge about child care
- too poor to have adequate food in the house.

Iwaniec et al (1988) pointed out that these mothers in particular had recognisable difficulties when they were compared with a group of mothers whose children did not fail to thrive.

Mothers of FTT childern (Iwaniec et al 1988)

- often reported a disturbance in their sense of the child belonging to them
- report that they have little or no pleasure in the baby
- spend less time interacting (talking, cuddling, etc.) with these children
- pick up FTT babies/children less often
- smile and talk less to these babies/children
- play less often with the child
- report that they get on better with their other children who do not fail to thrive.

A mother's perception of her child can be a crucial aspect of how the child is growing. One study (Stratton & Swaffer 1988) investigated the causal beliefs of mothers whose children had been physically abused and found consistent patterns of perception. The mothers tended to see themselves as helpless, and the child as being to blame when anything went wrong. In the same paper a case study of a mother whose child was failing to thrive revealed a remarkably strong tendency to believe that nothing would change in the future.

It is well worth knowing what mothers and fathers believe their children to be capable of. Sometimes parents have very high expectations which their children can not fulfil, but parents may believe that if only the child tried he would manage to do what the parents wanted. This can happen to the most experienced parents at times, and the child will not suffer from an occasional misunderstanding about his ability, but when the

pattern is repeated over and over again and the demands possibly even escalate, the child can not cope and may show distress (see also Ch. 7). Refusing to eat may be the channel through which the child expresses his anxiety.

Overweight or underweight mothers and fathers. The parents' struggle with their weight can have profound consequences on their children. Body image is an issue for both men and women, from a fashion point of view as well as from a health point of view. If a parent has a distorted image of his or her body shape this may not only result in difficulties for the parent but may also affect how the parent sees the child and how the parent teaches the child about size and shape.

Because women are usually the ones who prepare food and feed the children, their influence is most often crucial in the feeding situation. The mother's health may be at risk from obesity and she may have specific difficulties feeding her child. In treatment the problems of both mother and child must be addressed.

It is well recognised that a mother may feel resentment whilst preparing food for the child alone. Her own efforts to avoid thinking about food may deny the child's needs. This is not to say that these mothers are harsh or uncaring, though some can be, but to indicate the complexity of the interactions between parents and children. The father's role is essential and if the father is also dieting the difficulties may be multiplied. Parents may also believe that children will grow on minimal food intake — low calorie food, and salads, for instance. Also, in our society women's ideal figures are thin and mothers may attempt to reproduce this ideal shape in their child. Under such circumstances children simply may not get enough food as well as receiving the message that they are causing their mother psychological discomfort and putting her under pressure.

Thin and underweight mothers. Another group of mothers who may have children who are FTT are those who are very thin; they may also diet to keep thin or they may be very thin for other reasons such as poverty, worry, stress and distress. However, these mothers too may use their thinness as a yardstick for the children's growth. Distorted body images can be a result of dieting and the person who is either very thin or overweight may not only have a distorted view of her own body but also of those around her, including her children. It is hard for those mothers to recognise what is happening and an 'outsider' such as a doctor or health visitor can, in a supportive but firm way, point this out and help the mother to achieve a more balanced image both of her children and of herself.

MANAGEMENT OF FAILURE TO THRIVE

There can be little doubt that effective intervention is required in failure to thrive. As has been demonstrated, failure of growth and development primarily follows deprivation of calories and food. The thrust of the treatment programme must therefore be to address the nutritional problem, although inevitably there will be other issues arising during the course of treatment which will need to be addressed.

Aims of treatment

1. To correct malnutrition and induce catch-up growth.
2. To address general issues of parenting to provide the optimal environment for the nurturance and care of the child and his or her developmental needs.
3. To provide support and care for the parents to assist them in achieving the first two aims, except where it has been decided to seek alternative care for the child.

Hospitalisation versus outpatient treatment

The vast majority of children who fail to thrive can be very adequately treated as outpatients. Work with the parents in the home, during visits to outpatient clinics in hospital, in community based clinics, health centres and other facilities such as nurseries is most helpful.

Hospital treatment is useful when:

1. severe failure to thrive, especially in an infant, makes treatment urgent;
2. extreme anxiety in the parents renders them in need of greater support and some transfer of responsibility for the child;
3. there is coexistent physical abuse which requires investigation and treatment whilst the child is in a safe environment; or
4. there is concurrent infection or illness.

Advantages of hospitalisation

In theory, at least, the calorie intake of the child can be closely monitored and a carefully prescribed diet administered, having been calculated on the basis of that required for a healthy child of normal weight for the particular child's length, plus an amount for catch-up growth. This will vary but it is usual to calculate to a figure of 50% on top of the basic requirement above (Kempe & Goldbloom 1987). Thus

$$\text{calorie requirement} = \begin{array}{l}\text{usual requirement for} \\ \text{healthy child of normal} \\ \text{weight for length} \\ + 50\% \text{ extra}\end{array}$$

Another recommendation of daily calorie needs for catch-up growth in calorie /kg is:

$$\text{kcal/kg} = \frac{120 \text{ kcal/kg} \times \text{median weight for current length}}{\text{current weight}}$$

The infant's weight can be monitored daily if necessary and signs of associated physical illness monitored. Investigations can be ordered as required and samples such as stool cultures more readily obtained. The parents' responses to the child and their approach to feeding can also be observed although some parents find the hospital situation threatening and may feel that it serves to emphasise their feelings of inadequacy. However, a supportive and caring ethos can do a great deal to assist parents who are desperate and feel that they are failing in the care of their child. This can provide the initial boost to their confidence and rehabilitation with the child if approached in a way that does not 'take over' the feeding and care of the child. Naturally facilities for resident parents and a welcoming approach to their presence are taken for granted but parents should also be encouraged at times to get away from the sometimes dreary and boring hospital routine, and attend to their own needs. During the admission the parents' practical involvement in their child's care will increase and they will have an active role in discussions about the time for discharge.

Children with serious feeding difficulties who are slow or at times resistant to feeding may often fare best being fed by a particular member of staff and this can be a highly personal situation. It is often the particular nurse who the child eats and feeds best with who is also most able to help the parents. It is usually advantageous for the child to have few carers, especially at feeding times, although in a busy paediatric ward this may not always be possible.

Hospital admission can at best be viewed as the beginning of any treatment programme and a launch for the crucial part of treatment which involves the parents taking full responsibility for their child's nutrition (Haynes et al 1984).

Disadvantages of hospitalisation

If the hospital takes over the parents' role, successfully in that the infant thrives, or unsuccessfully (toddlers in particular may not thrive), this may only serve to reinforce the parents' feelings of hopelessness, frustration or powerlessness to nurture their child. When the child returns home the situation may return to that before the admission or even deteriorate further. If investigations (laboratory, X-rays) are undertaken and found negative, a false reassurance that all is well may be transmitted to the parents who may feel that the child 'has been treated'. Similarly, children should be on an ordinary diet without high density calorie supplements. Failure of the child to gain weight in hospital (not uncommon if wards are very busy with seriously ill children), may provide a reason for acceptance of continuing failure to thrive and discourage further intervention.

The reasons, aims and conduct of hospital admission must therefore be clearly considered and discussed with the parents and staff on the ward if useful outcomes are to be achieved from the short-term manoeuvre.

Outpatient treatment (Iwaniec & Herbert 1982, Iwaniec et al 1985, Hanks et al 1988, Ayoub et al 1989, Schmitt & Mauro 1989)

Nutritional assessment in the home

An assessment of the food intake of the child can be made in the home by the parents and forms an integral part of the programme. The parents are provided with an open diary card (see Table 3.1) with an instruction sheet which requests that they record as accurately as possible what the child eats and drinks, providing times, quantities and brands, if appropriate, of manufactured food. It is reasonable to ask for this to be completed over 2 or 3 days and then to be returned to the doctor for analysis. If the services of a paediatric dietitian are available then a detailed analysis can be undertaken.

Information from the daily dietary diary:

- Total calorie and protein intake (can be expressed as a proportion of the recommended dietary intake for an average child of that age),
- Range and variety of foods given,
- Frequency and pattern of feeding,
- Variation from day to day.

A dietary record can be a helpful source for discussion and the development of advice on a practical level as well as a baseline instrument which can show positive as well as negative results of feeding a failure to thrive infant or child.

A diet diary can be very simple, and may be repeated at intervals and comparisons made. Records may of course at times be falsified, and 'food lies' appear on the record sheet. There are ways of detecting this. A diet sheet which is placed in the kitchen usually comes into contact with food; through its use it becomes creased and the handwriting is neither even nor the same and differences from meal to meal can be spotted. The reasons for under-reporting and over-reporting can form the basis for important hypotheses. Why should this have occurred? Is the parent feeling uneasy and why? Has the parent an inkling that the child requires more food and that they should provide it? Could under-reporting point to listlessness, tiredness, helplessness and possibly depression in the parent? Could over-reporting indicate that the parent/s are concerned lest they be seen as not feeding their child adequately and are therefore now overcompensating? Are they hiding something, if so what and why?

It is well recognised that parents whose children are failing to thrive often have low self-esteem and the fact that they can not give their children adequate nourishment is another blow to their psychological wellbeing. Bringing these issues out in the open has been found to be a turning point in many cases.

A suitable dietary record and guidelines to occompany it are shown in Tables 3.1 and 3.2.

The help of the dietitian can be invaluable at this point. Once a diary has been kept, the items of food can be converted into calorie and energy units and form another discussion point with the parents, including giving them advice on how much a child needs at any given time in their development to grow adequately. Parents rarely find this threatening and usually manage to contribute considerably. It quite often stimulates their curiosity and a dietitian is then able to make helpful suggestions as to how diet can be varied, what foods are over-represented or under-represented in the existing diet, etc. This discussion adds a different dimension to the whole issue and can be made to be therapeutic for both parents and child.

Many mothers, and it is usually the mothers who fill in the diet sheets, will record what the children have eaten. However, as already indicated, this is emotionally a taxing task; it can lead to the mother having to face the feeding difficulty and this can be very upsetting. Some mothers find it very hard because on one hand they genuinely wish to cooperate with the task but on the other they can not face up to the stark realities of their child's food intake. This may lead to the mother filling in the record sheet just before coming to the clinic. A 'food lies' record, completed only shortly before discussion with a professional and compiled from memory rather than describing what was actually eaten, may look like the example in Figure 3.10.

When this pattern occurs it is usually a sign that the parents are more upset than has hitherto been recognised and it becomes essential that:

1. the diet sheet is discussed in detail (including parents' fears, anxieties etc.);
2. the professionals indicate that they realise that the record is not correct;
3. parents are helped to reconstruct, possibly more accurately, what the child did eat during the day (doing it with a professional can be of help);
4. parents are provided with further dietary information if this is required;
5. enquiry is made about their cooking facilities (Have they got a cooker, gas, electricity? How much money is available for food during the week? Is this a problem?);
6. the professional enquires whether mother filled in the sheet or did she have to ask someone else to do this because she can not read or write, or has difficulties with such tasks?

Table 3.1 Dietary record

Name:
Date of Birth:
Date Record Started:
Where is the child (Home, Hospital):

Time	Day One	Day Two	Day Three
(o'clock)			
1			
2			
3			
4			
5			
6			
7			
8			
9			
10			
11			
12 (midday)			
1			
2			
3			
4			
5			
6			
7			
8			
9			
10			
11			
12 (midnight)			

Table 3.2 Food chart guidelines

Keeping a food chart will help me to get a good idea of which foods your child enjoys eating.
  Please follow these guidelines when filling in the chart:
1. Record *everything* that your child eats *and* drinks on all three days, including anything during the night.
2. Record the time, type and amount of food eaten.
3. Use handy measures to give an idea of quantity, e.g. 1 cup/mug, number of tablespoons/dessert spoons/ teaspoons.
4. Only record what food is eaten or drunk even if you have offered more. e.g. 1 slice of toast — ate only half.
5. Record the brand name of the food if using ready made meals or foods, e.g. Findus Fisherman's Pie.
6. Record as you go along as it is difficult to remember at the end of the day.

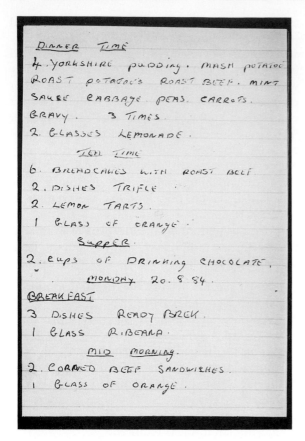

DINNER TIME
4. YORKSHIRE pudding. MASH potatoe
ROAST potatoe's ROAST BEEF. MINT
SAUSE CABBAGE PEAS. CARROTS.
GRAVY.   3 TIMES.
2. GLASSES LEMONADE.
     TEA TIME
6. BREADCAKES WITH ROAST BEEF
2. DISHES TRIFLE
2. LEMON TARTS.
1 GLASS OF ORANGE.
     SUPPER.
2. cups OF DRINKING CHOCOLATE,
     MONDAY 20.8.84.
BREAKFAST
3 DISHES READY BREK.
1 GLASS RIBEANA.
     MID MORNING.
2. CORNED BEEF SANDWICHES.
1 GLASS OF ORANGE.

Fig. 3.10 'Food lies — one page out of a diary kept by a mother of her child's eating habits. All the pages were in the same hand and pen. The child was seriously underweight.

Depending on the circumstances of the family, there may be further issues which are relevant and need further exploration. Such interventions can be powerful and help the mother/parents to develop ways and means to feed the child in such a way that the child gains weight.

Common patterns revealed by the diet diary

1. Reduced total daily calorie intake. This is the most usual finding, as expected, and results from infrequent meals and low total intake.

2. Strict 'three meals per day'. There are few opportunities for the child to feed between meals, with long intervals and no intake. 'Night starvation' is frequently a feature. Drinks may also be limited. Intervals of between 12 and 15 hours between intakes of food are not uncommon.

3. 'Healthy' diet. Food consists of low fat, low energy density foods. This has also been termed the 'muesli belt syndrome' as it tends to occur in those sections of society who are health conscious about what they eat. Dietary fibre may be high leading to satiation, but total energy intake is too low (Roberts et al 1979, Sinatra & Merritt 1981).

4. Chaotic pattern. This is characterised by little pattern and wide variation between the individual days. The child may receive sufficient on one day but substantially less on another.

5. Over-optimistic or 'food lies'. Occasionally parents express what they would like to think the child is eating or what they think the doctor or health visitor wishes to hear. Two Weetabix for an 18-month-old child for breakfast is a lot — some adults find this difficult to manage.

6. Refusal pattern. Parents repeatedly record that the child refuses what food is offered.

Timespans between meals. Children who are already failing to thrive do not manage well on three meals a day and need to have food offered more frequently. This can often conflict with what the parents have been taught to do, which is not to give children food between meals because it spoils their appetite for the main meals. Rigid frameworks and feeding schedules are still much more likely to be applied, particularly when one or both parents experience difficulties around the topic of eating. It is interesting to note how hard it can be for a mother to feed her child between mealtimes if she feels this is outside her normal routine.

The diary of food intake gives a clear view of the eating pattern for the child. It also shows the actual timespans between food intake. As illustrated in the case material, children who fail to thrive often can not manage without food for the entire night. This is more easily recognised for small neonates and babies in the first few months, but not for the child as he grows older. Two- or three-hourly feeding schedules are acceptable for the baby but may also have to be thought of when an older child is not managing to eat and grow.

There may be worries that the child might become spoilt and not give up the little meals and frequent feeding, spoiling the child's appetite for the main meals. However, once children gain weight and catch up, they themselves are more satisfied, less restless or listless and manage to learn new things, including the fact that mealtimes

Table 3.3 Observation of feeding practice

1. feeding behaviour,
2. interactions between parents and child,
3. hierarchy of family members, i.e. who is served first,
4. position and social arrangements for eating,
5. type and presentation of food,
6. quantity of food offered (including differences between members of the family).

will eventually become more spaced and fit into a routine which suits the whole family, not only the child. Both parents and professionals are often concerned with this 'spoiling' aspect and may need reassurance that children are adaptable and will learn to eat at different times.

Observation of feeding practice (Table 3.3)

An important aspect of management is observation of the child being fed. Where possible it is best to do this in the child's home and in the usual situation in which the child is fed. Recording of observations on videotape, if available, is also acceptable to many parents and enables the session to be played back and viewed and discussed with the parents if they wish. Sometimes additional information is available on reviewing which was not noticed when the feeding took place. Feeding observation allows information to be obtained on feeding behaviour, parent–child interactions and the emotions surrounding feeding. It also allows assessment of the child's eating patterns, intake, hunger and interest and any abnormal or unusual behaviour. How the child is held, whether he is allowed to participate, how hot or cold the food is, its appearance and presentation to the child are also noted. The parents should be asked to feed the child in the usual circumstances and setting which would occur if the observation was not being made.

CASE HISTORY 3
After seeing a 4-year-old girl who was failing to thrive in the outpatient clinic for some months without improvement, it was decided to visit the child's home and observe her feeding.

She was the middle child of five and her other four sisters appeared to be thriving well. The children ate in the dining kitchen, the food was distributed by the father and then eaten with the parents sitting apart in another room. The food was distributed in quantity according to a well-established formula which the father knew and could explain. The oldest child, aged 9, received the most and about 2–3 times that which the child who was failing to thrive received. The other three children, including a 2-year-old, also received more than her. The father explained that it was pointless to give her more food because she would not eat it and it would probably land on one of the other children's plates. The child confirmed the father's prediction and ate very little in comparison to her sisters.

CASE HISTORY 4
A boy of 15 months had been failing to thrive from about four months of age. He had had many infectious illnesses including bacterial meningitis but it was felt that his failure to thrive was primarily the result of inadequate feeding. His mother was a slim, unsupported single parent who negated most of the advice which had been offered, predicting that nothing would work. She said that he usually refused much of what was given him.

A feeding session was recorded in the home. The child was fed a large bowl of stew by spoon, initially with him standing with a toy in his hand. He started to refuse but his mother then held him tightly and encouraged him, eventually giving him a good-sized portion. Towards the end of the feeding both she and the child appeared to become more relaxed and she interacted in a warm and encouraging way with him. On viewing the film later, it was noticed that steam was rising from the food and it could be seen quite clearly that the child pulled back as the first mouthfuls of food touched his mouth. The mother said she did not wish to see the film but the temperature of the food was discussed. Shortly after this the child started to thrive quite dramatically after a long period with little weight gain. The reasons, however, were not clear.

CASE HISTORY 5
A 3-year-old girl was brought by her parents because she was failing to thrive and because there were a number of behaviours which made it difficult for the parents to care for her. The girl would not sleep, was restless day and night, clinging to her mother and generally a miserable little girl. The parents, from a middle class background, had an older child who had never presented them with such difficulties. The girl had recently begun to refuse food altogether and would go for long periods of time (e.g. breakfast to tea time) without taking nourishment. The mother had a difficult relationship with the child and she felt that this child did not give her half the pleasure the older one gave her at the girl's age or now. It was agreed that the child would be videotaped during feeding and her behaviour discussed with the parents. A suggestion to offer the child small amounts of food on an hourly basis for a short time was an easier task for father than for mother. The child went to bed at about 19:30 but would regularly wake up and cry. The father had begun to give the child food and drink if she woke up during the night, despite the fact that this caused

disagreement between the parents. However, they came back with the girl and reported that she was sleeping better when father was there to feed her at night. The child had indeed put on weight.

Sometimes the interventions seem unorthodox, as in this case, but what can also be observed is that behavioural and physical changes take place. The little girl in the last case was reported to sleep better, demand food, allow father to feed her, smile and play with her mother and other children. Mother in turn found the child easier and said that she had become a little more patient with her and no longer felt so helpless.

Most parents have no difficulties in recognising what kind of food children need at certain ages, even when they are failing to thrive. However it is important to check with the parents that they are aware of the dietary needs of their children and that they have adequate facilities to meet their children's needs. Again, a checklist can assist the practitioner and parents to look at what might be missing. Not every family has a cooker or electricity and gas, so it is important to know whether food can be cooked (Table 3.4).

Eating is a social activity during which much is learnt and experienced. Children do not often like to eat on their own, however difficult they may find the alternative. Hearing mother and father talking, and watching how the siblings interact with each other and the parents, grandparents and visitors are vital socialising factors. Learning how to eat food and what the rules are in the family makes eating into a very important experience. Children are influenced by this in many ways and their attachments shaped during such interactions. Mealtimes are much more crucial than one would at first glance believe, particularly in a family setting, and the ways of doing things are often reproduced in an intergenerational pattern. How mother and father were fed as babies and children, and how they experienced mealtimes while growing up will be remembered when they are parenting and feeding their children. In order to intervene and help the child to grow when he is failing to thrive, some if not all of these issues need to be understood in order to achieve change.

Type of food

Less emphasis is generally given to what is fed as it is usually quantity that is lacking. However, inappropriate diets, late weaning practice and overreliance on junk food snacks, e.g. sweets and the like, will need to be addressed at some stage.

Avoid substitute, synthetic or medicalised food supplements. Advice which relates to parent's financial and food preparation resources is essential. Cheap, value for money foods such as bread, milk, potatoes, eggs, baked beans, spaghetti, etc. should be emphasised rather than more expensive meat or manufactured food products. The ability to cook and prepare food must not be taken for granted and gentle exploration of the parents' knowledge and skills sought before advice is given. Advice must be coordinated if more than one professional is involved with the family, and networking is crucial. Contradictory statements lead to confusion and resentment.

Cultural issues need to be discussed sensitively and on an informed basis. Parents from different cultures are often only too willing to explain food values, customs and child care issues practised in their culture.

Table 3.4   Meal time and presentation of food

Is there a table,
is there a chair?
Is it fun for everyone there
and where is the TV?
Is there a plate?
Is there a spoon,
and a fork and a cup
to eat and drink with?
Is the food too hot,
or is it too cold?
Is there too much
or is there too little?
Is the food in too large pieces
or is it in liquid form?
Is it too spicy?
Is the child fed by mother
or father,
by siblings
or others (what relationship to child)?
Does the child eat alone?
Does the child eat with mother?
Does the child eat with father?
Does the child eat with siblings?
Does the child eat with others (relationship to child)?

The use of video recording meal times with the child

As already indicated in the section on observation of feeding practice (p. 37) video recordings of children and families eating can highlight a wonderful array of interactions and behaviours, which may provide many clues to the child's and family's problems about eating and failure to thrive. As mentioned earlier, mealtimes can be a socially highly rewarding time, and a platform for children to learn and communicate with their parents and each other. It has been recognised over time that the video recording as such can be a therapeutic process if undertaken sensitively.

The issues of recording the child's feeding situation, or the family's mealtime, must be discussed with the parents, and their anxieties about being scrutinised, watched and criticised must be dispelled. The video recording should not serve to criticise parents, but be used to explore aspects of the situation with them sensitively. Often, distraught parents do not realise how difficult mealtimes have become for everyone when a child is failing to thrive, will not eat, and is generally difficult at this time. Food is a powerful psychological weapon between children and their parents at the best of times and mealtimes can escalate into a battleground for all. It may also be important to make video recordings at intervals, so that progress can be noted, particularly when the progress is at first slow.

Watching the video together with the parents and the child can often be a moving experience, particularly when parents recognise their struggle as well as the child's difficulties. Video recordings can produce the same experience as one might have when looking at a painting for the first time, then coming back and looking at it again and discovering that something was simply not seen the first time round; was that apple really on the ground? Did the child really keep the food in her mouth for 3 minutes before spitting it out?

Some patterns of eating which can be highlighted:

1. Does the child eat on his/her own or with family?
2. Does the child eat off his/her own plate or off others?
3. How long does the child take to eat?
4. What does the child do when he/she has enough?
5. Does the child like to be fed or eat by him/herself?
6. What are the family patterns and rules during mealtimes?
7. Does the child use fingers or implements?
8. What do the parents prefer?
9. What likes and dislikes has the child?

There are many more patterns which can be gleaned from such a recording, both on a micro (details of interactions, feeding, etc.) and macro (family patterns, emotional atmosphere, etc.) level.

The parents sometimes request a copy of the recording and this can be an important moment. However, it should be stressed here, and explained to the parents, that it can be very painful for all concerned to have only a record of the poor feeding situation and that in such a case another recording showing the child eating when changes have taken place is vital. It might be possible to edit two parts of a video together and show the child at different periods in time. A video recording should not be kept by the parents in order to show how difficult mealtimes have been for parents and child, because this could be used punitively towards the child.

As with all interventions, when taking video recordings in order to help develop interventions and changes for the family, ethical considerations need to be thought through. The filming must be done in the child's and family's interest, and the family must know about it in advance and have the chance to give proper informed consent.

These considerations and the actual videotaping of mealtimes can bring parents and those who are attempting to help them together in a common quest to look at the difficulties and then attempt to work together in order to bring about change. This kind of intervention does not have to be threatening; it can be viewed positively, and even introduce some light-heartedness and fun.

The role of the father in interventions

Increasingly, more fathers wish to be involved when their child is failing to thrive and it cannot be sufficiently stressed how valuable their contribution in the intervention can be. It must be also pointed out that the father can of course be an important contributing factor to the child's failure to thrive. Though we have used the terms 'mother' and 'parents' predominantly, all our thinking applies to fathers as much as to mothers, whether one or the other parent figure is in the primary child caring role.

Management of denial

Many parents will maintain that the child receives sufficient food and may be angry at the implication that the child's nutrition is inadequate to encourage normal growth. It is as well to emphasise that there is no criticism or blame attached to this situation but that in order for the child to gain weight more quickly he will require additional food over and above his present intake. It is quite common, however, for parents to continue to deny the link with food even when the child begins to thrive. It is important not to be drawn into and accept the parent's denial. 'Everyone in our family is small and he is very healthy, so I don't know what all the fuss is about after all' may be taken as an open invitation to discharge the child from the clinic. It is obviously in the child's interest to resist this and maintain an objective professional view for the parents even if it attracts anger and disbelief.

The use of growth monitoring

An important part of management is the continued monitoring of the child's growth. At the initial assessment the parents will have been shown the child's growth pattern and his weight age given — for example a 4-year-old girl whose weight is 12 kg (about 1 kg below the 3rd centile) is said to have the weight of an average 2-year-old girl. Parents can be given their own growth charts and with the introduction of parent-held records this should become standard practice. At the commencement of treatment, intervals for further measuring should be discussed and agreed with the parents. In the initial stages weekly or fortnightly measurements are usual if the parent's efforts are to be sustained. As the situation improves less frequent weighing may be appropriate. Too much concern about weighing without other aspects of treatment can be counterproductive, and weighing by itself is unlikely to achieve much.

It is useful to give parents some idea of what is a reasonable weight gain so that they can have something to aim at. The improvement which may occur as weight increases provides feedback and further encouragement. The family may come to recognise good weeks and bad weeks and begin to understand how the child's weight fluctuates with the overall situation at home or with how the parents are feeling. Fluctuations in weight in children who fail to thrive are very common and these can be discussed. After a while parents learn to judge whether the weight gain is good or not even before the child is put on the scales and in this they come to feel more in control of the situation.

Targets are very important and the 3rd centile is often a useful one to aim for, although for most children there is still more catching up to do when that is reached. It must be recognised that the 3rd centile is only the lowest point on the centile chart and that for almost all children it does not represent their optimal chances for growth. The height centile can also be a useful guide to produce a target for weight in children with a wide discrepancy.

Whilst children are often weighed every two or three weeks, an opportunity to discuss the child's progress should in general be given every month. In practice less frequent attendances than this are not as helpful, especially at the most active stage of treatment. Once progress is being made and catch-up occurring consistently, less frequent appointments can be an encouragement but it is wisest to keep in touch for a while afterwards or ensure that continual help and advice is available from another source, e.g. health visitor, GP.

Education

There are many parents with children who fail to thrive who lack basic information about nutrition and malnutrition. Emphasis is put on the usefulness of teaching cooking skills and how to choose the appropriate food for children according to their age. Self-help groups can be of value, particularly if they can be housed in a community-based centre and supported by a professional like a dietitian or health visitor. Some of the reading material provided by the National Dairy Council or the Health Visitors Association, for instance, is helpful. However, when one considers the number of people at present who cannot read, who have difficulties reading or do not like reading, it becomes clear that providing information by such means alone will not assist all groups of parents. It simply can not replace the human contact, modelling and teaching which professionals and some voluntary groups have to offer.

Intervention

'Intervention' in this context is probably a more accurate term than 'therapy' or 'treatment', because it is easier to convey to parents and professionals alike that it is possible to be of help to this group of people, though this can sometimes be quite difficult. Chapter 15 outlines the different therapeutic interventions that can be offered and what is needed in the way of training to carry them out.

From what has been described so far, there is no doubt that complex medical, psychological and social dimensions are at work in cases of non-organic FTT. Intervention is essential for all concerned. The benefits for these children and their families when professionals have worked as a team have been particularly highlighted. Dietitians, health visitors, nursery nurses, doctors, psychologists and social workers all have something useful to offer (Table 3.5).

Strict vegetarian and bizarre diets

With a far greater acceptance of 'health foods' some parents have turned to vegetarian, vegan or other diets which are very restricting. While adults may experience no difficulties with such diets, children, particularly small ones, do not manage to thrive.

CASE HISTORY 6

Tina was 11 months when her parents, who were both strict vegetarians, realised their daughter was thinner and smaller than other children and was falling below the 10th centile on the weight chart. They were encouraged to feed Tina more food more often and to keep a food diary. It became clear from the food diary that Tina would be given cold cooked potato, carrot or other vegetable, which she did not like. Brown bread was also refused by her unless it had jam or honey on it, which the parents did not keep in the house. The parents reported that Tina did not want the food they were eating, despite the fact that they would mash it and select some of the things she seemed at times to favour. On observation it became clear that both parents brought variety and flavour into their diet by using hot spices, like curry, and it was only when mother cooked totally separate meals for Tina that they realised that Tina did not cope even with lightly curried foods. This caused a dilemma for the parents, because they did not wish to cook totally separate meals for their child.

This is an ongoing problem which is not easy to resolve. As already stated, the self-esteem of parents with children who fail to thrive is often already low and suggestions need to be carefully phrased at times so as not to further demoralise the parents. However it must be stressed that facing the issues is an important aspect of the intervention and professionals must be clear of the likely consequences for the child if there are no changes in management. Denial or thinking that the subject must only be raised very delicately would be detrimental for the child because in cases such as

Table 3.5 Multidisciplinary approach to failure to thrive

Professional group	Involved	Role
Health visitor	All cases	Recognition, prevention, advice re feeding, diet and child care. Empowerment of parents.
General Practitioner/Community health doctor	Most cases	Surveillance/recognition, referral. Support for family. Care of parents' and child's health.
Paediatrician	Referred cases (HV/GP)	Assessment, advice re cause and necessary treatment. Recognition of illness factors. Follow-up coordination.
Dietitian	Depends on availability Selected cases	Dietary assessment. Dietary advice. Support for other professionals and family.
Child psychologist/child psychiatrist	Complex cases Disturbed families	Management of complex parent–child relationships. Support and encourage positive parenting. Psychotherapy for family.
Social worker	Where associated with abuse, social deprivation	Child protection, case work, resource finding. Statutory function.
Others, e.g. nursery, family aide, home care worker, home-start	Selected cases	Promote parenting skills, support parents, assist with child's care.

Note: close cooperation between the professionals involved with the family is essential and joint working ideal.

Tina's the weight loss can be rapid and associated behavioural problems quick to follow.

Tina stopped crawling, would demand to be carried all the time, did not sleep easily at night, whined continually and became, more miserable and could only be pacified if mother offered her the breast. After a while she would refuse all solid food and only take the breast. Both parents needed considerable support at that time. They had become very angry and felt their daughter was rejecting them. There were times when they could cope more easily if it was suggested by a professional that Tina was probably ill and needed investigation in hospital, rather than accepting that what Tina needed was special food appropriate to her age rather than the food the parents ate. Once the 'deadlock', particularly between Tina and her parents, but also between the parents and professionals was broken and Tina received ordinary baby food, things eased. The food was vegetarian, but cooked with a baby's tastebuds and needs in mind. Tina began to smile again and generally became less clingy as she recovered and put on weight.

The balance of vegetarian or other specialised diets needs careful monitoring. Small children do not thrive on what are irreverently called 'muesli belt diets' or cult diets (Roberts et al 1979). Parents may need considerable help in preparing food for their children when they themselves are on such diets. Parents may often feel criticised if dietary changes are suggested and become defensive in a way that makes it difficult to find a way for their children to grow.

Diets related to failure to thrive in children

1. Parental food fads
2. Strict vegetarian/vegan or Zen macrobiotic diets
3. Diets high in carbohydrates, high in fibre, low in fat, and vitamin deficient
4. Breast feeding at an inappropriate age to the exclusion of other foods.

The doctor, dietitian, health visitor, or other professional may need considerable skills to discuss these issues with the parents and help them to work out a diet which will suit the child. The experience of grandparents can at times be very valuable, though the dynamics need to be understood by the professionals and great care has to be taken to empower the parents. If the family can be united in the task of helping with the feeding of the child it may relieve much of the tension that can develop in these situations. Not being able to feed one child can undermine the fundamental role of the parents and can lead to considerable lack of self-esteem, particularly in the mother.

Failure to thrive is often experienced as a major crisis which can escalate into a life-or-death situation for many babies, small children and their mothers. Mother's feelings of inadequacy have often reached a low ebb and may be worsened when others — nurse, friend or grandparent — can feed the child adequately. Parents often indicate that they have become demoralised and distressed by the feeding process. Some rally their psychological defences and come to believe that their children are the same as others in the neighbourhood, ignoring the evidence of the weight chart and other signs of their child failing to thrive. Professionals may join in this defensive manoeuvre and strengthen this parental belief, often by pointing out children who are thinner. This may produce comments like 'there are many children thinner in the neighbourhood and little Emma is just taking after her mother, who was small as a child too'. On the other hand, parents realise the seriousness of the situation and recognise the often destructive pattern they are in. These parents are often distraught and feel helpless to effect change in the eating behaviour of their child. A vicious circle is often the outcome for both groups, with an unhelpful preoccupation about food associated with a high level of tension. Neither position is conducive to change.

Attachment

The theme of attachment will emerge throughout this book and will be related to the different forms of child maltreatment. The concept of attachment is integral to any discussion of failure to thrive and parent–child behaviour. Bowlby (1969, 1973, 1980), Ainsworth et al (1978), Crittenden (1988), Ainsworth & Crittenden (1989) and Parkes et al (1990) have researched and written extensively on the attachments between human beings, and specifically about the attachment needs of the infant and child. The small child shows his attachment behaviour by insisting on close proximity to a few specific individuals, with mother and father figuring high on the list. Attachment needs relate to close, emotionally powerful relationships between two of more people in which each of them seeks for closeness. Children and adults alike feel more secure when they are close to an attachment figure. Attachment bonds between mother and child are particularly important, and how sensitively or insensitively a mother handles her child will have consequences both in the long and short term. For instance, the quality of attachment in infancy affects play and exploration on the one hand and cognitive, behavioural and social functions on the other. Attachment behaviours are crucial in the feeding situation and if they are distorted in this context anxiety and/or ambivalence feature strongly in the relationship and may lead to maltreatment or lack of adequate care. Because infants can form attachments to a number of close figures who take part in their early care, the mother is not the only one who shoulders the responsibility for her infant's attachment bonds. However, she is usually the key figure and the patterns of attachment which may develop depend largely on her care. Ainsworth et al (1979) showed that there are very clear patterns of attachment.

Patterns of attachment

1. Secure attachment
2. Anxious/Avoidant attachment
3. Anxious/Ambivalent attachment or Anxious/ Resistent attachment.

Any intervention needs to pay attention to the pattern between the infant/child and mother, and attachment figures other than the mother should be included in any assessment. Clearly if mother is the sole attachment figure, this can be an important indicator that support for her in her childcare duties is of relevance. How these concepts and the theory fit into our understanding of child abuse and its treatment are discussed in more detail in Chapter 15.

There are other writers and clinicians who have contributed to our understanding of the mother-infant dyad and Winnicott (1964) described beautifully the details in the interaction between mother and infant during the feeding situation in the early days and weeks of life.

Treatment failure

Success of treatment is measured by improvement in growth and development of the child, reduction of behavioural disturbance and a more positive nurturing and caring attitude towards the child.

Failure of treatment occurs when parents fail to comply, which usually means that they do not keep appointments or cooperate with treatment or the child continues to lose weight or to fall further behind in growth. These children are at risk of death or injury and active approaches must be taken. Removal of a child into substitute care requires statutory legal action in most cases; a case has to be made that the child is being harmed by his parents' continued failure to nourish him. Usually it is sufficient to show that his growth is seriously impaired and that there is no other cause that would absolve the parents of responsibility for this.

It is unusual for a court to make the necessary orders until the agencies involved have shown that they have offered all possible available practical help to the parents. This would include, for example, provision of necessary placement, family help and social work support as well as assistance with housing where appropriate (Table 3.5). Only then, and if the parents are either refusing or failing to use help, will an order be made. Sometimes legal proceedings have the effect of encouraging previously refractory parents to confront the situation of their child and provide the necessary intervention for them to start to work at improving matters. Rehabilitation will then need to proceed quickly and without the children being separated from their parents for very long. Use of the legal system to introduce external control in this way has produced significant results in some cases.

In the case of a very young infant who is failing to thrive in the care of an unsupported mother in very difficult social circumstances, early decisions about removal and adoption should be made, if at all possible. The outcome for the child is likely to be better if alternative care is found early.

It is always helpful to impose a time framework on difficult cases where the possibility of termination of parental care is considered. Older children with longstanding failure to thrive sometimes present, having been undiagnosed or untreated in infancy. These children frequently have associated behaviour disturbance and may show signs of serious emotional deprivation. They are often short as well as light and have bizarre or unusual eating habits.

CASE HISTORY 7 (Fig 3.3)

Josephine was aged 9 years when she was referred from school because she had said very little during the time that she had been a pupil. She had daytime wetting and appeared a quite shy child. Her weight of 16 kg corresponded to a weight age of 4 years and her height was 108 cm — also well below the 3rd centile.

She was uncommunicative but cooperated passively. Her mother acknowledged her poor growth and after counselling agreed that Josephine should be given a trial period in foster-care. She was fostered as the only child with an older foster-mother who gave her a lot of individual attention. Her wetting stopped and she began to communicate. She was moved to a school for children with moderate learning difficulties where she became much happier. She exhibited catch-up growth for both weight and height (Fig. 3.3) which have eventually reached the 3rd centile.

If a child is failing to thrive it is helpful to look at a variety of signs and recognise those behavioural and emotional patterns which are apparent in each individual case. This can be achieved by asking the parents, and/or by observing the child. These patterns are not meant to establish a diagnosis of FTT, rather they are there to help identify the particular difficulties which can accompany the failure to thrive. It is useful to establish when each of the behaviours first appeared. Whether the failure to thrive of the child is primary or secondary can be assessed and will be essential in the formulation and progress of treatment. As illustrated above, the relationship between various family members can be mapped and put together with the medical findings and the social factors that are part of the jigsaw.

Summary

1. Failure to thrive, whilst formerly only recognised in institutions, is now seen as part of the wider syndrome of child maltreatment.

2. Failure to thrive is failure to grow — physically, intellectually, emotionally, socially.

3. To thrive optimally, a child must be well fed and loved.

4. The consequences of FTT are profound and longlasting on health and development.

5. FTT should be recognised in primary care using standard techniques of growth measurement in a programme of health surveillance.

6. Non-organic FTT should be positively identified through a detailed assessment of the child and family. Laboratory investigations have a minimal part to play in investigation.

7. Treatment aims to improve the child's nutrition and promote satisfactory parenting whilst supporting the family.

8. Management is multi-disciplinary and close cooperation is essential.

9. Programmes of management should be developed around the child's home environment; hospitalisation should be seen as a last resort.

10. Intervention focuses on a detailed history of feeding and diet obtained through diaries and direct observation.

11. Parental and professional difficulties in acknowledging FTT may lead to denial, and this should be recognised.

12. FTT occurs in all sections of society, and can be associated with eating disorders in the parents, cult and bizarre diets as well as poverty, ignorance and neglect.

13. FTT is associated with other forms of abuse and can itself be considered a form of emotional abuse.

REFERENCES

Ainsworth M D, Blehar M C, Waters E, Wall S 1978 Patterns of attachment: a psychological study of the strange situation. Erlbaum, Hillsdale, NJ

Ayoub C, Pfeifer D, Leichtman L 1989 Treatment of infants with non-organic failure to thrive. Child Abuse and Neglect 3: 937–941

Batchelor J, Kerslake A 1990 Failure to find failure to thrive. Whiting & Birch, London

Berwick D M, Levy J C, Kleinman R 1982 Failure to thrive. Diagnostic yield of hospitalisation. Archives of Disease in Childhood 57: 347–351

Bowlby J 1969 Attachment and loss. Vol I Attachment. Basic Books, New York

Bowlby J 1973 Attachment and loss. Vol II Separation. Basic Books, New York

Bowlby J 1980 Attachment and loss. Vol III Loss. Basic Books, New York

Buckler J M H 1979 A reference manual of growth and development Blackwell, Oxford

Burgess H J L, Burgess A P 1969 A modified standard for the mid-upper arm circumference in young children. Journal of Tropical Paediatrics 189–192

Capitanio M A, Kirkpatrick J A 1969 Widening of the cranial sutures. Radiology 92: 53–59

Chase H P, Martin H P 1970 Undernutrition and child development. New England Journal of Medicine

282: 933–939

Cole T J, Donnet M L, Stanfield J P 1981 Weight for height indexes to assess nutritional status — a reminder on a slide rule. American Journal of Clinical Nutrition 34: 19–35

Coleman R W, Provence S 1957 Environmental retardation (hospitalisation) in infants living in families. Paediatrics 19: 285–292

Ellis R W B, Mitchell R G 1965 Disease in infancy and childhood, 5th edn. Livingstone, Edinburgh

Elmer E, Gregg G S, Ellison P 1969 Late results of the 'failure to thrive' syndrome. Clinical Paediatrics 8: 584–589

Evans D, Bowie M D, Hansen J D L et al 1980 Intellectual development and nutrition. Journal of Paediatrics 97: 358–363

Fomon S J 1974 Infant nutrition, 2nd edn. Saunders, Philadelphia

Frank D A, Zeisel S H 1988 Failure to thrive. Pediatric Clinics of North America 35: 1187–1206

Frisancho A R 1974 Triceps skin fold and upper arm muscle size norms for assessment of nutritional status. American Journal of Clinical Nutrition 27: 1025–1058

Glaser H H, Heagerty M C, Bullard D M et al 1968 Physical and psychological development of children with early failure to thrive. Journal of Paediatrics 73: 690–698

Goldbloom R B 1982 Failure to thrive. Paediatric Clinics of North America 29 (1): 151–166

Hall D M B 1989 Health for all children. A programme for child health surveillance. Oxford University Press, Oxford

Hanks H G I, Hobbs C J, Seymour D, Stratton P 1988 Infants who fail to thrive. An intervention for poor feeding practices. Journal of Reproductive and Infant Psychology 6: 101–111

Haynes C F, Cutler C, Gray J, Kempe R S 1984 Hospitalised cases of non-organic failure to thrive: the scope of the problem and short term lay health visitor intervention. Child Abuse and Neglect 8: 229–242

Homer C, Ludwig S 1981 Categorisation of etiology of failure to thrive. American Journal of Diseases of Childhood 135: 848–851

Hufton I W, Oates R K 1977 Non organic failure to thrive. A long term follow up. Paediatrics 59: 73–77

Illingworth R S 1981 Weight and height. In: The normal child, some problems of the early years and their treatment. Churchill Livingstone, Edinburgh, Ch 5, pp. 48–69

Illingworth R S 1983 The development of the infant and young child, 8th edn. Churchill Livingstone, Edinburgh

Iwaniec D, Herbert M 1982 The assessment and treatment of children who fail to thrive. Social Work Today 13: 8–12

Iwaniec D, Herbert M, McNeish A S 1985 Social work with failure to thrive children and their families. Parts I and II. British Journal of Social Work 15: 243–259, 375–389

Iwaniec D, Herbert M, Sluckin 1988 Helping emotionally abused children who fail to thrive. In: Browne K, Davies C, Stratton P (eds) Early prediction and prevention of child abuse. J Wiley & Sons, Chichester, pp. 229–244

Izuora G I, Epigbo P 1983 Emotional reactions of adult Africans to children with severe kwashiorkor. Child Abuse and Neglect 7: 351–356

Jellife D B, Jellife E F P 1969a The arm circumference as a public health index of protein calorie malnutrition of early childhood. Journal of Tropical Paediatrics 15: 253–260

Jellife E R P, Jellife D B 1969b The arm circumference as a public health index of protein calorie malnutrition of early childhood. Journal of Tropical Paediatrics 15: 176–188

Kempe R S, Goldbloom B 1987 Malnutrition and growth retardation ("failure to thrive") in the context of child abuse and neglect. In: Helfer R E, Kempe R S (eds) The battered child. University of Chicago Press, Ch 16, pp. 312–335

Krieger I, Sargent D A 1967 A postural sign in the sensory deprivation syndrome of infants. Journal of Paediatrics 70: 332–339

McDowell I, King F S 1982 Interpretation of arm circumference as an indicator of nutritional status. Archives of Disease in Childhood 57: 292–296

Mitchell W G, Gorrell R W, Greenberg R A 1980 failure to thrive. A study in a primary care setting. Epidemiology and follow up. Paediatrics 65: 961–977

Oates R K, Peacock A, Forrest D 1985 Long term effects of non-organic failure to thrive. Paediatrics 75: 36–40

Prader A, Tanner J M, Von Harnack G A 1963 Catch up growth following illness or starvation. Journal of Paediatrics 62: 646–659

Radbill S X 1987 Children in a world of violence: a history of child abuse. In: Helfer R E, Kempe R S (eds) The battered child. University of Chicago Press, Ch 1, pp. 3–22

Roberts I F, West R J, Ogilvie D, Dillon M J 1979 Malnutrition in infants receiving cult diets: a rare form of abuse. British Medical Journal 1: 296–298

Rosenn D W, Loeb L S, Jura M B 1980 Differentiation of organic from non-organic failure to thrive syndrome in infancy. Paediatrics 66: 689–704

Schmitt B D, Mauro R D 1989 Non-organic failure to thrive: an outpatient approach. Child Abuse and Neglect 13: 235–248

Sills R H 1978 Failure to thrive. The role of clinical and laboratories evaluation. American Journal of Disease in Childhood 132: 967–969

Sinatra F R, Merritt R J 1981 Iatrogenic kwashiorkor in infants. American Journal of Diseases in Children 135: 21–23

Skuse D H 1988 Personal communication

Skuse D H 1989 Emotional abuse and delay in growth. In: Meadow S R (ed) ABC of child abuse. British Medical Journal, pp. 26–28

Spitz R A 1945 Hospitalism. Psychoanal Stud Child 1: 53–74

Stratton P, Swaffer R 1988 Maternal causal beliefs for abused and handicapped children. Journal of Reproductive and Infant Psychology 6: 201–216

Sturm L, Drotar D 1989 Prediction of weight for height following intervention in three year old children with early histories of non-organic failure to thrive. Child Abuse and Neglect 13: 19–28

Tanner J M 1978 Foetus into man. Open Books, London

Taylor C R, Taylor E M 1976 Multifactorial causation of malnutrition. In: McClaren D (ed) Nutrition in the community. J Wiley & Sons, Chichester

Whitten C F, Pettit M G, Fischoff J 1969 Evidence that growth feeding from maternal deprivation is secondary to undereating. Journal of American Medical Association 209 (11): 1675–1682

Winnicott D W 1964 In: Davies, Wallbridge (eds) Boundary and space. Penguin Books

4. Physical abuse

Physical abuse (battering, 'Non-Accidental Injury' — NAI), refers in this chapter to violence directed towards children. A physically abused child is defined as 'any child who receives physical injury (or injuries) as a result of acts (or omissions) on the part of his parents or guardians'. The definition includes: actual or likely physical injury to a child, or failure to prevent physical injury (or suffering) to a child including deliberate poisoning, suffocation and Munchausen's syndrome by proxy.

Within these definitions, hitting a child does not constitute physical abuse unless it results in injury. The law states that parents may use reasonable force. However, several countries in Europe have passed laws against the hitting of children by parents. In the United Kingdom, corporal punishment in state schools is now prohibited, although it is permitted in private schools.

Corporal punishment

'Spare the rod and spoil the child' is firmly embedded in our culture. The use of physical pain for the purposes of discipline is long established. These views are still firmly held by a majority of the present day society. Although physical punishment has been outlawed in most other settings — for example prisons, military establishments — it persists with regard to children. With the banning of corporal punishment in state schools and codes of conduct to prohibit it in day nurseries, childminders' and children's homes and foster-homes, some progress has been made in acknowledging the limitations of this practice. Research however continues to show that hitting children is widely practised by parents of all social classes, involving children of all ages (Newson & Newson

1986). Supporters of corporal punishment claim it is simple, effective and often the only way of maintaining discipline. Opponents say it is associated with higher levels of delinquency, is ineffective and teaches violence (Newell 1989). It may create resentment and a desire in the child to hurt back. The child's self-esteem may be adversely affected. With regard to physical abuse, although there is clearly a difference between corporal punishment and physical abuse, it is obvious that the two are closely linked. Many parents who end up battering their children start out by disciplining them. The injuries resulted when things got out of hand.

Physical abuse varies from fatal to severe or moderate. All abuse is serious, and soft tissue injuries such as bruising involve considerable force in their production. This in turn inflicts pain and is invariably associated with some degree of emotional abuse, including harsh words, threats and rejection. The dangerousness of an injury relates especially to the age of the child. A small bruise in a baby may be a predictor of later serious or fatal abuse whilst a beating in an older child may denote no threat to life.

Failing to protect or deliberately placing in danger is as serious as deliberately inflicting injury. Such passive abuse may reflect a conscious or unconscious urge to be rid of a child. Acts of omission include failing to protect or deliberately placing a child in a dangerous situation (For example, leaving a baby in a bath unsupervised.)

Children are very vulnerable and few parents who shake, hit or slap a child intend to cause serious injury. Many injuries occur when parents lose control under stress, but some are sadistic and premeditated, for example some burns and scalds.

INCIDENCE AND PREVALENCE

Officially reported cases represent only a fraction of the total number of cases in the population as a whole. Reporting depends on awareness of the problem by the public and professionals including doctors, nurses, social workers, teachers and others in contact with children. Such awareness tends to increase following the reporting of a particularly serious, often fatal, case by the media. Referrals then tend to rise for a while.

The NSPCC's annual statistics (Creighton & Noyes 1989), based on a sample of registers covering 9% of the population of England and Wales, found an increase in registration rate from 0.63 per thousand (under 17 years) in 1983 to 0.82 per thousand in 1987. The figures suggest there were over 8000 cases of physical abuse registered in England and Wales in 1987. 0.6% were classified as fatal, 9% serious and 90% moderate. In Leeds, where cases have been recorded since 1969, Figure 4.1 shows the growth in diagnosed cases over the period 1969–88 (Figures by permission of M F G Buchanan, unpublished.)

It has been estimated (Creighton & Noyes 1989) that between 200 and 230 non-accidental deaths occur each year in Britain and that 1.5–2% of all children have been physically abused by the age of 17 years. Boys outnumber girls — for example, in the NSPCC's series from 1983–87, 55% were boys, 45% girls. Nearly half are aged 0–4 years, with about a quarter each of 5–9 and 10–14 years. 1 in 8 are aged less than a year, but 70% of serious head injuries occurred to children less than one year old (Creighton & Noyes 1989).

Physical abuse, however, rarely exists on its own and it is important to recognise links with other forms of abuse (Hobbs & Wynne 1990). 1 in 6 physically abused children have also been sexually abused and others have been neglected or are failing to thrive. Emotional abuse coexists in most cases. Physical abuse occurs to children of all ethnic groups, but possibly has different frequency between the groups. Handicapped children are seen to be at increased risk and, in one study (Smith & Hanson 1974), 13.5% of physically abused children had handicaps. In some instances, the abuse may be the cause of the handicap (Buchanan & Oliver 1972).

SOCIAL BACKGROUND

Physical abuse is reported more often from conditions of social deprivation and poverty, although it occurs in all social classes. In the NSPCC's figures (Creighton & Noyes 1989), only 4% of mothers and 5% of fathers were in non-manual occupational categories but, more significantly, 67% of mothers and 52% of fathers were unemployed and only 15% of mothers and 35% of fathers reported as being in paid employment.

15% of mothers and 43% of fathers had criminal records but often these were unrelated to crimes towards children. However, fathers were more likely than mothers to have a record of violence against adults.

There is a greater tendency for families in which there is a physically abused child to be larger than the national average — 25% of such families have four or more children. Very nearly half of the abused children are firstborn. Younger siblings also carry a significant risk, although the percentage of injured children falls with each succeeding child after the first.

Poverty

The dehumanising effects of poverty are well understood. Persons unlucky enough to be poor and not very bright are more likely to adapt to their survival in ways which are unattractive and harmful to others around them. Poverty where the

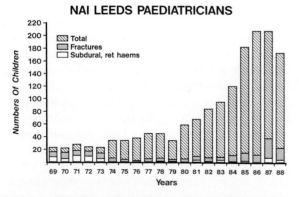

Fig. 4.1 Annual total number of cases of non-accidental injury seen by Leeds paediatricians between and including the years 1969–88.

characters are witty, resourceful and courageous is more likely to be found in the novels of Charles Dickens or George Bernard Shaw. Nelson Algren, a contemporary American writer reporting on what he personally saw of poor and dehumanised Americans with his own eyes, 'day after day, year after year' said 'Hey an awful lot of these people your hearts are bleeding for are really mean and stupid. That's a fact. Did you know that?'

The harshness of poverty is destructive to human values and child abuse is one of its legacies. That is not to say that all parents who are poor abuse their children, nor is it to say that abuse occurs only amongst the poor. But there is no denying the link. Low income is associated with a marked increase in violence. Detection rates are also linked to low socio-economic status, many times more cases being found in these groups.

PERPETRATORS

Natural parents or parent figures are responsible for causing the injury in over 90% of cases. Overall, natural mothers are responsible in one-third and natural fathers in slightly fewer (Creighton & Noyes 1989). If figures are analysed according to who the child was living with at the time, then natural mothers were implicated in 36% but natural fathers in 61% of cases where the child was living with them. Whilst mother substitutes appear much less often in the statistics, step-fathers and father substitutes, including cohabiting boy-friends of mother, account for almost 1 in 5 cases. Step-fathers appear to be implicated relatively more often than cohabitees. Occasionally other relatives or baby-sitters are implicated.

Less than half of physically abused children come from families with both natural parents present, but marital difficulties are common when both parents are present.

RECOGNITION

Presentation

1. Direct report

This may be made by a child, a parent or other interested third party. Most such reports are true and should, in general, be believed. Third party reports (often anonymous telephone calls to the NSPCC or social services) should be treated seriously but sometimes are found to have no basis, or to carry malicious intent. Worries by grandparents and other responsible family members also need careful assessment. The reasons for the reports must be identified, even if no obvious abuse is found.

CASE HISTORY 1
A boy of 8 told the teacher that he had not been to school because Daddy had given him a black eye. The injury had resolved and could not be verified, but there appeared to be no reason for the child to lie. A report was filed with the Social Service Department, who agreed to check any further absences from school through the Education Welfare Officer.

2. Presentation of an injury

Following abuse, parents frequently take the child for help — to hospital, to a health visitor or GP. Pointers to physical abuse include:

● Repetitive pattern of injury, but parents may use different hospitals to avoid detection.

● Injuries not consistent with the history — i.e. too many, too severe, wrong kind, wrong distribution, wrong age.

● Patterns of injury which strongly suggest abuse, e.g. bruising to a young baby (there are few reasonable explanations); multiple injuries following a moderate fall; severe head injuries in babies or toddlers; rib fractures; subdural haematoma and retinal haemorrhage from violent shaking; multiple cigarette burns; fractures in infants and toddlers.

● Presence of other signs of abuse — e.g. neglect, failure to thrive, sexual abuse.

● Unusual behaviour in the parents — e.g. delay in seeking medical advice, refusal to allow proper treatment or admission to hospital, unprovoked aggression towards staff.

3. Incidental discovery of injury

Abused children are frequently allowed to go to school, to nursery or to another person's care where injuries may be found and reported. It is not unusual for parents in this situation to deny knowledge of the injury and for there to be no satisfactory explanation.

Features in the history

It is unusual for the doctor to have all the information required in the history. The following is a checklist of important features assembled by the various professionals involved:

1. *Discrepant history* — does it change with telling or with who tells it? Is it vague or unclear? Exact details of time, place, person and actions are needed. For example, how did the child fall, how far, onto what? Compare your account with that of others — social worker, health visitor, policeman. Major differences need explanation. Do the father and mother give the same story?

2. *Unreasonable delay* in seeking help or care for the child, especially following a fracture or serious burn or scald, is a strong indicator. Denial that the child was in pain and minimisation of the symptoms are common. Following a serious head injury, a baby may be left tucked up in a cot, only to be brought hours later when he refuses a feed or begins to have seizures. One parent of a child with a serious burn said the doctor's surgery was closed so she didn't do anything for a week.

3. *Family crisis*. There may be a family crisis or a complicated home situation which has precipitated the injury. This could be, for example, a bereavement, break-up of relationship, loss of job or final demand for a debt. These stresses are usually revealed if parents are listened to.

4. *Trigger factors* are behaviours in the child which precipitate the parent's violence. Inconsolable crying in the night, difficult feeding or wetting are common; in older children, stealing or lying may provoke.

5. *Parental history of abuse*. Parent's traumatic experiences as children are important, but may be forgotten or repressed. Parents may admit to being beaten themselves as children. Some may have been in care.

6. *Unrealistic expectations* coupled to a poor understanding of child development. The child is expected to love and accept the parents. When he cries or won't take his feeds, it is because he is rejecting or punishing them. An expectation that a 2-year-old will behave in model and ideal ways is likely to lead to what parents perceive as a failure on the part of the child. Obsessional and rigid patterns of child-rearing may be expressed in other ways (for example a meticulously clean and tidy home) and can create stresses and tensions.

7. *Social isolation* from friends, extended family and professionals is a common finding in parents who abuse. 'Who can you turn to for help?' is a crucial question. As the abuse escalates, the parents find it increasingly difficult to allow anyone into their lives for fear of discovery. Abusing parents tend to attribute their problems to external factors rather than to their own difficulties.

8. *Past history of child*. The presence of high levels of parental anxiety, frequent admissions to hospital in the first months of life, frequent 'accidents', 'a tendency to bruise easily' are often found. The child's behaviour, growth and development and health may also be sources of anxiety. Much of this information will come from sources other than parents, who may minimise their difficulties in their eagerness to present themselves as perfect parents.

Summary of influencing factors in physical abuse

Socio-cultural:	attitudes toward physical punishment, values placed on children as individuals versus chattels, property, ownership.
Socio-economic:	poverty is a major stress which promotes violence, deprivation and child abuse. Not all poor families abuse.
Unemployment:	a special kind of social stress, linked with poverty.
Family breakdown:	unstable marital relationships, spouse violence, separation and divorce. Loss of extended family supports from increased social mobility.
Health:	poor health in parents, especially mother, reduces coping and tolerance levels. Psychiatric illness or poor psychological health including symptoms of stress. Alcohol and drug usage including prescribed psychotropic drugs.
Handicap:	one child factor that is important. Difficult children to care for — e.g. screamers, poor feeders — are other examples.
Education:	lack of education and the personal resources this brings results in fewer ways of coping. Low intelligence is another factor.
Poor parenting:	either from poor childhood experiences, or lack of opportunity to learn.

Individual:	youth, immaturity, isolation, criminality are all adverse factors.
Generational:	the tendency to repeat the cycle of abuse from generation to generation.
Environmental:	effects of cold, damp, overcrowded housing, nowhere for the children to play, enforced proximity.
Services:	lack of appropriate, accessible services — e.g. day care, nurseries, maternal and child health services.

Denial

As with all forms of abuse, denial that the injury arose non-accidentally is commonly encountered. Whilst it is the parents who are usually most actively involved in the denial, others — including the child, other family members and professionals, especially those who know the family — may also be involved.

Parents may convince themselves that there has been no abuse and may even go as far as claiming that there is no injury. This is to be distinguished from deliberate attempts to conceal or lie which are also commonly encountered. In denial the parents may appear remarkably unmoved and their simple logic 'If I'd done that to him, would I have been so foolish to have brought him to hospital?' can be quite appealing to the inexperienced. Denial is best seen as a coping mechanism to reduce the distress surrounding the crisis of the diagnosis. The seriousness of denial lies in the way that it very effectively prevents any intervention or change. Professional denial has the same effect.

PROCEDURES

Approaches to investigation

Key figures include:
- Social worker
- Paediatrician
- Police officer.

Vital sources of information:
- General practitioner
- Accident and Emergency doctor or nurse
- Health visitor, school nurse or midwife
- Paediatric nurse (if child in hospital)

- Other individuals — e.g. probation officer, obstetrician, adult psychiatrist and staff, pathologist — can occasionally help
- Other sources — other hospitals, towns, armed forces units.

It is usual for each team to have a central coordinator of information, usually a social worker, who will become the key worker. One task is to contact those with information and check the important facts and opinions, carefully drawing distinctions between the two types of information.

A general practitioner might say 'I've known this family for five years and I'm sure these parents couldn't injure their baby', but may go on to say that the mother has been on antidepressant medication following the birth of the baby and only last year lost her own mother with cancer. He may say 'I don't see much of the father, he rarely comes in but I was asked for a report for a recent insurance medical and he was overweight and had been drinking rather more heavily than usual recently'.

The health visitor might say 'This is the first baby and the pregnancy went reasonably smoothly, although the mother needed a lot of support at the time of delivery and was noted to be withdrawn and tearful whilst she was in hospital. We wondered about a psychiatric opinion, but decided to let the GP know on discharge. The father visited but didn't seem to be a great help. The home is usually very clean and tidy, perhaps a little spartan but recently mother hasn't been managing with the housework as the baby has been keeping them up a lot at night with crying. There was a brief admission to hospital when we thought he had pyloric stenosis because the mother described projectile vomiting, but he settled very quickly and took his bottles well. I've called two or three times when there has been no-one in, or at least no-one answered the door, but on one visit there was a tiny mark just by the side of his eye which his mother said she thought could have been caused by a rattle in his cot.'

The information must be collated quickly and accurately but will be discussed in more detail at the case conference. The police may or may not know the family, but if a name and date of birth are available they will be able to check if there is a history of violence or assault against children.

Medical examination (Buchanan 1989)

Medical examination is an essential step in the identification of physical abuse. Doctors should be experienced with children, understand growth and development and have forensic skills. They should be able to write clear and concise reports and give evidence in court.

Examination of physically abused children requires a calm, unhurried approach with attention to detail, good note-keeping and an ability to cope with distressed children and parents. The room should be appropriately equipped, including toys and soft furnishings, and be quiet and private.

Important points:

1. Full paediatric history, including careful note of explanations of injury, times, details, etc.
2. Developmental history.
3. Parents' expressed difficulties with child — behaviour, health, development.
4. Detailed examination of whole child to include:
   - Growth — height, weight, arm circumference, head circumference (plotted)
   - Nutrition
   - General demeanour and appearance
   - Signs of neglect, sexual abuse, emotional disturbance
   - Development including language, social skills.
5. Documentation of injuries. Diagnosis of physical abuse usually involves the assessment of lesions which are visible to the unaided eye. Accurate documentation should be by means of words, drawings and photographs. Each method has its own particular merits which are complementary. Accurate and detailed documentation permits others — including police officers, courts, social workers and other doctors providing additional opinions — the opportunity of assessing the injuries for themselves. Descriptions should be brief but detailed and include:
   a. Probable nature of the lesion and approximate age (colour for bruises)
   b. Site
   c. Shape
   d. Size (in cm)
   e. Any unusual distinguishing features
   f. Where possible, an estimate of its likely causation.

Injuries should be listed one by one and related to body drawings which give the best indication of patterns. Drawings should be outline with sizes (e.g. of bruises) marked.

Photographs

Taking photographs is now a routine part of the documentation of these cases, just as skeletal radiographs are routine records of skeletal injury. However, photographs are not in themselves diagnostic. It is usual to ask permission of both parent and child where appropriate.

Procedure for photography

Photographs should be taken as soon as reasonably possible after an injury has been observed. In some cases serial photographs may be required, for example in bite mark recognition, but this is exceptional.

Many hospitals have departments of medical photography with professionally trained photographers who are used to photographing medical subjects. However, the photographer is only able to achieve satisfactory results when he or she is working with clear and detailed instructions of exactly what is to be photographed and how the lesion would be best demonstrated; for example, if it is a torn frenulum it may not be sufficient to write 'mouth injury' on the request card. For best results it is preferable for the examining doctor to be present during the photography to ensure the best views are taken as well as a fully comprehensive set where there are many injuries. With small frightened children, the mother or a skilled nurse to hold and comfort the child will be essential. Again, for similar reasons, it is often best to photograph the child on the ward rather than have the child visit the photographic studio, although in some cases where this is appropriate better results can be achieved.

The doctor as photographer

With modern technology, moderately skilled

physicians can obtain excellent results by taking photographs themselves. Many doctors use a single lens reflex camera (SLR) to record injuries in the consulting room. There are a few points:

1. Modern fully automatic SLRs incorporating a programme for electronic flash exposure and utilising an interchangeable lens system are appropriate.

2. There should preferably be arrangements through a department of medical photography to handle exposed films so as to maintain quality control and support.

3. A system of recording patient's name, lesions and date is required using standard frame counters and/or data back information.

4. Slides or prints are acceptable. The police prefer and use prints. 35 mm slides can be used in court with a hand viewer or projector and screen, which gives the doctor the opportunity to demonstrate the injuries to the court, pointing out the important features.

Useful tips

1. A macro lens of longer focal length (90–105 mm) allows detailed photographs of individual lesions.

2. For bruises it is useful to take exposures at different distances to allow both detailed examination and an appreciation of the pattern and position of bruising in relation to the body as a whole. If the photograph is taken from too far away, small bruises will not be visible.

3. Use a neutral background when photographing. A non-reflective green surgical towel is ideal.

4. Faint and fading bruises may not show with electronic flash on camera. Studio lighting or reducing the exposure with an exposure compensation setting may be more effective. However, photography must not be used to enhance or exaggerate the trauma that is present.

Using photographic evidence in court

Photographs can and should on occasions be used in court to supplement oral evidence. It is necessary to verify legally that the photographs are of the child in question, when they were taken and by whom. Despite anxieties, medical photographers have not in our experience been asked to attend court. In cases where prosecution is likely, the police may arrange to have their photographer take photographs for them, but they may also use 'medical photographs' in evidence.

INJURIES IN PHYSICAL ABUSE

Classification of injuries

- Superficial (dermatological): bruises, abrasions, lacerations, scratches, bites, stab wounds, pin pricks, pinch marks, ligature marks, broken or avulsed hair or nails, burns or scalds (see Ch. 5), chemical injury.
- Deeper lesions: haematoma, cephalhaematoma, mouth injury (tear of lip frenulum), strangulation.
- Fractures, dislocations, wrenched limbs, periosteal injury.
- Thoraco-lumbar internal injury — stomach, gut, solid viscera, lung.
- Intracranial (including eyes) and spinal injury: whiplash, shaken, subdural haematoma, cerebral haemorrhage, contusion or oedema, spinal cord injury.
- Asphyxia, drowning and poisoning.
- Fabricated disorders (Munchausen by proxy).

Superficial injury

Bruises

Bruises are present in 90% of physically abused children. Bruises arise when blood is lost from the intravascular space into the skin and subcutaneous tissues. Except in rare cases of severe bleeding disorder, trauma is always implicated in their causation. Bruises do not blanch on pressure and have a characteristic colour. They can be mimicked by paint or pen marks, dye from clothes, birth marks, mongolian blue spots or café au lait spots. The configuration, delineation and colour evolve with and provide a guide enabling ageing to be attempted. If there is any doubt that a lesion is a bruise, serial examination will decide the matter.

These schemes in Table 4.1 were presented in

Table 4.1   Ageing of bruises

One scheme (Schmilt 1987):	Age	Colour
	0–2 days	swollen, tender
	0–5 days	red, blue, purple
	5–7 days	green
	7–10 days	yellow
	10–14 days (or more)	brown
	2–4 weeks	cleared
Another scheme:		
	Recent (24–48 hours)	reddish purple, swollen, tender
	2–3 days	brownish purple
	4–7 days	brownish green
	7 days +	yellow

well-known textbooks. The apparent discrepancies highlight the caution which doctors should adopt when discussing the ages of bruises in court.

Age of injuries. Multiple bruises have often been inflicted on a number of occasions and there will be different ages as well as size and shape. This polymorphic pattern of injury is typical of abuse. After a single accident, bruises will be of the same age and few in number. Falls downstairs are not associated with multiple bruises in many sites and of different ages.

Sites for inflicted bruises. Buchanan (1989) analysed sites for superficial injuries of all kinds in 251 abused children. The figures refer to the number of injuries and the total obviously exceeds the total number of children, denoting that injuries were present in several sites in some children. (Fig. 4.2).

General points about sites. Bruises on the buttocks, lower back and outer thighs are often related to punishment. Injuries to the inner thigh and genital area suggest either sexual abuse or punishment for perceived toileting misdemeanours. The penis may be pinched or pulled and sometimes tied with string, hairs or rubber bands.

Injury to the head and neck is common. Slap marks are found on the sides of the face and ears, extending onto the scalp. Bruises on the external ear are unusual following accidents because of the protective effect of the triangle created by the shoulder, skull and base of neck which greatly reduces injury to the ear following a fall. Bruises on the lower jaw and the mastoid are strongly associated with abuse. Other sites are round the

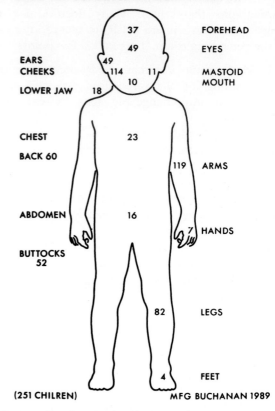

SITES FOR SUPERFICIAL INJURY IN N.A.I.

FOREHEAD 37
EYES 49
EARS CHEEKS 49 114 11
MASTOID MOUTH 10
LOWER JAW 18
CHEST 23
BACK 60
ARMS 119
ABDOMEN 16
HANDS 7
BUTTOCKS 52
LEGS 82
FEET 4
(251 CHILREN)   MFG BUCHANAN 1989

Fig.4.2   Sites for superficial injury in 251 non-accidental injury cases. Sites, not number of children, are totalled. (Reproduced by courtesy of Dr M F G Buchanan)

neck, suggesting choking, and the eyes and mouth. Black eyes can occur in normal school children from a direct injury but it takes a very hard blow to the forehead for blood to track down around one or both eyes. Injury to the upper lip and its frenulum may follow forced feeding, and an old tear of frenulum will persist.

Bruises distal to the elbow and knees generally carry less significance than those on thighs and upper arms. Bruises to the trunk (chest and abdomen) are also suspicious of abuse and lower abdominal bruises should suggest sexual abuse.

Patterns of bruises. Inflicted bruises show a number of different patterns:

- Hand marks
- Marks of implements — e.g. straps, sticks, buckles
- Bruises from throwing, swinging or pushing the child onto a hard object.

- Bites
- Bizarre marks
- Kicks.

Hand marks

1. Grab mark or fingertip bruises, for example on limbs, face, chest wall.
2. Hand print or linear finger mark.
3. Slap mark — often vaguely two or three finger-sized linear marks are seen with stripe effect. Rings may leave a tell-tale mark.
4. Pinch marks — a pair of crescent-shaped bruises, facing one another.
5. Poking marks — finger nail may cut the skin.

Marks from implements

The Newsons (Newson & Newson 1986) found, amongst a sample of 700 children, that by 7 years of age 26% of boys and 18% of girls had been hit with an implement of some kind. In both use and threat, the order of preference was: first strap or belt, second cane or stick, third slipper, fourth miscellaneous objects.

Belts or straps leave parallel-sided marks which tend to curve with the contours of the body, whereas stick marks are less clearly defined linear marks over prominent areas, usually thinner than strap marks. Loops of flex show circular closed-end thin lines. Large confluent areas of bruising, commonly on buttocks, arise from slipper beatings.

Ties or ligatures cause circumferential bands around limbs and gags abrasions from the corner of the mouth. Look for petechiae on the upper eyelids and face as well as bruising to the neck in strangulation.

Bite marks

Bites can be animal or human, adult or child (Bernat 1981). Identification of the perpetrator is possible if the mark is recent and clear. Animal bites e.g. dog or cat, result in puncturing, cutting and tearing of the skin by the carnivorous dentition. Recently, the importance of attacks by animals on children has finally been taken seriously. Dog bites should be preventable.

The human diet is omnivorous and the teeth similar in size, shape and prominence. The resulting bruises are crescent-shaped and individual tooth marks may be identified if the injury is recent. In a very aggressive bite, the skin may be broken. To differentiate between the bite of an adult and a young child (under 8 years) it should be remembered that the intercanine distance (measurement across the mouth between the third tooth on each side) is greater than 3.0 cm in the adult or older child and less than 3.0 cm in a young child with primary teeth.

Arch width differences between a 5-year-old child and an adult are 4.4 mm in the maxilla and 2.5 mm in the mandible, i.e. not great (Moores 1959). In the same study, the cumulative widths of the six upper deciduous teeth were 10 mm smaller in the primary than in the secondary dentition. In the lower arch, the difference was approximately 7 mm.

Suspect identification can be attempted with the help of a forensic dentist or odontologist. A series of photographs, starting as soon as the injury is identified, should be taken at intervals of 24 hours with a millimetre rule incorporated. Suspected perpetrators are asked to provide a dental impression to compare with the photographs.

ABO blood grouping can be determined from saliva washings of the skin surrounding a bite. Approximately 0.3 ml of saliva are deposited and it can be difficult to obtain sufficient by swabbing.

Bizarre marks

Unusual bruises may arise when a child is struck through clothes and then the pattern of the weave may appear. Puncture wounds (e.g. from a nappy pin), cord burns and self-inflicted injuries all produce unusual non-accidental marks. Petechial (pin-prick) bruises are common and arise when capillaries rupture, producing small haemorrhages around them. They can be seen on an arm if it has been held tightly, around the neck or between the fingers of a handslap.

Kicks

Usually on the lower half of the body, these are large, irregularly shaped bruises occasionally reflecting the shape of the shoe.

Injuries in a community population

In non-abused children, up to 12 bruises may be seen. In 400 children in the community aged from two weeks to 11 years, some injury was found in 37% but with increasing prevalence towards the end of the third year of life (Roberton et al 1982). The commonest sites were the lower leg (21.5%), thigh and buttock (9.25%) and arms (8.5%). In contrast, bruises to the head and face were found in only 6.5% of non-abused compared to 60% of 119 non-accidentally injured children. Accidental injury to the shins, bony prominences (e.g. foreheads) in toddlers and to the hands and feet were prominent, but bruising to the lumbar region showed a marked variation with age being unusual before the age of three, but present in 15% of children between the ages of 6 and 11 years. Bruising in young babies (two weeks to two months) was found in only 4 out of 60, and in 2 cases there was a clear history of injury. Bruising was uncommon between three and nine months (only 1 in 8 children affected) but increased as the children became more mobile and active, so that 50–65% of children aged between 12 months and 11 years had lesions, usually minor bruising. Injuries to genitalia (2 children, both easily explained) and to chest and upper back (maximum 5% in all the age groups) were uncommon, as were burns (3 only), and none had fractures.

Non-traumatic causes of bruising

Occasionally children are encountered where non-accidental injury is suspected and a bleeding disorder is encountered. Wheeler & Hobbs (1988), over 10 years, found that 23 out of 50 children with lesions suspicious of non-accidental injury were referred with possible bruising. Of these, 5 had bleeding disorders. Of the other possible causes of confusion, mongolian blue spots, capillary haemangioma, allergic periorbital swelling and dye ink or paint were described.

O'Hare & Eden (1984) reported that routine tests of clotting in every child with bruising suspected of being non-accidental in aetiology resulted in abnormal initial investigations in 16%. Whilst children with spontaneous bleeding or bleeding for trivial trauma were found, many other children had several features supporting a diagnosis of non-accidental injury. The coexistence of a bleeding disorder and physical abuse does occur and the diagnoses are not mutually exclusive. The risks from abuse to a child who has a bleeding disorder may well be greater, so that concern for the child's wellbeing may increase on discovering an abnormality.

Tests to exclude a bleeding disorder in suspected non-accidental injury include (Table 4.2):

1. full blood count film
2. platelet count (size and shape)
3. partial thromboplastin time
4. prothrombin time
5. thrombin time
6. fibrinogen
7. bleeding time.

In addition, the drug history is important — for example salicylates can induce a platelet disorder.

Other superficial lesions

Scratches are common in abused children and may result from finger nails, nappy pins, etc. Children have also been stabbed with knives. Finger or toe nails can be pulled out and trau-

Table 4.2 A child with bruises: is it a haematological disorder? (From Harvey D R, Kovar I Z Child health. Churchill Livingstone, Edinburgh, 1991 with permission.)

	Platelet count	Bleeding time	PTT	PT	Factor VIII level	Factor IX level
Idiopathic thrombocytopenic purpura	Low	N	Normal	N	N	N
Haemophilia	Normal	N	Prolonged	N	Low	N
von Willebrand's disease	Normal (defective platelet aggregation)	Prolonged	N or prolonged	N	Low	N
Factor IX deficiency	Normal	N	Prolonged	N	N	Low

N = normal; PTT = partial thromboplastin time; PT = prothrombin time

matic alopecia results if the child is grabbed by the hair. The hair may spiral, following over-stretching, at the broken end and the scalp may be tender with petechiae at the hair roots. Differentiation from alopecia areata which is common in deprived, poorly nourished children involves the absence of loose hair at the periphery, inflammation or scaling of the scalp. Violent traction forces on the scalp, such as those incurred by lifting the child by his hair, can lead to the diffuse extensive boggy swelling of a subgaleal haematoma between the scalp aponeurosis and the calvarium. These may present without history and then abuse should be implied.

Fractures and bony injury

Abusive fractures usually result from the more extreme forms of violence and represent serious injury. They may coexist with other signs of trauma: external, e.g. bruises, scratches, or internal, e.g. subdural haematoma, retinal haemorrhage or ruptured gut. Fractures may occur in any bone, being single or multiple, clinically obvious or occult and then detected only on radiograph. Bony injury in the presence of normal bones provides incontrovertible evidence of substantial trauma. Fractures are an important finding in fatal outcome following abuse.

The recognition of fractures prompted identification of what Caffey (1946) called the parent-infant stress syndrome, later renamed the battered baby syndrome (Kempe et al 1962). Caffey drew attention to the metaphyseal avulsion at the end of long bones which he thought resulted from indirect traction, stretching and shearing (i.e. acceleration and deceleration stresses on the periosteum and articular capsules rather than direct impact stresses on the bone itself). He linked this to the whiplash shaking syndrome. Since that time the spectrum of injury to the infant and young child's skeleton has widened. Injury to almost every bone has been described in abuse, but certain patterns have emerged and our understanding of the relationship between cause and effect has improved.

Prevalence of fractures — abuse and accident

4% of 4037 physically abused children had long bone fractures and 2% fractures in other bones (Creighton & Noyes 1989). The majority of abusive fractures occur in infants and pre-school children. One study (Herndon 1983) of physically abused children typically found that 58% were under the age of 3 years and sustained 95% of the fractures. In non-abused children Worlock et al (1986) found that 85% of fractures occur over the age of 5 years.

In the first year of life not only are fractures more likely to follow an assault but, looking at the whole population of infants with fractures, they are more likely to be the result of abuse than at any other time. A high index of suspicion is therefore required.

McClelland & Heiple (1982) studied 34 infants up to 1 year with 55 fractures. 15 patients were injured in accidents and 19 by abuse. Worlock et al (1986) calculated that one in 8 infants with fractures had been abused.

Various studies have emphasised that fractures are an unusual outcome following ordinary childhood accidents as studied in hospital and at home (Kravitz et al 1969, Helfer et al 1977, Nimityongskul & Anderson 1987; Levene & Bonfield 1991).

Helfer et al (1977), reviewing 246 children aged 5 years or less who fell out of bed (219 at home and 95 in hospital), found 3 who sustained skull fractures with no serious intracranial injury, 3 fractured clavicles and one fractured humerus. The height of the fall was around 90 cm or 3 feet, onto carpeted or non-carpeted floors. 17% of the children had bumps, lumps, bruises or scratches. Roberton et al (1982) recorded no recent fractures although, as discussed earlier, many had bruises. In infants and toddlers falls from up to 3–4 feet account for most accidents which reach medical attention but the chance of fracture is low at 1–2% or less. About half of such fractures are uncomplicated single linear fractures of the skull.

History

When fractures follow genuine accidents, the child is usually presented promptly, there is a clear history of an accident, and the development of immediate pain, loss of function and developing swelling. In abuse the history may be vague, inconsistent or absent. Medical attention is then more likely to be sought for swelling or loss of function after a period of delay. Sometimes the discovery of the fracture may be unexpected, e.g. rib fracture in an X-ray taken for a medical cause or in a skeletal survey after bruising has been noticed.

Correlation must be attempted between:

- the type of injury observed
- the known mechanisms required for its production
- the proposed mechanism of its production.

If there is a lack of correlation then abuse must be suspected.

Some common sense points:

1. Fractures are sudden, painful and lead to immediate loss of function.

2. If children are said not to cry or express pain, ask why. Abused children are sometimes too frightened to complain and the frozen and watchful child can be recognised in the Accident and Emergency department (Ounstead 1975).

3. Children do not continue to walk or play normally with a fracture, but parents who have abused may ignore the injury.

4. Pain is at a maximum at the beginning and swelling, bleeding and bruising take a while to develop in full. As these develop, pain may lessen.

5. Many fractures show no bruising.

6. As many of the fractures in abused children involve areas of bone dislodged from the main shaft or incomplete (greenstick) breaks, all the classic signs of fracture are not always present. Loss of function is the most important sign of a recent fracture. Once healing is under way there may be no clinical signs of fracture detectable, but radiology will reveal the old injury. In abuse, this is especially important because there may be fractures of different ages evident on the skeletal survey.

Patterns of injury in abuse

The fracture which follows abuse may be single or multiple, recent or old, or a combination and be found in one or more sites. Important patterns include:

- Single fracture, e.g. humerus with excessive unexplained bruising

- Multiple fractures in various bones, different stages of healing (classic battered baby syndrome)
- Metaphyseal-epiphyseal fractures at the end of long bones (these are often multiple after violent shaking and associated with head injury including subdural haematoma)
- Rib fractures, single or multiple
- Periosteal new bone formation
- Skull fracture with intracranial injury.

Whilst injuries are never interpreted in isolation, some fractures carry a higher and some a lower specificity for abuse. Examples of these are:

Higher specificity:

- Wide, complex, skull
- Metaphyseal/epiphyseal
- Rib
- Scapula and sternum
- Multiple fractures.

Lower specificity:

- Narrow, linear, parietal skull
- Shafts of long bones
- Clavicle
- Single fracture.

Long bone fractures

These are common fractures in children. A variety of different injuries are encountered:

- Metaphyseal lesions carry a high specificity for abuse (Silverman 1987). Radiologically, corner and bucket-handle fractures are described.
- Cartilaginous epiphyseal plate injury (Salter & Harris type I and II). These occur in both accident and abuse (Salter & Harris 1963).
- Transverse, oblique and spiral shaft fractures.
- Subperiosteal new bone formation. This is seen after injury but is also seen with other pathology, including infection and metabolic disease.
- Other fractures include compound, comminuted, impacted and pathological (underlying bone disease).

Metaphyseal fractures. Disruption through the relatively more fragile growing part of the bone results from indirect trauma. The fracture appears in a corner or bucket-handle configuration depending on the orientation of the X-ray beam. Most often a whole disc-like fragment results from complete separation. These injuries result from pulling or twisting forces and are often multiple. They have a strong association with non-accidental aetiology (Kleinman 1987). These fractures may be associated with soft tissue swelling. With healing, periosteal new bone formation may be seen in the more severe injuries. It is, however, frequently absent in milder injuries (Kleinman 1987).

Epiphyseal plate injuries. Although most injuries to the growing ends of long bones involve the primary spongiosa of the metaphysis, there are some which involve separation of the epiphysis as a result of disruption of the cartilage of the epiphyseal plate. The fracture may involve bone and cartilage or cartilage alone. In the latter case, detection of the fracture will be difficult until healing signs appear, usually at least 7–10 days later.

Transverse, oblique and spiral fractures. Worlock et al (1986) described 35 children with fractures which resulted from abuse and 826 with fractures following accidents. They commented that long bone injuries strongly associated with abuse were subperiosteal new bone formation and spiral or oblique fractures of the shaft resulting from gripping or twisting. In the study, spiral fracture of the humerus was significantly more common in abuse than in the control group. However, they concluded that the fracture alone in most cases would not enable differentiation.

The mechanisms of production of the four basic types of linear fracture (transverse, oblique transverse, spiral and oblique) are discussed by Alms (1961). This may be useful in checking the validity of a history. Alms concluded that the mode of production of the four basic fracture types is deduced on the grounds of simple mechanical theory:

- Transverse fractures are the result of angulation. This can occur following a direct blow.
- Oblique transverse fractures are the result of angulation (or bending) with axial loading (or compression).
- Spiral fractures are the result of axial twists with or without axial loading.

- Oblique fractures are the result of angulation and axial twisting in the presence of axial loading.

Axial loading applies to bones, e.g. tibia, which are weight bearing at the time of injury.

CASE HISTORY 2
A 14-month-old girl was brought to the Accident and Emergency Department with an obvious recent fracture of the forearm. A history was given that she had attempted to climb out of the high chair in which she was being fed and fell. In falling her arm had been caught in the structure of the side of the side of the chair.

In fact, one or two unusual bruises to the thigh, a pattern of failure to thrive and the child's frozen appearance raised concerns. Later it was admitted that during a frustrated feeding session the mother's boyfriend, who had been left to feed the reluctant child, swung her by the arm. In both instances angulation without axial loading could have produced the transverse fracture which resulted.

Periosteal new bone formation. The periosteum comprises inner osteogenic and outer fibrous layers. Subperiosteal haemorrhage causes elevation of the periosteum and separation of the osteogenic layer from the cortex of the bone. X-rays are initially normal (there may be soft tissue swelling) but after about 7–10 days a thin layer of subperiosteal new bone is formed. Earlier detection of these changes can be achieved by radionuclide bone scanning. The new bone formation may be localised or generalised. Whilst this is an important finding in abused children, being thought to occur when limbs are grabbed, pulled or twisted, it is itself a non-specific finding encountered in a range of other conditions. These include osteomyelitis, congenital syphilis, rickets, scurvy and vitamin A intoxication, Caffey's disease and leukaemia. In most instances differentiation will be straightforward leaving trauma as the probable cause which, if unexplained, will strongly suggest abuse. Caffey's disease is nowadays little heard of in clinical practice and careful differentiation from abuse is required.

Fractures in specific bones
Femur. Femoral fractures have a long association with abuse, the age of the child being an important variable. Abuse is the predominant aetiology in infancy (Anderson 1982, Gross & Stranger 1983). Anderson found that out of 117 children with 122 femoral fractures, 18 were under

Table 4.3 Significance of limb bone fractures

Bone	Fracture type	Abuse	Accident
humerus	spiral/oblique	+ +	+
	supracondylar	+	+
	metaphysis	+ + +	+ −
forearm	shaft	direct/indirect injury	common
	metaphysis	uncommon	rare
hand—small bones	shaft	occasionally described	uncommon
femur	shaft	< 2 years high risk	older child
	metaphysis	+ + + (lower end)	uncommon
tibia	shaft-periosteal	+	−
	spiral	+	+
	metaphysis	+ +	rare
fibula	shaft	kick +	+
	metaphysis	+	rare
foot—metatarsal	metaphysis	highly specific, uncommon pre-school	−
pelvis	pubic ramus	periosteal reaction	only after major trauma
scapula	various injuries	indirect force, high specificity	rare

13 months of age. Of these 15 (83%) were abused. Up to 2 years of age, 79% were abused including two-thirds in whom the fracture was the only injury. In older children abuse as a cause is less common. Gross & Stranger (1983) found that in 74 children up to 6 years of age with femoral fractures, abuse was identified in 34 (46%) but in 65% of infants under 1 year.

Obviously, making a certain diagnosis of abuse when a fractured femur is the only injury may be difficult but it is important to remember that trivial injury is unlikely to cause a fracture in an otherwise healthy child. In abuse the fracture usually occurs during violent twisting or swinging of the leg or child by the leg. A spiral fracture of the shaft could occur accidentally but only a major fall (e.g. from a first floor window) would generate sufficient force to injure this substantial bone.

Metaphyseal fractures occur more often in the distal end of the bone. Fractures of the femur account for around 20% of fractures seen in abused children.

Tibia. Fractures of the tibia are described less frequently than femoral fractures in abuse and are most often metaphyseal injuries or subperiosteal new bone formation. The tibial spiral shaft fracture may follow abuse or occur in toddlers learning to walk. More severe forces may produce a displaced spiral or oblique fracture (Kleinman 1987).

Humerus. This is one of the most frequently injured bones in abuse. The infant is violently grasped by the arm, pulled, swung or jerked, resulting in a range of fractures to the shaft and to both ends of the bone. In the shaft, oblique or spiral fractures usually result although a direct blow may produce a transverse break. Supracondylar fractures occur in both accidents and abuse. An apparent dislocation of the distal end may in fact be a displaced epiphysis.

Hands and feet. Injuries to the digits, metatarsals or metacarpals are occasionally found in abuse. There may be little indication of injury clinically, and direct impact is thought to account for some of these. Fusiform swelling of the digits may mimic juvenile arthritis.

Other bones. The clavicle is one of the most commonly fractured bones in childhood. Injury to the lateral part, less common than the midshaft fracture, may be more suggestive of abuse. Scapular and sternal fractures, which nearly always result from direct impact (blows), are highly suggestive of abuse although very uncommon.

Rib fractures

Rib fractures in infants comprise between 5 and 27% of fractures in abused children (Akbarnia et al 1974, Barrett & Kozlowski 1979, Herndon 1983). They can occur antenatally and a case is described of a woman who had attempted to abort her fetus by banging her abdomen against tables any by falling downstairs. Multiple healing rib fractures were discovered radiologically (Gee 1975). Care is needed in determining whether a rib fracture occurred as a result of birth trauma as, for example, when an over-vigorous assistant attempts to extract a breech delivery by grasping the child's thorax too hard. This must be very uncommon.

Cardiopulmonary resuscitation rarely, if ever, causes rib fractures and can be safely disregarded as a factor (Feldman & Brewer 1984). Other non-abuse causes of rib fractures include motor vehicle accidents, rickets, osteoporosis, surgery and osteogenesis imperfecta. If there is no history of specific major trauma and no radiological evidence of intrinsic bone disease, unexplained rib fractures are highly specific for abuse.

Diagnosis. Rib fractures, usually only diagnosed radiologically, are frequently multiple and bilateral and most often situated posteriorly near the costotransverse process articulation. Fractures can also occur further anteriorly and are sometimes multiple in the same rib. Kleinman (1987) suggests that rib fractures occur when a child is violently shaken. Anteroposterior compression occurs when the infant's chest is held with palms situated laterally, thumbs anteriorly and fingers posteriorly. In evidence of this, he quotes an abuser's confession and the findings of periosteal disruption and new bone formation on the ventral aspect of the ribs' surface. The rib cage is viewed as a single functional unit comprising a series of parallel struts, and forces are distributed widely throughout the cage leading to multiple fractures of similar age.

Radiology. Acute changes may be invisible, especially if they are situated posteriorly close to the costovertebral junction. Even with healing in this position, only slight widening of the neck of the rib will be seen.

Lateral and anterior fractures are less commonly seen and special oblique views may be needed to identify them, especially in the acute phase. Bone scans have been found to be useful where radiology has produced negative results. Callus formation enhances identification of the fracture and is usually well developed within two weeks. The only remaining evidence after a month may be slight cortical thickening.

Spinal injury

This usually results from forced extension and flexion injuries causing damage to several levels. Defects in the lucency of the anterior superior edges of the vertebral bodies, often in the lower thoracic and upper lumbar region, with narrowed disc spaces are typical. There may be no associated spinal cord injury (Swischuk 1969). Injury to the posterior element of the vertebra is less common and is usually associated with injury to the body; the most usual injury is fracture of the spinous process and posterior ligamentous injury.

Skull fractures

Diagnosis. Diagnosis of a skull fracture is usually only made after X-ray examination. Occasionally depressed or wide ('growing') fractures can be palpated and the presence of bleeding or cerebrospinal fluid (CSF) from an ear or nose may lead to a presumptive diagnosis of fracture. A swelling over the scalp may or may not be associated with a fracture of the skull but it should certainly suggest the possibility that one exists.

Skull fractures cannot readily be aged and, because they heal without callus, the usual timetable of events is not applicable. Because it is not usual practice to follow up skull fractures to check on healing, the rate at which they disappear is imperfectly understood. Except for medico-legal purposes, or occasionally when a fracture begins to 'grow', follow-up radiographs serve little useful clinical purpose.

Difficulties in diagnosis arise in infancy because of the presence of aberrant suture lines. Occasionally experienced radiologists may disagree in a difficult case, but usually consultation between the clinician and radiologist enables an accurate diagnosis to be made.

Significance of skull fractures. Injury to the skull is all too common in the severely battered child. Fracture of the skull implies an impact between a solid object and the head. When a child has been violently shaken there may be serious intracranial injury without skull fracture unless impact against a blunt object has also occurred.

Accidental skull fractures in young children usually follow falls, but it is as well to emphasise that this is an infrequent occurrence in the usual kind of accidents which occur. In two series (Kravitz et al 1969, Helfer et al 1977), with a combined total of 594 young children sustaining falls of up to 90 cm (about 3 feet) from table or worktop height, only 5 (1–2%) sustained a skull fracture — all single and linear. None sustained intracranial injury. The surface onto which the child falls is also relevant (Nimityongskul & Anderson 1987).

Patterns of skull fractures (Hobbs 1984). Fractures should be accurately described and measured, either on the radiograph or at post mortem. The following classification depends on these definitions:

Single linear: a single fracture consisting of an unbranched line in straight, zig-zagged or angled configuration. The fracture margins are closely opposed with the maximum width between them usually no more than 1–2 mm and often less than 1 mm.

Multiple or complex. This term applies where there is more than one fracture or where a single fracture has multiple components including a branching pattern. There may be a stellate configuration with several branching lines converging on a central point.

Depressed. This is a fracture where the normal curvature of the skull is interrupted by the inward displacement of bone. There may be comminution of the fracture with a fragment displaced inwards.

Growing fractures (Lende & Erickson 1961) are enlarged linear fractures, usually 3 mm or more at maximum width. They may continue to enlarge over time, sometimes with the formation of a leptomeningeal cyst.

Reports of skull fractures should include:

a. Site — which bone(s)
b. Whether suture lines crossed
c. Configuration — e.g. linear, crazy paving, stellate, branching
d. Orientation — horizontal, vertical, oblique
e. Length (cm) of each component, × maximum width (mm)
f. Other features — e.g. depression, growing
g. Presence of soft tissue swelling (use bright light source).

Comment should also be made on sutures,

Table 4.4 Anatomy of skull fractures in abuse and accident (Hobbs 1984)

	Accident (60 cases)	Abuse (29 cases)
Single linear	55	6
Multiple complex	3	23
Depressed	3	12
Maximum fracture width (3 mm or more)	4	10 (of 13 measured)
Growing	2	6

whether widened or not, with a measure of width.

Table 4.4 gives figures from a study of 89 children aged 0–2 years with skull fracture. 29 of the children were abused.

Site. The most commonly fractured bone, in either accident or abuse, is the parietal which is large, prominent, relatively thin and vulnerable to injury. Frontal fractures are much less commonly seen, either in abuse or accident, whilst occipital fractures have a special predominance in abused children. A depressed occipital fracture is virtually pathognomonic of abuse.

Fractures of the temporal bone and anterior and middle fossa are also uncommon and usually follow severe trauma.

It is frequently possible to recognise that, in the child accidentally injured with fracture(s) involving more than one bone or non-parietal bones, the history denotes a more severe fall. For example, one child with a fracture extending from the parietal across into the temporal bone sustained his injury when he fell from a first floor window (4 metres) onto the ground below. Such an injury would be most unlikely to arise from

Table 4.5 Site and extent of cranial fractures (Hobbs 1984)

	Accident (60)	Abuse (29)
Parietal	57	27
Occipital	3	16
Frontal	0	4
Temporal	1	5
Anterior or middle cranial fossae	1	4
Number of bones involved		
1	56	7
2	3	11
3 or more	1	11

a fall of 1–2 metres. This child suffered from disturbed consciousness for 2–3 days but made a full recovery.

Growing skull fracture (Lende & Erickson 1961). Most fractures which occur innocently following falls of a few feet are narrow, hairline cracks, usually in the parietal bone. The width can be measured on a radiograph with a millimetre rule. Occasionally wider fractures of 3 mm or more are seen and rarely a fracture may exceed 5 mm in width. These latter fractures are considered to be growing and require special consideration.

Growing fractures are uncommon, although they are reported in small numbers in the neurosurgical literature. The essential features are:

1. A skull fracture in infancy or early childhood
2. A dural tear at the time or injury
3. Brain injury beneath the fracture
4. Subsequent enlargement to form a cranial defect.

Out of 89 cases of skull fractures of all kinds in the children studied in Leeds (Hobbs 1984) aged up to 2 years, there were three growing fractures which required surgical treatment. By the time that this kind of treatment is required, the defect is obvious as a smooth swelling over the defect which is pulsatile. The edges of the skull defect are palpable. Growing fractures are linked to severe injury, and abuse should be suspected if such a fracture is found.

Dating fractures (O'Connor & Cohen 1987)

Fractures in child abuse often present late. Recognition of discrepancy between the claimed age and the age ascertained from radiological assessment is strong presumptive evidence of abuse. The presence of fractures of different ages and at different stages of healing is also strong evidence of abuse. In abuse, repeated trauma to the same site may complicate the process of healing.

Stages in the process of healing

1. Induction. The interval between instant of injury and appearance of new bone. During this phase haemorrhage and swelling occur and pain subsides — sometimes as early as 1–2 days after injury. The process of repair begins with ingrowth of capillaries, removal of non-viable tissue and cellular reorganisation.

2. Soft callus. Osteoblasts proliferate and lay down new bone, often seen first around the periosteum. In older children this takes 10–14 days, less in infants. This stage lasts around 3–4 weeks until the fracture line begins to obliterate.

3. Hard callus. The fracture is solidly united and lamellar bone replaces periosteal and endosteal bone. In adults this takes 2–3 months, less in children. Infants' fractures may unite in a quarter of the time of those in older children.

4. Remodelling. The gradual restoration of the original configuration of cortex and medulla can continue for 1–2 years after the original injury. The potential of this process to achieve extreme degrees is maximal in children.

Skeletal survey

It is not always necessary to undertake a full skeletal survey in every child where physical abuse is suspected. A skeletal survey should be considered in the following situations:

- presentation with a fracture which suggests abuse,
- physically abused child under 3 years of age,
- older child with severe soft tissue injury,
- localised pain, limp or reluctance to use a limb,
- previous history of recent skeletal injury,
- unexplained neurological symptoms or signs,

Table 4.6 Timetable for radiographic changes in children's fractures. Reproduced with permission of the authors and publishers from O'Connor J F, Cohen J 1987 In: Kleinman PK (ed) Diagnostic imaging in child abuse. Williams & Wilkins, Baltimore.

Category	Early (days)	Peak (days)	Late (days)
1. Resolution of soft tissues	2–5	4–10	10–21
2. Periosteal new bone	4–10	10–14	14–21
3. Loss of fracture line definition	10–14	14–21	
4. Soft callus	10–14	14–21	
5. Hard callus	14–21	21–42	42–90
6. Remodelling	3 months	1 year	2 years to epiphyseal closure

Repetitive injuries may prolong categories 1, 2, 5 and 6.

- child dying in suspicious or unusual circumstances.

Carty (1989) suggests that the following radiographs are required when conducting a survey for occult trauma:

1. skull anteroposterior and lateral,
2. chest, spine and pelvis anteroposterior
3. anteroposterior view of long bones including the hands.

Frasier and colleagues (1991) recommend the following:

- anteroposterior arms
- anteroposterior forearms
- anteroposterior femur
- anteroposterior lower leg
- anteroposterior and lateral skull
- anteroposterior pelvis
- lateral lumbar spine
- anteroposterior (grid) chest for ribs.

Note: all films on separate plates.

It must be emphasised that these are the minimum radiographs and must be supplemented with local views of any suspicious area to establish a firm diagnosis.

Differential diagnosis of skeletal abnormality in children

1. Normal variants, e.g. symmetrical periosteal new bone formation in healthy infants,
2. Pseudofractures, e.g. aberrant sutures on skull X-ray,
3. Accidental trauma including birth trauma (clavicle, humerus),
4. Osteogenesis imperfecta (Taitz 1987),
5. Infection, osteomyelitis, congenital syphilis, Caffey's disease,
6. Nutritional — scurvy, rickets, Vitamin A intoxication,
7. Malignancy — leukaemia, tumour,
8. Osteoporosis, copper deficiency (Shaw 1988),
9. Child abuse,
10. Others — e.g. congenital indifference to pain, Menke's syndrome.

Most of the above are rare. In a review of 10 years of non-accidental injury in Leeds (Wheeler

& Hobbs 1988), out of 2578 referrals there were 1912 children with suspected physical abuse. Of these, 50 children had lesions resembling abuse where another cause was found, excluding accidents. 8 of them had bony lesions as follows:

Birth injury (clavicle)	1
Calcified cephalhaematoma	1
Osteoporosis secondary to neuromuscular disorder	1
Caffey's disease	1
Congenital hydrocephalus	1
Normal skull variant	1
Scoliosis	1
Osteomyelitis	1

From a medico-legal point of view, osteogenesis imperfecta and copper deficiency are worth careful consideration. Abuse is common and both these conditions are rare, but they may occasionally cause confusion.

Osteogenesis imperfecta. Brittle bone disease comprises four main varieties which are divided into various subtypes and are genetically determined abnormalities of connective tissue.

Type I — autosomal dominant associated with blue sclerae.
Type II — very severe, multiple fractures at birth and early death.
Type III — similar to II, but less severe. Cortical thickening, tendency to fracture.
Type IV — Rare autosomal dominant with occasional mutations. Osteoporosis ±. Sclerae not blue.

Types I and IV enter into the differential diagnosis of child abuse. Easy bruisability is also a feature.

A diagnosis of osteogenesis imperfecta is encouraged by presence of blue sclerae, osteopenia, thin cortices, a tendency to bowing and angulation of healed fractures, a family history, dentinogenesis imperfecta, deafness presence of wormian skull bones. Whilst most children would have at least one or more of these associated findings, the possibility of encountering a sporadic type IV case with none does exist, but it has been estimated at between one in a million and one in three million births. The probability of encountering such a child in comparison to meeting one who has been abused is very small and, as Taitz (1987) points out, 'medical witnesses need to formulate their opinion in the light of such odds. Provided care is taken, osteogenesis imperfecta does not provide a satisfactory reason for unexplained fractures in otherwise healthy babies.'

Copper deficiency. This has also been raised as a possible cause of unexplained skeletal abnormalities, including fractures. Skeletal manifestations of copper deficiency are:

1. Retardation of bone age
2. Osteoporosis
3. Metaphyseal cupping
4. Increased density of the zone of provisional calcification
5. Metaphyseal sickle-shaped spurs.

The changes occur late and are distributed symmetrically throughout the skeleton. Copper deficiency is rare (100 reported cases) with fractures in 16 (5 term infants). Fractures usually occur in abnormal long bones, ribs in preterm infants only and never in skull.

Other features of copper deficiency include:

1. Preterm infants (40% of cases of copper deficiency are in preterm infants.
2. Abnormal feeding pattern, not in breast or formula-fed infants.
3. Psychomotor retardation, hypotonia, pallor, hypopigmentation of skin and hair, prominent scalp veins, sideroblastic anaemia resistant to iron therapy. neutropenia.
4. Low serum copper — all cases have levels below 43 μg/dl term, 33 μg/dl preterm.
5. Response to copper supplements.

An experienced radiologist should be able to differentiate between child abuse and the abnormal bones of copper deficiency, but it is wise to check the presence or absence of other features.

Intracranial injury (Billimire & Myers 1985, Hobbs 1989)

The prognosis of a head injury relates to the intracranial component. Injury to the brain is the commonest cause of death from physical abuse. 95% of serious head injuries in the first year of life result from abuse and serious head injury following an alleged minor fall in a baby should alert the clinician to the possibility of abuse. The pathology of head injury includes:

1. Scalp injury — bruises, traumatic subgaleal haematoma
2. Skull fracture
3. Subdural and subarachnoid haemorrhage
4. Cerebral contusion, haemorrhage and oedema.

Subarachnoid haemorrhage (Newton 1989)

This rarely occurs spontaneously in childhood and then follows rupture of an AV malformation or aneurysm in two-thirds of cases. No cases in children under one year old have been reported. Subarachnoid haemorrhage, detected by the finding of blood-stained cerebrospinal fluid, may occur as part of a wider pattern of injury following trauma.

Subdural haemorrhage (Caffey 1946, Newton 1989)

This is likely to give rise to concern over the possibility of non-accidental injury when it arises in infants and young children. It is invariably traumatic in origin, although a clotting disorder may present with subdural haemorrhage so appropriate investigation should be considered.

Over half the cases of subdural haemorrhage present without evidence of skull fracture or other sign of injury to the head. This gave rise to the notion of 'spontaneous origin' or arising from 'minimal trauma' until the mechanism by which these children had been abused was appreciated. It is now accepted that these children have been violently shaken. The infant's anatomy — with a large, heavy, relatively poorly supported head — predisposes to violent acceleration and deceleration forces in the 'whiplash shaken syndrome' (Guthkelch 1971, Caffey 1972) The soft, pliable skull and brain lead to stress on the bridging veins as they attach to the sagittal sinus, causing disruption and bleeding into the subdural space, often over a wide area bilaterally. The expanding intracranial mass produces symptoms which depend on its rate of growth and may be acute or chronic. In the chronic slowly accumulating case, failure to thrive, poor feeding, sporadic vomiting, un-explained anaemia and fever with late onset of fits and accelerated head growth may occur. In the acute case, irritability, vomiting, decreased responsiveness, irregular breathing and apnoea may suggest the diagnosis in the presence of a tense fontanelle. Diagnosis is made by CT scan whilst subdural taps through the anterior fontanelle used to be both diagnostic and therapeutic.

Retinal haemorrhage

The presence of retinal haemorrhage, which frequently coexists with subdural haematoma, is strongly presumptive evidence of abuse. Retinal haemorrhages occur in about 10% of newborn babies but rapidly disappear in a few days. In abuse, the haemorrhages persist much longer and probably occur secondarily to brain trauma which suddenly elevates the intracranial pressure causing compression of the central retinal vein and increased pressure at the choroidal anastomosis at the optic disc. This blockage of circulation leads to rupture of intraretinal capillaries which leak blood into the retinal tissues. Various patterns are described — flame, dot, etc. This subject has been reviewed recently and other rare causes need to be considered (Baljit Kaur & Taylor 1990). See also Warcourt & Hopkins (1971).

Cerebral contusion, haemorrhage and oedema

Areas of cerebral injury may be scattered throughout the brain leading to fits, raised intracranial pressure and long-term handicap. Between 3 and 11% (Buchanan & Oliver 1972) of children in hospitals for the retarded were handicapped as a result of physical abuse in one study. Epilepsy, post-traumatic hydrocephalus and changes to visual pathways, and cerebral infarction leading to atrophy and microcephaly result.

Children presenting without a history of trauma who have unexplained hydrocephalus, raised intracranial pressure or fits may have been abused. The fundi should be carefully examined for retinal haemorrhages and skeletal survey considered. Differential diagnosis of 'non-traumatic' presentation includes herpes simplex encephalitis, meningitis and tumour as well as the administration of drugs and poisons. Other useful investigations include a lumbar puncture and computed tomography.

Shaken impact syndrome

A recent experimental study by Duhaime and colleagues (1987) has suggested that the original hypothesis for the mechanism of injury in the 'the shaken baby syndrome' may be inadequate to explain the severity of the injuries often encountered.

The classic description has the assailant holding the infant around the chest wall between his or her hands. As the infant is violently shaken the head and limbs flail, so producing the subdural and retinal haemorrhages and the long bone fractures. Duhaime's team found difficulty in reconciling the injuries in 48 infants thought to have been shaken with the histories and clinical findings. In addition, when infant-sized dolls were shaken by

Table 4.7 Ophthalmic injuries in abuse (Allen Gammon 1981)

Structure	Result	Lesion	Effects
Eyelids, periorbital tissue	Blunt trauma, e.g. fist	Bruising — 'black eye'	Recovers
Cornea, conjunctiva	Blunt or penetrating trauma, burns, chemicals	Haemorrhage, laceration, abrasion, ulceration, scarring	Variable, depending on severity in visual axis
Lens, anterior structures	Blunt or penetrating trauma	Iris sphincter rupture. Dislocated lens	Vossius ring glaucoma, intraocular scar formation, cataract
Posterior structures, vitreous, retina	Anterior injury transmitted to back of eye. Whiplash, shaking	Vitreous haemorrhage, retinal haemorrhage. Retinal detachment	Retinal scarring, papilloedema, optic atroply
	Fractures of orbit	Optic nerve injuries	Resolution and visual loss variable
Visual cortex	Head injury. Contrecoup	Cerebral contusion, haemorrhage	Cortical blindness

Table 4.8 diagnosis of intracranial injury (Zimmerman et al 1979, Alexander et al 1986, Wissow 1990).

History: no injury or minor household accident ('rolled off settee')
Presentation: may suggest illness—fits, unconsciousness, lethargy, apnoea, delay in presentation.
Examination: may be no external findings of injury.
Child's condition suggests: meningitis, encephalitis, toxic state, metabolic disease and others.
Useful physical signs: full or bulging fontanelle;
            low haematocrit (earlier injury).
            separation of sutures;
            increased head circumference;
            retinal haemorrhages.
Investigations: skull X-ray, skeletal survey;
            lumbar puncture — may be bloody;
            CT scanning — diffuse cerebral oedema, subarachnoid haemorrhage, subdural haemorrhage;
            Magnetic Resonance Imaging — posterior fossa and intraparenchymal lesions.

adult volunteers, the forces measured by transducers were thought to be insufficient to account for the severity of injury expected in the clinical situation. In contrast, accelerations caused by impact exceeded shake accelerations by a factor of almost 50. Out of this work has grown the concept of the shaken impact syndrome.

A further aspect of this syndrome is its repetitive nature. Alexander et al (1990) described 24 children who had been shaken. 12 of these children had external head trauma in addition to being shaken. 71% had evidence of prior abuse, neglect or both. 33% were known to have been previously shaken. It is important therefore to recognise the complex factors responsible for head injuries in child abuse.

Radiological investigation of suspected intracranial injury

The detection of intracranial injury following child abuse depends on the threshold for investigation as well as the method of examination used. Prior to the introduction of CT, recognition of intracranial injury relied on clinical, surgical or postmortem findings. Many cases of intracranial injury are undoubtedly missed because the clinical signs are insufficient to warrant CT scanning. It is also believed that some intracranial injury is not detectable on CT. CT findings include:

- diffuse or focal cerebral oedema
- subarachnoid haemorrhage
- subdural haemorrhage (interhemispheric, convexity — acute or chronic)
- intraventricular haemorrhage
- contusional haemorrhage
- post-traumatic hydrocephalus and cerebral atrophy.

The reversal sign of anoxic/ischaemic encephalopathy is a finding which carries a poor prognosis indicating irreversible brain damage.

MRI (Alexander et al 1986) has certain advantages over CT in the detection of intracranial injury. In the subacute and chronic setting it is superior in detecting deep cerebral injuries and in dating extracerebral fluid collections. These include non-haemorrhagic white matter contusions and shearing injuries. Small subdural haematomas, particularly those orientated transversely or in difficult areas proximal to bone e.g. posterior fossa, are more readily detected (Frasier et al 1991). The technical details of MRI scanning are beyond this text but it is important to use the correct technique as well as being aware of the changes which take place over time.

Abdominal injury (McCort & Vaudagna 1964, Touloukain 1968, Cooper et al 1988)

Abdominal injuries are less commonly recognised in physical abuse than limb fractures or craniocerebral injuries. Their importance lies in the threat to life, particularly if there is a delay in diagnosis. Intra-abdominal trauma usually results from a kick or punch, and injury to gastrointestinal as well as solid organs may result.

CASE HISTORY 3
A 6-year-old boy's mother returned home to find him ill in bed. His step-father was in the house with his three siblings and no explanation was given for the injury initially. It was later stated that he had been playing on a nearby building site and that something may have fallen on him. Even later the step-father said that the child had returned from the building site, got himself in and out of the bath and then gone to bed.

On arrival at hospital it was immediately obvious that he had an acute abdominal catastrophe. A plain X-ray showed free gas in the peritoneum. Recent abrasions over the right lower chest wall and overlying the lumbar spinous processes were noted. At operation free blood, bile and pancreatic juice were found in the peritoneum. There was a laceration in the liver, and traumatic transection of the pylorus with complete transection of the head of the pancreas. The duodenum was devitalised, the common bile duct and pancreatic duct were transected. There was bleeding from the middle colic vein.

Diagnostic points

1. There may be no signs of external injury, e.g. bruising.

2. Delay in presentation and denial of a history of trauma make diagnosis difficult and mortality high.

3. Doctor's attention is attracted to other injuries, e.g. head and limbs.

4. Free gas is found in a minority of cases.

5. A high index of suspicion is required, especially if the general condition of the child is poor or shock is present.

Types of injuries

*   Perforation of gut — stomach, duodenum and duodeno-jejunal flexure, jejunum, ileum;
*   Haemorrhage — major vessel;
*   Laceration, contusion, haematoma — liver, spleen, duodenum, pancreas, mesentery, kidney.

Mechanics of injury

1. Compression. A punch or kick to the abdomen will squeeze the intestinal tract, especially the stomach or colon. Susceptibility to injury is greatest when the organs are distended by food or gas. The result is likely to be rupture if the organ is unable to withstand the increased pressure.

2. Crushing injury. If an organ is compressed against the spine or rib cage, crushing or shaking forces result which lead to damage. An example is in blunt abdominal trauma, certainly to the upper abdomen, where the relatively fixed duodeno-jejunal flexure is crushed against the spine producing shearing forces which result in rupture or bleeding into the wall. Other susceptible organs include the pancreas, liver, spleen and kidney.

3. Sudden acceleration/deceleration injuries, as where the child is swung or thrown into a solid object. This is likely to interrupt the vascular supply to the bowel with or without perforation.

Specific injuries

Stomach. (Case & Nanduri 1983, Schechner & Ehrlich 1974). Rupture is rare following both accidental and non-accidental injury, with the majority of cases in children, predominantly boys.

Gastric injuries may follow motor vehicle accidents, but a few cases have reputedly followed vigorous cardiopulmonary resuscitation. The injury was then assumed to be the result of the ventilatory dilatation of the stomach with air. The few cases in the literature relating to abuse are in children presumed to have received a blow to the upper abdomen. Cases of spontaneous rupture of the stomach are found almost exclusively in infants during the first two weeks of life and are related to birth trauma, congenital defects, peptic ulcer, septicaemia, hypoxia or oxygen therapy. However, the study relating to this predates our current knowledge of abuse, and cases of abuse would not have been recognised (McCormick 1959).

The usual site of laceration is along the anterior wall and greater curvature; the lesser curvature is less commonly involved. Other abdominal injuries — including to the liver, bowel, spleen and pancreas — often coexist. Severe shock may follow release of gastric contents and hydrochloric acid into the peritoneum; mortality varies from 10–66%. Delay in presentation, diagnosis and surgery increases morbidity and mortality.

CASE HISTORY 4
A 5 month-old baby was found dead by his grandmother around dawn, after his mother had left him and his 2-year-old sister alone and unattended overnight in her flat. At post mortem, he showed signs which suggested severe anoxia before death (petechial haemorrhage to thymus, brain and lungs) and greater curvature rupture of the stomach which contained milk solids. There was bruising to the liver and diaphragmatic tissues, but not to the skin of the abdomen. 36 hours earlier he had appeared to be a well, thriving, uninjured infant when presented to a paediatrician because his mother had claimed previous sexual abuse by the infant's father of her 2-year-old daughter. The grandmother stated that she had found the baby and could not wake him. She had pressed his abdomen and called an ambulance. No prosecution followed.

Duodenum and small bowel (Woolley et al 1978, Hamilton & Humphreys 1985). Injury to the duodenum and duodeno-jejunal flexure is well recognised in blunt abdominal trauma. As with abdominal injuries in general, the majority of children are under 4 years of age and, in a review of 21 small intestinal perforations in 17 abused children, the average age was 2 years. In the same series, 60% involved the jejunum, 30% duodenum and 10% ileum.

Perforation may be intraperitoneal, leading to different clinical pictures. Intraperitoneal perforation results in abdominal pain, distension, fever, shock, leucocytosis and signs of peritonitis. There may be free gas in the peritoneal cavity. It may be visible radiologically, although sometimes with difficulty. Supine and erect films should be taken where there is any suspicion of abdominal injury.

Retroperitoneal perforation from duodenal injury may not produce typical signs of peritonitis and the signs are more insidious. Radiology is often unhelpful. Intramural haematomas of the duodenum and jejunum have been recognised in abuse only recently. If a bleeding disorder is excluded, the aetiology is presumed to be trauma. The haematoma may be localised or diffuse, and present with vomiting and abdominal pain, sometimes delayed for hours or days after the injury. There may be significant blood loss and elevated white cell count.

Radiological examination may reveal signs of upper intestinal obstruction and a filling defect may be visualised in the lumen of the gut on barium examination. The mass encroaches on the lumen, is smooth and rounded and produces varying degrees of obstruction. Specialist radiological assessment is essential for accurate diagnosis. Providing there is no perforation, conservative treatment is indicated. When a duodenal haematoma is recognised in a child, child abuse should always be considered and appropriate search for other injuries and an appraisal of the child's and family's history undertaken. One author found clear evidence of abuse in 50% of cases of duodenal haematoma.

Pancreas (Hartley 1967, Slovis et al 1975, 1980). Acute pancreatitis is a rare condition in childhood. It may be due to drugs, viral infection, systemic disease or — most commonly — blunt abdominal trauma. Drugs associated with pancreatitis include high dosage corticosteroid therapy, valproic acid, sulfasalazine and thiazine.

Pancreatitis may occur in cystic fibrosis, systemic lupus erythematosus, antitrypsin deficiency, diabetes mellitus, Crohn's disease, glycogen storage disease type 1, hyperlipidaemia types I and V and familial (hereditary) cases, hyperparathyroidism, Henoch-Schonlein purpura, Reye's syndrome, and malnutrition. Alcohol-induced pancreatitis should be considered in older children. Obstruction to the pancreatic ducts by stones, tumours or choledochal cysts is a rare cause. Trauma may be accidental or non-accidental. Car accidents (as passenger or pedestrian), bicycle handlebar injuries and falls against objects are typical examples. The injuries are not always considered serious at the time and some children have been sent away from Accident and Emergency departments only to return later. The onset of pancreatitis may be rapid, or gradual and insidious. The commonest injury pattern seen is the pancreatic pseudocyst; contusion, laceration, disruption and complete transection are less common. 60% of pseudocysts are due to trauma and the origins of around 30% are unknown but almost certainly include some cases of unrecognised trauma. Increasing evidence linking pancreatitis and pseudocysts with blunt abdominal trauma indicates that, if there is no satisfactory history, abuse must be a strong possibility and should be investigated as such.

Lying across the spine, the pancreas is vulnerable to blunt trauma by crushing against the vertebral bodies. Pancreatitis develops when damage occurs to the glandular acini or ducts, leading to seepage of enzymes into tissue spaces and consequent autodigestion. Clinical features are persistent abdominal pain, bilious vomiting, fever, leucocytosis and elevated serum amylase. An epigastric mass is frequently palpable in patients with pseudocysts. Radiology, including computed tomography and ultrasonography, is useful in diagnosis, especially in defining the presence of a pseudocyst. Where there is peritonitis, high levels of amylase may be found in the fluid obtained by paracentesis. Pleural effusions may be present and bony lesions from fat necrosis consist of intramedullary necrosis and new bone formation, difficult to distinguish from leukaemia, sickle cell infarction or bony metastases. Involvement of a paediatric surgeon in consultation in management is valuable, although conservative management is successful in many children with acute pancreatitis.

Liver (Cooper et al 1988). Injury to the liver usually arises from direct injury from blows or following sudden deceleration. Major injuries are uncommonly seen and are identified at laparoscopy or post mortem. Smaller contusions and lacerations may go unnoticed and undiagnosed. Only if the newer imaging techniques are routinely used (ultrasonography, radionuclide or CT) are these injuries detected.

The most common injuries are laceration, capsular tear and haematoma. More serious injury can lead to vascular damage (e.g. to hepatic veins and vena cava) with massive haemorrhage. There will frequently be other evidence of injury elsewhere, but the mortality from liver trauma is high.

Spleen. The spleen is a commonly injured abdominal organ in childhood trauma. There is, however, little in the literature relating splenic injury to child abuse. It must be considered as a possible injury in the abused child with abdominal pain, especially in the left upper quadrant. Increased uptake of ^{99m}Tc methylene diphosphorate by the spleen in a 5-year-old child scanned to detect skeletal injury was related to a subcapsular haematoma outlined by ^{99m}Tc sulphur colloid scan.

Kidney (Morse 1975). As with the other solid abdominal organs, injury to the kidney is very uncommon in child abuse. Injury can be classified as contusion, laceration or rupture. The most serious injury may involve damage to the renal vessels. Posterior rib fractures may be noted together with bruising to the back and loin regions. There may be haematuria, loin pain and usually evidence of injury elsewhere. A tender mass in the flank may be palpable. In suspected renal trauma urine must be obtained for examination, by catheter if necessary, and imaging techniques including intravenous urography and radionuclide scintigraphy used to visualise the kidneys.

Recently it has been recognised that acute renal failure following major soft tissue injury in abuse may relate to myoglobinuria secondary to rhabdomyolysis.

Chest injuries

Bruising to the chest wall and rib fractures are common in abused children. Underlying injuries to the pleura, lungs, heart and mediastinal organs are rarely recognised.

CASE HISTORY 5
An abused infant of 3 months presented acutely ill. An empyema necessitatis was thought to be related to an inflicted puncture wound of the overlying chest wall. Other injuries included an avulsed toe nail and multiple bruises.

The flexibility of the rib cage in a young child appears to protect the intrathoracic organs from injury from compression or blows. Underlying pulmonary contusion is seldom clinically significant. Injury to bronchi has not been reported in child abuse and tension pneumothorax must be extremely rare. Injury to the heart is limited to single case reports, but the possibility of penetration injury should always be considered. One child with sewing needles lodged in the heart has been described.

REPORTING NON-ACCIDENTAL INJURY

If a doctor is worried about the possibility that an injury may have been inflicted, he should discuss this with others — including senior nurses and other doctors — and contact by telephone the social services department, either in the hospital or the area where the child lives. It is important to emphasise that the diagnosis of physical abuse involves both a medical opinion and social work assessment of the family. In some cases, where the doctor is worried, he may ask for the social services, NSPCC, health and others to check their records.

It is a matter of judgement when to involve the police in the investigation. It is important to match the level of concern with the level of response. Usual practice is to involve the police early with serious and certain abuse, but where the injuries are less severe practice might be to notify and discuss at the case conference, especially if the family situation favours this approach.

Medical reports

These are written for the social services department and NSPCC, who have a statutory responsibility to protect children. The child's GP and the Community Child Health Service, who may both have responsibilities to the child and family, should be notified.

Important areas to be included (not necessarily in order):

1. The doctor's name, qualifications and appointment; the date and place of the examination.
2. The child's name, date of birth and age at examination. Siblings can be included in the same report.
3. Referral pathway and requesting agency or individual.
4. Parents' or others' statements regarding how the injuries occurred.
5. Statements by the child using the child's words, including anything said to the doctor.
6. Other medical or social information relevant to the assessment.
7. The manner, demeanour and behaviour of the child, his physical and emotional state and indicators of poor care or neglect.
8. Height and weight, including percentile ranking, and a clinical statement of the growth and nutrition.
9. A developmental assessment.
10. Injuries listed and described.
11. Examination of the child's genitalia and anus.
12. The results of X-rays or blood tests.

The opinion

It is important to express an opinion about the injuries and an overall view of the child.

Example: It is my opinion that the pattern, number and distribution of injuries indicate that this child has been non-accidentally injured. The bruising to the left side of the face is not consistent with the parents' explanation of a fall downstairs, but is more likely to have resulted from a blow with an outstretched hand. The 1.0 cm circular cratered scarred lesion on the left thigh is consistent with an inflicted cigarette burn and not with the child scratching or picking himself.

Other concerns should also be listed,

Example: This child's weight is below the 3rd centile and he appears poorly nourished. It is my opinion that he is suffering from failure to thrive due to an inadequate intake of food. The fairly severe nappy rash and dirty fingernails and generally unkempt appearance suggest that he is being physically

neglected. Finally, it is likely that the child's poor language development, assessed as being about 12 months delayed at the age of 3, reflects inadequate stimulation.

Child protection conference (formerly case conference) (McMurray 1989)

The physically abused child may require urgent protection by means of an Emergency Protection Order (previously Place of Safety Order) and this should be sought from a magistrate as necessary. The case conference is available to allow discussions and exchange of information after abuse has been confirmed or is suspected. Case conferences followed recommendations incorporated in a 1980 Department of Health and Social Security circular which gave advice to social services on a systematic approach to the management of child abuse. One of its recommendations was that an interagency 'case conference' should be called where appropriate.

In cases of suspected or confirmed physical abuse, the timing of the conference is important. After an injury has been recognised, an investigation is instituted into the circumstances and an assessment made of the family situation and likely source of the abuse. The child will usually be placed in a safe location, be it hospital ward, foster-home or with a suitable relative. Occasionally the child remains at home with the abusing parent(s) where it is judged that the risk of further injury is low and the parents are showing appropriate cooperation. However, with severe injury, a period of separation is advisable to allow assessment of the risk of returning home and to enable plans for future management of risk to be made. It is advisable for the child to remain in a place of safety until such time as the conference has been held and decisions made. It is not always necessary to seek a court order to keep the child in a place of safety. If the parents are cooperative and show willingness to leave the child in hospital, this may not be necessary.

Attendance at the case conference involves (McMurray 1989):

- Social services — the Chairman may be a senior social work manager, depending on the local arrangements. He or she should not have direct decision-making responsibility for the case.

- The social worker and his/her team leader are always present.
- Other social workers who may be present include probation officers, if involved with either parent, and the education welfare officer who will liaise with school.
- Police — many areas now have trained and dedicated officers for child abuse work. The officer involved in the investigation will make a report.
- Health workers — GP, health visitor, school nurse, nurse manager. These are all important members with information about the child and family.
- Paediatrician — preferably of senior grade, either Consultant or SCMO or Senior Registrar.
- Other doctors from Accident and Emergency, Child Psychiatry, are occasionally required.
- Child Abuse Co-ordinator or advisor; is in an important position to advise on case management and is often in a neutral position, not having had contact with the family.
- Solicitor — will be present to advise and guide the conference on legal matters.
- Others — nursing staff, housing officer, teachers and members of voluntary organisations.
- Parents — under the new guidelines issued in 'Working Together' (1988,1991), parents may be invited where practicable to attend part or, if appropriate, the whole of the case conference at the discretion of the Chairman.

Whether parents are invited to the case conference or not, it is essential that they are kept fully involved and informed about the basis of an investigation or intervention as well as the outcome and decisions of the case conference. Parents and children (where appropriate) are asked to submit their views in writing if possible to the case conference.

Decisions of the child protection conference (Working Together 1988)

The conference should focus on the child as the primary client whose interests must transcend those of the parent where there is any conflict.

The conference will develop a plan for the child.

A decision will be taken regarding registration of the child's name under the appropriate category on the child protection register. Once this is done, the child automatically becomes the subject of an interagency protection plan with automatic review at least every six months. The conference will also decide who the key worker should be and discuss how the information regarding decisions will be imparted to and discussed with the parents.

The conference may wish to make recommendations regarding such matters as the institution of care proceedings and the appropriate immediate placement of the child, but the responsibility for these decisions does not lie with the conference.

Siblings

Where a child has been identified as suffering abuse within a family, it is always necessary to consider the position of any siblings. Information, including a paediatric assessment, should be collected and all siblings discussed at the conference. Very often there will be evidence of difficulties with siblings who, even if not injured, may well have experienced violence within the family and have lived within a stressful and dysfunctional situation. A conference may choose to register a sibling when another child in the household has been harmed.

Further protection for the child and siblings

Following a child protection conference and inclusion of a child's name on the register, an interagency protection plan is made which is subject to formal review at least every six months.

The statutory agency may decide to receive the child into care on a voluntary basis if the parents are agreeable for his protection but, in view of the nature of child abuse, parents frequently deny that their child is at risk of harm and a decision must then be taken to institute care proceedings. The local authority and NSPCC have the powers to bring care proceedings.

Emergency protection can be secured by obtaining, under the new Children Act (An Introduction to the Children Act 1989), an Emergency Protection Order which will provide protection for 8 days, renewable under exceptional circumstances, for another 7 days.

MANAGEMENT OF CHILD AND FAMILY

The aims of management are to secure a safe environment for the child, to provide for his future needs and prevent further abuse. After a period of assessment, the small number of children for whom substitute or alternative care is required should be identified. The majority of children will return or remain at home with a plan of management to protect the child.

Strategies include:

1. Addressing the source(s) of stress within the family
2. Alleviating material difficulties — housing, debt
3. Empowering parents to improve their parenting skills
4. Provision of day care
5. Improving community support
6. Use of family aides, home helps
7. Promoting non-violent ways of coping with stress
8. Facilitating improved relationships within family and extended family
9. Information about child development.

The plan should incorporate inputs from a variety of different agencies (e.g. statutory and voluntary) and be coordinated by the key worker. Concerns about the children must be honestly expressed to the parents and the need for change spelled out clearly. Expectations and standards of care must be explicitly stated. If there is a legal order, control is with the statutory authority within the terms of the order. Otherwise cooperation must be achieved voluntarily — often difficult in child abuse work.

In addition to addressing the needs of the child, it is important that the parents, needs are addressed; otherwise they will not be able to provide differently for their child. Sometimes a separate worker is assigned to give special attention, for example to a mother or a father, leaving the key worker to focus on the child's needs.

Part of successful management is the periodic assessment of the child's wellbeing and development. It is useful for the family and closely involved 'face workers' to have an assessment by a paediatrician who can comment on the child's progress, highlighting improvements as well as areas of development which need to be addressed. Encouraging the parents to make their own observations and assessments is also part of such programmes as the Child Development Project being used by health visitors in some areas (Barker et al).

When satisfactory progress has been made, and the family appears to be functioning at an acceptable level, the child's name may be removed from the register and the intensity of work reduced, although contact will usually be maintained after this time.

Summary

1. Accidental injury is extremely common in childhood.

2. Differing patterns of injury allow distinction of accidental injury from abuse, in the majority of cases.

3. 1–2% of children are recognised as being physically abused at some time during their childhood.

4. There is a strong relationship in reported cases with adverse social circumstances.

5. Mothers are more often implicated as perpetrators than men, because they are the principal carers.

6. Bruises are the most commonly encountered injury followed by fractures and brain injury.

7. Subdural haemorrhage and retinal haemorrhage are almost always the result of abuse.

8. Rib, certain patterns of skull and long bone metaphyseal fractures are all strongly suggestive of abuse.

9. Abdominal injury is the second most common cause of death and is frequently missed in diagnosis. Injuries to the stomach, duodenum and pancreas are most often seen.

10. Differential diagnosis includes bleeding and clotting disorder, bone disease, congenital abnormalities and skin conditions.

11. Physical abuse commonly coexists with other abuses e.g. 1 in 6 are also sexually abused.

12. Acute injury is often a crisis in a childhood of violence.

13. The importance of minor injury in babies cannot be overstated.

14. Interventions aimed to protect children and support families must be mindful that children may be permanently damaged or die.

15. When giving evidence in court, build up the diagnosis to explain the final opinion.

REFERENCES

Akbarnia B, Torg J S, Kirkpatrick J, Sussman S 1974 Manifestations of the battered child syndrome. Journal of Bone and Joint Surgery 56A: 1159–1166

Alexander R C, Schor D P, Smith W L 1986 Magnetic resonance imaging of intracranial injuries from child abuse. Journal of Pediatrics 109: 975–979

Alexander R, Crabbe L, Sato Y, Smith W, Bennett T 1990 Serial abuse in children who are shaken. American Journal of Disease in Childhood 144: 58–60

Allen Gammon J 1981 Ophthalmic manifestations of child abuse and neglect. In: Ellerstein N S (ed) Child abuse and neglect. A medical reference. J Wiley & Sons, New York, pp. 121–139

Alms M 1961 Fracture mechanics. Journal of Bone and Joint Surgery 43: 162–166

Anderson W A 1982 Significance of femoral fractures in children. Ann Emerg Med 11: 174–177

An Introduction to the Children Act 1989 HMSO

Baljit Kaur, Taylor D 1990 Retinal haemorrhages. Archives of Disease in Childhood 65: 1369–1372

Barker W and others. Evaluation Documents 9 & 11. Obtainable from: Early Childhood Development Unit, University of Bristol, 22 Berkeley Square, Bristol BS8 1HP

Barrett I K, Kozlowski K 1979 The battered child syndrome. Australian Radiology 23: 72–82

Bernat J E 1981 Bite marks and oral manifestations of child abuse and neglect. In: Ellerstein N S (ed) Child abuse and neglect. A medical reference. J Wiley & Sons, New York, pp. 141–164

Billimre M E, Myers P A 1985 Serious head injury in infants: accident or abuse? Pediatrics 75: 340–342

Buchanan A, Oliver J E 1972 Abuse and neglect as a cause of mental retardation: A study of 140 children admitted to subnormality hospitals in Wiltshire. British Journal of Psychiatry 131: 458

Buchanan M F G 1989 Physical abuse of children (video tapes and accompanying booklet). University of Leeds Audio-Visual Service

Caffey F 1946 Multiple fractures in the long bones of infants suffering from chronic subdural haematoma. American Journal of Roentgenology 56: 163–173

Caffey J 1972 on the theory and practice of shaking infants. American Journal of Disease in Childhood 124: 161–169

Carty H 1989 Skeletal manifestations of child abuse. Bone 6: 3–7

Case M E S, Nanduri R 1983 Laceration of the stomach by blunt trauma in a child: a case of child abuse. Journal of Forensic Sciences 28: 496–501

Cooper A et al 1988 Major blunt abdominal trauma due to child abuse. Journal of Trauma 28 (10): 1483–1487

Creighton S J, Noyes P 1989 Child abuse trends in England and Wales 1983–87. NSPCC, London

Duhaime A-C, Gennarelli T A, Thibault L E, Bruce D A, Margulies S S, Wiser R 1987 The shaken baby syndrome: a clinical, pathological and biomechanical study. Journal of Neurosurgery 66: 409–415

Feldman K W, Brewer D K 1984 Child abuse, cardiopulmonary resuscutation and rib fractures. Paediatrics 73: 339–342

Frasier L D, Smith W L, Alexander R C 1991 Clinical presentation and imaging studies in child abuse. Hospimedica May 1991: 28–35

Gee D J 1975 Radiology in forensic pathology. Radiology 41: 109–144

Gross R H, Stranger M 1983 Causative factor responsible for femoral fractures in infants and young children. Journal of Pediatric Orthopedics 3: 341–343

Guthkelch A N 1971 Infantile subdural haematoma and its relationship to whiplash injuries. British Medical Journal 11: 430–431

Hamilton A, Humphreys W G 1985 Duodenal rupture complicating childhood non-accidental injury. Ulster Medical Journal 54: 221–223

Harcourt B, Hopkins D 1971 Ophthalmic manifestations of the battered baby syndrome. British Medical Journal 3: 398

Hartley R C 1967 Pancreatitis under the age of five years: a report of three cases. Journal of Pediatric Surgery 2: 419

Helfer R E, Slovis T L, Black M 1977 Injuries resulting when small children fall out of bed. Paediatrics 60: 533–535

Herndon W A 1983 Child abuse in a military population. Journal of Paediatrics and Orthopaedics 3: 73–76

Hobbs C J 1984 Skull fracture and the diagnosis of abuse. Archives of Disease in Childhood 59: 246–252

Hobbs C J 1989 Head injuries. In: Meadow S R (ed) ABC of child abuse. British Medical Journal, pp. 12–14

Hobbs C J, Wynne J M 1990 The sexually abused battered child. Archives of Disease in Childhood 65: 423–427

Kempe C H, Silverman F N, Steele B F, Droegmueller W, Silver H K 1962 The battered child syndrome. JAMA 181: 17–24

Kleinman P K 1987 Diagnostic imaging of child abuse. Williams & Wilkins, Baltimore

Kravitz H, Driessen G, Gomberg R, Korach A 1969 Accidental falls from elevated surfaces in infants from birth to one year of age. Paediatrics (suppl) 44: 869–876

Lende R A, Erickson T C 1961 Growing skull fractures of childhood. Journal of Neurosurgery 18: 479–489

Levene S, Bonfield G 1991 Accidents on hospital wards. Archives of Disease in Childhood 66: 1047–1049

McClelland C Q, Heiple K G 1982 Fractures in the first year of life. A diagnostic dilemma? American Journal of Disease in Childhood 136: 26–29

McCormick W F 1959 Rupture of the stomach in children. Archives of Pathology 67: 416–426

McCort J, Vaudagna J 1964 Visceral injuries in battered children. Radiology 82: 424–428

McMurray J 1989 Case conferences. In: Meadow S R (ed) ABC of child abuse. British Medical Journal, pp. 42–44

Moores C F A 1959 The dentition of the growing child. Harvard University Press, Massachusetts, pp. 79–110

Morse T S 1975 Renal injuries. Pediatric Clinics of North America 22: 379

Newell P 1989 Children are people too. The case against physical punishment. Bedford Square Press, London

Newson J, Newson E 1986 Findings on use of physical punishment on 1, 4, 7 and 11 year old children, together with some sequel in later life. University of Nottingham, Child Development Research Unit

Newton R W 1989 Intracranial haemorrhage and non-accidental injury. Archives of Disease in Childhood 64: 188–190

Nimityongskul P, Anderson L D 1987 The likelihood of injuries when children fall out of bed. Journal of Paediatric Orthopaedics 7: 184–186

O'Connor J F, Cohen J 1987 Dating fractures. In: Kleinman P K (ed) Diagnostic imaging in child abuse. Williams & Wilkins, Baltimore, pp. 103–113

O'Hare A E, Eden O B 1984 Bleeding disorders and non-accidental injury. Archives of Disease in Childhood 59: 860–864

Ounstead C 1975 Gaze aversion and child abuse. World Medicine 12: (17) 27

Roberton D M, Barbor P, Hull D 1982 Unusual injury? Recent injury in normal children and children with suspected non-accidental injury. British Medical Journal 285: 1399–1401

Salter R B, Harris W R 1963 Injuries involving the epiphyseal plate. Journal of Joint Surgery 45A: 587–622

Schechner S A, Ehrlich F E 1974 Gastric perforation and child abuse. Journal of Trauma 14: 723–725

Schmitt B D 1987 The child with nonaccidental trauma. In: Helfer R E, Kempe R S (eds) The battered child, 4th edn. University of Chicago Press, Chicago

Shaw J C L 1988 Copper deficiency and non-accidental injury. Archives of Disease in Childhood 63: 448–455

Silverman F N 1987 Radiology and other imaging procedures. In: Helfer R E, Kempe R S (eds) The battered child. University of Chicago Press, Chicago, pp. 214–246

Slovis T L, Berdon W E, Haller J O et al 1975 Pancreatitis and the battered child syndrome. Report of two cases with skeletal involvement. American Journal of Roentgenology 125: 456

Slovis T L, VonBerg V J, Mikelic V 1980 Sonography in the diagnosis and management of pancreatic pseudocysts and effusions in childhood. Radiology 135: 153–155

Smith S M, Hanson R 1974 134 Battered children: a medical and psychological study. British Medical Journal : 666–670

Swischuk L E 1969 Spine and spinal cord trauma in the battered child syndrome. Radiology 92: 733

Taitz L S 1987 Child abuse and osteogenesis imperfecta. British Medical Journal 295: 1082–1083

Touloukain R J 1968 Abdominal visceral injuries in battered children. Paediatrics 42: 642–646

Wheeler D M, Hobbs C J 1988 Mistakes in diagnosing non-accidental injury, 10 years' experience. British Medical Journal 296: 1233–1236

Wissow L S 1990 Head and internal injuries. In: Child advocacy for the clinician, an approach to child abuse and neglect. Williams & Wilkins, Baltimore

Woolley M M, Mahour G H, Sloan T 1978 Duodenal haematoma in infancy and childhood. Changing aetiology and changing treatment. American Journal of Surgery 136: 8–14

Working Together 1988 A guide to arrangements for inter-agency co-operation for the protection of children from abuse. HMSO

Working Together under the Children Act 1989 A guide to arrangements for inter-agency co-operation for the protection of children from abuse. HMSO, London 1991

Worlock P, Stower M, Barbor P 1986 Patterns of fractures in accidental and non-accidental injury in children: a comparative study. British Medical Journal 293: 100–102

Zimmerman R A, Bilaniuk L T, Bruce D, Schut L, Uzzell B, Goldberg H I 1979 Computed tomography of craniocerebral injury in the abused child. Radiology 130: 687–690

5. Burns and scalds

Burns and scald injuries to children are common. The majority result from accidents which involve varying degrees of parental inattention, including cases of neglect. A small number involve deliberate abuse and their detection poses an important challenge to doctors who see large numbers of children. Doctors in the front line of accident and emergency work see the more severe injuries at the all-important time of presentation and their records and observations are vital to assessment. They work closely with paediatricians as well as surgeons who are responsible for treatment. Less severe injuries may never be seen in hospital; general practitioners, health visitors and school nurses may be the first to see them and question how they have been caused.

The parent who abuses may wish to hide the consequences, which are then only discovered by the vigilance of others, for example nursery nurses or school teachers. It is interesting to note how often concealment is partial or imperfect and this seems to reflect the ambivalence of the parents.

STATISTICS

11.1% of all accidental deaths (Jackson 1985) are classified as burns or scald injuries but these include children who die in house fires where the inhalation of smoke may play an important part. Children in house fires may have been left alone, unattended or unsupervised, and have played with fires or matches. Repeated fire-setting is also seen in children who have been abused. Some learn that it is a sure way of raising concerns which can lead to removal into safety.

In England and Wales each year there are over 5000 discharges and deaths from hospital of children with burns and scalds; four-fifths of these are in children aged 0–4. Accidental injuries of this type are very much a problem in younger children, who have to be taught of the risks and dangers of heat and fire. Attendance without admission to hospital is even more common — one estimate from a Home Office Surveillance system run by the Department of Trade and Industry puts the number of attendances at all Accident and Emergency departments offering 24-hour cover in 1983 at 13 900 for burns and 21 900 for scalds, with a similar age distribution as for children admitted. As in virtually all childhood accidents (horse-riding excepted), boys outnumber girls in the cases of burns and scalds by 6:4.

The majority of these injuries occur in the home, which for young children is understandably the most dangerous environment. It is against this background — in which burns and scalds are common injuries, particularly in the younger child — that one faces the task of identifying abuse. The proportion of children with burns and scalds resulting from abuse is not accurately known, with estimates from 4–39% (Stone et al 1970, Phillips et al 1974, Hight et al 1979, Showers & Garrison 1988). The few British studies (Raine & Azmy 1983) suggest 1–2% of admitted children, whilst a typical study from America in one hospital found 8% of suspected inflicted injury with 4.2% later substantiated (Phillips et al 1974). In Melbourne the figure of 6% was found, whereas in Michigan — in one of the largest studies over six years and involving 872 children admitted to a burn centre in the Children's Hospital — 16% were thought to have been inflicted (Hight et al 1979). It is suspected that under-diagnosis is the rule, as with abuse in general.

Burns and scalds occur in around 10% (Martin 1970) of physically abused children, occasionally in association with other injuries such as bruises or fractures. The highest proportion of physically abused children with burns or scalds is the early UK study of Smith & Hanson (1974) in Birmingham, where 20% had burns and scalds. These figures of course reflect hospital experience and serious abuse. Bruising is still far commoner than burns or other injuries.

ACCIDENTAL BURNS AND SCALDS

A great deal could be done further to reduce accidental burns and scalds which occur principally to young children (Jackson 1985). Kitchens, and to a lesser extent bathrooms, remain the focus of danger; the living room fire is much less a danger in these days of central heating and improved safety conscious gas and electric fires, but it must still be viewed as negligent for there to be an unguarded fire with young children in the house.

The peak age for these accidents is between the first and second birthdays, when children acquire mobility without the means to protect themselves. Exploratory behaviour is at a peak and cups of tea, kettle flexes or pan handles all pose dangers. Washing machine hoses can be pulled out of sinks and an older toddler may be able to climb into a bath into which scalding hot water has been run. Even a spilled cup of tea contains a considerable amount of heat if freshly poured and the presence of clothes will keep the liquid in contact with the skin for longer and with larger volume and hence heat.

Some of the most serious accidents ensue

Table 5.1 Common accidents admitted to a children's surgical ward (adapted from Hobbs 1986)

Scalds	
Total	134
Drinks, food, pans, kettles	112
Baths, sinks, domestic hot water	22
Contact burns	
Total	12
Room heaters	9
Tools, appliances	3
Other	
Fat, caustic, flame, electrical	17

when a flex from an electric kettle or jug is pulled, dragging the kettle and contents off a table or work surface above a child. As the water cascades down, the child's head, shoulders and upper trunk bear the brunt of injury with possible secondary injury to arms and feet. The use of coiled kettle flex is being introduced as a means of reducing this kind of accident.

Tap water scalds

Although the pour scald injury still accounts for the majority of scalds, accidents involving domestic hot water from taps or showers in baths and sinks are also important. It is often in these circumstances that the possibility of abuse is raised.

The relationship of time and surface temperature in the causation of burns was explored by Moritz & Henriques many years ago (1947). The relationship is expressed in the graph (Fig. 5.1), which shows the time taken at a particular temperature to produce a full thickness burn. For example, at 65 °C it may only take around 0.5 seconds to produce a full thickness burn on the inside of the thigh, to 10 seconds at 54 °C for a child, although perhaps three times as long for the

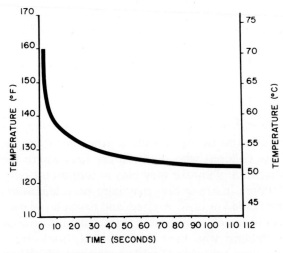

Fig. 5.1 Relationship between temperature and time required to cause full thickness scalds of adult skin. (From Feldmam K W 1987 Child abuse by burning. In: Heffer R E, Kampe R J (eds) The battered child. University of Chicago Press, Chicago)

adult who has a thicker skin. The relationship is logarithmic and holds until 44 °C when injury becomes less predictable. At temperatures above 70 °C scalding becomes almost instantaneous. The importance of this information will become apparent when careful forensic assessment of bath scald injuries is undertaken and it also enables us to estimate the potential dangerousness of a domestic hot water system for a child (Table 5.2).

Accidents from tap water are serious because they are frequently extensive and severe, requiring the care of a special burns unit. Over one-third in one study involved a quarter or more of the body surface area. The major factor causing these injuries is the high temperature of domestic hot water in many homes. Studies in North America have confirmed that many homes have water temperatures higher than 54 °C, which will produce a full thickness scald in 10–30 seconds. Obviously, if thermostats are not working properly, the temperature may be even higher than 65 °C. A safe temperature of 49 °C has been proposed for domestic baths and showers to avoid accidents, but this is unlikely to be widely adopted and a maximum of 54 °C seems to be a more realistic figure adopted by bodies concerned with safety in the home. There appears to be no study of hot water system temperatures in homes in Britain.

Contact burns

The third major group of accidental thermal injuries has shown a reduction in recent years. Room heaters are important as causes of burns in accidents, neglect and non-accidental injury. Whilst properly designed and fitted fireguards protect children, loose or poorly fitted guards may be circumvented by exploring hands, resulting in serious burns, especially from the electric bar fire. Contractures caused by deep palmar burns may occur if the hand adheres to the element.

Other sources of contact burns, both accidental and non-accidental, include irons: the flex is grasped by the young child who pulls the iron off the ironing board. A variety of do-it-yourself appliances including soldering irons, hair crimpers and rollers are potentially dangerous. The external surfaces of cookers and cooker doors may be hot enough to produce a burn.

Other accidents causing burns

Conflagrations and flame burns

Smokers' materials — matches, cigarettes, lighters — can all be responsible for fires which result in injury or death. Paraffin heaters and liquid petroleum gas cylinders are other potential sources of hazard to families. Deaths from clothes and nightdresses catching fire from open fires have fallen dramatically with improved safety regulations.

Faulty wiring, bare wires and faulty appliances may be responsible for fires or electrocution; children are at high risk if these problems are left unattended or go unnoticed. Older children may be burned making fires in the open or playing with fireworks.

NON-ACCIDENTAL BURNS

It is disturbing to think of an adult deliberately inflicting a burn on a child. Because of this, it is less likely that the possibility will be considered and the inflicted injury may be overlooked.

Burning a child may be an impulsive immediate response — to a child playing with a fire, for example. One parent held her child's hand against the fire to demonstrate to the child that it was hot when she found the child playing with the fire's controls: a superficial burn resulted. In other instances there may be deliberate premeditation, as when the child who has wet or soiled is plunged into a bath of hot water. It takes time to run the water and undress the child. Where burns are linked to sexual abuse (Hobbs & Wynne 1990) it seems likely that there is a wish to inflict pain, sometimes as a way of threatening the child into silence. Here the adult may obtain gratification from sexual aggression. Children who have been abused in this way are often terrified and find difficulty in relating what has happened to them. Inflicted burns are sadistic and may be part of ritual abuse.

Diagnosis

Presentation is either as:

- acute injury
- neglected or old injury
- healed burn or scar.

Table 5.2   Proforma for immersion scalds (modified from an evidence worksheet provided by P J Peltier, Office of District Attorney, San Diego, California)

CASE NO:_____ POSSIBLE PERPETRATOR'S NAME:_____

PRESENT DATE:_____ CHILD'S NAME:_____

PLACE WHERE INJURY OCCURRED _____

BATH OR SINK MEASUREMENTS:

    Width: _____ Inches

    Top length _____ Inches

    Bottom length: _____ Inches

    Inside depth: _____ Inches

    Construction _____ (porcelain, fibreglass, metal, plastic etc.)

RUNNING WATER TEMPERATURE - HOT:		RUNNING WATER TEMPERATURE - COLD:	
Seconds	Degrees	Seconds	Degrees
0		_____	_____
5	_____		

RUNNING WATER TEMPERATURE (FULL HOT AND COLD):

Seconds	Degrees
10	_____
20	
_____	_____ Peak Temp.

Seconds	Degrees
_____	_____ Peak Temp.

FULL HOT WATER STANDING 5 INCHES DEEP (TEMPERATURE MEASURED IN MIDDLE OF BATH/SINK AT MID-DEPTH):

Inches	Fill Time Minutes	Seconds	Minutes 0	Degrees
1	_____	_____		_____
2	_____	_____		_____
3	_____	_____		_____
4	_____	_____		_____
5	_____	_____		_____

PARENT RAN A TUB OF WATER ON MY REQUEST. RESULTS: DEPTH 5 INCHES — 1 MINUTE AFTER WATER OFF — TEMPERATURE _____ DEGREES. MEASUREMENT WAS MID-BATH/MID-DEPTH.

INVESTIGATOR #1: _____ I. D. # _____ DIVISION: _____

INVESTIGATOR #2: _____ I. D. # _____ DIVISION: _____

Following a non-accidental burn the parents may:

- rush to hospital
- self treat (acceptable if minor)
- ignore
- take steps to hide injury
- present after a delay for treatment or if complication develops (Purdue et al 1988).

History

As with all non-accidental injuries, the cardinal point is a history which does not match the injury. It has to be said that the more carefully taken the history, the clearer the picture will be of how the injury supposedly happened. Until there is a completely clear picture further questions should be asked and information sought. Sometimes only a visit to the scene or an examination of the fire or bathroom enables an understanding of the incident and if there are doubts after the usual history taking it is better to wait, admitting the child to hospital until it is clear.

Delay or avoidance of treatment is common and the reasons must be explored. One family said the doctor's surgery was closed so they did nothing. This might be just about acceptable in a minor burn but most families know that Accident and Emergency departments at hospital stay open 24 hours a day. If the burn looks older than the history claims, then the views of an experienced nurse are sought.

Nurses dress burns often, and soon get an idea of how old a burn is. Their experience is vital in recognising the abused burned child.

Many parents say they did not witness the incident, perhaps being in another room or attending to another child. This was the case in two out of every three abused children seen in Leeds, but in only about 10% of true accidents in another study (Martin 1970). It should be borne in mind that most of the children burned are under 5 years of age, and the commonest age for burns from abuse is less than 3 years. These children are normally close to their parents and there is usually little doubt about what has happened when an accident occurs. In abuse the parent may state accurately as to the cause of the injury but obviously not about the way it happened. Where parents say they do not have any idea how the injury occurred, they should be encouraged to speculate, to list all the sources of heat in the house and to suggest possibilities. In this way the source of injury will often be mentioned. Persistent inability to explain the injury may sometimes indicate that the parent has left the child alone or poorly supervised: in families who abuse their children this is not uncommon.

In abuse, parents rarely take responsibility. They usually feel that the child deserved it and may even blame the child for the injury. He may have tripped over, been pushed by the dog or a sibling or be playing with the taps yet again despite his being told repeatedly not to do so.

Sometimes of course these stories are true, but concern should always be aroused if the parent is hostile towards the child. Even though the child obviously contributes to many of the accidents we see, parents usually feel guilty and blame themselves. Parents of children with accidental injuries naturally feel uncomfortable about being questioned and their feelings of guilt should not be misinterpreted.

Denial of the injury is another important clue. This can be manifested by non-presentation or trivialisation of the injury or the child's response. 'It wasn't bad, he didn't even cry' is not uncommon. Sometimes the denial is complete. One mother swore that the deep circular ulcer on one buttock of her child was a nappy rash when her health visitor, general practitioner, a paediatrician and paediatric nurse all said it couldn't be and had to be a burn. She steadfastly refused to accept their diagnosis. In the case of another child, the mother stated firmly that the child had scraped his back playing in the garden when the lesion was

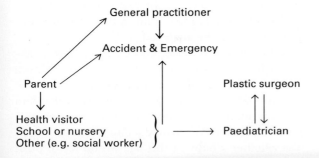

Fig. 5.2 Pathway of referral for non-accidental burns.

obviously a burn. The finding of an old, healing, unpresented burn across his younger sister's bottom provided further evidence with which to confront the family. Of course there are some lesions which look like a burn but about which it is impossible to be certain. This is particularly true of small, poorly defined, healing lesions which could have a number of causes.

Confessions are not common but are sometimes made to doctors who gently confront parents' concerns about injuries which don't add up.

CASE HISTORY 1

One mother talked for an hour about the burn on her baby's hand, finally saying

'You don't believe it was an accident do you? Well I'm having some difficulty but if someone did that on purpose I think they must need help. Would they go to prison if they did that?'

'It's not possible to predict that and the police would have to know but it's not automatic and where someone has taken responsibility and accepted help, there is more likely to be a sympathetic response.'

'Well I did it and I deserve what's coming. I can't cope with my children any more.'

This mother took responsibility, accepted a period with her two children away from her and then, with their return home, accepted help and support and continues to care for them. She herself was sexually abused as a child between the ages of 6 and 8 but never told her mother, whose father had been the abuser.

Other parents are unable to admit what has happened but make sure they are found out.

CASE HISTORY 2

One mother who had been struggling for some time with two children brought her 3-year-old daughter with glove scalds to both hands. The history that the child had fallen full length and fully clothed into a bath of hot water without sustaining scalds elsewhere was clearly so inconsistent with the injury that abuse had to be suspected. Despite having had the inconsistencies pointed out to her, the mother stuck rigidly to her story but did not deny very vigorously the suggestion that the child had been abused.

These case histories are important because they demonstrate the help-seeking behaviour shown by parents who are abusing their children. Failure to recognise and intervene leaves the children at further risk.

Child's history

Unprompted statements made by the child in hospital undergoing treatment are common. 'Mummy did it' may not imply abuse as such but 'Mummy did it because I was bad' is more significant.

CASE HISTORY 3

One mother who had five boys, two of whom in the past had had worrying burns (one on his bottom and the other on his abdomen), came to the hospital because a third, 3-year-old, child had been noticed in nursery school to have an oblong-shaped burn at the top of his thigh. His mother agreed it was a burn but steadfastly refused to offer an explanation, although after some time she said it could have been the iron but would say no more. Judging that little progress was being made, it was decided to address a question to the boys, who were all in various parts of the room playing with toys. 'Do any of you know how this burn happened?' One by one the children slowly shook their heads, quietly and avoiding eye contact. However, a voice from one corner of the room from beneath a chair said 'Mummy did it'. The hostility with which she turned on this child left all concerned about his safety. Although it could not be ascertained what had happened, it was a worrying exchange.

Child's developmental ability

This can be a crucial part of the history when, for example, it is alleged that the child took an active part in producing the injury. In one case (Plate 4.1) three closely opposed burn marks on the upper thigh from a heated ring at the end of an expandable curtain wire were very unlikely to have been caused by the 2-year-old child concerned. Clearly the necessary fine motor skills had not yet developed. In another case, where it was alleged that a child had climbed over the edge of a bath, it was shown that the child did not have the necessary skills to do this.

Whilst a general understanding of child development is essential to making clear decisions about what it is possible for a child to do, an alternative is to observe the child in this situation and gauge what can be achieved.

A 9-month-old baby allegedly crawled backwards into a central heating radiator, sustaining burns to the soles of both feet. Whilst the radiator was not particularly hot, it was envisaged that had the feet maintained contact for several seconds a burn could have ensued. The question raised was whether a baby of this age would try to push away from the radiator, thus maintaining contact for longer. In practise, it was found that a rapid withdrawal response from his feet was observed when placed in contact with an aversive stimulus, this indicating the unlikelihood of the proposed theory.

Types of thermal injury (Characteristics of different thermal injuries are shown in Table 5.3)

Depending on the age, it is often possible to make a reasonable assessment of the likely type of burn present.

In abuse several patterns have been recognised:

1. Dip scald or forced immersion injury (Lenoski & Hunter 1977, Feldman et al 1978)

This is a relatively common non-accidental-injury and affects hands, feet, buttocks or sometimes the whole child. As the child is held in the hot water, unable to struggle, clear demarcation lines are found between scalded and spared skin. This gives the glove and stocking distribution, modified if the fist is clenched or if the sole of the foot presses against the cooler base of the bath. With the child's buttocks, the central area may be spared if pressed to the cool bath base, leaving the 'hole in the doughnut effect'. Such children will not have the splash marks expected of children who accidentally fall into the bath. Water will find its way into hollows in the child's body but where surfaces are opposed, the skin will be spared. If, therefore, the legs are flexed and the child dunked, confluent areas of non-scalded skin in opposition will be seen.

2. Splashed, thrown or pour scald injury

Unusual sites for these injuries, for example genitalia, or a pattern of separated areas, as when fluid is thrown, may suggest abuse, although examination will be less conclusive than with the forced immersion scald. The backs of the hands are uncommonly scalded in accidents but are affected when the hand is held under a flow of hot water.

3. Food burns

If a child is accidentally given hot food with a high moisture content, the lips and mouth are the likely sites to be burned. If a beaker or dish of food is pushed into a reluctant child's face, the burns are centred around the mouth but are also present on the face, including the cheeks. Sticky foods such as hot porridge can concentrate heat and produce unpleasant scalds.

Scalds in the groin have been seen, when a bowl was tipped into a child's lap and a scalded foot when a child put his foot in his bowl of porridge on the floor. Although unusual, these were accepted as accidents.

4. Contact burns

Holding a hot object against a child's skin is possibly the commonest way of abusing a child. The child may also be pressed against a hot object, such as a fire or hotplate. If there are multiple burns, particularly if they are on different 'sides' of the child such that contact must have occurred on several occasions, abuse is more likely. Children

Table 5.3 Characteristics of various types of thermal injury

SCALD	Variable thickness between and within different lesions. Contouring of depth, tendency to be deepest in the middle. Dip, splash or pour patterns. Smooth circular edges. Peeling and sloughing. Skin loss in sheets. Moist, macerated, soggy lesions spread into flexures, depressions, e.g. natal cleft. Blisters pronounced.
CONTACT BURN	Shape conforms to the object. Sharply delineated margins. Square and straight edges. Depth variable but generally uniform. Dry, scabbing.
Cigarette	Circular 0.5–1.0 cm diameter. In abuse often full thickness cratered, leaving circular, depressed, paper thin scars. In accident superficial, eccentric with tail from brushed contact.
Flame	Tissue charred. Hair singed.
Chemical, e.g. caustic liquid	Scald-like distribution, staining ±. May be deep with underlying tissue destruction.
Friction	Occurs over body points, e.g. nose, point of shoulder. Usually superficial. Intact blisters not seen.
Electrical	Deep, small, localised. Exit and entry points. Common site — hands and fingers. Tissue charring and deeper necrosis. Nuclear streaming on microscopy.
Microwaves	Unusual, sharply demarcated, full thickness burns widely distributed on body (opposite microwave emitting devices). Deeper burns to muscle described.

soon learn to avoid hot objects and the intense pain which accompanies a burn.

Common objects used to inflict burns include fire grills, irons and curling tongs; the heated top of a cigarette lighter was mentioned in one study (Keen et al 1975). Objects may be heated in the fire and applied like a brand. The distinct configurations allow one to compare the object with the injury, giving positive identification. The depth of burn depends on the temperature and factors preventing the child from escaping the heat. The commonest sites are the backs of hands, outside of legs, buttocks and feet.

5. Cigarette burns

Cigarette burns are increasingly seen as a manifestation of child abuse. A proportion of children referred with suspected cigarette burns turn out to have other skin pathology, frequently impetigo (Wheeler & Hobbs 1988).

It is not known how long it takes to produce a deep, cratered, circular, full thickness burn, but it is suspected that it is a second or two or possibly more. This is far longer than the milliseconds which will elapse in a brushed contact which leaves an area of reddening, often with a tail or elliptical shape.

Cigarette burns may be single or multiple; a look-out should be kept for scars. Cigarette burns carry a particularly high emotive significance; it is wise to be clear of the certainty that the lesion is a cigarette burn before giving evidence in court.

Other burns

Flame, caustic, radiant, electrical and friction burns are all seen in abuse. Their features are described in Table 5.3, but none is common. Children have been forced to stand in front of a fire until their legs were burned from radiation, children are dragged across a carpet on their faces producing friction burns, or burns occur where ropes have been used to restrain a child. If a caustic substance is placed on the skin, destruction of the tissue may continue for some time and lead to deep injuries with considerable scarring. Fortunately this must be extremely rare in child abuse. Severe and extensive sunburn in a young child is

not uncommon and could be viewed as indicating poor care. Erythema and blistering result. Recently microwave ovens were reported to produce full thickness burns in children placed inside them (Alexander et al 1987).

Sites in abuse

It is always essential to consider the part of the child's body affected. There are no sites which are specific to abuse, but the hands (Johnson 1990), buttocks, genitalia and feet are especially important (Fig. 5.3). Isolated burns on the buttocks commonly arise from abuse. The backs of hands can be burned accidentally, but as the child explores it is usually his fingers that are burned, not

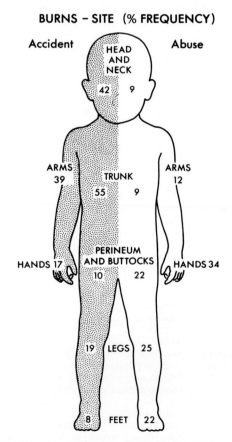

BURNS – SITE (% FREQUENCY)

Accident / Abuse

	Accident	Abuse
HEAD AND NECK	42	9
ARMS	39	12
TRUNK	55	9
HANDS	17	34
PERINEUM AND BUTTOCKS	10	22
LEGS	19	25
FEET	8	22

Fig. 5.3 Percentage frequency of sites involved in burn and scald injuries in accident and abuse. Data from 195 children (165 accidents, 30 abused) with burns and scalds. (Reproduced with permission from Hobbs C J 1986 When are burns not accidental? Archives of Disease in Childhood 61: 357–361.)

so much the flat of the dorsum or the back of the wrist.

Burns on the soles of the feet should also cause concern unless of course there is a sensible history. Any site can be the target and nowhere is spared. In one seriously abused infant, the cornea was burned, probably by a cigarette. The child was presented to the family doctor and treated for an eye infection but only later when the child had been seriously bruised around the face and sustained a skull fracture was the corneal ulcer demonstrated with fluorescent staining.

Self-inflicted burns are sometimes encountered in disturbed children who have usually also been abused. As with scratches and bruises, the arms and hands are the predominant sites; recurrent injury to these sites should raise the possibility of this cause.

Often, further evidence later clarifies the picture. Where suspicion is high, a full investigation is warranted and requires coordination of a team response for the child.

Differential diagnosis

Conditions confused with burns include:

- Impetigo — crusted (golden), irregular, rapid response to antibiotics. No scarring.
- Severe eczema or nappy rash. Sometimes difficult to distinguish but distribution and presence of pain assist.
- 'Scalded skin syndrome' (toxic epidermal necrolysis) is occasionally seen in newborn babies. Large superficial blisters with separation of upper layers of skin. Child may be ill from staphylococcal infection. Separation of the skin with minimal trauma (Nikolsky's sign) present.
- Contact dermatitis — may be localised (e.g. to wrist nameband).
- Acrocyanosis or 'deprivation' hands and feet.

Exotic and unusual burn accidents

There are situations in which the history sounds unlikely or there is no satisfactory explanation. One child had lesions which resembled scalds around both ankles. The explanation that this was a vinegar burn was doubted until the vinegar was found to be glacial acetic acid (pH 1.5) which required dilution at 1 in 10 before use. Another case was described where a baby placed in a car seat in a car that had stood in the sun sustained a burn on his abdomen, for which at first no explanation was forthcoming. The belt buckle had been hot enough to burn him and, as he had often cried before on being placed in the seat, his distress had not been heeded. Black vinyl plastic seats have been implicated in similar circumstances.

The most common differential diagnosis remains between accident and abuse.

MANAGEMENT

The primary consideration in treatment of most burn or scald injuries is the medical or surgical treatment of the injury and child. In small healing or healed burns, the issues of child protection may be the prime and sole concern. Medical and surgical management are not discussed in this text and the reader is referred to other sources for details.

Close cooperation of paediatricians with surgical teams undertaking the management of the injury is vital if the future safety of the child is to be ensured. Where abuse is suspected, early assessment by the paediatrician experienced in physical

Table 5.4 Checklist of points in diagnosis of abuse

History does it explain: extent, depth, pattern, type, age — of injury

- Is there a more likely explanation if history doesn't fit?
- Is burn compatible with child's ability and development?
- Are there other injuries which might suggest abuse?
- Are there signs of sexual abuse, or failure to thrive, or neglect?
- Has the child given a history: in parents' presence? elsewhere?
- Have the parents responded reasonably to the injury and are they cooperating with treatment?
- Who is taking responsibility? Are the parents detached or lacking concern for the child?
- How is the child behaving? May need to wait for initial panic and shock to subside before child's more normal behaviour becomes apparent. Is he withdrawn, frozen, or hyperactive, anxious, aggressive?
- Has anyone visited the home, seen the fire, bath, etc?
- Is there information from other professionals, e.g. at a case conference?

abuse in conjunction with the surgical and nursing staff treating the injury should allow discussion of the likely mode of injury to take place. Examination as soon as possible after arrival of the child at hospital, coupled with further examinations as the boundaries of the injury become clearer, is valuable and can be coordinated with dressing changes if required. Photography, both close-up and whole body to show overall pattern, is invaluable for later reference and study and to assist with the presentation of evidence in court. Drawings are also helpful. The usual assessments of developmental level, growth and behaviour of the child are made.

PRESENTATION OF EVIDENCE IN COURT

Where a child has bruises or other typical non-accidental injuries, the bruises should be included in the evidence, although the exact aetiology may remain open in terms of medical opinion unless it is clear exactly how the injury was inflicted. It would be unusual for the doctor to be able to be dogmatic about the exact nature of many of the burns in this situation. Where the injury is exclusively a burn, which may be extensive or serious, and where the history permits a clearer opinion to be formed, it is often the best policy to present to the court the reasoning behind the diagnosis.

CASE HISTORY 4
The mother's story was that a 4-year-old child with stocking distribution scald had been left alone and happy for a few minutes in the bath in warm water which could not have scalded him. On his mother's return he had got out of the bath, was dripping wet and his feet were badly scalded in a symmetrical stocking distribution.

It is reasonable to examine the various possible scenarios one by one for the court, starting with the accidental version (e.g. he turned the tap on, the water got hot and he got out) followed by what it is thought really happened. The pros and cons of each argument are weighed up with a final statement of which one — on the balance of probabilities — seems most likely.

In this way the court is able to follow the reasoning and explore the possibilities, hopefully coming to an agreement as to what is likely to have happened. Using this method, a direct statement

of an opinion is avoided that the child has been abused too early in the evidence, and the phrase 'I found it difficult to see how it could have happened in the way stated' is useful. Another useful phrase is 'one is left with few other reasonable alternatives than that this burn was deliberately inflicted on the child'. Caution is required but cases can be brought for child protection on the balance of probability rule if there is general agreement that the history is not adequate.

FOLLOW-UP

This is often undertaken with a paediatrician or plastic surgeon with an interest in burns. Behaviour problems are common in this group of children. Foster-parents may come to recognise the signs and symptoms of other forms of abuse, notably sexual. Psychological help may be necessary for the most disturbed children.

Psychological effects of injury

The psychological and emotional consequences of inflicted burns are likely in general to be more severe than the physical effects. They may have a devastating effect on the psychological health of the child, who may show persistent behavioural difficulties extending into adult life.

Sequelae

Burns and scalds in children are associated with acute and chronic physical and psychological sequelae. The child with physical scars will have a constant reminder of his abuse, which may reinforce the emotional difficulties and interfere with psychological healing. Adults have sometimes revealed scars which they acquired in childhood burns, expressing confusion and anxiety when attempting to remember how they might have been caused.

Repetition of burns in childhood

Burns cause extreme pain, and repetition of accidental injury is uncommon. In contrast, repeated incidents are not uncommon in abuse and should arouse suspicion. Children with several separate burns which could not have arisen at the same time are likely to have been abused.

Summary

1. Most burn and scald injuries in childhood occur in preschool children and should be prevented.

2. Accidents follow brief lapses in protection, neglect as part of a pattern of inadequate parenting and abuse when injury is deliberately inflicted.

3. Burns and scalds following abuse are under-reported.

4. Evaluation is difficult requiring a careful and detailed history. A visit to the home may be necessary.

5. Non-accidental thermal injuries include forced immersion and pour scald, contact, friction and chemical burns.

6. Sites in abuse particularly include backs of hands, buttocks, genitalia and feet. No site is exempt.

7. Significant points in the history are un-witnessed incidents, delayed presentation, mini-misation of severity of injury, surprising lack of pain, repeated burns.

8. Differential diagnosis includes other skin pathology, especially infections.

9. There is a particular association between sexual abuse and burns.

10. Repeated burns are a dangerous form of neglect.

11. Burns may be associated with any form of abuse.

12. Medical assessment is often complex and requires the opinion of plastic surgeons, A & E surgeons and nurses experienced in treating burns.

13. Emotional sequelae are expected to be severe and longlasting.

14. When giving evidence in court, build up the diagnosis to explain the final opinion.

REFERENCE

Alexander R C, Surrell J A, Cohle S 1987 Microwave oven burns to children: an unusual manifestation of child abuse. Pediatrics 79: 255–259

Feldman K W, Schaller R T, Feldman J A, McMillan M 1978 Tap water scalds in children. Pediatrics 62: 1–7

Hight D W, Bakalar H R, Lloyd J R 1979 Inflicted burns in children. Recognition and treatment. JAMA 242: 517–520

Hobbs C J 1986 When are burns not accidental? Archives of Disease in Childhood 61: 357–361

Hobbs C J, Wynne J M 1990 The sexually abused battered child. Archives of Disease in Childhood 65: 423–427

Jackson R H (Chairman) 1985 Report of a working party on burn and scald accidents to children. Child Accident Prevention Trust. Bedford Square Press, London

Johnson C F 1990 The hand as a target organ in child abuse. Clin Pediatr (Phila) 29 (2): 66–72

Keen J H, Lendrum J, Wolman B 1975 Inflicted burns and scalds in children. British Medical Journal 4: 268–269

Lenoski E F, Hunter K A 1977 Specific patterns of inflicted burn injuries. J Trauma 17: 842–846

Martin H L 1970 Antecedents of burns and scalds in children. British Journal of Medical Psychology 43: 39–47

Moritz A R, Henriques F C 1947 Studies of thermal injury: the relative importance of time and temperature in the causation of cutaneous burns. American Journal of Pathology 23: 695–720

Phillips P S, Pickrell E, Morse T S 1974 Intentional burning. A severe form of child abuse. Journal of the American College of Emergency Physicians 3: 388–390

Purdue G F, Hunt J L, Prescott P R 1988 Child abuse by burning — an index of suspicion. J Trauma 28: 221–224

Raine P A M, Azmy A 1983 A review of thermal injuries in young children. Journal of Pediatric Surgery 18: 21–26

Showers J, Garrison K M 1988 Burn abuse: a four year study. J Trauma 28: 1581–1583

Smith S M, Hanson R 1974 Battered children — a medical and psychological study. British Medical Journal iii: 666–670

Stone N D, Rinaldo L, Humphrey C R, Brown R H 1970 Child abuse by burning. Surg Clin North Amer 50: 1419–1424

Wheeler D, Hobbs C J 1988 Mistakes in diagnosing non-accidental injury, 10 years experience. British Medical Journal 296: 1233–1236

FURTHER READING

Hobbs C J 1989 Burns and scalds. In: Meadow S R (ed) ABC of child abuse. British Medical Journal

6. Neglect

Working Together defines neglect as 'The persistent or severe neglect of a child, or the failure to protect a child from exposure to any kind of danger, including cold or starvation or, extreme failure to carry out important aspects of care, resulting in the significant impairment of the child's health or development, including non-organic failure to thrive' (Working Together 1991).

Kempe & Goldbloom (1987) wrote 'neglect can be a very insidious form of maltreatment. It implies failure of the parent to act properly in safeguarding the health, safety and well being of the child'.

Helfer (1987) widened the definition to beyond an individual's (parent's) responsibility to that of society, when he described the 'litany of smouldering neglect' whereby many children in the USA are brought up in poverty, do not have access to health care, do not finish their education, can not read, and drift into drugs, crime and jails.

In 1991 the UK government became a signatory to the United Nations Convention on the Rights of the Child (1989). The first General Declaration on the Rights of the Child was in 1924 — but Declarations are not binding, Conventions are. Thus broad statements such as Article 24 'the right of the child to the enjoyment of the highest attainable standard of health and the facility for the treatment of illness and rehabilita-tion of health' are agreed. Countries should take measures to diminish infant and child mortality, promote health education and prevent accidents. It is also stated in Article 19 that legislative, administrative, social and educational measures should be taken to protect children from all forms of physical and mental violence, injury and abuse (including sexual abuse) and negligent treatment.

In the UK The National Children's Bureau (1987) had already written of the social measures necessary to have a real impact on the welfare of children and in particular to affect:

- perinatal and infant mortality
- immunisation
- child health
- child abuse
- cigarette smoking
- drug abuse.

The improvements in social conditions required attention to:

- unemployment
- homelessness
- poverty.

Clearly very many social issues are raised and it is not surprising that Helfer (1990) wrote of the increasing ' "de-emphasis" on the neglect of the children whereby even those professionals mandated to report neglect may not, feeling nothing will be done (or can be done) by overwhelmed under resourced child protective service agencies'.

But, as Helfer comments, the needs of children are known and understood and the consequences of a neglected childhood predictable. Childhood is a vulnerable time and needs not met during the child's period of growth may have irreversible consequences.

INCIDENCE OF NEGLECT (Table 6.1)

It is difficult to know how many children are neglected in the UK. Certainly those who are registered represent only the tip of the iceberg. In a survey of Child Protection Registers in 1988

Table 6.1   Children on Child Protection Registers (% in category) (Creighton & Noyes 1990)

Year	Neglect	Neglect and physical or sexual abuse	Emotional abuse
1983–87	6	—	—
1988	6	7.5	2.0
1990	8	10.0	3.0

(Children and Young Persons on Child Protection Registers 1988) 13% were registered because of neglect, 2% because of neglect and physical abuse, less than 1% because of neglect, physical abuse and sexual abuse, and less than 1% neglect and sexual abuse.

The NSPCC statistics from 1983–87 (Creighton & Noyes 1989) record only 6% of children on registers because of neglect in their sample of 10 areas. This figure was static over the 5-year period, which clearly needs explanation. Were all the workers engulfed in the rise of recognition of child sexual abuse? Conditions for children had not improved during those years.

In 1988, 6% of registrations again were because of neglect, rising to 8% in 1990. If neglect in association with physical or sexual abuse or both is included, the percentages are 7.5% in 1989 and 10% in 1990. An additional 2% and 3% were registered because of emotional abuse (Creighton & Noyes 1990). The average age of children registered because of neglect was 4 years 9 months. As with physical abuse, neglect continues throughout childhood but professionals (and society) find it too difficult to manage and so fail to acknowledge neglect in older children.

Family factors in cases of neglect

The NSPCC statistics (Creighton & Noyes 1990) record only 15% of mothers and 39% of fathers in paid employment, mostly semi-skilled and unskilled manual jobs. 'Debt' was a significant stress in 22% of families, 'marital problems' were the commonest recorded stress factor noted in 30% of families. 38% of children registered because of neglect were living with their mother alone. The professional assessment in neglect cases was most likely to be that the primary stress factor was 'inability to respond to the maturational needs of the child'.

The serious consequences of neglect should not be dismissed in the short or the long term. Although this chapter emphasises the insidious long-term damage caused by neglect, the factor of neglect is not always recognised in mortality figures.

CASE HISTORY 1
A 4-year-old boy was found dead in bed. He had had measles and autopsy showed he had died of bronchopneumonia. The family were well known to professional agencies. The boy had 'failed to thrive', and was not immunised. The family had recently moved into temporary housing known to be cold, with a leaking roof. They were not registered with a general practitioner and when the Emergency Call Service (Emergency Doctor Service) arrived it was too late. It was Christmas Day.

CASE HISTORY 2
A single mother and her children aged 3 and 1 years lived in sheltered housing. The mother was very independent and known to be 'difficult'. She had a past history of drug abuse but was not currently abusing drugs or alcohol. Her 3 older children were in the care of their father. When the younger child became ill his mother said that the doctor was not needed. Three days later his mother arrived screaming at the warden's office that her son was dead. He died in the ambulance. Autopsy showed that the 14-month-old child had died of septicaemia secondary to otitis media.

CASE HISTORY 3
4-year-old twins were playing on the railway line. Their mother had left them for the afternoon with their father and his partner, neither of whom wished to share the care of the boys. One boy was hit by the foot plate on a passing express train and killed. The Coroner commented on the need for British Rail to keep their fences in better repair.

In the first case death was recorded as due to 'natural causes', that is 'measles'. There are 15 deaths each year in the UK due to measles. Some may be inevitable but others are preventable. In the second case proper medical care was denied to the child, and the twins were not protected from danger.

These three deaths were due to neglect; many like these go unrecorded and unrecognised as part of Helfer's (1990) neglected neglect.

FAMILY LIFE AND CHILD-REARING IN A CHANGING SOCIETY

Child-rearing is difficult in a complex, rapidly

changing society. The effects of these changes will be evident in the well-being of children. Disadvantage in one aspect of life begets disadvantage in other fields. The UN Convention (1989) in the preamble states 'that the child, for the full and harmonious development of his or her personality, should grow up in a family environment, in an atmosphere of love and understanding'.

What is the state of the family in the UK in 1991? Current statistics (Population Trends 1991, OPCS 1990) show that:

- almost one-third of births were outside marriage in 1991 compared with 12.5% in 1981.
- over half of these 'illegitimate' babies are registered in the name of both parents.
- marriage rates and remarriage rates are falling as cohabitation rates rise.
- divorce rates are rising; an estimated 153 000 children under 16 years were affected in England and Wales in 1990.
- 17% of all families in the UK are lone parents (over 90% lone mother) and one-third of children will experience lone parenthood in childhood.
- around 1.6 million children have a lone parent in the UK.
- around half of lone parents marry or re-marry within 5 years (Ermisch 1986).
- cohabitation, reconciliation and the non-dependence of teenagers contribute to 'outflow' from lone parenthood (Edwards 1991).
- 100 000 14–16 year-old children disappeared from home in 1989 (24 000 more than in 1987).

The Children Act 1989 emphasises that children need families. A main principle of the Act is that 'wherever possible, children should be brought up and cared for within their own families' and parents are to be supported to help bring up their children (in need).

Research shows that children do better when cared for by their natural parents and that children are hurt when this relationship breaks down. The divorce rate in the UK is currently one-third of all marriages and rising. Remarriage fails to repair the damage caused by divorce; 'grief and disruption' is long lasting (Phillips 1991).

It is evident that social policy must take account of these new patterns of family life. Children need stability and security but adults need assistance to provide for the needs of children. Phillips (1991) suggests that, to improve support, family relationship measures would include:

- improving the economic position of families,
- educating all children about relationships and parenthood,
- a network of counselling services to help family relationships in trouble.

Poverty is a major stress in many families, and particularly single parent families, but improving the economic status of families will not resolve the rejection many children feel following divorce. The consequences of the breakdown of emotional relationships within families lead some children to leave home early, to premature cohabitation, marriage, parenthood and divorce. Education and ultimate career prospects for some children are jeopardised by the divorce of their parents.

SOCIAL DISADVANTAGE, CHILD HEALTH AND CHILD REARING

There are clear links between ill health and social deprivation. Adversities tend to be multiple and further adversity compounds disadvantage.

Wedge & Essex (1982) showed the overlap between:

- one parent or large family
- low income
- poor housing.

and to this should be added:

- impaired health
- poor growth
- school failure
- history of accidents.

Childhood deprivation is used to describe the condition of children whose needs are not met — whether emotionally, socially or in terms of learning opportunity. Patterns of disadvantage tend to continue from one generation to the next as children from impoverished families become inadequate parents themselves. However children are resilient and many, in spite of difficult childhoods, do survive and become successful adults. The less lucky or more susceptible do not.

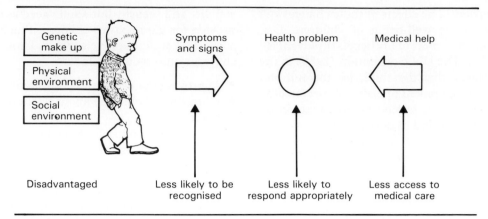

Fig. 6.1   The disadvantaged family. The members of a family at disadvantage are more likely to fall ill, they have fewer personal and material resources to cope with illness, and there are fewer medical resources available to them. (Reproduced from Polnay L, Hull D 1985 Families and homes. In: Community paediatrician. Churchill Livingstone, London.)

Childhood poverty is increasing in the UK:

● 1 in 4 or 1 in 5 children live below the poverty line (Delamothe 1991).

● Over 65% of lone parent families depend entirely on income support (HMSO 1991).

● Except for Ireland and Portugal the UK has the highest proportion of children in the EC living below 50% of average expenditure level (Smith P 1991).

● 10% of families do not have money for out-of-school activities and 14% lack an outing for children once a week (Smith P 1991).

Childhood poverty and health are closely associated (Smith P 1991). Table 6.2 summarises some of the statistics relating child mortality to occupational class.

Neonatal deaths are related to maternal age, poverty, social class, place of birth and region, birth weight, and legal status of the infant (Madeley 1991). Although the levels of neonatal mortality reflect the effectiveness of maternity services, a closer relationship, particularly worldwide, is with income.

Even in the UK there are marked regional differences. (Table 6.3)

The perinatal mortality rate, stillbirths and infant deaths are high in disadvantaged Asian communities (Table 6.4). Whilst consanguinous marriage, high maternal age and parity have an

Table 6.2   Occupational class and mortality (OPCS 1987)

	Social class I	Social class V	Illegitimate	New Commonwealth Pakistan
Still birth/1000 live births [1]	3.4	6.8		
Neonatal mortality/1000 live births	3.9	5.9	6.1	6.8
Post-neonatal mortality/ 1000 live births	3.0	5.9	9.0[2]	6.5[3]
Infant deaths/1000 live births (< 1 year)	7.0	11.8		
Children (1–16 years) Standard mortality rate [4]	< 80	> 160		

1. Births within marriage, England and Wales 1988
2. Mother < 20 years and lives in N.W. England
3. Mother born in Pakistan
4. England and Wales 1978–79 and 1982–83

Table 6.3 Infant mortality 1986–1988 by geographical situation

	*Perinatal deaths	†Infant deaths
Bradford	13.5	14.3
Gateshead	12.1	10.2
Powys	12.3	7.3
Huntingdon	5.1	5.1
England and Wales	9.1	9.3

*per 1000 stillbirths and deaths in first week of life
†per 1000 live births

influence on these figures, poverty, poor nutrition and housing are likely to be more important (Black 1991). Access to appropriate medical care is more problematical, especially to families where English is a second language.

Post-neonatal deaths have a marked seasonal variation in the UK, not mirrored in Scandinavian countries which are colder but have better, warmer housing. The potential for prevention is in good child care, especially during cold weather, improved nutrition, and housing. Sir Donald Acheson (the retiring Chief Medical Officer) in launching 'The Health of the Nation' said 'Health inequalities will be eradicated only by government measures to tackle poverty and improve conditions in which people live' (Smith F 1991). It has been assessed that if all children in the UK enjoyed the same survival chances as the children of professionals and managers over 3000 deaths a year might be prevented (Whitehead & Dahlgren 1991).

Infant deaths, and particularly deaths from Sudden Infant Death Syndrome (SIDS), are related to social disadvantage. Over-represented are families with young, single mothers, living in socially disadvantaged areas. The baby is more likely to have been born preterm, of low birth weight, twin pregnancy and been bottle fed, and live in a household with smokers. The incidence of SIDS

Table 6.4 SMR ratios by mother's country of birth (Balarajan et al 1989)

	UK	India	Bangladesh	Pakistan
Standardised mortality rates, stillbirths and deaths up to one year	96	134	118	237

in families where there has been previous child maltreatment is higher than might be expected.

CASE HISTORY 4

Mr and Mrs A had 3 children living at home; the youngest was a baby of 3 months. Mrs A's first child was neglected and made the subject of a Care Order and adopted aged 4 years.

The parents had a fierce argument, about Mr A's excessive drinking. Mrs A stormed out and disappeared (as she had done many times before). Mr A went to collect the two older children from day nursery. He told the staff he needed help with the baby. Social Services arranged for the baby to go to foster-parents.

The baby arrived at the foster-parents' home at 19:30, brought by the social worker. When the baby failed to take his feed this was put down to a change of routine. The baby was put in his cot by the foster-mother who noticed he was hot and had a 'funny cry'. Half an hour later the baby was found dead in his cot. Autopsy revealed the baby had an upper respiratory tract infection but nothing more.

Did the foster-parents, without prior knowledge of the baby or his behaviour, fail to recognise the symptoms of an ill baby? (Stanton et al 1978).

CASE HISTORY 5

A baby aged 6 months was found dead in his cot. He was very thin, had numerous bruises on his chest and back, scratches on his face and he was dirty with severe nappy rash. Two children were subsequently born to this family. They were severely neglected and Care Orders were made at the age of 2 and 1 years.

Following the death of the first child an autopsy report commented on the poor growth and superficial injuries of the baby. No cause of death was found. The parents were reassured and told 'they had nothing to reproach themselves for'.

Why did he die?

Cot death, neglect or filicide?

The difficult task of the differentiation between Sudden Infant Death Syndrome (SIDS) and smothering is reviewed in more detail in Chapter 12. (Emery & Taylor 1986, Meadow 1990, Newlands & Emery 1991).

The rate of SIDS in the UK is approximately 2 per 1000 live births. A small proportion of these are thought to be due to filicide (Emery 1985). The features which may assist in the recognition of smothering have been suggested by Meadow (1989):

• previous episode of unexplained apnoea, seizures or 'near miss cot death',

- an infant over 6 months of age,
- previous unexplained disorders affecting the child,
- other unexplained deaths of children in the same family.

Oliver (1983) explored these unexplained deaths in childhood by studying the deaths of children from families known to Social Services because of abuse or neglect, over a 20-year follow-up period. 41 children died out of a total 560 children in 147 families. This is about 7% of the children, all before they were 8 years old and the majority under 1 year. 29 of the deaths were thought to be due to abuse or neglect.

It is difficult to tease out the various strands which contribute to the excess mortality of babies and children in socially disadvantaged families. Important factors are:

- low birth weight
- poor nutrition
- lack of immunisation
- damp, cold housing
- cigarette-smoking carers
- increased rate of respiratory disorders
- poverty (causing stress, poor diet, bad housing, etc.).

Access to medical care is often less than ideal in socially disadvantaged families and this adds to the difficulty in providing optimum care. As many as 1 in 7 families in inner-city areas are not registered with a GP. This is partly due to frequent house moves, which are themselves disruptive to family life. Medical care is thus limited to 'emergencies' and health visitors have the difficult task of contacting these highly mobile families where statistics show there is an increased incidence of medical and developmental disorders in the children.

It is estimated that 'preventable' causes of infant death are three times as common in social class V as social class I (Spencer 1991).

Child-adult morbidity and poverty

Whitehead & Dahlgren (1991) wrote '. . . social inequalities in health are evident for most diseases and from birth to old age . . . .' Barker (1990) also saw the continuum of poor socioeconomic circumstances in childhood leading into disease developing in later life. Smith (1990) described adults in social class V with a life expectancy 8 years shorter than social class I, three times as much mental illness, more coronary heart disease, lower self-esteem and lower immunisation rates. The origins of these disparities in health were in:

- perinatal and infant morbidity
- low birth weight
- infectious disease, respiratory disease
- accidents
- height (an indicator of nutrition in childhood)
- dental health.

Low birth weight is a major cause of morbidity and has a strong social class gradient. Additional evidence is accumulating that social disadvantage may effect the development of diseases in later life (Smith F 1991). The standardised mortality ratio for men in social class V is twice that for men in social class I, much the same picture as for children in social class V compared with social class I (OPCS 1988). The effect of social disadvantage is shown particularly in respiratory, circulatory and musculoskeletal disorders. Thus not only do the poorest have shorter lives but their health is worse from childhood onwards (Davey Smith et al 1990).

CASE HISTORY 6
A boy of 6 years was admitted to a children's ward very ill due to pneumonia. He was wasted, stunted and anaemic. A tracheo-oesophageal fistula had been repaired at birth. Early surgical follow-up showed good progress. At 3 years he was referred to a paediatrician because of 'asthma'. He was lost to follow-up at 4½ years. The family were known to various agencies as a 'problem'.

On admission aged 6 years his mother said he had been unwell for more than a year. He weighed less at 6 years than at 4½ years. The pneumonia proved untreatable and lobectomy was performed.

Was this neglect? Could the family, GP, school health service have recognised this earlier? Did the hospital fail to pass on to primary care the need for follow-up?

CASE HISTORY 7
A boy of 7 years was admitted to a children's ward 'acutely' with empyema and septicaemia. He nearly died. He has been left with impaired respiratory function. At review various other medical problems were identified in the boy and his 5-year-old brother:

- severe dental caries requiring extractions and dentures
- failure to thrive
- untreated hypospadias and undescended testes.

As in Case 6, a 'difficult' family, and an inadequate health surveillance system conspired to impair the health of these boys.

Nutrition is related to growth and health. Low income families have not only to spend a high percentage of their money on food (30%), calorie for calorie 'unhealthy' foods are cheaper (Spencer 1991).

Housing is clearly related to health and social disadvantages. Nearly 100 000 households involving children were registered homeless in 1988 (Lowry S 1991). Over half the bed and breakfast, bedsit and hostel accommodation fails to meet health and safety standards (Gillen 1991). Thus not only are children living in cramped, unsuitable housing — it is also damp, cold, unhygienic and unsafe. High-rise flats are unsuitable for children, young and older, who need safe, supervised playing areas. Mothers too become depressed and isolated when separated from friends and family.

Accidents are a major child health problem in the UK and many more children from socially disadvantaged homes are killed or maimed, adding disability to disadvantage. Half of the deaths in children aged 1–15 years are due to 'accidents' and over half of these are caused by road traffic accidents. Much of the serious morbidity due to accidents follows traffic accidents.

Deaths from road traffic accidents where the child is usually a pedestrian, drowning in canals or deaths on railway tracks show a 5–10-fold variation with social class. This reflects not only lack of supervision of children but also the inadequacy of

Table 6.5   Accidents in children

- More than 50% of deaths in childhood are due to accidents, poisoning, violence.
- 20% of children have a significant injury each year.
- More than 60% of pedestrian deaths are on minor roads (near home).
- Peak age for pedestrian deaths is 4–6 years (majority under 10 years).
- Peak time for pedestrian deaths is late afternoon.
- Twice as many deaths due to road traffic accident (RTA) in boys as compared to girls.
- Twice as many deaths due to RTA in social class 5 as compared to 1.

play areas in many inner-city areas, and the failure to protect children from traffic by road planners.

Accidents within the home are related to lapses in supervision, for example another child is ill and the mother is distracted. Antecedents of accidents are that the family have just moved, the parents split up or the mother is depressed. Accidents also happen to more boys, especially those described as over-active, distractable or 'accident-prone', often in socially disadvantaged families (Tables 6.5 and 6.6).

CASE HISTORY 8
A boy of 10 years was admitted to the Intensive Care Unit unconscious having been involved in a road traffic accident. His sister, aged 8 years, and he had been chased home by a 'gang' of boys, from the same school, and in their escape had run across a busy road and into a car. The boy had learning problems and was supported in mainstream school, having an Educational Statement of Special Needs. He was tall, clumsy and poorly cared for, being dirty and smelly. His single parent mother was out at work when the children came home from school. The family were constantly harassed in the neighbourhood; the eldest boy was in prison.
The injured boy recovered but has suffered permanent brain damage.

The rates of death from injury have changed very little in the UK in the last 20 years. Disagreement continues as to who is responsible but the Child Accident Prevention Trust (Jackson et al 1988) advocates the need for education and a multi-disciplinary approach to the problem of accidents in children.

A suggested model is given in Figure 6.2.

CHILD-REARING AND NEGLECT

In 1991 the UK Government became a signatory to most of the UN Conventions on the Rights of the Child. Under Article 27 the Convention is clear on the need for family and State responsibility.

Table 6.6   Repeated accidents

- More boys
- More inner city, no garden
- Children described as restless, fidgety, disobedient, enuretic, nail biters, destructive, aggressive
- Families known to Social Services Department
- Frequent house moves
- Young, depressed, stressed mothers

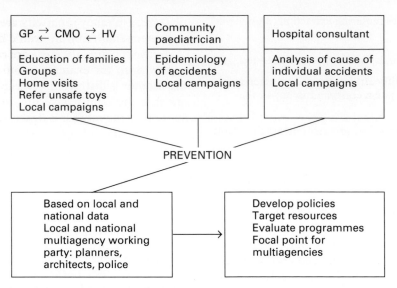

Fig. 6.2 Coordinated accident prevention within a health district. GP = general practitioner, CMO = clinical medical officer, HV = health visitor.

• The parents have the primary responsibility to secure the conditions of living necessary for the child's development.

• The State shall assist parents, and in cases of need provide material assistance, particularly with regard to nutrition, clothing and housing.

Society therefore has a view as to child-rearing practice but is the responsibility for children to be shared, with parents enabled and empowered, or is the current trend in the UK to prevail with an increasing devolution on the individual? Helfer (1987) has written of the consequences of a society which neglects its children, at the family and societal level.

Poverty makes child-rearing difficult; the least able in society are the poorest and thus they have to function particularly efficiently to overcome the effects of social disadvantage and be successful parents.

Money is a buffer which is taken for granted by those with adequate means, whilst poverty increases stresses on the often impoverished emotional resources of the family, which further impairs coping skills.

Child health clinics and paediatric out-patient clinics are populated with parents of all social classes who are experiencing difficulty in child-rearing. Whilst neglect in the terms outlined in this chapter is associated with poor physical care and often poverty, emotional abuse and deprivation occur at all income levels and also lead to unhappy, disturbed, under-achieving children (Ch. 7).

Parents who neglect their children fail to care for their children physically or to supervise them and do not engage the developmental needs of the child in terms of cognitive stimulation (Skuse 1989). As the child grows the parents do not respond to him or provide for his complex and changing needs.

Childhood — which should be joyful, exciting and full of promise — becomes an existence, the child being cold, hungry, tired, uncomfortable, unloved and consequently showing a lack of interest in people and his surroundings. Neglected children are emotionally deprived children and may also suffer other abuses, such as physical or sexual abuse.

In infancy, neglected children will be recognised by their poor physical state and their failure to thrive and achieve age-appropriate developmental skills. The pre-school child may not only be small, thin, poorly cared for and developmentally delayed, but may also have difficulty in forming relationships and show behavioural problems. At school the neglected child will have learning (especially language and attention) problems, as well as increasingly evident emotional difficulties.

Emotionally abused children may be physically well cared for but suffer the same consequences in terms of learning and emotional development. Neglected children are physically neglected and emotionally deprived. The progress neglected and emotionally deprived children make when moved into well-functioning alternative families may be dramatic. The longer a child is neglected, the worse the outcome in terms of emotional competence and the acquisition of educational and social skills needed in adult life. (Table 6.7)

What are a child's needs? (Table 6.7)

Children have differing needs at different ages, but all children need adequate nutrition, warmth, housing, love, understanding, security, education and health services. Children need protection from illness, accident, cruelty, neglect, exploitation (child labour) and discrimination (colour, race, gender). In the UK this is best provided by two caring adults who care for each other as well as the children.

What does a newborn baby need?

Food, warmth, comfort, company, sleep, grooming and movement are the essentials. How will the parents meet the newborn baby's needs? This will depend on their knowledge and understanding of child-rearing, social and cultural influences and whether they themselves were warmly nurtured as children. Parents who have been neglected them-

Table 6.7 The needs of children

- Food
- Warmth
- Clothing
- Shelter/protection
- Grooming
- Fresh air/sunlight
- Activity/rest
- Prevention of illness and accident
- Affection
- Continuity of care
- Security of belonging
- Personal identity
- Opportunity to learn
- Opportunity to achieve success
- Opportunity to achieve independence

selves may have great difficulty in parenting but this is not inevitable. Education in schools is essential to supplement deficits in knowledge provided at home.

The practical needs of the baby include:

- Milk — breast/bottle (sterilisation equipment)
- Warm room
- Access to hot water
- Access to feeding 3–4 hourly.

Emotional needs. Rearing a baby is a 24-hour commitment, 7 days a week. Was the child planned? Was the baby wanted in order to be a provider of love? Is the baby difficult, a slow feeder needing small (2–3 hourly) feeds, irritable and so relentlessly testing his mother's skills? Is the mother tired, young, educationally slow, inexperienced, alone? Is the house adequate or is it difficult to keep warm or clean, or obtain hot water? Does the mother get help, both physically and emotionally? If she gets tired or becomes depressed, can she respond to the needs of the baby? Does the baby become cross and more irritable or apathetic and disinterested? Is this baby just one stress too many in the household?

It is easy to see how babies become too much for parents without support or with inadequate support systems, and care deteriorates as the parents struggle with their own unmet needs and difficulties, as well as the increasing demands of the baby.

What do older babies and toddlers need?

As the baby grows it is no longer appropriate that he sleeps so much; he sits up, wants to move and explore, uses his hands and begins to talk. Feeding is more difficult as he needs solids, a variety of foods, and to be spoon-fed. All these needs require more planning, time and patience on the part of the parents. As he becomes mobile the home needs modifying to enable him freedom to explore, but it also needs 'child-proofing'. Stairgates, fireguards, cookerguards are simple protective devices which are often not used, yet may allow the child space in safety. By eye contact, smiles, laughs and coos the child communicates his pleasure. Waving and clapping are early signs in communication. It is expected that the child is taken to the well-baby clinic to be weighed, to be immunised, to have his development screened and his hearing checked and any problems discussed. Babies are seen in clinic most frequently in the first 12 months of life, on average 6 times, but social class I and V mothers attend least frequently.

As the child grows older he is dependent on his carers to continue to provide materially, but also to talk, play and show interest.

Needs of the pre-school child

A child who is not spoken to, or only hears occasional commands, does not learn to listen and pay attention. Visual and auditory attention are essential if the child is to benefit from the learning opportunities about him. Sitting on his mother's knee from 12–15 months, looking at pictures in a book, pointing, listening, experimenting with sounds, the child will learn to look, hear, pay attention and communicate. Delay in language development is universal in neglected children.

At mealtimes a child has to learn to sit at the table, not to wander and to use implements rather than finger-feed. He has to be toilet trained and shown how to dress. If he has not learned these basic skills by school entry he will already be grossly disadvantaged.

Needs of the school child

At school children are required to sit, listen to a story or follow complex instructions, hold a pencil, cope with dinner and playtime, change for PE and use the toilets appropriately. A child's language should be at the level of 'reading readiness'. He needs to be able to separate from his mother. He also needs to be able to form relationships with his peer group and previously unknown adults.

Children need to belong and be the 'same'. At school the child needs to be clean, tidily dressed and not to smell. He does not want to look or feel different from his peers. He does not want his parents to dress or behave differently, especially in school, from other parents.

Children need home to be organised with a routine for getting up, having meals, baths, clean clothes, going to bed. To succeed at school a child needs to be on time and to attend regularly. Poor school attendance, whether due to intercurrent illness or family disorganisation, leads to a discontinuity which slows academic progress. Neglected visual or auditory impairments disadvantage the child who is trying to learn to read.

Children of all ages need encouragement and success to allow them to develop confidence and self-esteem. Parental support and their appreciation of the value of education is essential to help motivate the child.

Children need to start to take responsibility to help in the home, care for pets, and visit Granny. They need increasing experience and activities outside the home to develop greater independence as they learn more of their world.

The child's development, both in social skills and emotionally, is largely determined by his relationship with his main caretakers, usually his mother. Clearly, relationships with the other parent, siblings and grandparents are also important, as is the relationship between the parents. It is of great importance in the long term for the child to form at least one close, positive and secure relationship. This does not have to be with his mother, but the relationship with the caring adult should be long-term and close. The lack of such a relationship does not mean that the child will inevitably become stunted emotionally but it makes it more difficult for the child to form good secure attachments in the long term.

It also appears that some children are less vulnerable than others in that they are more able to form other relationships and develop social networks outside the emotionally neglecting home. This gives the child the opportunity to have alternative social experience and aid his emotional growth. Thus, although many emotionally neglected children have problems initially with peer relationships which continue to affect adult relationships, this is not inevitable.

Needs of the teenager

Teenagers need much the same, and more in many ways than younger children. They continue to need family organisation and routine but also boundaries to test, to discover the tolerable limits of their behaviour. They need constant love and emotional support to help them cope with the demands of peers, school and their own aspirations.

They need adults who can cope with the excesses of their behaviour and do not reject them.

They need adults to help with school work and to provide an environment in which it can be done. They also need adults outside the home in whom they may confide. Teenagers worry about health, sex, sexuality, careers, everything, and need informed caring adults, not always parents, to advise.

CLINICAL ASPECTS OF NEGLECT

Neglected children present in many ways to the doctor (Table 6.8): the baby with severe cradle-cap who is failing to thrive, the toddler of 2 years who has ingested his mother's iron tablets, the 5-year-old suffering the complications of measles or the 8-year-old child who is failing at school. Essentially, neglect and its consequences are preventable and so present a challenge to all who work with children and their families, especially in primary care.

The clinician's task is primarily that of assessment of the child's growth, development and physical health (Table 6.9). This is put in the context of a family assessment in collaboration

Table 6.8 Physical manifestations and consequences of neglect

Deprivation	Result	Long-term effect
1. Supervision/safe environment	Accidents — falls, scalds, ingestions, RTA, drowning, house fires	Morbidity from accidents, e.g. brain damage
2. Lack of seat belt in car/helmet when cycling	Accidents/death	As above
3. Medical care:		
— fail to immunise	Measles, rubella, mumps whooping cough etc.	Deafness, brain damage, death, lung damage, fetal damage
— fail to seek advice for ill child	Illness recognised when child seriously ill/dying	Persisting morbidity e.g. empyema, suppurative otitis media, brain damage
— fail to attend for developmental surveillance	Squint, deafness, other disorders not recognised	Amblyopia, poor speech, learning difficulties
— refuse medical care	Prolonged illness, avoidable complication, death	Avoidable death and morbidity
4. Hygiene in home	Repeated episodes of gastroenteritis, skin infections, head lice, zoonoses,	Fail to thrive. Poor self-esteem. Ostracised at school.
Clean (smoke- and mould-free) air	Dirty child. Infection: especially respiratory, asthma	Chronic respiratory disease
Clean water	Increased lead burden	Behavioural and learning disorder
5. Warmth	Cold injury — red, swollen hands and feet. Hypothermia, hypostatic pneumonia. Infection, especially chest	Frostbite — loss of part of toes rarely.
6. Food Inadequate calories, inadequate feeding, inappropriate diet (including fads)	Malnourished — small, thin, protuberant, abdomen, may be stunted 'emotional dwarf' with apparent adequate nutrition: impaired brain growth (especially < 2 yrs), vitamin deficiencies	Impaired physical wellbeing, apathy. Learning difficulties. Stunted as adult (adapt to smallness)
7. Drink	Inappropriate patterns of drinking — e.g. from WC, drains — causing GI infections	
8. Physical care — grooming	Dry, thin, sparse hair, alopecia, cradle-cap, nappy rash, spotty skin, maceration in skin folds. Thickened, yellow nails. Dirty, smelly body with infestations, e.g. nits. Vulvovaginitis, especially young girls. Clothing inappropriate, inadequate, dirty.	Socially unacceptable at nursery/school — shunned by peers, i.e. additional emotional deprivation

Note: other environmental pollution
- lead from motor vehicle exhaust, old lead paint
- radioactivity from nuclear power plants
- toxocara in parks, playing fields
- dog-bites.

Table 6.9   Clinical assessment of neglect

Child's appearance	Note clothing, hair, skin, nails, odour
Growth	Height ⎫ serial measurements Weight ⎬ to check growth rate Head circumference Mid-upper arm circumference (MUAC)
Physical examination	Signs of disorder, e.g. squint, asthma, heart murmur, dental caries, undescended testes, CDH (congenital dislocation of hips), signs of physical or sexual abuse
Development	Gross motor skills Fine motor skills Vision ⎫ by age-appropriate Hearing ⎬ technique Language — receptive and expressive Play Behaviour — observed in clinic — information from third party

with the health visitor. It is always necessary to have a clear idea of normal development and not to accept 'his language is the norm for the area' when told of a neglected child with language delay. Usually children are seen over a period of time and by undertaking careful assessments it is possible to monitor the child: is he progressing at an adequate rate or is he slipping even further behind? Good records are essential to allow review and if the extra nursery time, health visitor and social work support are not effecting a change for the child, is it time to discuss alternative care? (Table 6.10).

Some doctors will wish to join the parents and other professionals in looking at any feeding problems, behavioural and learning difficulties and work together to plan a strategy to help the child within his family. Others will offer to monitor (objectively) the effects of the intervention.

PATHWAY TO NEGLECT

Why are children neglected and what are the ante-

Table 6.10   Additional information for assessment

1. Report from day nursery or school	Nursery nurse or teacher
2. Assessment of care at home	Health visitor or school nurse or social worker
3. Physical state of home	As above
4. Care of other children	As above

cedents? There clearly is a 'cycle of deprivation'. Neglected children are at risk of growing up into adults with limited skills in all sorts of areas and becoming inadequate, neglectful parents.

In the community there are many families being monitored by health and social work professionals: an example case history is given below (Fig. 6.3).

Assessing families

Much useful work has been undertaken recently to look at why parents may neglect children and how they may be helped to parent more adequately. The result of assessment may be that the particular parent or parents are not able at this point to provide adequate care.

A framework for categorising families is given in Table 6.11 (Crittenden 1988). Why are the parents failing? Are they able or motivated to change? What can be done to support the child and parents and improve their environment? Is the extended family helpful or destructive? Before statutory proceedings are considered, a thorough assessment and programme of support should be implemented to see if the family can change in time for this child. Parents do mature, do learn new skills and, if their material position improves, they may feel success is possible. Mild to moderate depression is endemic in mothers in inner cities. Their feelings of hopelessness — coupled with the enormity of the task of rearing children well, often alone, usually in poverty, in an impoverished environment — are real.

In some circumstances it is too dangerous to leave a baby at home and statutory proceedings have to be initiated early in the assessment. Rehabilitation to the home is always an option after a full review.

Which families are resistant to change?

Some families have overwhelming problems which are multiple; given that resources are limited the overall outcome may be dependent upon the presence of:

1. mental retardation of the adults
2. severe difficulty with interpersonal relationships

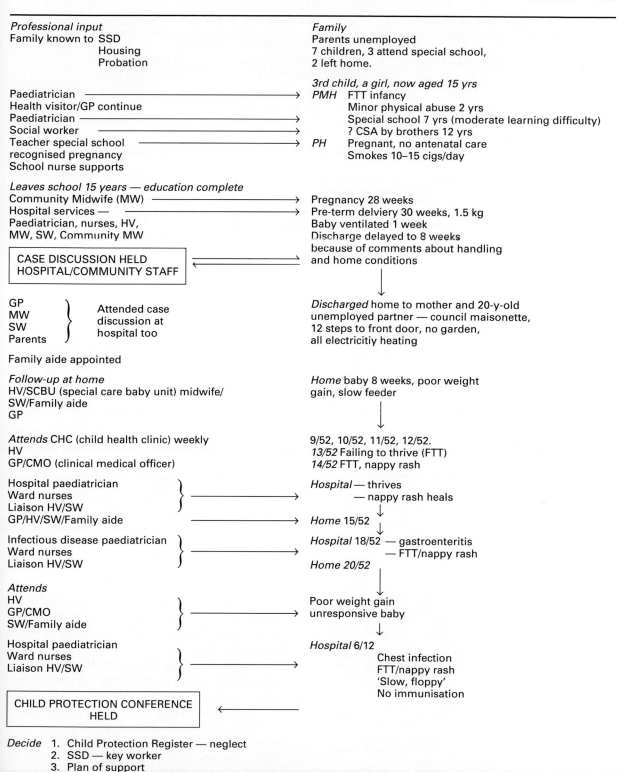

Professional input
Family known to SSD
              Housing
              Probation

Paediatrician ————————————————→
Health visitor/GP continue
Paediatrician —————————————————→
Social worker   ————————————→
Teacher special school   ———————→
recognised pregnancy
School nurse supports

Leaves school 15 years — education complete
Community Midwife (MW) ——————————→
Hospital services —   ——————————→
Paediatrician, nurses, HV,
MW, SW, Community MW

| CASE DISCUSSION HELD |
| HOSPITAL/COMMUNITY STAFF | ⇐══════════

GP
MW   } Attended case
SW   discussion at
Parents } hospital too

Family aide appointed

Follow-up at home
HV/SCBU (special care baby unit) midwife/
SW/Family aide
GP

Attends CHC (child health clinic) weekly
HV
GP/CMO (clinical medical officer)

Hospital paediatrician }
Ward nurses   } —————————→
Liaison HV/SW   }
GP/HV/SW/Family aide   —————————→

Infectious disease paediatrician }
Ward nurses   } ———————→
Liaison HV/SW   }

Attends
HV
GP/CMO   }
SW/Family aide } ———————————→

Hospital paediatrician }
Ward nurses   } ———————→
Liaison HV/SW   }

| CHILD PROTECTION CONFERENCE |
| HELD | ⇐————————

Family
Parents unemployed
7 children, 3 attend special school,
2 left home.

3rd child, a girl, now aged 15 yrs
PMH   FTT infancy
         Minor physical abuse 2 yrs
         Special school 7 yrs (moderate learning difficulty)
         ? CSA by brothers 12 yrs
PH   Pregnant, no antenatal care
         Smokes 10–15 cigs/day

Pregnancy 28 weeks
Pre-term delviery 30 weeks, 1.5 kg
Baby ventilated 1 week
Discharge delayed to 8 weeks
because of comments about handling
and home conditions

Discharged home to mother and 20-y-old
unemployed partner — council maisonette,
12 steps to front door, no garden,
all electricitiy heating

Home baby 8 weeks, poor weight
gain, slow feeder

9/52, 10/52, 11/52, 12/52.
13/52 Failing to thrive (FTT)
14/52 FTT, nappy rash

Hospital — thrives
             — nappy rash heals
Home 15/52

Hospital 18/52 — gastroenteritis
              — FTT/nappy rash
Home 20/52

Poor weight gain
unresponsive baby

Hospital 6/12
         Chest infection
         FTT/nappy rash
         'Slow, floppy'
         No immunisation

Decide   1. Child Protection Register — neglect
         2. SSD — key worker
         3. Plan of support
         4. Reconvene in 3/12 to see outcome (or sooner)

Fig. 6.3   Case history to illustrate management (cont'd overleaf).

HV, GP, CMO, SW, Family aide nursery
nurse — all anxious — all continue to be involved.

Baby now 7/12 at day nursery, attends with mother
and father, starts to become more alert.
IMMUNISED AT NURSERY

All continue except Family aide withdrawn.

Baby slowly puts on weight and development
accelerates.

OP appointment missed.

Squint diagnosed — fails to attend for first appointment.

2nd OP appointment taken by SW.
Nursery nurse takes mother to hospital and
learns to do therapy at nursery

Baby now 12/12
Mild cerebral diplegia — weekly physiotherapy
arranged.

Summary 1. Unplanned, unsupervised pregnancy leads to preterm delivery for unprepared young mother.
2. Consequences:
   (i) for baby — cerebral palsy, squint, possible learning problems later, poor parenting leading to undernutrition, impaired learning opportunities, ill health (Table 6.8).
   (ii) for mother — pregnancy when 15 years, has few coping strategies, becomes dependent on professionals, will she be able to learn in time to meet this child's needs?
   (iii) for father — pitched into parenthood with as few skills as mother.
   (iv) for professionals — vast use of resources, will change be effected? What are their responsibilities to the child and the parents? When does parenting become 'not good enough'?

Fig. 6.3   Case history to illustrate management. PMH, past medical history; PH, presenting history.

3. limits of resources; neglecting families may consume vast amounts of professional time and other resources.

The parents may have little awareness of their inadequacies in child-rearing and the longer the neglect continues, the more difficult it is to help the children effectively. Parents may also feel unable to change and are overwhelmed by their day-to-day poverty and struggle to survive. If the adults have mere survival as their goal, their aspirations for their children will be low too. Their extended family and neighbours may feel a similar hopelessness and parents and children are enmeshed in an impoverished family and social system resistant to change.

Neglecting parents often feel bad about themselves, do not laugh much or have fun. They do not know how to play with their children. They often find difficulty in showing and receiving affection from partners and children.

Intervention is directed towards:

1. enabling the adults to feel change is possible,
2. reducing the level of family dysfunction and improving parenting skills in a structured but supportive way,
3. fostering normal emotional development, including skills of communication between the adults as well as the children,
4. focusing on the family as a whole, rather than the child alone, and improving the quality of life of the adults, which it is hoped will be of lasting benefit to the children,
5. giving attention to the extended family but with sensitivity so as not to alienate, as without the

Table 6.11   Neglecting families (after Crittenden 1988)

1. 'Neglected' parents	Neglected in own childhood. Slow, even mentally handicapped. Unemployed or unskilled work. Partner similar. Several children when young. Extended family large but poor support. Few expectations for self or children. Live from day to day.
2. 'Secondary incompetence' of parents	Become neglectful due to adverse circumstance, e.g. head injury, psychiatric illness, drug or alcohol abuse. Extreme beliefs, e.g. nutritional, religious, cultural.
3. Environment	Poor, overcrowded housing, unfenced gardens. Cold, damp, poor repair. Bed and Breakfast accommodation. Temporary housing e.g. Caravans. Unsafe surroundings e.g. dangerous or no play areas, busy roads, unfenced railways, waterways. Poverty, insufficient food, electricity or gas disconnected.
4. Over-reliance on/rejection of professionals	May have large numbers of professionals. Professionals' anxiety may be very high. Professional help may be totally rejected.

support of those wider networks any change in the family is liable to be rendered ineffective,

6. providing support, which will be needed for years.

Specific help for the child is also necessary:

1. He needs an interesting environment where he can learn to focus his attention and to talk, e.g. a good day nursery.

2. Enable him to feel competent, responsive to others, be an individual in his own right and able to have an effect on his future — this involves individual work as in good day care.

3. Ideally the child's mother is not only involved in (1) and (2) but also in work at home with coordinated home visits by social worker, nursery nurse, teacher, etc.

CONCLUSION

Neglect is a prevalent form of maltreatment in the UK. It is insidious and adversely affects children in many ways including retardation of growth and development, as well as poor general health. Neglected children may also be abused in other ways. A summary is given in Table 6.12 (Skuse 1989).

Neglecting families have a poor prognosis for change. The earlier intervention takes place, the greater the chance for progress. The whole family, including the mother's partner, should be involved. Separation, even in day care, should be careful and involve the mother as, with weak bonds in the family, dissolution can occur. Support should be structured and supportive, but not unduly coercive as this often provokes anger and withdrawal from services. Professional help will be needed in the long term.

Ongoing assessment of the growth, development and health of the children in neglecting families is needed. If, despite support, the children continue to fail, alternative care (foster-care) may be needed, with early planning towards permanency if the prospects for change at home remain poor.

The paediatric assessment in neglect must include (Table 6.9):

1. Physical state — skin, hair, nails, clothes
2. Growth — growth rate
3. Development — gross motor, fine motor, speech, hearing, vision
4. Emotional wellbeing
5. Information from other professionals (Table 6.10).

A paediatrician may review the child's progress. Detail is important: include notes of failed hospital appointments, failure to immunise, poor attendance for speech therapy or nursery. Is this child failing to grow because of a lack of calories? Why doesn't he get enough food? Has anyone observed a mealtime? It is necessary to compile a logical detailed report which demonstrates why this child is failing to grow and develop in the absence of a medical disorder. In the first instance

Table 6.12 Key features of neglect and emotional deprivation (after Skuse 1989)

	Infant	Pre-school	School child	Teenager
Physical	FTT Recurrent infection Repeated admissions Severe nappy rash	Short, ± underweight Unkempt, dirty Microcephaly	Short, ± underweight Unkempt, dirty	Short + underweight + obese Poor general health, unkempt, dirty, delayed puberty
Development	General delay	Language delay Poor attention Emotional immaturity	Learning difficulties Poor attention Lacks confidence Immature	School failure
Behaviour	Attachment disorder: anxious, avoidant Socially unresponsive	Over-active Aggressive, impulsive Indiscriminate friendliness Physical comfort from stranger	Over-active Aggressive Withdrawn Lacks confidence Poor relationships Poor school progress Wettting, soiling Destructive	School non-attendance, smoking, drinking, substance abuse, run away, sexual promiscuity, stealing, lying, destructive (self, others, property)

the aim of paediatric intervention is to help the parents care for their child, to assess the child's needs (by a thorough physical and developmental check) and then suggest how these needs might be met. Referrals for audiometry, the dentist, support of a nursery place and advice on sleep problems are positive ways in which the child and parents may be helped.

If the child still fails to grow and develop the doctor must say so and be prepared to tell the parents and other professionals. Finally it may be necessary to give evidence in court. This is difficult, especially when parents are clearly disadvantaged by their own past. However, protection of the child is paramount; children have rights too, and failure to grow and develop is a denial of every child's inheritance.

Summary

1. Neglect is insidious, pervasive and the commonest yet least recognised form of child maltreatment.

2. Neglect, as defined in the Children Act (1989), will be considered as to whether it involves actual or likely 'significant harm' and whether it involves 'ill treatment' or 'impairment of health or development' (in each case as defined by the Act).

3. 8% of children on Child Protection Registers are categorised as neglected (1990). Most of the children reported are under 5 years of age but neglect extends throughout childhood.

4. There is a strong relationship in reported cases with adverse social circumstances.

5. Whilst neglect reflects wider social issues, it is the microcosm of the family in which it achieves expression.

6. Children have emotional, physical and social needs; neglected children have these needs inadequately met.

7. Patterns of neglect are recognisable clinically and by the parent's behaviour.

8. The hallmark of neglecting behaviour is non-compliance or the failure to recognise the child's needs.

9. Preventable accidents are a major cause of morbidity and mortality in neglectful families. The significance of repeated accidents should be recognised in the Accident and Emergency Department.

10. The cycle of deprivation is well demonstrated in neglecting families.

11. Interventions in neglecting families must be goal directed, time limited, and always involve the parents. Progress is often slow.

12. Prevention of neglect must be broad based, involving social policy as well as education and development of parenting skills.

13. Presentation of evidence in court demands a comprehensive assessment over time with reference to attempted interventions.

14. 1989 marked the thirtieth anniversary of the Declaration of the Rights of the Child. The aims of this basic statement of human rights have not been achieved in practice.

REFERENCES

Balarajan R, Raleigh V S, Botting B 1989 Mortality from congenital malformations in England and Wales; variations by mother's country of birth. Archives of Disease in Childhood 64: 1457–1462

Barker D J P 1990 The fetal and infant origins of adult disease. British Medical Journal 301: 1111

Black J A 1991 The medical needs of ethnic minority children in Britain. Current Paediatrics 1: 53–58

Children and Young Persons on Child Protection Registers. Year ending March 31 1988. Government Statistical Service, ISBN 1 85 197 4148 DoH

Creighton S J, Noyes P 1989 Child abuse trends in England and Wales 1983–87. NSPCC

Creighton S J, Noyes P 1990 Child abuse in 1989. Research briefing, No 11. NSPCC

Crittenden P 1988 family and dyadic patterns. In: Browne K, Davies C, Stratton P (eds) Prediction and prevention of child abuse. J Wiley & Sons, Chichester

Davey Smith G, Bartley M, Blane D 1990 The Black Report on socio-economic inequalities in health 10 years on. British Medical Journal 301: 373–377

Delamothe T 1991 Social inequalities in health. British Medical Journal 303: 1046–1050

Edwards R 1991 Lone parent families poverty and employment highlight, No 102. NCB

Emery J L 1985 Infanticide, filicide and cot death. Archives of Disease in Childhood 60: 505–507

Emery J L, Taylor E M 1986 Investigation of SIDS. New England Journal of Medicine 315: 1676

Ermisch J 1986 The economics of the family: applications to divorce and remarriage (Discussion Paper No 140). Centre for Economic Policy Research

Gillen D 1991 Poor housing, vulnerable people. Leading Article in British Medical Journal 303

Helfer R E 1987 The litany of the smoldering neglect of children. In: Helfer R E, Kempe C H (eds) The battered child, 4th edn. University of Chicago Press, Chicago

Helfer R E 1990 The neglect of our children. In: Child abuse. Pediatric Clinics of North America 37/4

HMSO 1991 House of Commons Security Committee. Low income statistics: household below average income tables 1988

Jackson R H 1988 The doctor's role in the prevention of accident. Archives of Disease in Childhood 63: 235–237

Jackson R H, Cooper S, Hayes H R M 1988 The work of the Child Accident Prevention Trust. Archives of Disease in Childhood 63: 318–320

Kempe R S, Goldbloom R B 1987 Malnutrition and growth retardation in the context of child abuse and neglect. In: Helfer R E, Kempe C H (eds) The battered child, 4th edn. University of Chicago Press, Chicago

Lowry S 1991 Housing and health. BMJ Publications, London

Madeley R J 1991 Recent trends in infant, neonatal and post-neonatal mortality rates. Current Paediatrics 1: 49–52

Meadow S R 1989 Suffocation. In: Meadow S R (ed) ABC of child abuse. British Medical Journal

Meadow R 1990 Suffocation, recurrent apnoea and sudden infant death. The Journal of Pediatrics 117; 3: 351–357

National Children's Bureau, Policy and Practice Review Group 1987 Investing in the future: child health 10 years after the Court Report. National Children's Bureau

Newlands M, Emery J S 1991 Child abuse and cot death. Child Abuse and Neglect 15: 275–278

Office of Population, Censuses and Surveys 1987

Occupational class and mortality

Office of Population, Censuses and Surveys 1988 Occupational mortality 1979–1980 and 1982–1983. (Childhood Supplement Series B5 No 8.) HMSO, London

Office of Population, Censuses and Surveys 1990 Mortality statistics, perinatal and infant: social and biological factors. Series DH3, No 21. HMSO, London

Oliver J E 1983 Dead children from problem families in NE Wiltshire. British Medical Journal 286: 115–117

Phillips M 1991 Divorce and its burden of pain. The Guardian 6–12–1991

Polnay L, Hull D 1985 Families and homes. In: Community paediatrician. Churchill Livingstone, London

Population Trends 66 1991 HMSO

Skuse D 1989 Emotional abuse and neglect. In: Meadow R (ed) ABC of child abuse. British Medical Journal

Smith F B 1990 The BMJ and poverty. British Medical Journal 301: 734

Smith P 1991 Child poverty who says? Concern 78: 4–5

Spencer N J 1991 Child poverty and deprivation in the UK. Archives of Disease in Childhood 66: 1255–1257

Stanton A N, Downham M A P S, Oakley J R, Emery J L, Knowledon J 1978 Terminal symptoms in children dying suddenly and unexpectedly at home. British Medical Journal 2: 1249–1251

Wedge P, Essen J 1982 Children in adversity. Pan, London

Whitehead M, Dahlgren G 1991 What can be done about inequalities in health. Lancet 338:

Working Together 1988 A guide to arrangements for inter-agency co-operation for the protection of children from abuse. DHSS Working Together 1991. HMSO, London

7. Emotional maltreatment

Though emotional abuse is an accepted category in the registration of children who have been abused it is probably the most complex form of abuse in terms of definition, recognition, management and registration. It is rarely absent when a child has been abused physically, sexually, is failing to thrive non-organically, or has been neglected and yet the statistics point to a very low incidence rate both in the USA and Britain (Creighton & Noyes 1989). As Garbarino et al (1988, p. 7) so aptly stated, 'rather than casting psychological maltreatment as an ancillary issue, subordinate to other forms of abuse and neglect, we should place it as the centrepiece of efforts to understand family functioning and to protect children'.

The long-term effects for children are described by Egeland & Erikson (1986, p. 667); 'The sharp decline in the intellectual functioning of these children, their attachment disturbances and subsequent lack of social/emotional competence in a variety of situations is cause for great concern. The consequences of this form of maltreatment are particularly disturbing when considered in the light of a careful re-examination of our society's definition of child abuse and a consideration of means for early identification and intervention to help prevent the cumulative malignant effects of this form of maltreatment'.

CASE HISTORY 1

Martin, aged 6, woke up every morning with a bucket in the corner of his sparsely furnished room. '. . . and I went to do my pee in the bucket, then my dad would come and unlock the door'. Martin was not allowed to touch his father because his father had told him that he, Martin, had the devil living in him. Father also told him that anyone who touched Martin could catch 'it'. Martin was often referred to as 'devil' by all members of his family and his father had told Martin that he was the son of the devil. Martin was not allowed to sit at the table with the rest of his family but had to sit on the floor. He had his own cup and plate and had to wash them up separately, so as not to 'contaminate' the others. Martin was often beaten by his parents as part of drumming the devil out of him. He was criticised continually and often had to sit with the large dogs in the garden. Martin was terrified of the dogs, because his father had told him that the dogs would 'get him'. Martin only ran away from home once and hid but his father and the dogs found him and Martin was threatened that they would tear him to pieces if he ran away again. When the school became very concerned about Martin the parents took Martin to a Social Services Office and said that the child was out of control and that they would not take him back home with them. Martin, looking dirty, clad in ill-fitting clothes, thin and unable to speak, was taken into care. It took considerable time before this story emerged.

HISTORY OF CHILD CARE

Ill-treatment, punishment and even child killings are recorded in the history of many societies and civilisations; for the child the years of infancy were the most dangerous ones, not only because the infant's life was not a very valued one. The period of childhood was always poorly defined — the infant would be seen as a nonentity with no feelings and treated with little understanding. The most important thing a child had to do was to grow up and become an adult. Adult values pertained on this path of growth and the fact that children might have age-appropriate needs did not occur to most people. Plato advocated that children would learn through play but for the most part it was believed that the only way children would grow up was by repressing their spirits, the foolishness of the child, by beating them severely with

107

the aim of driving this spirit/devil out of them. Scott (1977) showed that in medieval times child-care practices fell back into benightedness; 'If babyhood was survived, all but the most favoured children became little adults and a convenient source of labour. Instances of barbarous treatment of children, infanticide, exploitation, starvation, flogging and mutilation abound; and until comparatively recently these seemed to have caused little public reaction'.

Even in the 19th century the attitude towards children was one of stern materialism. Infants were killed in order to limit the size of the family and 'baby farming' was a well-known practice whereby children would be handed over to such baby farms if the parent(s) could not care for them. Many children born illegitimately received this treatment.

In England the Education Act and the Children and Young Person's Act were formulated during the 1930s and 1960s, growing out of a wish to grant children rights. However, in general people remained firm in their beliefs that children had no rights and that they remained the property of their parents to do with as they pleased, or rather as they were best able. With the advent of a more child-centred society parents began to speak of their own often appalling childhoods. It was then that professionals working in the field of child care began to realise that many of the parents of abused children had themselves been maltreated as children. It was also quickly realised that it did not seem to matter in which social class a child grew up. Kempe & Kempe (1978) wrote; 'In each generation we find, in one form or another, a distortion of the relationship between parents and children that deprives the children of the consistent nurturing of body and mind that would enable them to develop fully'. Slowly, children's needs have been realised and in some parts of the world a more child-centred attitude has been accepted. However translating this knowledge into practice is still a difficult task for most societies.

DEFINITION OF EMOTIONAL MALTREATMENT

The working group of the recent document *Working Together* and of the Children Act 1989 define emotional abuse as: 'actual or likely severe adverse effects on the emotional and behavioural development of the child caused by persistent or severe emotional ill treatment or rejection. All abuse involves some emotional abuse' (p. 49).

Lourie & Stefano (1978) defined emotional maltreatment as: 'an injury to the intellectual or psychological capacity of the child, as evidenced by an observable and substantial impairment in his or her ability to function within his or her normal range of performance and behaviour with due regard to his or her culture'.

Some authorities find emotional abuse too difficult to define (Helfer & Kempe 1980) preferring to choose verbal abuse as a specific category and otherwise pointing to the fact that all maltreated children are victims of emotional harm.

Garbarino et al (1988) discuss 'What psychological maltreatment?' at length and provide definitions from a number of professional angles, including clinical and legal. On page 2 they quote Whiting (1976) as making a useful distinction between emotional abuse and emotional neglect. She indicates that 'emotional neglect is a result of subtle or blatant omission or commission experienced by the child, which causes handicapping stress on the child' and when 'meaningful adults are unable to provide necessary nurturance, stimulation, encouragement, and protection to the child at various stages of their development, which inhibits his optimal functioning'. She also points out that it 'applies when parents resist or refuse cooperative intervention for a child diagnosed as disturbed'. Of course not only children who are already disturbed come into this category, but also those who, for instance, are not sent to school or referred for medical attention when they are not well. Whiting feels that emotional abuse relates to, and is distinguished from, neglect by the 'deliberate parental action' against a child which causes emotional disturbance.

INCIDENCE OF EMOTIONAL ABUSE

The American Humane Association reported in 1984 that their statistics collected between 1976 and 1982 showed emotional abuse as occurring in 17% of children registered. In England the NSPCC register of cases between 1983 and 1986 showed 1.5% of all abused children to have been registered under the category of emotional abuse; by 1987 the figure had fallen to 1%. From clinical practice it is known that these figures reflect gross under-reporting in this area. It is difficult to interpret such data. It probably highlights the difficulties professionals have in registering this form of maltreatment.

In most cases emotional abuse is not the central reason for the registration of children and other more visible signs of maltreatment have to be present, despite the increasing evidence that emotional maltreatment has considerable effects in the long term on cognitive and emotional development as well as on the capacity to form relationships and other social effects.

NORMAL EMOTIONAL DEVELOPMENT OF CHILDREN

In some sense there is no such thing as 'normal' emotional development; individual differences exist and for the ordinary child, depending on what care he receives, his emotional growth will proceed. However, good emotional development is crucial not only for the individual but also for intergenerational patterns and society as a whole.

It is important to stress that a classification can only be achieved if the age of the child is taken into consideration. What does need to be stated clearly, even though we now have a far better

Table 7.1 Child development, related to Erikson's (1963) stages

Age	What the child learns
0–1	to trust
1–3	to be autonomous — age-appropriate independence
3–6	about 'initiative v guilt', the child starts to explore, test boundaries, learns that breaking the rules creates conflicts and guilt, begins to recognise that others have rights
6–12	this is the stage of 'industry v inferiority' — establishing himself as competent and achieving; most importantly he acquires social and academic skills
12–20	this is the stage of 'identity v role confusion' — transition from childhood into adulthood, seeking for an identity, coming to terms with being male or female, confusion about sexual and social position. Peers are most important during this stage

understanding of the child's emotional development, is that the internal (emotional) world of the child is structured by his environment and particularly the parents and caretakers surrounding him. This process occurs from the earliest days of development and structures the individual's personality through attachments, love and care as well as anxiety and trauma (Bowlby 1969, Winnicott 1988).

Different forms of emotional maltreatment will affect children differently at various ages. It is possible to draw an analogy from fetal development, in which an infection like rubella causes most damage to those organs that are developing rapidly at the time of the infection. Similarly, emotional abuse will affect those psychological functions that are developing at the time. Erikson's (1963) well-known classification of developmental tasks can be used as a way of structuring what is known about age-related effects of emotional maltreatment.

Erikson's theory of psychosocial development centres on the developmental life span of human beings. He proposed eight stages through which all human beings need to develop. These eight stages, five of which cover 'childhood', occur at specific age ranges, during which certain tasks will have to be achieved. Erikson (1963) also believed that children actively explore all aspects of life and that they have a considerable capacity to adapt to people and situations. Children are not just passive beings who are shaped by their parents, they actively seek to control their environment.

The developmental stages of childhood are briefly as set out below.

First year of life

During the first year of life the infant has the 'task' to achieve basic *trust v mistrust*. Clearly this 'task' is highly influenced and shaped by the adults surrounding the child. It involves learning to trust others to supply basic needs like food, warmth, love, consistency, etc. If, during this phase, the parents are incapable of providing reasonable care or are rejecting the baby, including giving inconsistent care, the infant is likely to grow in experiencing the world as a dangerous place with untrustworthy or unreliable people in it.

Age 1–3 years

The child grapples with the issues relating to *autonomy v shame and doubt*. Children need to learn to be autonomous, to begin to do things for themselves and have a sense of adequacy (putting their clothes on, feeding themselves, etc.). If he does not achieve a certain amount of age-appropriate independence the consequences will lead the child to doubt his abilities and so feel shame as well as doubt. At this stage the parents are still the main figures in the child's life.

Age 3–6 years

The child is in the stage of *initiative v guilt*. This stage includes the beginnings of exploration beyond what the child is sometimes capable of and where the child tries to take on responsibilities he often can not handle. It is the time when he wants to be grown up and to do things, or set himself goals, that he knows his parents will not approve of or think are unsafe or even dangerous. Through such excursions the child will come into conflict with parents and siblings and this is likely to lead to feelings of guilt. In order to leave this stage successfully a balance has to be achieved whereby the child can both stay in this exploratory mood and take initiatives but also learn not to interfere with the rights and goals of others. The positive outcome is a child who is purposeful and able to initiate his own activities.

Age 6–12 years

Here *industry v inferiority* is the issue. The peer group becomes an important factor in the child's life. Competition, particularly in the academic and social sphere, is central during this stage in development. The child needs to establish himself as a competent, self-assured person. Failure to succeed will induce inferiority.

Age 12–16 years

This stage can extend up to the age of 20. The youngster learns about growing up, becoming an adult and about his identity and sexuality. Making relationships, particularly with the opposite sex, is essential. The peer group is most influential in shaping the young person's social and occupational path, though the parents remain crucial models.

THE IMPORTANCE OF ATTACHMENT THROUGHOUT CHILDHOOD

Discussion of emotional maltreatment without taking into account what we now know about attachment theory and attachment behaviours (specific individuals providing a secure base for the infant) would be incomplete. Secure, anxious, and avoidant attachments as described by Bowlby (1969) and Ainsworth et al (1978) grow out of the need of the child to be in close proximity to a responsible and responsive adult during his development. Bowlby (1969) pointed out that the survival of human beings, in particular of the very small baby, is optimally secured when the infant and child can maintain proximity to one attachment figure or several. As in Erikson's first stage, the baby learns to trust an adult who reacts appropriately to the baby's needs. If all goes well in a family then the baby's cries will elicit the proximity of his mother or caretaker. Since the baby usually cries only because of some form of need (e.g. hunger) or distress the mother's presence, behaviour and her consequent action are essential to help the baby develop a feeling of security.

The view of Crittenden & Ainsworth (1989) has been influenced and shaped by psychoanalytic theory as well as ethology and evolutionary theory which influenced that aspect of attachment theory which deals with the adaptation of the infant through interactions with the parental system and environment. Further discussion of this concept can also be found in Chapter 15.

For the mother/parents to behave in a consistent, loving and nurturing way it is essential that they themselves have experienced something approaching this pattern in their own childhood. When Ainsworth et al (1978) researched attachment patterns in a 'strange situation' they found that children react differently not only at different ages but also depending on their experience of mothering. The major patterns established from this now very well-known research are:

1. a secure attachment to specific adults

2. an anxious/avoidant pattern of attachment
3. an anxious/ambivalent or anxious/resistant attachment.

The baby of about 7–8 months will have formed his first attachments, usually to his mother, but also to other people who have been close to him up to that time. As already indicated, if all goes well the baby will have experienced consistent, loving care and will be securely attached, able to explore in the presence of the attachment figure(s) even in a strange situation and with a stranger present. Children who have been maltreated often show the anxious/avoidant or anxious/ambivalent pattern or an unusual combination of this pattern.

If the ordinary baby comes to the hospital or is observed at home he will be somewhat hesitant at first in exploring his surroundings in the presence of a stranger but this will ease with the mother/attachment figure close by. There children may become distressed and cry, but are comforted by their mother and can be reassured. Children who have been abused show different patterns. They may cling to their parents, they may cry and whine, and they may become distressed out of all proportion. These children may cause irritation to the parental figures and receive little of the understanding and care which might help them to feel more secure. At the other end of the continuum the child may become agitated, charge around, get into every corner, cupboard or drawer, touch everything in sight without any real interest and seem restless and aimless. In a third pattern of behaviour the child tiptoes away and watches what goes on from a safe distance; these children often show what is well described as frozen watchfulness. Crittenden & Ainsworth (1989) describe their recent research in this area where they examined the attachment patterns in families where child maltreatment occurred.

Failure of attachment consequent on early maltreatment

Many children who are being maltreated experience emotional abuse from an early age, quite often as a precursor of other forms of abuse. One way which this interaction between mother and child can develop is recognised in the attachment literature (Bowlby 1969, 1975, 1981, Belsky & Nezworski 1988) and in the writings by Kempe & Kempe (1978). Specific groups of parents may be more likely to abuse their children generally, however emotional abuse can occur in all social strata. Children of very young, inexperienced mothers who come from a deprived background themselves and who may have children in the hope and belief that at last there will be a human being that will love them are at high risk. The bitter disappointment and resentful feelings that arise as it becomes clear that the baby does not provide the longed-for care and love surface in the parent's frustration against the child. The fact that the mother has to provide for the needs of the baby and give him affection rather than receive it can lead to considerable confusion in the mother. The recognition of the necessity of providing care and love rather than receiving it from the baby may be a very early beginning to a poor relationship. As a consequence the baby becomes the object of the mother's disappointment and her consequent resentment can lead to physical abuse, neglect, failure to thrive and sexual abuse. Egeland (1988) indicated that one-third of parents who were abused as children are at risk of abusing their own children.

THE CHILD'S SYMPTOMS AND ADAPTATION

Understanding the expressions of emotional abuse in a child is a difficult process. In families children and parents will have to work out between each of them how they respond and behave to each other and those outside the family. These responses and behaviours have been called the 'transactions' between people; this model was described by Sameroff & Chandler (1975) and further developed by Stratton (1977, 1982a) highlighting the complexity of interactions as they occur between the caretaker and child.

An infant experiencing feeding difficulties may not only be tense and anxious himself but also have a tense and anxious mother. The infant may adapt to the anxious mother by attempting to avoid the traumatic feeding situation and become passive and resistant to taking in food. In turn the mother may become even more tense and anxious and also avoid all aspects of the feeding situation. Once this pattern has been established the result can be that the child loses weight and becomes difficult to handle, possibly even leading to physical abuse as well as rejection and failure to thrive. The transactional process is easy to describe in this kind of example, and it is a common sequence in cases of non-organic failure to thrive. What is so striking is that, even with a clear example like this, at the time it demands a considerable effort of imagination to recognise the pattern of behaviour as an attempt at adaptation within a transactional relationship. Often an outsider has more chance of observing this pattern and recognising it as a result of the baby's adaptation, than the mother has to detect it and intervene in such a way that the interaction between them is changed.

The term 'adaptation' acknowledges the fact that the child is not a passive recipient of influence. Under the pressure of maltreatment, the child will take whatever route seems to offer the best chance of minimising risk and pain. Children do not have a long-term perspective on the effects of their behaviour, particularly when they are under the stress of abuse. A tragic consequence is that the attempts of the child to adapt to the abusive situation may actually increase the probability of further abuse. Stratton (1982b) in his section 'transactional adaptation' unravels some of the complexities in which an infant's adaptations can be understood and how the baby responds to the care-giving environment in which he finds himself. Bringing the two concepts of transaction and adaptation together gives an insight into how any care-giving situation can elicit responses from the child. These responses then will set up the conditions which will influence the parent's behaviour towards the child.

The underfed child will adapt to the need to conserve energy, and to the anxiety or even antagonism shown by the parents during feeding. On observation of the baby's behaviour it may seem as if he is uninterested in food and feeding. This behaviour (turning away, screaming, keeping the mouth firmly shut, spitting food out, etc.) adaptive in the short term, will make it more likely that the parents can attribute the low food intake to the child being a 'poor feeder'. Parents of children with the label 'poor feeder' are more likely to

have little investment in thinking of what the child might like to eat, they may be impatient and give up after only a short time of trying to feed the child or they may become despondent and depressed at their lack of success. All of this or any one of these responses may reinforce the parent's avoidance of the feeding situation. The process of transactional adaptation, which normally works to keep healthy patterns self-sustaining, can also be responsible for the continuation of maltreating behaviours.

In children who have been sexually abused the pattern applies equally, leading to confusion and emotional distress which hinder the child's development and can impair health. Summit (1983) describes the adaptations made by many of the children who have been sexually abused in terms of accommodating the abuse. Their sexualised behaviour towards others (children and adults alike) and themselves is one such example. As these children move through the different developmental stages and grow older, specific aspects of their abusive experiences may become clearer to them. As this happens they may have to adapt once more to the anxieties which are produced by the understanding they have gained. The adaptation may again be in terms of relieving their anxiety and for instance lead the child to behave aggressively towards anyone who tries to befriend him or come close. The effort of 'accommodation' itself leads to short-term as well as long-term emotional difficulties which are quite unacceptable in terms of adequate child care.

What professionals need to achieve is a recognition of the patterns of disturbed or disturbing behaviours by children encountered in families, clinics, children's homes, foster-families, schools, etc., and that these disturbing behaviours can be adaptations which first developed in the child's original environment or home. Professionals need to work back and discover the circumstances in which these adaptations originated. To practise and become fluent in such reconstructions it is essential that the signs of a history of emotional or sexual abuse, for instance, are recognised in the behaviour of the child — not just one form of behaviour but the way a child reacts in many situations. As Stratton (1977) pointed out, 'main effect' models are simply unproductive in terms of understanding the negative influences during development. In child sexual abuse the 'main effect' model takes the form of viewing the abuse as a damaging event inflicted on a passive child from outside and that this 'damage', in all its manifestations, should be directly observable. Without in any way diminishing the responsibility of the adult, it is still totally misleading to view the child as a passive recipient of influence, whether good or bad. Moment by moment the child adapts to what is happening, and if there is any sense in which the relationship is transactional, the adult will be influenced by the child's adaptation. The longer-term strategies which the child adopts in order to minimise trauma and immediate threat are the 'characteristics of sexually abused children', described elsewhere in this book, and are known to expose the child to further risk. The importance for treatment of the psychological and emotional consequences in such abusive situations is that the maltreating adult and the maltreated child need interventions to break the cycle of their behaviour with each other. Children transfer the behaviours learnt in one setting to another setting. If they are taken into care or are fostered the adaptations will continue and the carers in these situations may also need early and active support to care for these children.

Crittenden (1988), observing parenting behaviours in maltreating families, described physically abusing parents as interfering and hostile, including becoming verbally hostile and in this way abusing their children both in a physical and emotional way. Neglecting parents seemed to behave differently towards their children. Rather than being active and interfering they did not respond to their children's attempts for attention and were withdrawn. The consequences for the children of neglecting parents were vividly described and are only too easily recognised in clinics. The children under one year of age coming from neglecting parents presented as passive and cognitively delayed. It was easy to ignore these children, they were almost 'invisible' to both parents and professionals. However, once they were a little older and able to move about the pattern changed and these children became 'uncontrolled seekers of novel experiences'. They are into everything, quite out of control, and can often be found in dangerous situations (e.g. in the road, exploring dangerous objects, exposing themselves to heights, etc.). At times it can appear as if they are making up for lost (passive) time. The families and, sometimes, professionals may label the child 'hyperactive' and so make the child responsible for the behaviours without considering the interactions and possibly adaptation which will have taken place and which have been described above. Crittenden's research confirms the work undertaken by Dix (1991) quoted below.

PATTERNS OF EMOTIONAL ABUSE

Much child abuse includes the verbal degrading of the child as well as the fact that children understand from their poor treatment by their carers that they are not valued members of their family or environment. Their self-esteem is often pitifully low and these children develop ways of expressing their emotional disturbances which can range from daydreaming and withdrawing, to becoming aggressive and antisocial; aggression and anger may be directed against themselves and others (Hanks & Hobbs 1992) and some of the children may become mute and depressed. It is not surprising that the behaviours children show when they have been maltreated overlap and do not always appear to be specifically related to the form of maltreatment. Behavioural problems such as wetting, soiling, poor educational attainment, poor concentration, stealing, lying, depression, etc.; may all be expressions of a child's distress caused by being maltreated. In children who have been sexually abused a specific form of emotional distress may show. These children often behave in sexualised ways towards peers, siblings and adults alike, showing and repeating not only what has happened to them but also their confusion and emotional distress.

The child's sexualised behaviour towards others can be interpreted as part of an expression of their feelings, their confusion, guilt and emotional distress. The feelings and behaviours follow one another and accumulate; one moment the behaviour might be followed by feelings, the next moment the feelings may cause behaviours — whichever way round, further disturbance will be the outcome. This relentless cycle will have further damaging effects as the child grows up.

The guilt often develops out of a mistaken belief by the child that he alone has initiated the abuse and is to blame.

How the different components of emotional abuse can be defined and separated is not clear at present. Let us take verbal abuse as an example. How can this be defined? How often and to what degree does the child have to be subjected to verbal abuse by parent figures before this becomes damaging? Are there critical ages at which some forms of emotional maltreatment are much more damaging than at other developmental stages? As already indicated, Garbarino et al (1988) made an important contribution to assessing emotional maltreatment in that they identified components of emotional abuse in terms of rejecting, terrorising, isolating, corrupting and ignoring. This classification has proved a valuable tool in understanding psychological maltreatment in a developmental context. It also helps in viewing the behaviours that many children show as the consequences of abuse in a more meaningful way.

● *Rejecting* — the adult refuses to acknowledge the child's worth and the legitimacy of the child's needs.

● *Isolating* — the adult cuts the child off from normal social experiences and contacts and prevents the child from forming friendships, and makes the child believe that he is alone in the world.

● *Terrorising* — the adult verbally assaults the child, creates a climate of fear, bullies and frightens the child, and makes the child believe that the world is capricious and hostile.

● *Ignoring* — the adult deprives the child of essential stimulation and responsiveness, stifling emotional growth and intellectual development.

● *Corrupting* — the adult 'mis-socialises' the child, stimulates the child to engage in destructive antisocial behaviour, reinforces that deviance, and makes the child unfit for normal social experiences (Garbarino et al 1988).

Table 7.2   Components of emotional abuse (Garbarino et al 1988)

rejecting	— child's needs not acknowledged
isolating	— child cut off from normal social interaction
terrorising	— verbal assault on child
ignoring	— child deprived of essential stimulation
corrupting	— child involved in inappropriate behaviour

Dix (1991) has provided an up-to-date and comprehensive study 'about the emotions parents commonly experience, about when and why they occur' and, importantly, what the consequences for parenting are once specific emotions have been aroused. He concludes that parents'

positive and empathic emotions motivate attunement to children, facilitate resposiveness to the child's wants and needs, and enables parents and children to coordinate their interactions to the benefit of both. In contrast, distressed parents perceive that they are doing poorly. For complex reasons their concerns are continually undermined. They are unable to select and manage interaction plans so that their concerns are promoted, and, as a result, they experience aversive events and negative emotions at high rates. . . . Because the negative emotions of distressed parents are chronic and intense, they can promote inattention, negative perceptions of children, and poor problem solving. Negative emotions can lead to parenting that is hypersensitive, avoidant, punitive, overly controlling and focused on self- rather than child concerns (pp 19–20).

CLINICAL ASSESSMENT

At the stage of the professional assessment Garbarino's et al. (1988) five forms of psychological maltreatment (rejecting, isolating, terrorising, ignoring and corrupting) are particularly helpful. By using these stages one can begin to recognise how the parents behave towards the child and what the parents' interactions with the child are like. The interactions reported or observed can be recorded under the 5 headings. The next step is to register any visible and observable signs. These may be physical signs: the child may have swollen, red hands and feet, physical delay in growth may be noted, motor movements and/or language may be impaired. There may be bruises or injuries, and alongside these the child may show a number of emotional signs and behaviours which indicate that he is unhappy, disturbed, unable to concentrate and learn, unable to interact with others, is unable to play, and has poor attachment behaviours toward parents or caretakers (Ainsworth 1985, Crittenden & Ainsworth 1989). These observations should be noted and the parents should be asked what their observations are about the child and what they perceive as being the difficulties.

Once the interactions between parent and child,

Table 7.3

Child's age	Guidelines to child's symptoms or maladaptations
0–1	sleep/feeding problems. irritability, apathetic, dull, anxious attachments
1–3	as above; overactive, apathetic, aggressive, attention deficit, language delay, indiscriminate affection, fearful and anxious, inability to play, irritable, anxious and ambivalent attachments
3–6	as above; peer relationship difficulties, attention seeking, clingy, school failure begins, poor social skills
6–12	as above, though sleep and feeding problems may resolve, inappropriate attachment to carers, rejected by peers, school failure, developing delinquent behaviours, running away, truanting, school failure, wetting, soiling, stealing, bullying
12+	as above; depressions, escalated aggression, anxiety, overdosing selfharm, poor self-image, may continue or begin to wet and or soil, psychosomatic illness, drug and substance abuse, criminal activities

the child's presentation, the possible delays and the physical state of the child have been established, the psychological and behavioural signs can be mapped and so provide a picture of the child's difficulties and possible delays at any given age. The next stage is to indicate, age-appropriately, what the short- and long-term consequences are most likely to be for the child.

Psychological assessment of emotional maltreatment in the child

- Behavioural signs shown by the child (positive, negative, delays, etc.)
- Emotional signs observed in the child
- Physical signs noted about the child
- Parental behaviour towards the child
- Likely consequences of the above on the child.

These broad categories may be further examined by recording:

1. The child's learning difficulties, age-appropriately. Can the child read, count, tell the colours; does he know the days of the week, know his address, etc?

2. The level of the child's concentration. Do the parents *report* that it is good or poor? Does the examiner *observe* good or poor concentration?

3. Can the child play age-appropriately? Can the child use fantasy in play (e.g. pretend to speak through a toy telephone, become engrossed with dolls, cars or trains etc. and construct a situation), play a game with another (adult or child)?

4. Can the child carry out instructions (age-appropriate)?

This list can be developed by the individual clinician and used to comment on the child's state of wellbeing. Garbarino et al's assessment instruments (1988, p. 234) may be used, however a universal checklist has not been developed as yet and comparisons are difficult to make.

A recent development of the dimension of emotional abuse has been described by Glaser (1991). These 'dimensions of emotional abuse' are as follows:

1. Persistent negative attitudes expressed verbally and non-verbally
   a. negative attributions and attitudes
   b. harsh discipline and over-control
2. Promoting insecure attachment
   a. conditional parenting
   b. inconsistency and unpredictability
3. Inappropriate developmental expectation and considerations
   a. premature impositions
   b. failure of protection or containment

Table 7.4   Assessment of child and family

- Provide a child-centred room with toys and drawing materials.
- Take the history — develop a family tree (genogram) and map the child's development, his milestones and problems from birth.
- Observe and make notes on: mother's affect, the child's affect and any interaction between the two, also interactions between siblings and other people present.
- Continue with a further detailed history including description of the current difficulties and previous interventions by family and professionals.
- Talk with the child, either with parent(s) or alone, recognising the problem for the child, and at least some of the consequences; emotional, behavioural, cognitive disturbances and the child's description of his family.
- Collect further information, before or after the interview, from the GP, or school nurse, health visitor, teacher, social worker.
- Collate the information and:
  1. assess what the problems are
  2. assess the motivation for change both in the family and professional system
  3. plan for intervention including therapy.

c. overprotection

d. failure to explain

4. Emotional unavailability
5. Failure to recognise the child's individuality and psychological boundaries
6. Cognitive distortions (double binds) exist in the child.

Besides these observations, developmental tests such as the Denver Developmental Scale and intelligence tests such as the Wechsler Intelligence Test of Children or the British Intelligence Scale, reading tests, or specific tests for those children with learning difficulties will help to assess the cognitive stage the child has reached.

The recognition of attachment patterns described earlier in the chapter may also be of assistance here.

CONSEQUENCES OF EMOTIONAL MALTREATMENT

Different forms of emotional maltreatment will produce different short- and long-term effects on children, but it is also important to consider what the effects of such maltreatment are at the different ages and stages of development for the child. Spitz (1948) showed clearly how important the emotional care of the very young child is and that infants need an emotionally rich environment to function and grow appropriately. Infants and children who grow up lacking physical care and nurturance at every level, including lack of consistency in the love they are given, will suffer not only at the time but will also carry the long-term consequences of such lack with them into the future. This can manifest itself in many ways, from total withdrawal at one end of the continuum to more active disturbances like hostility and aggression at other end. It will continue to have an influence on their lives and often express itself in the poor relationships these children make as adults, and intergenerationally in the poor relationships they often make with their own children.

Table 7.5 Psychological consequences for emotionally maltreated children

- Often perform below average on IQ tests
- Have low self-esteem and confidence
- Have problems in social relationships with peers and adults
- Anxious attachments
- Difficulties in accepting and giving affection
- Show a high degree of avoidance
- Are often aggressive and lack impulse control
- Show non-compliance
- Are often frustrated, anxious and non-compliant
- Poor relationships within the family and at school
- Fail to make transitions into adulthood

PRESENTATION IN COURT

Cases of emotional maltreatment rarely result in early statutory intervention. This is not because the consequences are not severe but mainly because they are much more difficult to establish in a legal setting than, for instance, physical abuse. Before taking legal steps to protect the child there is usually a need for a long period of assessment and attempt at intervention by multidisciplinary groups. If evidence is to be presented it must be done logically and as objectively as possible. The application of the 'jigsaw puzzle of abuse' described in Chapter 9 is as valid in this form of abuse as in any other.

The court will often wish to know from the social worker, psychologist or psychiatrist what is likely to be the outcome for the child if he stays at home. The court is also likely to want to know what the child's needs might be in the family or in alternative care.

In terms of significant harm the impairment will show particularly in the areas of emotional development, growth and behaviour. These areas need to be clearly described. Comparing the child's ability to learn and his achievements may show a realistic gap between what the child would be capable of achieving if the emotional pressure and consequent impairment was reduced or stopped altogether.

REFERENCES

Ainsworth M D 1985 Patterns of infant-mother attachment: antecedents and effects of development and, II Attachments across the life-span. Bulletin of New York Academy of Medicine 61: 771–791

Ainsworth M D, Blehar M C, Waters E, Wall S 1978 Patterns of attachment: assessed in the strange situation and at home. Lawrence Erlbaum, Hillsdale, New Jersey

Belsky J, Nezworski T 1988 Clinical implications of attachment. Lawrence Erlbaum, Hillsdale, New Jersey

Bowlby J 1969 Attachment and loss. The Hogarth Press and Institute of Psycho-Analysis, London

Bowlby J 1975 Separation: anxiety and anger. Penguin Books, Harmondsworth

Bowlby J 1981 Loss: sadness and depression. Penguin Books, Harmondsworth

Bowlby J 1988 A secure base. Tavistock, London

Creighton S J, Noyes P 1989 Child abuse trends in England and Wales 1983–87. NSPCC, London

Crittenden P 1988 Family and dyadic patterns of functioning in maltreating families. In: Browne K, Davies C, Stratton P (eds) Early prediction and prevention of child abuse. Wiley & Sons, Chichester

Crittenden P, Ainsworth M D S 1989 Child maltreatment and attachment theory. In: Cicchetti D, Carlson V (eds) Child maltreatment. Cambridge University Press, Cambridge

Dix T 1991 The affective organisation of parenting: adaptive and maladaptive processes. Psychological Bulletin 110: 3–25

Egeland B 1988 Breaking the cycle of abuse: implications for prediction and intervention. In: Browne K, Davies C, Stratton P (eds) Early prediction and prevention of child abuse. J Wiley & Sons, Chichester

Egeland B, Erikson M 1986 Deprivation of attachment. In: Bassard M, Germain R, Hart S (eds) The psychological maltreatment of children and youth. Pergamon Press, Elmsford NY

Erikson E H 1963 Childhood and society, 2nd edn. Norton, New York

Garbarino J, Guttman E, Seeley J W 1988 The psychologically battered child. Jossey-Bass Publishers, San Francisco

Glaser D 1991 Emotional abuse — identification and treatment. Paper presented at BASPCAN First National Congress on the Prevention of Child Abuse and Neglect,

University of Leicester

Hanks H, Hobbs C 1992 Self abuse and suicide. Current Paediatries 2, 1: 57–59

Helfer R E, Kempe C H 1980 The battered child (3rd edn.) University of Chicago Press, Chicago

Kempe R S, Kempe C H 1978 Child abuse. Fontana Books, London

Kempe R S, Kempe C H 1984 The common secret; sexual abuse of children and adolescents. W H Freeman, New York

Lourie I, Stefano L 1978 On defining emotional abuse. In: Proceedings of the Second Annual National Conference on Child Abuse and Neglect. U S Government Printing Office, Washington DC

Sameroff A J, Chandler M 1975 Reproductive risk and the continum of caretaking casualty. In: Horowitz F D, Hetherington M, Scarr-Salapatek S, Siegel G (eds) Review of child development research, Vol. 4. University of Chicago Press, Chicago

Spitz R A 1948 The importance of mother-child relationships during the first year of life, Mental Health Today 13

Stratton P M 1977 Criteria of assessing the influence of obstetric circumstances on later development. In: Chard T, Richards M (eds) Benefits and hazards of the new obstetrics. SIMP, London

Stratton P M 1982a Significance of the psychobiology of the human newborn. In: Psychobiology of the human newborn. J. Wiley & Sons, Chichester, p. 17–52

Stratton P M 1982b Emerging themes of neonatal psychobiology. In: Psychobiology of the human newborn. J. Wiley & Sons, Chichester, p. 391–414

Summit R C 1983 The child sexual abuse accommodation syndrome. Journal of Child Abuse and Neglect 7: 177–193

Whiting L 1976 Defining emotional neglect. Children Today 5: 2–5

Winnicott D W 1988 Babies and their mothers. Free Association Books, London

8. Sexual abuse — the scope of the problem

We have learned during the Inquiry that sexual abuse occurs in children of all ages, including the very young, to boys as well as girls, in all classes of society and frequently within the privacy of the family.

Report of the Inquiry into Child Abuse in Cleveland 1987 (Butler-Sloss 1988)

It is only very recently that child sexual abuse has emerged into public consciousness in a way that has allowed for open discussion within society. Media reporting and increasing adult disclosure have provided the first glimpses of what Roland Summit (1988) has termed 'society's blind spot'. If one was allowed only a single epithet to describe child sexual abuse, it might be 'hidden'. In a society increasingly willing to examine itself in all its aspects, both good and bad, it was inevitable that sooner or later child sexual abuse would be discussed, but it is important to reflect that our knowledge and understanding of the problem is at a comparable stage to that of the early aviators who had just managed to become airborne but who were in imminent danger of falling from the sky. If we think of these individuals with their early aircraft, they seemed to have grasped the basic concepts of flight but did not have the resources to do other than attempt to establish the principles and point the way forward. Comparison to our modern aviation industry of these early attempts to fly seems almost absurd, for the progress in less than a century has been spectacular. The purpose of this analogy is to indicate that there is often a significant point, following which progress in understanding becomes rapid; some would say this point has been reached in addressing the issue of child sexual abuse. This is not to deny that there have been earlier far-sighted attempts to address the problem but, like the men who jumped off

towers in various winged contraptions, they usually ended in disaster.

As with flying, there have always been those who point out the difficulties of even attempting to tackle something which on the face of it appears inconceivable — there are those who will deny the existence of child sexual abuse, preferring to believe that such things could not happen to children.

The debates and controversy are bound to continue for a long time to come until there is a much clearer understanding of the issues. Child sexual abuse provokes powerful emotions, leading to the normal defence reactions of denial and avoidance. 'Yes, of course sexual abuse occurs, but not in our school '. 'No, you can't tell a person who abuses children from one who doesn't, but I am sure this person, who I know well, couldn't possible have abused and the child must be wrong.'

In England, within a brief interval of the first reports of child sexual abuse reaching public awareness, a major crisis developed in Cleveland, involving the community in upheaval and controversy. A public inquiry (Butler-Sloss 1988) was called because the social order had been disturbed. Society had to face the possibility either that large numbers of children in its midst were being sexually exploited by their trusted caregivers, or that there had been a witch hunt by misguided professionals including doctors, social workers and psychologists. Neither option was particularly attractive, but in the end opinion has slowly come round to the view that child sexual abuse does exist as a significant problem. We acknowledge that there are other views—that sexual abuse is uncommon or that, though common, is essentially harmless. However, this chapter is

119

written from the viewpoint of those who hold that child sexual abuse is a major social problem which has long-term consequences and implications, not only for the individuals involved (perhaps more than we may wish to contemplate) but for the whole of society. Evidence to support this view is accumulating at an extraordinarily rapid rate through books, articles in professional and lay literature, radio and television programmes, conferences, meetings and public debate, Committees of Inquiry, debates in parliament, standing committees of the professions, professional associations, children's rights and parent's rights groups. What is written here will almost certainly be surpassed before it reaches publication, such is the rate of new learning and the explosion of knowledge about this subject.

A historical perspective on the way children have been treated and maltreated is given in Chapter 2. Just as Freud (1954), Tardieu (1860) and others struggled to grasp the facts of the sexual abuse of children in the context of a prevailing social attitude of disbelief, so others, more recently, have begun to understand the wider psychological resistances which have kept this problem hidden for so long. Sgroi (1978) says that 'those who try to assist sexually abused children must be prepared to battle against incredulity, hostility, innuendo and outright harassment. Worst of all, the advocate for the sexually abused child runs the risk of being smothered by indifference and a conspiracy of silence'.

The pressure from one's peer group as well as the community to ignore, minimise or cover up the situation may be extreme. These words may seem to have more than a faint ring of paranoia to them but are written from an experience which is repeatedly described by people who work in this field. Anyone who has not shared these experiences is unlikely to have entered into close dialogue with this area of abuse and certainly has not identified with the child's position in this situation.

DEFINITION OF CHILD SEXUAL ABUSE
(see Glaser & Frosh 1988)

Issues:

- What is sexual?

- When does what has occurred become abuse?
- How important is age?
- How relevant is consent?

Essential characteristics of child sexual abuse:

    a. Children in general do not like it.

    b. Sexual gratification of the abuser is the usual aim of the abuse.

    c. There is a power/age differential which effectively removes meaningful consent.

    d. The activity is usually secretive, collusive and perpetuated by the more powerful person. However, sometimes the strong needs of the child for physical affection, attention and dependency lead to the child's apparent complicity or willingness to initiate and maintain the abuse.

Sexual abuse, therefore, is interactive but the responsibility rests entirely with the adult. 'Sexual' relates to any activity which leads to sexual arousal in the adult. It includes a wide range of activities.

There are many definitions, for example:

1. 'The sexual exploitation of children is referred to as the involvement of dependent, developmentally immature children and adolescents in sexual activities that they do not fully comprehend, are unable to give informed consent to and that violate the social taboos of family roles' (Schechter & Roberge 1976).

2. 'A child (anyone under 16 years) is sexually abused when another person who is sexually mature involves the child in any activity which the other person expects to lead to their sexual arousal' (Baker & Duncan 1985); or, even simpler,

3. 'Sexual abuse is the exploitation of a child for the sexual gratification of an adult' (Fraser 1981).

No single definition is entirely satisfactory, but the essential aspects are to be found in the ones quoted. Obviously a 10-year-old boy (child) who is attempting to have anal intercourse with a 3-year-old cousin is sexually abusing her. A 10-year-old is not sexually mature, but is sexually capable although still developmentally immature. The issue should be seen from the child victim's viewpoint.

The issue of force or coercion is also important. A child may express power differentials through size in drawings (Fig. 8.1). Whilst some abuse is clearly the result of violent or forcible acts producing physical injury and best described as rape, molestation refers to a more cautious if equally determined approach to the child who is abused by the use of threats, bribes, trickery and emotional manipulation. In both situations there are powerful emotions at play which overcome any resistance the child may have. Violence is an appropriate description for this abuse of power. The issue of coercion is related to the age difference consideration, although it is almost impossible to define this precisely. Clearly, mutual sexual exploratory play between children of similar ages is not abuse, but where coercion is involved the situation is perceived differently.

CASE HISTORY 1

A 10-year-old boy hero-worshipped his 13-year-old cousin with whom he spent time at holidays and weekends. However, his cousin taught him how to masturbate and later involved him in oral sex and attempted buggery. When the younger boy resisted, he threatened to beat him up. The 10-year-old repeatedly asked his mother whether he had AIDS and eventually she elicited the story of what had happened with his cousin. Along with the boy's disclosure, his 12-year-old sister admitted that she had repelled the cousin's attempts to fondle her breasts, although he had masturbated and smeared semen on her, to her disgust.

This case, despite the narrow age difference of the children, clearly indicates that the behaviour is abusive and, from a detailed family assessment, a generational family history of child sexual abuse was elicited from the adults.

Clinical aspects of definitions

It is unusual in clinical practice for long discussions to take place on what does or does not constitute sexual abuse. It is as though the boundary is so clearly defined that serious difficulties do not arise. Of course, there must be encounters between adults and children which might appear worrying and somewhere between normal physical contact and sexual abuse. For example, french kissing seems more prevalent amongst families involved in sexual abuse, but in itself might not be described as sexual abuse. If the activity is leading to sexual arousal of the adult, then this is more

Fig. 8.1 Drawing by a 7-year-old sexually abused girl of her family. The girl is far left with her younger brother, mother and mother's boyfriend in that order on her right. Do the sizes of the figures reflect the child's perceptions of personal power?

likely to have significance. If the activity is perceived as unpleasant or to be avoided by the child, then we should take note. As Glaser & Frosh (1988) have noted, 'the general rule that equates "sexual contact" with some form of genital involvement is a useful one where questions of the appropriateness of physical encounters are raised'. The bathing costume areas are well understood and whilst the sensitivity about other parts of the body, for example breasts and thighs, varies from culture to culture, genital awareness is universal.

INCIDENCE AND PREVALENCE OF CHILD SEXUAL ABUSE

Definitions

Incidence: the number of new cases occurring in a given time period, usually one year (expressed as numbers of cases per year or as a rate per 1000 children). Figure 8.2 shows the numbers of children diagnosed by paediatricians in Leeds in the years 1978–88.

Prevalence: the proportion of the population that has been sexually abused at some time during the course of childhood (usually expressed as a percentage).

'How common is the occurrence of child sexual abuse?' is one of the first questions raised in every discussion. At present in the UK we have no reliable answers, but available information indicates that it is certainly not a rare or exotic condition worthy of a single case report in the literature (Markowe 1988). What we as paediatricians do not know at present are the answers to these and similar questions:

1. Is child sexual abuse as common a childhood problem as asthma or febrile convulsions?

2. What proportion of paediatricians' time is spent treating and advising on the immediate symptoms and disorders of childhood which arise from this kind of abuse (for example behaviour disorders, psychosomatic problems, recurrent abdominal pains, disorders of elimination, recurrent vaginal and anal conditions)?

3. What proportion of bed-wetting children who fail to respond adequately to our tried and tested therapies are wetting as a consequence of child sexual abuse?

4. How many children with recessive genetic or unexplained congenital disorders have been born as a result of an incestuous relationship?

5. Why are so many mothers vague and evasive about the identity of their child's father?

6. How many of the intractable and difficult behavioural problems of handicapped children, both home-based and institutionalised, are related to sexual abuse?

These and other questions require answers if we are to apply some of the knowledge which is now beginning to emerge about this hidden problem.

International comparisons

Information on prevalence is available from several developed countries, including the USA, Canada (Badgley 1984, Bagley & Ramsay 1986), England (Baker & Duncan 1985), Sweden (Ronstrom 1985) and New Zealand (Mullen et al 1988). More information is available from North America than elsewhere: the child prevalence rates range there from 6–62% for females and from 3–31% for males (Peters et al 1986). These figures are derived from research studies of adult victims designed to elicit retrospective disclosure, constituting the principal methodology that has been adopted in the last 10 years. In Britain national studies are required but have not yet been undertaken. The most widely quoted survey is the Mori Poll published in 1985 (Baker & Duncan 1985) which provided a figure of 10% of subjects reporting having been sexually abused before the age of 16 years (12% females, 8% males). Data from other countries does not show results that

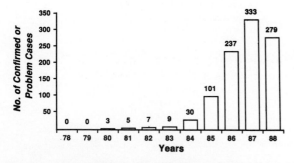

Fig. 8.2 Annual total number of cases of sexual abuse seen by Leeds paediatricians in the years 1987–88.

differ in major orders of magnitude, although the variations between individual studies are large and probably relate to differences of methodology, definition and sample. Some of the major differences in the studies relate to the way in which the information was obtained, with higher rates reported in face to face interviews with selected sensitive interviewers (Russell 1983) than in self-administered questionnaires or telephone interviews. Another important observation which was made (Peters et al 1986) in reviewing the various prevalence studies was that the number of screen questions within the protocol aimed at uncovering sexually abusive experience was related to the prevalence rate. Questions such as 'Were you ever sexually abused as a child?' or 'Did anyone ever touch your private sexual parts when you didn't want this'? seem more likely to elicit a positive response if there are more of them in the questionnaire.

In one sense it is surprising not just how many people have been sexually abused but how many are willing to reveal this in the context of a research study. It is in the private and anonymous situation where there are no further consequences that the individual may feel able to disclose. In reviewing the reasons for success in these studies it is clear that if the respondents are questioned with multiple screen questions which avoid labels like 'sexual abuse' and which give respondents more time and opportunity to remember forgotten experiences or gather courage to reveal embarrassing ones, then responses will be more complete. Recall is also aided by including relationship-specific questions, such as 'Did your brother ever touch you on your genital area when you didn't want it?'

Findings of the Mori Poll (Baker & Duncan 1985)

The poll, conducted by female interviewers of a nationally representative sample of 2019 men and women, used as its definition: 'A child (anyone under 16 years) is sexually abused when another person who is sexually mature involves the child in any activity which the other person expects to lead to their sexual arousal. This might involve intercourse, touching, exposure of sexual organs, showing pornographic material or talking about sexual things in an erotic way'. As with most studies, abuse both within and without the family were measured separately, as well as the number of episodes to indicate whether this was a one-off or a repetitive pattern of encounter.

10% of subjects reported being sexually abused before the age of 16 years (12% of females, 8% of males) with no special risks in specific social class categories. Whilst 63% of respondents reported only a single experience, 23% were repeatedly abused by the same person and 14% subjected to multiple abuse by a number of people. Of the abusers, 49% were known to the victims and 14% of all abuse took place within the family. 51% of the experiences reported as abusive involved no physical contact, 44% involved physical contact but not sexual intercourse, and 5% full sexual intercourse.

These findings are not atypical of the kind of results obtained in this kind of research. Females tend to report abuse more often than males, but it is very likely that men under-report. The highest prevalence rates are to be found in studies using the most searching and sensitive methods of questioning, suggesting that lower rates in some studies are underestimates of the problem.

The figures include a wide range of abuses and relationships of abuser to child. Figures for specific patterns of abuse, e.g. father/son, will be correspondingly lower. Important factors which appear not to influence the rates include education and socio-economic status or class, ethnicity or age. Within the USA, where there are sufficient numbers of studies to draw some conclusions, geographical region appears not to be a significant factor. The claims 'Well, the problem is more common in place A than place B', or 'We don't have incest in this town' seem unlikely to withstand close scrutiny.

Possible factors accounting for differences in prevalence rates in research studies (Peters et al 1986)

1. Definitions:
   - type of abuse — contact, non-contact
     - — exposure to pornography
     - — verbal acts
   - upper age limit of childhood

- criteria to define encounter as abusive
- difference in age between perpetrator and victim
- experiences with peers included.

2. Sampling differences:
  - age (differences may reflect fluctuating real prevalence rates or changing attitudes towards disclosure
  - social class, ethnicity, education, geographical region, inner v outer city v rural.

3. Methodology:
  - sampling techniques
  - response rates (usually many non-responders)
  - Method of administration of questionnaires/ interviews — face to face, self administered, telephone
  - type and number of questions
  - skill and experience of questioner
  - opportunity for follow-up and support of interviewers.

PATTERNS OF ABUSE

Child sexual abuse occurs in a variety of situations and social settings:

1. Intrafamilial: (Bentovim et al 1988): includes abuse within the nuclear and extended family and may incorporate family friends, lodgers or close acquaintances with the knowledge of the family. Abuse within adoptive or foster-families is also included here.

2. Extrafamilial: includes abuse with adults frequently known to the child from a variety of sources including neighbours, family friends, schoolfriend's parents, as well as abuse within 'sex rings'.

3. Institutional: includes abuse occurring within schools, residential children's establishments, day nurseries, holiday camps — e.g. cubs, brownies, boy scouts and other organisations both secular and religious.

4. Street or stranger abuse: assaults on children in public places, child abduction.

Intrafamilial abuse

As sexual abuse is a secretive activity where the risks of detection are minimised by the offender, the family offers the safest option. The opportunity to control and manipulate the child into silence, the avoidance of discovery and the taboos which prevent society from believing that parents could sexually abuse their own children provide insurance against discovery.

In the author's experience (Hobbs & Wynne 1987) two-thirds of children are abused by a family member (see Fig. 8.4, p. 129): this includes not only natural parents but also step-parents, unrelated boyfriends and cohabiting friends as well as grandparents, uncles, aunts, cousins, brothers and sisters. Relations who do not live under the same roof as the child will use the collusive secrecy of the family and easy access to the children, often in preference to abusing children outside the family. However, evidence from in-depth amnesty studies (Abel et al 1981) in the USA of committed sexual offenders indicate that as many as half of them have abused children both within and without their families.

Abuse occurs when an abuser has access to an available and vulnerable child. In a family setting it is more likely that all the children will be involved, but in institutional settings individual vulnerability may have more influence on the choice of the child.

Intrafamilial abuse is likely to be chronic, to begin in many cases soon after the birth of the child and to extend throughout childhood (Bentovim et al 1988). For some children the abusing relationships continue into adult life; women may bear their father's children and continue to live within their family, participating in the ongoing abuse of the next generation. Intrafamilial abuse, therefore, is more easily perceived as a pattern of relationships in which all the family participates and in which the normal boundaries within and between generations do not exist. The paediatrician who is working in this area should be aware of these generational cycles of abuse (Kaufman & Zigler 1989). When an angry grandmother writes or calls to proclaim her son or daughter innocent, she may be trying to protect them, but it is also likely that she is thinking of the whole family including herself and her husband and all the uncles, aunts, nieces and nephews who will feel threatened and exposed by the uncovering of abuse in a single child. For this reason, it has been the author's experience that arrangements to foster sexually abused children within the wider family have often met with difficulty, including further abuse by other family members. It is common when investigating sexual abuse in a family to make links with other related families where abuse has been recognised. The work of Oliver (1983) in Wiltshire has shown how abusing and neglecting families are connected through extensive kinships and how so much childhood morbidity and mortality is found in these families.

Extrafamilial abuse

The boundaries between intrafamilial and extrafamilial abuse are often blurred and the recognition of one must lead to a consideration of the other. A boy who has been abused at home by his father may unconsciously allow himself to be in dangerous situations with other men, who may take the opportunity to abuse him away from his family.

Many of the children in sex rings (Wild & Wynne 1986) were found to have been abused at home, but some had not. Often it was the ringleaders who had been victims of parental abuse and had recruited other children into the situation. Whilst some of these children had been deprived of attention at home and were vulnerable to the rewards of 'prostitution', they had not been sexually abused within their homes as far as one could tell (Wild & Wynne 1986).

In extrafamilial abuse a wide variety of adults, usually known to the child, establish relationships and lure him or her into situations where the child is abused, often in return for something which the child is not receiving at home. The child remains silent because disclosure might evoke parental anger with the child for allowing him or herself to become involved in the relationship. Baby-sitters and others who claim a genuine interest in helping the family may manoeuvre themselves into positions of trust so that they achieve contact with children in their own or the abuser's home. Some parents are happy that the child is willing to be away for a while to relieve them of the endless responsibility of child care. Others seem less concerned about where or with whom their child

spends time. Children who truant from school seem especially vulnerable and this should be viewed in some cases as a warning sign.

Child sex rings (Burgess et al 1981, Burgess 1984, Wild & Wynne 1986)

Characteristics:

● One adult (or small group) and several children. Men and women, boys and girls, usually in separate rings.

● Elaborate socialisation process binds and locks children into the ring

● Ringleaders are also often abused within their families.

● Children aged 6–16 years including siblings (i.e. school age).

● Adult abusers appear benevolent and encourage children to act out, pitting child members of the ring against one another.

● Older children may abuse and manipulate younger ones.

● Children are sexually abused individually or as a group with a range of activities from masturbation to intercourse.

● Pornography binds children more firmly to the ring and establishes commercial links with other abusers.

● Extreme secrecy is maintained by threats, peer group pressure and the fear of discovery.

● Discovery depends on dedicated and experienced police officers working closely with other community agencies.

● Rings have a life of years, may break and rejoin around another abuser. Children join and leave the rings, maintaining secrecy.

● Children are emotionally damaged by the abuse, experiencing subsequent sexual difficulties, acting out behaviour, alcohol or drug abuse. Identification with the abuser is common.

● Child sex rings have been discovered in Britain in several cities and in the USA. It is likely that they are a common and widespread form of abuse. Around 300 children were involved in Leeds (Wild & Wynne 1986).

● The term 'child prostitution' has been used because in some cases the abuser will reward the children with cups of coffee, attention and small monetary gifts. For this reason, children from materially or emotionally depriving families may be at greater risk.

Ritualistic abuse

This can be intrafamilial or extrafamilial and is discussed in Chapter 13.

SEXUALLY ABUSED CHILDREN

The traditional view of the sexually abused child implied that there was often something within the child's make-up which contributed to abuse. These so-called 'child factors' have been much discussed within the context of physical abuse as well as neglect and failure to thrive. It was hypothesised that either the child's behaviour, manner or appearance triggered off interest on the part of the adult. In sexual abuse a mythology existed that only certain children at certain ages were abused and that this was related to their 'mini' adult sexuality: hence the view that a teenage girl blossoming into puberty provided a stimulus which to a stepfather, not bound by incest taboos, could be irresistible. Recognition that this scenario was little more than a comforting attempt to normalise deviant behaviour has led to a reappraisal of this.

Children of all ages are abused, including babies. Reported cases of girls still outnumber boys (2:1) (Hobbs & Wynne 1987) but boys are less likely to be suspected, to report or to be believed (Rogers & Terry 1984). In view of these confounding variables, it has been suggested that boys are sexually abused to the same extent as girls (Kempe & Kempe 1984, Hanks et al 1988). Age at diagnosis does not inform us of age of onset of abuse, but the mean age at diagnosis is around 7 years with the peak at 2–7 years according to data on children diagnosed in Leeds (Fig. 8.3). Age at diagnosis depends more on the ease of diagnosis, willingness to disclose and frequency of physical findings which assist diagnosis. There are good reasons for believing that older children learn the consequences of disclosure, are better able to conceal the fact of their abuse and have a greater sense of the perceived harm which they may suffer if they tell. As well as finding abused children of both genders and all ages, it is quite usual to find

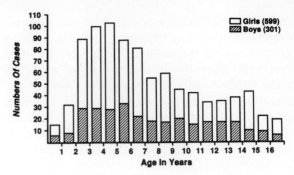

Fig. 8.3 Age/sex distribution of 900 sexually abused children seen by paediatricians in Leeds in the years 1986–88.

that all the children in the family have suffered abuse (Hobbs & Wynne 1986).

Rather than child factors being important in determining whether or not abuse occurs when they come into contact with the abuser, it is the indiscriminate behaviour of the abuser which appears to be more important. If this is the case, differences between sexually abused children and non-abused children are more likely to be the result of the abuse than its cause. Recently a 5-year-old girl took to having make-up and nail varnish, having her hair done in a grown-up style and wearing earrings. Sexual abuse by her father and brother was discovered and her transformation to a sexual object gave important clues to her foster-mother that all was not well. If she had been 12 or 13, the alternative explanation that she was sexually precocious and inviting inappropriate attention could easily have been preferred.

These children are groomed and trained to respond sexually, the process occurring gradually over a long time. Loss of childhood innocence and the appearance of a child too wise for his or her years are common effects.

Accommodation syndrome (Summit 1983)

When a child is caught up in sexual abuse, that child develops an adjustment pattern to the abuse which is known as the accommodation syndrome. An understanding of this 'normal' behaviour pattern is vital to be able to assist children, including explaining in court why a child is relating in a particular way. The five charateristics of the child sexual abuse accommodation syndrome are:

- Secrecy
- Helplessness
- Accommodation
- Delayed disclosure
- Retraction.

This pattern is most clearly seen when the abuser is a trusted care-giver, for example a parent or parent figure.

Secrecy

Children are told not to tell. Threats of physical violence, but often promises of withdrawal of love and affection, are all that are needed to secure a dependent child's silence. The child fears disapproval or punishment, and attempts to tell often confirm these worst fears. Retaliation certainly occurs. One 5-year-old child who told her aunt that her stepfather was putting his fingers in her bottom was given a good hiding. Another child, who complained to her mother that her 'tuppence' was sore, told her mother it had happened because daddy took her into the bedroom with him. The mother responded by hitting the child across the face, leaving bruises on her cheek and ear which, when noticed by the grandmother, led to detection.

Older children understand the implications for the family of a police investigation: possible imprisonment of father, loss of income, stigmatisation, shame and the possibility that they may be held responsible for all this. The logical solution for most children is to maintain the conspiracy of secrecy and silence.

Helplessness

Children are unable to stop the abuse in most cases. Although they may resist at least initially, they find that it is less trouble to lie still, pretend to be asleep and switch off. In this way they attempt to protect themselves. This behaviour is often reflected in the ease with which children are medically examined; during the examination some children even go to sleep. Children will not cry out or struggle to protect themselves and this is often misinterpreted as willing compliance, both by the abuser and society at large. The cost that the child pays for the abandonment of active resistance is insecurity, victimisation and a loss of psychological well-being. The child is helpless, powerless and has no-one to turn to.

Entrapment and accommodation

In the position of helplessness and secrecy, the child feels trapped and feels there is no way out of the situation. The only active role the child can play is to hold herself responsible and, in sensing the wrongness and badness of what is happening, attempt herself to make amends. The victim therefore scapegoats herself, leaving the abuser free of experiencing the child's hostility. Self blame and guilt are almost universal feelings shared by sexually abused children.

In addition the child faces other pressures:

1. The need to protect other children. The abuser may tell the child that if he stops abusing her he may have to turn to other, possibly younger children.

2. The need to protect the other parent.

3. The need to protect the family home and integrity of the family.

The child has the power to destroy the family, but the responsibility to keep it together. Parent and child roles have been subtly reversed and in doing so the child has accommodated to the situation at the expense of herself and her needs. The loss of childhood is a useful concept to describe the way in which the child is forced into a pseudo-adult role.

Once in this position, other adults easily view the child as a consenting and willing participant in the situation and come to doubt the child's statements if later the truth is revealed. The child who is able to accommodate effectively to the abuse will cover up the reality in order to protect the parent, but also to allow herself space for survival. It is not unusual for children, for example, to flourish at school where they feel protected and safe, effectively splitting off that part of their life from the threats and insecurity of home. Children's capacity to develop different personalities to cope with their complex feelings leads to psychological disintegration and the multiple personality states seen in some adult survivors (Goodwin 1989a).

Delayed disclosure and retraction

It is likely that many children never disclose their sexual abuse. They may attempt to within the family, but less often outside. Many adult victims disclosing in later life indicate that they never told. Disclosure is favoured by:

1. Overwhelmingly impossible situation at home.
2. The presence of a sensitive friend or helper, e.g. school teacher.
3. Abuser no longer in contact (e.g. divorce)
4. Education strategies, telephone lines.
5. Good luck.

Many disclosures seem to arise almost by chance. Incidents where a chance remark is made by a child when defences are down, picked up by a sensitive listener and carefully expanded upon are not common. However, it is very simple to inhibit a child's attempts at disclosure by not hearing, disapproval or disbelief.

Our experience suggests that disclosure is not particularly favoured at any age (Hobbs & Wynne 1987, Hanks et al 1988). Contrary to the popular view that when the child enters adolescence he or she is more likely to disclose, we find that this is not a particular peak for referrals. At that age children can begin to get out of the situation and that is an option that may be simpler than disclosure and exposure. Disclosure is, however, often delayed (school children present more often through disclosure than pre-school children — Hanks et al 1988), the abuse will have been going on for some time and the child fears that he or she will not be viewed sympathetically. The disclosure is, therefore, often retracted, may sound unconvincing, often includes details of only one or two incidents and is almost never exaggerated. The types of activity described will often be the less intrusive and upsetting ones for the child. There may be ambiguity which the child does not readily resolve.

CASE HISTORY 2
10- and 8-year-old girls in foster-care visited their alcoholic mother regularly at weekends. She failed to protect them from her violent boyfriends and eventually the older girl said to her social worker that one of the boyfriends had touched her once through her clothes between her legs. Thinking that it was unlikely that there would be any medical evidence and that the abuse did not seem so serious, the social worker delayed a while, but mentioned it to the child's paediatrician when he next routinely saw the children. On questioning the older girl further, she revealed that she had been hurt between her legs and that she was sore for several days. Her younger sister, who up to this point had denied that she had been involved in any way, then reminded her foster-mother that she had on occasions complained of a sore bottom. Both the children readily agreed to medical examination, where signs were found which strongly suggested that the older girl had experienced intercourse. The younger girl also had signs suggesting that vaginal penetration had been attempted.

Even, therefore, when children are being protected and given consistency and security, disclosure can be a slow gradual process, taking months and sometimes years. All these factors, of course, make criminal investigation difficult and often unrewarding; the current conviction rate is 5% in Leeds (Frothingham et al 1991). It is easy to suggest that the child is not being truthful when of course the child will usually conceal more than he or she is willing to reveal. Only an understanding and sensitive interpretation of the psychological processes involved allows the evidence to be properly assessed.

Retraction

Whatever children, adults and even sometimes professional witnesses say about sexual abuse, there is a strong likelihood that they will reverse it under pressure.

For the child, the whole subject is loaded with ambivalence, guilt and self doubt. A hostile response by family or the outside world soon lets children know that they had better take it all back and say they made it up. The fact that children cannot and do not readily make up stories of explicit sexual activity is quickly forgotten by all concerned as the threat of the child's disclosure recedes. The retraction reassures, encourages disbelief of the original disclosure and may lead to inaction. While it should be viewed as a normal and expected part of the psychological adjustments of sexually abused children. People are happier to believe that children lie than that they are sexually abused (Goodwin 1989b).

Anger and rage. These emotions are common in abused children and may find expression in many ways:

1. Self destruction, self hate, self mutilation, suicidal behaviour, promiscuity and running away.

2. Exploitation of others, e.g. as ringleader may manipulate younger children in the ring.

3. Rejection of non-abusing parent, usually the mother if the father is abusing. There may be good easy to hand reasons, for example, 'Why didn't mother stop it, she must have known!'.

4. Aggressive, antisocial behaviour, wanton destruction, vandalism.

5. Depression, drug and alcohol abuse.

6. As the child becomes older, abusing or raping others less powerful.

ABUSERS

Quotations:

Everyone hates a child molester until it's someone you know. (American Police Officer)

In response to an article in the *Observer* in August 1989 entitled 'Why do men do it?' we asked 'why do women do it', or even 'Why do people do it?' Perhaps the answer is much more simple than it appears — what could be easier than abusing a child?

Sexual offenders will only tell you the minimum of what they need to say to avoid responsibility for what they have done. The only characteristic that offenders have in common is that they commit deviant sexual acts — and also thought it was okay to do it. (Judith Becker, in a paper presented to a child abuse conference in Glasgow, 1987)

Child sexual abusers include white-collar workers, priests, doctors, attorneys, judges, blue-collar workers and those who have no job (S Wolf, at a conference on child protection, Leeds University, 1988)

Facts about abusers

Most abusers or perpetrators are related to or known to the child. Figure 8.4 demonstrates these relationships in a study of 337 children. Most abusers commit large numbers of offences involving large numbers of children. In one study 232 abusers guaranteed confidentiality admitted that they had attempted 55 250 acts of child abuse and completed 38 727 of them (Abel et al 1985). Abusers include both men and women. Our expectations and the teaching given to us as children

(don't speak to strange men) mean that we underestimate and fail to recognise female abusers. The numbers being recognised are steadily increasing.

The majority of abusers start behaving in this way as adolescents. Many abusers themselves report sexual abuse as children, but not all (Knopp 1984). Most, however, recall difficult and damaging experiences as children (Becker 1988).

In one study of convicted abusers' childhood experiences (Wolf 1987): 17% witnessed sexual abuse, 23% were victims of emotional abuse, 27% were victims of sexual abuse, 30% were victims of violence and 37% had witnessed violence. In addition, 47% had feelings of isolation and 100% grew up in dysfunctional families.

25% of children diagnosed in Leeds were abused by teenagers (Hobbs & Wyne 1987). Whilst many of the boy abusers have been sexually abused, recent work suggests that female teenage abusers have all been sexually abused (Tranter — personal communication 1991).

Rationalisations and distortions

Abusers may say to defend their actions (Donleary & Goodwin 1989):

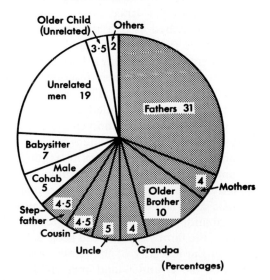

Fig. 8.4 Pie chart to show relationship of perpetrators to children in 337 cases of sexual abuse. Shaded area represents relatives of child. Percentages are shown. (Reproduced with permission from Hobbs C J, Wynne J M 1987 Child sexual abuse — an increasing rate of diagnosis. Lancet ii: 837–841)

- 'The child was sexually provocative, she came and sat on my knee'.
- 'If she didn't want to be raped, why did she start developing breasts'?
- 'I only did it to teach him about sex'.
- 'I just knew she wanted to by the way she was looking at me'.

Models for viewing abusive behaviour (Salter 1988)

1. Sexual addiction — high levels of sexual arousal leading to need for frequent gratification and cycle of addiction. Breaking the habit is extremely difficult. Abusers tell themselves they won't do it again. As with other addictions, the need for increasing 'dosage' leads to escalation of the abuse.

2. Paedophile — child sexual fixation (Groth 1982). 'Children are missing out if they don't have the opportunity to enjoy sexual relations'. Everyone else has got it wrong. The paedophile has no sexual interest in adults. His interest is the world of the child. The paedophile's defences are so unchallengeable that he may never be able to start on the difficult process of treatment. Paedophiles are increasingly organised and may be in touch with others, exchanging information and publications.

3. Family models (Furniss 1984) — incestuous families are described as patriarchal and authoritarian but within them the individuals have strong needs and personal weaknesses. Patterns of male or female dominance are often described and the marital relationship is poor. The emotional and sexual difficulties are controlled by the development of inappropriate sexual and emotional bonds with the children. In some families this serves to avoid conflict, in others it seems to regulate the violent and disturbed patterns of family life. It is postulated that these families, however, maintain their fragile and dangerous existence because the terror of abandonment is so much greater. The members of the family collude and keep the secret to maintain the integrity of the family unit. This model helps us to understand that child sexual abuse occurs within the context of emotional deprivation and neglect and never as an isolated finding in an otherwise well-functioning family.

4. Sociological — within society power is one aspect of relationships between individuals and groups of individuals. Men are typically seen as possessing more power than women and of assuming dominant roles in families. Rich have more than poor and whites more than blacks. Adults have power over children. A misuse of adult power for the achievement of adults' needs, denying the child's own needs, is at the centre of child sexual abuse. Sociologists would say that while these major power differentials exist, the potential for abuse is inherent. Only when society is more fair and just will this be reflected in individual and family relationships.

Abusers and denial

Abusers are amongst the best liars and deniers. There is no such person as an abuser who does not deny. Salter (1988b) listed the various components of denial as follows.

1. Denial of the acts themselves (type and period of time the abuse occurred)
2. Denial of fantasy and planning
3. Denial of responsibility for the acts
4. Denial of the seriousness of the behaviour
5. Denial of internal guilt for the behaviour
6. Denial of the difficulty of changing abusive patterns.

There is a continuum from admission with justification to admission with guilt. The more the abuser shifts towards the latter, the less pathological is his behaviour. Treatment of abusers is seen as enabling them to move gradually from the position of denial to acceptance of the responsibility for what they have done, together with a sense of the seriousness of their actions.

ACTS IN SEXUAL ABUSE — TYPES OF ABUSE (Fig. 8.5)

Sexual abuse involves:

1. Contact:
   - Touching, fondling or oral contact with breast or genitals.
   - Insertion of fingers or objects into vulva or anus.
   - Masturbation: by adult of him/herself in the presence of the child, including ejaculation

onto the child; by adult of child or by child of adult.

- Intercourse: Vaginal, anal or oral intercourse whether actual or attempted in any degree. This is usually with adult as the active party but in some cases a child may be encouraged to penetrate the adult.
- Rape is attempted/achieved penile penetration of the vagina (Fig. 8.6).
- Other genital contact; intracrural intercourse where the penis is laid between the legs or genital contact with any part or the child's body, e.g. rubbed penis on thigh.
- Prostitution: any of the above abuse which includes the exchange of money, gifts or favours and applies to both boys ('rent boys') or girls.

2. Non-contact:
- Exhibitionism (flashing).
- Pornography of many kinds; photographing sexual acts or anatomy.
- Showing pornographic photographs, films, videos.
- Erotic talk, telling children titillating or sexually explicit stories.
- Other sexual exploitations. Sadistic activities.
- Burning a child's buttocks or genital area.

At the present time we have no sure way of assessing or predicting the harm or upset which is caused to a child from these varying activities. The child's responses are individual. Whilst we all have

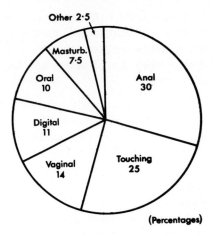

Fig. 8.5 Pie chart to demonstrate percentage frequency of different types of sexual abuse in 337 children. (Reproduced with permission from Hobbs C J, Wynne J M 1987 Child sexual abuse — an increasing rate of diagnosis. Lancet ii: 837–841)

our own ideas as to which activity is more serious and which likely to be more damaging, it is as well to remember these difficulties. Most people view intercourse as the most serious and exhibitionism the least.

Many children suffer more than one abuse, for example genital fondling, oral and anal intercourse, and it is often considered that the abuses may escalate over time from, say, exposure, involvement in masturbation and intracrural intercourse to vaginal intercourse. However, the high frequency of oral and anal intercourse in preschool children suggests that this slow seduction is often shortened where children have less ability to resist.

Figure 8.5 gives the relative proportions of the different abuses seen in our series. Types of abuse will vary depending on the way children are selected; clinical series are likely to have fewer non-contact cases for obvious reasons.

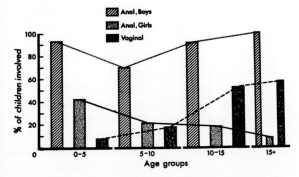

Fig. 8.6 Penetrative sexual abuse. Percentage of children involved in anal and vaginal penetration by age group and gender from a study of 337 sexually abused children. (Reproduced with permission from Hobbs C J, Wynne J M 1989 Sexual abuse of English boys and girls: the importance of anal examination. Child Abuse and Neglect 13: 195–210)

EFFECTS OF SEXUAL ABUSE (Finkelhor & Browne 1986, Wyatt & Powell 1988)

It is widely believed that sexual abuse is harmful. At best it is unpleasant, at worst extremely frightening and painful, physically and psychologically, for the child. Even older children, physically mature enough to experience pleasurable sexual sensations, are hurt and suffer from its effects. Children tell us that they do not like it, they wish it to stop and usually convey pain and discomfort when attempting to tell us about it. Evidence that child sexual abuse has deleterious effects comes from:

a. Observation of sexually abused children from around the time of diagnosis.

b. Follow-up of children following recognition of sexual abuse.

c. Studies of the population of adults to assess the frequency of mental health problems in abused and non-abused populations (Mullen et al 1988).

d. Observations of adult psychiatric patients who have been abused (Whitwell 1990).

Effects may be short-term or long-lasting.

Broad aspects of effects

Short-term — child

1. Emotional and behavioural effects.
2. Educational and learning.
3. Social relationships.

Children may exhibit disturbed behaviour, e.g. soiling , wetting, self injury or abnormal emotional states such as anxiety, depression and withdrawal. They may have difficulty with learning and require special educational provision or assistance. His relationships with adults and other children may be distorted in that they may only be able to relate to adults of one sex and have no class friends, or alienate themselves by involving other children in sexual activities.

Long-term — adult (Briere & Runtz 1988)

1. Mental health problems: depression, suicide, self injury, poor self-esteem, alcohol and/or drug abuse.
2. Sexual adjustment difficulties: prostitution, marital difficulties, aversion to sexual contact, fertility control.
3. Child-rearing difficulties: repeat cycle of abuse, over protectiveness, fear of closeness.
4. Social dysfunction: delinquency, criminal behaviour/offending, acts of violence, victim role.

Another way of looking at the harmful effects has been proposed by Finkelhor & Browne (1986) and includes four separate but inter-related areas of traumagenic dynamics. These different dynamics — traumatic sexualisation, betrayal, stigmatisation and powerlessness — account for the variety of symptoms and effects which we see. For each of the dynamics one can envisage:

- the abusive component,
- the shaping effect it has on the child through its impact,
- the manifestations which are incorporated into the child's and subsequently adult's behaviour.

Sexual traumatisation. A child may find that he or she receives attention and affection in exchange for sex; for example, many receive gifts for allowing daddy to get his way. The child then confuses sex with love and receiving care and attention. The long-term result will be that as the child grows up he or she may attempt to sexualise all relationships from which affection and attention are expected. The result will be seen as sexual promiscuity, possibly prostitution, and a tendency to sexualisation of relationships with their own children.

At the other end of the spectrum, sexual activity may be perceived as associated with entirely negative emotions and memories, leading to sexual aversion and difficulty in arousal or orgasm, or complete avoidance of sexual intimacy.

Betrayal. Betrayal stems from the loss of trust and disillusionment which a child feels when abused or not protected by a parent. This can produce dependency, clinging in young children or a search for a trusted person. The impaired ability to judge people may lead to mistrust or misjudgment in relationships with obvious disastrous implications for marriages.

Stigmatisation. In child sexual abuse, the wrongfulness of the activity is soon perceived by a child as well as the offender and feelings of being dirty or damaged are common, leading to a sense of worthlessness or poor self-esteem. Such individuals, as they grow up, can become outcasts prone to alcohol or drug abuse, self injury, criminal activity and isolation (Bagley & Ramsay 1986).

Powerlessness. Sexual abuse is clearly an abuse of the power which all adults have over children. Inability — through weakness born out of dependency and developmental immaturity — to stop the abuse leaves the child feeling powerless, anxious and unable to influence his or her own life. The child, as he or she grows up, may feel anxious, inefficient with impaired coping skills, a tendency to run away from problems, or sometimes despair and depression. Revictimisation is always a possibility but compensatory mechanisms to overcome these feelings include a need to control or dominate and a potentiality for aggression and becoming an abuser (Rogers & Terry 1984).

This model is useful in understanding some of the basic psychological mechanisms occurring in sexually abused children. It is derived from understanding of a great many facts, for example that prostitutes were very often sexually abused as children (James & Meyerding 1977), that there is a high frequency of a history of abuse in depressed women, and that victims may also become abusers.

What is also clear from the testimony of adults abused as children is that the feelings which accompany thoughts or recollections of these experiences remain hidden for many years and often for a lifetime. Letters from ageing grandparents who disclose abuse for the first time bear witness to the pain and suffering which these individuals have had to deal with all their lives. The process of coming to terms with this may be protracted, slow and incomplete. Repression and denial can be very powerful and the individual unable to confront these feelings except through these defensive mechanisms.

Factors which affect outcome in child sexual abuse

The degree to which a child is emotionally harmed by child sexual abuse in influenced by such factors as the child's prior history, current developmental level and age, as well as the nature of the sexual abuse.

Aspects of the sexual activity:

a. type of sex act
b. frequency and duration
c. degree of force/violence and degree of bribery and coercion used
d. relationship with offender

e. age of child when contact first occurred
f. multiple abusers.

Other important factors are linked to these questions:

a. Did the child disclose the abuse?
b. To whom did they reveal it?
c. Have family and institutions responded?

Type of sex act

In our culture there is a perceived hierarchy of 'seriousness' of sexual activity ranging from kissing, breast touching, genital touching to intercourse. A similar hierarchy has been suggested for the prediction of trauma in child sexual abuse. Russell 1986 found the following percentage of women traumatised according to the type of act: clothed contact, unwanted kissing — 22%; touching of unclothed genitals, breasts — 36%; vaginal intercourse, oral or anal intercourse — 59%.

Penetrative abuse is considered more harmful than non-penetrative (Russell 1986, Briere 1988, Harter et al 1988). In addition to research findings, it is clear that professionals working in this field share this perception. Davenport (1988) interviewed 19 doctors (paediatricians, psychiatrists), social workers and clinical psychologists, all of whom were working actively in this field. She found that penetration was considered most abusive of all the various acts. This is also reflected in the way in which the law views the seriousness of various offences. The term rape itself implies penetration. The victim's perception (what he or she feels about what has been done to them) and the harm which results are closely and aetiologically related.

Frequency and duration

The balance of evidence favours the view that harmfulness is related to frequency and duration (Tsai et al 1979, Russell 1986). However, chronicity is likely to lead to accommodation which may be associated with fewer symptoms in the short term although it may be associated with greater long-term psychological harm. In chronic abuse, the child is more likely to suffer long-term distortion in development.

Degree of force and violence

Society perceives physical force or violence as abusive, whereas more subtle inducements resulting in the same outcome are often not viewed in the same way. Conversely, whilst initially force will be immediately traumatising there may be some solace for the victim who is able to perceive later the wrongfulness of the experience and his/her own lack of involvement. Children who are tricked, bribed or seduced to comply may feel complicity and their view of themselves may be distorted in other ways. They often feel more intensely that they are at fault and should have stopped the abuse. The reality — that they would not have been able to do this easily — is lost. However, the degree of violence, according to research studies, remains an important factor although it will certainly interact with other variables (Finkelhor 1979, Bagley & Ramsay 1986, Russell 1986).

Relationship with offender

The relationship with the offender includes family links, quality and closeness, age, gender and maturity of the abuser.

Abuse by close relatives, especially if in a parental or caring role, is generally felt to have the most harmful effects (Finkelhor 1979, Adams-Tucker 1982, Russell 1986). However, no straightforward connection between the closeness of the relationship (nuclear family, versus relative, versus friend, versus stranger) and the effect on the child has been established (Finkelhor 1979). In the long term the quality of other, non-abusing, relationships will also influence the outcome.

Age of child

This is an important and complex factor. With young pre-school children the view that the child does not understand or perceive the wrongfulness of the act is often quoted to indicate that less harm will result. However, many young children exhibit signs of emotional disturbance indicating that, whether or not they have an understanding of right and wrongfulness, the negative effects have been perceived and responses have occurred. In developmental terms the effects are likely to be related to the developmental processes occurring at the time. In the younger child, the development of trust may be harmed and if the abuse continues relationships will become distorted in fundamental ways.

Thus it is our view (Hanks et al 1988) that:

Sexual abuse strikes at the foundation of the child's development as an individual. Abuse occurring in the early stage of a child's life (from birth to five years of age) is more likely to lead to major and fundamental changes in normal development and from what we have seen so far to have life long consequences. These children have been deprived of trust and security within a relationship. What is more they have come to regard human relationships in a distorted way — a distortion that they are at first not aware of and that cumulatively grows. As they grow older and reach the age of around nine years they become clearly aware of the taboo which exists about incest and withdraw in shame and guilt, or turn to aggressive or abusive behaviour themselves.

Adolescents have also been considered to be especially vulnerable psychologically to sexual abuse. Adolescence is characterised by a search for identity and an understanding of the meaning of normal and deviant sexual relationships as well as drives towards autonomy and independence. Sexual identity is at the height of its development and will be distorted by sexual abuse. It is often said that guilt is especially common and may be compounded by the pleasurable effects which may at times be felt from the sexual contact. Isolation from peers may also be enforced by the perpetrator. Perpetrators often object to the child having other relationships and prohibitions mount at the possibility of other sexual relationships. Age is therefore an important complex variable, with different effects expressed at different developmental stages.

Multiple abusers

The effect of being abused by multiple perpetrators is to convince the child that the blame for the abuse lies in himself, rather than with the offenders. The harmful effects are therefore compounded and patterns of revictimisation into adulthood may result.

Effects of disclosure

Children are harmed not only by the abuse, but

also by the response of the family and professional system. Disbelief or denial by someone (e.g. mother or father) in a position of responsibility regarding the child is clearly a major source of harm to a child already suffering the effects of sexual abuse. Obviously it will add to the child's sense of betrayal. Even when a disclosure is believed, the immediate effects of disclosure on the family may be extremely traumatising. Disruption of family relationships, suicide and emotional turmoil and distress are all potentially harmful, certainly in the short term. A positive response and support of disclosure may be therapeutic in assisting the child and may have effects on such outcomes as the 'attitude to men' following abuse (Wyatt & Ray Mickey 1988). Many children still receive little in the way of therapeutic help or positive support, the most usual reaction, even when the abuse is acknowledged and acted upon, being 'to forget about it as quickly as possible' (Frothingham et al 1991).

Iatrogenic harm

It is important to distinguish between the crisis and distress following discovery, which in themselves have not been caused by the professional response, and true components of iatrogenic harm which certainly have (Jones 1991). Jones lists these as:

1. Overzealous professional intervention: the crusader who may end up alienating parents and children alike.

2. Repeated interviewing, multiple interviews. To this can be added extended, pressured interviews.

3. Repeated physical examinations (physical examinations conducted against the wishes of the child or insensitively are also included).

4. Social and economic effects on the family. These cannot in all fairness be called iatrogenic and society needs to confront the needs of families where enforced break-up has led to loss of income, loss of job, etc.

5. Defensive decision making. Refusal to take any risk leading, for example, to unwarranted removal of the child from the family. It is preferable when possible of course, to remove the perpetrator, leaving the child at home.

6. Attendance in court. There is evidence that this adds to the harm experienced by a sexually abused child (Flin & Bull 1989, Goodman et al 1989).

7. Withholding of treatment (often it is simply not available or is withheld to spare the short-term distress often experienced at the beginning of therapy).

8. Overtreatment for too long where change is impossible. This compounds the situation and the helplessness of the family where earlier use of statutory intervention would have been more helpful.

9. Foster and residential care. Further abuse may occur in care and this can be devastating for children placed there for protection. Children who have been sexually abused may be moved around as they are more difficult to care for. Lack of support for foster-parents and drift in placements all have professional components.

Summary

1. Child sexual abuse has recently been recognised as a major cause of morbidity in children of all ages, boys and girls.

2. Prevalence studies of adult survivors suggest substantial under-reporting by children, although reports have been increasing in many countries in recent times.

3. The abuse is an abuse of power and can be perpetrated by male and female adults, teenagers, as well as older children.

4. Definitions emphasise the developmental immaturity of the child, the lack of consent and the sexual needs of the abuser as well as the deviant and coercive nature of the behaviour.

5. The abuse occurs within and without the family, in institutions, in organised rings, by perpetrators known or unknown to the child. Ritualistic abuse frequently involves sexual abuse.

6. There appear to be few factors which predispose the child to become a victim of sexual abuse, and all children are potentially at risk. The effects of sexual abuse on the child may predispose them to further abuse.

7. Investigators of child sexual abuse need to be aware that children develop complex adjustment behaviours to accommodate to the abuse.

Although regular gross abuse is occurring the child may openly present as happy and coping well.

8. The accommodation syndrome includes: secrecy, helplessness, accommodation, delayed disclosure and retraction.

9. Abusers commit large numbers of deviant sexual acts, usually accompanied by denial and justification. The types of abuse include contact and non-contact, penetrative and non-penetrative acts. Prosecution is infrequent.

10. The available evidence indicates the harm-ful nature of sexual abuse and models for under-standing the effects are helpful in helping children's and adults' problems. The harm may be short- or long-term.

11. Many factors influence the harm which children suffer after sexual abuse. The long-term outcome is affected by the child successfully revealing the abuse, being believed and being protected.

12. Professional interventions, while seeking to secure protection and support for the child, must avoid themselves adding to the child's distress.

REFERENCES

Abel G G, Becker J V, Murphy W D, Flanagan B 1981 Identifying dangerous child molesters. In: Stuart R B (ed) Violent behaviour. Brunner/Mayed, New York

Abel G G, Mittelman M S, Becker J V 1985 Sexual offenders: results of assessment and recommendations for treatment. In: Ben-Aron M H, Huckle S J, Webster C D (eds) Clinical criminology: the assessment and treatment of criminal behaviour. MM Graphic, Toronto, pp 191–205

Adams-Tucker C 1982 Proximate effects of sexual abuse in childhood. A report on 28 children. American Journal of Psychiatry 139: 1252–1256

Badgley R et al (Committee on sexual offences against children and youth) 1984 Sexual offences against children, Vol 1. Canadian Government Publishing Center, Ottawa

Bagley, Ramsay 1986 Disrupted childhood and vulnerability to sexual assault. Long-term sequels with implications for counselling. Social Work and Human Sexuality 4: 33–48

Baker A, Duncan S 1985 Child sexual abuse: a study of prevalence in Great Britain. Child Abuse and Neglect 9: 457–467

Becker J V 1988 The effects of child sexual abuse on adolescent sexual offenders. In: Wyatt G E, Powell G J (eds) Lasting effects of child sexual abuse. Sage, London, pp 193–207

Bentovim A, Elton A, Hildebrand J, Tranter M, Vizard E 1988 Child sexual abuse within the family: assessment and treatment. Wright, London

Briere J 1988 The long-term clinical correlates of childhood sexual victimization. Annals of the New York Academy of Sciences 528

Briere J, Runtz M 1988 Post sexual abuse trauma. In: Wyatt G P, Powell E J (eds) Lasting effects of child sexual abuse. Sage, London

Burgess A V 1984 Child pornography and sex rings. D C Heath, Lexington M A

Burgess A W, Groth A N, McCausland M P 1981 Child sex initiation rings. American Journal of Orthopsychiatry 51(1): 110–119

Butler-Sloss E 1988 Report of the Inquiry into Child Abuse in Cleveland 1987

Davenport C 1988 The traumatizing effects of child sexual abuse. Public and professional opinion. BSc thesis, University of Leicester

Donleavy J, Goodwin J 1989 What families say: the dialogue of incest in sexual abuse. In: Goodwin J (ed) Sexual abuse: incest victims and their families. Year Book Medical Publishers, Chicago, pp 65–82

Finkelhor D 1979 Sexually victimized children. New York Free Press

Finkelhor D, Browne A 1986 Initial and long term effects. A conceptual framework. Ch 6 in: A sourcebook on child sexual abuse. Sage, London, pp 180–198

Flin R, Bull R 1989 Child witnesses in Scottish criminal proceedings. In: Spencer J R, Nicholson G, Flin R, Bull R (eds) Children's evidence in legal proceedings. Faculty of Law, University of Cambridge, pp 193–200

Fraser B G 1981 Sexual child abuse: the legislation and the law in the United States. In: Mrazek P B, Kempe C H (eds) Sexually abused children and their families. Pergamon, Oxford, pp 55–73

Freud S 1954 The origins of psychoanalysis: letters to Wilhelm Fliess. Drafts and notes 1887–1902. Bonaparte A, Freud A, Kris E (eds). Basic Books, New York

Frothingham T E, Barnett R, Hobbs C J, Wynne J M 1991 Child sexual abuse in Leeds before and after Cleveland. Paper presented at the 1st National Conference on Child Abuse and Neglect, Leicester, England, September 1991, and submitted for publication

Furniss T 1984 Conflict-avoiding and conflict regulating patterns in incest and child sexual abuse. Acta Paediatrica Scandinavica 50: 299–313

Glaser D, Frosh S 1988 Child sexual abuse. Ch 1 Myth and reality: the dimensions of child sexual abuse. Practical Social Work Series, Macmillan, London

Goodman G S, Pyle E A, Jones D P H, England P, Port L K, Rudy L, Prado L 1989 Emotional effects of criminal court testimony on child sexual assault victims. Final report submitted to US National Institute of Justice, Grant number 85-IJ-CX-0020

Goodwin J M 1989a Recognising multiple personality disorder in adult incest victims. In: Goodwin J (ed) Sexual abuse: incest victims and their families, 2nd ed. Year Book Medical Publishers, Chicago

Goodwin J M 1989b Credibility problems in multiple personality disorder patients and abused children. In: Goodwin J (ed) Sexual abuse: incest victims and their families, 2nd ed. Year Book Medical Publishers, Chicago

Groth A N 1982 The incest offender. In: Sgroi S (ed) Handbook of clinical intervention in child sexual abuse. Lexington Books, Lexington MA, pp 215–239

Hanks H G I, Hobbs C J, Wynne J M 1988 Early signs and recognition of sexual abuse in the pre-school child. In: Browne K, Davies C, Stratton P (eds) Early prediction and prevention of child abuse. J Wiley, Chichester

Harter S, Alexander P C, Neimeyer R A 1988 Long term effects of incestuous child abuse in college women. Social adjustment, social cognition and family characteristics. Journal of Consulting and Clinical Psychology 56(1): 5–8

Hobbs C J, Wynne J M 1986 Buggery in childhood — a common syndrome of child abuse. Lancet iii: 793–796

Hobbs C J, Wynne J M 1987 Child sexual abuse — an increasing rate of diagnosis. Lancet ii: 837–841

James J, Meyerding J 1977 Early sexual experience and prostitution. American Journal of Psychiatry 134: 1381–1385

Jones D P H 1991 Professional and clinical challenges to protection of children. Child Abuse and Neglect 15 (suppl 1): 57–66

Kaufman J, Zigler E 1989 The intergenerational transmission of child abuse. In: Ciccheti D, Carlson V (eds) Child maltreatment. Cambridge University Press, Cambridge

Kempe R, Kempe C H 1984 The common secret: sexual abuse of children and adolescents. W H Freeman, New York

Knopp F H 1984 Retraining adult sex offenders: methods and models. Orwell V T: Safer Society

Markowe H 1988 The frequency of child sexual abuse in the UK. Health trends, No 1. DHSS, Vol 20: 2–6

Masson J M 1984 The assault on truth: Freud's suppression of the seduction theory. Farror, Strauss & Giroux, New York

Mullen P E, Romans-Clarkson S E, Walton V A, Herbison G P 1988 Importance of sexual and physical abuse on women's mental health. Lancet ii: 841–845

Oliver J E 1983 Dead children from problem families in N E Wiltshire. Bristish Medical Journal 286: 115–117

Peters S D, Wyatt G E, Finkelhor D 1986 Prevalence. Ch 1 in: Finkelhor D (ed) A sourcebook on child sexual abuse. Sage, Beverley Hills, California

Rogers C M, Terry T 1984 Clinical interventions with boy victims of sexual abuse. In: Stuart I, Greer J (eds) Victims of sexual aggression. Von Nostrand Rheingold, New York, pp 91–104

Ronstrom A 1985 Sexual abuse of children in Sweden. Perspectives on research, intervention, consequences. Unpublished manuscript. Rodden Barren, Box 27320, Stockholm, Sweden

Russell D E H 1983 The incidence and prevalence of intrafamilial and extrafamilial sexual abuse of female children. Child Abuse and Neglect 7: 133–146

Russell D E H 1986 The secret trauma: incest in the lives of girls and women. Basic Books, New York

Salter A C 1988a The role of the offender. Ch 3 in: Treating child sex offenders and victims. A practical guide. Sage, London, pp 43–53

Salter A C 1988b Offender denial. Ch 8 in: Treating child sex offenders and victims. A practical guide. Sage, London, pp 91–110

Schechter M, Roberge L 1976 Child sexual abuse. In: Helfer R, Kempe C (eds) Child abuse and neglect: the family and the community. Ballinger, Cambridge, Mass

Sgroi S M 1978 Introduction: a national needs assessment for protecting child victims of sexual assault. In: Burgess A W, Groth A N, Holmstrom L L, Sgroi S M (eds) Sexual assault of children and adolescents. Lexington Books, Lexington, USA, pp xx–xxii

Summit R 1983 The child sexual abuse accommodation syndrome. Child Abuse and Neglect I: 177–193

Summit R C 1988 Hidden victims, hidden pain, societal avoidance of child sexual abuse. In: Wyatt G E, Powell G L (eds) Lasting effects of child sexual abuse. Sage, Beverley Hills, California

Tardicu A 1860 Etude medico-legale sur les services et mauvais traitments exerces sur des enfants. Ann Hyg Pub Med Leg 13: 361–393

Tsai M, Feldman-Summers J, Edgar M 1979 Childhood molestation: variables related to differential imparts on psychosexual function in adult women. Journal of Abnormal Psychology 88(4): 407–417

Whitwell D 1990 The significance of childhood sexual abuse for adult psychiatry. British Journal of Hospital Medicine 43: 346–352

Wild N J, Wynne J M 1986 Child sex rings. British Medical Journal 293: 183–185

Wolf S 1987 Personal communication

Wyatt G E, Powell G J 1988 Lasting effects of child sexual abuse. Parts II, III and IV. Sage, London

Wyatt G E, Ray Mickey M 1988 The support by parents and others as it mediates the effects of child sexual abuse. In: Wyatt G E, Powell G J (eds) Lasting effects of child sexual abuse. Sage, London

FURTHER READING

Arnold R P et al 1990 Medical problems of adults who were sexually abused in childhood. British Medical Journal 300: 705–708

Brown R M et al 1989 Child sexual abuse presenting as organic disease. British Medical Journal 299: 614–615

Leventhal J M 1988 Has there been a change in the epidemiology of sexual abuse of children during the 20th century? Pediatrics 82: 766–773

Wilkins R 1990 Women who sexually abuse children. British Medical Journal 300: 1153–1154

9. Clinical aspects of sexual abuse

PART 1
PRESENTATION, RELATED SYMPTOMS, MEDICAL EXAMINATION

Wherever there are children, there will be sexually abused children; an increasing proportion of those children recognised to have been abused will have been sexually abused (in 1983, 5% of registered abused children had been sexually abused, in 1987 the proportion was 28%). In 1988, the Government published figures of 12% of children on the Child Protection Registers as having been sexually abused, the National Children's Homes (in 1988) 15%, and the NSPCC figure for 1987 38.6% (Creighton & Noyes 1989).

The recognition of child sexual abuse (CSA) depends upon the adult ability to acknowledge that abuse might occur and so be prepared to see and hear. This means not only recognising the warning signs or hearing a disclosure, but also knowing how to handle this concern, or cope with an apparently clear allegation. It is evident that some seriously sexually abused children may not manifest any signs or symptoms; this, however, does not mean that all is well with the child, as is seen for example when one child in a family discloses and it becomes apparent that others in the family have also been abused. When children disclose it is sometimes obvious in retrospect that there were signs which could have been seen. The non-disclosing child may be the more damaged child in a family, and all siblings should be examined (Muram 1991).

The emotional distress of a child does of course vary with the child, the abuse, the abuser and the frequency of the abuse, but almost all children subsequently say how much they disliked the abuse. (see Ch. 8). Children have a right to a childhood free of abuse: that they do not complain, appear clinically distressed or disturbed does not mean that they are not suffering.

There is an increasing debate concerning the role of CSA in the subsequent physical and mental health of women; of course most of this abuse was undisclosed in childhood (Peters 1988, Arnold et al 1990; Whitwell 1990). It is probable that boys suffer equally with girls and find disclosure even more difficult. Ideally, children would have the confidence to speak out and expect their parents to protect them; if the abuse is intrafamilial a child's mother may not protect, and then others must listen and act.

Historically it has always been known that some children are victims of CSA but the usual notion has been of a teenage girl complaining of sexual abuse by her step-father. The recognition that sexual abuse may involve the very young, boys as well as girls, and may involve serious assault such as oral, vaginal or anal abuse, is relatively new, although the forensic literature does contain much that is relevant to the current debate (Paul 1984, de la Haye Davies 1987). It was against a background of the increasing recognition of CSA and the difficulties of management that the Cleveland Inquiry reported (Butler-Sloss 1988). There has subsequently been much advice to professionals: 'Working Together' (1988, 1991) and 'Diagnosis of Child Sexual Abuse: Guidance for Doctors' (1988) give a framework for doctors to work within clinically. The American Academy of Pediatrics has published comprehensive guidelines (1991). The Royal College of Physicians of London also reported on the physical signs of sexual abuse in children (RCP 1991).

REFERRAL

Adults are increasingly recognising and listening to children when they speak of abuse. Until professional management improves, children may well feel that it is safer to keep quiet, and abusers have much invested in denial. For the minority of children who are identified, there should be access to a system which is supportive, accepting and helpful in the long term, even if the short term may be emotionally distressing.

All professionals dealing with children should understand local procedures. A flow chart from 'Diagnosis of Child Sexual Abuse: Guidance for Doctors' (1988) is shown in Figure 9.1. A doctor may see a child because of concern voiced by another professional, the child, or his family, or

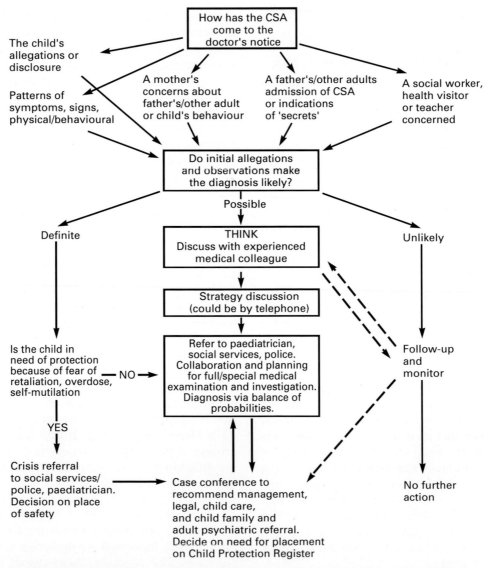

Fig. 9.1 Child sexual abuse. The initial medical contact's role (i.e. family doctor, A/E, STD etc). (Reproduced with permission from Diagnosis of Child Sexual Abuse: Guidance for Doctors 1988 DHSS, HMSO.)

another third party. The complaint may be of abuse or one of several presentations for which CSA may be the underlying cause. The general practitioner will see the child in a health centre, and the paediatrician in a local clinic or hospital. If the parents initially take the child to a police station, the child should not be examined there but referred on, usually to the local District Hospital for examination within the Child Health Department. The child is the victim and should not be examined in a police station.

Doctors should not work alone in this field. They should seek advice, cooperate with other agencies and take appropriate responsibilities (Table 9.1).

A decision whether to refer a particular case of possible CSA to Social Services will depend upon the level of concern following the paediatric assessment, and discussion with the health visitor or general practitioner, for example. Table 9.2 gives

Table 9.1 Responsibility of examining doctor

---

1. Take a full history
2. Physically examine the child if appropriate.*
3. 'Whole child' examination to include growth and development.
4. Take swabs as indicated:
   a. STD screen
   b. forensic swabs.
5. Arrange further investigations as indicated:
   a blood count
   b. clotting screen
   c. skeletal survey
   d. pregnancy test
   e. HIV antibody test
   f. hepatitis B antibody test.
6. Talk to child and carers and explain findings.
7. *Check results* of 4 and 5.
8. Talk to other professionals, often before examination has been arranged; include SSD and police as indicated.†
9. Write report for GP, Child Health (Community Services) and SSD.
10. Write police statement on request.
11. Attend case conference.
12. Attend court.
13. Arrange follow-up paediatrically.
14. Refer for treatment of:
    a. mental health, e.g. child psychologist or psychiatrist
    b. physical complications, e.g. anal warts to paediatric surgeon.
15. Refer for second (paediatric) opinion.

---

* If the initial doctor does not feel confident to undertake the physical examination, refer to an appropriate colleague or arrange a joint examination with an experienced colleague.
† If the child has presented by disclosing, e.g. to a teacher, a 'planning meeting' should be held (Fig. 9.1).

guidelines to help make this decision.

For other children — referred by teachers or nursery nurses to Social Services, or children referred directly to the police — the decision whether a full Child Protection Investigation is indicated may be made before or after referral to the paediatrician, depending upon the circumstances. 'Working Together' (1991) gives details of interagency working.

Consent to examination should be informed and is equally valid whether given orally or in writing. If a child is capable of understanding the nature and purpose of the examination then he or she is capable of giving consent. The DoH Guidance to the Children Act (DoH 1991) makes it clear that it is the doctor's responsibility to help the child to understand and also to come to a decision as to the child's capability.

The components of informed consent have been described (BAAF 1991) as an understanding of:

- the nature of the examination
- the immediate purpose of the examination
- to whom the resulting information will be given
- the implications for others (this is not the child's responsibility).

From the age of 16 years a child is regarded at law as capable of giving consent. Depending on the level of understanding, younger teenagers or children may give consent. Parental consent must be sought in all situations apart from the above, unless parental responsibilities are invested elsewhere. If in doubt, seek legal advice and remember that if court proceedings are in process the court's permission is needed.

The commonest form of lack of consent is by teenagers, who find physical examination particularly difficult. A follow-up appointment is usually offered in these circumstances.

The more detailed aspects of consent are described in Chapter 14.

Joint medical examinations

Joint examinations are examinations undertaken by more than one medical practitioner where the practitioners have separate clinical responsibilities. The police surgeon is employed by the police

Table 9.2   Guidelines for making the decision to report CSA to Social Services (after American Academy of Pediatrics 1991, Royal College of Physicians 1991)

History	Examination	Lab.	Concern	Report
None	Normal	None	None	None
Behavioural changes	Normal	None	Low	+/– FU
None	Supportive	None	Possible	+/– FU
History from parents	Supportive	None	Possible	+/– FU
None	Diagnostic	None	Probable	Refer
Clear statement	Normal	None	Probable	Refer
Clear statement	Diagnostic	None	Probable	Refer
None	Normal ⎫ Supportive ⎬ Diagnostic ⎭	Gonorrhoea ⎫ Semen ⎬ Pregnancy ⎭	Definite ⎫⎬⎭	Refer ⎫⎬⎭
Behavioural changes	Supportive	Other STD	Probable	Refer

Notes:
1. A supportive physical examination includes signs, e.g. enlarged hymenal opening, scar at posterior fourchette (RCP 1991).
2. A diagnostic sign includes signs, e.g. laceration extending beyond the anal mucosa onto the perianal skin (RCP 1991).
3. '+/–' Consider reporting on basis of information gathered.
4. 'FU' i.e. follow up all cases if there are continuing concerns or unexplained behaviours or physical signs.
5. If in doubt discuss with colleagues and Senior Social Worker.
6. 'Refer' suggests that the case should be referred to social services; these children are usually followed up, at least in the short term.

authority to examine the child and to provide a report for possible criminal proceedings. The paediatrician has a wider responsibility in the short and longer term (Table 9.1). However there are advantages in working with a colleague with complementary skills, although the indications for such examinations are likely to become fewer as paediatricians have more experience of examining sexually abused children.

One example where a paediatrician is likely to request the help of an experienced police surgeon is in a case of stranger rape, when collection of forensic samples, for example fibres, is very important and better done by an experienced practitioner.

Ultimately, as in physical abuse, neglect and all other forms of child abuse, paediatricians will accept responsibility for the examinations, not least because of the long-term sequelae of abuse and consequent need for ongoing care.

It is also necessary to evaluate the efficacy and cost of medicals. Two doctors cost more, there is often considerable waiting time for the child, family and professionals and the child has two doctors examining her (it is a 2 in 1 examination, rather than a single one). If there is a conflict of medical opinion, usually over the interpretation of physical signs, rather than the actual signs, it may be very difficult for the SSD to protect and the police to proceed.

Also, if a police surgeon is present the parents must know and this may escalate the investigation in an unhelpful way when it is at a preliminary stage.

Confidentiality

The doctor may be referred a child where there has been a clear disclosure; alternatively the suggestion of CSA may arise during the course of the interview or examination. In the case of the latter, the doctor may have immediate concerns and feel it necessary to refer to the statutory agencies at once, or in other situations to follow up over weeks or months while collecting further information (Table 9.2).

Once the doctor has reached a point of some concern he should report; confidentiality to child or family is secondary — the General Medical Council's Annual Report in 1987 states '. . . if a doctor has reason for believing that a child is being physically or sexually abused, not only is it permissible for the doctor to disclose information to a third party, but it is the duty of the doctor to do so'.

The diagnostic process in child sexual abuse

This does not differ from the diagnosis of any disorder in medicine, except that it is usually complex and sooner or later involves information gathering by other agencies such as social services and the police (Working Together 1988, 1991). As in other disorders, a diagnosis is built up gradually, starting with the history, followed by physical examination and laboratory investigation. Physical, emotional and sexual abuse may all co-exist, and the child's growth, development and behaviour should also be considered. Consider the diagnosis as a 'jigsaw' and piece together all the information (Table 9.3).

There are, however, certain points which must be taken into account. The examination of a child who may have been abused is essentially a *forensic examination*. Although the examining doctor may think he is dealing with a child who presents to him with bed-wetting, he may find signs suggesting that the child is a victim of CSA. He may refer the child on for a more specialised examination but *his* notes may be required by the court at a later stage.

Table 9.3 The clinical jigsaw in child sexual abuse

Child's story or disclosure	+ Parents' history	+ Other third party e.g. nursery nurse observation
Child's past medical history	+ Family history	+ Child's development
Child's physical growth	+ Child's emotional/ behavioural state	+ Physical examination
Medical investigations e.g. STD	= Initial medical opinion	+ Social work investigations
Police investigation	+ Further opinion	= Proven abuse (rarely) or Probable abuse or Possible abuse or Abuse unlikely

Medical notes

These should:

1. Be written at the time of examination (contemporaneously) or immediately afterwards.

2. Be clear, concise and contain details or questions asked: for example 'no urinary symptoms' is better than nothing, but 'no dysuria, frequency, urgency or haematuria' is better still. Initials such as NAD are not helpful when discussing the physical examination later — what actually was done?

3. Record verbatim any spontaneous remarks made by the child during the examination, as with any answers to questions: e.g. 'What made your tuppence sore?', answered by 'Daddy with his finger like this . . .' and record what the child demonstrates.

4. Record injuries appropriately: line drawings with annotations are the clearest, suitable charts are available. Describe bruises by position, size, colour (rough age) and think how they may have been caused. Burns, scratches and lacerations are also measured and described (Chs 4 and 5).

5. Record abnormalities of the genitalia or anus, again a line drawing is helpful.

6. In the rare cases of recent assault, usually stranger rape, other factors are important to avoid losing valuable contact evidence. A good description is given in forensic medicine textbooks. A joint medical examination with an experienced police surgeon is useful here (Paul 1984, McLay 1990a, RCP 1991).

7. Record which investigations were performed; and ensure results are obtained. Were photographs taken? If used in court proceedings these may need to be sworn by the photographer (Ch. 4).

8. Record any treatment given.

9. Indicate if follow-up was arranged.

PRESENTATION OF CHILD SEXUAL ABUSE (summarised in Table 9.4)

1. Disclosure

Disclosure of abuse by the child is of itself the most important piece of the 'diagnostic jigsaw'. When work in CSA began, the majority of investigations were instigated by an allegation of

Table 9.4   Presentation of child sexual abuse (Vizard & Tranter 1988)

1. Disclosure	By child or third party
2. Physical indicators	Rectal or vaginal bleeding, pain on defaecation Sexually transmitted disease (STD) Vulvovaginitis/vaginal discharge/'sore' Dysuria and frequency? UTI Physical abuse, note association of burns, pattern of injury, death Pregnancy
3. Psychosomatic indicators	Recurrent abdominal pain Headache, migraine Anorexia or other eating disorders Encopresis Enuresis Total refusal syndrome

4. Behavioural indicators
    (i)   Pre-school
 	
    (ii)   Middle years
 	
    (iii) Teenagers
	
	Sexually explicit play, 'excessive' masturbation, insertion of foreign bodies (girls), self-mutilation, withdrawn, poor appetite, sleep disturbance, clingy, delayed development, aggression.
	Sexualised play, sexually explicit drawing or sexual precocity, self-mutilation, anxiety, depression, anger, poor school performance, mute
	Sexually precocious, prostitution, anxiety, anger, aggression, depression, truancy, running away, solvent/alcohol/drug abuse, self-destructive behaviour, overdoses, self-mutilation suicide

5. Learning or severe learning problems. Physical handicap (see Ch. 10)	May present with depression, disturbed (including aggressive) behaviour. Sexualised behaviour. Attempts at disclosure not understood. May be physical and psychosomatic indicators as above.
6. Social indicators (see Ch. 8)	Concern by parent or third party, sibling, relative or friend of abused child. Schedule 1 offender in close contact with child.

See also Table 9.13 for specific emotional and behavioural indicators.

abuse by the child. But, as professionals have recognised other signs which may be indicative of abuse, the concept of 'disclosure work' began. Jones defined such work as 'the process by which professionals attempt to encourage or hasten the natural process of disclosure by a sexually abused child' (Butler-Sloss 1988 — Pt 2 Ch 11, Jones & McQuiston 1988 — p. 204).

Some children 'disclose' spontaneously. Disclosure is defined by Jones as 'a clinically useful concept to describe the process by which a child who has been sexually abused (within the family) gradually comes to inform the outside world of his plight'.

The young child may speak innocently of behaviour which the adult recognises as abuse. Older children decide to tell, usually in an attempt to stop the abuse and maybe to protect younger siblings. A spontaneous unprompted statement by a child is the most reliable way in which CSA may be acknowledged. It is generally recognised that very few children lie about sexual abuse, and the few that do will tend to be emotionally disturbed teenagers. If children complain of re-abuse, they are also to be believed in the first instance, as evidence suggests that they rarely lie. The simple rule is: believe the child initially, and test the statement later.

In disputed custody cases allegations of CSA should be taken seriously and evaluated rigorously. Many allegations are subsequently validated (MacFarlane 1986).

Children usually tell someone whom they trust, whether this is initially a friend, family member or professional (teacher, school nurse, doctor). After initial 'disclosure' and a strategy discussion between professionals, a formal interview will take place; recently this has usually taken the form of a joint interview conducted by a social worker and police officer from a Child Abuse Unit.

Interviewing should be undertaken by staff who have undergone appropriate staff development and training (Working Together 1991). The number of investigative interviews should be kept to a minimum (Butler-Sloss 1988) but whilst some children who are ready to talk are able to disclose the details of their abuse in 1–2 interviews, other children 'frozen' by fear or anxiety may only come to talk of their abuse over months to years. This is an unresolved clinical dilemma. There are also children with communication difficulties or who have English as a second language who need interviewers with particular skills.

If an assessment is undertaken in the course of court proceedings the court's agreement is needed as the evidence may not be used in court unless the court agrees.

Recording of interviews should be accurate and differentiate between fact, hearsay and opinion.

Video or audiotapes have been made of interviews with the intention of avoiding repeated interviews, and the Pigot Committee (Pigot 1989) had hoped that they would be admissible in criminal court without the need for the child to be present and to be cross-examined. Under the Criminal Justice Act 1991 a video-recording may be used as the child's main evidence in certain circumstances but the child must also be available for cross examination. The child in court may be helped by the use of screens and contemporaneous video-links.

The Home Office is preparing a code of practice in the use of videotapes including appropriate interviewing technique. There may well be conflict between issues concerning the child's welfare and legal requirements. Hearsay evidence is allowable in family proceeding courts but not in criminal courts.

If videotapes are not made to a very high standard they will not help the child as legal arguments dismiss the evidence. Similarly, minor inconsistencies in evidence given in court when compared with the videotape will imply that the child is unreliable or lying.

Current research in the UK shows that children who do give evidence have more anxiety symptoms up until the trial than those who do not give evidence, and this manifest anxiety persists for the following 12 months before their levels of anxiety fall to levels of the non-evidence-giving victims.

If the alleged abuser is convicted this may be enabling to the child, but if he is acquitted, for whatever reason, the child may be devastated. He feels that this is a public statement that he was lying (Pigot 1989, Spencer & Flin 1990, Smith & Wilson 1991, Spencer 1991).

In a comparative study in Leeds of practice in

Table 9.5 Anatomically complete dolls

1. Sexually explicit play is suggestive of CSA.
2. Non-abused children do not enact adult sexual behaviour.
3. Abused children may play non-sexually with dolls.
4. Abused children are more likely to treat the male doll roughly.
5. Helpful to elucidate abuse in young, shy, developmentally slow children.
6. May cause abused child great distress.
7. Should be used by skilled professional.

1985–6 and 1989 the percentage of cases where the perpetrator was convicted fell from 25% to 5% (Frothingham et al 1992). The reasons for this are speculative.

The current position in the UK remains that children may be better protected in family proceedings court by the use of videotapes of well-conducted interviews but many parents and professionals caring for children are wary about submitting them to the trauma of an appearance as a prosecution witness in a criminal court.

Interviewing young children

Children may be helped to talk using play materials, including anatomically complete dolls, drawing, and Plasticine (Tables 9.5 and 9.6; Figs 9.2–9.5). However it must be remembered that in helping the child to tell (Bentovim et al 1988, Glaser & Frosh 1988, Jones & McQuiston 1988, Siran et al 1988, Glaser & Collins 1989) the possibilities are:

1. the abuse has occurred and the child is speaking of it,
2. the abuse has occurred and the child is unable to speak of it or is denying it,
3. the abuse has not occurred and the child cannot speak of it.

There are several levels at which this work may be done and the use of leading, alternative or hypothetical questions should be left to those with

Table 9.6 Use of line drawings

1. May enable child to describe abuse.
2. Sexually explicit drawings may be the child's way of disclosing abuse.
3. The child may find it easier to complete outline figure provided by examiner.

Fig. 9.2 Sexualised drawings by a girl aged 7 years who later disclosed CSA by her father after reception into care following physical abuse of her brother aged 5 years.

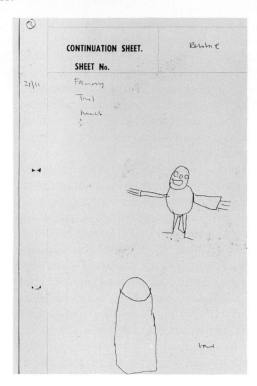

Fig. 9.3 A girl aged 8 years, unable to talk of abuse but in answer to the question 'Why are you sore?' drew a man with a phallus and, by way of further explanation, the enlargement.

special expertise. This may also apply to the use of the anatomically complete dolls. There are major problems inherent in disclosure work. Firstly, the child may not be ready to tell. Children formerly have told when *they* have been ready — unfortunately the need for a 'completed' investigation within a few days (the usual requirement of the police) means children may be under pressure to tell their story and, rather than being encouraged to tell, just clam up or retract. Investigations should be conducted at the child's pace not the professional's. Secondly, the use of the term 'disclosure interview' assumes abuse has occurred when this may not be the case.

Table 9.7 lists some of the research findings into the accuracy of children's statements.

Interviewing. This should feel safe and re-laxed for the child and be uninterrupted. Children should be interviewed in a suitable and sensitive environment (Butler-Sloss 1988).

Interviews are inevitably part investigation, part assessment, and part therapeutic. The dilemma of

this situation has not been resolved. The therapeutic needs of the child are not the same as the requirements of the legal system, and the interviewer has to focus on the aim of the interview whilst recognising the need to be sensitive to the child's feelings.

The interviewer should be trained and on

Table 9.7 The child's disclosure — is it true?

1. The more detail that is recalled the more likely it is to be truthful.
2. Do the core elements of the story remain consistent?
3. Distinguishing details, e.g. taste of semen, smell, 'knife in bum', are not learned from watching sexually explicit material on TV or videos.
4. Children are known to recall events accurately from pre-verbal stage of development.
5. Children's memory is no less accurate than adults but children tend to recall less detail. Children relate events within the limits of their language and understanding.
6. Children can place events in correct temporal order.
7. Recantations are uncommon, stereotyped, and often use incongruous language.
8. Children may be silenced by fear, coercion or anxiety.
9. Children can not fantasize sexual acts of which they have no experience.

Fig. 9.4 Drawing by a girl aged 6 years with recurrent vaginal discharge and nightmares involving a monster who came to her bed. She later disclosed abuse by her grandfather.

Fig. 9.5 Drawing by a girl aged 7 years explaining that she only felt safe from sexual abuse while her father was in prison.

occasion have special skills, for example be fluent in sign language for a severely hearing impaired child. The gender of the interviewer is important — most teenage girls would prefer to talk to a woman. If joint interviews are undertaken one worker leads the interview and the other observes. Children from a young age are interviewed apart from their parents but often one of the interviewers has a relationship with the child, albeit a very recent one.

The interviewer should be well briefed before the session and have a relevant knowledge of the child and his family. The interview should have a structure which allows later analysis. There are good descriptions of interviewing technique available (Glaser & Frosh 1988, Jones & McQuiston 1988, Vizard & Tranter 1988, Furniss 1991).

Recording is important and may be by contemporaneous note taking, video or audiotaping.

The function of the interview is to:

- Investigate the possibility of CSA
- Validate the child's allegations
- Assess the child's need for protection
- Assess the need for ongoing therapy.

The interview. As previously described the interview should be child-centred and child-led. Most sessions start with a free play session and then move on to a more structured session, when drawing is often helpful in children of 5 years and over. At this stage the use of anatomically complete dolls with younger children (under 7 years) or developmentally delayed or very shy children may be very helpful.

The session includes direct enquiry about events, people and places; whichever method is used, the child must know the context of the interview but care is needed to avoid asking leading questions.

The number of interviews needed to make a proper assessment varies but primarily investigative interviews are usually limited to 1–3. Therapeutic work is described in Chapter 15.

Additional disclosures may be made over the intervening months to years in therapy. Severely traumatised children may be unable to communicate until they feel safe, and then only after months of specialist help. Whilst they are in contact with their abuser they may never speak, which presents the SSD with a real dilemma. Likewise, information disclosed in therapeutic sessions may not be acceptable to the courts because of the techniques employed (Vizard & Tranter 1988).

At the end of the initial investigative interview(s) the questions which should be asked are:

- Is it likely that abuse has occurred?
- Is it known who perpetrated the abuse?
- Will the child be protected?
- How is the child affected, what are the plans to continue the support of the child, what are his therapeutic needs?

Paediatricians are used to talking to children and it is not uncommon for children to talk of their abuse during the course of their examination. This information needs later validation.

CASE HISTORY 1
Stephen, aged 7 years, was seen at the request of Social Services as bruising had been noticed by the school nurse. The NSPCC had previously had an anonymous allegation about a 'beating'. Stephen presented as a frightened, underweight, quiet boy with a swollen upper lip and scattered bruises on his back, and physical signs compatible with anal abuse.

After examination Stephen was asked 'What makes your bottom sore?'. He said, without further questioning but with palpable anxiety, 'Daddy does it . . . lean over bed . . . puts willy in bum, puts willy in mouth . . . willy stands up — goes big...sticky stuff comes out . . . it's different from wee, it's got a bad taste — I spit it out. In Daddy's bedroom, lean over bed . . . Mummy knows — seen him do it. Daddy does it.'

CASE HISTORY 2
Sarah, aged 4½ years, was seen at the request of SSD following referral by her school. She had been playing in the Wendy house when she told the teacher that she went in bed with Daddy and he had a stick and hurt her. There was also a history of daytime wetting, occasional soiling and delayed language development. Sarah was a small, sad girl with signs compatible with anal abuse.

She was spoken to alone and would not engage in free play. She repeated 'I want Debbie' (her mother). When asked 'Did anyone hurt you?' she said 'I want

Debbie' but went on 'I was crying, in my room, David (her father) hurt it with a stick — he puts his finger . . . (pointed to genital area) — David did it, sore on bum, it was a stick, in bum, lots of times. He takes off my clothes to look at my bum. David gets in bed, David wees in my bed, David wees in my hole, he puts stuff in there ... He hurts my hole. Mummy does not hurt my hole. Debbie does not hurt my hole. I love Mummy and Daddy. Daddy says sorry in my room, in my bedroom. David is nice after'.

CASE HISTORY 3
Lucy was seen initially when 4½ years old. She was referred because of concerns by her GP and health visitor. The referral letter described her poor language, that she avoided eye contact and was day-wetting. At an initial outpatient appointment in August the history was unchanged but physical examination showed some anal abnormality. In September physical examination was much the same, a child protection conference was held and as a result Lucy's mother was told of the professionals' concern as to possible sexual abuse and work was started in school with Lucy by the social worker.

In October physical examination was entirely normal and Lucy was more talkative and confident. In December she was so bright and outgoing that physical examination was thought unnecessary.

By February, although Lucy had been making good progress generally, there had been two episodes at school when she had been very withdrawn and it was noticed she was becoming aggressive towards her mother. As her behaviour had changed a physical examination was performed and there were minimal genital signs but marked anal signs consistent with abuse. When asked directly what had happened, Lucy said 'A man has hurt my bum and my tuppence. He hurt it with a knife. He didn't say he was sorry. In my bedroom. It's my Daddy'.

CASE HISTORY 4
Susan and Elizabeth were aged 4 years and 6 years and seen because of anonymous allegations to the NSPCC about CSA. They were very frightened. Neither child would talk and physical examination was normal. When given the anatomically complete dolls, Elizabeth demonstrated oral sex and said the names of her two elder brothers and father. She then put the penis of the man doll between the girl doll's legs and said 'Daddy'. She became very upset and started to cry. The younger sister would not hold the dolls and just looked frightened.

Elizabeth said 'Mummy knows what happens'. The older brothers (aged 8 and 10 years) subsequently made full disclosures of abuse involving both parents and all four children.

Note. Currently few paediatricians would use the dolls in an interview like this because of the need for later validation. However with young or developmentally delayed children paediatricians do have skills which are of use in assessing such children where others are unable to successfully communicate due to lack of experience and expertise.

CASE HISTORY 5

Naseem, an Asian girl aged 9 years, was noticed to be unhappy at school. She was thin and rocked to and fro. She was referred because of her unhappy behaviour, low weight and vaginal discharge. Physical signs were compatible with vaginal interference. Work with the family was unsuccessful and eventually Naseem was taken into care because of emotional abuse and failure to thrive. The question of CSA was unanswered.

Three days before the final hearing at court, Naseem wrote to the social worker and told of the sexual abuse by her father at home. The fear of returning home following the court hearing was finally greater than the fear of her father.

2. Physical indicators of CSA

Physical indicators are important as they may give the first sign that all is not well with the child. They may be the only sign in infants or young children or in other children who, for whatever reason, cannot communicate. They may corroborate the child's story. The significance of a particular indicator is variable, for example vaginal bleeding is a symptom which should always be thoroughly investigated and a sign such as laceration of the hymen is of the highest significance (in the absence of a history of accidental penetration). Caution is needed in the interpretation of signs and symptoms and time is often needed to build up the diagnostic jigsaw (Table 9.3).

It is much easier for a doctor when examining a child who has disclosed abuse to explain that certain physical signs are consistent with abuse; it is much more difficult if similar signs are found incidentally (Table 9.2). Management of such cases needs careful planning and it may be only after weeks to months or even years that the whole picture emerges. In the meantime the child lives in a possibly abusive home, but the limitations of medical examination must be acknowledged (Butler-Sloss 1988, RCP 1991).

Information should be shared (Table 9.2) as appropriate with other professionals at a planning or strategy meeting and responsibility shared (Diagnosis of Child Sexual Abuse: Guidance for Doctors 1988, Working Together 1988, 1991).

Figures 9.6 and 9.7 show the relative impor-

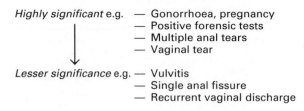

Fig. 9.6 Which signs are significant in CSA?

tance of the various signs and the effects of healing or re-abuse on the signs found on examination.

An examination where no abnormality is found cannot exclude CSA. In a study to evaluate the physical signs associated with CSA, 382 sexually abused girls, mean age 5.8 years, were examined — 71% had normal findings, including 48% who had been penetrated (inter labial not vaginally) (Marshall et al 1988). Other authors have emphasised the same point (Muram 1989b, RCP 1991).

Healing takes place rapidly and scarring is uncommon (Hobbs & Wynne 1987). Changing physical signs suggest healing, re-abuse, or that a disease process is evolving.

A differential diagnosis of vulvovaginitis, genital and rectal bleeding is given in Table 9.8.

(i) Genital bleeding

This is an important symptom and must always be investigated. Common causes include:

- accident — but there should be a history of a painful fall, most frequently a straddle injury (see later, p. 178);
- early puberty — investigate as precocious puberty;
- other regular bleeding, such as each Friday night when the baby-sitter comes;

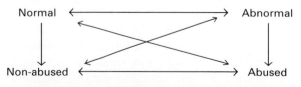

Fig. 9.7 Healing and physical signs: examination.

Table 9.8   Causes of vulvovaginitis, vaginal and rectal bleeding

Vulvovaginitis	Genital bleeding identical to bloody discharge	Rectal bleeding
1. Poor hygiene 2. Local irritation — bubblebath, soap, tights 3. Candidal infection (after broad spectrum antibiotics) 4. Threadworms 5. Part of systemic infection — measles, varicella, streptococcal 6. STD (see Table 9.10) 7. CSA — causing superficial trauma with secondary infection 8. CSA — self-mutilation 9. Associated skin disorder, e. g. eczema, lichen sclerosus 10. Foreign body — RARE, ? CSA	1. Onset menses (n.b. pseudo-menses ≡ trauma) 2. Precocious puberty 3. Accidental trauma 4. Foreign body — RARE, ? CSA 5. Infection, e. g. streptoccal 6. STD (see Table 9.10) 7. Tumour 8. Skin disease	1. Fissure 2. Infective diarrhoea e.g. salmonella, shigella 3. Inflammatory bowel disorder, e.g. ulcerative colitis 4. Rectal polyp or other tumour 5. CSA — penetrative, penile or foreign body 6. Foreign body — ? CSA

- lichen sclerosus, vulval haemangioma and other rarities.

(ii) Rectal bleeding

This also warrants investigation; organic causes have recently been well reviewed (Raine 1991). In general paediatric practice bleeding is commonly only seen secondary to fissures and infective diarrhoea.

Fissures are usually caused by the painful passage of a large hard stool, and faecal masses are palpable in the child's abdomen. A fissure is defined as 'a break in the lining of the anal canal, usually extending from inside the canal to the anal verge, and travelling vertically to the verge'.

Anal fissures, as is clear from the definition, differ from the superficial breaks in the skin which are seen where there is perianal soreness for whatever cause — diarrhoea, threadworms, seborrhoeic dermatitis (McCrae 1985) — where the break in the skin does not cross the anal verge into the anal canal.

Anal fissures are caused by the stretching of the anal margin to a point where splitting occurs, giving a triangular tear with the apex within the anal canal. The aetiology of the fissure — whether it is organic or caused by a foreign body being inserted forcibly — can not be deduced from its appearance. Fissures are also seen in inflammatory bowel disease, for example Crohn's disease,

but other signs and symptoms will be apparent in the presence of systemic illness.

Anal fissures cause pain on defecation and may be associated with anal spasm. They bleed initially but usually heal over 1–3 weeks. Healing is impaired if the fissures are being persistently stretched, as in untreated constipation or continuing anal abuse. In these circumstances, a fissure may be seen as a deep, wide cleft, often placed posteriorly. Healing of such a chronic fissure may take months and is more likely to heal with scarring. Large fissures may leave a skin tag as a marker of previous trauma. Such chronic fissures are not painful (RCP 1991) and the skin tag is considered to represent an overgrowth of skin in the healing process.

Anal fissures are seen most commonly in infancy, associated with significant constipation and are usually superficial and may be multiple. They are seen with decreasing frequency after infancy and are uncommon in the school-aged child (Shandling 1987). In older children fissures are usually single and posterior (McCrae 1985).

In one study of 20 children attending a gastroenterology clinic because of severe constipation, 8 children had fissures and they were all in the age group 1–3.5 years (Anderson 1975).

In Clayden's (1981) review of severely constipated children referred to a Regional Constipation Clinic, 1 out of 18 children on presentation had a fissure. Another review by the same author showed that 3 out of 30 children at follow-up had fissures and 16% had a past history of fissure (Clayden 1988). However Agnarsson et al (1990), in a survey of 136 children with mild to moderate constipation, reported that 35 children had fissures and, most unusually, 10 had 2 fissures and 8 multiple fissures.

In McCann et al's study of children selected for non-abuse, average age 5 years 7 months, none of the 267 children had fissures (1989). By contrast, in a series of children who had been anally abused, 59/69 children aged 0–5 years and 53/143 children of all ages had anal tears or fissures (Hobbs & Wynne 1989).

Fissures following abuse become less likely with increasing age of the child, particularly if lubricant is used. If the child is examined some time after the abuse has occurred fissures may have healed and few leave scars.

Children who have been abused and have fissures often do not complain of as much pain as might have been expected. Some abused children do become constipated.

Fissures are associated with anal abuse (Hobbs & Wynne 1986, American Academy of Pediatrics 1991, RCP 1991). In the absence of constipation or inflammatory bowel disease, the presence of fissures needs explanation. If a child has two or more fissures (not excoriations) and especially if there are other signs of anal trauma such as bruising, swelling of the anal verge, laxity or dilatation, enquiry into the possibility of abuse should follow.

Bleeding in the absence of fissures may be due to other disorders such as rectal polyp (Raine 1991).

(iii) Vulvitis and vaginitis in pre-pubertal girls

This is partially dependent on the oestrogen status of the child. At birth the influence of maternal oestrogen causes the mucosa to be thick and the secretions slightly acidic. The maternal hormonal effect ceases after about 4–6 weeks and the mucosa becomes thin and the pH neutral until puberty.

Pre-pubertal girls are prone to vulvitis and this is said to relate to this relative oestrogen deficiency. Specific infections are also influenced by the child's oestrogen status: trichomonas grows poorly in the absence of oestrogen and the reverse is true for gonorrhoea and chlamydia.

Causes of vulvitis include:

- Poor hygiene
- Sensitivity, e.g. to bubblebath, soaps
- Threadworms (cause irritation and the child scratches)
- Atopic eczema, seborrhoeic dermatitis
- CSA — causing local trauma and secondary infection
- Excessive and inappropriate washing
- STD
- Other specific infections, e.g. streptococcus
- candida — rare except after a course of antibiotics
- *NOT* masturbation, unless self-mutilation seen in some sexually abused children (see later).

Symptoms caused by vulvitis:

- Soreness
- Itchiness
- Burning on micturition.

Causes of vulvovaginitis:

- Non-specific
- Group A, β-haemolytic streptococcus, *Staphylococcus aureus*, *Haemophilus influenzae*
- *Gardnerella vaginalis*
- Sexually transmitted disease
- Rarely, foreign body.

Symptoms of vulvovaginitis:

- As vulvitis
- Discharge.

Sexual abuse and vulvitis and vulvovaginitis. A high proportion of pre-pubertal girls who have been sexually abused complain of 'soreness' and have a vulvitis or vulvovaginitis on examination. This is probably due to rough handling leading to abrasions of the mucosa which may become secondarily infected. Hence, when symptoms of the lower genitourinary tract occur — including vulvovaginitis associated with soreness and discharge, or recurrent dysuria in the absence of proven urinary tract infection — CSA should be considered (Diagnosis of Child Sexual Abuse: Guidance for Doctors 1988).

Management of vulvitis and vulvovaginitis

- Take a detailed history.
- Include in the history details of usual bathing practices: recent work recognises situations where cleansing becomes excessive and inappropriate causing soreness and even discharge. The child's genitalia may be handled and inspected with resulting physical and psychological harm (Herman-Giddens 1989).
- Enquire into the possibility of CSA, if not at the first visit then at follow-up — parents increasingly expect this.
- Perform a complete physical examination of the child (remember anus).
- Consider appropriate microbiological investigations: suggest a full STD screen (see Fig. 9.8) in older sexually active girls and girls with recurrent symptoms (even if little discharge is present).
- Treat specific infections and threadworms.
- Advise on
  - daily baths — no scrubbing of genitalia, 'sit and soak'
  - avoidance of irritant soaps and bubble-baths
  - no disinfectant in bath
  - cotton pants; avoid tights and closely fitting clothes.

(iv) Dysuria

Following CSA, pain on micturition or even traumatic haematuria may be seen in boys and girls. There may also be frequency of micturition. These symptoms occur when a girl (or boy) has a traumatised urethra which may be evident on examination by bruising, swelling, inflammation or dilatation. Microscopy of the urine and culture should differentiate a urinary tract infection from local inflammation. A history of recurrent dysuria is common in girls who have been sexually abused, particularly young girls aged less than 6 years, when 20% have genitourinary symptoms (Klevan & De Jong 1990). Difficulty in passing urine is also seen in boys and girls, and even retention where there has been more serious trauma.

Proven urinary tract infections are not a good marker for CSA; in one series of such infections 2/428 children had been sexually abused (Mehl 1990). However recurrent genitourinary symptoms are an indicator of possible CSA, which should be considered in the differential diagnosis.

Urethral pathology is uncommon but includes urethral caruncle, haemangioma, prolapse and polyp.

(v) Masturbation

Masturbation does not ordinarily cause any abnormal physical signs. As a pleasurable activity in boys and girls it usually involves rubbing, and is universal in young children. Girls usually rub around the clitoris and so achieve an orgasm. Vaginal penetration, involving stretching and often tearing of the hymen, is painful and not a usual part of masturbation in young girls. Young girls are usually unaware that they have a hymenal orifice.

'Excessive' masturbation is described in some abused children (Corwin 1988). This may be the child's response to the need for sexual arousal, or comfort, or due to vulval irritation secondary to trauma or infection. If masturbation alone causes a vulvitis this is abnormal and should be thought of as self-mutilation and highly correlated with CSA. Parents and teachers use the expression 'excessive masturbation' to describe the behaviour of children who are continually rubbing their genitalia in public, both digitally and also rubbing against furniture, knees or any firm surface. It should be asked 'Why does this child masturbate so much?'.

(vi) Self-mutilation

Self-mutilation has been long recognised in abused adolescents and is increasingly appreciated, even in young children, where excessive scratching may cause deep lacerations which bleed or become secondarily infected. Children burn, pinch and cut themselves. The mutilation may affect face, neck, arms, abdomen and arms, for example, as well as the genitalia or anus (Hanks & Hobbs 1992).

(vii) Foreign bodies

Insertion of foreign bodies into the vagina is unusual in children (Paul 1986). This is because

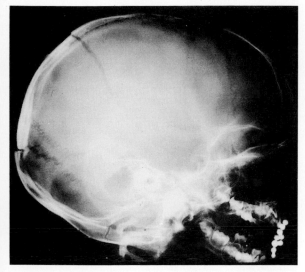

Plate 1 Abused 18-month-old child. History of fall from chair. Depressed occipital fracture with two components. Maximum width 2 mm. Bruises to both ears, buttocks and spine. Right hemiplegia.

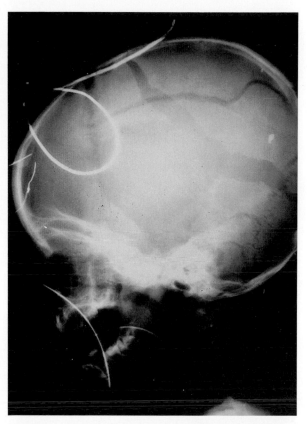

Plate 3 15-month-old fatally abused child. Failure to thrive, bilateral retinal haemorrhages, multiple bruises to forehead, ears and limbs, torn frenulum, fracture of metaphysis left knee. Large subdural haematoma evacuated through large central craniotomy. Five fractures including extensive bilateral parietal fractures, one 14 mm in width, and three occipital fractures. (Reproduced with permission from Meadow S R, ed 1989 ABC of child abuse. British Medical Journal)

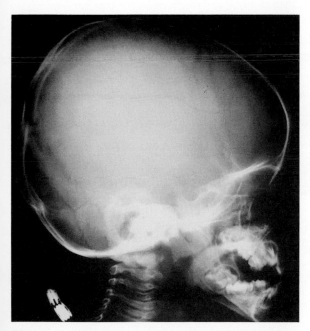

Plate 2 Accidentally injured 13-month-old child; fell 3 feet from kitchen unit onto concrete floor. Linear horizontal parietal fracture 10.5 cm × 1–2 mm in width. Haematoma above ear. No other injuries and no cerebral complications.

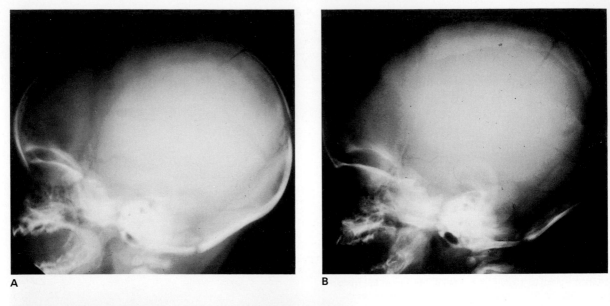

A

B

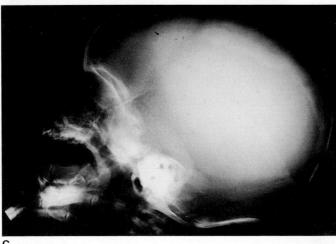

C

Plates 4a–c 7-week-old abused child with a parietal growing fracture. Child allegedly fell from father's arms onto the floor and immediately became unconscious and limp. Child developed fits and required ventilation. Fractures of ribs and femur and unilateral retinal haemorrhage present with haematoma in rectum and small bruise at top of natal cleft. **(a)** 11 mm at presentation. **(b)** 20 mm at 17 days. **(c)** 26 mm at 42 days. Cystic collection of fluid and underlying necrotic brain found at operation. (**c** Reproduced with permission from Meadow S R, ed 1989 ABC of child abuse. British Medical Journal)

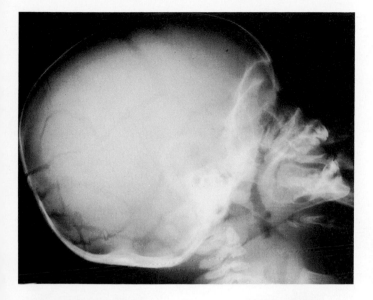

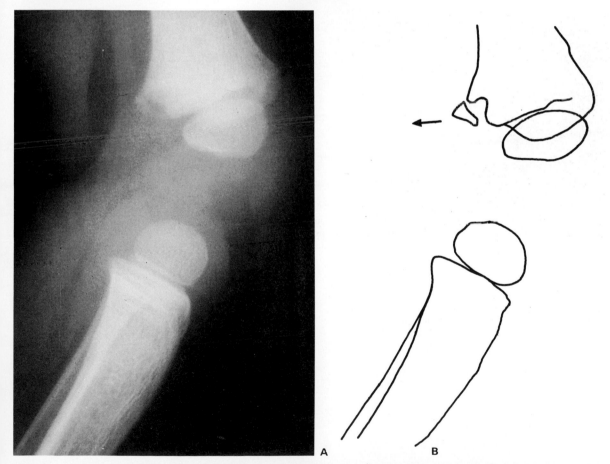

A   B

Plate 6a, b Radiograph **(a)** and line drawing **(b)** of metaphyseal (corner) fracture of the lower end of the femur (same child as Plate 3). (Reproduced with permission from Meadow S R, ed 1989 ABC of child abuse. British Medical Journal)

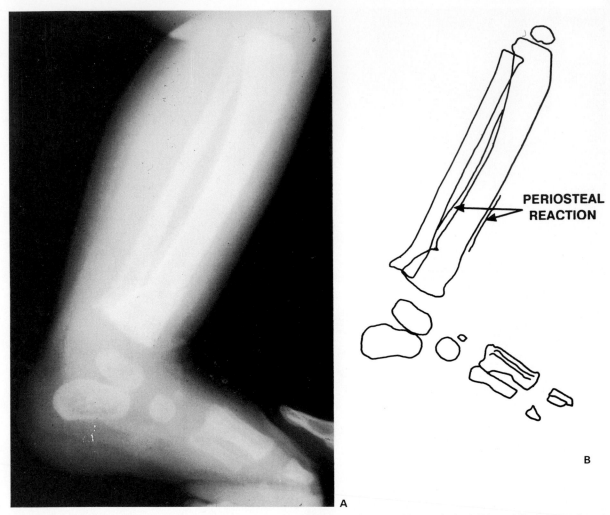

PERIOSTEAL
REACTION

A

B

Plate 7a, b Radiograph **(a)** and line drawing **(b)** of distal non-displaced fracture of lower shaft of tibia and fibula in an abused child of 6 months, with evidence of periosteal reaction along tibial shaft. Fracture is probably 10–14 days old. Other injuries included multiple rib and complex skull fractures. (Reproduced with permission from Meadow S R, ed 1989 ABC of child abuse. British Medical Journal)

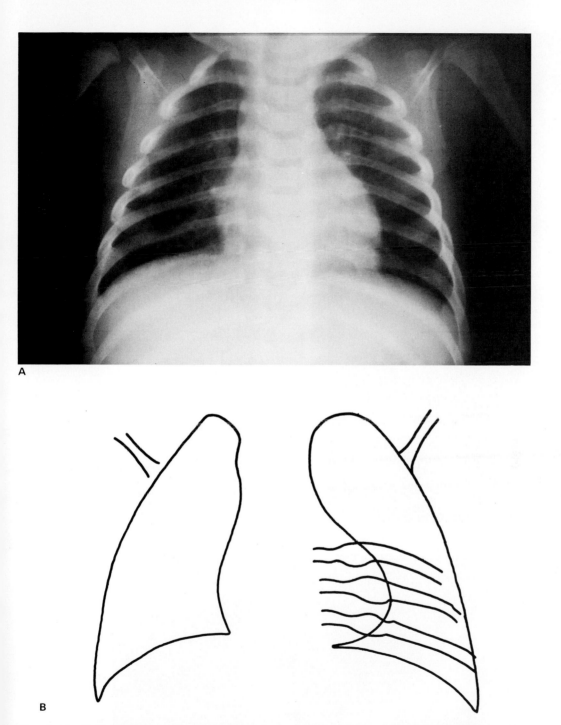

A

B

Plate 8a, b Radiograph **(a)** and line drawing to illustrate findings **(b)** in posterior healing rib fractures of left sixth, seventh and eighth ribs behind cardiac shadow in abused infant. Presence of callus and unclear fracture line suggests fractures are less than two weeks old. (Reproduced with permission from Meadow S R, ed 1989 ABC of child abuse. British Medical Journal)

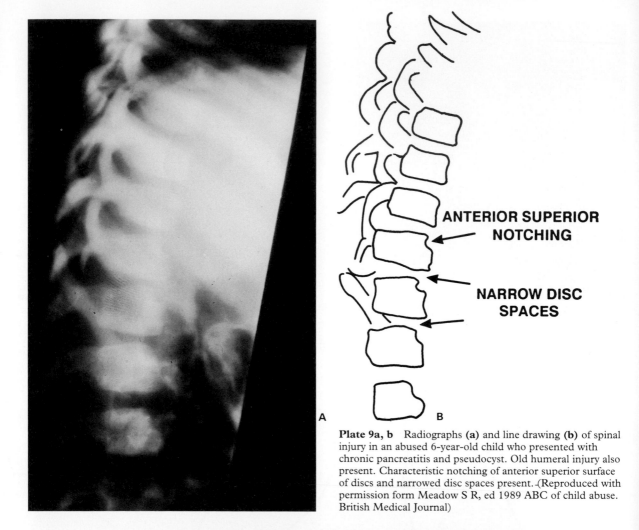

ANTERIOR SUPERIOR NOTCHING

NARROW DISC SPACES

A   B

Plate 9a, b Radiographs (**a**) and line drawing (**b**) of spinal injury in an abused 6-year-old child who presented with chronic pancreatitis and pseudocyst. Old humeral injury also present. Characteristic notching of anterior superior surface of discs and narrowed disc spaces present. (Reproduced with permission form Meadow S R, ed 1989 ABC of child abuse. British Medical Journal)

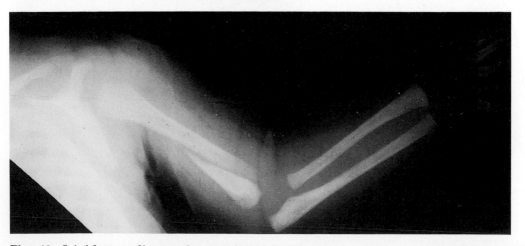

Plate 10 Spiral fracture of humerus in a 6-week-old infant whose mother said the arm broke as she dressed the child. No other injuries, so diagnosis of abuse not certainly established, but suspected.

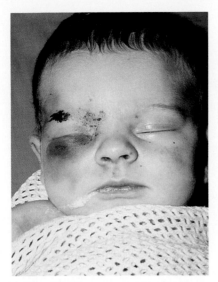

Plate 11   Battered baby aged 2 months. Facial, ear and mouth bruising. Fractured skull, corneal burn.

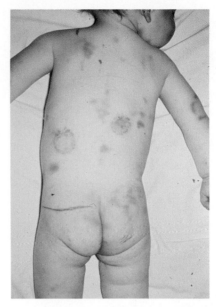

Plate 12   Battered baby. Various lesions including bites, bruises and healing laceration.

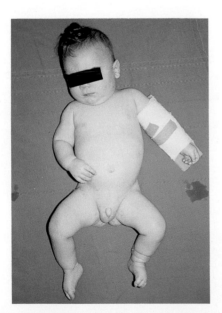

Plate 13   Battered baby with over 20 individual injuries. Presentation with injured elbow. Fractures of skull, ribs, humerus, tibia, of various ages on skeletal survey. Faint bruises on arm, fingertip bruising to chest and face just visible. Nappy rash. Nutrition good.

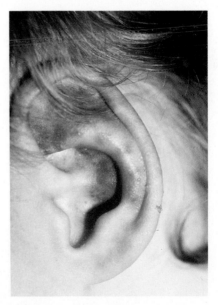

Plate 14   Bruising to ear from blow to the side of the head in a 12-month-old boy.

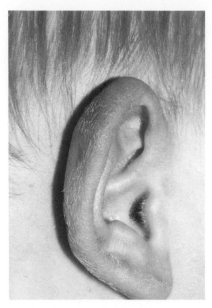

Plate 15 Bruising to rim of ear resulting from ear being forcibly pinched in a 15-month-old baby.

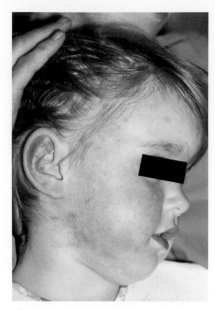

Plate 16 Diffuse recent bruising to side of face, including lower jaw and neck with linear pattern, and ear. Admitted hand slap. Child of 3 years.

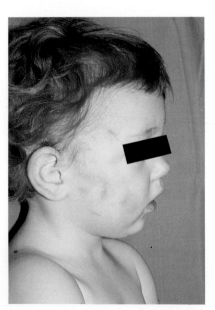

Plate 17 Patchy bruises, several days old, over the side of the face of a 20-month-old abused boy.

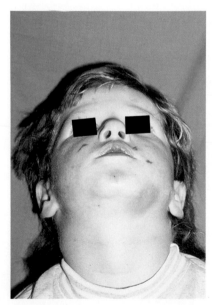

Plate 18 Jawline bruise in a 3-year-old abused girl. Several scratches are present on her face.

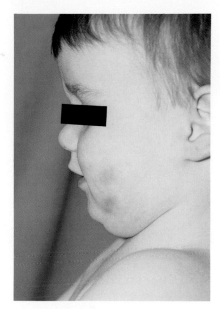

Plate 19 Fingertip facial bruising in a boy of 11 months.

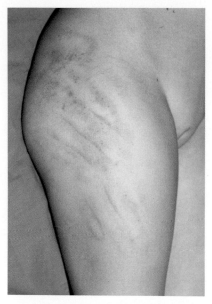

Plate 20 Hand marks on the thigh of a 4-year-old repeatedly abused girl. Mother admitted causing the injury.

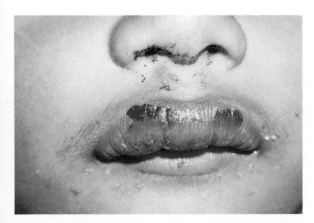

Plate 21 Swollen, bruised lip from a punch in the mouth in an older boy.

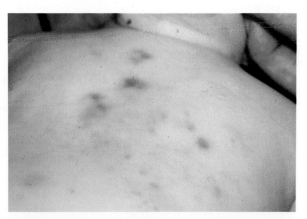

Plate 22 Pinch marks on the chest of a fatally abused 5-month-old infant. The bruises are paired and may be of varying ages.

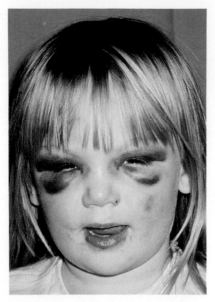

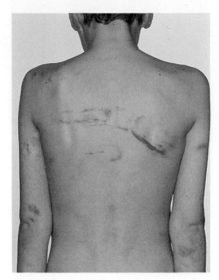

Plate 23 Bilateral periorbital haematoma in a 3-year-old girl resulting from a blow to the forehead where fainter bruising and swelling was also noted. A total of 60 bruises were found on the child's body. History of an unwitnessed fall downstairs.

Plate 24 Belt mark in 11-year-old boy.

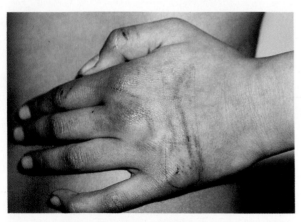

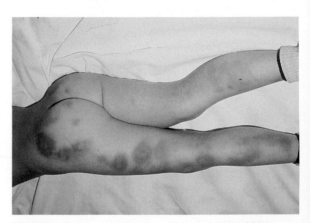

Plate 26 Bruises resulting from kicks in 5-year-old boy.

Plate 25 Mark caused by a stick beating in older Asian boy. Hand held up to protect face.

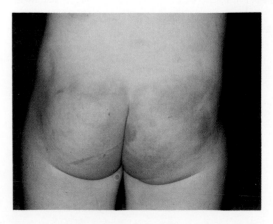

Plate 27 Bilateral fading buttock bruises in 3-year-old child from slipper beating, admitted by mother.

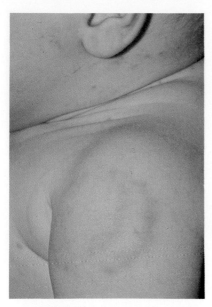

Plate 28 Large radius double bite mark of recent origin. Individual teeth marks can be made out. Father admitted biting this 12-month-old girl.

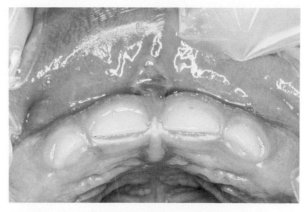

Plate 30 Torn frenulum in an 18-month-old girl who presented with a 2-day-old fracture and bruises to buttocks and face.

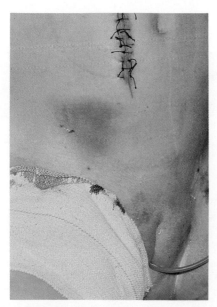

Plate 29 Abdominal bruising in an infant who sustained duodenal rupture. History that child had fallen across a table seemed unlikely to be true.

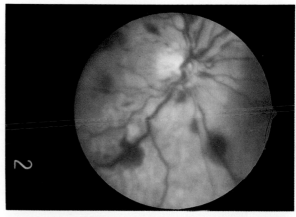

Plate 31 Retinal haemorrhages in a 4-year-old boy shaken to death. Evidence of anal abuse and bruises to back and face. No skull fracture.

Plate 32 Traumatic hair loss in abused 2-year-old boy.

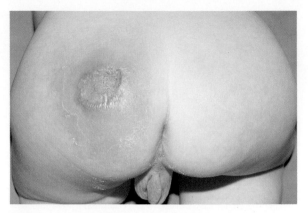

Plate 33 Lesion found on buttocks in a 12-month-old handicapped boy. Mother strenuously insisted that it was nappy rash. Lesion consistent with burn.

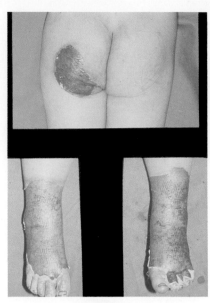

Plate 34 Forced immersion scald with deep areas around both ankles in 4-year-old abused child. Stocking distribution, no splash marks. Mother admitted to holding child in the bath. (Reproduced with permission from Meadow S R, ed 1989 ABC of child abuse. British Medical Journal)

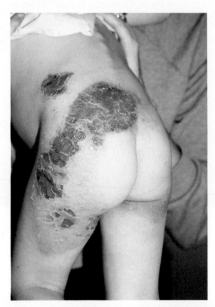

Plate 35 Extensive bath scalds in 3-year-old girl failing to thrive. Central part of buttock spared where pressed onto cool base of bath — 'hole in doughnut' effect. Abuse suspected but not proven. (Reproduced with permission from Meadow S R, ed 1989 ABC of child abuse. British Medical Journal)

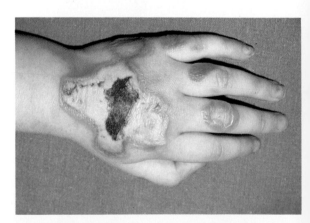

Plate 36 Full thickness burn from an iron in a 2-year-old child. Alleged that older brother was responsible. Incident unwitnessed by mother. Labial fusion and multiple anal fissures present.

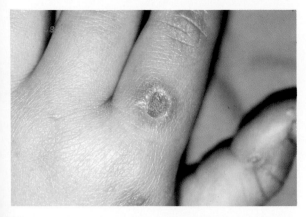

Plate 37 Cratered deep cigarette burn in typical site on the back of the hand of a 5-year-old boy who also said 'Mummy put her fingers in my bottom'. (Reproduced with permission from Meadow S R, ed 1989 ABC of child abuse. British Medical Journal)

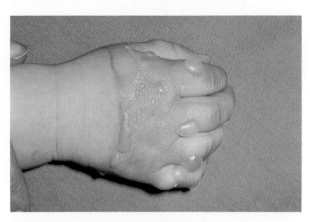

Plate 38 Forced immersion scald of the hand of a 3-year-old who 'sat in a bath of hot water'. No scalds were found elsewhere.

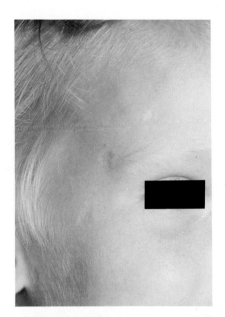

Plate 39 Depressed scars in a 4-year-old boy. Both he and his brother had multiple cigarette burns of varying ages over their foreheads.

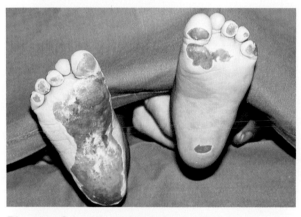

Plate 40 Contact burns in a 9-month-old who, when left with father, allegedly crawled against a central heating radiator. Story not consistent with explanation. Delay in presentation.

Plate 41 Contact burns on thigh in a 2-year-old boy with developmental retardation inflicted by his mother. Burns were also present to penis. (Reproduced with permission from Meadow S R, ed 1989 ABC of child abuse. British Medical Journal)

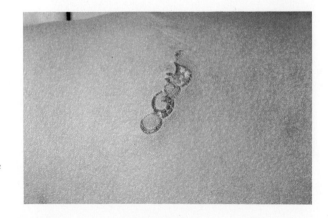

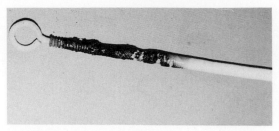

Plate 42 Curtain wire heated in fire and used to inflict burns shown in Plate 41. (Reproduced with permission from Meadow S R, ed 1989 ABC of child abuse. British Medical Journal)

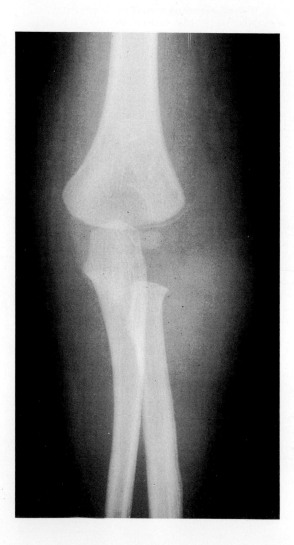

Plate 43 Metaphyseal fracture of the lower end of the humerus in an abused 2-year-old boy who allegedly fell onto his elbow. Multiple bruises, penile and anal injury also present. A thin fragment of bone is seen separated from the metaphyseal end of the shaft.

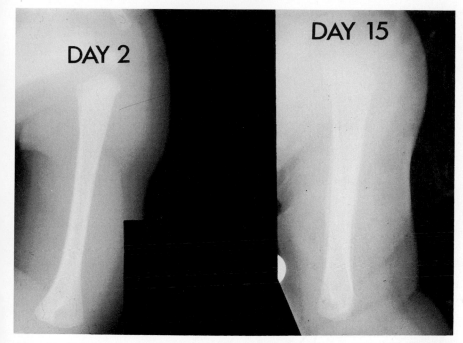

Plate 44 Development of radiological periosteal reaction in humerus of 3-month-old infant who presented with painful non-moving arm. No history offered. Abuse thought likely. At age 5 years, sexual abuse by father recognised when parents' marriage ended (see also Plate 50).

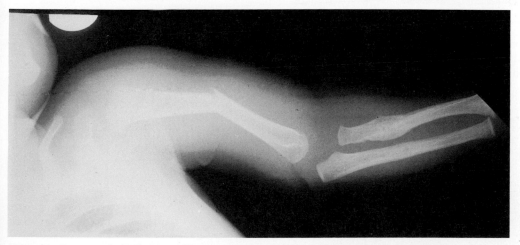

Plate 45 Recent and old fractures of humerus, radius and ulna in a 5-month-old abused infant.

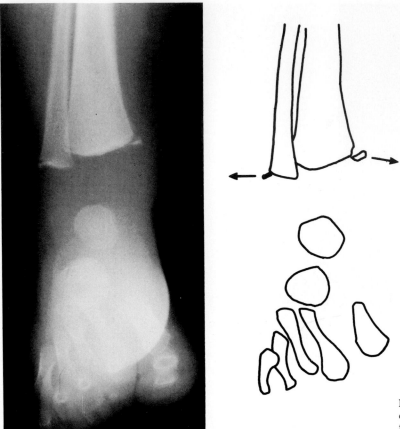

Plate 46a, b Radiograph (**a**) and line drawing (**b**) of distal metaphyseal chip fracture of the lower end of tibia and fibula in an abused infant.

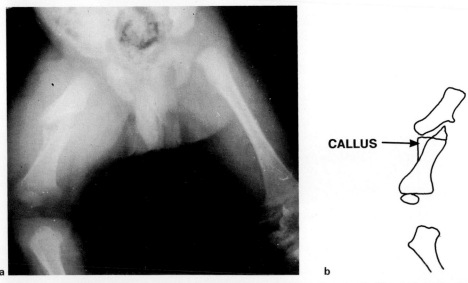

CALLUS

Plate 47a, b Radiograph (**a**) and line drawing (**b**) of refracture of previously fractured and healing femur of a 13-week-old abused infant who presented after the second injury.

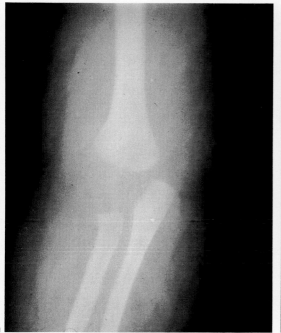
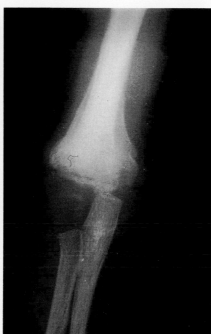

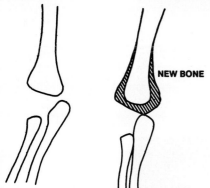

NEW BONE

Plate 48a, b Radiographs **(a)** and line
drawings **(b)** of distal humerus epiphyseal
separation in a 5-month-old abused infant
(same case as Plates 5 and 13). Initially injury
was confused with dislocation but on follow-up
4 weeks later (right-hand radiograph) extensive
formation of new bone confirmed displacement
of epiphysis. (Reproduced with permission from
Meadow S R, ed 1989 ABC of child abuse.
British Medical Journal)

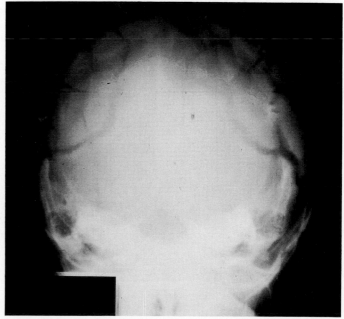

Plate 49 Multiple wide skull fractures in 'crazy paving' pattern in
11-month-old boy who allegedly fell from settee onto carpeted floor.
Enlarged ventricles on CAT scan. Father admitted abuse to police.

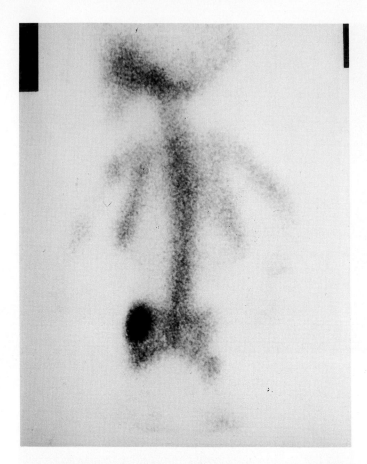

Plate 50 ⁹⁹ᵐTechnetium bone scan of 3-month-old infant (same case as Plate 44) on day 5, showing increased uptake in the left humerus relative to right.

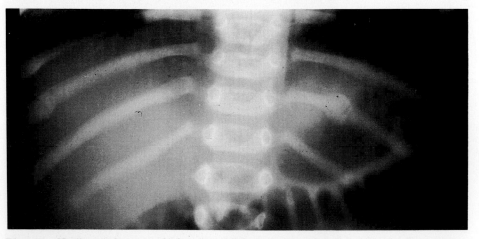

Plate 51 Healing rib fractures of left 11th and right 10th ribs with well-developed callus (same case as Plates 5, 13 and 48).

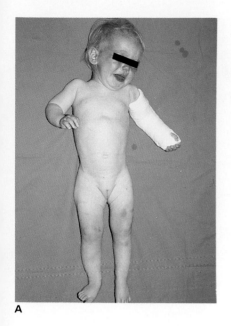

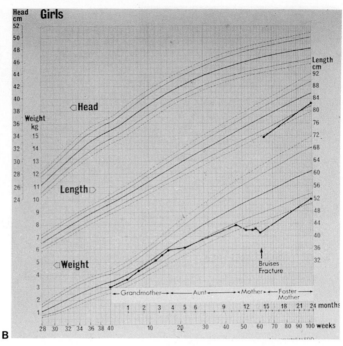

A

B

Plate 52a, b (a) 14-month-old child with a non-accidental mid-shaft fracture of radius and ulna and fingertip bruising to thigh. (b) Growth chart confirms a pattern of failure to thrive which commenced at between 3 and 4 months when care was transferred from grandmother to aunt. Loss of weight followed the further move of the child to her mother's care. Catch-up growth is demonstrated in the foster-mother's care. (Reproduced with permission from Meadow S R, ed 1989 ABC of child abuse. British Medical Journal)

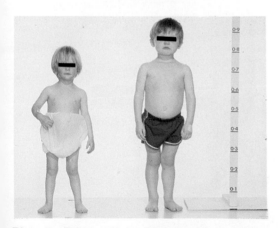

Plate 53 Failure to thrive children are small. An average-sized 4-year-old is shown on the right in comparison with a child of the same age on the left who has failed to thrive. There is also developmental delay.

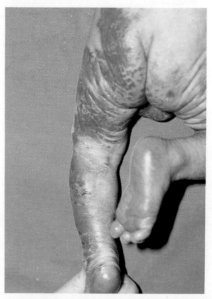

Plate 54 Neglect. Severe ammoniacal dermatitis in an infant of 4 weeks left in a wet cot for days on end. Rapid resolution on admission to hospital.

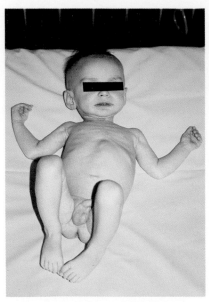

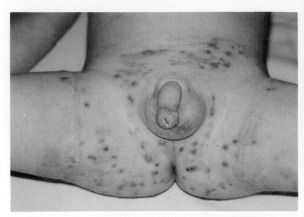

Plate 56 Severe nappy rash in 2½-year-old neglected child.

Plate 55 Emaciated appearance, flexed posture and bright, alert, radar-like gaze in 6-month-old ruminating infant. Note prominent ribs and sunken eyes.

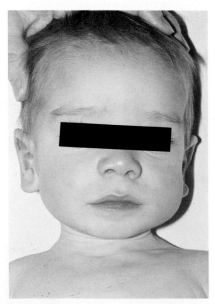

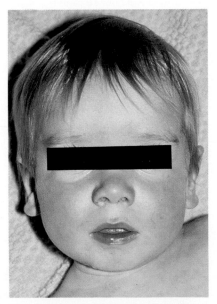

Plates 57, 58 Before (left) and after (right) nutritional rehabilitation, faces in a child at 4 and 6 months. Note difference in expression and hair.

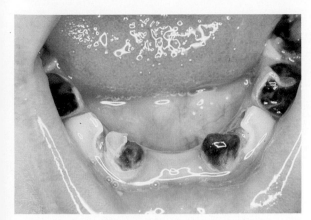

Plate 59 Grossly neglected carious teeth in a 4-year-old neglected child who presented with neglected pneumonia and empyema.

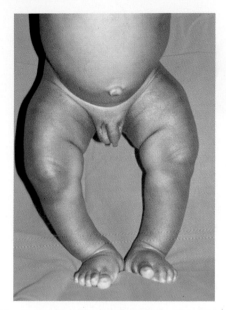

Plate 60 Rickets in a 12-month-old neglected child of West Indian origin.

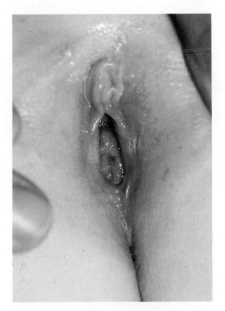

Plate 61 Normal infantile genitalia. Age 15 months.

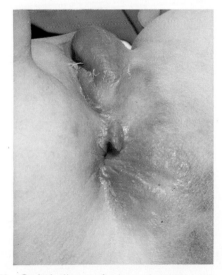

Plate 62 Crohn's disease of vulva and anus in a 10-year-old girl. (Courtesy of Mr P C Buchan and colleagues)

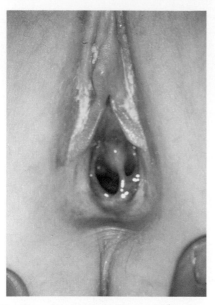

Plates 63 Hymenal septum in a 5-year-old.

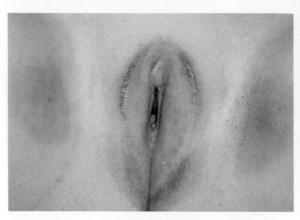

Plate 64 Patchy tram-line reddening of both labia majora and inside of thighs in a 7-year-old. Gaping hymenal opening is visible without separation of labia. History of intracrural intercourse (penis between thighs) and digital penetration.

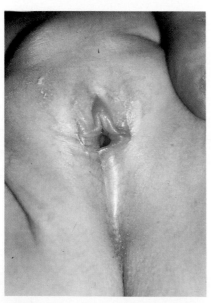

Plate 65 Extensive posterior labial fusion in an abused 2-year-old with anal findings and an old burn on the thigh.

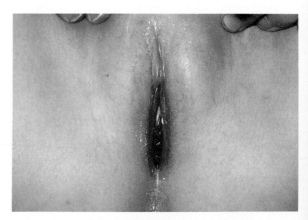

Plate 66 Marked reddening of labia minora and tissues of introitus in 4-year-old who disclosed digital vulval interference.

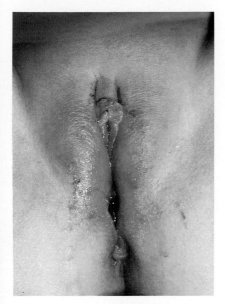

Plate 67 4-year-old abused child with recent bruising, reddening and swelling of labia majora and a midline tear extending posteriorly through the vaginal wall, perineum and as far as the anus. Anterior anal haematoma. Findings consistent with violent penetration of vagina.

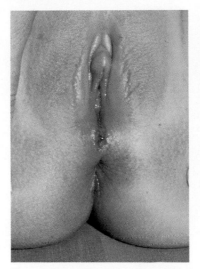

Plate 68a Fresh midline unexplained tear through posterior fourchette, abuse presumed, in 20-month-old child.

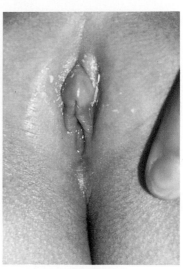

Plate 68b Same child as Plate 68a three weeks later. Pale midline scar now present. Hymen appears normal.

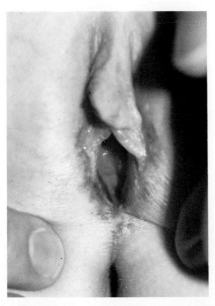

Plate 69 Abrasions/bruises of the inner aspect of labia majora, fourchette and labia minora in a 7-year-old who presented with unexplained genital bleeding.

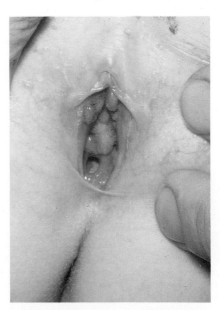

Plate 70 Florid, large, mature genital warts in a 3-year-old. Father had penile and anal warts and admitted contact in the bath. (Reproduced with permission from Hanks H, Hobbs C J, Wynne J M 1988 Recognition of sexual abuse in the pre-school child. In: Browne K, Davies C, Stratton P (eds) Early prediction and prevention of child abuse. John Wiley & Sons, Chichester)

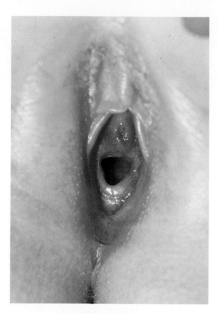

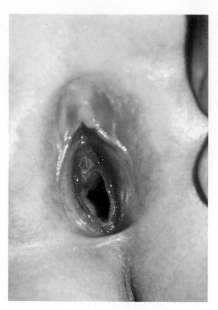

Plate 71 8-year-old girl who presented in school with a love bite on her neck. Dilated hymenal orifice with smooth, rolled edge, excessive reddening and prominent urethra. (Reproduced with permission from Hobbs C J, Wynne J M 1987 Child sexual abuse — an increasing rate of diagnosis. Lancet ii: 839)

Plate 72 7-year-old girl who presented with unexplained vaginal bleeding. The hymen is irregular and attenuated and the orifice dilated with probable tears, including one at 6 o'clock. There is vascular hyperaemia and extreme reddening with contact bleeding. Swabs for culture were negative for bacteria and viruses. There was no disclosure of abuse with the child in protective care.

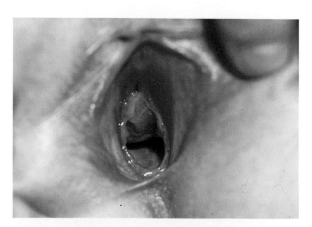

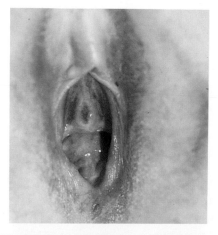

Plate 73 10-year-old girl who presented with day-time wetting in school. Child flirtatious and overweight, living in the care of her father following marital breakdown. Excessive reddening of hymenal orifice and vagina with healed tears in hymenal ring. Hymen attenuated. (Reproduced with permission form Hobbs C J, Wynne, J M 1987 Child sexual abuse — an increasing rate of diagnosis. Lancet ii: 839)

Plate 74 9-year-old girl with history of anal warts at age 4 years, history of vaginal wall tear following alleged fall at age 7 and persistent soiling, self-mutilation and emotional problems. Generalized reddening, prominent urethra, dilated vagina (1.5 cm). There is virtually no hymen visible with few remnants posteriorly. The posterior fourchette is poorly defined and a superficial abrasion is present in the skin in the midline at 6 o'clock.

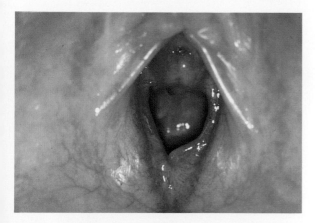

Plate 75 5-year-old with intermittent vulval soreness, withdrawn behaviour and fluctuating physical signs, both anal and genital. Hymenal opening is dilated, 1 cm horizontal diameter and there is a sharp V at 6 o'clock. The hymen edge is irregular, rolled and there is anterior asymmetry. The symptoms and signs regressed when the child's step-father left the family home. The parents accepted that abuse had taken place, but by another child in the street.

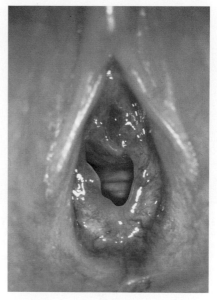

Plate 76 6-year-old girl with a history of abuse by step-father. Appearances suggest an old healed tear at 11 o'clock anteriorly. Hymenal opening is asymmetrical and measures 0.7 cm transversely across the widest point.

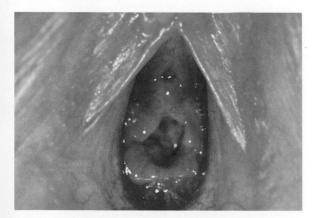

Plate 77 4-year-old girl with a history of vaginal abuse. There is a healed transection of the hymen at 9 o'clock.

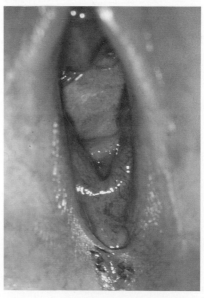

Plate 78 Fresh tear of fourchette in a 4-year-old child with a clear history of penile/vaginal abuse. The hymenal opening is enlarged with a deep healed transection at 6 o'clock.

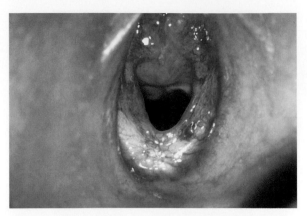

Plate 79 9-year-old girl who gave a history of painful vaginal penetration abut 12 months previously whilst in care of mother. Hymenal opening is 1 cm anteroposteriorly × 0.8 cm transversely and there is thickening of the posterior hymen between 5 and 7 o'clock with new vessel formation at 5 o'clock.

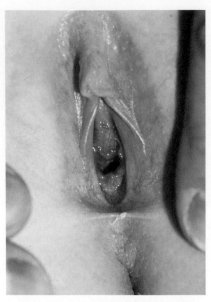

Plate 80 5-year-old girl with history of digital abuse by father. Irregular hymenal opening, clefts at 3, 5, 7 and 9 o'clock and anterior tear at 1 o'clock.

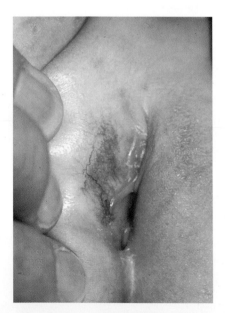

Plate 81 Vascular naevus of right labium majus in a 2-year-old child with suspicious anal findings and a worrying family history. On follow-up these findings were persistent.

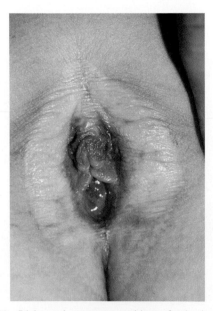

Plate 82 Lichen sclerosus et atrophicus of vulva in 6-year-old girl who presented with persistent irritation, scratching and bleeding of the anogenital area. Pale atrophic skin surrounds normal mucous membrane.

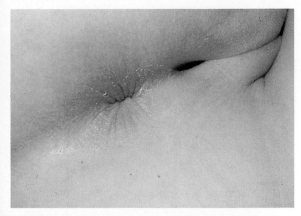

Plate 83 Normal anus in 2-year-old child, out of nappies. Line of anterior – posterior closure with smooth regular radiating folds seen.

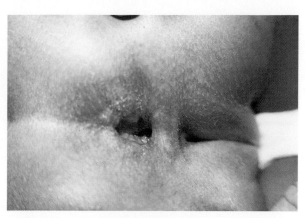

Plate 84 2-year-old black girl with sudden onset of nightmares, wetting and clinginess noted at home and in day nursery. Anus shows dilatation, 'tyre sign' and some perianal venous congestion. Signs had healed in one week. Child said 'Daddy's snake bited my bottom". (Reproduced with permission from Hobbs C J, Wynne J M 1986 Buggery in childhood — a common syndrome of child abuse. Lancet ii: 795. Hobbs C J, Wynne J M 1989 Sexual abuse of English boys and girls. The importance of anal examination. Child Abuse and Neglect 13: 201–202)

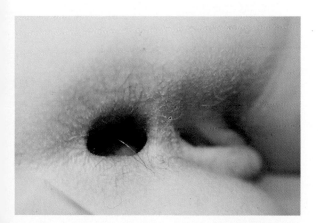

Plate 85 Wide dilatation in a 12-year-old girl who had a history of anal intercourse with father over a 6-year period. Resolution of signs was gradual over about 12 months. (Reproduced with permission from Hobbs C J, Wynne J M 1986 Buggery in childhood — a common syndrome of child abuse. Lancet ii: 795)

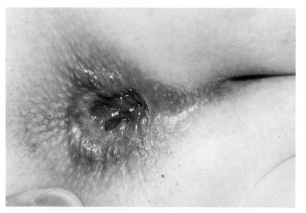

Plate 86 Gross anal abnormality in 3-year-old girl who had exhibited aggressive biting of younger brother. Lax dilated anus with deep fissures, swollen rim and venous (dark) congestion in a half-circle around the posterior anus. Prominent skin papillae are noted, suggesting oedema of the tissues. Two other children in family with similar findings discovered. (Reproduced with permission from Hobbs C J, Wynne J M 1989 Sexual abuse of English boys and girls. The importance of anal examination. Child Abuse and Neglect 13: 201–202)

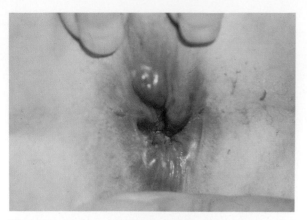

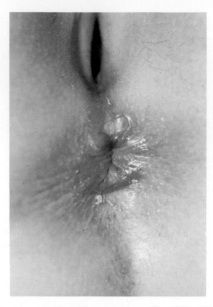

Plate 87 Gross venous dilatation, multiple anal fissures and reddening in a 5-year-old boy with scalds in his groins, bruised ear and frozen watchfulness. He disclosed physical and sexual abuse by his father. (Reproduced with permission from Hobbs C J, Wynne J M 1987 Child sexual abuse — an increasing rate of diagnosis. Lancet ii: 839. Hanks H, Hobbs C J, Wynne J M 1988 Recognition of sexual abuse in the pre-school child. In: Browne K, Davies C, Stratton P (eds) Early prediction and prevention of child abuse. John Wiley & Sons, Chichester)

Plate 88 8-year-old girl (same case as Plate 71) with abnormally dilated hymenal opening. Anus shows pale, wide, deep anterior tear with swollen prominent fold adjacent to it. The anus is closed and the other folds are reasonable normal. There is a posterior band of dark venous congestion and the whole of the anus is darkened by venous discoloration. (Reproduced with permission from Hobbs C J, Wynne J M 1987 Child sexual abuse — an increasing rate of diagnosis. Lancet ii: 839. Hobbs C J, Wynne J M 1989 Sexual abuse of English boys and girls. The importance of anal examination. Child Abuse and Neglect 13: 201–202)

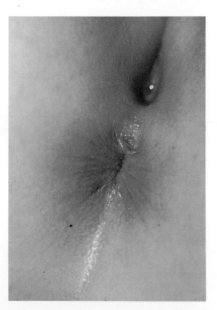

Plate 89 Same child as Plate 88, 4 months later, to demonstrate healing. Anterior scar with prominent V-shaped ridges present. Dusky colouration but no evidence of localised venous congestion present.

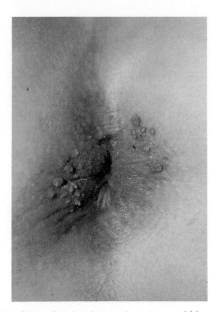

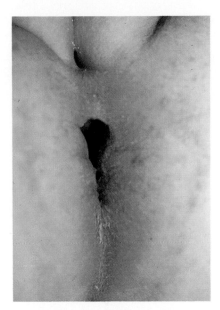

Plate 90 Crop of perianal warts in a 6-year-old boy showing emotional difficulties and poor concentration at school. Child indicated that there was something distressing about which he could not talk. Parents separated, father bisexual. Mother had history of genital warts. The anus showed dusky venous congestion, posterior scar and venous prominence at 6 o'clock. The fold pattern is irregular. Abuse suspected but not confirmed. Parents cooperated with child protection plan.

Plate 92 Lax gaping anus in an 18-month-old left in the care of an alcoholic violent cohabitee while mother had her second child in hospital. The child had suffered serious non-accidental injury at the hands of her natural father, who was imprisoned. There was a vulval abrasion and these anal findings, which resolved fully within 7 days. (Reproduced with permission form Hanks H, Hobbs C J, Wynne J M 1988 Recognition of sexual abuse in the pre-school child. In: Browne K, Davies C, Stratton P (eds) Early prediction and prevention of child abuse. John Wiley & Sons, Chichester)

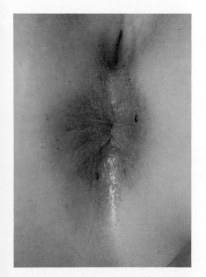

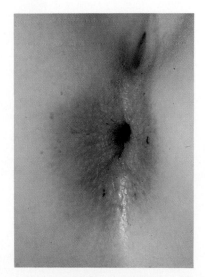

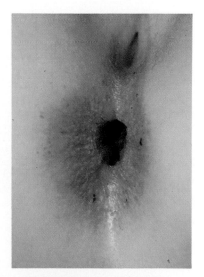

Plate 91a–c These three figures demonstrate the sign of reflex anal dilatation. They were taken in succession with brief intervals between them. Following dilatation the anus will usually close again. 5-year-old child sexually abused by her older teenage brother. The anus is reddened. Vulva showed evidence of multiple abrasions, swelling and reddening.

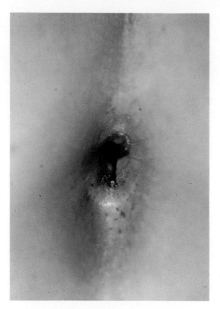

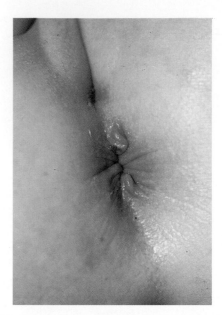

Plate 93   Anal appearance in a 9-year-old boy with previous history of failure to thrive, non-accidental bruising, toddler scald following neglect, severe behavioural and learning difficulties requiring residential special education. There is anal dilatation, a deep chronic posterior fissure and smooth pink skin around the anal margin. Venous discoloration and funnelling are also present. (Reproduced with permission from Hobbs C J, Wynne J M 1986 Buggery in childhood — a common syndrome of child abuse. Lancet ii: 795)

Plate 94   Skin tags in a 5-year-old girl involved in sexual acting-out at school. History of sexual abuse by grandfather who also abused the child's mother. There are no signs of recent abuse.

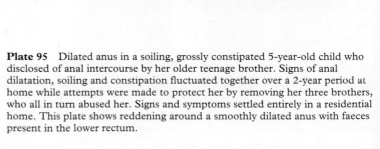

Plate 96   Multiple fissures in a lax disrupted anus in a 12-year-old girl with multiple abusers. The examination was undertaken 3 weeks after she was taken into protective care and after abuse was thought to have stopped.

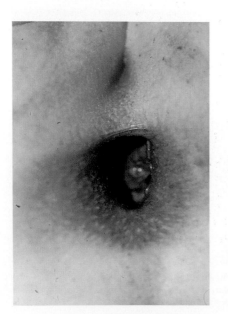

Plate 95   Dilated anus in a soiling, grossly constipated 5-year-old child who disclosed of anal intercourse by her older teenage brother. Signs of anal dilatation, soiling and constipation fluctuated together over a 2-year period at home while attempts were made to protect her by removing her three brothers, who all in turn abused her. Signs and symptoms settled entirely in a residential home. This plate shows reddening around a smoothly dilated anus with faeces present in the lower rectum.

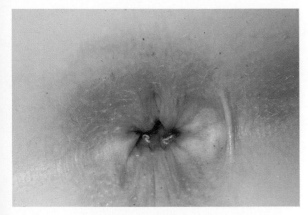

Plate 97 Anal scarring in an abused boy of 5 years. Two threadworms are also present.

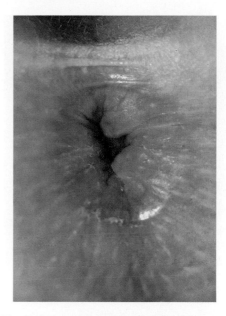

Plate 98 Anal verge deficit at 3 o'clock in a chronically abused child aged 4 years. There is also a ring of veins around the anus.

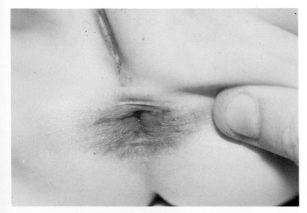

Plate 99 Lax everted anus of 3-year-old abused girl. There was labial fusion, vulval reddening, failure to thrive and emotional disturbance.

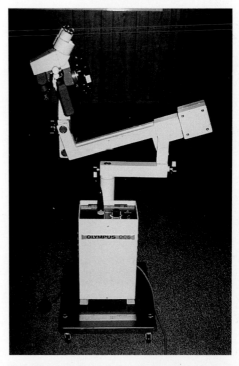

Plate 100 Olympus OCS Colposcope with 35 mm camera attached. The camera shutter can be fired by remote release, e.g. by foot.

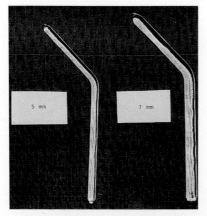

Plate 101 5 and 7 mm glass rods, used to assess hymenal opening size and configuration. (Courtesy of Dr Ellis Fraser)

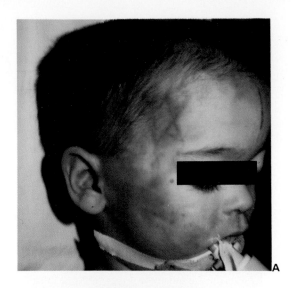

Plate 102 Healing of anal signs in a deeply unconscious 2-year-old boy. **(a)** Facial signs on admission; **(b)** & **(c)** anal signs at 2 days; **(d)** & **(e)** anal signs at 5 days.

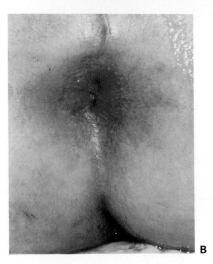

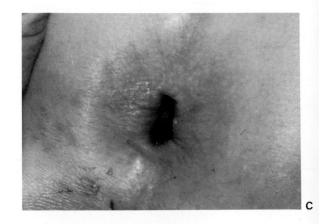

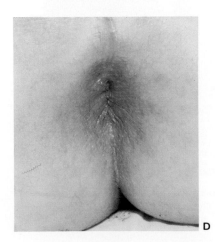

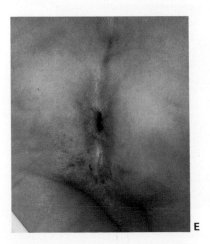

many younger pre-pubertal girls are unaware they have a vagina and by the time they are more aware of their anatomy they are beyond the age of this kind of behaviour. The symptoms produced by a foreign body are bleeding and purulent discharge (Paradise & Willis 1985). If insertion of a foreign body has caused stretching of the hymen it will have caused pain and often bleeding.

Always consider CSA if a child is seen with a foreign body in the vagina, and particularly if there are repeated episodes (RCP 1991). This is learned behaviour — where did the child learn to put pencils, Lego bricks or other objects inside herself?

Rectal foreign bodies are only rarely found and are usually associated with sadistic rape of older children.

(viii) Threadworm infestation (oxyuriasis)

This is extremely common during childhood and the incidence is higher in school children from 5–14 years, with boys and girls equally affected. Incidences as high as 40–50% have been reported in London children (Goldsmid et al 1985).

The gravid female worm emerges from the child's anus at night and usually lays her eggs perianally, but may also migrate to the vulva. The child suffers intense irritation perianally and in the vulval area, and scratches. The perianal skin and vulva become reddened and on occasion excoriated. The eggs may be trapped under the child's nails, the fingers are then sucked and the child re-infects herself or her classmates by touching toys and so on.

Symptoms of threadworm infection:

- No symptoms
- Pruritus in perineal area
- Vulval irritation leading to scratching, vulvitis and occasionally pyogenic infection of excoriations leading to vulvovaginitis and discharge
- reinfestation rates are high.

Diagnosis

- If a child is heavily infected worms may be seen perianally.
- A piece of Sellotape is applied perianally in the morning before washing or toileting and then placed adhesive side down on a slide. The adhering eggs are visible under a microscope.
- Stools show eggs in 5–10% of cases.

Treatment:

- Mebendazole (Vermox) 100 mg stat (over 2 years)
- Piperazine (Pripsen) repeat after 14 days
- Treat the whole family.

(ix) Infantile eczema and seborrhoeic dermatitis

Children with these disorders have a tendency to develop vulvitis and perineal soreness.

(x) Lichen sclerosus et atrophicus (LSA)

This is an uncommon skin disorder, but may present with symptoms of vulvitis, the girl complaining of soreness, burning, itching, dysuria, genital bleeding and, if the perianal area is affected, pain on defecation and anal bleeding. It usually affects girls in mid-childhood but boys may be affected and present with phimosis.

The physical signs may be quite dramatic and superficially appear like trauma — hence CSA may be considered. However the long history of intense irritation and burning sensations, coupled with the signs of LSA, should make the differentiation from CSA. There are on examination white atrophic areas on the vulva and perianal skin, but also areas of vasculitis or purpura with ecchymoses. Fissures are common perianally. There may be a superadded infection leading to a vulvo-vaginitis (Handfield-Jones et al 1987).

The possibility of frictional trauma from CSA being an aetiological factor in some cases has been suggested but there is as yet no evidence to support this (Priestley & Bleehan 1990).

(xi) Sexually transmitted disease (STD)

The increased recognition of STD in children parallels the recognition of CSA in general. Non-sexual transmission of STD is rarely an issue in adults and when STD occur in children, sexual abuse must be suspected (RCP 1991). Acquisition or transmission of STD in childhood is more complicated than in adults, particularly in infancy.

Table 9.9   STD and the probability of abuse

STD	Incubation period	Vertical transmission — neonatal disease	Probability of abuse (after RCP 1991)
Gonorrhoea	3–4 days	Neonatal ophthalmia Neonatal vaginitis (rare)	xx (xxx if child > 2 years)
Trichomonas	1–4 weeks	Rare but occasionally seen, usually clears spontaneously	xxx
Chlamydia	7–14 days	Neonatal conjunctivitis Neonatal pneumonitis	xx (xxx if child > 3 years and organism cultured is child's)
Warts	Several months	Laryngeal papillomata (HPV-II) Genital/perianal?	x
Herpes	2–14 days	Localised or disseminated	xx
Bacterial vaginosis	2–14 days		x
HIV	Majority convert in 3 months	If maternal	Sexual assault
Hepatitis B	Up to 3 months	Infection	Recognised
Syphilis	Up to 3 months		xxx

Footnotes:
1. Key: x — possible CSA
         xx — likely CSA
         xxx — almost certain CSA.
2. The former presumed importance of fomites is decreasing (Clarke & Lacey 1990).
3. Full penetrative sexual intercourse (vaginal or anal) is not necessary for infection. Orogenital sex and intercrural contact may transmit pathogens (Branch & Paxton 1965).

For example, the long incubation period of human papillomavirus or chlamydia makes for difficulty in diagnosis during the first two years of life. The presence of a STD does give corroborative evidence of CSA and Table 9.9 gives a guide to the probability of abuse (Clarke & Lacey 1990, RCP 1991).

The infections seen commonly in the UK are gonorrhoea, warts, chlamydia, trichomonas, herpes and bacterial vaginosis; rare infections are hepatitis B, syphilis and HIV. A STD is diagnosed in 3–13% of sexually abused children, the higher rates being in older children (White et al 1983). Presenting signs and symptoms are given in Table 9.10.

Investigation must be carried out meticulously and checked, given the far-reaching consequences of the diagnosis. It is usual to work in close association with a GU physician. Table 9.11 summarises the tests needed.

Gonorrhoea in childhood is almost always

Table 9.10   Presenting signs or symptoms of STD

1. No signs or symptoms e.g. chlamydia
2. Discharge (vaginal, penile, rectal) e.g. gonorrhoea
3. Itch or soreness (vulval, penile or perianal) c.g. candida
4. Pain (vulval or rectal) e.g. herpes
5. Ulceration, vesicles, warts (genital, oral, perianal) e.g. condylomata
6. Systemic illness e.g. gonorrhoea

due to abuse. In one series 44/45 1–10 year-olds and 115/116 10–14-year-olds had suffered abuse (Branch & Paxton 1965). Neonatal infection is the only exemption to this rule.

Only just over half the infected children are likely to have symptoms, Table 9.11, and those with pharyngeal infections are likely to be asymptomatic (De Jong 1986).

Trichomonas is a less common infection in CSA but is found in older girls in particular (Herman-Giddens et al 1988). *Trichomonas vaginalis* does not survive long in the pre-pubertal vagina and so if infection is found the abuse is recent (RCP 1991).

Genital herpes is likely to have resulted from CSA (Kaplan et al 1984). Typing of the virus does not help in identification of CSA as HSV-1 causes as much genital herpes as HSV-2, and in any event oral sex is common.

Chlamydia trachomatis (CT) was found in 4–17% of sexually abused children who had been routinely screened for STD (RCP 1991). The diagnosis is ideally made on culture but this is not always available.

Most girls with CT infection are asymptomatic. The usual neonatal presentation is ophthalmia, and persistence of CT beyond infancy is controversial, CSA being strongly suspected beyond the first 1–2 years of life.

Table 9.11 Summary of sexually transmitted diseases

	Signs and symptoms	Epidemiology/incubation	Microbiological investigation ALWAYS REPEAT
1. Gonorrhoea *Neisseria gonorrhoeae*, Gram-negative intracellular diplococci	*Newborns* — conjunctivitis *Prepubertal* — vulvovaginitis c/o itchy, discharge, dysuria. Rarely systemic — urethritis is uncommon *Adolescent girls* — asymptomatic, discharge, cervicitis, salpingitis *Adolescent boys* — urethritis, epididymitis, prostatitis *Anorectal* — pruritis, mucopurulent discharge, bleeding	*Incubation* 3–7 days Transmission — requires intimate contact with epithelial or mucus-secreting cells, dies 1 hour 1. sexual contact 2. birth canal (up to 1 month)	1. Gram stain — intracellular diplococci, Gram-negative 2. Culture — *always repeat* 3. Serological typing, types 1–16, specialised lab 4. Investigate trichomonas chlamydia *Diagnosis* requires culture of the organism
2. Trichomoniasis *Trichomonas vaginalis* protozoon	*Newborn* — low risk — 0.5% nasal discharge, vaginitis *Older children* — vulvovaginitis, urethritis, cystitis, asymptomatic	*Incubation* 4 days–4 weeks *Transmission* 1. sexual contact 2. birth canal	1. Microscopy 2. Culture 3. Investigate for gonorrhoea, chlamydia
3. Chlamydia *Chlamydia trachomatis* sub-group A	*Manifestations* as for gonorrhoea, may be asymptomatic, n.b. conjunctivitis in newborn	*Incubation* 7–21 days *Transmission* 1. sexual contact 2. birth canal (up to 1 month)	1. Culture mandatory for diagnosis 2. Enzyme immunoassay and immunofluorescence not reliable 3. Check for gonorrhoea
4. Genital herpes *Herpes simplex* virus, DNA-containing, Types 1 and 2 (HSV-1 and HSV-2)	*HSV-1* primary infection — usually aged 1–5 years, 'cold sores', 10% gingivo stomatitis. Occasionally other parts — skin, eye, genital tract. Rarely encephalitis Tendency to recur Heal 10–14 days *HSV-2* primary infection, small, painful vesicles develop either singly or in groups, general malaise, lesions usually on penis or vulva, vagina, cervix in women, also perineum, anus, rectum. Recurs but attacks tend to come at longer intervals and be less severe *Newborn* — similar spectrum to above. Disseminated disease is often fatal	*Incubation* 2–7 days *Transmission* 1. HSV-1 direct contact 2. HSV-2 direct contact 3. Neonate by birth canal 4. Autoinoculation of genital area with HSV-1?? 5. Children with genital herpes, HSV-1, consider CSA especially in absence previous cold sores. HSV-2, consider CSA	1. Cervical cytology i.e. pap smear, see multinucleated giant cells and eosinophilic nuclear inclusions 2. Tissue culture, also enables typing of virus 3. Serological methods 4. Electron microscopy
5. Genital and anal warts (condylomata acuminata) Human papilloma virus, over 50 types, types 6 and 11,18, live on keratinising surfaces, types 16 and 18 only on mucous membranes	Soft verrucous lesions on genital and anorectal area. Rarely adjacent thigh or trunk. May extend to vagina, cervix, anal canal *Complications*: 1. invasive carcinoma of cervix 2. carcinoma of anal canal *Children*: 1. high index of suspicion CSA 2. non-venereal transmission suggested in early infancy, or lesions distant from anogenital area *Differential diagnosis* — clinically from molluscum contagiosum	*Incubation* — average 2–3 months, up to one year *Transmission* 1. in utero 2. birth canal 3. direct contact 4. sexual abuse 5. autoinoculation of some types	1. Biopsy/histology 2. Genotyping — genital types HPV 6, 11, 16, 18, 31. Common warts HPV 1–4 3. Screen for other STD

Warts are the most frequently seen STD in paediatric practice and management is often difficult. They are indicators of CSA but certainty is less than with, say, gonorrhoea (Neinstein et al 1984, Herman-Giddens et al 1988). Recent work suggests that the more thorough the investigation, the more likely it is that CSA will be identified (Gutman 1990). Tests should be done to exclude other STD.

Typing of warts demonstrates only partial site specificity — that is, genital warts are associated with type 6 and 11 and less often 16, 18 and others. Types 1 and 2 have been found in perianal warts.

Data from children does not yet make the clinical picture clear. Children with anogenital lesions rarely have warts elsewhere but one boy has been reported who had warts on his hands and perianal warts, and type 2 virus was detected in both (Flemming et al 1987).

It is likely that with greater multi-agency experience in investigation of venereal warts in children over the age of 2 years that CSA will be increasingly recognised in these children.

In order to postulate a non-sexual acquisition of venereal warts there should be (Rock et al 1986):

- a negative social enquiry
- no other signs of abuse
- lesions somewhat distant from the anus or introitus
- child under 9 months when lesions noted.

Bacterial vaginosis (BV) is a cause of vulvovaginitis and has been found in association with CSA, especially if there has been multiple abuse. A review in 1985 of 54 pre-pubertal girls showed BV in 8/31 abused girls and 1/23 non-abused girls (Hammerschlag 1988); another review in 1987 showed BV in 14% of abused girls compared with 4% of non-abused (Bartley et al 1987).

BV is uncommon in non-abused girls; the probability of abuse on BV infection alone is not high but is supportive of the diagnosis.

HIV infection has been recognised in CSA and the cases due to sexual assault are likely to rise (Gellert 1989). Screening for HIV needs careful consideration and the following protocol is suggested. In general terms:

- If a child is unwell with signs and symptoms suggestive of HIV infection he should be tested.

- If a child has been involved in high-risk activities, e.g. prostitution or drug abuse, he should probably be tested.
- If a child (usually a teenager), parent or carer insists on testing this needs careful consideration.
- A single act of stranger abuse, a coexistent STD, previous anal or oral abuse do not currently warrant screening.
- HIV antibody testing would be done at the time of the initial examination and after 3 and 6 months.
- Counselling for the child and his carers is mandatory.

Hepatitis A and B may be transmitted by sexual contact, hepatitis A by oral–anal contact and hepatitis B by homosexual and heterosexual intercourse. Hepatitis B has been seen in CSA in Leeds (1991).

Recovery is the rule after hepatitis A but hepatitis B may lead to an infective carrier state and chronic hepatitis. This clearly has implications for the child and his carers.

Screening for hepatitis B is not routinely done in the assessment of sexually abused children but should be considered in the same circumstances as for HIV testing.

Carers and siblings should be tested if the child is found to have HBsAG and HBeAg in his serum, indicating an infective carrier state. If carers are non-immune they should be offered hepatitis B vaccine.

Concomitant infections with hepatitis B and HIV are common.

Molluscum contagiosum is an infection caused by a DNA pox-containing virus. Whilst children usually have non-venereal infections with lesions on the face, trunk and limbs, in a minority there is an association with other STD and CSA.

Criminal injuries compensation is available to victims of CSA. A consequent STD may well have serious long-term health implications for the child and should be documented in the report for the Board (see Ch. 14).

A protocol for investigation of STD is given in Figure 9.8. If the child is young the application of swabs may cause distress. The use of small, nasopharyngeal swabs dampened with tap water may limit the discomfort. The protocol has been planned to use a minimum of swabs, as indicated

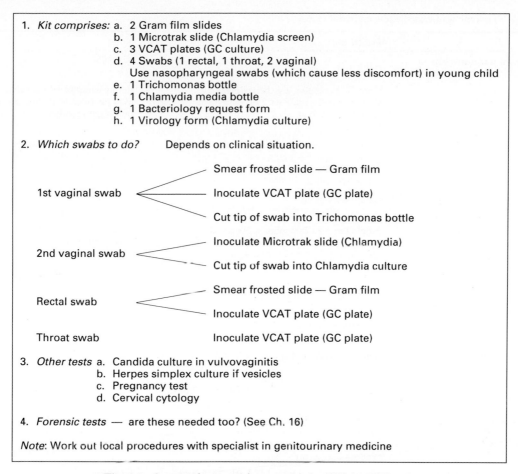

1. *Kit comprises:* a. 2 Gram film slides
   b. 1 Microtrak slide (Chlamydia screen)
   c. 3 VCAT plates (GC culture)
   d. 4 Swabs (1 rectal, 1 throat, 2 vaginal)
   Use nasopharyngeal swabs (which cause less discomfort) in young child
   e. 1 Trichomonas bottle
   f. 1 Chlamydia media bottle
   g. 1 Bacteriology request form
   h. 1 Virology form (Chlamydia culture)

2. *Which swabs to do?*   Depends on clinical situation.

   1st vaginal swab
   — Smear frosted slide — Gram film
   — Inoculate VCAT plate (GC plate)
   — Cut tip of swab into Trichomonas bottle

   2nd vaginal swab
   — Inoculate Microtrak slide (Chlamydia)
   — Cut tip of swab into Chlamydia culture

   Rectal swab
   — Smear frosted slide — Gram film
   — Inoculate VCAT plate (GC plate)

   Throat swab   Inoculate VCAT plate (GC plate)

3. *Other tests* a. Candida culture in vulvovaginitis
   b. Herpes simplex culture if vesicles
   c. Pregnancy test
   d. Cervical cytology

4. *Forensic tests* — are these needed too? (See Ch. 16)

   Note: Work out local procedures with specialist in genitourinary medicine

Fig. 9.8 Suggested protocol for screening for STD in childhood.

clinically. However, if the child cannot cooperate and clinically there is concern, sedation or even a general anaesthetic should be considered. Always consider whether forensic swabs are indicated — usually only if the most recent sexual assault was within the last 72 hours.

An outline of treatment is given in Table 9.12.

(xii) Physical abuse

Physical abuse and CSA are closely related (Reinhardt 1987, Hobbs & Wynne 1990, RCP 1991). Approximately 1/6 of 769 physically abused children and 1/7 of sexually abused children had been physically abused and deaths occurred (Hobbs & Wynne 1990).

The injuries may be of the kind seen in physical assault, but there are patterns associated with CSA (Fig. 9.9). Grip marks on the inner aspect of the upper arms, the thighs and around the knees are common. Signs associated with partial suffocation, such as petechiae around the orbit and linear marks around the neck, are seen — presumably the assailant in an attempt to quieten the child has put a hand over the child's mouth or squeezed the neck.

Bruises on the lower abdomen, particularly over the pubis, and also around the hips where the child has been grasped are seen in CSA.

'Love-bites' are of concern whatever the age of the child and are usually on the neck, or breasts of older girls. Other bites are also relatively commonly seen, often on the back or shoulders.

Deliberately sadistic acts such as laceration of the dorsum of the penis are also seen or cuts to the

Table 9.12   Treatment of sexually transmitted diseases

	Treatment	Notes
Ophthalmia neonatorum — conjunctivitis within 21 days of birth:		Notifiable
1. Gonococcal	Systemic penicillin, e.g. benzylpenicillin 50 000 units/kg body wt/24 h in divided doses, b.d., 3 days Saline eye baths	Rarely generalised infection May be associated with chlamydia Investigate mother
2. Chlamydia	Systemic antibiotics, e.g. erythromycin ethylsuccinate 50 mg/kg body wt/24 h in divided doses, 14–21 days Saline eye baths	May be associated with pneumonia Severity of ophthalmia varies Investigate mother
	Adult doses given	
1. **Gonorrhoea** a. uncomplicated	Ampicillin 3 g orally with probenecid 2 g orally	Contacts ? Other infection ?
b. penicillinase-producing gonococcus or allergy to penicillin	Spectinomycin 2 g i.m. or co-trimoxazole 4 tab orally b.d. 2 days	
2. **Trichomonas**	Metronidazole 200 mg 8-hourly for 7 days or 2 g as single dose	Do not drink alcohol on drug Contact?
3. **Chlamydia**	Oxytetracycline 500 mg q.d.s. 7–14 days or erythromycin 500 mg q.d.s. 7–14 days	
4. **Herpes** Types 1 & 2	Primary attack — Acyclovir 200 mg 5 times/day, 5 days *Topically* Acyclovir cream *Secondary* attack — Septrin 2 tabs b.d. 7 days *Topically* Nystaform-HC cream t.d.s.	Check cervix cytology annually What is appropriate for children?
5. **Genital and anal warts**	*Adults* — podophyllin 10–25% twice a week *Cervical warts* — laser treatment *Children* — refer to paediatric surgeon for excision/diathermy	May be associated with malignancy, especially Types 16 and 18 Follow-up?
6. **Gardnerella or bacterial vaginosis**	Metronidazole 400 mg 12-hourly for 5 days	Contact?
7. **Candidiasis**	*Adults*, e.g. clotrimazole as local cream or pessary; systemically, e.g. fluconazole 150 mg *Children* — local cream, e.g. clotrimazole	Predisposing factors, e.g. diabetes, antibiotics
8. **Molluscum contagiosum**	Liquefied phenol or saturated solution of trichloroacetic acid applied to base of lesion with sharp stick	
9. **Viral hepatitis**	Prevention in high risk groups — hepatitis B vaccine Contacts — specific immunoglobulin Infant — active and passive immunisation at birth	Hepatitis A and B may be transmitted sexually
10. **HIV infection**	No method of immunisation No specific treatment AZT orally Treat opportunistic infection promptly	

labia or perianally. Burns and scalds are one of the least well recognised manifestations of abuse and clinical assessment may be difficult. Sadistic burns are inflicted to the genitalia and other 'abusive' sites such as the back of the hand, buttocks or back of the neck.

An important feature in the history is a description of repeated incidents of burning, each burn on its own perhaps having been dismissed as 'minor'.

Sexually abused children are murdered either in the course of the abuse or in order to silence them.

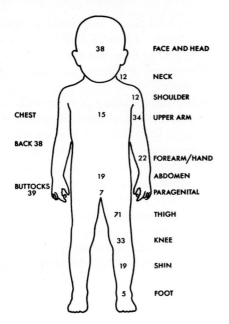

38	FACE AND HEAD
12	NECK
12	SHOULDER
CHEST 15	
34	UPPER ARM
BACK 38	
22	FOREARM/HAND
19	ABDOMEN
BUTTOCKS 39	
7	PARAGENITAL
71	THIGH
33	KNEE
19	SHIN
5	FOOT

Fig. 9.9 Distribution of bruises by site in 110 physically and sexually abused children. Figures refer to the number of children. (Reproduced with permission from Hobbs C J, Wynne J M 1990 The sexually abused battered child. Archives of Disease in Childhood 65: 423–427.)

CASE HISTORY 6

A girl aged 14 years told her mother that her step-father had been sexually abusing her since she was 6 years old. All the appropriate agencies were involved and the girl left to live with friends, the mother undertaking to protect her. She returned home. The girl was found dead with her mother; both had been involved in sexual intercourse before they were killed and the step-father was hanging from the bannister.

CASE HISTORY 7

A boy aged 4 years was found unconscious and bruised when his mother returned from shopping His father said he had been bouncing on his bed and fallen. On examination he had a badly bruised swollen face, retinal haemorrhages and anal signs of recent buggery. He died 5 days later of his head injury.

(xiii) Pregnancy

Pregnancy in girls should always be questioned and the girl be given time to talk and be counselled apart from her mother. This may be difficult to achieve.

Testing of blood groups, including DNA profiling, may help identify or confirm the alleged father or exclude others.

CASE HISTORY 8

A girl aged 12 years was taken to see a paediatrician when a schedule 1 offender moved into the family home. She was too embarrassed to allow a genital examination. The social worker and doctor were very concerned. Six months later she presented 28 weeks pregnant.

(xiv) Psychosomatic indicators

These are important because this may be the only way in which a child demonstrates his distress. The stresses on a child may be very many and range from the weekly spelling test to bullying in the playground or an alcoholic father; added to the list must be 'Is there any CSA?'

Recurrent abdominal pains. These are particularly common in the 5–10-year age group. The child usually complains of central abdominal pain and nausea, looks pale and may vomit. The pain may last from minutes to hours. The child feels unwell enough to need to lie down but then after a period of rest is completely well and resumes activity. There are no abnormalities on physical examination between attacks. Up to 10% of children complain of such pains at some time and there is often a family history of abdominal pain and also migraine.

Organic causes for the pain should be considered and, although more than 90% of children have no pathology, urinary tract infections and duodenal ulcers occasionally present in this way.

CSA is one of the stresses which should be explored, especially in children where the pain persists in spite of reassurance by the doctor.

Headaches. These become more common as children grow into adolescence and on enquiry the majority of teenagers will report recurrent headaches.

A child with severe recurrent headaches may have an underlying disorder such as an intracranial space-occupying lesion; a detailed history and examination are needed. The younger child, with morning headaches not relieved by analgesia and which worsen over weeks to months, clearly needs thorough investigation.

Migraine is the commonest recurrent headache in childhood and is usually associated with nausea or vomiting, visual disturbance, lethargy and unilateral headache. There is often a strong family history. Other 'tension headaches' are described with a heaviness or tight band, or sharp pain, including pain in the neck. Migraine and other headaches are usually a symptom of stress, although there may be an additional association with certain foods such as chocolate, or hunger, or excessive tiredness. Management involves looking into the child's lifestyle for identification of stress factors, one of which may be CSA. Treatment of headaches involves reassurance about lack of an organic cause (brain tumour) and simple analgesics, but essentially should deal with the stress precipitating the attacks.

CASE HISTORY 9

A boy of 11 years presented with migraine which was becoming disabling. He was a keen athlete but had had to withdraw from training because of headache. When examined he was underweight and had scars of self-mutilation on his forearms. Later he disclosed anal abuse by his older brother.

(xv) Anorexia and eating disorders

This is a relatively common disorder in adolescence but in its extreme form has a significant morbidity and mortality. CSA is now being recognised as one of the important antecedents to this disorder. Although girls are recognised to have anorexia more often than boys, if affects both sexes.

The age of onset is usually in the early teenage years but children as young as 10 or 11 years are also identified. It may begin with the teenager being very particular about her diet, the total calories and content, but then she eats less and less. She hides food, has tempers about eating food yet remains well and active, whilst becoming progressively thinner. Many children with anorexia have sessions of bingeing (bulimia); more recently recognised is their physical activity — they may swim, run and exercise in a similarly obsessive way. The girl's periods stop, or may never start.

Management is complex; in serious cases hospital admission is needed and individual family work with a child and family psychiatric team is usual.

(xvi) Constipation, soiling and encopresis

Constipation involves difficulty or delay in the passage of faeces. Soiling is the frequent passage of liquid or semi-solid faeces into clothing (Agnarsson & Clayden 1990). Encopresis is the passage of faeces of normal or near normal consistency into socially inappropriate places (including clothing) (Graham 1991).

Constipation and soiling is commonly seen in paediatric practice but encopresis, which is likely to be associated with considerable emotional trauma (including emotional abuse and CSA), is more commonly seen in child psychiatric clinics. There are emotional difficulties for any child who is not continent of faeces, and the groups overlap.

Soiling associated with constipation is usually seen in children of 3–6 years. It often follows a febrile illness and the constipation gradually worsens over months with child passing painfully, and infrequently, large stools, and soiling intermittently. Fissures may be caused with consequent pain and further retention of faeces.

Physical examination shows a well child with a distended abdomen and faecal masses easily palpable. Examination of the anus reveals soiling and a large faecal mass above the sphincter. A fissure may be visible but is uncommon, although excoriation and reddening of the perianal skin is a frequent finding.

Organic causes of constipation are uncommon and include:

- anorectal stenosis
- aganglionosis (Hirschsprung's disease)
- spinal cord lesion.

The diagnosis of the above disorders may be made on anal examination, with a tight sphincter and empty rectum in aganglionosis and an abnormally lax sphincter in spinal cord lesions.

Psychological factors in constipation (Graham 1991):

- parental factors (training too young, punitive, disorganised household)
- factors in child (delayed development, anxiety, fear)
- association with CSA (retention of faeces as a response to stress, especially in anal abuse).

Constipation also occurs in severely physically and mentally handicapped children. Whilst this may be due to dietary and other factors, handicapped children may be abused (Ch. 10).

Management of constipation:

- Consider pathology — organic, dietary or functional.
- Empty bowel — laxatives and faecal softeners.
- Enemas are best avoided but occasionally needed.
- Begin a re-training programme — relaxed, positive, gradual.
- Laxatives and softeners may be needed for several months.

Encopresis. At 3 years of age, 16% of children show signs of faecal incontinence once a week or more but at 4 years only 3% (Richman et al 1982), and at 7 years only 1.5% and by 10–11 years 0.8% (Graham 1991).

More boys than girls are affected by encopresis and there are no consistent social class differences. Encopresis usually starts before 5–6 years and may or may not be associated with constipation. The soiling occurs several times a day and may be at school and home or just at home.

Factors in encopresis (Graham 1991):

- parental (little significance or aggressive, punitive, conformity, high standards)
- child (developmental delay, fear, part of emotional disorder)
- family factors (tension, disharmony)
- life stress (bullying).

Abused children (CSA, emotional abuse) may be very angry; encopresis may be an expression of this anger and associated with smearing of faeces and other destructive behaviour. Other children, who may be depressed and fearful, express their distress through soiling. It may also be rationalised by the child 'If I'm smelly and dirty he'll leave me alone'.

Management

- Look at probable cause — if the abuse stops, the encopresis may be dramatically cured
- Look at child–parent relationship
- Positive encouragement and reward
- Behaviour modification
- Psychotherapy.

(xvii)   Enuresis

Enuresis is the involuntary emptying of the bladder at an age when continence is expected. This may be a problem during the day or night. Over 10% of children aged 5 years wet the bed and at least 10% of the bed-wetters wet during the day. Around 5% of 10-year-olds wet the bed, diminishing to 1% of adults. Children who have been dry and start to wet have often had an emotional upset, for example parental divorce.

Abused children may only become dry when they feel safe and are protected. Amongst persistent day-wetters there are increasing numbers of recognised victims of CSA (Bentovim & Boston 1988).

Factors associated with wetting:

- More often boys, and often family history of bedwetting
- More often socially disadvantaged, insecure or unstable family unit
- Behavioural problems in child
- Other signs of emotional distress in child (particularly in secondary wetting)
- Developmental delay
- Rigid, intolerant parental attitudes and high expectations
- Neglectful parents
- Angry child who deliberately wets as a hostile gesture.

Clinically:

- Exclude urinary tract infection.
- Ensure anatomy is normal, e.g. ectopic ureter.
- Check neurologically there are no signs.
- Look for signs of CSA (and other abuse).

Management (Graham 1991):

- Enquiry into signs of emotional disturbance, abuse
- Depends on age and motivation of child and family
- Reassurance of child and parents
- Positive rewards
- Bladder training
- Enuresis alarm
- Medication
- Psychotherapy.

(xviii)   Total refusal syndrome

This is a recent clinical description of the behaviour of a group of seriously psychologically disturbed children, usually adolescents, who take to their beds and in extreme cases will not feed, wash or toilet themselves. Inevitably the differential diagnosis has been with myalgic encephalomyelitis but clinical investigation suggests that a severe traumatic event(s), such as serious emotional and/or sexual abuse, is more important in the aetiology (Tranter, personal communication). Management involves admission to a specialist adolescent psychiatric unit to tackle the practical (i.e. food refusal) as well as the psychological disorder.

(xviii) Behavioural indicators

CSA may present as one of the 'ordinary' emotional and behavioural problems in childhood, such as bed-wetting, anxiety symptoms, or school failure (Lusk & Waterman 1986, Diagnosis of Child Sexual Abuse 1988, Sgroi et al 1988, Brown et al 1989).

The range of behaviours associated with CSA is wide as children express their distress in different ways. Occasionally children present with psychotic symptoms apparently precipitated by the stress of coping with sexual abuse in a vulnerable personality.

As with physical signs, some behaviours are relatively specific for CSA, such as sexually explicit play, whereas others are non-specific, such as nightmares or deterioration in school performance (Table 9.13) (Corwin et al 1988). An increasing proportion of children seen in child guidance and psychiatry clinics are now recognised victims of CSA (Lusk & Waterman 1986, Brown et al 1989). Children attending special schools for children with emotional problems are a group of children of whom the question 'why?' should always be put: could it be CSA (or other maltreatment) that is causing this child's deviant behaviour?

Recently three cases have been described of children demonstrating apparent mental deterioration where the cause was considered, initially, to be a deteriorating organic mental state, but was later shown to be the child's extreme reaction to sexual abuse (Brown et al 1989). The cardinal features of such states have been described as mental deterioration with loss of skills in language and play and general social withdrawal (Corbett et al 1977). The differential diagnosis in these

Table 9.13 Specific emotional and behavioural indicators of victimisation (Corwin 1988)

Pre-school (0–4 years)
1. Nightmares triggered by place, person, objects related or including physical movements or vocalisations that are consistent with sexually abusive experience
2. Premature eroticisation
   a. Preoccupation with genitals
   b. Repetitive seeking to engage others in differentiated sexual behaviour
   c. Excessive or indiscriminate masturbation or masturbation with objects
   d. Precocious, apparently seductive behaviour
   e. Depiction of differentiated sexual acts in doll play
3. Fearfulness
   a. Over-determined denial of genital anatomy and exposure to normal nudity
   b. Avoidance and anxiety in response to specific questions about differentiated sexual behaviour
   c. Unexplained person, gender, place, or object avoidance or fearfulness
4. Child's age-appropriate and circumstantially congruent description of being sexually abused
5. Dissociative phenomena

School age (6–11 years)
1–5. As for Pre-school, plus:
6. Sexual aggression and coercion towards other children
7. Cross dressing
8. Prostitution

Adolescents (12–18 years)
1–8. For School Age, plus:
9. Extreme sexual inhibition

children was considered to be autism, schizophrenia and neurodegenerative conditions such as lipidosis. The three children, all girls aged 5–6 years, improved and disclosed CSA on admission to a residential psychiatric unit.

THE MEDICAL EXAMINATION

The mechanics of any medical examination are important in order to minimise trauma for the child and family, but also to ensure that the maximum amount of information is learned from the examination.

The paediatrician may be asked to see a child who has made a clear disclosure. In these circumstances a social worker will usually give details of the disclosure to the doctor, who may need to clarify details of pain felt, or bleeding, but essentially accepts the history presented. A full medical history should still be taken (see below) but the child should not be expected to re-tell what may have been a distressing story.

On other occasions the child presents 'incidentally' (Table 9.4). In these circumstances some paediatricians will have developed skills in talking to children concerning abuse and feel able to use the anatomically correct dolls, line drawings, and so on. Other doctors prefer to note the physical signs and discuss their findings with colleagues (including a social worker) as described in Figure 9.1. Increasingly social workers and police officers, conduct 'disclosure interviews'. It may well be that the social worker needs to work for weeks or months with a child before the clinical picture does become clear. It has been shown that a too-rapid escalation of investigations may lead the child to refuse to talk, and although the child may be left unprotected in the short term, experienced workers learn to pace the interviews. This may be difficult for police officers if pressurised by senior colleagues to conduct one or two interviews and then make a decision, 'yes or no?'.

Increasingly too, videotapes are made of interviews with children. Again these require skilled interviewers as a poorly conducted interview may be used 'against' the child by lawyers. Few paediatricians have facilities to videotape their conversations with children, which is unfortunate as the spontaneous disclosures made by children during physical examinations are often not only clear but of good evidential value.

The facilities needed by doctors examining children who may have been sexually abused are described later in Chapter 14. The physical environment needed by children and families is equally important. But, however good the facilities, if the examining doctor is not sympathetic to the child's needs, is rushed, or is impatient the therapeutic contribution of the examination is lost.

The medical examination begins with a history. This may have been presented by the child's GP in a referral letter, by a parent or by a social worker or police officer. Older children may give their own medical history but younger children should (almost) always be accompanied by a parent, otherwise the medical background inevitably will be incomplete.

Forensic aspects of the medical examination

The entire medical examination is in essence a forensic one in that all aspects from the history to the physical examination to any investigations performed, for example to screen for STD or the presence of semen, may be used as evidence in court.

The term 'forensic examination' has become associated with the taking of swabs for evidence of sexual assault, for example looking for the presence of saliva, sperm, blood or fibres. As most abuse is ongoing and intrafamilial abuse such 'forensic tests' are uncommonly positive, and one study of 205 girls resulted in 2 positive swabs (Muram & Elias 1989). Another study performed particularly to evaluate the forensic aspects of CSA found that 40% of children had physical abnormality thought to be important evidentially and around 10% had positive swabs (Enos et al 1986). The advice given by forensic scientists in the UK (Frances Lewington, personal communication) has been to swab if there has been probable abuse within 48–72 hours (or 3–4 days in older girls); the results from this selected group show that around 10% of specimens will be positive.

However, careful physical examination is much more likely to give corroborative evidence of sexual assault. The physical signs seen vary with the type of abuse and when the last assault took place (Paul 1977). There will also be a difference in the recognition of physical signs depending upon the group of children seen, and their mode of presentation. Various studies show that between 10% and 80% of children will have abnormality (Enos et al 1986, Hobbs & Wynne 1987, 1989, Lindblad et al 1989, Muram 1989a, Muram & Elias 1989, Frothingham et al 1991).

Paediatricians will wish to build up a clinical picture based on the history, the investigations and presence of physical signs in order to have an opinion based on probability. It is on this balance of probability that children may be protected. The concept of the 'jigsaw of sexual abuse' in medical practice is established in Figure 9.3 (Butler-Sloss 1988 — letter from Professor Forfar p. 203, RCP 1991). In a criminal court, however, the Court will only want to hear what the physician found. What were the physical signs? What were they consistent with? The Court will not listen to hearsay evidence, what the child said to the doctor or teacher, whereas such evidence is admissible in family proceeding courts.

The doctor should record in his notes the place, date and time of examination, the reason for the examination and at whose request it took place. In these litigious times it is necessary to say who gave consent (even if verbal) and record who was present (Steiner et al 1988). The details of history, examination, but also which investigations (microbiological, haematological or forensic) were asked for should be recorded; for forensic swabs sent to the Regional Forensic Laboratory it should be noted to whom the specimens were given. This is the first step in the 'chain of evidence', the details of which must be maintained for court. The doctor should also label the specimens and sign the label (Paul 1984). This is discussed in more detail in Chapter 14. Clearly, forensic sampling depends upon the clinical situation. Paediatricians will usually need the assistance of a police surgeon in 'stranger rape', when a complete collection of swabs is mandatory.

Medical history

This includes the usual headings:

1. *History* of presenting complaint or allegation (see below).
2. *General health* — include emotional wellbeing, appetite, urinary and bowel history, symptoms of depression and menstrual history.
3. *Drug history.*
4. *Past medical history* of significant illness, such as hospital admissions for unexplained abdominal pain.
5. *Developmental history* or school progress.
6. *Immunisation history.*
7. *Family history* — do other siblings need examining?
8. *Social history* — what is known? Is the father a Schedule 1 offender (i.e. has he a previous conviction for offences against children)?

If the allegation is one of abuse, several points should be considered:

1. Has the child already made a clear disclosure, is it necessary to repeat the questioning? There may be specific information the doctor needs to know about the abuse (e.g. pain during abuse or bleeding) which is not available from the

professionals who have previously interviewed the child.

2. If the child has not made a clear disclosure, the doctor with paediatric skills is usually able to form a rapport with the child and may obtain a fuller history. Ideally the history includes details as to when, where, what, who, how often, over what time span, *did it hurt* (this is important when interpreting signs), when was the last assault, was there anyone else there, was lubricant used, what lubricant was it, where was it kept, was there ejaculation, where? The list is considerable but the more details there are, the more likely the police are to find corroborative evidence. Doctors may also feel able to ask about masturbation, oral sex, and anal sex, which others have avoided. Leading questions such as 'Was it in your bedroom?' are to be avoided, rather 'Where did it happen?'. It is, however, permissible to ask 'Did he put it (penis) anywhere else?'. If the direct question is asked 'Did he put it (penis) in your mouth?' record a nod, 'Did he put it (penis) in your bottom?' record a head shake, make clear notes of what was said. It is usual to talk to the child without parents present at some time during the history taking, even for children as young as 3–4 years.

3. The child may be unwilling to talk initially, but during and after the physical examination he may begin to talk; ask 'What made it sore?'.

4. For young, mentally slow or withdrawn children, the anatomically complete dolls are helpful in skilled hands.

5. Use of drawing in children may allow them to explain more easily.

6. Children may not want to repeat their story, they may feel they have said it once and should be believed. Pressure may lead to retraction, as children are effectively silenced by early disbelief, as they may be by threats from the abuser or even those they might expect to help, such as their mother.

7. Difficulty in history taking also arises with very young children. Although they remember the sequence of events their concept of a period of time and of number is immature. Thus a child of 2–3 years may understand one, two, a lot. If pressurised to give, for example, the number of times he was abused, he may guess a number which may well change and the child is dubbed

'unreliable'. Similarly a week, a month, a year are all a long time to a young child. Children do know who Daddy is, not all men are Daddy and children under 12 months know Daddy from other men. Colours are used to discredit children as witnesses — a child may helpfully guess 'red', at 3 years he is not untruthful, or confused, he just does not know.

8. If abuse has gone on over a prolonged period, particularly if the child is stressed by anxiety or fear, memories merge, especially if the abuse is by the same perpetrator(s) in the same environment. However rape by an uncle of an 8-year-old on her birthday will be fixed in time and place. If the abuse is by Dad, and involves touching, masturbation, oral sex, the child may remember the time when Mum caught him doing it, the first time he attempted vaginal intercourse and hurt her badly making her bleed, and so on. Children do not exaggerate as a rule. Clinical experience shows that they are more likely to understate their abuse.

9. It is necessary to ask older children if they are sexually active, and what this has entailed. Often teenagers have not discussed such matters with their parents and privacy should be ensured for this interview. Ask about the use of tampons. Remember to take a menstrual history and consider the possibility of pregnancy. Is the 'morning-after pill' needed?

10. Many children will only disclose months to years after the abuse has stopped, when they feel safe to tell. Children received into foster-care because of physical abuse may months later disclose sexual abuse. Children may disclose abuse by fathers when parents separate and they feel secure. Likewise children in residential schools or homes or in alternative care away from their abuser may tell, as long as they do not have to, or to avoid, return to the abusive home or school.

11. Traditionally children will only tell when they are ready, and this may be after months, years or never. An unresolved clinical problem for professionals is early recognition of the signs of CSA before the child is ready to talk. At one time it was thought that children confronted with the suspicion would be able to disclose, but this is clearly not so. The power of abusers to keep children (and wives) quiet should not be underestimated.

It may be that with recent publicity abusers are using greater threats than ever to keep their victims quiet — this would correspond with the age distribution of children who do disclose, either the very young, less than 5 years old, or teenagers. The younger ones may not be aware of the significance of telling and the older teenagers can run away, or move away, having some independence. Around 30–50% of teenage runaways say that they have been sexually abused at home (Ch. 17).

12. Children may feel a doctor 'can tell' during the physical examination and so disclose; this misunderstanding can be useful in allowing the child to talk.

13. If there is a history of assault with ejaculation in the last 2–3 days, it may be useful to do forensic tests: an appropriate examination should be arranged.

The past medical history. If practicable take a history from birth. Relationship problems between mother and child may have begun very early on. Record any significant illnesses, hospital admissions and operations. Children have their appendices removed because of persistent abdominal pain which may, in reality, have been a psychosomatic disorder. Has there been any other maltreatment in the past? There is not infrequently a history of physical abuse, particularly burns, failure to thrive, neglect, emotional deprivation or previous sexual abuse. Abused children are especially vulnerable to re-abuse, and several types of abuse may coexist. Have there been urinary tract symptoms in the past? Recurrent vaginal discharge? Have there been bowel problems, soiling, bleeding, pain on defecation? Is there a history of other trauma: broken limbs, burns, scalds?

Has the child had emotional problems, been referred to a psychologist or psychiatrist? The common problems of soiling, wetting, as well as school refusal, temper, anxiety, depression, anorexia and all the 'conduct disorders' — stealing, lying, fighting, glue-sniffing — have their origins somewhere.

How is the child coping socially? Does he have friends, how does he find school or nursery, can the child separate or is he clingy, does he separate too easily? How is he progressing academically?

A developmental history should be taken in younger children. Include in particular language development, social skills and emotional well-being — all of which may be adversely affected in CSA. Is he making progress is school?

A family history is important, as a picture of the child in the context of his family needs to be built up. The parents' ages, occupations and health are enquired into, followed by other children's ages, sex and wellbeing. Do the other children need to be interviewed and examined? It is uncommon for only one child in a household to be abused (Muram et al 1991). It is clearly of great importance if any adult within the household has a previous record of offences against children. These are designated Schedule 1 offences.

PART 2
THE PHYSICAL EXAMINATION

Historically doctors have not routinely examined girls' genitalia or children's bottoms after an initial inspection in the neonatal period. Although the vast majority of boys' testes have descended by 3 months of age (over 96%), boys' genitalia will be repeatedly re-examined whereas girls' only when there is a clinical indication, for example daytime wetting. The result is that most doctors, even children's doctors, have little experience of this examination and do not know the range of normality when inspecting genitalia (of girls) or bottoms (of children).

Current teaching suggests that to examine children routinely in this way is too intrusive although some would disagree (Meadow 1987). However, in the UK at present, practitioners should perhaps recognise the many ways in which CSA may present and so have a lower threshhold for examination. In this way doctors will examine more children and quickly learn the normal variants and which physical signs should cause concern. Therefore, whilst an allegation of CSA is clearly an indicator for physical examination, so also are wetting, soiling, vaginal discharge and unexplained abdominal pain, as well as other behavioural indicators.

When and why should children be physically examined?

There may be reticence on the part of parents and professionals to allow a child to be examined. Adults readily identify with the child and feel this is yet another intrusion into the child's privacy. Yet a well-conducted physical examination may have therapeutic as well as investigational attributes. The examination is clearly performed in the context of the history, and experience has shown that all children alleging sexual abuse should be seen by a paediatrician.

The examination is comprehensive, and includes an assessment of the child's growth, development, recognition of other forms of abuse, as well as the usual physical examination. The child's behaviour throughout should be noted, does it change when the genitalia are examined? Children may be over-active and excitable, only to become passive and frightened during the examination.

Six main reasons have been suggested as to why the possibly sexually abused child should be examined (Bamford & Roberts 1989):

- to detect traumatic or infective conditions which may require treatment,
- to evaluate the nature of any abuse,
- to provide forensic evidence,
- to reassure the child, who may feel serious damage has been done,
- to start the process of recovery,
- as the sibling of the index child.

When should the examination take place?

Examination should normally be arranged during the child's usual day. There is little place for evening examinations, at a time to suit the doctor rather than the child. If the assault is recent, that is within 48–72 hours, it may be that forensic specimens should be collected and the examination is arranged accordingly. There may be advantages to waiting a few days before examining a child, so work can be done to prepare the child for examination.

Where should the child be examined?

As discussed earlier, examination should usually take place at a local hospital with:

1. Quiet, child-orientated waiting room and examination rooms with appropriate toys and books.

2. Proper equipment:
    a. couch and usual examination tray
    b. bright light source
    c. STD screening pack
    d. forensic pack
    e. hand-held illuminated magnifying glass
    f. ± glass rods
    g. ± colposcope
    h. refrigerator (for specimen storage)
    i. camera.

3. Nursing staff to reassure child, weigh, measure the child, collect urine specimens, assist in the collection of other specimens, care for accompanying adults, and *chaperone the doctor* (essential medicolegally).

4. Adequate number of rooms to separate any parties as necessary. Separate interviewing facilities are also often needed. Ideally there should be a room with a one-way screen and sound and videotaping facilities.

The manner of the physical examination

The time taken over the history usually gives children the opportunity to settle and become accustomed to the unusual surroundings. The examination should be uninterrupted and taken at the child's pace. Many children aged 1–3 years find it more upsetting to have their ears looked into than their bottoms examined. However, this changes and by 5–6 years children are beginning to be clear about privacy and, as they are no longer in nappies, have become unused to being exposed. For young children the gender of the examining doctor seems less important than the manner of the examination. This also changes as the child grows older and ideally the child should have a choice, older girls often preferring a woman doctor and older boys a male doctor. The child should also choose who accompanies him during the examination. Older children may prefer to be examined alone, others may prefer a friend rather than a parent to be present. There is no reason why a police officer should be present, unless the officer has befriended the child and the child requests her presence.

Reassurance should be given to the child during the history taking and examination. The doctor should:

1. explain who he is.

2. explain all stages of the examination as he proceeds. There is no need to say 'It will not hurt'; this causes apprehension.

3. if appropriate, reassure that the child has been right to tell, and it is not his 'fault'.

4. reassure that there has been no 'damage'. Children and parents often have delusions about this, even to the extent of the effect on subsequent child-bearing.

5. if the girl is still technically a 'virgin' (i.e. the hymen remains) say so — this may be very important socially and culturally.

6. explain that unfortunately a lot of children are abused and it is never the child's fault.

7. avoid using terms such as scarring, which may cause unnecessary alarm.

Sedation or general anaesthetic

It is unusual to have to sedate a child although there are circumstances when it is essential (Table 9.14). Written consent should be sought before a child is sedated or anaesthetised.

Forensic specimens

The collection of forensic swabs is discussed in Chapter 14.

THE PHYSICAL EXAMINATION

The physical examination follows the normal paediatric routine. Children are usually weighed and measured by the nurse before the examination

Table 9.14 Indications for general anaesthetic or sedation

1. Distraught child where examination considered essential in order to further protect the child.
2. Painful injuries, e.g. vaginal wall tear, which need evaluation, i.e. for possible surgery.
3. Risk of STD and child unable to allow adequate screening (swabs).
4. Strong possibility forensic swabs would be useful and child unable to comply.
5. Foreign body.
6. Older child who wishes to comply but cannot due to anxiety.

(unless the child is distressed). This initial contact with the nurse may be very helpful to establish some rapport if specimens are to be collected later. The measurements should be taken in a standard way, on equipment that is regularly checked. The values are plotted on centile charts.

In order to gain the child's confidence examine the child gently from head to toe. It is also useful to screen for squint, dental caries, heart murmur and so on as the child may have been neglected medically as well as maltreated in other ways. When examining the abdomen note carefully if there are faecal masses. Does the child have dry skin, eczema or any other skin disorder?

If there are any signs of recent physical assault, bruises, burns or lacerations record the findings carefully. Measure any lesion in cm, describe colour, depth of scald or laceration and also the dimensions of any scars. Sexually abused children may present as though they have been physically abused, see Chapter 8, or with bruises perhaps more specific for CSA (Fig. 9.9; Hobbs & Wynne 1990). Record any signs of self-mutilation: usually cuts, bites, or nips of arms, upper chest or face.

The physical examination of pre-pubertal girls' genitalia

Children under the age of 3 years are usually best examined on their mother's knee and older girls in a similar supine frog-legged position on a couch. The prone knee–chest position may give a better view of the posterior margin of the hymen but is undignified and is only used in the UK if felt essential for the completeness of the examination.

Digital examination is rarely indicated although some practitioners use graduated glass rods which allow evaluation of the hymenal margin and the size of the hymenal opening. In skilled hands rods provide useful information, particularly in demonstrating tears, but their use has been questioned recently as measurements may be inaccurate because of the elasticity of the hymen (RCP 1991). Rarely it is necessary to pass a speculum to find the source of bleeding, but in this circumstance a general anaesthetic is needed.

The genitalia should be examined in a good light; an auriscope with the speculum removed provides light with magnification.

A colposcope gives the examiner a good light source, magnification, and a built-in camera. It allows the examiner a clear view of vascular patterns and minor abnormality as well as accurately measuring the hymenal opening. The use of a colposcope is further discussed on page 176. Although useful, a colposcope is certainly not essential.

The physical signs associated with genital abuse are listed in Tables 9.15 and 9.16.

The Tanner stages of puberty are given in Table 9.17, and the stage should be recorded.

The external genitalia should be inspected first for bruises, lacerations, burns, scars, skin disorders, or warts, vesicles and molluscum contagiosum.

The labia majora are gently separated and the urethra, perihymenal regions, hymen, posterior fourchette, and labia minora are visualised (Fig. 9.10).

The hymen, perihymenal tissues and posterior fourchette have a clear, lacy, vascular pattern. The mucosa appears much redder in pre- than post-pubertal girls. The normal introitus should be free

Table 9.15 Signs associated with genital abuse (for more complete description by site see Table 9.16)

---

1. Bruising, abrasions, reddening, oedema of external and internal genitalia
2. Recent or healing lacerations of labia, posterior fourchette
*3. Lacerations or scars on hymen which may extend to posterior vaginal wall
4. Dilated hymenal opening
*5. Attenuated hymen with loss of hymenal tissue
6. Multiple healed hymenal tears seen as clefts, rounded remnants, deficits in margin (n.b. congenital variants)
*7. Sexually transmitted disease
8. Vulvovaginitis (not STD)
9. Dilated and/or traumatised urethra
10. Labial fusion, of variable degree (usually posterior)
*11. Scars e.g. at posterior fourchette, vaginal wall
12. signs of uncertain significance are:
    - hyperpigmentation of perineum, inner thighs, perianally
    - periurethral and perivaginal synechiae
    - adhesions to vaginal wall
    - increased vascularity of hymen (Emmans et al 1987)
13. Remember to look for signs of:
    - other physical abuse
    - anal abuse/oral abuse
    - self-mutilation
    - eating disorder
14. Pregnancy

Note Signs marked * are highly correlated with abuse and in some instances diagnostic (see text).

Table 9.16 Signs associated with genital abuse

Site	Lesion	Description	Aetiology
Labia majora	Erythema	Reddening of skin	Inflammatory response to local irritation or skin disorder, or infection
	Bruising	Extravasation of blood into skin, initially red or reddish purple and undergoes colour change with time	Local trauma
	Burns/scald	Skin loss of varying degree, blister	Local trauma
	Oedema	Swelling of tissues	Associated with infection or trauma
	Abrasion, scratch, laceration	Superficial skin loss, initially pink or red, and moist, before healing with scab formation	Superficial trauma, e.g. finger-nail, scratches, frictional injury
	Scars	Area of altered skin, i.e. depigmented, thinned or thickened	Lacerations usually heal with a linear white scar which fades with time; burns or scalds, if partial thickness or deeper, scar in shape of initial lesion
	Vesicles	Small, painful vesicles surrounded by erythema — look at vulva	Is it HSV-1 or HSV-2 infection? Chicken pox
	Warts	Soft, white, broad-based or pedunculated lesions variable in size and number — look at vulva and anus	Usually a STD (see section on STD)
Vulvo vaginitis	Erythema, oedema	Swelling, reddening of vulval tissues may extend onto labia majora. Discharge yellow, greenish, white, watery, sticky, scanty, profuse.	Often no pathogenic organism is grown. If indicated, full screen for sexually transmitted diseases should be performed. Common in 2–5-year age group. Increased incidence of non-specific vulvovaginitis in CSA.
Labia minora, perihymenal area	Erythema	Reddening of mucous membrane	Inflammatory response to local irritation, e.g. bubblebath or infection, or trauma such as rubbing, also skin disorders
	Bruising	Areas of extravasation of blood which initially appear a darker red and after 24 hours are seen as deep red/purple	Trauma
	Oedema	Swelling of tissues	Associated with infection or trauma
	Abrasion, scratch, laceration	Loss of superficial layer of mucous membrane, appears as a red area of variable shape, n.b. seen better with colposcope	Trauma. Lesions heal very quickly in 1–7 days
	Warts, vesicles	As before	
	Labial adhesions	Agglutination of labia minora at posterior fourchette	Acquired lesion due to unknown cause or trauma
Posterior fourchette	Erythema, oedema, bruising	As vulva	
	Laceration	Tear usually running vertically from below	Distinguish scar from congenital midline streak
	Friability	Tissues readily tear and bleed	
	Scarring	Altered vascular pattern. Thickened white area, irregular shape	Important area of trauma in CSA
Hymen	Erythema, oedema, abrasion, bruising	As vulva, due to trauma; or superficial infection	
	Dilatation of hymenal opening	a. Attenuation with loss of hymenal tissue b. Wider than expected horizontal diameter for age: • 0.5 cm is upper end of normal at 5 years • 1.0 cm is not seen in pre-pubertal girls (labial separation — not traction)	Penetrating trauma with blunt force (RCP 1991) Stretching of hymen as in digital penetration Hymen is elastic and recovery may take place Different methods of examination important

Table 9.16 *Cont.*

Site	Lesion	Description	Aetiology
	Deficit	Discontinuity in margin. Differentiate from notch in crescentic hymen at 11 and 1 o'clock	Penetrative tear
	Mound or bump	Seen in margin of hymen, may be multiple: • associated with disruption of hymen • often posterior	Trauma causing tears to hymen with healing causing the irregularity Often associated with dilated hymen
	Tears	If very recent (< 24 hours) may see bleeding. Complete or incomplete transection of hymen, may extend to vaginal wall	Penetrative stretching
	Shape of hymen	Attenuated	Penetrative trauma (may be gradual rubbing away or more acute disruption)
		Posterior rim or heart or crescentic shape (all variants of same) Annular Fimbriated	Congenital variants
		Horse-shoe shape	May represent anterior tears, but hymen often deficient anteriorly: look for other signs — scarring, dilated hymen
		Asymmetry of shape e.g. 'V' at 6 o'clock, sharp angle, square angles, any major distortion	May represent healed tears in hymen, look for scarring, disruption of hymen
	Scar	White, irregular, thickened area	Previous trauma — RARE
Vagina	Bruising, abrasion	Areas of darker red on vaginal wall	Penetrative trauma
	Dilated/gaping	To accommodate 1 or more fingers (1.5 cm–4.0 cm) at puberty	Repeated dilatation leads to widening, lengthening of vagina with eventual loss of rugae
	Loss of rugae	Flattening of rugae	
	Tears	Extending from hymen to posterior vaginal wall	Severe penetrative trauma leading to tear which may scar
	Scar	Posterior wall scarring	
Urethra	Erythema, oedema, bruising, dilatation	Reddened, swollen periurethral tissues, pouting urethral meatus	Rubbing — see as part of vulvitis Urethra may also be penetrated by foreign body
Perineum, inner thighs, perianally	Pigmentation	Increased pigmentation of skin	Due to repeated friction as in intercrural intercourse. Non-specific sign also seen in obesity

from all scarring. Bands of tissue may be seen running across the periurethral, perihymenal tissues or within the vagina. These are called 'support bands' and their significance is not clear but they are probably a normal variant.

If the child has been masturbated roughly there may be uniform erythema, swelling of the tissues and even superficial lacerations of the labia minora or posterior fourchette caused by finger-nails.

Blunt trauma, as in inter-crural or attempted vaginal intercourse, gives marked erythema, which may extend onto the labia majora, and oedema which may obscure the hymenal opening. There may be bruising, but this is uncommon. Localised abrasions, often lateral to the hymen, are seen in digital and penile abuse.

The urethra should be inspected. The orifice may appear to 'pout' after vigorous rubbing and occasionally abusers thread objects into the urethra, causing actual dilatation and trauma to the tissues.

When the labia are separated the hymen may be clearly visible, but often the hymen appears closed and in order to see the hymenal margins it is necessary to apply gentle pressure downwards and laterally or to lift the labia and apply gentle downward pressure for a few seconds (Figs 9.11 and 9.12). These manoeuvres affect the dimensions of

Table 9.17 Stages of puberty (after Tanner 1978)

Breast development

Stage 1 Pre-adolescent: elevation of papilla only.

Stage 2 Breast bud stage: elevation of breast and papilla as small mound. Enlargement of areola diameter.

Stage 3 Further enlargement and elevation of breast and areola, with no separation of their contours.

Stage 4 Projection of areola and papilla to form a secondary mound above the level of the breast.

Stage 5 Mature stage: projection of papilla only, due to recession of the areola to the general contour of the breast.

Pubic hair

Stage 1 Pre-adolescent. The vellus over the pubes is not further developed than that over the abdominal wall, i.e. no pubic hair.

Stage 2 Sparse growth of long, slightly pigmented downy hair, straight or slightly curled, chiefly along labia.

Stage 3 Considerably darker, coarser and more curled. The hair spreads sparsely over the junction of the pubes.

Stage 4 Hair now adult in type, but area covered is still considerably smaller than in the adult. No spread to the medial surface of thighs.

Stage 5 Adult in quantity and type with distribution of the horizontal (or classically 'feminine') pattern. Spread to medial surface of thighs but not up linea alba or elsewhere above the base of the inverse triangle (spread up linea alba occurs late and is rated stage 6).

Genital (penis) development

Stage 1 Pre-adolescent, testes, scrotum and penis are of about the same size and proportion as in early childhood.

Stage 2 Enlargement of scrotum and testes. Skin of scrotum reddens and changes in texture. Little or no enlargement of penis at this stage.

Stage 3 Enlargement of penis, which occurs at first mainly in length. Further growth of testes and scrotum.

Stage 4 Increased size of penis with growth in breadth and development of glans. Testes and scrotum larger, scrotal skin darkened.

Stage 5 Genitalia adult in size and shape.

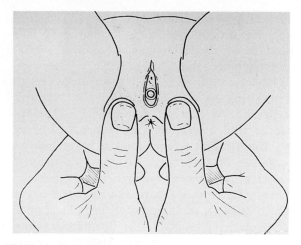

Fig. 9.11 Diagram to illustrate separation as a means of achieving relaxed visualisation of the hymenal opening.

the hymenal opening and the method of examination should be noted. A gaping orifice on labial separation is suggestive of abuse (RCP 1991).

Occasionally the posterior part of the hymen is not visible by this method or it appears rolled; examining the child in the knee–chest position will allow better visualisation.

McCann (1990) found, by using a combination of examination methods in 172 pre-pubertal girls aged 10 months to 11 years, that in only 2 children did the vaginal introitus not open. Labial traction was more successful than labial separation and the knee–chest position was the most successful.

The hymen is the membrane across the opening of the vagina. In the newborn period and infancy

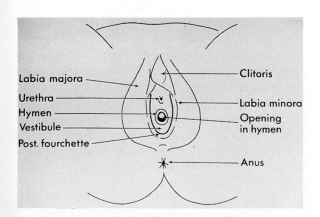

Fig. 9.10 Anatomy of normal pre-pubertal female genitalia.

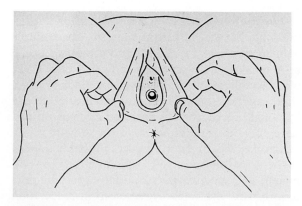

Fig. 9.12 Diagram to illustrate labial traction as a means of achieving relaxed visualisation of the hymenal opening.

it is relatively thick under the effects of maternal oestrogen but changes, being thinner and less redundant during childhood until puberty, when it once again becomes oestrogenised.

Consequently, until the age of 2–3 years the hymen remains redundant, fleshy and sometimes sleeve-like. As the girl grows older it becomes thinner until, again under the influence of oestrogen, the hymen becomes thicker, redundant and sleeve-like or fimbriated. Hymenal elasticity increases with pubertal development.

Imperforate hymen is rare and *congenital absence* of hymen very rare. In one study in 1131 newborn infant examinations, all 1131 infants were noted to have a hymen (Jenny et al 1987). Between 3 and 4% had hymenal variants such as tags and transverse hymenal bands. The highest possible frequency of congenital absence of hymen was calculated as less than 0.3%. The authors conclude that if hymenal tissue cannot be identified traumatic disruption should be considered as the likely cause.

The central opening varies in shape between thin and crescentic, annular, frilly, midline bar, cuff-like and punctate (Herman-Giddens & Frothingham 1987). The margin may be smooth, thin or rounded. The hymen is often more pronounced posteriorly and relatively deficient anteriorly.

The annular hymen and posterior ring configurations (crescentic) are the commonest two variants (McCann 1990). The posterior rim appears to be commoner in older girls (RCP 1991).

Rarely a bifid hymen is seen and this may be in association with a septate vagina and bicornuate uterus.

The hymenal opening is usually symmetrical in mid-childhood. Marked asymmetry, for example a small notch at 11 o'clock and a marked notch at 1 o'clock, may represent a healed tear at 11 o'clock. Likewise a 'V' shape at 6 o'clock or other sharp angles, square angles or distortions of the hymenal margin should be noted as signs of possible previous trauma.

Minor bumps in the margin are probably normal variants but bumps in association with a distorted hymen and vascular pattern, seen especially posteriorly and also laterally, are seen in association with abuse. The hymenal rim is usually thin and smooth with a clear vascular pattern.

The hymenal opening may appear to wink during examination; this is normal.

Measurement of the hymenal opening depends on the method used to examine the child (McCann 1990) and the measuring device. A rigid tape measure placed adjacent to the child's genitalia gives an adequate assessment of the horizontal dimension. Photographs taken using a colposcope may be accurately measured. Graduated glass rods are also more precise as measuring instruments but their use has recently been questioned, given the elasticity of the hymen (RCP 1991). However, if the smallest rods are used, the point at which stretching occurs should be evident.

The horizontal diameter of the hymenal orifice increases only a little with age, up to 0.4 cm at 4 years (Woodling 1986). The opening in a girl of 5 years is rarely more than 0.5 cm (Huffman et al 1981). When early signs of oestrogen effects are visible the hymenal orifice 'will measure 7 mm or more in diameter by the time a reaction to oestrogen is grossly visible' and is around 1 cm when puberty is complete (Dewhurst 1988).

The above figures are from standard gynaecology texts but what are recent research findings? Research findings in pre-pubertal girls are summarised below:

• Cantwell (1983): 74% of children with a vaginal introital opening greater than 0.4 cm had a history of CSA.

• Herman-Giddens & Frothingham (1987): 4% of children with a vaginal introital opening of greater than 0.4 cm denied a history of CSA.

• White et al (1989): 94% of children with an introital diameter greater than 0.4 cm had a history of sexual contact.

• Goff et al (1989): a study of 373 girls at routine health checks showed that in supine frog-leg position the mean diameter in the first year of life was 0.17 cm rising to 0.25 cm at 7 years.

• Emmans et al (1987); in a study of 3–6-year-old girls ('normals'), recorded measurements of 0.29 ± 0.13 cm (with a range 0.1– 0.6 cm).

• McCann et al (1990b): in a study of girls selected for non-abuse

2–4½ years	Labial separation	0.39 ± 0.14 cm (range 0.1–0.55 cm)
	Labial traction	0.52 ± 0.14 cm (range 0.2–0.8 cm)

5–7 years   Labial separation 0.42 ± 0.17 cm
                                    (range 0.1–0.8 cm)
              Labial traction   0.56 ± 0.18 cm
                                    (range 0.1–0.9 cm)

8 – Tanner Labial separation 0.57 ± 0.16 cm
stage 2
                                    (range 0.3–0.8 cm)
              Labial traction   0.69 ± 0.20 cm
                                    (range 0.25–1.5 cm)

(Measurements in knee–chest position are greater)

- McCann et al (1990a): in a study of girls in a CSA evaluation clinic,

Pre-school Labial separation 0.35 ± 0.14 cm
                                    (range 0.1–0.7 cm)
              Labial traction   0.57 ± 0.16 cm
                                    (range 0.1–1.0 cm)

Early   Labial separation 0.40 ± 0.16 cm
school
                                    (range 0.25–1.0 cm)
              Labial traction   0.59 ± 0.17 cm
                                    (range 0.25–1.0 cm)

Pre-   Labial separation 0.50 ± 0.20 cm
adolescent
                                    (range 0.2–0.9 cm)
              Labial traction   0.65 ± 0.21 cm
                                    (range 0.3–1.0 cm)

(Measurements in knee–chest position are greater)

- Paul (1990), in a commentary on his experience as a police surgeon, records that diameters of 0.2–0.9 cm may be normal.
- Bamford & Roberts (1989) say that the unstretched hymenal orifice in most young girls is no more than 0.5–0.6 cm.
- RCP (1991) suggest that at puberty the horizontal diameter is approximately 1 cm, that a diameter of more than 1 cm is not seen in normal pre-pubertal children, and a hymenal size of 1.5 cm in association with other trauma would be highly suggestive of abuse. The report emphasises that this is supportive evidence of CSA but not diagnostic on its own.
- Heger & Emmans (1990) in a useful paper summarised the findings:

    a. Healing is rapid and even in cases where there has been penetration there may be normal findings (Muram 1989b).

    b. A horizontal diameter of >0.4 cm is associated with abuse (Cantwell 1987, White et al 1989).

    c. Care must be taken in over-emphasis of measurements of only a few mm (Paradise 1989).

    d. The size of the hymenal opening depends on:

       — the age of the child
       — the pubertal development
       — the position of the child
       — the degree of labial traction
       — the relaxation of the child
       — obesity of the child.

    e. The usual shape of the opening is annular (that is encircles the hymen) or crescentic (absent 11–1 o'clock).

    f. Healing may lead to contraction of the opening as a result of scar formation (Cantwell 1987).

    g. Healing may take place when the child is protected from further CSA (Cantwell 1987) unless the hymen is attenuated, when it cannot recover.

    h. A diagnosis of CSA is made on all the evidence, not one single sign.

    i. A normal hymenal opening does not exclude CSA and minor abnormality does not prove CSA.

Hymenal tears (transections or lacerations) may occur at any site. Those caused by penile or attempted penile penetration are likely to cause greater damage than those caused by digital penetration and are commonly found at 5–7 o'clock and may extend on to the posterior fourchette and occasionally the posterior vaginal wall. *Synechiae* or bridging scars may be seen following these penetrative injuries. *Scars* at the posterior fourchette are thickened, white irregular areas, which disrupt the usual lacy vascular pattern. They are to be differentiated from the congenital flat, white, midline streak (Herman-Giddens & Frothingham 1987) or the area of relative pallor seen in the midline in some non-abused girls (McCann 1990).

Tears caused by digital penetration may be caused circumferentially but are commonly seen between 9 o'clock and 3 o'clock anteriorly.

In association with tears there are often other signs of abuse, such as a gaping hymenal orifice or abrasions to the perihymenal area but it is uncommon to see tears bleeding as they heal so rapidly, that is in 1–3 days. When tears heal they may leave:

- V-shaped notches in the hymenal margin,

- clefts (note that the hymen is often deficient anteriorly and clefts at 12 o'clock are a normal variant),
- a bump (where a tear has healed and the apposed sides have not been accurately aligned — there is often some thickening and disruption of the hymen),
- an asymmetrical, square or distorted shape to the hymenal orifice (differentiate from the notches at 10 and 2 o'clock of a crescentic hymen).

Physical signs and the reported abuse do not always correlate as expected (Muram 1989b). Tears are the most common finding in girls who describe penile or digital penetration. If the disruption of the hymen is more forcible, causing multiple tears, only remnants or tags of hymen may remain. However, even if there has been a history of vaginal penetration, up to one-third of girls have no abnormality on examination (57% if digital penetration, 3.5% if penile; Muram 1989b). With continued healing fewer and fewer signs are evident. Definite scars in the hymen are rare, but a thickened, irregular margin of a distorted hymen is seen — the changes are usually laterally or inferiorly.

Earlier teaching based on gynaecological practice suggested that hymenal tears do not heal. Experience of CSA shows that if abused girls cease to be involved in sexual activity healing does take place unless the hymen is attenuated (rubbed or worn away by chronic abuse). An attenuated, scarred hymen is never seen in normal children (RCP 1991).

Occasionally a traumatised hymen will heal to obliterate the orifice, hence the term 'acquired' imperforate hymen (Berkowitz et al 1987).

Labial fusion — the partial or complete adherence of the labia minora — is seen in infancy and early childhood. McCann et al (1988) described adhesions seen in non-abused children aged 2 months to 7 years as very superficial, semi-transparent and easily ruptured by lateral traction. The majority were diagnosed under the age of 2 years, disappearing by puberty. The incidence of these adhesions was 1.4%. In a later study of girls selected for non-abuse (McCann 1990) the incidence of labial fusion was reported as 39% but

in 19/35 girls the fusion was 2 mm or less and only seen on magnification using a colposcope. The incidence of labial fusion in sexually abused girls has been reported in 3–18% of girls (Berkowitz et al 1987, Emmans et al 1987).

Labial fusion occurs secondary to denudation of the upper squamous epithelial layer of the labial mucosa with the formation of a thin connective tissue bridge (Rimsza & Feingold 1989) and is caused by inflammatory disorders, including vulvitis and nappy rash, or trauma.

McCann et al (1988) described injury to the posterior fourchette by intracrural or intralabial intercourse causing trauma to the tissues which varied in severity from reddening to deep laceration, leading to labial fusion.

Labial fusion in CSA often follows trauma which is more violent than the irritation or infection associated with nappy rash, but the adhesions may be indistinguishable clinically.

In CSA labial fusion may be:

- Longer, 0.2–1.0 cm (or more)
- Superficial, semi-transparent, easily ruptured
- Thick, irregular (more like a scar) in more severe injury
- Not necessarily in the midline (distinguish from midline raphe)
- Associated with a disrupted vascular pattern
- In older girls (Bays & Jenny 1990)
- Indistinguishable from the 'innocent' labial adhesions secondary to nappy rash (RCP 1991).

Other signs associated with genital abuse include:

- Vulvitis (erythema ± oedema)
- Vulvovaginitis
  a. non-specific
  b. STD
- Pouting or dilated urethra
- Areas of friability, e.g. posterior fourchette
- Foreign body in vagina
- Self-mutilation of genitalia (not caused by ordinary masturbation; Bays & Jenny 1990)
- Pregnancy.

Foreign body in vagina. Foreign bodies in the vagina are unusual (Paul 1986); less than one case is seen each year in over 600 children examined annually because of possible CSA in Leeds.

The child may complain of pain, there may be bleeding and later a purulent vaginal discharge.

Young children know about micturition and defaecation but not of the presence of a vagina. Masturbation involves rubbing the clitoris. Insertion of objects through the hymen hurts; they are likely to have been inserted by a third party. If the child has inserted objects herself CSA should be seriously considered.

The physical examination of pubertal and post-pubertal girls

Children do not like being examined for physical signs of possible CSA and in general the older they are the more distressed they feel. Although examining children in different positions — knee–chest, supine with traction and supine with separation of the labia — may lead to a very thorough examination (McCann et al 1990) it must be considered whether the extra upset to the child is justified. If there is concern about the posterior aspect of the hymen, consider asking the girl to be examined in the knee–chest position, but do not 'flip' children over automatically.

Maintain as much privacy for the girl as possible by the use of screens, a sheet, and only have present a minimum of adults (discuss with the girl).

As with younger girls, a full physical examination is necessary: note bruises, bites and lacerations as well as signs of trauma to the genitalia and anus.

In many instances it is possible to gain adequate information with the girl examined supine in the frog-legged position, without use of stirrups or specula. However, assessment of the hymenal margin and dimensions of the opening is not possible by inspection alone. The orifice may appear deceptively small despite penetration having occurred, due to the elasticity of the hymen (RCP 1991). A gentle digital vaginal examination is necessary to look for hymenal tears in the oestrogenised, more redundant hymen. Glass rods or a small plastic syringe may also be used to display the margin of the hymen. Vaginal examination is needed to assess the size of the hymenal opening and the vagina.

The hymenal opening will admit just the tip of the fifth finger (about 1 cm) at around menarche. If this causes discomfort it suggests that nothing larger has penetrated the child. If an index finger (1.5–2.0 cm approximately) can be inserted without discomfort, this would be compatible with previous digital penetration or use of tampons. A two-finger examination without discomfort (that is 3.5–4.5 cm) would be compatible with penile penetration, although if the child has been infrequently penetrated she will complain of discomfort. Repeated vaginal intercourse leads to a widened, lengthened vagina with loss of vaginal rugae.

This examination can be completed quite quickly and although girls dislike digital vaginal examination it is easier for them than a full gynaecological examination. However, if it is necessary to swab the cervix (if, for example, there is a risk of gonorrhoea), the smallest appropriate speculum should be used and in these circumstances a paediatrician would usually work in association with a gynaecologist or genitourinary specialist.

When interpreting physical signs it is important to know if the girl has used tampons, and whether or not she is sexually active. A recent study (Curtis et al 1989) showed that 19% of girls and 16% of boys have had intercourse at 15 years. Girls who have been sexually abused previously are more likely to be sexually active than their peers.

Use of tampons is not associated with bruising, abrasion, laceration or other hymenal damage but repeated use may lead to minor stretching of the orifice (Woodling & Kossoris 1981, RCP 1991).

It is important to recognise when to screen girls for STD and abnormal cervical cytology. Clearly, sexually active girls with many partners are at risk but do they take precautions? A recent study (Clarke et al 1990) showed that such girls were anxious about HIV infection but they continued to behave in a high-risk way. Half of the group of 56 sexually active 12–16-year-old girls never used a contraceptive.

Although anal abuse is less common in older girls, always look at the anus. The incidence of anal intercourse between adults is not known; it is illegal but is probably much more widely practised than is acknowledged. The relatively common occurrence of additional anal abuse in rape is also recognised.

Rape and STD (Forster 1992)

The prevalence of STDs amongst rape victims varies, and is greater where there has been an attack by a stranger or multiple assailants. Also, because of the long incubation period, for example of warts, follow-up may be needed over 6 months if all infections are to be recognised, and HIV infection is to be excluded.

It is suggested that all rape victims be screened for STD (after forensic tests) and:

- post-coital contraception offered
- follow-up at 3 months
- HIV testing as indicated
- prophylactic antibiotics avoided unless it is known that the assailant was infected
- girls referred for emotional support and counselling.

The colposcope (Woodling & Heger 1986, Muram & Elias 1989, McCann 1990)

The colposcope is an instrument for visualisation of the adult cervix and for the management of cervical disease, including neoplasia. The instrument was first used in sexual abuse diagnosis by Teixeira, and some examiners in the USA have begun to use it.

The instrument consists of a powerful and adjustable light source and binocular and variable magnification. One of the most important advantages of the equipment is that an integral camera permits simultaneous photographs to be taken during the examination without the use of an additional light source. The instrument is most valuable for detailed examination of the female genitalia including the hymen, although visualisation of the anus is, of course, also possible. The instrument, however, is expensive, relatively non-portable and requires some skill in its use, particularly with young children who usually are unable to lie perfectly still.

35 mm single lens reflex, Polaroid and video cameras can all be used, with still photographs obtainable from video film. 35 mm probably provides the best quality results in the form of slides or prints.

Evaluation. Reports, of the usefulness of the colposcope in improving the quality and precision of diagnosis in child sexual abuse work are few. The initial impression is that other simpler forms of magnification and lighting (e.g. the otoscope) may provide broadly similar results and should be viewed as generally acceptable methods of examination. By providing a higher quality image and a simple means of recording this, however, it is likely that the colposcope will assist, especially in the more difficult cases. Further evaluation is needed, but it is likely that where funds permit, the colposcope will be a useful alternative tool.

What is clear, however, is that this is not an essential item of equipment and does not supplant other methods. In the end it is the experience and observational skills of the examiner which are the most important factors. Initial use in Leeds indicates that the instrument is acceptable to parents and children, who can usually be involved by inviting them to look down the eyepieces.

As the use of photography increases as a means of recording and avoiding further examination, the colposcope is likely to come into its own. Another development is the incorporation of a graduated measure in order to assess directly the diameter of the hymen.

Physical signs — genital abuse, healing and other disorders

Disclosure remains the most common form of presentation of CSA, occurring in 40% of children in the 1989 Leeds series, with a further 20% disclosing during the initial investigation (Frothingham et al 1991).

Abnormal genital physical signs were found in 58% of the girls in the abuse series (mean age 6.9 years). This is a higher figure than in other series and probably reflects the easily available appointments for physical examinations in Leeds (RCP 1991). Within days to weeks healing may be complete and Marshall et al (1988) reported normal findings in 71% of sexually abused girls, including 48% with a history of interlabial penetration. Muram (1989b) in his review of sexually abused girls found definite signs in 16% of girls who gave a history of digital abuse and in 86% of girls who reported penile penetration, but only 57% and 3.5% of these two groups were felt to have normal genitalia. Clearly, serious CSA

Table 9.18 Differential diagnosis of genital signs

1. Recent trauma due to sexual interference
2. Accidental injury, e.g. straddle injury
3. Vulvitis, e.g. threadworms, bubblebath, trauma
4. Skin disorder, e.g. lichen sclerosus, eczema
5. Congenital abnormality, e.g. vascular lesion
6. Infection, e.g. candida after antibiotics
7. Infection complicating trauma as in CSA
8. Previous trauma with scarring
9. Urethral caruncle, haemangioma, prolapse, polyp

including penetration may occur without there being persistent physical abnormality, such as tears.

All signs (diagnostic or supportive) must be assessed in the context of the history and a clinical judgement made as to their significance. It must be remembered that normal physical examination is to be expected in as many as two-thirds of sexually abused girls (RCP 1991).

Interpretation is made more difficult if there is coexisting disease or infection (Table 9.18) or if the examination has taken place some days or weeks after the last assault when healing will have occurred (Table 9.19).

Some physical signs, such as erythema, are non-specific, but a child who complains of soreness, perhaps dysuria, and says that she has been 'rubbed by Grandpa' is presenting a history consistent with the clinical signs.

Supportive signs of genital abuse include (American Academy of Pediatrics 1991, RCP 1991):

- an enlarged hymenal opening
- a notch in the hymenal edge which may be associated with scarring, distortion of hymen
- a bump in the hymen, plus some disruption
- localised erythema, oedema, pouting urethra, minor abrasions
- mounded scar at posterior fourchette
- labial fusion
- chafing, abrasions of inner thighs, genitalia.

Other signs which are highly significant or diagnostic (American Academy of Pediatrics 1991, RCP 1991):

- lacerations or scars in hymen, which may extend to posterior vaginal wall
- attenuation of the hymen with loss of hymenal tissue
- pregnancy
- STD
- positive forensic tests.

Healing (Table 9.19) and the *resolution of physical signs* are not yet adequately researched. As has been described earlier, hymenal tears may heal in different ways, and the hymenal orifice once stretched may again diminish in size (Cantwell 1987) unless there has been loss of hymenal tissue (attenuated or disrupted hymen).

An attempt has been made to correlate the relationship between sexual acts and genital findings (Muram 1989b) and the outcome of anogenital trauma (Finkel 1989).

In Muram's (1989b) study the girls examined

Table 9.19 Approximate guide to healing of genital signs

Time	Stain bruises	Labia majora bruises	Vulval abrasion/ bruising lacerations	Vulval oedema	Tears in hymen	Deficit/scar in hymen	Scars at posterior fourchette	Dilation of hymen
Hours	Red-purple	+	+	+	+	+	−	+
1–3 days	Purple-swollen Yellow 3+	+	±	+	+	+	−	+
3 days	Yellow Fading Brown	±	±	±	±	+	−	+
2 weeks	±	−	−	−	−	+	±	±
3 weeks	±				−	+	+	±
Longer	±					+	+	may reverse completely or remain fixed, gaping

Note: Bruising of mucous membranes may be difficult to detect clinically — there is no good clinical method available; photography and follow-up may help.

were victims of CSA and the assailant had confessed to the type of assault. The mean age of this group of 31 girls was 9.1 years (range 1–17 years). In 29% of the girls there was no abnormality, 26% had non-specific changes (erythema, vulvovaginitis, labial fusion) and only 45% had abnormal findings (vaginal tears, hymenal opening greater than 1 cm). It is also important to note that even when the assailant admitted digital or penile penetration, 37% of the girls had no abnormalities at all or only non-specific abnormalities. This was true of pre-pubertal as well as more sexually mature children.

Hymenal tears are the commonest persisting sign of genital abuse. Inflammation, bruising and superficial lacerations heal in less than one week (Table 9.19).

Scars are rarely seen, and the common site is the posterior fourchette (Hobbs & Wynne 1987a, McCann et al 1988). It is important to differentiate scars at 6 o'clock from a congenital midline raphe or linear white streak. Scars are usually thicker and irregular, and healing has left a distorted vascular pattern. The reasons why supportive evidence of CSA is only seen in a minority of children are due to:

- the type of abuse
- the frequency of abuse
- the force used
- the age of the child
- the presence of infection
- the stage of the healing process.

Muram (1989c) in his evaluation found that fewer than a third of children had signs considered specific for a diagnosis of CSA and even these altered with time, for example hymenal opening greater than 1 cm, hymenal laceration, bites.

Healing involves regeneration and repair (Finkel 1989). Superficial lacerations and abrasions heal by regeneration only. The process begins with thrombosis and inflammation followed by regeneration of the epithelium with new cell formation and then differentiation into a new surface epithelium. The wound heals by 48–72 hours and differentiation is complete in 5–7 days. The superficial injury has thus healed without residue in a week.

If, however, the laceration has been deeper and healing involved repair with formation of granulation tissue, there will subsequently be scar tissue. Regeneration in this situation is followed by organisation, which is the replacement of coagulated blood by granulation tissue, and wound contraction. The granulation tissue appears red initially but with time, as the cellular and vascular components of the tissue decrease, its colour changes to become paler and it becomes smaller. Most scars mature in around 60 days. However, as the scar contracts it may distort the surrounding tissues in an unexpected way. The final scar is much smaller than the original injury.

Appreciation of the effects of healing by secondary intention may help to explain the grossly distorted architecture seen in abused girls on occasion. It should also be remembered that the prolonged incubation period of some STD also leads to new signs appearing even when the child was thought to be protected.

Accidental genital injuries. West et al (1989) described three types of injury:

- By far the commonest injury seen was straddling.
- Accidental penetration of the labia minora was the next commonest. In West's series no accidents involving penetration of the hymen were seen.
- Tearing due to forced abduction of the legs, such as in gymnastics and some falls, was rare.

The history should be of a sudden, painful injury with immediate bleeding. The history is usually dramatic (Bays & Jenny 1990).

Physical examination

- Straddle injuries are caused by the forced compression of soft tissues between the object straddled and the underlying bone, that is the pubic symphysis and rami. The injury may affect the mons, clitoris, urethra and the anterior part of the labia majora and minora. The soft tissue injury may be linear, asymmetrical and coincide with the bone. The hymenal opening is not dilated (Muram 1986, West et al 1989). There may be marked swelling and bruising in the traumatised tissue, and on occasion lacerations (Enos et al 1986).
- Accidental penetration of the labia is seen more often in young girls, from 18 months to

3 years, who fall astride toys. There is often only minor bruising but a small 0.5–1.0 cm laceration in the labia minora which may bleed profusely. The hymenal opening is unaffected. The laceration usually heals rapidly in 2–3 days, and usually heals without scarring. Surgery is rarely needed. These lacerations are indistinguishable from those caused by fingernails in the course of CSA.

• Tearing due to forced abduction of the legs is rare. Bays & Jenny (1990) describe the splitting of the midline structures but the only patient report was Finkel (1989) where the child's legs were forcibly abducted during sexual abuse.

West et al (1989) wrote that superficial laceration of the posterior fourchette was a rare accidental injury and CSA should always be considered in this situation.

Other genital injuries are seen in:

• female circumcision — illegal in the UK under the Prohibition of Female Circumcision Act 1985
• seat belt injuries in road traffic accidents — thus in exceptional circumstances.

Masturbation does *not* cause injury except in the rare cases of self-mutilation in children with or without learning difficulties, when CSA must also be excluded from the aetiology (Muram 1986, Bays 1991). Tampons do *not* cause injury to the hymen, but may cause slight stretching (Bays 1991).

Skin disorders are common in childhood and may coexist with CSA.

• Nappy rash due to prolonged contact with wet or soiled nappies, perhaps exacerbated by diarrhoea, is common.
• Children with atopic eczema or seborrhoeic dermatitis may have sensitive skins; the genital and perianal skin becomes red and sore and there may be superficial linear breaks in the skin.
• Lichen sclerosus may initially look like trauma (Jenny et al 1989) but careful examination will show the typical appearance of white atrophic plaques and speckled purpura (Ridley 1987). The anogenital area is the commonest area affected in young girls and it is this distribution which helps make the diagnosis. The pale atrophic area often extends from the genital area across the perineum

to perianally in a figure of eight pattern. There may be frank bleeding from haemorrhagic blisters, but differential diagnosis from trauma may be made by the distribution of the lesions (Priestley & Bleehan 1987, Ridley 1987). Treatment is with bland emollients, good hygiene and a mild corticosteroid cream.

Congenital vascular lesions may occur in the genital area, but if in doubt it is as well to review the child in a couple of weeks. The vascular lesion will remain whereas trauma heals.

Genital infections due to STD should be investigated as possible CSA. Non-specific inflammation may be associated with trauma and sometimes the oedema of the tissues is so great as to make it impossible to view the hymenal orifice. Follow-up examination is necessary to review the physical signs. CSA should be considered in cases of recurrent vulvitis or vulvovaginitis (Diagnosis of Child Sexual Abuse, HMSO 1988).

Examination of boys

Boys need treating with the same respect as girls during history taking and examination. Boys of 7 and 8 years, and under, are usually amenable to examination by either a male or female doctor but older boys often prefer a man. Boys frequently feel very humiliated by being victims of CSA. The image of male invulnerability is strong in our culture and should be recognised. Boys may be examined on their mother's knee or on the couch; sedation is very rarely needed. The same examination technique as for girls is applicable to boys.

Points specific to the examination of boys

The usual examination is completed to review the descent of testes and presence of hydrocele or hernia, but also signs of recent trauma or scars. Burns to the penis or scrotum or lacerations of the penis or urethra have been seen but, in general, trauma to the genitalia is uncommon (Hobbs & Wynne 1989 (Fig. 9.13). Describe the stage of puberty (Table 9.17) the child has achieved. A urethral discharge is abnormal; it should be described and appropriate swabs taken (Fig. 9.8).

The boy's demeanour should be described. Was he calm and cooperative or was he angry? Did his

MALE GENITALIA

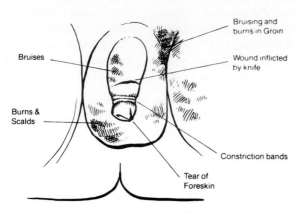

Fig. 9.13 Diagram to show injuries of the male genitalia encountered in abuse.

behaviour change during the examination? Did he behave in a sexualised way, masturbate or have an erection? An immediate, sustained erection on removal of a boy's pants is uncommon. Also masturbation during the examination requires explanation. Why is he so sexually excitable?

Examination of the anus and perianal region

Children are most comfortably examined in the left lateral position, curled up, and older children prefer to be covered with a sheet. Young children and babies are reassured by being examined on their mother's knee, and the examining position is then with the child lying on his back with his legs lifted vertically.

When asked to turn on to their side, a significant proportion of sexually abused children turn prone: is this how they were abused?

Although the knee–chest position allows good visualisation of the anus, this is an undignified position for children to maintain, and humiliating, especially if they have been abused in this posture: Also, if physical signs are to be compared it is clear the mode of examination must be known. Hence, when eliciting signs, for example (reflex) anal dilation, or observing for dilated veins, the child would normally be in the left lateral position, the buttocks gently parted with minimal traction and the anal sphincter observed for 20–30 seconds (Hobbs & Wynne 1986). Other examiners have placed the child in the knee–chest position for up

to 8 minutes (McCann et al 1989) and recorded their findings. The findings are not comparable and the recommendation in the UK is that the period of perianal inspection should not normally exceed 30 seconds (RCP 1991).

Standardisation is also needed in the terms used. The Cleveland Inquiry found doctors should 'agree a consistent vocabulary to describe physical signs which may be associated with CSA' (Butler-Sloss 1988, p.247(a)). Table 9.20 gives a description of signs and Table 9.21 an approximate guide to healing, from experience in Leeds.

On examination the anus is shut (Fig. 9.14), there are radiating skin folds to give a puckered appearance and the perianal skin is dry. If hygiene is good there is no erythema of the surrounding skin unless there is an additional disorder such as diarrhoea. In younger children particularly, there is often perianal erythema due to a combination of factors:

- poor hygiene, soiled nappy
- threadworms
- nappy rash
- candidiasis
- skin disorders such as atrophic eczema, seborrhoeic eczema, or rarely lichen sclerosus
- excessive washing and cleansing, which may be a form of CSA (Herman-Giddens 1989)
- rarely a β-haemolytic streptococcal skin infection presents as angry, red, swollen skin perianally, and there may be an associated vulvitis
- trauma, as in intracrural intercourse when the erythema extends forwards to involve the perineum, labia, scrotum and upper inner aspects of the thighs (RCP 1991).

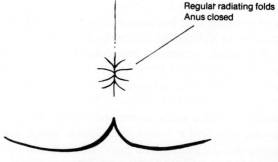

Fig. 9.14 Normal anus.

Table 9.20   Examination of anus and perianal region

Site	Lesion	Description	Aetiology
1. Skin	Erythema	Reddening of skin	Non-specific response to local irritation (infection, trauma, skin disorder)
	Thickening, pigmentation, lichenification	Swelling which may be associated with erythema, superficial cracks, darkening of tissues	Damage to skin as a result of skin disorder, e.g. eczema, scratching, rubbing (as in CSA) but non-specific response over prolonged period
	Loss of anal skin folds	Thickening of folds, leading to smooth, often pink, shiny skin with loss of fold pattern	Uncommon in childhood. Reported in adults where longstanding anal abuse
	Scars	Fan-shaped, linear, of heaped-up skin. Distort usual skin folds	May be secondary to fissures from any aetiology. *Uncommon* in childhood. N. B. wedgelike smooth areas in the midline with or without depression are to be differentiated from scars
	Faecal staining	Soiling of liquid faeces about anus	Imperfect hygiene. Seepage of liquid faeces in chronic constipation. Lax anal sphincter
	Perianal warts, vesicles	As genital warts, vesicles	
	Threadworms	Cotton-like worms, cause intense local irritation, hence erythema and superficial excoriation	
2. Anal margin	Oedema of anal margin	'Tyre sign' i.e. swollen anal margin (see notes)	Recent trauma to anal margin by forcible stretching
	Bruising	As other skin bruising	Suggests severe trauma
	Haematoma anal verge	Discrete red swelling on anal margin	Suggests severe trauma
	Skin tag	Mound of skin on anal verge	Deep fissures may heal leaving a skin tag. Anterior skin tags or folds were found in 11% of children
	Fissure	Break in the lining of the anal canal usually extending from inside the canal to the anal verge and travelling vertically to the verge. It is an open lesion. May be narrow and superficial or deep and wide when usually chronic, and often posterior. Variable number and position. Occasionally heals with scarring if deep	Due to stretching of anal margin as in severe constipation or anal penetration. Occasionally inflammatory bowel disease is seen in childhood and associated with fissures and other skin signs. Uncommon even in constipation, when usually children 1–3 years and single fissure seen. Multiple fissures, especially in absence of constipation, strong possibility CSA. Fissures commonly seen at 6 or 12 o'clock in CSA or other causes
	Anal verge deficit	Indentation covered with skin in anal verge, i.e. not a fissure	Does it represent an old anal verge injury? Is it a normal variant? Clinical follow-up may be needed.
Perianally	Venous congestion	Purple, blue to black discolorations perianally, vary from grape-like swellings to flat areas. May exist as a ring or just segmental (may be related to fissure, 6 or 12 o'clock usual site)	Mechanism unsure, seen in association with anal penetration. Do not observe anus for longer period than 20–30 seconds as may be normal findings in non-physiological position, e.g. knee–chest for 5 minutes
Configuration of anus	Funnelled anus	The anus appears deeply set. It is a fixed funnel shape.	Recorded in older forensic texts. Is occasionally seen usually mid-childhood or teenagers; reflects chronic anal abuse
	Shortening or eversion of anal canal	The anorectal junction with its characteristic star-shaped folds becomes approximated to the anal orifice.	Seen in first 2–3 years of life and likely to reflect repeated anal abuse. Associated with laxity and reduced anal tone
External sphincter	Laxity (open anal canal)	On gentle traction or merely parting the buttocks the anus appears open and gapes	The anus should be shut on inspection. A patulous anus is described in neurogenic disorder. Digital assessment of anal tone is unreliable, unnecessarily intrusive and should be abandoned

Table 9.20 *Contd.*

Site	Lesion	Description	Aetiology
	Gaping	A widely gaping anus, up to 2 cm, may be seen shortly after anal abuse	Within hours of abuse the anus may dilate widely, but this is a transient phenomenon
	Twitchy	External sphincter alternately contracts and relaxes every 2–5 seconds	Manipulation of the anus, for example repeated digital penetration or use of suppositories
External and internal sphincter	Anal dilatation	When the buttocks are separated the external and internal sphincters relax and a central hole is seen which allows the observer to look through the anal canal to the rectum. The relaxation is such that the orifice is roughly round, of 0.5–2.0 cm in A-P and horizontal planes. The opening may close, only to re-open, sometimes repetitively. The opening is smooth. The anal skin folds are clearly visible. Faeces may be clearly visible in the rectum. Occasionally children will demonstrate the sign, 'I can make my bottom get big'. The sign will go after days to months, once the abuse ceases	Passage of wind during the examination may demonstrate anal dilatation — but the dilatation is usually seen once, i.e. it is not repeated. Manual evacuation of faeces, instrumentation may, theoretically, give transient signs (RAD, laxity) but there are no clinical studies. Theoretically use of suppositories may cause twitchiness. Anal dilatation has been described in inflammatory bowel disorder, haemolytic uraemic syndrome. Severe chronic constipation may give a 'visibly relaxed anus'. If associated with anal abuse there will usually be other physical signs evident. Whether the sign is due to damage by stretching of the internal sphincter or a learned behavioural response or other mechanism is not known

Table 9.21 Approximate guide to healing of anal signs

Time	Bruising erythema, perinium, perianally	Abrasions anal verge	Oedema anal verge (tyre) sign)	Spasm anal sphincter	Anal fissures	Dilated veins	Anal dilatation	Laxity	Gaping anus
Hours	Red-purple +	+	+	+	+	+	+	+	+
1–3 days	Purple-swollen + yellow 3+	+	+	+	+	+	±	+	±
7 days	Yellow + Fading – Brown	±	±	+	±	+	±	+	–
2 weeks	±	–	–	–	±	±	±	+	
3 weeks	±		–		±	±	±	+	
Longer	±				deep fissures may remain unhealed for months	± may be seen over months	± usually disappears in few weeks if child separated from abuser	±	

Other signs:
1. haematoma anal verge
2. skin tags
3. scars (take up to 2 months to organise)
4. thickening of perianal skin and loss of skin folds (chronic abuse)

Perianal erythema is a non-specific sign but may be one of several signs which are associated with CSA or the only sign, for example in intra-crural intercourse.

If there is repeated friction of the perianal tissues the skin thickens, there may be loss of skin folds and the skin looks pink, smooth and sometimes shiny (Goff et al 1989).

Hyperpigmentation of the inner thighs and perianal region may occur in longstanding intra-crural intercourse but is a non-specific sign, being more common in pigmented skin and also in association with obesity.

If there is faecal soiling or seepage is it due to:

- constipation with overflow (large faecal masses may be palpable in the abdomen and visible rectally)
- encopresis
- a lax anus as in neurological disorder, e.g. spina bifida
- a lax anus due to chronic anal abuse (Reinhardt 1987)?

It has been suggested that these skin changes are reversible, as opposed to scarring, which is not (Butler-Sloss 1988, p.247 6a).

Scarring. The perianal skin should be free of scars, although there may be a midline raphe. Superficial fissures usually heal without scarring but deeper fissures may scar. Healing may be delayed by infection, continued passage of hard stools or further anal abuse. Scars may be linear, fan-shaped or in association with areas of heaped-up skin or skin tags. Fan-shaped scars should be differentiated from the depressions seen at 6 and 12 o'clock in some non-abused children (McCann et al 1989). However scars are unusual and are found in less than 10% of children who have other signs of anal abuse (Hobbs & Wynne 1989). Scars outside the midline were not seen in children selected for non-abuse (McCann 1990).

Skin tags may form at the end of a fissure. The interpretation of these skin tags is difficult. In a review of 164 children selected for non-abuse, skin tags or abnormal folds were found at 6 or 12 o'clock in 11% (18) children but no child had such a lesion outside the midline (McCann et al 1989). Clearly fissures due to abuse or severe constipation may occur at 6 or 12 o'clock and result in a skin

tag or abnormal fold. Hence an explanation should always be sought (but may not be forthcoming) for tags or folds, especially if outside the midline.

Smooth areas, which may be depressed and are wedge-shaped, are not infrequently seen at 6 and 12 o'clock (McCann et al 1989). These should be differentiated from the thickened, more irregular fan-shaped scars which may form at the site of a large fissure. Caution is therefore needed in the interpretation of skin changes at 6 and 12 o'clock, as for skin tags.

Swelling of the perianal tissues, seen as an oedematous ring around the anus, has been called the 'tyre sign' (Hobbs & Wynne 1989). Used in this sense it reflects acute trauma to the anal sphincter, as after forcible penetration (digital or penile), and is seen 24–48 hours after abuse. The same term 'tyre sign' has been used to describe a muscular hypertrophy of the external sphincter (Bamford & Kiff 1987). It has been postulated that this is caused by the child trying to maintain continence in spite of a dilating internal sphincter.

Fissures (also called tears) are breaks in the lining of the anal canal caused by over-stretching of the tissues. Their position with reference to the face of a clock should be described, as should length, depth and state of healing. Constipation may lead to fissure formation. However many severely constipated children do not have any fissures (Clayden 1988) and in the Leeds experience a child who has multiple fissures is likely to have been abused (Hobbs & Wynne 1989). Children selected for non-abuse did not have any fissures (McCann et al 1989) (see p. 151). Tears which extend into the surrounding perianal skin are of particular concern (Plate 88) (American Academy of Pediatrics 1991). Deep fissures may heal as described earlier with scarring and leave a skin tag as a marker of earlier trauma. There may also be a sentinel vein on either side of the fissure. Linear or fan-shaped scars may be seen (Paul 1986).

Tiny cracks in the skin, as caused by scratching (threadworms) or in eczema or nappy rash, are to be differentiated from fissures. When a child has been anally abused there may be scratches due to the abuser's finger-nails tearing the anal margin; this excoriation may be a localised lesion, but interpretation depends upon the history.

Perianal venous congestion may be evident

immediately the child is examined, but it is usual to observe the child in the left lateral position for 20–30 seconds. Dilated veins may be seen as grape-like clusters, through to flat areas of discoloration. The veins may be purple, blue or black and extend as a ring around the anus or just in segments, perhaps associated with a fissure. 24% of children in the Leeds study (Hobbs & Wynne 1989) of children with abnormal signs had venous congestion.

Haemorrhoids are extremely rare pre-pubertally and are not likely to cause confusion (Shandling 1987, McCann 1990). However, venous congestion may be seen in any condition which interferes with the normal vascular drainage in the area — an example would be a sacral tumour. Once anal abuse has ceased, the dilated veins will gradually disappear but it may take many months. Excessive traction, positioning and long periods of observation (over 30 seconds) may lead to venous congestion in normal children. 52% of children in one study showed engorgement if left for more than 2 minutes in the knee–chest position (McCann et al 1989). As with reflex anal dilatation, venous congestion as described in the McCann et al 1989 study is not comparable to the Hobbs & Wynne 1989 paper, as the conduct and timing of the medical examination differed so markedly (RCP 1991). There may also have been unrecognised CSA in the McCann et al study due to the protocol used in which the children were not interviewed.

Laxity and reduced tone of the anal sphincter is associated with repeated stretching (Paul 1986, McLay 1990a) in the absence of a neurological disorder. Gross faecal loading as seen in severe chronic constipation also leads to a visibly relaxed sphincter (Clayden 1988). The assessment of anal tone is a matter of controversy. Many paediatricians feel digital examination is unnecessary and of doubtful value (Butler-Sloss 1988, p.192). Tone is recovered rapidly after acute stretching, as is known to paediatric surgeons who have performed four-finger anal stretches. If anal tone does not recover rapidly this suggests the abuse was long-standing or continuing.

Shortening or eversion of the anal canal occurs in abuse so that the anorectal junction with its characteristic star-shaped folds becomes approximated to the anal orifice. This finding is only seen in the first years of life, up to around 3 years. It is likely to reflect repeated anal intercourse and is associated with laxity and reduced anal tone (Hobbs & Wynne 1989).

Gaping of the anus may be seen shortly after anal penetration. The anus is fixed open, 1–2 cm, and there may be associated signs of acute trauma, erythema and oedema. The sign may only persist for several hours but on other occasions the anus may gape for days.

Bruising to the perianal area is rare but bruising to the buttocks, thighs and lower abdomen, common (Reinhardt 1987, Hobbs & Wynne 1990).

Anal dilatation (or reflex anal dilatation or 'O' sign) has been long known to forensic physicians (Ganz 1962, Paul 1986, Butler-Sloss 1988 p. 247 6a, McLay 1990a, b). It is not a known reflex and appears to be related either to stretching of the internal sphincter or as a modifiable behavioural response. The external sphincter usually contracts when the surrounding skin is stimulated. This sphincter is under conscious control; when examining children tightening of the sphincter is seen but the child can only maintain this state for 10–20 seconds before relaxing and the anus may 'wink'. Both internal and external sphincters are normally in a state of constant contraction and continence is maintained. The internal sphincter is under autonomic control; distension from above causes it to dilate. It is usually therefore 'closed' and remains so even when the external sphincter relaxes, therefore the interior of the anal canal is not seen. If the child passes flatus during the examination both sphincters will relax and the anus will briefly dilate.

The usual method of eliciting this sign is to gently part the buttocks with the child in the left lateral position and observe for up to 30 seconds. If the sign of (reflex) anal dilatation is present the observer sees the anus open into a circular tube down which the examiner can often see through the anal canal to the rectum. The opening may close and open repetitively, and the degree of dilatation may be up to 2.5 cm measured horizontally. Minor degrees of dilatation may be observed, and the significance is not clear. If the child has a loaded bowel and wishes to defecate he should be re-examined later. However the presence of stool is not in itself an explanation for the dilatation.

Gross faecal loading, as previously described, leads to a 'visibly relaxed sphincter' (Clayden 1988) but this is a different sign, and of course the absence of severe chronic constipation will be evident on examination.

Anal dilatation has been described following manipulative surgery to the anus, for example stretching or instrumentation (Paul 1986). Similarly, repeated use of enemas may, theoretically, cause dilatation. There is clearly no logic to the theory that threadworms, or poor hygiene, cause the internal sphincter to dilate.

If the buttocks are gently parted it is not possible to reproduce the sign, and even with traction on the buttocks it is unlikely (RCP 1991). Controversy has raged around the significance of the sign of reflex anal dilatation (RAD). The view of the Cleveland Inquiry (Butler-Sloss 1988, p. 247 6a) was 'We are satisfied from the evidence that the consensus is that the sign of anal dilatation is abnormal and suspicious and requires further investigation. It is not in itself evidence of anal abuse'. This was also the view of the Police Surgeons Association (Butler-Sloss 1988, p. 247 6a). 'While not pathognomonic of sexual abuse it (anal dilatation) should give rise to suspicion that sexual abuse may have occurred.'

The sign, as described by Hobbs & Wynne (1986) and elicited as described in this chapter, was seen in:

- 4% of 1368 children referred for possible abuse (physical, neglect, CSA)
- 18% of 337 children considered to have been or probably to have been sexually abused
- 42% of sexually abused children with anal signs (Hobbs & Wynne 1989).

It is difficult to compare these Leeds findings with other studies because of:

- different examination technique (McCann 1990)
- different definition of sign (Clayden 1988, Agnarsson et al 1990)
- no description of method (Stanton & Sunderland 1989)
- inclusion of unknown numbers of sexually abused children in study (Clayden 1988, Stanton & Sunderland 1989, Agnarsson et al 1990, McCann 1990).

A summary of findings of the prevalence of RAD:

- Wright et al (1987): 8.5% of children referred to police surgeons because of possible CSA.
- McCann et al (1989): 15% of 267 children selected for non-abuse during first 30 seconds, 49% subsequently.
- McCann (1990): 9% of non-abused children displayed RAD in the first 30 seconds of examination, and of these in 62% it was a dynamic sign. 49% at 4 minutes.
- Stanton & Sunderland (1989): 14% of 200 presumed non-abused children in a community health clinic, general paediatric clinic and renal clinic.
- Priestley (1987): 4% of 100 children seen in general paediatric practice with no suggestion of abuse.
- Agnarsson et al (1990): 8% of 136 children with mild to moderate constipation.
- Clayden (1988): 15% of 129 children with severe chronic constipation had 'visibly relaxed sphincters' (and had received enemas, suppositories).

Bamford & Roberts (1989) wrote that abnormal patency of the anus in the absence of a neurological disorder was indicative of something hard and large having passed through the anus, upwards or downwards.

The relevance to RAD of faeces in the rectum is unclear. A loaded rectum is thought to increase the prevalence of RAD (RCP 1991). Certainly a chronically distended rectum is associated with leakage of soft stool around the anus through a 'visibly relaxed anus' (Clayden 1988).

Clinical experience of anally abused children shows it is unsafe to dismiss the sign of RAD because faeces are seen in the rectum. Children with faecal loading and RAD may also have been abused.

Summary of RAD:

- An agreed description of the sign is needed (p. 182).
- A standard technique is needed for eliciting the sign (left lateral position, buttocks gently parted and anus inspected for 30 seconds).
- RAD is commoner in anally abused groups than other groups (RCP 1991).
- The sign may vary from day to day.

• When abuse ceases the sign disappears (over weeks to months), and during the period of healing lesser degrees of dilatation are seen.

• RAD in an otherwise normal child is cause for concern and justifies follow-up.

• RAD has been described in inflammatory bowel disease and after anal manipulation.

• RAD of > 1 cm is supportive evidence of abuse.

• RAD of > 2 cm indicates penetrating trauma (Heger to RCP 1991) or 'is more likely than not to be associated with abuse' (RCP 1991).

• Even if the child is ill, ventilated or dying, do not dismiss RAD as a consequence of the child's general condition (see below).

• When infants or children die the anus usually remains closed (Batcup G, personal communication — a review of the anus at autopsy confirms this, 1992) In unexplained death, possibly due to asphyxia, if there is a dilated anus at autopsy CSA should be considered.

CASE HISTORY 10
A 2½-year-old boy was brought to the hospital after he had had a period of apnoea. He was badly beaten and had one fixed dilated pupil; emergency neurosurgery was performed to remove a large blood clot. He had been sexually abused (admitted by assailant) and his anus was lax, with RAD to 1.5 cm and multiple fissures.

Over the next 2 weeks his condition remained critical, he was ventilated and survival was thought unlikely. In spite of his poor general condition his anus showed signs of healing — the slides were taken on Day 2 and Day 5 (see Plate 102).

Anal dilatation is accepted as a sign associated with anal abuse, but (Hobbs & Wynne 1986) 'Diagnosis of buggery is made from the history, the physical findings and associated evidence.' Unfortunately some of the media (and some practitioners), in order to simplify and also to deny the existence of CSA, looked to 'reflex anal dilatation' as a 'fingerprint' test for CSA which could then be discredited.

Twitchy anus describes an anus in which the external sphincter repeatedly and rapidly contracts and relaxes. The sign is observed in children disclosing anal abuse and it may be related to repeated digital penetration.

Funnelling — a deep-set, dished anal appearance — is seen in older children and has been

well described in earlier literature (Mant 1960). It is not seen in younger children.

Haematomas of the anal verge are uncommon but are seen after forcible anal penetration. They are purple/red localised, round swellings of the anal verge which distort the normal skin folds. They are painful.

Bruising of the anal margin and perineum is also seen, but is not common.

Anal warts are the most common STD seen in children. If present, and particularly in children beyond infancy, the possibility of CSA should be explored.

Herpes and gonorrhoea may be seen.

Rectal abscess or fissures may be the presenting sign of CSA, albeit a rare one.

Perforation. CSA may lead to perforation of the bowel. In the Leeds experience a boy, aged 6 weeks, was admitted seriously ill with peritonitis, secondary to a rectal tear. The father admitted causing the injury by digital penetration whilst abusing the baby.

Accidental perforation is rare. A boy of 9 years perforated his rectum when leap-frogging over the snooker table and landing on a cue. Other injuries caused accidently by sitting on spikes or glass have not been difficult to differentiate from CSA.

Skin disorders should not cause much confusion to paediatricians. Atopic eczema, seborrhoeic dermatitis and candidiasis are common, and may coexist with CSA.

Lichen sclerosus (see p. 179) has a characteristic appearance and new signs develop over time making follow-up examination useful in the diagnosis (Plate 82).

Chronic inflammatory bowel disease has been felt to mimic CSA (Hey et al 1987) but the clinical picture as a whole will enable the diagnosis to be made. The published case was of Crohn's disease asymmetrically affecting the genitalia and anus.

Haemolytic uraemic syndrome (Vickers et al 1988), presenting in 3 girls under 3 years with bloody diarrhoea and very abnormal anal signs, has been described.

Clearly, any sick child with signs and symptoms of inflammatory bowel disease should be investigated for an organic disorder. CSA may present acutely as a surgical emergency, for example bowel perforation, but the clinical picture would suggest trauma rather than a disease process.

Chronic constipation is a relatively common complaint and may be related to CSA. Warning signs of possible CSA have been suggested to alert doctors to this possibility (Clayden 1987). These included a history of emotional disturbance with history of possible abuse, passivity during examination, laxity of the anus, bruising perianally and the presence of an STD. Clayden noted that anal abuse may occur with no physical sign being evident, but also, if signs are seen, there may be an alternative diagnosis to that of CSA.

Laxity of the anus, due to neurological disease such as spina bifida, should not be difficult to recognise. Children with Down's syndrome have normal anal tone (Dr F Bamford, personal communication). It should be remembered that physically and intellectually disabled children may be victims of CSA.

Congenital anomalies are relatively uncommon in terms of median raphe and smooth wedge-shaped areas, anterior or posterior, in the midline of the anal verge (McCann 1990). These smooth areas may be depressed. They do not have the thickened, irregular and distorting features of a scar.

Perianal folds or tags of tissue, in the midline, anterior to the anus only, were found in McCann's study but, curiously, only in girls (in 11% of subjects). McCann felt it was possible to differentiate these tags from the sentinel tags which form in relation to a fissure as there was no disruption beneath the fold.

Assessment of anal signs

Anal abuse appears to be common because it is possible to penetrate the distensible anus and rectum even at a young age. Experience in Leeds shows there is little disturbance of function as a result, and constipation, diarrhoea, or faecal incontinence are uncommon. The younger the child, the more likely there are to be abnormal physical signs (Hobbs & Wynne 1989). 60% of children aged 0–5 years who were considered victims of CSA had abnormality compared with 42% of the total of 337 cases of confirmed CSA.

The frequency of physical signs in anal abuse is shown in Table 9.22 with a description of the

Table 9.22 Signs which are likely to be significant in the assessment of anal abuse

	RCP (1991)	'Abused children' % frequency Hobbs & Wynne (1989)	'Non-abused children' % frequency McCann (1990)
1. Laceration or healed scar extending beyond the anal mucosa onto perianal skin with no reasonable history e.g. major trauma	Diagnostic	Few	0%
2. Anal laxity	Supportive	38%	0%
3. Reflex anal dilatation > 1 cm (30 seconds *left lateral* position)	Supportive (0.5–2.5 cm)	42%	—
4. Reflex anal dilatation (30 seconds *knee–chest* position)	—	—	9%
5. Reflex anal dilatation > 2.0 cm	Penetrating trauma (Heger 1991)	—	1.2%
6. Fissures	Supportive	53%	0%
7. Erythema	Supportive	53%	41%
8. Swelling	Supportive	8%	0%
9. Venous congestion (30 seconds left lateral)	Supportive	24%	7% (?)
10. STD/warts	Supportive/diagnostic	4%	0%
11. Scars/tags/folds	Supportive	8%	0% outside midline 0% boys 11% anterior skin tags, folds in girls
12. Haemorrhoids	Very unusual	0%	0%

Notes
1. Venous congestion was seen at the beginning of the examination. Knee–chest in 7%.
2. Signs of chronic anal abuse include skin changes, with the perianal skin thickened and smooth (Paul 1990).
3. Many older children who have been anally abused are normal on examination (RCP 1991).

Table 9.23   Signs associated with anal abuse (Hobbs & Wynne 1989, Paul 1990, American Academy of Pediatrics 1991, RCP 1991)

'Acute' signs (within hours)	'Chronic' signs
Swelling perianally (tyre sign)	Thickened perianal skin, with loss of skin folds
Bruising	
Haematoma anal verge	Anal laxity
Fissures, may bleed	Anal dilatation
Gaping anus	Venous congestion
Linear abrasions of skin	Chronic fissures
Genital signs	Scarring (linear, fan-shaped)
Other signs of physical injury	Skin tags
	Warts or other STD
	Funnelling (teenager?)
	Hyperpigmentation
	Self-mutilation

signs in Table 9.20, and a guide to rates of healing in Table 9.21. Acute signs, as compared with signs associated with chronic abuse, are listed in Table 9.23. Table 9.24 gives a differential diagnosis of anal signs.

Some patterns of physical signs such as multiple anal fissures, a gaping anus (as seen in the early hours following buggery) or gonorrhoea are clearly highly significant in the assessment of possible anal abuse, whereas reddening or a superficial single fissure are much less specific (Table 9.24). However, given a clear disclosure by the child of anal penetration, erythema and a single fissure are consistent with such a history. Alternatively a single deep fissure (usually at 6 o'clock) in a toddler, in the absence of constipation, may be the only sign of anal penetration and the doctor may have to recognise the severity of this injury (equivalent in physical abuse terms to a fracture) in order to protect the child. What could a deep tear extending 2 cm or more up the anal canal be caused by, other than excessive stretching? The

Table 9.24   Differential diagnosis of anal abuse

1. Accidental trauma
2. Skin disorder, e.g. atopic eczema, lichen sclerosus
3. Congenital abnormality, e.g. midline raphe, wedge-shaped area in midline
4. Infection, e.g. candidiasis, streptococcal cellulitis
5. Inflammatory bowel disease, e.g. Crohn's disease
6. Severe, chronic constipation causing anal laxity
7. Single anal fissure, e.g. constipation
8. Neurological disorder, e.g. neurogenic bowel in association with spina bifida
9. Rectal tumour

RCP report finds that a laceration or healed scar extending beyond the anal mucosa on to the perianal skin in the absence of explanation, e.g. major trauma, is diagnostic of blunt force penetrating trauma — that is, anal abuse (RCP 1991).

It is also useful to note that skin tags or scars outside the midline position, haematomas, fissures, haemorrhoids and abrasions are not found in the 'normal' population (McCann 1990). But clinically it is well known that there may be no abnormal signs in spite of a clear history, and other corroboration, of abuse (Bamford & Roberts 1989). The older the child, the less likely it is that there will be abnormality, and if the abuser is gentle and uses lubricant, the trauma of buggery or digital penetration is lessened. Over 50% of teenagers with a clear history of anal abuse have no abnormal signs on examination. Paediatricians may also see the child only weeks or months after the last assault; hence the low percentages of physical findings in some series (Reinhardt 1987). However, if the abuse has been ongoing, although acute signs such as erythema, fissures or bruising may have healed, other signs such as laxity may persist (Spencer & Dunklee 1986).

The only definite proof of buggery is the presence of sperm in the rectum. Scars are uncommon, 11% (Bamford & Roberts 1989) and in less than 10% of the Leeds series (Hobbs & Wynne 1989). It should be borne in mind that a STD may subsequently develop after the due incubation period.

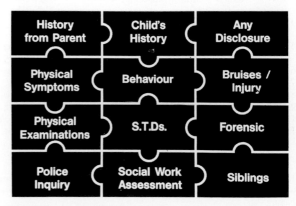

Fig. 9.15   The jigsaw of sexual abuse. A model of the complex interlocking nature of sexual abuse diagnosis. A multi-disciplinary approach is implied in this model.

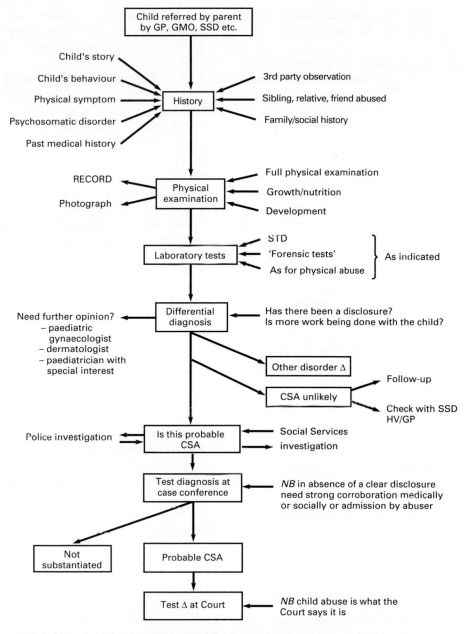

Fig. 9.16 The diagnostic process.

Summary

A variety of signs may be associated with anal abuse in children. The signs vary with the type of abuse, the frequency of abuse, the age of the child, the force used, the use of lubricant, the presence of infection and, most importantly, the time since the last assault, as healing may be completed, scarring being exceptional. In association with anal abuse may be seen the signs of genital abuse or other physical assault. There may also be associated STD.

Forensic tests are uncommonly positive in CSA because of the chronicity of the abuse (i.e. the child is not usually seen within 1–2 days of abuse). The child will usually have bathed, changed clothes and defecated before the physical examination. The presence of sperm in the rectum is the only proof of sodomy.

Physical signs must always be assessed in the context of the history, physical examination and investigation. If there is a possibility of CSA further discussion and usually investigation will be undertaken by the social worker and the police (Figs 9.15, 9.16) (Zeitlin 1987). However, doctors may wish to see the child again before instigating a full investigation. The timing of such an investigation is important and, although children may be left unprotected in the short term, ill-advised haste may leave the child unprotected in the long term if the case collapses before it begins.

Paul has written of the pitfalls of medical examination (1990) but if a careful history is taken, the diagnostic jigsaw is built up of all its component parts and the diagnosis is put in the context of the social services and police investigations, mistaken diagnoses are usually avoided. The diagnosis of CSA has far-reaching consequences for the child and his family, and a thorough, validated clinical practice is needed.

Summary

1. The recognition of CSA is increasing as adults listen to children and acknowledge the protean manifestations of CSA in childhood.

2. Doctors who work in this field should not work in professional isolation and should also understand the need for interagency cooperation.

3. Consent is needed before any medical examination.

4. The diagnosis of CSA is made by building up the pieces of the diagnostic jigsaw: the medical examination is one part of this process.

5. Children's disclosures of abuse should be initially accepted and subsequently skilled validation is required.

6. Physical indicators of CSA are important because they may be the first sign of child abuse. Physical signs also corroborate the child's story.

7. Normality on physical examination is common even when a child has been a victim of CSA.

8. Follow-up examination is often helpful in the evaluation of physical signs to note healing or the evolution of an organic disorder, e.g. lichen sclerosus et atrophicus.

9. Single physical signs may support the diagnosis of CSA but are rarely proof of CSA. Pregnancy, gonorrhoea or the presence of sperm in the vagina or rectum are exceptions to this generalisation.

10. Physical abuse and CSA are seen together in around 15% of cases. Burns and bites are particularly associated with CSA.

11. All sexually abused children have been emotionally abused.

12. Penetrative abuse in young children involves oral or anal intercourse — vaginal penetration being seen in older girls (although sodomy may persist).

REFERENCES

Agnarsson U, Clayden G 1990 Constipation in children. Maternal and Child Health 15: 252–256

Agnarsson U, Gordon C, Wright C et al 1990 Perianal appearances in childhood constipation. Archives of Diseases of Children 65: 1231–1234

American Academy of Pediatrics 1991 Guidelines for the evaluation of sexual abuse in children. Paediatrics 87: 254–260

Anderson C 1975 Constipation. In: Anderson C, Burke V (eds) Paediatric gastroenterology. Blackwell, Oxford

Arnold R P, Rogers D, Cook D A G 1990 Medical problems of adults who were sexually abused in childhood. British Medical Journal 300: 705–708

BAAF 1991 Implications for medical practitioners. Children Act 1989. Practive note 28. BAAF, London

Bamford F W, Kiff E S 1987 Child sexual abuse. Letter. Lancet ii: 1396

Bamford F, Roberts R 1989 Child sexual abuse. In: Meadow S R (ed) ABC of child abuse. British Medical Journal, p. 31

Bartley D L, Morgan L, Rimsza M E 1987 Gardnerella vaginalis in prepubertal girls. American Journal of Diseases of Childhood 141: 1014–1017

Bays J, Jenny C 1990 Genital and anal conditions confused with child sexual abuse trauma. American Journal of Diseases of Childhood 144: 1319–1322

Bentovim A, Boston P 1988 Sexual abuse — basic issues — characteristics of children and families. Ch 2 in: Bentovim A, Elton A, Hildebrand J, Tranter M, Vizard E (eds) Child sexual abuse within the family. Wright, London

Bentovim A, Elton A, Hildebrand J, Tranter M, Vizard E 1988 Child sexual abuse within the family. Chs 5 & 6 Helping children to describe experience of child sexual abuse. Wright, London

Berkowitz C D et al 1987 Labial fusion in pre-pubertal girls:

a marker for sexual abuse? American Journal of Obstetrics and Gynecology 156: 16–20

Branch G, Paxton R 1965 A study of gonococcal infections amongst infants and children. Public Health Reports 80: 347–352

Brown R M et al 1989 Child abuse presenting as an organic disease. British Medical Journal 299(6699): 614–615

Butler-Sloss E 1988 Report of the Inquiry into Child Abuse in Cleveland 1987. HMSO

Cantwell H 1983 Vaginal inspection as it relates to child sexual abuse in girls under thirteen. Child Abuse and Neglect 7: 171–176

Cantwell H B 1987 Update on vaginal inspection as it relates to child sexual abuse in girls under thirteen. Child Abuse and Neglect 11: 545–546

Clarke J, Lacey C 1990 Sexually transmitted diseases in sexually abused children. Community Paediatric Group Newsletter

Clarke J et al 1990 The sexual behaviour and knowledge about AIDS in a group of young adolescent girls in Leeds. Genitourinary Medicine 66: 189–192

Clayden G S 1981 Chronic constipation in childhood. University of London, pp. 118–120

Clayden G 1987 Anal appearance and child sexual abuse. Letter. Lancet i: 620

Clayden G S 1988 Reflex anal dilatation associated with severe chronic constipation in children. Archives of Disease in Childhood 63: 832–836

Corbett J et al 1977 Progressive disintegrative psychosis in childhood. Journal of Child Psychology and Psychiatry 18: 211–219

Corwin D L 1988 Early diagnosis of chid sexual abuse: diminishing the lasting effects. In: Wyatt G E, Powell G J (eds) Lasting effects of child sexual abuse. Sage, London, pp 251–269

Creighton S J, Noyes P 1989 Child abuse trends in England and Wales 1983–1987, NSPCC

Curtis H et al 1989 Teenage sexuality: implications for controlling AIDS. Archives of Disease in Childhood 64: 1240–1245

De Jong A R 1986 Sexually transmitted diseases in sexually abused children. Sexually Transmitted Disease 13: 123–126

de la Haye Davies H 1987 Protocol for the forensic examination of the sexually abused child. The Police Surgeon 32 (Dec 1987)

Department of Health 1991 An introductory guide to the NHS. DoH, London

Dewhurst J 1988 Evidence. In: Butler-Sloss E Report of the Inquiry into Child Abuse in Cleveland 1989. HMSO

Diagnosis of Child Sexual Abuse: Guidance for Doctors 1988 DHSS, HMSO

Emmans S et al 1987 Genital findings in sexually abused, symptomatic and asymptomatic girls. Pediatrics 79: 778–785

Enos W F et al 1986 Forensic evaluation of sexual abuse in children. Pediatrics 78: 385–398

Finkel M A 1989 Anogenital trauma in sexually abused children. Pediatrics 84(2): 317–322

Flemming K A, Venning V, Evans M 1987 DNA typing of genital warts and diagnosis of sexual abuse in children (letter). Lancet ii: 454

Forster G 1992 Rape and sexually transmitted disease. British Journal of Hospital Medicine 47(2): 94–95

Frothingham T, Barnett R, Hobbs C, Wynne J 1991 Child sexual abuse in Leeds before and after Cleveland. Submitted for publication

Furniss T 1991 The multi-professional handbook of child sexual abuse. Routledge, London

Ganz E 1962 Signs of sodomy. Letter. British Medical Journal 1: 263

Glaser D, Collins C 1989 The response of young non-sexually abused children to anatomically correct dolls. Journal of Child Psychology and Psychiatry 30(4): 547–560

Glaser D, Frosh S 1988 Child sexual abuse. Macmillan, London, Chs 4–6

Goff C W et al 1989 Vaginal measurements in pre-pubertal girls. American Journal of Diseases of Childhood 143: 1366–1369

Goldsmid J, Kibel M A, Mills A E 1985 Diseases due to infection. In: Forfar J O, Arneil G C (eds) Textbook of paediatrics. Churchill Livingstone

Graham P 1991 Child psychiatry. A developmental approach. Oxford Medical Publications

Gutman L T 1990 Sexual abuse and human papilloma virus (letter). The Journal of Paediatrics 116(5): 495–496

Gutman L T et al 1991a Diagnosis of child sexual abuse in children with genital warts. Archives of Diseases in Childhood 145 (2): 126–127

Gutman L T et al 1991b HIV transmission by child sexual abuse (letter). Archives of Diseases in Childhood 145(2): 137–141

Hammerschlag M R 1988 Sexually transmitted disease in sexually abused children. Adv Paediatr Infect Dis 3: 1

Handfield-Jones S E, Hinde F R J, Kennedy C T C 1987 Lichen sclerosus et atrophicus in children misdiagnosed as sexual abuse. British Medical Journal 294: 1404–1405

Hanks H, Hobbs C J M 1992 Self abuse and suicide. Current Paediatrics 2: 57–59

Heger A 1991 (In evidence to RCP.) Physical signs of sexual abuse in children.

Heger A, Emmans S J 1990 Introital diameter as the criterion for sexual abuse. Paediatrics 85: 222–223

Herman-Giddens M 1989 Harmful genital care practices in children. Journal of the American Medical Association 261(4): 577–579

Herman-Giddens M E, Fronthingham T S 1987 Prepubertal female genitalia: examination for evidence of abuse. Pediatrics 80(2): 203–208

Herman-Giddens M E, Garmann L T, Benson N L 1988 Association of coexisting vaginal infections and multiple abusers in female children with genital warts. Sexually Transmitted Diseases 15: 63–67

Hey et al 1987 Differential diagnosis in child sexual abuse. Letter. Lancet i: 283

Hobbs C J, Wynne J M 1986 Buggery in childhood: a common syndrome of child abuse. Lancet ii: 792–796

Hobbs C J, Wynne J M 1987a Child sexual abuse — an increasing rate of diagnosis. Lancet ii: 837–841

Hobbs C J, Wynne J M 1987b Management of sexual abuse. Archives of Diseases in Childhood 62: 1182–1187

Hobbs C J, Wynne J M 1989 Sexual abuse of English boys and girls: the importance of anal examination. Child Abuse and Neglect 13: 195–210

Hobbs C J, Wynne J M 1990 The sexually abused battered child. Archives of Disease in Childhood 65: 423–427

Huffman J W et al 1981 The gynaecology of childhood and adolescence. W B Saunders, Philadelphia, p. 25

Jenny et al 1987 Hymens in newborn female infants. Pediatrics 80(3): 399–400

Jenny C, Kirby P, Fuquay D 1989 Genital lichen sclerosus mistaken for child sexual abuse. Paediatrics 83: 597–599

Jones D P H, McQuiston M G 1988 Interviewing the sexually abused child. Gaskell

Kaplan K M, Fleischer G R, Paradise J E, Friedman H N 1984 Social relevance of genital herpes simplex in children. Archives of Diseases in Childhood 138: 872–874

Klevan J L, DeJong A R 1990 Urinary tract symptoms and urinary tract infection following sexual abuse. American Journal of Diseases in Childhood 144: 242–244

Lindblad F et al 1989 Child sexual abuse: physical examination. Acta Paediatrica Scandinavica 78(6): 935–943

Lusk R, Waterman J 1986 Effects of sexual abuse on children. In: MacFarlane K et al (eds) Sexual abuse of young children. Holt Rinehart & Winston

McCann J 1990 Use of the colposcope in childhood sexual abuse examinations. Pediatrics Clinics of North America 37(4): 863

McCann J et al 1988 Labial adhesions and posterior fourchette injuries in childhood sexual abuse. American Journal of Diseases in Childhood 142: 659–663

McCann J et al 1989 Perianal findings in prepubertal children selected for non-abuse: a descriptive study. Child Abuse and Neglect 13(2): 179–194

McCann J, Wells R, Voris J et al 1990a Comparison of genital examination techniques in prepubertal girls. Pediatric Clinics of North America 85: 182–187

McCann J, Vovis J, Simon M 1990b Genital findings in prepubertal females selected for non-abuse: a descriptive study. Paediatrics 86(3): 428–439

McCrae W M 1985 Disorders of the alimentary tract. In: Forfar J O, Arneil G C (eds) Textbook of paediatrics, 3rd edn. Vol 1. Churchill Livingstone, pp 472–474

MacFarlane K 1986 Child sexual abuse allegations in divorce proceedings. Chapter 7 in: MacFarlane K, Waterman J, Conerley S, Damon L, Durfee M, Long S (eds) Sexual abuse of young children. Holt, Rinehart and Winston

McLay W D S (ed) 1990a Sexual abuse of children. Ch 13 in: Clinical forensic medicine. Pinter, p. 234

McLay W D S (ed)) 1990b Sexual offences against adults. Ch 14 in: Clinical forensic medicine. Pinter, p. 263

Mant A K 1960 Forensic medicine. Lloyd, London, p. 243

Marshall W N, Puls T, Davidson C 1988 New child abuse operation in an era of increased awareness. American Journal of Diseases in Childhood 142: 664–667

Meadow S R 1987 Editorial. Staying cool in child abuse. British Medical Journal 295: 345

Mehl A L 1990 Urinary tract infection and sexual abuse (letter). American Journal of Diseases in Childhood 144: 1073

Muram D 1986 Genital tract injuries in the prepubertal child. Paediatric Ann 15: 616–620

Muram D 1989a Anal and perianal abnormalities in prepubertal victims of sexual abuse. American Journal of Obstetrics and Gynecology 161(2): 278–281

Muram D 1989b Child sexual abuse: relationship between sexual acts and genital findings. Child Abuse and Neglect 13: 211–216

Muram D, Elias S 1989 Child sexual abuse — genital tract findings in prepubertal girls. II. Comparison of colposcopic and unaided examinations. American Journal of Obstetrics and Gynecology 160: 333–335

Muram D, Speck D M, Gold S S 1991 Genital abnormalities in female siblings and friends of child victims of sexual abuse. Child Abuse and Neglect 15: 105–110

Neinstein L S et al 1984 Non-sexual transmission of sexually transmitted diseases: an infrequent occurrence. Paediatrics 74: 67–76

Paradise J E 1989 Predictive accuracy and the diagnosis of sexual abuse: a big issue about a little tissue. Child Abuse and Neglect 13: 169–176

Paradise J, Willis E 1985 Probability of vaginal foreign body in girls with genital complaint. American Journal of Diseases in Childhood 139: 472–476

Paul D M 1977 Medical examination in sexual offences against children. Med Sci Law 17: 251–258

Paul D 1984 Examination of the living. In: Mant A K (ed) Taylor's principles and practice of medical jurisprudence. Churchill Livingstone

Paul D M 1986 What really did happen to Baby Jane? The medical aspects of the investigation of alleged sexual abuse of children. Medicine, Science and Law 26: 85–106

Paul D 1990 The pitfalls which may be encountered during an exam for signs of sexual abuse. Med Sci Law 30(1): 3–11

Peters S D 1988 Child sexual abuse and later psychological problems. In: Wyatt G W, Powell G J (eds) Lasting effects of child sexual abuse. Sage, Beverley Hills, CAL, pp 107–117

Pigot, His Honour Judge T C 1989 Report of Advisory Group on Video Evidence. Home Office, London

Priestley B 1987 Reflex anal dilatation and abuse. Lancet ii: 1396

Priestley B L, Bleehan S S 1987 Lichen sclerosus et atrophicus in children misdiagnosed as sexual abuse. British Medical Journal 295: 211

Priestley B L, Bleehan S S 1990 Lichen sclerosus in sexual abuse (letter, comment). Archives of Disease in Childhood 65(3): 335. Comment on Archives of Disease in Childhood 1989 64(8): 1204–1206

Raine P A M 1991 Investigation of rectal bleeding. Archives of Disease in Childhood 66: 279–280

Reinhardt M 1987 Sexually abused boys. Child Abuse and Neglect II: 229–235

Richman N, Stevenson J, Graham P 1982 Pre-school–school: a behavioural study. Academic Press, London

Ridley C M L 1987 Editorial. Lichen sclerosus et atrophicus. British Medical Journal 295(21): 1295–1296

Rimsza M E, Feingold M D 1989 Labial fusion. Picture of the month. American Journal of Diseases of Childhood 143: 381–382

Rock B, Naghasfar Z, Barnett N, Buscerna J, Woodruff J D, Shah K 1986 Genital tract papillomavirus infections in childhood. Arch Dermatol 122: 1129–1132

Royal College of Physicians 1991 Physical signs of sexual abuse in children (report of working party of RCP)

Sgroi S et al 1988 Children's sexual behaviours and their relationship to sexual abuse. In: Sgroi S (ed) Vulnerable population. Vol 1. Lexington Books

Shandling B 1987 Surgical conditions of anus, rectum and colon. In: Behrman, Vaughan (eds) Nelson Textbook of pediatrics, 13th edn. W B Saunders

Siran A B et al 1988 Interaction of normal child with anatomical dolls. Child Abuse and Neglect 12: 295–304

Smith P, Wilson A 1991 Children as witnesses. Seen and heard. Vol 1, p.25

Spencer H, Dunklee P 1986 Sexual abuse of boys. Pediatrics 78: 133–138

Spencer J 1991 Reformers despair. New Law Journal 787

Spencer J, Flin R 1990 The evidence of children, the law and psychology

Stanton A, Sunderland R 1989 Prevalence of reflex anal dilatation in 200 children. British Medical Journal 298: 802–803

Steiner H et al 1988 Description of recording physical signs in suspected child sexual abuse. British Journal of Hospital Medicine 40(5): 346–351

Tanner J M 1978 Physical growth and development. Ch 7 in: Forfar J O, Arneil G C (eds) Textbook of paediatrics. Churchill Livingstone

Vickers D et al 1988 Anal signs in haemolytic uraemic syndrome. Letter. Lancet i: 998

Vizard E, Tranter M 1988 Recognition and assessment of sexual abuse. Ch 4 in: Bentovim A, Elton A, Hildebrand J, Tranter M, Vizard E (eds) Child sexual abuse within the family. Wright, pp 59–88

West R, Davies D, Fenton T 1989 Accidental vulval injuries in children. British Medical Journal 298: 1002–1003

White S T et al 1983 Sexually transmitted diseases in sexually abused children. Paediatrics 72: 16–21

White S T et al 1989 Vaginal introital diameter in the evaluation of sexual abuse. Child Abuse and Neglect 13: 217–224

Whitwell D 1990 The significance of childhood sexual abuse for adult psychiatry. British Journal of Hospital Medicine 43: 346–352

Woodling B 1986 Sexual abuse and the child. Em Med Serv 15: 17–25

Woodling B A, Heger A 1986 The use of the colposcope in the diagnosis of sexual abuse in the pediatric age group. Child Abuse and Neglect 10: 111–114

Working Together 1988 A guide to arrangements for inter-agency co-operation for the protection of children from abuse. HMSO

Working Together under the Children Act 1989 1991 A guide to arrangements for interagency co-operation for the protection of children from abuse. HMSO, London

Wright C et al 1987 Detection of sexual abuse in children. Letter. Lancet ii: 218

Zeitlin H 1987 Investigation of the sexually abused child. Lancet ii: 842

10. Sexual abuse of children with special needs

Kvents & Atkins (1986) wrote 'a disabled child may be incapable of disclosing the abuse even if he or she is upset and realises it is inappropriate. It is crucial that these children have a way to report abuse.'

The recognition of the sexual abuse of children with special needs is emerging as a major concern whether the child is at home, at school, fostered, or in residential care. It is difficult, but necessary, for professionals working with disabled children and adults to accept the unacceptable fact that is occurs (School 1987). The sexual abuse continues into adult life and the indications are that the rates of abuse in handicapped people are higher than in the general population (McCormack 1991).

It has long been known that children may be damaged by abuse (Ammerman et al 1988). This has usually been described in terms of permanent neurological damage, for example, following head injury, but the disabling consequences of emotional and sexual abuse are increasingly recognised. Abused children may present with learning difficulties which themselves make the child more vulnerable.

Lynch & Roberts (1982) wrote of the vulnerabilty of mentally handicapped children, recognising that, becuase they may be difficult to rear, abusive and neglectful behaviours might be triggered in otherwise competent parents.

PREVALENCE (Table 10.1)

Estimates from America suggest that between 1 in 3 and 1 in 4 teenagers with learning problems have been sexually abused (Chamberlain et al 1984), with an even higher prevalence amongst hearing impaired children (Sullivan et al 1987); this compares with a ratio of 1 in 10 estimated for all children in Britain (Baker & Duncan 1985).

A preliminary study in Britain of consultants caring for mentally handicapped adults suggested that 4–5% of these adults were being abused, sexual abuse being more common than neglect or physical abuse (Cooke 1990). This is thought to be an underestimate; if selected groups of mentally handicapped adults are considered, 50% of those referred to the Tavistock Clinic in London for psychotherapy have been sexually abused (Sinason 1992).

A study in Seattle (Ryerson 1984) reported over 400 cases of sexual abuse involving children and adults with special needs over a 4-year period. Chamberlain et al (1984) described a group of 87 girls aged 11–23 years, all of whom had learning problems — 14 of 41 mildly handicapped and 2 out of 23 of the severely handicapped girls were thought to have had unlawful sexual intercourse.

39% of 150 multihandicapped children admitted consecutively to a residential hospital had been or were thought likely to have been abused (Ammerman et al 1989). Physical abuse was more common than sexual abuse but important features of the CSA were:

- in 50% the abuse began under 2 years of age
- 66% involved penetration
- 40% had been abused by multiple perpetrators.

Hearing impaired children appear to be one of the most vulnerable groups, with boys involved as frequently as girls, and up to 50% of children having been abused at home, during transport to school, or at school (day or residential) (Sullivan et al 1987, Kennedy 1989).

Table 10.1 Estimates of the prevalence of CSA in various groups

Adults with learning difficulties (UK)	5%
Teenagers with learning difficulties (USA)	25%
Children with learning difficulties and behaviour problems referred for therapy	50–70%
Hearing impaired children	50%

Thorough assessment of all children with emotional difficulties will reveal a high level of abuse. It was assessed that over half the children attending a Child and Family Psychiatric Unit had been abused, sexual abuse being the main form of abuse (Hallas M 1990 personal communication).

A study of a small residential school for emotionally disturbed children aged 8–12 years found that half had been sexually abused (Wadsworth & Abel 1987).

WHY ARE CHILDREN WITH SPECIAL NEEDS SO VULNERABLE ?

In 1986 Finkelhor & Baron wrote that any child disabled or disadvantaged is at once more vulnerable to abuse and, once abused, is more vulnerable.

The vulnerability of the disabled child may begin from very early in life if his attachment to his parents is impaired. The child was not the hoped-for child, and research shows that lack of appropriate support at this difficult time is associated with later physical abuse. Parents' relationships with their disabled child are inevitably different because of the added dependence and may become distorted. The sexual abuse of older sons by their mothers is an increasingly recognised example of this.

Finkelhor (1984) also wrote of the preconditions of CSA:

- motivation to abuse
- overcoming societal inhibitions
- overcoming situational inhibitions
- overcoming the child's resistance.

Schor (1987) explains these preconditions with reference to the developmentally delayed child (Tables 10.2, 10.3).

Not only are the children available and abusers have many opportunities to abuse, but also it is

Table 10.2 Why are children with special needs vulnerable to CSA? (Schor 1987)

1. Difficulty in communication:
   - learning problem
   - language disorder
   - emotional difficulty
   - hearing impaired.
2. Can't get away — physical disability.
3. Age-inappropriate dependency (for dressing, bathing, toileting) means sense of privacy meaningless:
   - learning problem
   - physical disability
   - visually impaired.
4. Isolated and inexperienced, do not know 'norms'.
5. Need for affection, friendship which is exploited.
6. Use of transport to school, residential placements, foster-homes.
7. Multiple carers.
8. Previous abuse.
9. Distressed behaviour wrongly attributed to intrinsic disorder when cause is CSA:
   - 'excessive' masturbation
   - self-mutilation.
10. Not seen as sexually attractive (whether adult or child).
11. Low self-image of disabled child compounded by guilt discourages disclosure.
12. Denial by abuser and disbelief by carers may precipitate psychotic breakdown and prevent further communication and provide 'evidence' of the childs unreliability.

easier to maintain secrecy if the child has communication difficulties. Even if the child tries to communicate he may be misunderstood. His language or behaviour may be explicit but alternative explanations are preferred. An example would be 'excessive' masturbation — is it due as is often said to the disability or is this a presenting sign of CSA?

The dependency of the child who relies on others to bathe, dress or toilet him makes the notion of privacy meaningless. Handicapped children are often compliant, they may fear abandonment, feel guilty at being handicapped and not the child their parents wanted, and may wish they had never been born (Sinason 1992).

Table 10.3 Factors of which abusers of handicapped children are aware

1. Easy targets — immature, dependent, inexperienced, inarticulate, needy, previous abuse.
2. Recognition of the low status of children and especially handicapped children: does this lower taboo levels?
3. Families may become isolated, stressed, involved in inappropriate roles such as bathing sexually mature adolescents.

There are many myths about the sexual abuse of children with disability (Marchant 1991). One important one is that they are not sexually attractive or desirable and by virtue of their handicap will be protected. This vulnerability and powerlessness may be appealing, as is their lack of assertiveness.

Abusers are well aware of the low status of handicapped children and rationalise the abuse claiming that this is inevitably the only sexual relationship the child will have — it's not harmful, it's educational and even a good experience.

A further hazard for children with learning difficulties is that if they do disclose and the perpetrator denies the abuse they are more vulnerable to psychotic breakdown. Verbal and physical symptoms may then be seen as psychotic features (Sinason 1992).

Finally, by the time the CSA is recognised it is often of long standing, the child may have accommodated to the abuse and as with other children may not be able to speak of the abuse even if the abuse has become evident to others.

CLINICAL PRESENTATION (Vizard & Tranter 1988)

1. What the child says

Children with learning or communication problems, for whatever reason, have difficulty in telling of their abuse and being understood. Skilled professionals who understand the nature of the child's handicap or developmental disorder may be able to communicate with the child but must be able to use the appropriate method(s). These include play, sign language(s), use of dolls and puppets, line drawings, or the child's drawings. The child may need engaging in sessions over months to even years in the most traumatised cases.

Direct and leading questions are often needed, as for very young children, which will have implications for court purposes, but this is inevitable. As long as the entire clinical picture is presented and explained, the interview with its limitations should be accepted.

CASE HISTORY 1
A girl of 13 years with severe learning problems

presented at school with a chemical burn on the back of her hand and signs consistent with vaginal penetration. There was a clear history of escalating abuse by the taxi driver who took her to school daily. The police investigation was dropped because of inconsistencies in her story; she 'named colour of curtains wrongly in room assaults took place'.

2. Behavioural signs (Vizard 1989)

- Sexualised behaviour
  — explicit sexual behaviour
  — excessive masturbation
- Change in behaviour
  — anger, aggression
  — withdrawn, mute
- Persisting anger or disturbed behaviour
  — temper tantrums which are unexplained
  — self-destructive behaviour
  — violence to other, to animals
  — destructive of toys, belongings, room, bedding
- Problems associated with urination and defecation
- Eating disorder.

3. Physical signs

- Vaginal or rectal bleeding
- Sexually transmitted disease
- Pregnancy
- Non-accidental injury.

PHYSICAL EXAMINATION

This should be a full examination and the child should be supported by an adult with whom the child feels comfortable. An adult in authority, such as a headteacher, is not usually this person. General anaesthesia or sedation is sometimes needed. Issues of consent should be discussed: it is usually the parent who has the authority to consent, see Chapter 9.

Physical abnormality may on occasion be diagnostic of abuse (gonorrhoea or pregnancy) but is more often supportive of the diagnosis of CSA (Royal College of Physicians 1991). 35 highly dependent females aged 13–35 years were examined when one of their number was found to be pregnant; 13 had signs which were consistent with penetration (Elvick et al 1990).

Forensic tests should be done if there is a possibility of recent assault. Children may have a poor sense of time and be unable to say when the last abuse occurred unless the abuse occurred on a memorable day such as a birthday.

CASE HISTORY 2

A girl aged 16 years with severe learning problems was seen at school to have two 'love bites' on her neck. Physical examination showed signs compatible with repeated vaginal penetration. Forensic swabs were positive for semen. The father admitted to the police a long history of vaginal intercourse.

CASE HISTORY 3

A girl aged 14 years with Down's syndrome said to a teacher following respite care with foster-parents that she did not like it when Uncle Terry touched her 'boo-boos'. Her father, a police officer, would not make a complaint fearing that investigation would cause his daughter unnecessary upset as the complaint was unlikely to reach court.

CASE HISTORY 4

A boy aged 9 years with moderate learning problems and aggressive, uncontrollable behaviour was referred because of 'excessive masturbation'. When examined he had an immediate and sustained erection. Investigation revealed repeated abuse and probable prostitution involving his mother's many male partners. Aged 12 years he sexually abused any available younger child and at 13 years was placed in a secure unit.

CASE HISTORY 5

A girl aged 3 years and her brother aged 6 years, mute and thought to have severe learning difficulties, were referred by the school nurse when the girl had possible burns on her abdomen. Both children had anal signs compatible with anal penetration. In an adoptive home both children have made remarkable progress. The girl, aged 8 years, attends mainstream school with support and her brother, now 11 years, attends a unit for children with moderate learning problems.

CASE HISTORY 6

A boy aged 15 years with moderate learning problems presented to the paediatrician because of recent onset of soiling. He immediately disclosed sexual abuse involving a male member of staff at the assessment centre he attended.

CASE HISTORY 7

A girl aged 10 years with moderate learning problems and some behavioural difficulties was seen to have a bruised face and burns on her hand and neck. Her step-mother was emotionally, physically, and sexually abusing her.

CASE HISTORY 8

A boy aged 11 years with Duchenne muscular dystrophy and his sister, 13 years, who had moderate learning problems were both sexually abused by their 19-year-old foster-brother. Previously their father physically abused them and their mother had abandoned them.

CONSEQUENCES OF CSA

By virtue of their coexisting disability children with special needs respond in protean ways to the additional trauma of abuse. There is debate as to how far this trauma actually causes learning problems (Vizard 1989).

- CSA caused anxiety and impairs the child's ability to pay attention and learn. Even when the CSA stops, the degree of recovery is uncertain; children with learning problems are particularly vulnerable to psychological damage when they are abused (Sinason 1992).
- Disclosure of abuse may engender great anxiety in the child and disbelief precipitate frank psychosis.
- There is a continuing increased risk of mental health problems in the survivors of CSA, notably depression (Mullen 1991).
- CSA may have an adverse effect on the child's developing personality, in particular in the ability to make stable relationships.
- Children who have been sexually abused may become abusers, and this is also true of children with learning difficulties (Dunne 1990).
- Children born as a result of an incestuous union have a 30–60% risk of inherited abnormality (Illingworth 1987).
- Specialist clinics for treating victims and abusers are few and only a minority receive adequate help.

Summary

1. The sexual abuse of children with special needs is emerging as a major concern.

2. The prevalence of abuse in disabled children and adults is greater than for the general population.

3. Particular groups such as the hearing impaired are at especial risk, but no group is exempt from CSA.

4. Children may be abused at home, on transport, at school, in foster or respite care, in a hospital or hostel, or anywhere.

5. CSA will only be recognised if parents and professionals are prepared to see and hear.

6. Children are vulnerable because of their dependency, difficulties in communication and need for companionship.

7. Traditionally, sexually explicit behaviours have been considered as part of the disorder rather than learned.

8. Abusers recognise disabled children as easy targets of low status with whom they may have sex with relative impunity.

9. Children are distressed by the abuse but their attempts to communicate may be misinterpreted as fantasy or challenging behaviour; disbelief may lead to psychotic breakdown in the children with learning disorders.

10. Skilled professionals with particular communication skills are needed, and usual methods of interviewing are not always appropriate. Direct questioning and leading questions may be necessary if the child is to be understood.

11. Criminal proceedings are rare unless there is an admission by the abuser or there is additional corroborative evidence.

12. Family Courts are able to hear evidence not admissible in other courts in order to ensure the welfare of the child.

13. Child victims may become abusers, in adolescence or earlier.

14. Prevention lies in:
- acceptance that disabled people have ordinary sexual needs
- sex education for all children
- education of carers and professionals.

REFERENCES

Ammerman R T, Van Hasselt V, Hersen M 1988 Abuse and neglect in handicapped children: a critical review. Journal of Family Violence 3: 53–72

Ammerman R, Van Hasselt V, Hersen M, McGonigle J J, Lubetsky M J 1989 Abuse and neglect in psychiatrically hospitalised multihandicapped children. Child Abuse and Neglect 13: 335–343

Baker A W, Duncan S P 1985 Child sex abuse: a study of prevalence in Great Britain. Child Abuse and Neglect 9: 457–467

Chamberlain A, Rauh J, Passer A, McGrath M, Burket R 1984 Issues in fertility control for mentally retarded female adolescents. Sexual activity, sexual abuse and contraception. Pediatrics 73(4): 445–450

Cooke L B 1990 Abuse of mentally handicapped adults. British Medical Journal 300: 193

Dunne T P, Power A 1990 Sexual abuse and mental handicap. Preliminary findings of a community based study. Mental Handicap Research 3: 111–125

Elvick S L, Berkowitz C D, Nicholas E, Lindley Lipman J, Inkelis S H 1990 Sexual abuse in the developmentally disabled: dilemmas of diagnosis. Child Abuse and Neglect 14: 497–502

Finkelhor D 1984 Child sexual abuse. New theory and research. The Free Press, New York

Finkelhor D, Baron L 1986 High risk children. In: Finkelhor D (ed) A sourcebook on child sexual abuse. Sage, p. 83

Illingworth R S 1987 The development of the infant and young child. Normal and abnormal. Churchill Livingstone, Edinburgh, pp. 20, 342

Kennedy M 1989 The silent nightmare. Soundbarrier, March 1989

Kvents E J, Atkins D V 1986 Guide to "No-Go-Tell" New York. The Lexington Center, New York

Lynch M, Roberts J 1982 Ill health and physical handicap. In: Lynch M, Roberts J (eds) Consequences of child abuse. Academic Press. New York

McCormack B 1991 Sexual abuse and learning difficulties (leader). British Medical Journal 303: 143–144

Marchant R 1991 Myths and facts about sexual abuse and children with disabilities. Child Abuse Review 5 (2): 22

Mullen P E 1991 The consequences of child sexual abuse (leader). British Medical Journal 303: 144

Royal College of Physicians 1991 Report. Physical signs of sexual abuse in children. The Royal College of Physicians, London

Ryerson E 1984 Sexual and self-protection education for disabled youth: a primary need. SIECUS Report XIII; 1: 1–7

Schor D P 1987 Sex and sexual abuse in developmentally disabled adolescents. Semin Adolesc Med 3; 1: 1–7

Sinason V 1992 Therapy. Paper presented 7-1-1992 in study day "Abuse of young people with learning difficulties", Salford, to Paediatrics Child Abuse Interest Group

Sullivan P M, Vernon M, Scanlan J M 1987 Sexual abuse of deaf youth. AAD October 1987

Vizard E 1989 Child sexual abuse and mental handicap: a child psychiatrist's perspective. In: Brown H, Craft A (eds) Thinking the unthinkable. FPA Educational Unit, London

Vizard E, Tranter M 1988 Recognition and assessment of child sexual abuse. In: Bentovim A, Elton A, Hildebrand J, Tranter M, Vizard E (eds) Child sexual abuse within the family: assessment and treatment. John Wright, Bristol

Wadsworth D J, Abel K 1987 Some aspects of the primary identification of sexual abuse in children: experiences from a residential setting. Child Abuse Review 1 (6)

11. Fetal problems

Being the fetus of a woman who abuses alcohol or drugs is clearly harmful, but definitions of fetal maltreatment are difficult to formulate. The law in the UK permits research on embryos up to the age of 14 days and elective abortion until 24 weeks (in some circumstances 28 weeks). The rights of the fetus as a separate being may thus be considered to begin at 28 weeks or when the mother has decided to continue with the pregnancy.

For a pregnancy to have the best outcome it should be planned, the parents be healthy and mutually supportive, and the mother's diet be good. Mother and baby have the right to receive good obstetric and neonatal care. The principal adverse factors affecting outcome are maternal poverty, youth and unmarried status. It would therefore be unjust to blame the outcome of a pregnancy solely on the mother's alcohol or drug abuse; the reasons why women abuse drugs are many and often socially determined.

The situation under the law is complex. In 1987 Berkshire County Council sought to remove at birth a child, who was the victim of drug withdrawal, from her heroin-addicted mother (D [a minor] v Berkshire County Council 1987). The case was eventually heard in the House of Lords who found that 'X is being neglected or ill treated' could be interpreted under the Child and Young Persons Act, 1969, to include the intrauterine phase of life. The argument was that child care was a continuum and that, if neglect was part of this continuum, the court could consider conditions occurring before the child was born.

However, many babies born in the UK to a mother who abuses alcohol or drugs do go home with their mother, after a multidisciplinary assessment, with continuing support. The position is increasingly difficult with the association of HIV infection and intravenous drug abuse, and alternative care is inevitable for some babies. The situation is now so critical in the USA that many babies remain in institutional care owing to the difficulty in finding foster-parents who are able to cope not only with the risk that the baby may develop HIV infection but also the fact that babies of addicts may be extremely difficult to care for due to brain damage sustained in utero (see later).

Men may be involved in fetal maltreatment by physically assaulting the mother. Family violence studies show that spouse abuse occurs with increased frequency and intensity during pregnancy (Gelles 1987).

Table 11.1 Factors which affect fetal health

1. Maternal abuse of drugs (non-therapeutic)
2. Maternal abuse of alcohol
3. Maternal tobacco abuse
4. Physical abuse: ● directed at mother
   ● directed at fetus
5. Mother's non-attendance at antenatal clinic
6. Father's neglect of mother's needs
7. Poverty, poor housing, poor nutrition of mother
8. Unwanted, unplanned, uncared-for pregnancy
9. Teenage pregnancy.

CASE HISTORY 1

A woman, aged 22 years, 24 weeks pregnant was admitted because of multiple stab wounds to her abdomen. Her partner, in a temper, had sought to injure her and her unborn baby. The abdominal wounds were explored and although initially it was thought the fetus was unharmed, subsequent radiology and premature delivery of the baby 2 weeks later revealed that the fetus too had been stabbed, causing extensive intra-abdominal injury. The baby died aged 3 weeks.

Men may also be emotionally abusive or negative

201

about the pregnancy. They may facilitate the mother's access to drink or drugs. They may fail to provide materially. A woman who is anxious or depressed (as many drug abusers are) needs emotionally supportive friends and family about her if she is to cope with her own drug withdrawal to better preserve the pregnancy. Unfortunately her partner and friends often also abuse alcohol or drugs which makes it all the more difficult for the pregnant woman to alter her lifestyle. Women who abuse alcohol are also notoriously secretive in their habits and frequently do not seek help. Society appears to be more disapproving of women who drink, which may also inhibit some women from asking for help; certainly there are few facilities for alcoholic women.

DRUG AND ALCOHOL ABUSE BY THE MOTHER

Drug and alcohol abusing women who become pregnant have several characteristics in common which make it difficult to assess the importance of the various factors involved in damaging the fetus. It is difficult to obtain a clear, accurate history as to which drugs have been abused, at what dose and how often. Many women abuse several drugs and in addition drink too much alcohol and smoke tobacco. They tend to neglect their own health and their nutrition is suboptimal. They are frequently poor attenders at antenatal clinics. There is often a history of several previous pregnancies

ending in spontaneous abortion. The women may have abused drugs for several years, be anaemic and have sexually transmitted diseases, hepatitis or HIV (Fig. 11.1).

The effect on the pregnancy may be early miscarriage, fetal damage, preterm delivery, stillbirth, neonatal illness or death, and consequences reaching into infancy: increased risk of SIDS, developmental delay and learning problems, behavioural disorders, neglect, and physical abuse (Fig. 11.2). However, some infants appear to survive unscathed. There are recognisable clinical patterns relating to the drug which is abused. These are listed in Tables 11.2 and 11.3.

Women who abuse drugs tend to be socially disadvantaged and tackling the reasons for their alienation is more likely to be helpful than attempting to curb drug barons. Education on the effects of drug abuse (which are little appreciated) will be successful only if women feel secure, confident and in control of their lives; then, they may listen.

Alcohol abuse — fetal alcohol syndrome (FAS)

In the UK, alcohol abuse is the commonest form of substance abuse. Fetal alcohol syndrome was initially recognised in 1968 by Lemoine et al and re-described independently in 1973 in the children of chronically alcoholic women by Jones et al 1973. The syndrome represents a clinical continuum

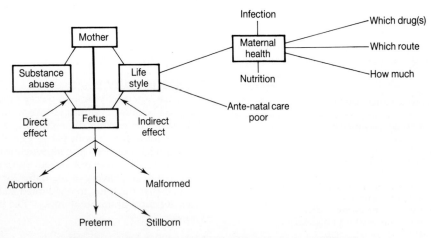

Fig. 11.1   Relationship between substance abuse and lifestyle.

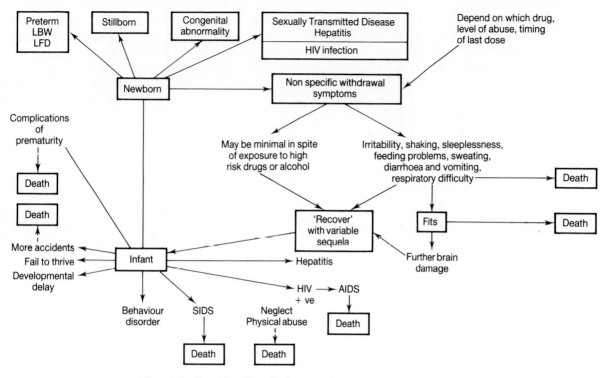

Fig. 11.2   Possible effect of substance abuse on newborn and infant.

from the severe cases described by Lemoine to those less seriously damaged (Smith 1982). 'Fetal alcohol effects' (FAE) describes the consequences of alcohol abuse without the morphological features listed in Tables 11.2 and 11.3 (Murray-Lyon 1989), and below.

The learning problems in FAE and FAS vary from mild difficulty to mental retardation. The severity of the intellectual handicap is correlated to the severity of the physical characteristics. Infants may be hypotonic and irritable whilst older children have learning problems, poor coordination, and are hyperactive. The growth deficiency may be marked and catch-up growth is not generally achieved postnatally. Microcephaly also persists.

Table 11.2   Intrauterine effects of drug and substance abuse

Drug	Congenital malformation	Impaired intrauterine growth	Abortion, preterm labour	Neonatal withdrawal symptoms
Alcohol	+	+	+	+
Cigarettes	–	+	+	–
Cannabis	–	+	–	+
Opiates	–	+	+	+
Cocaine	+	+	+	+
Amphetamine	–	–	–	+
Benzodiazepine	–	+	+	+
Barbiturates	–	–	+	+
Phencyclidine	+	+	–	+
Heroin	+	+	+	+
Methadone	–	–	–	–+

Table 11.3 Consequences of intrauterine intoxication for infant

	Respiratory distress	Jittery, hyperactive	Lethargy	Poor feeding	Irritable	GIupset	Fits	Congenital malformation	Behavioural abnormality	Developmental abnormality	SIDS	Failure to thrive	HIV
Alcohol	+	+	–	+	++	–	+	+	+	+	+	+	–
Cigarettes	–	–	–	–	–	–	–	–	–	–	+	–	–
Cannabis	–	+	–	–	–	–	–	–	–	–	–	–	–
Opiates	+	+	–	+	+	–	+	–	+	+	+	+	+
Cocaine	+	+	+	+	++	–	+	+	+	+	+	+	+
Amphetamine	–	+	+	–	–	–	–	–	–	+	–	–	–
Benzodiazepine	+	–	+	+	+	–	–	–	+	–	–	–	–
Barbiturate	+	+	+	+	–	–	+	–	–	–	–	–	–
Phencyclidine	–	+	+	–	–	+	+	+	–	–	–	+	–
Heroin	+	+	–	+	+	+	+	+	+	+	+	+	+
Methadone	+	–	–	–	–	–	+	–	+	–	+	–	–

Summary of signs and symptoms of fetal alcohol syndrome:

1. Growth deficiency — pre- and postnatally,
2. CNS defects — microcephaly, learning problems,
3. Distinctive facies — short palpebral fissures, flat midface, indistinct philtrum, short upturned nose,
4. Congenital anomalies — heart, eye, renal, skeletal defects,
5. As fetal alcohol effects.

Fetal alcohol effects (FAE):

1. Learning problems,
2. Increased risk of perinatal death,
3. Increased risk of epilepsy.

Long–term effects of fetal alcohol syndrome. The dysmorphic features of FAS become less obvious over time, but growth failure and learning problems are permanent even when subsequent child care is good. The continuing high level of psychosocial problems includes, in addition to learning difficulties (average IQ 63 in the 'classic form of FAS'), hyperactivity, impulsiveness and antisocial behaviour (Bays 1990).

What is, or is there 'safe' drinking in pregnancy? Drinking patterns amongst women are changing in the UK and as women drink more the effects of increased consumption are seen in the number of women where excessive drinking is a problem (around 10% of all drinkers), the increased death rate from alcohol-related disorders, and admissions to mental hospital due to alcoholism (increased by 23% in 7 years).

How much alcohol is 'safe'? To non-pregnant women 14 units per week is considered nontoxic. 1 unit is equivalent to 10 g of alcohol, 1/2 pint of beer or 1 glass of wine, sherry or whisky. 26 units per week is thought to be harmful.

During pregnancy, consumption of more than 8 units a day is associated with FAS. More moderate consumption is reported to result in an increased rate of spontaneous abortion, fetal malformation and fetal growth retardation. Moderate consumption was defined as up to 10 units per week, although there are reports of problems at lower levels of alcohol intake.

How many pregnant women do drink more than 10 units (100 g) of alcohol per week? This varies between 6 and 20% in different parts of the UK. In one study (Barrison et al 1985):

- 20% of mothers drank more than 10 units a week in the early stage of pregnancy.
- 5% of mothers drank more than 5 units a day and were at risk of liver damage.
- Very few drank 8–10 units a day and were at risk of delivering a child with FAS.
- Consumption of alcohol falls in pregnancy except for heavy drinkers, and once pregnancy was confirmed only 6% of women drank more than 10 units a week.

The prevalence of FAS in different countries — 1 in 100 live births in Northern France, 1 in 600 in Sweden, 1 in 750 in Seattle and 1–2 per 1000 in the UK — reflects drinking patterns. In the UK women from ethnic minorities drink less than Caucasians, but not uniformly so (Barrison et al 1985).

The picture is not clearcut; there are variable effects even for heavy drinkers — for example, one sibling of a chronically alcohol-abusing mother may be severely affected while other siblings are unharmed. The frequent association of cigarette smoking and poor maternal nutrition also complicates the clinical picture.

Education is important. Around the time of conception women should ideally drink no alcohol; this is difficult unless pregnancies are planned. It is not known whether persistent heavy drinking or peaks (binges) or both are more teratogenic. Logically, alcohol abstinence around conception is advisable, with only a limited amount of drink throughout the rest of pregnancy.

Cigarette smoking during pregnancy

Cigarette smoking is even more common than alcohol consumption and young women have been smoking more whilst the overall trend in the UK is towards a decrease in smoking.

Smoking of 5 cigarettes a day has been associated with symmetrical growth retardation in the fetus (Wieburg et al 1985). Babies may be light for dates for many reasons but the additive effect of alcohol and cigarette smoking has been noted. However, up to 30% of the low birth weight has been attributed to cigarette smoking. It has also been suggested that cigarettes are associated with spontaneous abortion, stillbirth and prematurity.

Heroin abuse

The effects of heroin abuse are given in Tables 11.2 and 11.3. Infection with HIV is prevalent amongst intravenous drug users (see later).

There are high rates of fetal death, stillbirth and increased neonatal death, the latter due to respiratory distress and seizures. Withdrawal symptoms may persist for months. The neonate may have a coarse tremor, shrill cry, be very irritable, have diarrhoea, vomiting and fever, be hyperactive, sneeze and yawn.

The shrill cry, feeding and sleep problems make the baby difficult to care for; developmental and behaviour problems persist. Children born to heroin-abusing mothers are described as hyperactive, having temper tantrums and a low threshold for frustration. They are clumsy, cannot concentrate, and have delayed language development and later learning difficulties at school. These problems continue through adolescence, with persisting behavioural and learning disorder.

Cocaine

Cocaine abuse has overtaken heroin abuse in the USA and is rapidly rising in the UK, with the derivative 'crack' being increasingly available. The effects on the fetus are equally, if not more, serious than those due to heroin. The drug is used intranasally, intravenously and in cigarette form. As with all drug abuse, several drugs may be abused simultaneously, and HIV infection is common in intravenous drug abusers. Maternal abuse of cocaine and its effects are shown in Tables 11.2 and 11.3.

Cocaine causes a 10-fold increased rate of haemorrhage or placental abruption, around 30% spontaneous abortion rate, premature labour and fetal distress. Cocaine-induced vasospasm may be responsible for the placental effects as well as the congenital anomalies seen in the infant (Bays 1990). The neonate is small with microcephaly,

lethargic and may have considerable respiratory problems (RDS and meconium aspiration).

Congenital malformations have been associated with cocaine abuse, including cerebral and renal, cardiac and skeletal anomalies (Larson 1989).

Withdrawal symptoms may be delayed and only after discharge from hospital does the baby become irritable, jittery and cry uncontrollably. These symptoms may persist day and night for weeks or longer. There may also be an increased risk of infection in infancy. As many as 15% of such babies are said to succumb to SIDS. Crack makes the adult abusers more aggressive, and the level of family violence and child abuse and death has risen markedly in the USA. Behaviour and learning problems persist through childhood and beyond, much as for the offspring of heroin addicts. The extreme hyperactivity in association with poor understanding makes children damaged by cocaine difficult to care for even in good social circumstances. It is thought that structural damage occurs in utero and causes brain damage including other severe neurological deficits such as hemiplegia and Parkinsonian dystonia (Bays 1990).

THE CONSEQUENCES OF ADDICTION FOR THE FAMILY

As has been described, the affected neonate may not only have serious physical problems but also behavioural patterns which make caring for him difficult. Like any child, the baby needs care, attention and physical comfort but the carers find it difficult to look after a child who won't feed, or sleep, and cries endlessly. If the parents are still abusing drugs or alcohol they will not cope, but neither do many foster-parents who are driven to total exhaustion by the child's behaviour. Breakdown with change of carers occurs and the damaged child has further suboptimal care.

In an addicted mother, if the pregnancy was wanted, and she intends to withdraw and remain off drugs or drink, rehabilitation may be successful. If she has a partner or friends around her who are still abusing, the task is virtually impossible. The older the woman, and the longer her history of abuse, the less likely is she to succeed in staying off drugs or drink. Some cope for months but then relapse, and the child is received back into care. If this happens repeatedly the child will suffer harm.

If parents are trying to manage their baby, but both they and the child have withdrawal symptoms together, it is very hard. The child is unwell and the parents feel guilty, then angry, as they are tired and stressed. The parents are then seen not to be coping but foster-parents may equally be very stressed by dealing with such an infant. The child may have been damaged in utero, then neonatally (especially by seizures), and finally postnatally if his care is inadequate.

However, not all babies are so severely affected and many have been well cared for and eventually adopted. Not all babies born to HIV-positive mothers will become infected with HIV (see later).

HIV INFECTION IN CHILDREN

Although acquired immune deficiency syndrome (AIDS) was only recognised in 1981 it is a major health problem worldwide. In the UK the clinical picture has been that children infected have been from 'at risk groups', as described below, but this is likely to change. In Africa heterosexual transmission is widespread and the effects are already devastating, as babies may be born infected or become ill in childhood as their parents die. The World Health Organization estimates that 5–10 million people worldwide are infected with HIV, and AIDS will become an increasing cause of morbidity and mortality in childhood (Lissauer 1991).

HIV infection in children in the UK

Cases of the acquired immune deficiency syndrome (AIDS) in children account for less than 2% of the total number of reported cases, and 80% of these cases arise through vertical transmission (Mok 1990). The risk of HIV transmission from infected mother to child varies from 10–40% (Mok et al 1989). Factors influencing the risk may include maternal immune function and the gestational age of the infant.

Methods for diagnosing HIV infection in young infants lack specificity and sensitivity. Maternal IgG antibodies also limit the usefulness of antibody testing in the first 18 months. None of the laboratory tests have been correlated with eventual clinical outcome, and silent HIV infection may occur in children (Mok 1990). Current transmission rates may therefore need to be revised after further follow-up of these children. As the child reaches 18 months, a positive HIV antibody test is likely to indicate the presence of infection, although a negative test does not necessarily exclude infection. Antibody detection is by an ELISA screening test, confirmed by a Western Blot.

If the child has a negative antibody test but infection is strongly suspected clinically, the tests should be repeated or viral culture or antigen detection tests undertaken.

Risk factors

The majority of cases of paediatric HIV infection in the UK are the children of mothers from high-risk groups, that is intravenous drug users, prostitutes or women from countries where the prevalence of HIV infection is high. Around 20% of initial cases were children with haemophilia or recipients of blood transfusions. This group should reduce as donor units have been screened for HIV antibodies since 1985.

The clinical situation is changing rapidly as the pool of HIV infection increases in the general population. However, although currently the majority of HIV-positive teenagers are haemophiliacs, as their numbers fall the number of teenagers who are positive due to sexual abuse, intravenous drug use and unprotected sexual activity will rise.

HIV infection has been reported in Australia and the USA as a consequence of sexual abuse and the question of testing sexually abused children is increasingly raised (Berkowitz 1986, Leiderman 1986, Hobbs & Wynne 1987). It is probable that a significant proportion of young adults who have HIV infection have been sexually abused as children, as even if they were not infected as children the behavioural consequences of CSA, including sexual promiscuity and the teenage runaway lifestyle, put them at high risk.

The clinical manifestations of HIV infection are extremely variable. They are summarised in Table 11.4. A diagnosis of possible HIV infection should be considered in any child with these non-specific

Table 11.4 Clinical spectrum of HIV infection

1. *Variable course*: a. May remain asymptomatic
   b. Mild symptoms for several years
   c. Rapidly deteriorating course and death in months
2. *Presenting symptoms*: a. Failure to thrive
   b. Generalised lymphadenopathy, hepatosplenomegaly
   c. Oral thrush
   d. Frequent URTI, otitis media
   e. Weight loss, anaemia, fever.
3. *Symptomatic phase*: a. Bacterial peneumonia — usual childhood pathogens but also opportunistic infections: *Pneumocystis carinii*, CMV (lung biopsy often needed)
   b. Septicaemia, osteomyelitis, septic arthritis
   c. Neurodevelopmental abnormalities — poor development, dementia, ataxia, due to infection and HIV encephalopathy or brain tumour
   d. Skin, renal, hepatic and haematological abnormality
   e. Lymphoma, Kaposi's sarcoma is rare.
4. *Prognosis*: Uncertain. Children who develop opportunist infection in early life have a mortality of 60–80%.

---

or more specific symptoms, and a history of maternal or other risk factors for HIV infection. However, the social implications of testing must be considered: do not test unless it can be justified.

Practical issues in treating HIV-infected or at-risk children (HIV Infection in Infancy and Childhood 1989)

1. HIV is not transmitted by respiratory or enteric routes or casual person–person contact (households, school, prison).

2. HIV has not been shown to be transmitted by insects, food, water, toilets, swimming pools, sweat, tears, shared utensils.

3. Deep needle stick injuries with injection of infected blood have, very rarely, resulted in transmission of HIV infection (1 in 500 incidents). Needles should always be put in suitable disposal boxes.

4. Resuscitation of the neonate with an HIV-positive mother should be anticipated so that all necessary equipment is in the delivery room. The paediatrician should wear a mask, disposable gown over a plastic apron, surgical gloves and eye protection. Mouth-to-endotracheal tube suction should not be used for any delivery. The baby should be washed with soap and water and the cord swabbed with alcohol swabs.

5. Equipment, when used on potentially HIV-positive infected patients, should be disposable or disinfected by soaking in freshly prepared 0.1% sodium hypochlorite solution for 10 min or autoclaved.

6. Infected or potentially infected specimens (blood, excreta, respiratory secretions) if spilled should be cleaned up by staff wearing gloves, using sodium hypochlorite solution. Specimens for the laboratory should be placed in screw-top containers, marked with a bio-hazard label and double-bagged. They should be handled by staff wearing gloves or waterproof plasters over any open scratch.

7. Neonates, if healthy, should be nursed with their mother and not isolated. Usual care should be taken when dealing with blood specimen, cord, etc., when gloves should be worn.

8. Sick neonates need not be isolated. Care as previously described.

9. Breastfeeding is potentially a source of transmission of HIV, which has been isolated from breast milk. Women known to be HIV-positive are currently discouraged from breastfeeding. Such mothers clearly should not donate breast milk to human milk banks, where milk should be pasteurised.

10. Older children should not be isolated unless there is significant external bleeding, diarrhoea or the child is immunocompromised and needs reverse barrier nursing.

11. Immunisation is important for all HIV-infected children. The advice from the Department of Health (Memorandum on Immunization against Infectious Disease 1988) is unexpected in that it differs from the usually accepted teaching of withholding live vaccines from immunocompromised people. Children should receive:
   a. live vaccines: measles, mumps, rubella, polio
   b. inactivated vaccines: whooping cough, diphtheria, tetanus, polio, hepatitis B (if appropriate).
HIV-positive people should *not* receive BCG vaccine. The hepatitis B status of seropositive mothers should be tested and the infant given vaccine and gammaglobulin where appropriate. If

there are doubts the consultant in public health or infectious diseases will advise.

Management of HIV infection

Specific therapy for children with HIV infection should be discussed with units where there is experience of treating infected children as the drugs used are toxic and the outcome uncertain. General management involves aggressive treatment of infections and maintenance of nutrition.

All HIV-positive and high-risk infants should be followed up carefully. The first symptom of HIV infection may be a life-threatening illness. However, as in all chronic disorders of childhood, an attempt should be made to ensure that the child has as ordinary a life as possible. Practical issues of caring for children with HIV infection are listed above (HIV Infection in Infancy and (Childhood 1989).

Testing for HIV infection

This is a contentious issue and involves issues of confidentiality, consent and counselling (Swinburne 1989). Understanding of HIV infection in the community is limited and many myths exist as to the mode of transmission. Initially, infected people were advised to tell their GP, dentist, school and nursery. The consequence was that treatment was sometimes refused, children excluded from nursery and so on. Insurance com-panies may deny cover to anyone who has been tested for HIV infection, whether the result was positive or negative. This then affects the person's ability to obtain a house mortgage, for example. Parental consent is usual before testing a child for HIV infection; older children should also be asked (Gillick Principle; Gillick v West Norfolk and Wisbech Health Authority 1986).

The British Medical Association has stated (on the basis of General Medical Council advice) that children can be tested without parental consent if this is essential (even though in practice this means testing the mother's status too). Who else should know the result? Again, current advice is:

1. parents
2. the child's GP
3. think before informing school, nursery and

only do so with the parents' consent (see later).

Counselling is necessary before any test for HIV infection is undertaken and this is a particularly difficult and sensitive task.

Fostering, adoption, schooling

Education is the initial step when working with foster-parents and pre-adoptive parents willing to care for HIV-positive children. They must understand the risks, the potential course and outcome of HIV infection in childhood (Batty 1987).

In practice, emphasis is placed on good personal hygiene — handwashing with soap and water and covering open lesions. Health care issues such as immunisation and seeking early medical care if the child is ill are discussed. Household bleach, diluted 1:10 (sodium hypochlorite), is used to clean up spilled blood from cuts, vomit and so on.

Day nursery, play or nursery school are a necessary part of a young child's social life and development and should not be denied to at-risk or HIV-infected children. Most institutions already have measures for dealing with hepatitis B control and these should be adequate. Biting children are the subject of much concern. The risk of transmission is extremely low (Swinburne 1989) and effective management of the behaviour rather than exclusion of the child is preferable. Likewise, children should attend ordinary day school. If the child becomes unwell his educational needs should be reviewed in the light of his illness.

The Department of Education and Science has stated that there is no need for school staff to be informed of the HIV status of the child (Children at school and problems related to AIDS 1986). All schools should have advice on infectious disease and hygiene matters and the school health service should be involved in this aspect of education. The problem remains, when to tell the school or nursery? Ideally, if all personnel were trained and a uniform response could be assured, sooner rather than later would be the answer. If a child is ill and has increasing needs this is probably the time to discuss his condition, but all cases are different.

Sexually abused children are currently at low risk from HIV infection, although the clinical

Table 11.5 A suggested protocol for HIV testing of children who have been sexually abused (after Gellert et al 1990)

Child	or	Assailant
1. *Testing usually indicated if:*		
a. Symptomatic? HIV infection		a. HIV-seropositive
b. Adolescent with high-risk behaviour (drugs, prostitution)		b. symptomatic? HIV infection
		c. High-risk behaviour
c. Parent/adolescent insistent on test		d. Multiple assailant
2. *Testing may be indicated if:*		
a. Pre-pubescent with STD		a. Single unknown assailant
b. Adolescent with STD		
c. Anal or vaginal or oral penetration		

Note: The main purpose of early diagnosis:
(i) potential use of therapeutic drugs
(ii) Public health issues.

picture should be monitored. There are clear exceptions to this, such as a boy of 13 years working as a rent boy. Foster-parents may thus generally be reassured. Routine testing of all victims of CSA is not currently advisable. A recent paper has suggested a protocol for testing for HIV in sexually assaulted children (Table 11.5, Gellert et al 1990).

Foster-parents usually do need to know if a child they have been asked to care for is at risk of HIV infection or is HIV-positive. Foster-parents take children into their own homes, they may have children and grandchildren, and they should be informed of the risks, even if minimal, that they and their family are being asked to undertake on behalf of the child. With training and good selection of foster-parents placements are found and are often successful given good support.

Adoption is a difficult issue, especially when the child is an infant born to a HIV-positive mother. Only by around 15 months will diagnosis of HIV infection ordinarily be confirmed and even then an HIV-positive child may remain well for many years (Fig. 11.3). The baby needs a mother and a home, whether with his family or in care, from day 1 — not 15 months or 3 years. Experience in the UK is primarily in Lothian, Scotland, because of the high incidence of intravenous drug users in Edinburgh coupled with their high HIV infectivity rate (50–60%). Contrary to experience in the USA, both foster-homes and adoptive placements have been found for these babies.

For those babies who go home there must be

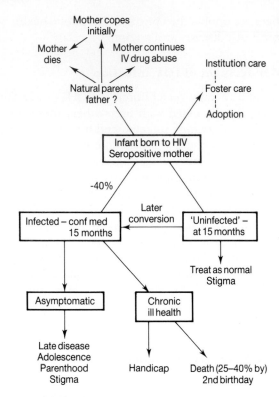

Fig. 11.3 What does the future hold? (After Mok 1987.)

support from all agencies. Their families are often severely disadvantaged, live in poverty, may be homeless and if the parents continue to abuse drugs the outlook for the child is even worse. Even when the mother is well motivated the prognosis is uncertain as she too has HIV infection, as probably does her partner. Parents receive prison sentences, become ill and die. Not surprisingly the risk of neglect and physical abuse of the baby, who may also be damaged by drug intoxication in utero, is high. The uninfected children in such households are also at risk of neglect and maltreatment and should be monitored.

In the USA many children remain in hospital beds, unwanted by their families (if they still exist) with failure to attract adequate foster-parents. This may also happen in the UK if the numbers of infected babies rise rapidly and there is not adequately resourced planning.

Counselling of children

The situation for older children who are HIV-seropositive is very difficult. Younger, asymptomatic children should be able to live as normal a life as possible, given the complication that their parent(s) may be ill. Generally it is reasonable for the family of a well child not to disclose that their child has HIV infection. Stigmatisation is inevitable given current attitudes and this will clearly cause the child and family unnecessary additional distress.

However, as HIV-positive children reach adolescence they will have to have understood the implications of their condition. These children should understand why they, especially, should have a healthy life-style, preferably before sexual maturity and teenage rebellion ensue. It is particularly important that they do not abuse drugs intravenously as this will contribute to the development of symptomatic disease, but it is in sexual relationships and parenthood that there will be the greatest upset and conflict. It is difficult for a teenager to come to terms with 'safe sex and no children'. The teenager too will be party to whether his HIV status should be kept confidential.

For symptomatic children decisions will be taken variably as to what to tell the child and when, as with any child with a chronic disorder. When older children realise the severity of their illness they will ask about death. Carers must be prepared for these questions and answer truthfully.

Summary

1. The fetus is vulnerable to a wide range of adverse influences which relate to the mother's health and lifestyle.

2. For the best outcome for the fetus a pregnancy should be planned, wanted and cared for.

3. Cigarettes are the most commonly used substance and affect birth weight.

4. Alcohol and other drugs of addiction cause fetal damage and disrupt lifestyle.

5. Drug abusing parents in addition often drink and smoke, and the cumulative effects increase the harm to the fetus.

6. Ongoing poor care in infancy is superimposed on the already harmed child who is also at risk of further abuse and neglect.

7. Brain damage caused in utero leaves the infants with persisting behavioural and learning difficulties. They may be difficult to care for requiring special parenting skills.

8. HIV infection is an increasing problem. Most cases result from infection acquired in utero. The social consequences are complex.

9. In this society where the pool of infected mothers is increasing, clinicians will become more aware of the consequences of infection. Early diagnosis may improve morbidity.

10. Legal interventions are required if the parents are unable to care adequately for their child.

REFERENCES

Barrison I, Waterson E J, Murray-Lyon I M 1985 Adverse effects of alcohol in pregnancy. British Journal of Addiction 80: 11–22

Batty D (ed) 1987 The implications of AIDS for children in care. BAAF

Bays J 1990 Substance abuse and child abuse. Pediatric Clinics of North America 37 (4)

Berkowitz C D 1986 Sexual abuse of children and adolescents. Advances in Paediatrics 34: 294

Children at school and problems related to AIDS 1986 DES and Welsh Offices

D (a minor) v Berkshire County Council 1987 1 All ER20

Gellert B G A, Durfee M J, Berkowitz C D 1990 Developing guidelines for HIV antibody testing among victims of paediatric sexual abuse. Child Abuse and Neglect 14 (1): 9

Gelles R J 1987 Family violence, 2nd edn. Sage Publications, Newbury Park

Gillick v West Norfolk and Wisbech Health Authority 1986 AC112

HIV Infection in Infancy and Childhood 1989 Report of a BPA working party. BPA, 5 St Andrew's Place, Regents Park, London NW1 4LB

Hobbs C J, Wynne J M 1987 Management of sexual abuse. Archives of Diseases of Childhood 62: 1182

Jones K L, Smith D W, Ulleland C N, Streissguth A P 1973 Pattern of malformation in offspring of chronic alcoholic mothers. Lancet 1: 1267

Larson E J 1989 Intoxication in utero. In: Mason J K (ed) Paediatric forensic medicine and pathology. Chapman & Hall Medical

Leiderman I Z 1986 A child with HIV infection. JAMA 256: 3094

Lemoine P, Harrousseau H, Borteyro J P 1968 Les enfants de parents alcoolique. Crest Med 21: 476

Lissauer T 1991 Infectious diseases. In: Harvey D, Kovar I (eds) Child health. Churchill Livingstone?

Memorandum on Immunization against Infectious Disease 1988 DHSS

Mok J 1987 HIV seropositive babies — implications in planning for their future. In: The implications of AIDS for children in care. BAAF

Mok J 1990 Leader. HIV infection in children. British Journal of Hospital Medicine 43: 247

Mok J Y Q, Haque R A, Yap P L et al 1989 Vertical transmission of HIV: a prospective study. Archives of Diseases of Childhood 64: 1140–1145

Murray-Lyon I M 1989 Adverse effects of alcohol in pregnancy. Gastroenterology in Practice, June/July

Smith D W 1982 Recognizable patterns of human malformation. W B Saunders, p. 411

Swinburne L M 1989 Medico legal implications of HIV infection in childhood. In: Mason J K (ed) Paediatric forensic medicine and pathology. Chapman & Hall Medical

Wieburg P, Marks J S, McLaren W M, Remington P L 1985 The fetal tobacco syndrome. Journal of American Medicine 253: 2998–2999

12. Poisoning, suffocation and Munchausen syndrome by proxy

INTRODUCTION

Poisoning, suffocation and Munchausen syndrome by proxy (MSBP) are related forms of child maltreatment which have recently been increasingly recognised. Poisoning may be accidental, neglectful or due to single acts of omission, whereas deliberate poisoning, suffocation or the fabrication of illness (MSBP) by a parent are clearly forms of child abuse. Whilst a depressed mother may leave her pills within the reach of her exploring toddler, other mothers deliberately poison or asphyxiate their child — either as a single event or over time as in Munchausen syndrome by proxy.

A relationship between these abuses is suggested in Figure 12.1. Current research clearly demonstrates that, as in other forms of child abuse, the very young are at greatest risk. It is evident also that if a previous child in a family has died an 'unusual or suspicious death' or from sudden infant death syndrome (SIDS), recurrent apnoeic spells in the new baby must be viewed very urgently as possible suffocation or MSBP (Emery 1985, Meadow 1990).

Repeated poisoning may be due to negligence but the consequences for the child may be equally as catastrophic as poisoning by intent or in order to fabricate illness (MSBP) and should be assessed as possible abuse.

POISONING

Accidental poisoning

Accidental poisoning of children is a major child health issue in the UK. Although it is seldom fatal, 15% of children do develop symptoms related to the ingestion and many children are seen in the Emergency Room of hospitals, made to vomit and have a very unhappy few hours which may include a brief admission to hospital.

A large multicentre study (Wiseman et al 1987) was set up to look at the causes of accidental poisoning, the outcome and also the type of packaging used by manufacturers. The peak age for ingestion was 2–3 years, adult supervision was faulty and ingestions took place at home. In 60% of cases the substance ingested was not in its usual storage place and 60% of substances were not in child-resistant containers; 22% of children were admitted to hospital, <10% needed intensive care and there were no fatalities.

Research has also been directed to consider the circumstances in which the ingestion took place (Sibert 1975). Environmental factors such as failure to use locked drug cupboards, bleach and turpentine stored under the kitchen sink and poor parental supervision with parents stressed by marital discord, poverty, several small children in

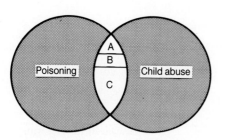

A. Acts of Commission (deliberate)
B. Repeated acts of Commission (MSBP?)
C. Acts of Omission (Neglect)

Fig. 12.1 Overlap of population of poisoned and abused children (adapted from Kresel & Lovejoy 1981).

the house and recent house move are commonly recorded.

Accidents may occur in well-regulated homes but repeated ingestion should be looked at as neglectful, and deliberate poisoning considered. It is also appropriate to look at parental behaviour: is the mother depressed, or impaired by the use of drugs or alcohol? Are there other signs of neglect within the family?

The drugs ingested are those often available at home — analgesics, anxiolytics, the contraceptive pill, cough medicine and iron. Bleach, detergents and petroleum products account for most of the household substances ingested.

If symptoms are severe — for example seizures, coma, intractable vomiting — consider whether an unusual substance such as salt, insulin or anticonvulsants has been administered.

The age of the child is also important. Toddlers aged 18 months to 3 years explore, test and taste whatever they find; by 4–5 years most children will know not to eat pills, although if weedkiller is kept in a lemonade bottle even much older children may be poisoned.

Parents may misread instructions on a bottle and overdose a child but the history is clear, whereas if parents deliberately overdose their child they will conceal the history. Children from 3 years are able to give a history and tell if they 'ate' Grandpa's 'sweeties' or if Mummy gave them herself. Children as young as 6 years do deliberately overdose, but this is rare under 10 years. If any child or adolescent does overdose a careful evaluation is necessary: what is making life so unbearable?

Intentional poisoning

Kempe (Kempe et al 1962), in his original description of the battered child syndrome, recognised deliberate poisoning by parents as a form of serious child abuse (Rogers et al 1976, Dine & McGovern 1982). Table 12.1 lists features of poisoning, whether due to accident, neglect or wilful intent by caretaker. There is considerable overlap but the more bizarre the clinical situation the greater the likelihood of intentional poisoning, whether as an attempt to kill the child or fabricate illness (MSBP). Drugs are also used to keep children quiet, for example use of sedatives at

Table 12.1   Poisoning – is it accident, neglect or deliberate?

	Accident	Neglect	Deliberate
Age	2–3 years Rarely older child	2–3 years Rarely older child	Infancy–3 years May be any age
History	Usually clear — makes sense	Variable — due to social chaos	a. None — but ill child b. History of accidental ingestion c. Recurrent symptoms
Symptoms	Uncommon < 15% < 1% need intensive care Rarely fatal	Uncommon < 15% < 1% need intensive care Rarely fatal	Common a. seizures, drowsy, vomiting diarrhoea b. Dead
Substance	*Drugs* — analgesics, anxiolytics, cough medicine, oral contraceptive, iron *Household* — bleach, detergent, petroleum product		*Drugs* — analgesics, antidepressants, anxiolytics, anticonvulsants, insulin, etc. *Other* — salt, bicarbonate of soda, corrosives, etc.
Past history	Nil	Repeated ingestions Increased incidence SIDS Known to SSD	Other unexplained child deaths in family including SIDS Other abuses
Diagnosis	History equates with clinical signs Confirmed if necessary by toxicological investigation	As Accidental	History usually at variance with clinical signs Ask advice of toxicologist — blood, urine samples THINK OF POSSIBILITY — PARENTS BEHAVIOUR MAY BE BIZARRE — BUT PRESENT AS CARING AND CONCERNED

night, or compliance, for example high doses of anxiolytics to allow sexual abuse to occur.

Adults who abuse drugs may also involve even very young children in their habit, and a child may present to hospital stuporose on the parent's heroin. There are many examples of children of all ages dangerously intoxicated with alcohol. This may be deliberate poisoning, or unsupervised drinking, often in a house where heavy drinking occurs. The number of deaths from solvent abuse increases annually in the UK and is nearing 200 per annum. Children as young as 8–9 years become involved in alcohol, drug and solvent abuse, usually with older teenagers (hence un-supervised) or at home with addicted parents.

Recurrent poisoning as part of Munchausen syndrome by proxy is discussed later in this chapter.

SUFFOCATION (see also Ch. 18 — Fatal child abuse)

As a form of physical assault on a baby, suffo-cation is difficult to detect because in spite of the violence of the act there may be no signs of injury, even at autopsy. Differentiation from sudden in-fant death syndrome (SIDS) may not be possible in the absence of any external sign of injury or foreign material in the mouth or airway (Pullar 1984, Bowen 1989). The clinical features of suffo-cation have been described (Meadow 1989a, 1990) and Table 12.2 lists the history and Table 12.3 the clinical features.

If suffocation is by use of a pad of material the child may not be injured. A hand across the child's face or around his neck would usually cause bruising but there may be just a few petechiae of the upper eyelids which disappear in 24–48 hours (in 'near-miss' or a non-fatal episode of strangula-tion). SIDS is defined as 'the sudden death of an infant or young child which is unexpected by history, and in which a thorough postmortem examination fails to reveal an adequate cause of death' (Bergman et al 1970).

Suffocation and SIDS largely involve very young infants. The older the child, particularly if there has been a history of recurrent episodes of apnoea, the more thought should be given to the possibility of deliberately induced asphyxial episodes.

The association between SIDS and social fac-tors is well established (Knowelden et al 1985). There is a strong trend which increases steeply in the poorest families. Unsupported families and unemployed families are 2–3 times more at risk than professional or managerial families. The inci-dence is greatest in inner city families, in areas of poor housing and social deprivation (Golding

Table 12.2 Clinical features of suffocation in infants and Sudden Infant Death Syndrome (SIDS)

	Suffocation (infancy)	SIDS
Incidence	Not known Emery (1985) suggests > 1/10 but < 1/15 'SIDS' due to abuse	2/1000 live births
Age	Infant < 12 months (but up to 3 years and rarely older)	Infancy, peak 3–4 months old, 90% before 8 months
History	*Presents* — maybe as 'near-miss cot death' or dead *Previously* — episodes cyanosis or floppiness accepted as apnoea or seizure Investigations all negative Other unexplained symptoms of ill-health	*Presents* — occasionally 'near-miss cot death', usually as SIDS *Previously* — healthy
Family	*Siblings* — unexplained disorder or death Other evidence of abuse in family, especially physical abuse or Munchausen by proxy	*Siblings* — recurrence of SIDS (2% risk) increases possibility of abuse (Emery 1986)
Socially	*Known* to SSD because of person's history of abuse	Children from known abusing families are at greater risk of SIDS (Baldwin & Oliver 1975, Roberts et al 1980). Children from socially deprived inner city areas at greater risk of SIDS (Golding et al 1985, Taylor & Emery 1988) and some abuses (Creighton 1989)

Table 12.3 Clinical features of babies who are suffocated and those who died of SIDS

Physical examination
1. *Suffocated infant*
    a. May appear well nourished with no signs of injury.
    b. Signs of physical neglect, bruising, scratches, healing fractures.
    c. Child may be underweight (check clinic growth chart).
    d. Signs of suffocation:
        (i) petechiae on face, especially eyelids
        (ii) bruises on lips and gums
        (iii) bruises around neck, part of neck, pressure marks at back of neck, upper chest and arms
        (iv) nail marks around face and neck
        (v) foreign material stuffed in nose and throat.
2. *Infant dying form SIDS* — usually well nourished, no signs of injury.

---

et al 1985, Taylor & Emery 1988). There is also an increased association noted in families known to Social Services Departments because of previous abuse (Baldwin & Oliver 1975, Roberts et al 1980, Newlands & Emery 1991).

Clinical investigation and management

Clearly it is of utmost importance to recognise if a child has been murdered, not least because of the welfare of other children in the family or as yet unborn children. On the other hand a SIDS death is a major tragedy for a family and at a time of such grief ill-considered investigation and intrusion are to be avoided.

The differential diagnosis must also be considered. Has the baby been ill, has there been contact with whooping cough? Was the baby preterm with a history of recurrent apnoea or has the mother mistaken exaggerated periodic respiration for apnoea, in a 'near-miss' cot death? Is there evidence of cardiac or respiratory disorder? Does the child have marked gastro-oesophageal reflux?

If the child is still alive, and there are features suggestive of Munchausen syndrome by proxy, management is as described on page 219, with the ultimate investigation being that of video-monitoring of the mother (Hilton 1989). If there are other signs of child maltreatment the management is as for other cases of possible serious abuse (see Ch. 14). If the final opinion is that this is a case of MSBP or physical assault, the baby is at real risk of death and usually would not return to his parent's care. Murder or attempted murder

is clearly a matter which should be urgently discussed with the police.

Most sudden and unexpected deaths in infancy are due to SIDS and not to suffocation or poisoning. Investigation of all deaths should be sensitive, a child death is always a tragedy. The police and coroner's officer are involved in all cases of sudden or unexpected death and a paediatric pathologist should ideally perform all autopsies on such infants. The details of the pathology of SIDS have recently been well described (Hilton 1989). Parents need to know as much as possible about the cause of death and any abnormality which may affect subsequent pregnancies. The pathologist will also use forensic skills in looking for signs of recent trauma or healing from previous assault.

Much has been written of the support needed by parents in the short and long term to come to terms with an infant death, and to help with their distress, especially in the first 12 months. Paediatricians have a role, particularly in discussing the autopsy report with the parents and later on in planning the care of subsequent children following a SIDS death.

Summary

Death by suffocation is not a rare form of child abuse. The victim is usually an infant and differentiation from death due to SIDS is difficult. The aetiology of SIDS is unknown — is there an entity 'SIDS' or is it a diagnostic dustbin (Emery 1989)? If 5–10% of sudden infant deaths are due to infanticide, is the label SIDS facilitating infanticide? If careful and thorough investigation takes place the number of completely unexplained deaths falls to around 1 in 5 deaths (Emery 1989). If a neutral confidential enquiry took place in these instances perhaps the final opinion would have a greater accuracy and parents would be more appropriately counselled.

Repeated episodes of partial asphyxiation are likely to be a manifestation of Munchausen syndrome by proxy and are further discussed under this heading. Older children may also be suffocated, for example, an older child who is screaming whilst her assailant sexually abuses her. A hand across her face will keep her quiet and may kill her. The physical evidence of the physical and sexual abuse as well as the child's testimony (if old enough, and still alive) will make the diagnosis.

MUNCHAUSEN SYNDROME BY PROXY

Dr R Asher, in 1951, described a disorder in which adults described fictitious illness. He named it after Baron K F H Von Munchausen, an 18th century mercenary who described his adventures in a way which bore little semblance to reality. Munchausen's syndrome has since become a well-recognised medical entity.

In 1977, Munchausen syndrome by proxy (MSBP) was described by Meadow in a girl of 6 years with apparent haematuria.

The definition of MSBP includes the following (Rosenberg 1987):

1. illness in a child which is faked and/or produced by the parent (or carer),
2. presentation of the child for medical assessment and care, usually persistently and resulting in multiple medical procedures and *multiple medical opinions*,
3. denial of knowledge by the perpetrator of the cause of the child's illness,
4. acute symptoms and signs in the child abate when the child is separated from the perpetrator although sequelae of the disorder may persist.

Clinical features

Clinically the range of symptoms produced is wide and the child suffers the 'illness' and inevitable disruption of his life both in the short and longer terms. The distress due to the fabricated illness is compounded by the increasingly complex and invasive medical investigations and associated hospital admissions which are imposed on the

Table 12.4 Clinical presentation in Munchausen syndrome by proxy

- Bleeding (haematuria, haematemesis)
- Seizures
- CNS depression (drowsy, coma)
- Apnoea
- Failure to thrive
- Diarrhoea
- Vomiting
- Fever
- Rashes
- Hypertension

Table 12.5 Warning signs of Munchausen syndrome (after Wissow 1990)

- Persistent or recurrent illness — even a new syndrome?
- Discrepancy between child's apparent good health and history of grave symptoms or seriously disordered laboratory tests.
- Overly attentive mother, will not leave child, appears surprisingly cheerful in face of grave clinical situation.
- Signs and symptoms settle on *separation* from mother.
- Routine treatment or medications never seem to work well.
- Several medical opinions previously – notes are lost.

child. The symptoms are as varied as the insults visited on the child. The commoner presentations are listed in Table 12.4. Many children have several symptoms, few signs, but disordered laboratory tests. The warning signs are listed in Table 12.5.

A review of the literature (Rosenberg 1987) lists the commonest reported symptoms in MSBP as seizures, followed by apnoea and unconsciousness. These are important in the morbidity and mortality associated with the condition. Diarrhoea, vomiting, fever and haematuria have also been repeatedly reported but over 65 symptoms have been recorded, from arthralgia to ventricular tachycardia (Meadow 1989b).

Clinical features, as given in Table 12.6, probably describe the severe end of the spectrum of MSBP. Substances used to fabricate illness may be unusual, such as salt leading to dehydration and seizures, or sedation due to barbiturates or antidepressants. Parents may not only lie when telling the history but also falsify charts of the child's vomiting, temperature, or urine output.

Emotional abuse is inevitable in this disorder and, as the child becomes drawn into the deception, he too lies and fabricates illness and may as an adult have the syndrome of Munchausen in his own right. Psychiatric disorder is well described

Table 12.6 Clinical features in Munchausen syndrome by proxy (data from published cases — Rosenberg 1987)

Gender	Boys and girls equally affected
Age at diagnosis	Average 3 years (1 month–21 years)
Length of illness	Average 14 months (days–20 years)
Morbidity	? 8%
Mortality	? 10–20% (most at risk under 3 years)
Other abuses	14% failure to thrive, 1% physical abuse, 1% sexual abuse. 100% emotional

in survivors of MSBP, and a particular concern is of chronic invalidism (Meadow 1989b). Separation anxiety (from the mother) and school refusal may become part of the syndrome.

Many of the children have also failed to thrive and have a history of non-accidental injury, inappropriate medication or neglect. Within the families there is also an excess of unexplained deaths. It is not unusual for more than one child in the family to have suffered from illnesses fabricated by the mother (Bools et al 1992). Sexual abuse may also occur.

There is little information on the relationship between the abused child and his mother but these families are clearly dysfunctional with relationships between all family members disturbed. Other children in the family are at risk, too, of emotional and physical abuse as well as unexplained death — Table 12.7.

There is little understanding of the aetiology of the disorder. Why do apparently caring mothers injure their children in this prolonged, perverse and calculating manner? The majority do not have a recognisable psychiatric disorder or a history of childhood abuse. They may be lonely and isolated, and certainly thrive on hospital wards with the attention their child's illness brings. But how they dissociate from their children to allow for their damaging behaviour is unknown.

Outcome

The outcome of MSBP for the child varies with the history. Of the cases described in the literature (Rosenberg 1987) a mortality rate of 10–20% is given, with the greatest danger to the very young, due to maternally induced asphyxia. This figure is

misleading as clearly only the severe end of the syndrome is diagnosed and many less dramatic cases go unrecognised.

Long-term morbidity is probably underestimated, but little is known in the long term of these children. 8% are said to have significant sequelae (Rosenberg 1987) including psychiatric disorder, the gastrointestinal consequences of surgery, cerebral palsy, joint disease and chronic invalidism which may persist into adult life. Again there are insufficient studies to show the true extent of disability following a childhood of fictitious illness.

Professional involvement

Professionals, mainly doctors, become enmeshed and manipulated by the mothers, who have been described as 'slick but sick'. The professionals can only avoid becoming part of the abusive cycle by talking to each other and not being piloted by the mother who will use them to abuse the child further (Fig. 12.2).

Diagnosis

The diagnosis of MSBP is difficult to make but for some children, for example infants where the history is one of repeated apnoea, there is considerable urgency and sophisticated investigation using video cameras may be needed (Hilton 1989). An experienced toxicologist will advise on an appropriate toxicological screen; meticulous nursing with careful observation, checking and re-charting will reveal maternal falsification of records, for example faked pyrexia.

But MSBP is only diagnosed after a delay of months to years, or even after a child has died. Only by considering the diagnosis will professionals make the necessary connections (Kaufman et al 1989) but why is it so difficult? The mothers are competent, anxious and attentive but also extremely devious. Doctors do not expect parents to trick them, let alone injure their own child and allow them to suffer unnecessary, painful and sometimes dangerous investigations. Once MSBP is considered, further management is carefully planned to collect the information necessary to make a definitive diagnosis and protect the child from further harm.

As in other forms of child abuse, management

Table 12.7 Families in Munchausen by proxy

Mother	Father	Sibling
Usual perpetrator	< 2% collude	—
'Model' parent on ward	Seen rarely in hospital	Physical abuse
Intelligent, caring, attentive	Detached, uninvolved, passive, in spite of child's serious illness	Unexplained deaths and illnesses
'Normal' psychiatrically Munchausen syndrome (self)		

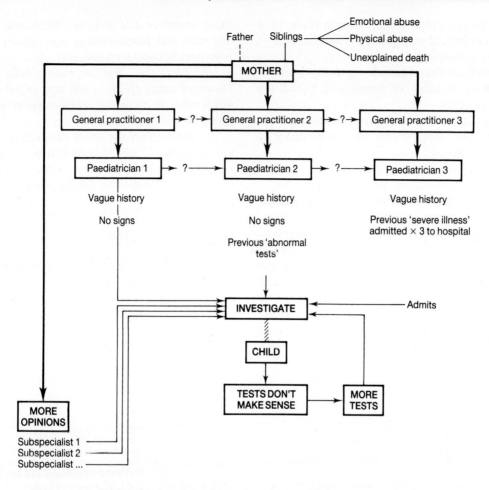

Fig. 12.2   Professional entrapment in Munchausen syndrome by proxy.

Note (1) MOTHER loves all her medical attendants until they fail to comply then she moves to opinions new.

(2) The child is incidental but necessary for the Mother's manipulation.

(3) Do the various doctors talk to each other?

of MSBP is not for the doctor alone. Confronting the mother with her own behaviour is not enough, as deaths have occurred after parents have been confronted and the child then allowed home (Rosenberg 1987).

Suggested management approach

Rosenberg (1987) describes in detail a protocol for managing a case of suspected MSBP:

1. Remember that MSBP occurs and also that there is a considerable mortality — the child's safety is paramount.

2. Mothers may be very attentive, caring, anxious and positively enjoy being resident in hospital.

3. Why can't you make a diagnosis? The fabrication of disease is such that any possibility should be considered. But consider MSBP in any 'rare' disorder.

4. Hospital admission is usually necessary for evaluation. Remember, a majority of mothers continue to abuse in hospital. The nursing staff must be fully involved, as the diagnosis of MSBP is often confirmed by their observations.

5. Take a detailed history, check verbally where possible with GP, HV, and other family members.

6. Talk to the child alone. Should there be a formal psychological or psychiatric assessment?

7. When in hospital:
   a. check all observations, e.g. temperature
   b. retain samples of urine and blood for toxicology
   c. may need to supervise parental visits or even stop them, by court order if necessary.

8. Keep careful, detailed nursing and medical notes. Check all laboratory investigations.

9. Have a strategy meeting with social worker and other appropriate professionals early on to facilitate understanding and information gathering.

10. Arrange to meet again to ensure there is further exchange of information with continuing communication between the professionals. When the parents are confronted with the diagnosis be prepared to take immediate action to protect the child. Parents react differently, and all will need support (including psychiatric help for some).

Many mothers will deny the deception but some will take full responsibility and others acknowledge part of their responsibility. A case conference is held to ensure that the case is fully explored. However many children will stay in parental care, albeit with good social work support and continuing medical surveillance.

11. Remember the other children in the family are at risk too. They should also be examined and be involved in the social work assessment as well as any long-term family work and medical follow-up.

Summary

MSBP is likely to be far more common than has been acknowledged hitherto. Most paediatricians will have 'minor' cases on their caseloads and the published examples represent just one end of a clinical continuum which may end in serious disability or death of the child.

REFERENCES

Asher R 1951 Munchausen's syndrome. Lancet 1: 339–341
Baldwin J A, Oliver J E 1975 Epidemiology and family characteristics of severely abused children. Br J Prev Soc Med 29: 205
Bergman A B, Beckwith J B, Ray C G (eds) 1970 Sudden infant death syndrome: proceedings of the second international conference on the causes of sudden death in infants. University of Washington Press, Seattle, WA
Bools C N, Neale B A, Meadow S R 1992 Co-morbidity associated with fabricated illness (Munchausen syndrome by proxy). Archives of Disease in Childhood 67: 77–79
Bowen D A 1989 Concealment of birth, child destruction and infanticide. In: Mason J K (ed) Paediatric forensic medicine and pathology. Chapman & Hall Medical
Creighton S J 1989 Child abuse trends in England and Wales, 1983–1987. NSPCC
Dine M S, McGovern M E 1982 Intentional poisoning of children — an overlooked category of child abuse: report of seven cases and review of the literature. Pediatrics 70: 32–35
Emery J L 1985 Infanticide, filicide and cot death. Archives of Disease in Childhood 60: 505–557
Emery J L 1986 Families in which two or more cot deaths have occurred. Lancet 1: 313–315
Emery J L 1989 Leader. Is sudden infant death syndrome a diagnosis? British Medical Journal 299: 1240
Golding J, Limerick S, Macfarlane A 1985 Sudden infant death; patterns, puzzles and problems. Open Books
Hilton J M N 1989 The pathology of sudden infant death syndrome. In: Mason J K (ed) Paediatric forensic medicine and pathology. Chapman & Hall Medical
Kaufman K L et al 1989 Munchausen's syndrome by proxy: a survey of professionals knowledge. Child Abuse and

Neglect 13: 141–147
Kempe C H, Silverman F N, Steele B F et al 1962 The battered child syndrome. JAMA 181: 17
Knowelden J, Keeling J, Nicholl J P et al 1985 Postneonatal mortality. A multicentre study. HMSO, London, p. 12
Kresel J J, Lovejoy F H 1981 Poisonings and child abuse. In: Ellerstein N S (ed) Child abuse and neglect: a medical reference. Wiley, Ch 17, p. 307
Meadow R 1977 Munchausen syndrome by proxy: the hinterland of child abuse. Lancet 2: 343–345
Meadow R 1989a Suffocation. In: ABC of child abuse. British Medical Journal, p. 21
Meadow R 1989b Munchausen syndrome by proxy. In: ABC of child abuse. British Medical Journal, p. 37
Meadow R 1990 Suffocation, recurrent apnoea, and sudden infant death. Journal of Pediatrics 117: 351–357
Newlands M, Emery J L 1991 Child abuse and cot deaths. Child Abuse and Neglect 15: 275–278
Pullar P 1984 Mechanical asphyxia. In: Mant A K (ed) Taylor's principles and practice of medical jurisprudence. Churchill Livingstone
Roberts J, Lynch M A, Golding J 1980 Postneonatal mortality in children from abusing families. British Medical Journal 281: 102, 1215
Rogers D, Tripp J, Bentovim A, Berry D, Goulding R 1976 Non-accidental poisoning: an extended syndrome of child abuse. British Medical Journal i: 793–796
Rosenberg D A 1987 Web of deceit: a literature review of Munchausen syndrome by proxy. Child Abuse and Neglect II: 547–563
Sibert J 1975 Stress in families who have ingested poisons. British Medical Journal 3: 87
Taylor E M, Emery J L 1988 Trends in unexpected infant

deaths in Sheffield. Lancet ii: 1121–1123

Wiseman H M, Guest V H G, Volans G N 1987 Accidental poisoning in childhood: a multi-centre study. General

Epidemiology 6: 293–301

Wissow S L 1990 Munchausen by proxy. In: Child advocacy for the chinician. Williams & Wilkins

13. Other forms of child abuse

DAY NURSERIES AND SEXUAL ABUSE

Finkelhor et al (1989) document sexual abuse in day care in their detailed research study. Whether the abuse took place in nurseries or family-based child care it was found that, by its very nature, more than one child was involved in being abused sexually, and in a number of institutions many children were sexually and ritually abused for years. The incidences have risen sharply and the consequences seem considerable, particularly since children in day care are young. Finkelhor et al (1988, p. 25) also point out 'the young age of the children, the unusual problems posed for investigation and prosecution, and the reports of particularly bizarre and damaging forms of multiple-victim/multiple-perpetrator abuse in some cases', which make it a priority to understand this form of abuse.

The sexual abuse of the children does not differ in these circumstances from sexual abuse in intra-familial or extrafamilial contexts. The perpetrators use the same means of involving the children in sexual abuse and the children are bribed, coerced and or threatened into the abusive situation. Summit's (1983) accommodation syndrome applies in these cases as much as elsewhere, and the spectrum of abuse ranges from fondling to intercourse and child rape. Finkelhor et al (1988) described some added dimensions to this form of abuse. They have found that, because the day care facility is a public one, the bathroom is the most frequently used place where the children are abused. 'Like the location the timing of the abuse is often determined by the need for secrecy and privacy'. A shift of emphasis lies in the fact that most of the children are sexually maltreated during the day time and working hours; beds are not often a feature in this form of abuse. However, the opportunity to separate children, during a lunchtime sleep for instance, where one child at a time can be selected, woken, and taken out to another room, so that the perpetrator can be alone with a child is a pattern now better understood. Further dynamics have been identified which are more specific in these cases. They include the form of coercion, the type of abuse, the duration and frequency of the maltreatment and the recognition that pornography is often used.

While vigilance and careful checking of child care facilities by parents and licensing authorities should be advised, Finkelhor et al are keen to point out that an overreaction to 'nursery crimes' would not help the working mother and child.

NETWORK ABUSE

Network abuse and ritual abuse have more recently become the focus of attention in many countries. Much has still to be learnt about how to understand this form of abuse. To protect children from this form of maltreatment has proven to be a difficult task and a legal nightmare. In an attempt to define ritual and network abuse it is essential to be clear about the meaning of both. Network abuse is defined as the abuse of a number of children (more than one) by adults from different families, institutions or organisations when they come together for the purpose of maltreating children.

Structure of rings

1. Solo rings
2. Syndicated rings
3. Transitional rings

4. Rings with female victims
5. Rings with male and female victims
6. Rings with male victims.

The literature on sex rings — Burgess et al (1981, 1984), Wilde & Wynne (1986) and Wilde (1986, 1989) — have highlighted organised and sometimes systematic attempts to exploit children sexually and abuse them in this way. Burgess (1984) points out that:

'*Solo rings* consist of one adult who is sexually involved with a number of children.' Burgess et al (1984) and Wilde & Wynne (1986) describe this form of sex ring as one where there is no transfer of the children or of photographs, but that children may be recruited by each other and become members of groups of children involved with different adults.

Syndicated rings include several adults who form a well-structured organisation for the recruitment of children, the production of pornography, the delivery of direct sexual services, and the establishment of an extensive network of customers (Burgess et al 1984).

Transitional rings may consist of more than one adult with several children but without the organisation of the syndicated rings. The transitional rings may eventually become syndicated and, for instance, sell pornographic photographs of children.

Rings with single sex children involved. It has been recognised that girls and boys may be selected for specific rings and specific purposes and/or clients. It was at first thought that female sex rings and female prostitution were more often connected. However more recently it has become firmly established that male children are as vulnerable and the concept of 'rent a boy' is far more usual than had been anticipated.

Child sex rings have been known for centuries and as Wilde (1989) points out there are examples in ancient history, for instance the Emperor Tiberius who abused groups of children sexually on the Isle of Capri. There are also reports by Wells (1958) and by Radzinowicz (1975) which included descriptions of sex rings.

Ritual abuse

Child abuse has acquired yet another dimension of child maltreatment in ritual abuse. This is a particularly unpleasant and brutal form of child maltreatment involving children, some of them very young, adolescents and adults. This form of abuse is always a part of group activity, often related to a cult, and frequently includes physical, sexual and emotional maltreatment.

A society which has difficulties in acknowledging that child sexual abuse occurs has even more difficulty in contemplating the existence of ritual abuse. The same descriptions 'vile, horrible, hysterical' which are used to deny the reality of ritual abuse are also still being put forward to deny all child sexual abuse.

There is still controversy over how to define ritual abuse. Definitions have been developed though there is confusion over distinguishing network abuse, ritual abuse, and satanic abuse. Finkelhor et al (1988) identified three types of ritual abuse:

1. Type I is defined as *true cult-based*, and it involves child abuse as an expression of an elaborate belief system. The abuse is part of a social system or a cult and includes physical, sexual and emotional abuse. By using children the adult reaches a mystical state, which allegedly is the goal, rather than the sexual abuse of the children. The children are indoctrinated into a different belief system which discredits parents and traditional teaching. The group is kept together as adults and children are corrupted and dare not disclose forbidden practices.

2. Type II is defined as *pseudo*; here the primary motivating factor is the sexual abuse of children, as seen in the ritual abuse case in Holland. Costumes and animals may be part of getting children interested, intimidating them into participation and deterring disclosure.

3. Type III is defined as *psychopathological*; here the abuse is a part of an obsessional or delusional aspect of an individual or a group.

Finkelhor et al (1989) defined ritualistic abuse as: 'abuse which occurs in a context linked to some symbols or group activity that have religious, magical or supernatural connotation, and where the invocation of these symbols or activities, repeated over time, is used to frighten and intimidate the children' (p. 59).

Lloyd (1990) defined this form of abuse as: 'the intentional physical abuse, sexual abuse or psychological abuse of a child by a person responsible for the child's welfare when such abuse is repeated and/or stylised, and is typified by such other acts as cruelty to animals, or threats of harm to the child, other persons and animals'.

A working group in Leeds (including the authors) has developed the following definition from the existing material in an effort to further understanding of this very complex issue. The Leeds working group defined ritual abuse as: 'physical, psychological, and/or sexual abuse of children, associated with repeated activities (i.e. ritual) which relate the abuse to contexts of a religious, magical, or supernatural kind. These activities include the use of particular language, imagery and symbols as well as the performance of certain acts' (Mc Fadyen et al 1993).

Snow & Sorensen (1990) consider ritualistic abuse in a neighbourhood setting and show that it emerges in both intra- and extrafamilial settings. They quote from research undertaken with individuals suffering from multiple personality disorder, indicating that many have been ritualistically abused as children.

The Report of the Ritual Abuse Task Force Los Angeles County Commission for Women, September 1989 (p. 1), stated that

Ritual abuse is usually carried out by members of a cult. The purpose of the ritual elements of the abuse seems threefold: 1. rituals in some groups are part of a shared belief or worship system into which the victim is being indoctrinated; 2. rituals are used to intimidate victims into silence; 3. ritual elements (e.g. devil worship, animal or human sacrifice) seem unbelievable to those unfamiliar with these crimes that these elements detract from the credibility of the victims and make prosecution of the crimes very difficult.

Jones (1991) examines reports of children having been ritually abused and highlights the difficulties in bringing these cases to prosecution. The description of brutal, perverse and sadistic behaviour towards children often makes the accounts sound unreal and fictitious. This is an added complication in the work of child protection for the legal profession (Lanning 1991).

In the UK, descriptions of ritualistic abuse have appeared in the press. The *Independent* newspaper (18.3.1990) described 5 criminal trials over the previous 2-year period. These trials all included the abuse of children in groups, with associated ritual, satanic and witchcraft practices.

The NSPCC have attempted to monitor the evidence for child pornography, sex rings and ritual abuse. In March 1990, C Brown, Director of the NSPCC, said that members of 7 NSPCC protection teams (out of a total of 64 teams) in England and Wales were currently working with children who were the victims of ritualistic abuse.

One of the best documented cases of ritualistic abuse in Western Europe occurred in Gude Pekela, a small Dutch town with a population of 8000 people. In Spring 1987 more than 100 children aged 3–12 years were subject to violent and sadistic abuse, often as part of satanic rituals. The cases came to light when a 4-year-old boy presented with anal bleeding and only after several days told his parents of his anal abuse, 'sticks in bottom', which had happened to his friends too. The children were lured by men and women dressed as clowns and animals, who took them to 'parties' and gave them ice-cream and drugged lemonade. The children were told to undress and made to take part in sexual acts with adults and with each other. The children described lying naked on tables, a church, candles, headless dolls and photographs and videos being made. The adults also dressed up in white robes and threatened the children that if they told they would be killed or their house set on fire. To emphasise the threat animals were killed, a 'baby killed', 'babies' were beaten.

When the Dutch case came to light the media response was that it could all be explained by 'mass hysteria'. Similarly, when in 1990 Mr Brown made his statement to the Press, a police spokesman for the CID in London said there was 'no evidence of the ritual abuse of children in England'.

Ritual abuse does appear to be uncommon; it represented around 1% of the total CSA cases recognised in the UK in 1988–89. However, it clearly does occur and it is likely that over the next few years the true extent of the problem will become evident. Whether the groups are linked and form a well-organised network across the country is less certain, although there is evidence for child pornography and child prostitution networks and it is likely that there are links between some groups. The position in the USA is no less contentious but is better recorded (Finkelhor et al 1989).

The elements of the Dutch case of young children who were badly scared, the use of drugs, candles, symbols, 'killing babies', pornography and so on are repeated over and over again in disclosures by abused children but meet with scepticism by adults. In the USA there is a continuing debate as to whether ritualistic abuse occurs; one side claims that it is multidimensional multi-abuser sexual abuse and cannot be defined, whereas the other describes the similarities between the identified cases of ritualistic abuse and how they differ from the usual intrafamilial abuse (although there may be elements of ritualistic abuse in any sexual abuse).

Summit (1990) describes groups of very young children, 2–6 years, with multiple abusers including many women, often based in day-care facilities from which the children are transported to 'big' houses, the use of pornography, video film making, drugs, violence, pain, sadism, threats and the abuse of children by children, cruelty to animals involving children too, turning the children into (albeit unwitting) abusers. Summit says that children are tricked into believing that adults have magical powers and believe what they see — babies being killed and beaten, and the more bizarre events. But by the use of drugs, fear and abnormal practices, such as smearing of faeces or eating excrement, children may be disorientated: reality and fantasy blend, they lose any sense of time and place and become confused. This does not mean that, when several children describe similar events it is mass hysteria and because investigating authorities have not found any dead babies, nothing has happened. If adults do not understand the child, who may appear illogical and his disclosures unbelievable and contradictory, he may be suspected of false allegation. While the clinical picture is disentangled the child, family and investigators (usually social worker, psychologist or psychiatrist) need support and the resources to investigate effectively. If society, the police or individual agencies 'do not believe in ritual abuse' the child, families and professionals are undermined and their credibility is attacked as the child is further damaged.

The data is disturbing, but it requires evaluation not dismissal. Polarisation into 'believers' and 'non-believers' is unhelpful, as are concepts of 'satanists running rampant' or 'therapists generating hysteria'. An open rational resolution of the difficult problems raised by the data is needed.

Characteristics of these rings are listed in Table 13.1 and Table 13.2 (Gould 1987, Finkelhor et al 1989, Summit 1990).

Effects of ritualistic abuse

The impact of ritualistic abuse on children is, not surprisingly, severe. The bizarre and coercive elements terrorise children and there is always severe emotional, as well as physical and sexual abuse. This leads children to dissociate experiences, which may have a lasting effect on their mental health (Pelcovitz 1990, Waterman et al 1990).

The longer the abuse lasts, the greater the physical force used, the larger the number of perpetrators and the greater the insistence on participation between children, the more likely to lead

Table 13.1 Ritualistic abuse — characteristics of 'sex rings' in the USA

1. Many in day-care facilities
2. Multiple perpetrators (5% single abuser)
3. Women abusers are as common as male abusers
4. Women may be sole abusers
5. Abuse may have occurred over long periods (20 years)
6. Abuse involves all forms of serious penetrative CSA
7. Adult–adult, adult–child, child–child abuse
8. High rate of pornography use
9. Drugs used to make children comply
10. 'Cult families'
11. All have religious, magical or supernatural belief system

Table 13.2 Ways in which children present and describe (USA experience)

1. May present with vomiting, nightmares, extreme anxiety, feeling 'bad'
2. Aggressive behaviour — sexually abuse peers
3. Extreme fear — terrorised to remain silent
4. 'Supernatural powers' — magic
5. Symbols used to frighten, and intimidate
6. Wear masks, costumes, including animal disguise
7. Drink blood, urine, eat faeces
8. Kill animals, 'babies', mutilation
9. Dig up graves, devil worship, crosses, religious implements
10. Pregnancy

to increased distress for the child in the future. Children who have been in the abuser role are likely to be more aggressive and act out sexually towards their peer group or with dolls. Other children regress, become very clingy and lose toilet training skills. Some children become obsessed with monsters, death and dying. Others are deluded that they have a spider, or monster within their body. They become confused with concepts of God, the Devil and evil, and their own beliefs are chaotic. Not only are the victims of ritualistic abuse more disturbed than in other cases of CSA, but their parents are upset and need considerable help.

Although much of the abuse in the USA has been described in day nurseries, various criminal trials in the UK show that teenagers are involved too and the effects on them must be equally as complex and far-reaching as sexual maturity is reached. There are particularly disturbing descriptions of teenage girls being made pregnant by cult elders and even criminal induction of abortion.

The ritualistic sex rings should be differentiated from 'historical child sex rings' (Burgess 1984). In these rings offenders are almost all male, often paedophiles, and child pornography is commonly used. Boys are equally abused as girls and pornography is used to corrupt — particularly adolescent boys who are easily sexually aroused. Ritual abuse is not a usual component of these rings, which are focused on the seduction of children and sexual activities.

CHILD PORNOGRAPHY

Pornography is an international multibillion dollar industry, and children are thought to be featured in around 6% of the published material.

There is a huge production of 'soft' porn from Page 3 pin-ups in the tabloids to Playboy, Mayfair, etc. The distribution of such material through high-street stationers is open; clearly different outlets are needed for illegal and child pornography. Organisations such as Paedophile Information Exchange exist to manage this side of the industry.

Currently there is a debate as to the role of pornography in the abuse of women and children. Men are also affected by pornography, whether in its production or as users. The effect of a combination of violence and sex, as depicted in the particularly nasty video, is of great concern, especially as the number of rapes and sexual assaults reported to the police rises each year. 'Snuff videos' where the hapless victim is murdered on camera have also been made — with what effect on the viewer?

Pornography trivialises sexual relationships by separating sex from its normal social context and reduces the depicted person to a recipient object. Children are therefore used in the representation of sex and sexuality with the aim of arousing sexual desire and providing or provoking sexual gratification (Ennew 1986). This material may be primarily for the use of paedophiles but others abuse children sexually as part of their incontinent sexual behaviour.

The images that are presented include a single child, or groups of children, sometimes with adults or animals. The children are variously dressed and posed in sexual acts involving other children, adults, animals or inanimate objects. One difficulty is that the appeal of child pornography lies in the eye of the beholder. Adults who sexually abuse children may find catalogues of children's clothes with child models sexually arousing. Holiday snaps of children on the beach or James, aged 2 years, naked in the bath are coveted images to some. This, however, does not alter the need for serious debate about the role of pornography in our society, including the tabloid pin-ups as well as more obviously offensive publications. Many women dislike pornography, and as men recognise the deviancy and the degradation of women such pictures portray, perhaps more men will reject it too. It is also important to look at the role pornography plays in the sexual development of teenagers in the UK. What are teenagers learning about sexual behaviour from these publications?

A study (Itzin & Sweet 1990) of 4000 women respondents to a questionnaire on pornography run by Cosmopolitan (a women's magazine) showed that 36% had seen pornography at less than 12 years old and 14% were under 10 years. Of this pornography 69% saw 'men only' magazines but 28% saw 'illegal magazines' depicting rape, animals or children in various sexual acts. This is abusive in itself: is this how children in the UK are to learn about 'adult' sexual behaviour?

64% saw the pornography at home or in a friend's or relative's house. More seriously there was an association between childhood exposure to pornography and sexual experience below the age of consent (16 years). More than 25% of children who saw pornography under 12 years had sex before the age of 16 years. Does this also relate to issues of child protection?

Pornography is commonly used by abusers. Offenders know that the typical adolescent is sexually curious and easily sexually aroused, if sexually inexperienced. Pornographic material may be made available in the seduction process by offenders, whether in 'historical sex rings' or intrafamilial abuse. In ritualistic abuse children have commonly described films, photographs and video-making equipment. The greater availability of video cameras has enabled amateur film makers to create their own pornography.

For children involved in the making of pornographic material there are additional consequences, although these are dismissed by the children (Pelcovitz 1990). Compared with sexually abused children who were not involved in pornography this group were found to be more stigmatised, felt 'gay' or 'damaged', guilty, had greater difficulty in trusting and were angry, especially about their powerlessness.

The use of pornography by adolescent abusers is also worrying. These teenager abusers are a significant group, and the corrupting effect of pornography should not be underestimated. Neither should the 'teaching' of these immature children be of such abnormal practices which may also introduce the idea of teenager–child sexual activity. In this context teenagers as baby-sitters may see a video, become sexually excited, use it as a model, and then experiment on their young charges.

The law in England and Wales is represented by the Protection of Children Act 1978, which makes it an offence for a person or body to take indecent photographs (including film or video) of children under 16 years to show or distribute these, or to publish or advertise them. The Criminal Justice Bill 1988, under Section 160, makes possession of pornographic material an offence.

Pornography is not harmless, and although the evidence needs substantiating, there appear to be links between violent sex videos and violent sexual assault. It is the depiction of the misuse of power, and degradation of one person by another, usually a woman by a man, that is harmful. Erotica, which is also available, is different in that love and partnership are portrayed rather than the isolation of the body from the person. It is in the former context that children and adolescents need to understand sexual relationships. When young children see pornography it appears to desensitise them to sexual activity and lead them into inappropriate behaviour. It also suggests ways of behaving which are not tolerated by ordinary social mores. In this way pornographic material may delay and distort sexual development rather than promote it.

In the UK, with increasing awareness of the adverse and insidious effects of all pornography on developing children and adolescents and the misuse of sexuality by adults, there are an increasing number of campaigns, such as 'Off the Shelf', to control its production and distribution (Itzin & Sweet 1990).

OTHER FORMS OF SEXUAL EXPLOITATION OF CHILDREN

Sexual exploitation of children takes many forms (Ennew 1986). All these forms of abuse exploit not only the power differential between the adult and child but also the social domination of male over female and elder over junior, and, in addition, class and wealth.

Sex tourism usually involves the abuse of poor, non-white, young, non-Western girls by rich, white, Western adult males.

'White slavery' usually concerns the use of young poor women by Western males. The girls are kidnapped, or forced by poverty into vice rings run for profit by racketeers. Very young girls, 8 or 9 years old, are used in 'kiddie-porn' or 'Baby prostitution'.

Boys have long been known to be involved in prostitution and sex rings. Again, youth and attractiveness are valued by their abusers.

Prostitutes in developing countries may be street children, often the children of impoverished rural families who have moved to towns and are unable to care for all their children. They may also be runaways, running from abuse or exploitation at home. Girls in particular may have been hired from their fathers to work in dancing, cabaret or bar work and forced into the sex trade. Similarly, girls are hired as servants and are sexually exploited by their employers.

A particularly sinister trade has been in children adopted from poor developing countries. Some children have been adopted by paedophiles and pimps running child prostitution rings, using the cover of an adoption agency.

Children will continue to be sexually abused in all these ways as long as there are gross social inequalities in society and corrupt men and women who will use the bodies of powerless children for their own gratification.

REFERENCES

Burgess A W 1984 Child pornography and sex rings. Lexington Books, Lexington M A

Burgess A W, Groth A W, McCausland M P 1981 Child sex initiation rings. American Journal of Psychiatry 51: 110–119

Burgess A W, Hartmann C R, McCausland M P et al 1984 Respone patterns in children and adolescents exploited through sex rings and pornography. American Journal of Psychiatry 141: 646–662

Ennew J 1986 The sexual exploitation of children. Polity Press

Finkelhor D et al 1988 The trauma of child sexual abuse: two models. In: Wyatt G E, Pomell (eds) Lasting effects of child sexual abuse. Sage

Finkelhor D, Williams L M, Burns N 1989 Nursery crimes. Sexual abuse in day care. Sage,

Gould C 1987 Symptoms characterizing Satanic ritualistic abuse not usually seen in s.a. cases. Paper presented at a National Conference on Affirming Children's Truth, Manhattan Beach, California

Itzin C, Sweet C 1990 What you feel about porn. Cosmopolitan Magazine, Spring 1990. Campaign against Pornography and Censorship, PO Box 844, London SE5

Jones D T H 1991 Commentary: ritualism and child sexual abuse. Child Abuse and Neglect 15(3): 163–170

Lanning K V 1991 Ritual abuse: a law enforcement view or perspective. Child Abuse and Neglect 15(3): 171–173

Mc Fadyen A, Hanks H, James C 1993 Child Abuse Review, 1, 1

Pelcowitz D 1990 Child pornography and extrafamilial sex abuse. Child Maltreatment 1990, conference San Diego, California

Radzinowicz L 1957 Sexual offences: a report of the Cambridge Department of Criminal Science. McMillan, London

Summit R C 1983 The child sexual abuse accommodation syndrome. Journal of Child Abuse and Neglect 7: 177–193

Summit R 1990 Cults and rituals: relationships to child abuse. Child Maltreatment 1990, conference San Diego, California

Waterman J, Kelly R, Oliveri M K, McCord J 1990 Specificity of effects on children of ritualized and non-ritualized sexual abuse. Child Maltreatment 1990, conference San Diego, California

Wells W M 1958 Sexual offences as seen by a woman police surgeon. British Medical Journal 2: 1404–1408

Wild W J, Wynne J M 1986 Child sex ring. British Journal of Medicine 293: 183–185

Wild W J 1989 Prevalence of child sex rings. Pediatrics vol 83: 4: 553–559

Address

'Off the Shelf' Campaign. c/o Campaign against Pornography, 9 Poland Street, London W1v 3DG

14. The management of child abuse

INTRODUCTION

As earlier chapters have shown, the field of child maltreatment is vast. Professionals may be involved in work in prevention but management leads right through to helping the damaged teenager struggling with the sequelae of an abusive childhood. Following the publication of the Report of the Inquiry into Child Abuse in Cleveland 1987 (Butler-Sloss 1988) several guides and papers appeared:

- Working together: a guide to the arrangements for interagency cooperation for the protection of children from abuse (1988)
- Working together under the Children Act 1989: a guide to the arrangements for interagency cooperation for the protection of children from abuse (1991)
- An introductory guide for the NHS: the Children Act 1989 (DoH 1991a)
- Diagnosis of child sexual abuse: guidance for doctors 1988
- Protecting children: guidance for social workers 1988
- Child sexual abuse: principles of good practice (Kolvin 1988)
- Management of sexual abuse (Hobbs & Wynne 1987)
- Physical signs of the sexual abuse of children (RCP 1991)
- Guidelines for the evaluation of sexual abuse of children (American Academy of Pediatrics 1991).

Inquiries into child abuse

18 inquiries were held from 1973–1981 and 19 inquiries from 1980–1989. Reports describe working with families resistant or hostile to professional intervention, the need to see children, good supervision and support of workers and good interagency working and communication.

The most recent study of inquiry reports, from 1980–1989 (DoH 1991b) identifies key lessons to be learned from the 1980s. It also notes the limitations of the studies:

- Inquiries focus on child abuse as a product of family interaction and service delivery and do not analyse the associated effects of environmental disadvantage.
- Analysis of the effectiveness of services delivered excludes what services, if available, might have helped.
- Analysis of the family as people rather than recipients of services might give a better understanding as to why children are killed.
- The adversarial process of inquiries overseen by lawyers leads to procedural wrangles and a view as to what happened rather than why.

Inquiries do look at the relationship between policies, procedures and practices of individual agencies and how they relate to the law and how effectively they work together.

- Governmental guidelines are needed and are they adequate? At the time of the Cleveland Inquiry there was minimal professional advice available in the management of CSA and little support for workers as clinical practice moved on rapidly.
- Local Area Child Protection Committees need guidelines as to practice, including conduct of reviews by individual agencies and interagency inquiries by the ACPC.

- An integrated standard of practice is needed for child protection, integrating it with child care and monitoring it locally and nationally.
- Individual agencies should establish standards of practice.
- Child protection must be seen as a priority by all the relevant agencies.
- There is a need for local and national training strategies which are coordinated to allow best training practice to be established.
- The most important recent outcome of enquiries is the need for a set of principles for professional relationships between adults and children.

Child care and child protection are not the sole prerogative of the welfare agencies, and it is not the professionals who kill children. The public is ambivalent about intrusion into family life, the cost of services and the need to protect children. The professionals, the public, parents and children must work together to protect children and prevent child abuse (DoH 1991b).

Social workers carry the statutory responsibility for children in the management of child abuse but other professionals also have a role to play. Interagency cooperation is required by the Children Act 1989, both in providing services to children in need, but also in the protection of children. Cooperation and collaboration between the different agencies is essential but is a difficult and complex process, as the Inquiry Reports show. With the growth of knowledge and understanding of child maltreatment, policy and practice evolve and there is a need to adapt and change whilst maintaining this close collaboration (Working Together 1991).

Child care legislation

Legislation attempts to achieve a balance between the need to protect children and respect parental responsibility whilst not allowing undue interference by the State in family life.

The Children Act 1989 creates a whole new framework to provide for the care and protection of children with a new range of court orders. The main principles of the Act are (DoH 1991a):

- The child's welfare is paramount.

- Wherever possible children should be brought up and cared for within their own family.
- Children should be safe and protected.
- Courts should avoid delay when dealing with children.
- Courts should only make an order if to do so is better than no order.
- Children should participate in decision-making and be kept well informed.
- Parents continue to have responsibility even when their children are no longer living with them.
- Parents with children in need should be helped to bring up their children.
- This help should be provided as a service to parents and children:
  — in partnership with parents
  — to meet the child's identified needs
  — to be appropriate to the child's race, culture, religion, language
  — to be open to effective independent representations and complaints procedures
  — to draw upon effective partnership between the local authority and other agencies including voluntary agencies.

Area Child Protection Committees (in England and Wales)

In order that all the agencies involved in child protection may work closely together there must be a joint forum for developing, monitoring and reviewing child protection policies. This is the Area Child Protection Committee (ACPC).

The ACPC members are accountable to the agencies they represent, and the agencies are jointly responsible for ACPC action. Social services, police service, health service (community and hospital, nursing and medical), education, probation, voluntary agencies and others are represented.

The functions of the ACPC include (Working Together 1991):

- Establishing, maintaining and reviewing local interagency guidelines
- Monitoring the implementation of legal procedures
- Identifying significant issues arising from the handling of cases and reports from enquiries

- Scrutinising arrangements to provide treatment, expert advice, and interagency liaison and making recommendations to the responsible agencies
- Scrutinising progress on work to prevent child abuse and making recommendations to the responsible agencies
- Scrutinising work related to interagency training and making recommendations to the responsible agencies
- Conducting reviews
- Publishing an annual report about child protection matters.

The ACPC may also set up working groups to:

- carry out specific tasks, e.g. provide a training programme, review cases
- provide specialist advice, e.g. advise in relation to specific ethnic and cultural groups.

The health service commitment

Each district health authority is responsible for the provision of a comprehensive service for children at risk of abuse and their families. Health professionals need their own professional guidelines on procedure which are compatible with those of the local ACPC procedure. Chief officers at a district and regional level of NHS have responsibility for ensuring appropriate arrangements are in place.

A designated doctor (Working Together 1991)

All provider units concerned with children should have child protection policies and procedures in place. A senior doctor experienced in child protection should advise on the content of contracts with provider unit commissioning authorities.

The designated doctor should be able to ensure that:

- child protection policies are in line with local ACPC policy (important since the White Paper on the NHS, 1989, with danger of fragmentation of services)
- there is effective communication between the different provider units including an efficient transfer of records
- advice is available to all doctors and health professionals

- doctors know how and when to refer children to SSD and how to use the Child Protection Register
- adequate training is available (usually multidisciplinary)
- provision of information and advice on child protection is disseminated
- he acts as a referral point for other agencies, i.e. SSD, Education
- he works with a designated senior nurse and midwife.

Doctors and child protection

Any doctor who sees children, or adults who are in contact with children, has a direct part to play in

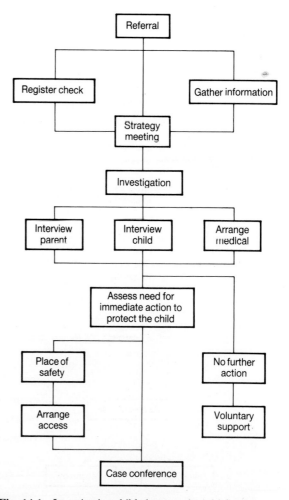

Fig. 14.1 Investigating child abuse — the initial stages.

the protection of children. This means that every general practitioner, clinical medical officer or paediatrician, through to the psychiatrist who hears a patient explain that he 'has to touch his little boy's genitalia from time to time' is necessarily involved.

Family doctors

Family doctors may recognise all forms of abuse. Figure 14.1 demonstrates a suggested pathway of referral for possible CSA but would also apply to other forms of abuse. To have further consultations with a professional colleague experienced in abuse work is the most important advice given. The management of a case of child abuse should not be the responsibility of a single professional. 'It is unwise for family doctors to keep a suspi-cion of child sexual abuse to themselves and take full responsibility without consulting others . . .' (Diagnosis of Sexual Abuse: Guidance for Doctors 1988, p. 24).

Family doctors often have an important role in cases of child abuse as their knowledge of the child and family is likely to be of longer standing and include an in-depth understanding of the family dynamics. Few will wish to take responsibility for the total clinical management of the case, Table 14.1 (Butler-Sloss 1988). It is important that family doctors attend child protection conferences or at least discuss the situation with the chairman of the child protection conference (Diagnosis of Sexual Abuse: Guidance for Doctors 1988)

Recording of findings and provision of reports by family doctors is as for other doctors (see p. 248).

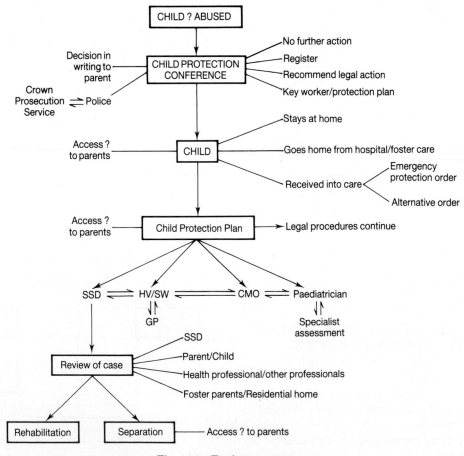

Fig. 14.2 Further management.

Table 14.1 Medical tasks in child abuse (after Butler-Sloss 1988)

1. Take a full medical history
2. Make a thorough medical examination
3. Arrange appropriate investigations for:
   a. sexually transmitted diseases
   b. forensic tests
   c. pregnancy
   d. bruising
   e. bony injury
4. Complete full and accurate records (at the time of examination)
5. Prepare medical report for GP, SSD or NSPCC, child health
6. Prepare a statement for police on request
7. Ensure results of investigation are recorded
8. Arrange appropriate referral for psychiatric, psychological or paediatric follow-up
9. Attend child protection conference, court
10. If there are differences of medical opinion endeavour to resolve these differences or at least identify area of dispute (Butler-Sloss 1988)

Family doctors may also be requested to attend court. Many family doctors will be anxious about confidentiality and this is explored later in this chapter.

Clinical medical officers

Clinical medical officers have a particular responsibility towards neglected and abused children. CMOs who visit SSD day nurseries will see children who are failing to thrive, who have delayed development and are neglected. Staff will refer children with 'sexually explicit behaviour' to them and they should know how to act. As is being increasingly recognised, there are many abused children in special schools and CMOs may be the only doctors with regular access to this group (Ch. 10). CMOs share the same responsibility as other doctors in recording and attending child protection conferences and court appearances. However, as with junior medical staff in hospital, there should be adequate training, supervision and support of all CMOs.

Psychiatrists

Child and adolescent psychiatrists are increasingly involved in child abuse work. In the UK there is a serious lack of provision of therapeutic services and in practice only the more difficult cases are therefore referred.

Psychiatrists may be involved in two main ways. Firstly in assessment as to whether, particularly, CSA has occurred, which also includes an assessment of the functioning of the family. Secondly psychiatric teams work with children and families to look at and treat emotional and behaviour disorders, the sequelae of abuse.

Psychologists

Clinical psychologists are increasingly involved in child protection work and their involvement varies, as for psychiatrists. There have been suggestions that psychologists are better able to conduct investigations than less well trained colleagues, but there are few psychologists available for this work and most are involved in therapy.

Paediatricians

All general and community paediatricians have a responsibility to work with abused children and their families. In each health district there should be a designated doctor, usually a consultant community or general paediatrician, who serves on the ACPC, ensures that there is an accessible and efficient service and is actively engaged in multi- and single discipline training in child abuse (see p. 232).

Police surgeon

Most police surgeons are family doctors who undertake a small number of sessions as a Deputy Police Surgeon each week. The Senior Police Surgeon advises the police authority.

Police surgeons must work closely with paediatricians, and if police surgeons examine children alone they must understand the need for a 'whole child examination' de la Haye Davis 1987, Butler-Sloss 1988), the use of appropriate investigations, for example to screen for sexually transmitted disease, and the need for follow-up (paediatrically or psychiatrically). Police surgeons should also write reports for and attend the child protection conference.

Nursing staff

Health visitors, midwives, hospital or school nurses and nursery nurses are well trained to recognise risk factors and warning signs of abuse but also have skills to support children and families when abuse is identified and to be able to continue to work with them subsequently.

It is important that GPs, CMOs and paediatricians all work closely with nursing colleagues in hospital and the community.

Child protection team

There are advantages in having a Child Protection Team based at each district general hospital. This would comprise paediatricians (hospital and community), psychologists, psychiatrists, liaison health visitor (from accident and emergency department, the ward, the child development team), social workers and colleagues in training.

1. **The core of professionals provides:**

- An expert clinical team
- A link with other health service colleagues (community and hospital)
- Support for members of the team
- Teachers and trainers
- Social work to the hospital and advice to the team
- A weekly review of current practice and longer-term audit.

2. **Administration of the Child Protection Team** requires a skilled secretary who is able to:

- Provide easy, open access to the doctors on the rota by SSD, police, other health professionals or carers (parents, grandparents and others). Children should be seen by appointment: physically abused children or children at risk of further harm are usually seen the same day. Children thought to have been sexually abused, with the exception of rape victims, may often be seen by arrangement to the advantage of child, parents and professionals. There is little justification for seeing children in the late evening at the convenience of a doctor.
- Provide efficient typing and distribution of reports.
- Support the committee work involved in ACPC, training, review of clinical practice (audit) and service development.

3. **Accommodation** needed at each district general hospital includes:

- quiet waiting area with toys
- interview/examination room: more than one room is needed if there are angry or upset relatives
- admission to a ward for a few children (see later).

Few health centres are adequately equipped. Children should *not* be examined in police stations; it is clear that there are only rare circumstances in which a child should be seen at a police station (Diagnosis of Child Sexual Abuse: Guidance for Doctors 1988).

4. **Nursing staff** are essential and should be trained (RSCN or nursery nurse) for work in the clinic or on the ward:

- to receive and support the child and family
- to chaperone the doctor (male or female)
- to weigh and measure the child
- to collect specimens, e.g. urine, and assist at collection of swabs, e.g. for STD, forensic
- to support the child during photography.

5. **Equipment:**

- Usual examination trolley
- Microbiological swabs, etc.
- Sexual offences pack (from police)
- Good illumination/magnification
- Camera/photography service
- Access to haematology, biochemistry, radiology
- Colposcope, glass rods, etc are optional
- Domestic refrigerator for appropriate storage of swabs used in STD screen and some forensic specimens.

6. **Access to hospital beds** is needed for admission of injured infants, investigation of infants failing to thrive and occasionally sexually abused children.

7. **Clinical advice** from colleagues such as genitourinary, orthopaedic, paediatric surgical or gynaecological consultants.

8. **Therapeutic service**

- Child and family psychiatrists and teams which may include play therapists, occupational therapists, dance and art therapy
- Child psychologist
- Child psychotherapist
- Adult service to support carers.

INTERAGENCY WORK IN CHILD PROTECTION (Working Together 1991)

Individual cases

There is a sequence of events in the investigation of an individual case, and some of these stages overlap. Doctors may be involved at all stages, and, rather than using medical skills only during the initial recognition and assessment, children and families may be helped by ongoing paediatric involvement. The doctors involved also need to understand how cases are to be handled (ACPC procedures).

The stages, as in 'Working Together', are:

1. Referral and recognition
2. Immediate protection and planning the investigation
3. Investigation and initial assessment
4. Child protection conference and decision-making about the need for registration
5. Comprehensive assessment and planning
6. Implementation, review and, where appropriate, deregistration.

1. Referral and recognition

- Any person who has knowledge of, or a suspicion that a child is suffering harm or is at risk of significant harm should refer to one of the statutory agencies (SSD, NSPCC, police).
- Referrals may be from the child's family, other members of the public or professionals working with the child and family.
- All professionals working with children and families should be adequately trained to recognise signs of abuse and how to respond.
- Professionals who receive the referral have to balance the need for action to protect the child with the harm which may be caused by unnecessary intervention.
- Except in cases of extreme urgency professionals will discuss referrals with other colleagues in child protection agencies and the referrer before acting. A specialist opinion may be needed here to carry the work on.
- If the child protection agency decides that a formal investigation is not needed the referrer should be informed.

2. Immediate protection and planning an investigation

- If there is a risk to the life of a child or a likelihood of serious injury the child's immediate safety must be secured by the statutory agency. Does the child need removing to some other place, either on a voluntary basis or by obtaining an Emergency Protection Order (EPO)?
- If the child is removed there is a requirement to return the child as soon as it is safe to do so.
- Could the child's safety be secured by the alleged abuser being removed from home or agreeing to leave?
- Are the other children in the home safe?
- The parents should be given appropriate opportunity to participate in the process and efforts made to facilitate contact between the family and child if there is an EPO.
- *A Strategy Discussion* between the statutory agencies, usually SSD and police, is needed at a very early stage to plan the investigation and the extent to which this will be a joint investigation. If the police are undertaking a parallel investigation which may lead to the prosecution of an alleged abuser there are issues concerning the child and his needs versus legal requirements. Working Together (1991) says very clearly, 'the welfare of the child must be of the first importance'. Psychologists, psychiatrists and the Crown Prosecution Service may take part in these discussions.

3. Investigation and initial assessment

- SSD have a duty to investigate where there is reason to suspect a child is suffering from or is likely to suffer significant harm. This includes children in a local authority placement (foster-home, residential home, school).
- The four prime tasks are:
  - to establish the facts giving rise to the concern
  - to decide if there are grounds for concern
  - to identify sources and level of risk
  - to decide protective or other action in relation to the child and any others.
- Interviewing of children requires staff who are competent and trained. Investigative interviews should be kept at a minimum. If court proceedings have been started the court's agreement

is needed for examinations for the purposes of expert evidence. Interviews should proceed at the child's pace. Recording of the interviews should be accurate and differentiate between fact, hearsay and opinion (see Ch. 9).

- If allegations are found to be unsubstantiated the carers with parental responsibility, the child (if appropriate) and the referrer should be told in writing, and a suitably worded apology offered which does not leave the investigations open to challenge.

4. Child protection conference and decision-making (Table 14.2)

The CPC is held following an investigation of an incident of possible abuse. It is convened by SSD or NSPCC. 'The child protection conference (CPC) provides the prime forum for professionals and the family to share information and concerns, analyse and weigh up the level of risks to children and makes recommendation for action' (Working Together, p. 31).

- The conference may decide:
  — if the child's name shall be put on the Child Protection Register
  — which statutory agency will carry ongoing child care responsibility and when the child protection review will be (if necessary)
  — to designate key workers for the child (SSD or NSPCC).

Table 14.2   Child protection conferences

---

a. *Initial child protection conference*
- Brings together the family and professionals to exchange information and plan together.
- Convened by SSD or NSPCC.
- Called after an investigation under Section 47 of the Children Act of an incident of or suspicion of abuse.
- Decide: (i) level of risk to child(ren)
          (ii) need for registration
         (iii) plans for future
- Key worker appointed (SSD or NSPCC) to:
          (i) fulfill the statutory responsibilities
          (ii) lead interagency work.

b. *Child protection review*
- Review arrangements for protection of child.
- Examine current level of risk.
- Is the child adequately protected?
- Should registration be continued or ended?

- Conferences should take place within 8 working days of referral (maximum 15 days)
- Parents are increasingly invited to the CPC in line with the emphasis of professionals working in partnership with parents and other family carers, and the concept of parental responsibility. The welfare of the child remains the over-riding factor and there are occasions when parents are excluded.
- The people involved at a CPC should be limited to those who need to know and have a contribution to make: these include SSD, NSPCC, police, education, the health authority, GP, health visitor, probation, voluntary organisations, lawyer (for local authority).
- Contributions are increasingly written and submitted to the CPC. Medical reports are usually presented in this way, although with parental attendance the format of these may need to change.
- Minutes are distributed to those who attended the CPC, but parents should receive, as a minimum, the findings of the CPC, who attended and the recommended plan.
- If a professional is unable to attend the CPC he may still submit a report.

Child Protection Register (Table 14.3)

- This is kept by SSD in each area.
- It is not a register of all children who have been abused but of children for whom there are unresolved child protection issues and for whom there is an interagency child protection plan.
- These plans are reviewed every 6 months.
- Professionals concerned about a child can quickly learn of any child protection plan by making enquiries to the CPR.
- Criteria for registration. Before a child is

Table 14.3   Child Protection Register

- Control Register in each SSD area.
- Only lists children about whom there are unresolved child protection issues and there is an interagency child protection plan.
- *Not* a register of all those children who have been abused.
- Only registered after child protection conference.
- Categories are neglect, physical injury, sexual and emotional abuse.
- Deregistration considered at each child protection review.

registered the conference must decide that there is, or is a likelihood of, significant harm leading to the need for a child protection plan.

One of the following requirements needs to be satisfied:

(i) There must be one or more identifiable incidents which can be described as having adversely affected the child. They may be acts of commission or omission. They can be either physical, sexual, emotional or neglectful. It is important to identify a specific occasion or occasions when an incident has 6ccurred. Professional judgement is that further incidents are likely.

or

(ii) Significant harm is expected on thc basis of professional judgement of findings of the investigation in this individual case or on research evidence. The conference will need to establish so far as is possible a cause of the harm or likelihood of harm. This cause could also be applied to siblings or other children living in the same household so as to justify registration of them. Such children should be categorised according to the area of concern.

Categories of abuse for registration. The following categories should be used for the Register and for statistical purposes. They are intended to provide definitions as a guide for those using the Register. In some instances, more than one category of registration may be appropriate. This needs to be dealt with in the protection plan. The statistical returns will allow for this. Multiple abuse registration should not be used solely to cover all eventualities.

Neglect. The persistent or severe neglect of a child, or the failure to protect a child from exposure to any kind of danger, including cold or starvation, or extreme failure to carry out important aspects of care, resulting in the significant impairment of the child's health or development, including non-organic failure to thrive.

Physical injury. Actual or likely physical injury to a child, or failure to prevent physical injury (or suffering) to a child including deliberate poisoning, suffocation and Munchausen's syndrome by proxy.

Sexual abuse. Actual or likely sexual exploitation of a child or adolescent. The child may be dependent and/or developmentally immature.

Emotional abuse. Actual or likely severe adverse effect on the emotional and behavioural development of a child caused by persistent or severe emotional ill-treatment or rejection. All abuse involves some emotional ill-treatment. This category should be used where it is the main or sole form of abuse.

5. Comprehensive assessment and planning

After registration of a child the initial plan includes a comprehensive assessment in order fully to understand the child and family and so plan further action. This is principally carried out by SSD but there may be a need for contributions from a paediatrician (FTT, development), psychologist or psychiatrist.

A written child protection plan with the contributions expected of the carers and professionals is agreed, and the key worker is responsible for coordinating the plan.

6. Implementation, review and deregistration

The interagency child protection plan requires regular review to ensure that it provides protection from abuse for the child. Reviews are held at a minimum interval of 6 months. The first one is usually held at the end of the child and family assessment where the full child protection plan is produced. Deregistration may only be decided at a child protection review.

Children in foster-homes or institutions

Investigation of possible abuse of children in a foster-home or residential setting must be as rigorous as in other circumstances. Similarly, extrafamilial abuse should be referred as for intrafamilial abuse, and child protection issues assessed on their merits.

Where the alleged abuser is a child or young person both abused and abuser are investigated.

Organised abuse

Investigation of organised abuse needs, ideally, a carefully worked-out plan, as by definition there will be a number of abusers involved and also a number of children and/or young adults. There may be a very tight organisation within the group and investigation will need to be at least as well-organised and sophisticated as that of the group. The type of ring varies: further description is found in Chapter 13.

Investigation of organised abuse (Working Together 1991):

- Should be coordinated at a senior level of each agency.
- The timing of the intervention must be planned and agreed by all agencies.
- Media management should be agreed locally (ACPC procedures).
- Agreement is necessary over adjoining geographical boundaries.

Case reviews (by ACPC)

A case review is held whenever a case involves an incident leading to the death of a child where child abuse is confirmed or suspected, or a child protection issue likely to be of major public concern arises. There should be an individual review by each agency and a composite review by the ACPC.

Doctors involved in case reviews should seek advice from a senior colleague, usually the designated doctor, and professional advice is also available from the Medical Defence Union or the Medical Protection Society.

Details of case reviews are found in Working Together (1991).

Clinical review of practice is essential and requires good record-keeping and computerisation to produce accurate statistics. Quality of service as well as numbers should be reviewed to record the service provided and to detect any clinical trends. In-house clinical review of cases by a senior midwife, health visitor and paediatrician is an important way of improving clinical practice and highlighting training needs.

HOSPITAL ADMISSIONS OF CHILDREN WHO MAY HAVE BEEN ABUSED

Indications

- Any child who is ill and warrants hospital care, for example for a severe head injury

- Infants with unexplained injuries and requiring further investigation, for example skeletal survey (Ch. 4)
- Severe failure to thrive in infancy
- Investigation of failure to thrive where the usual outpatient strategies have been unsuccessful (Ch. 3)
- Need for sedation or general anaesthetic to examine a child who may have been sexually abused (Ch. 9)
- Children admitted because of anorexia nervosa, self-poisoning.

Care in hospital

The nursing staff bear the brunt of the problems associated with the admission of abused children to the ward. Angry and distressed parents shout at the nearest person in authority. They may have many unmet needs themselves, are demanding and may be reluctant to be in hospital. Nursing and medical staff need training to see the child as a child in need and not as 'another social problem'. Attitudes are passed on from medical staff and it is reasonable to expect all paediatricians to be able to care for abused children.

Children should not be cared for in side-rooms as further abuse may occur whilst they are in hospital. All accidents should be properly monitored; children thought to be victims of Munchausen syndrome by proxy present (with their parents) a particular management problem (Ch. 12).

Parents must be kept informed, treated courteously, given necessary privacy and usually involved in the care of their child. Visiting restrictions and supervision of visiting in situations where the child is thought to be at further risk on the ward are the responsibility of SSD, not the nursing staff.

The nursing staff are able to record family visits, observe the care parents are able to give to their children and comment on the parent–child relationship. It is important that a senior nurse from the ward is able to attend any child protection conference held.

Junior medical staff should be assisted by their colleagues and should never handle a case of abuse alone. Senior house officers should not be the 'paediatrician' in court. Interviewing parents is a skilled art — the most junior doctor may take an initial, non-confronting history, but a senior doctor should be the one to explain why the history does not explain the injuries or other physical signs. Joint interviews with the parents involving the social worker and paediatrician are a very useful method of investigation.

Good communication between the parents, nursing and medical staff and the social worker is essential. The nurse in charge of the ward should know:

1. why the child is on the ward and what is the clinical plan of investigation
2. what the parents have been told
3. if there is any statutory order
4. what is the short-term plan (SSD)
5. what to do, and who to contact if the child is removed from the ward (tell SSD and after-hours emergency SSD and police)
6. that although it is reasonable to try and dissuade the parents from dramatic action, staff should not become involved in any physical restraint.

Medical notes

Hospital medical notes are the property of the health authority although the contents are 'owned' by the doctor. The courts may order the release of notes and all comments in the records should be capable of later scrutiny and interpretation.

Points to remember include:

1. All medical notes should be clearly written; entries should be dated and signed.
2. If investigations are requested these should be listed and the results should have been recorded. It is the doctor's responsibility to record results and to ensure that any appropriate information is passed on to parents, GP and others who 'need to know'.
3. Contemporaneous records (i.e. written at the time of interview or examination) are usual. This leads to maximum accuracy in recall. The court may ask whether notes are contemporaneous.
4. Notes should be detailed, record verbatim remarks made by the child or adult and be an ac-

curate and objective record of the interview. Persons present at the interview should be identified.

5. Physical examination should be well described, using diagrams and measurements to explain the clinical picture.
6. The reasons why a diagnosis is made should be listed.
7. The management plan should be clearly recorded; for inpatients include guidance as to what to do if parents do not cooperate. The social worker's name and telephone number should be clearly recorded in the notes.
8. A summary of the outcome of the child protection conference compiled by the attending doctor is written in the notes.
9. When the child leaves the clinic or hospital ward the notes should record where he went, with whom, and if paediatric follow-up has been arranged.
10. When parents seek a second opinion, paediatricians may send notes to the selected paediatrician, at the request of the paediatrician. It is not usual to send notes to solicitors unless directed to do so by the court. It is important that all paediatricians recognise that their first duty is to the child and that this over-rides all other obligations. Paediatricians may decide to agree to requests by solicitors for reports if they are to be disclosed, that is made available to all parties. Otherwise solicitors may only use 'favourable' (i.e. to their clients) reports, which is not in the interest of the debate as to the welfare of the child.
11. Medical reports and police statements are also written — see page 248.

Second medical opinions

There is a danger that a child may be referred for repeated physical and psychiatric assessments, a practice deplored by the Cleveland Report (Butler-Sloss 1988, p. 245). The Report also states clearly (p. 248) 'Medical Practitioners who have examined a child for suspected sexual abuse and disagree in their findings and conclusions should discuss their reports and resolve their differences where possible; in the absence of agreement identify the areas of dispute, recognizing their purpose is to act in the best interests of the child'. In an adversarial system it is unlikely that this will be possible as doctors may be appointed because of their known clinical perceptions of abuse. Clearly, if professionals are working in the best interest of the child:

1. All records and reports should be available to the paediatrician or psychiatrist asked for second opinions.

2. If the doctor wishes to examine the child, photograph or video the interview, the child's consent is needed. The doctor should justify why the child must be seen, rather than making a report from the records.

3. The guardian ad litem (a senior social worker appointed by the court to represent the child's interests) may be the most appropriate person to request second opinions—the child's welfare is his or her sole responsibility.

4. Social work reports and police statements are an essential part of the information needed to provide a thorough second opinion.

CLINICAL MANAGEMENT OF POSSIBLE CHILD ABUSE

All cases of child abuse are different but the same clinical skills are used on each occasion. A diagnosis of child abuse means that the doctor's opinion is that abuse has probably occurred. He may think it is a highly probable diagnosis but he can rarely be 100% certain. The diagnosis is built up, as a jigsaw, in parts. The history, the examination and the results of investigations lead to a provisional diagnosis, which is assessed in the light of investigations by social workers and the police. A child protection conference will further scrutinise all the evidence and a minority of cases will then be heard in court. In care courts the evidence is tested against the 'balance of probability', not 'beyond all reasonable doubt' as in criminal courts. The standard of proof required by care courts is high; necessarily so given their statutory powers to remove children from their families.

Doctors should be aware that non-doctors often do not appreciate that an opinion describes the doctor's conclusion on the basis of received information and is not a certainty. If a doctor diagnoses a myocardial infarction is he correct in 60%, 70%, 80% of cases? It is difficult to explain this concept,

yet doctors in child abuse cases are expected to get the diagnosis right every time, without appearing to be so arrogant as to suggest they cannot make mistakes.

If the doctor builds up the jigsaw carefully, can justify each piece of the picture and works closely with colleagues from other agencies, the child protection conference and courts become a safety-net to ensure mistakes are recognised. If the standards of proof are too high, children will not be protected but neither is there a place for inadequate investigation and assessment by doctors, social workers and police which may also lead to children suffering. The following examples suggest how cases might be initially managed. The clinical picture is described in the left-hand column and the management notes to the right, leading up to the time of the child protection conference. There may then be ongoing paediatric involvement and assessment, whether or not a diagnosis of probable child abuse has been made, if the investigation has demonstrated ways in which the child and family could be supported.

ALLEGATIONS OF ABUSE BY PROFESSIONALS

All professionals working with children are at risk of allegations concerning the abuse of children in their care, but professionals may also abuse children. Professionals should question why they are doing their particular job and ensure they do have clear boundaries. It is also necessary to recognise that paedophiles are attracted to jobs which involve child contact and are often 'good with children'. Thus it can be a difficult task for teams of adults working with children — whether teachers, social workers, doctors or voluntary workers — to recognise that colleagues may and do abuse children.

Procedures should be established for each professional group in order to protect children and adults as far as is possible. For doctors this will usually involve forethought when setting up clinics or situations where a child is to be examined. However if doctors spend time in specialist holiday camps for children, for example, guidelines are as for other residential workers.

Resources are needed to implement these procedures, but the medical defence unions are clear

EXAMPLE 1

Clinical problem
3-month-old infant brought by teenage parents to casualty department — 'stopped breathing'

↓

o/e Pale, quiet baby. Badly bruised chest. Well nourished. Clean. Bilateral retinal haemorrhages. No signs sexual abuse.

↓

Blood test — blood film normal
— clotting normal
Skeletal survey fracture 5th and 6th ribs bilaterally and shaft of left femur.
Photographs injuries.

↓

Opinion Ill baby—needs admission. Probable physical abuse.

↓

ADMIT

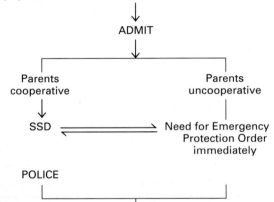

He needs a CT brain scan. Any evidence bony disorder (copper, osteogenesis imperfecta)? Other Δ Δ considered.

Management notes
This baby is clearly ill and needs immediate medical evaluation. The first doctor should take a simple history and avoid confrontation. Later a more senior doctor should explore this inadequate history. The parents should be involved and understand the need for medical tests; implied consent is usually considered adequate unless a general anaesthetic is to be given. The need for skeletal survey and photographs should be explained. Parents will usually allow admission, especially when the baby is clearly unwell.

A senior doctor should become involved at this stage. Social services are contacted, asked to become involved and, in a case of serious physical assault, they will inform the police early in the investigation (strategy discussion). The parents must know that the SSD and, later, the police have been informed. Once the child is in hospital the medical and social investigations continue towards child protection conference and plans for longer-term management.

---

in their advice and on the real possibility of allegations against practitioners. Flexibility is possible when the child is young, the doctor a woman and so on, but sexually abused children in particular may have sexually provocative behaviour and have been damaged by earlier abuse.

Once procedures have been agreed locally the managers of the unit should become responsible for their funding and implementation. It may be necessary to seek advice from the appropriate professional body if a doctor does feel vulnerable.

The procedures should have the weight of procedures rather than guidelines. Table 14.4 lists some strategies.

Table 14.4 Abuse by professionals? Avoidance strategies

1. Record and witness any injury, e.g. fall on floor
2. Record allegations of anything
3. Ensure touching is appropriate, as perceived by child too
4. Record any inappropriate touch or suggestion by child
5. Witness allegations if possible
6. *Do not physically examine child on own*
7. If interviewing child on own for long period consider use of two-way mirror, leave door ajar, etc
8. Do not 'cover up' for a professional colleague
9. Before interviewing or examining any child, ensure consent has been obtained from child and parents

EXAMPLE 2

Clinical problem

4-year-old child seen in day nursery to have bruised face.

Seen by doctor in health centre, OP clinic, *not* busy casualty department, *never* police station.

History — child 'wet the bed on purpose, so I hit him' — stepfather.

o/e Frightened, thin boy. Height 10 pc, weight < 3 pc.
4 parallel bruises left cheek, 'finger-tip' bruises upper arms. Different ages of bruising. Poor language development.

Opinion Physical assault—slap mark and grip marks.
Underweight.
Appears frightened, poor speech needs evaluation.
Bedwetting — age appropriate.

↓

Further medical evaluation needed — growth, development, emotional wellbeing — but as an outpatient.
Emotional maltreatment is seen as a central issue.
Other siblings need assessment too.

Management notes

Officer in charge of day nursery contacts SSD. Social worker visits nursery, sees parents and arranges to take the child and parents for a medical (often with a community paediatrician). Social worker contacts health visitor for up-to-date report. Family already known to SSD, marital and financial problems. Previous unexplained bruising 2 months ago.
Two younger siblings in nursery will need to be examined. Is it safe for this boy to go home? Strategy discussion (police and SSD). Further social worker investigation needed before a child protection conference within the next week.

EXAMPLE 3

Clinical problem

14-year-old girl tells friend who tells teacher 'I'm fed up with my Dad getting into my bed and making me have sex'. Teacher tells girl she cannot keep this 'secret' but will help her.
Social worker (SW) and police officer (PO) see girl in school.
Arrange medical with paediatrically qualified doctor at health centre or OPD (*not* police station).
Examining doctor takes history as appropriate — *n.b.* date LMP, use of tampons, other sexual activity, vaginal discharge. Full physical examination, finishing with genitalia and anus.
Are: a. pregnancy test needed?
b. STD swabs needed?
c. forensic swabs needed?
d. photographs needed?
Physical examination compatible with repeated vaginal intercourse.

Management notes

Schoolteacher accepts initial story, informs educational welfare officer or SSD (child protection agencies). Immediate investigation by SSD of any previous information and strategy discussion that day between SSD police and education.
SW and PO visit mother and seek her cooperation. Mother usually attends medical, but mother and daughter should give consent. The girl may prefer to see a woman doctor, this should be arranged, Do not make child repeat history unnecessarily.
The girl should decide who she wants to have in the examination room. Teenagers often prefer to be seen alone.
Reassure the girl that she is 'normal' anatomically, there is no 'damage', but remember possibility of pregnancy or presence of a STD.
Police decide to arrest father from work.
Will mother protect her daughter? What of other teenage daughters and son, aged 9 years?
Child protection conference arranged.

EXAMPLE 4

Clinical problem	Management notes
School refers 9-year-old boy ('P') to school doctor. He is failing to learn, wets, occasionally soils, and has no friends. Seen with mother at school medical. 12 months earlier 'Uncle John' moved into the family. P's behaviour has always been a problem but worse in last 6 months. o/e Restless, fidgety child, with a frequent brief smile. Height 75 pc, weight 50 pc. Physical examination normal. Follow-up arranged by CMO in 2/12 but as no improvement referred to consultant paediatrician. Seen in clinic — findings as above. *Opinion* Emotionally disturbed boy — needs further assessment, is this child sexually abused? Seen by clinical psychologist for 3 sessions. P tells mother Uncle John is abusing him — mother tells uncle.	The school and school nurse should have useful background knowledge on this boy. Past records describe an intelligent child, initially did well at school but always problems of concentration, poor peer relationships, gets bullied. Educational psychologist confirms that the boy has no specific learning problems and is underachieving. Could he have more support in school? School hears child is wandering around the estate until late into the evening. Sexually explicit drawings found in his school jotter. Paediatrician discusses concern with child abuse coordinator who will gather the known information and review—child's disclosure precipitates an early strategy discussion and investigation by SSD and police. Child protection conference arranged.

CASE HISTORY 1

A 12-year-old girl who had severe learning problems had been referred because of sexually provocative behaviour towards male teachers at school. A female paediatrician examined her alone. The child suddenly sat up, flung her arms around the doctor and kissed her passionately on the lips. What would a third party have made of this encounter?

PRACTICAL ISSUES OF MANAGEMENT

Confidentiality

Doctors are anxious about issues of confidentiality but the General Medical Council in its annual report of 1987 (Working Together 1991) gave unequivocal advice in cases of child abuse and child sexual abuse, 'if a doctor has reason for believing that a child is being physically or sexually abused, not only is it permissible for the doctor to disclose information to a third party but it is a duty of the doctor to do so'. The doctor may feel a responsibility towards the whole family; when there is a conflict of interest between the child and parents what should he do? The advice again is clear, 'the rights of the child should prevail' (Diagnosis of Child Sexual Abuse: Guidance for Doctors 1988).

No professional should work in isolation in this field, and inexperienced doctors should all have access to more senior colleagues for advice. The professional secretariat of the medical defence societies is always available for advice.

In the USA there is mandatory reporting of possible child abuse cases. All professionals are required to tell the child protection agencies if they have concerns of possible abuse. There are advantages for professionals in that they are obliged to report and the balance is towards early reporting. In the UK doctors will hesitate — can they justify their actions, is enough known, is it really serious? If there are good interagency links, with respect between professionals, a doctor may feel able to ring the local social services office, discuss the case with the child abuse coordinator and work out a plan of investigation. Doctors should share appropriate information as building up a diagnosis of abuse is like putting the pieces of the jigsaw together and other professionals often have information which clarifies the clinical picture. The police too have a legitimate interest in child abuse, and as part of a team will usually work in conjunction with other professionals.

Confidentiality at child protection conferences is also a legitimate concern. It should be the responsibility of local trainers under the auspices of the Area Child Protection Committee to ensure that there is a common ethical code. Information must be shared but members of the case conference need to be confident that confidentiality will be respected; the degree of confidentiality will be governed by the need to protect the child (Working Together 1991). Written reports are increasingly laid before child protection conferences, and medical reports should be factual considering that later they may be used in court.

If parents attend part or the entirety of a child protection conference care should be taken not to infringe a third party's confidentiality.

Consent for medical examinations

Consent for medical examination in paediatric practice is often implied. When a parent takes a child to see a doctor because the child has earache, help for the child is being sought. Parents expect the doctor to take a history, to ask the parent and child about symptoms and to examine the child. In this circumstance the examination would involve examining ears, nose, throat and chest, but the examination would depend upon the history. Whilst it is courteous to ask the child 'Is it alright if I look in your ears?', parents, by their presence, are assumed to be willing for the examination to take place.

Examination of children referred because of possible abuse

Whilst the examination of a child who may have been abused is triggered by the issue of maltreatment, an assessment of the whole child should be included in the examination. Health, growth or developmental problems should be recognised as the examination serves the purpose of a full health check. Consent (usually verbal) is required for this examination as well as for any necessary medical investigations or treatment. The Cleveland Report said 'The child is a person and not an object of concern' (Butler-Sloss 1988). There is also emphasis, later taken up by the Children Act 1989, on listening to children, hearing their views and seeking their (appropriate) consent for medical examination.

Children, except very young children, should always be asked for their permission by the doctor before examination. In practice physical examination is not possible without the child's cooperation. However, depending on the child's age and understanding, the nature and purpose of the examination should be discussed so that the child's consent is informed (see later). The Children Act (1989) considers the child's welfare to be paramount, and the child may be vulnerable when

given the choice to consent to or to refuse medical examination in the context of abuse. Abusers recognise this and may pressurise the child to refuse, fearing the consequence of corroboration of the allegations. The Act rightly leaves the consent with the teenager, but adults (parents or professionals) must be careful how they counsel children in these circumstances and should not offload their anxiety on to the child.

The current law

The Children Act therefore is clear that children, depending on their age and ability to understand, should be asked for their consent to examination. Parents must be fully involved in any procedures. Since the Gillick ruling older children have been able to give their own consent to medical treatment. Also, although parents must be involved, this does not mean that they may pressurise older children or insist on being present during the interview with the doctor or at the examination. In 1988 doctors were given clear advice as to the basis for medical consent (Diagnosis of Child Sexual Abuse: Guidance for Doctor 1988, pp 13–14). Examination without consent may be held in law to be assault. But for consent to be valid it must be informed, which means that the person must be aware of what he is consenting to and the possible consequences. The consent must be freely given without fear, threats, fraud or coercion. By the age of 16 years, children are regarded at law as capable of giving consent. Clearly there are exceptions, for example a child with significant learning difficulties.

Current practice

If a medical appointment has been requested by a parent, social worker or police officer in a case of possible maltreatment the doctor should formally ask for consent from the person with that authority (usually the parent or child) to talk to the child and examine him. Paediatricians usually rely on verbal consent and this practice is rarely challenged. In contentious cases practitioners may prefer a signed and witnessed consent to be taken. Police surgeons follow this latter practice.

However, consent is equally valid whether given

orally or in writing as long as it is informed and freely given. Consent is needed for any investigation, for example skeletal survey, and written consent is always sought before a general anaesthetic is given. If consent is witnessed by a professional witness it carries greater weight but in many instances there is no such witness, however preferable in law.

Teenagers and older children need a more detailed preparation than younger children with a different level of understanding of the medical and the consequences of the full investigation of any allegation. It should be emphasised, though, that the 'medical evidence' is but a part of the greater 'jigsaw' which includes the social work and the police investigation. The medical should rarely be seen as the final arbiter — 'yes, there has' or 'no, there hasn't' been abuse.

CASE HISTORY 2
A concerned mother, on discovering that her 16-year-old nephew had been abusing her 12-year-old daughter for 4 years wanted her girl examined. The mother was worried about 'damage or infection', and the girl as to whether she was 'normal'. The mother wanted 'proof' and it helped the girl to have medical corroboration of her story. The paediatrician helped with these concerns and referred the girl on for counselling.

Consent in cases such as the above should be informal and is unlikely to be problematical. Photography also requires consent. Photography may cause additional distress but if a colposcope is used (a piece of equipment with a light source, magnification and an integral camera) this may be minimised. Also, good photographs coupled with clear clinical notes and diagrams should make it difficult to justify further medical examinations. This must be in the child's best interest as the child is not submitted to a further examination but a competent second opinion may be provided nonetheless.

Other issues of consent

• Rarely, doctors will examine children without consent, but this is limited to emergencies of life or limb.

• If children are living at home, in the care of their parents and the children are too young to decide for themselves, the parent has the power to consent to medical treatment.

• When parents have delegated the care of their child to others they can also delegate their power to consent to medical treatment.

• When a local authority has parental responsibility for a child, it may, in appropriate cases, delegate the power to consent to medical treatment to others, for example the carers. In most cases where a local authority has parental responsibility. It is obviously important that in these circumstances the local authority and the parents discuss medical consent, covering various contingencies, before it becomes needed.

Notes have been prepared for doctors (DoH 1991a) which advise them to consider before medical examination:

• Who has the right to consent to this examination or assessment?

• Is the child subject to a court order?

• What are the directions of the court, if any, in relation to the order?

• Who has parental responsibility?

• Will the assessment be used in court proceedings?

• What are the views of the child, and has a guardian ad litem been appointed?

• Does the child have any difficulty in communicating for which special arrangements need to be made?

All the above questions must be addressed — if in doubt ask a lawyer. The British Agencies for Adoption and Fostering have produced a useful leaflet for practice which refers to children placed by local authorities and adoption agencies (BAAF 1991). All carers (persons providing day-to-day care) need to know what to do in an emergency, for prophylactic or other care.

In general terms:
1. *Emergency Protection Order.* Once proceedings have been started always ask the court's permission for medical examination; the applicant of the EPO has parental responsibility as long as the order lasts and may consent for emergency treatment, although this should be discussed where practicable with the parents.
2. *Child Assessment Order.* The court authorises medical examination.
3. *Care Order.* The local authority had parental responsibility and may give consent. This power may be delegated to carers in certain circumstances. The parent(s) also hold parental responsibility but

the local authority may determine the extent to which they exercise this. However, older children in care may also give consent or refuse as for other teenagers who understand the issues.

4. *Children in local authority accommodation* under Section 20 of the Children Act. The local authority has no power to consent to medical treatment unless this has been delegated by the parent or other person with parental responsibility.

5. *Children placed for adoption.* Birth parents retain parental responsibility for children of any age placed under the adoption agencies until they have been freed for adoption. The degree to which the parents are able to exercise this responsibility varies with the legal status of the child, arrangements made with the parent and any Section 8 order which is in effect. Clearly it is essential to plan with the birth parent if they would prefer to withdraw from this responsibility and the adopters need to be given delegated responsibility as long as they inform the agency of any treatment. Once children have been adopted they differ from foster-children in that all parental responsibilities are transferred to the adopters.

6. *Wards of court* differ in that the High Court has the right and power to consent to medical treatment and directions must be sought on the ward's behalf. Under the Children Act, children will no longer be made wards of court.

Summary

Children should never be denied emergency treatment because of the lack of formal consent. However, some forethought is needed when children are with carers other than their parents to ensure that the carer has authority to consent to examination and treatment when a child becomes less acutely ill. Consent for other medical examinations, for example an assessment concerning neglect and possible other abuse, may be problematical. Who has parental responsibility? What does the court authorise?

Tread warily! Do not be in contempt of court — likewise courts may refuse to accept medical reports from examinations they have not authorised.

Medical reports

Medical reports are written for a variety of pur-

poses and their format will vary. If a child is seen because of possible abuse a report should automatically be written and sent to other agencies on a 'need to know' basis. This usually means the child's GP, local SSD and child health (community). The written report will confirm the findings which will have been discussed earlier with the family and their social worker and others. It is important that a written report is available at the child protection conference, compiled by the paediatricians, clinical medical officer or police surgeon who examined the child.

Only if there is good communication will children at risk be protected, and doctors need to establish an efficient practice for provision of reports.

Types of report:

1. Initial medical report
2. Full medical report
3. Police statement
4. Affidavit/affirmation.

1. Initial medical report

If an emergency protection order is sought from the court, for example if parents are threatening to remove a 6-week-old baby with multiple fractures from the ward, a short report may be written just to confirm the injuries and state that a provisional diagnosis of physical abuse has been made. The social worker can present this at court as 'evidence of harm', and that, given the age of the child, 'significant (further) harm' is likely, and so satisfy the conditions for the order. This report should be dated and have the name, date of birth and address of the child and professional address, name, signature and degrees of the doctor. It should be followed up by a more complete medical report. This is a legal document, and all opinions will be open to scrutiny later.

2. Medical report

A medical report should be written to be available at the child protection conference on each child. There will be occasions, for example complex cases of failure to thrive or emotional abuse, when a longer, more detailed report is needed and the doctor needs more time to gain all the relevant information. In these circumstances an interim report should be written and an additional report written later.

In cases of child abuse it is not usual for the doctor to wait to write a report until asked to do so by the local authority's solicitor. This would cause unnecessary delays and difficulty for the child protection conference. In other situations a solicitor, representing the child (on behalf of the guardian ad litem) or the parents, may ask for a second opinion. This may be a paper exercise — that is, commenting on reports and notes — or the child and family may be seen. The medical report will state which papers the doctor has had made available to him and then comment on the findings and the interpretation of these findings. This should be an objective comment, remembering that the child's welfare is the main responsibility, not the protection of adults or vilification of colleagues.

Format of medical report (Fig. 14.3)
a. *The presentation* of the report should be clear — typed double-spaced with wide margins and headed 'Medical Report, Private and Confidential'.
b. *The purpose* of the report should be remembered; also that it is to be read by non-medical professionals. What does the doctor think and why? The doctor does not have to be 100% certain, and can rarely be so, but he can give an assessment of probability. Courts interested in child welfare have a different standard of proof based on 'the balance of probabilities', as compared with criminal courts where the standard of proof has to be 'beyond reasonable doubt' (Criminal Justice Act). In criminal cases the terms 'consistent' and 'not consistent' are used as opposed to 'probable' (Diagnosis of Child Sexual Abuse: Guidance for Doctors 1988, p. 39).
c. *The content* includes:
(i) Brief, relevant history, including circumstances and explanation of the injury. Only significant past medical history is included.
(ii) Description of the physical examination to include the child's demeanour, height, weight, cleanliness. All lesions (bruises, lacerations, burns, scars) described by size (cm), colour, depth, etc. Systems examination including genitalia and anus.
(iii) Investigations and results (dated).
(iv) Any further spontaneous comments by child

during examination, e.g. 'Kenny stuck me with a knife'.
(v) Opinion as to what has happened and why. The injury may be unexplained — in a baby of 3 months is this abuse, probably, or is abuse unlikely? Discuss the findings in the light of the other information, build up the 'jigsaw' which has led to your opinion so that you are able to justify it at the child protection conference or in court.
(vi) The professional address of the doctor, qualifications, and maybe also a list of experience with children or child abuse: this will be confirmed if the case goes to court. Always date reports and sign the top copy for court.
(vii) Distribution to family GP, local SSD, child health service and others as appropriate, such as other paediatricians, NSPCC, local authority solicitor.

Always keep a copy of the medical report; it may be appropriate to have a separate secure filing cabinet for 'abuse notes'. In these circumstances it is important that other relevant records (hospital notes, child health notes, general practice notes) contain a copy of the report for reference. The report may later be used in various courts and made available to lawyers representing the child, local authority or parents. *Think* before circulating the report: inexperienced doctors are well advised to discuss the contents with a colleague. If still in doubt, contact the medical defence organisations. If the case goes to court the medical report may or may not be agreed by the various parties; if it is contested the author will be asked to attend court.

Note that in some circumstances the child's address e.g. in fostercare, where there may be a risk of removal should be withheld

4. Affidavit/affirmation

An affidavit is a written report which is a statement of evidence and is set out in a standard way, although exhibits to the affidavit may include, for example, earlier medical reports. A solicitor will usually set out the affidavit which then must be sworn or declared before a commissioner for oaths or other authorised officer. In practice, a solicitor (acting as an authorised officer) usually does this for a small fee, payable by the requesting solicitor.

```
┌─────────────────────────────────────────────────────────────┐
│  ┌───────────────────────────────────────────────────────┐  │
│  │            Leeds Western Health Authority             │  │
│  │ ┌──────────────┐  ┌──────────────┐  ┌──────────────┐  │  │
│  └─┤              ├──┤              ├──┤              ├──┘  │
│    │ Child Abuse  │  │ Version 1.01 │  │    Report    │     │
│    │   System     │  │              │  │   Printout   │     │
│    └──────────────┘  └──────────────┘  └──────────────┘     │
└─────────────────────────────────────────────────────────────┘
```

Department of Community Paediatrics   Date: 12/04/90
Leeds General Infirmary
Leeds
LS2 9NS
Tel: LEEDS 432799 — ext: 2152   **PRIVATE AND CONFIDENTIAL**

Name: SNOW, JOHN   Alias:
Date of Birth: 06:06:87   Gender: M
Address: 12 ICE STREET
          LEEDS 30
          YORKSHIRE
Telephone:

GP: DR. BLOB
Address: 122 BLOOMER ROAD
          LEEDS 30

Social Worker: SUSAN WRIGHT
Telephone:

Social Service: BUCKSHAW ROAD
Telephone:

Health Visitor: JUNE SMITH
Telephone:

Consultant: DR BLANK

School: BELMONT PARK NURSERY

Police: NOT APPLICABLE
Telephone:

History: I examined John aged 2 years on 3.3.90 at .... Hospital at the request of .... Social Services
          Department. He was brought to the hospital by his mother Ms. Snow and S. W. Susan Wright.

          Ms. Snow told me that she had gone out to Bingo the previous evening leaving John in the care of a
          16-year-old girl baby-sitter. John was asleep on her return and it was not until the following morning she
          found he had two black eyes and bruising around his face. She immediately contacted her Health Visitor
          who referred him on to S.S.D.

          The family are not previously known to S.S.D.

          There is no past medical history of note.

          Immunisation — complete.

Examine: Well cared for boy, nutrition good. Height 90 cm (50 pc) weight 14 kg (> 50 pc) Lively and playful.
          Injuries
          1. Left black eye with red-purple bruising extending 4 cm × 1 cm below eye, associated with some
              swelling.

  2. Right black eye with red-purple bruising extending 4 cm × 0.5 cm below eye
  3. Left angle of jaw a row of red-purple bruises 4 × 0.5 cm
  4. Anterior aspect both shins × 3 0.3 cm yellowing bruises

Heart: Heart sounds I & II nil added
Chest: clear
Abdomen: soft
Genitalia: normal
  testes descended
Anus: normal
Investigations — Blood film normal
  Clotting tests normal
Photographs were taken

Opinion: Physical abuse.

The bruises around the face are recent and likely to have been caused within the previous 48 hours. The two black eyes are consistent with blows from a fist and the bruises below the jaw finger marks (grip.) Considerable force has been used and accidental injury is improbable given two black eyes, and the site of bruising below the jaw which is rare in accidental injury. There are three discreet areas of injury, all likely to have been caused at the same time.

The bruises on the shins are as seen in ordinary play.

John's general care, growth and development appears normal.
The blood test shows that John does not have an unusual tendency to bleed.

Signature: JOHN BLANK CONSULTANT COMMUNITY PAEDIATRICIAN

C.C. G.P.:
    Social Services: local office
    NSPCC
    Mr. Barnett, Sweet Street (Child Protection Coordinator)
    Dr. Robertshaw, Child Health
    Miss M A P Carlton, Child Health (Nursing)
    Dr. C J Hobbs if Western Child/Dr. J Wynne if Eastern Child

Fig. 14.3 A sample medical report.

The affidavit is made available to the judge and all parties to the case. If it is agreed the witness may not be called to give evidence. Oral evidence is given when the evidence is not agreed but may be limited to the reports.

More usually in proceedings under the Children Act 1989, the professional will be asked to sign a statement on the understanding it will be placed before the court.

Forensic evidence

Forensic medicine seeks to explain the relevance of clinical signs, such as bruising, in a legal context. Each doctor who presents evidence of a physical assault to a court is giving forensic evidence. There is clearly overlap between forensic medicine and pathology; some practitioners are involved in both fields.

Although most children's doctors will feel confident to examine children who may have been physically abused or neglected, extra training is needed in the collection of certain specimens, for example in a case of recent rape. There has been considerable debate as to the role of paediatricians and police surgeons. Some paediatricians have been adequately trained to collect specimens but few police surgeons will feel confident to care for the child and his family paediatrically and will ask for a joint examination. It is likely in the future that, as for physical abuse, paediatricians will undertake the bulk of all child abuse work, calling on specialist police surgeon colleagues for help in appropriate cases. The appointment of women as police surgeons solely to examine women and children who may have been sexually assaulted is a welcome initiative as long as there is close cooperation with paediatricians in child cases, and children are not examined in a police station.

This section will concentrate on evidence which may be found in cases of sexual abuse; interpretation of bruising and other injuries is discussed in Chapter 4, and Figure 14.4 is an outline approach to medical and forensic investigation of child sexual abuse.

Forensic tests are based on Locard's principle which states 'every contact leaves a trace'. For example, if an abuser has ejaculated over the child semen stains may be found on the child's body or clothes. If the child has scratched his assailant blood may be found on either party. Fibres from the clothes worn by the child or assailant may be found on the other, and so on.

Clearly, the evidence which is obtained and its relevance depends on the type of abuse, where it occurred and how long ago. In practice positive laboratory forensic tests are found in few victims of child sexual abuse (CSA). This is because most CSA is intrafamilial and ongoing. The child may disclose at any time following the most recent assault which may have occurred days, months or years earlier. This will allow healing to occur and the physical examination may be entirely normal. Detection of semen varies with time too. Ideally swabs are taken from the mouth, vagina or anus within 24 hours of the assault. Spermatozoa have been identified in the mouth after 24 hours, the anus after 65 hours and the vagina after 6 days, but most laboratories suggest a time limit of 72 hours for such specimens (Table 14.5). If the child has bathed, changed his clothes or had his bowels opened evidence will have been destroyed. Even semen stains on the child's bedclothes may be explained — I slept in his bed because he was frightened after a nightmare'. Transfer of fibres within a household is inevitable due to contact between people and furniture (Table 14.6).

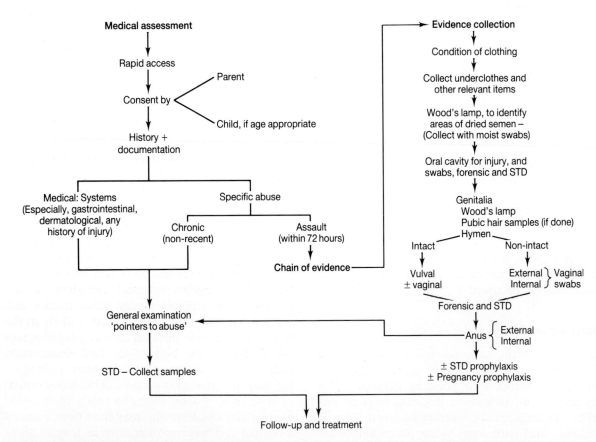

Fig. 14.4   An outline approach to medical and forensic investigation of child sexual abuse (Jenkins & Lewington 1991).

Table 14.5 Time limits for the detection of spermatozoa and seminal fluid (RCP 1991)

	Spermatozoa	Seminal fluid
Vagina	6 days	12–18 hours
Anus	3 days	3 hours
Mouth	12–14 hours	3 hours
Clothing/bedding	Until washed	Until washed

Forensic samples:

1. Evidential samples
2. Control samples (blood and saliva) for comparison purposes.

Stains may include:

- blood
- semen
- saliva
- lubricant
- vaginal fluid
- faeces.

Plain cotton wool swabs (dampened with water if necessary) are used to remove stains.

The other evidential trace material is loose material or debris, and forceps or swabs are used to remove these. Clothing is inspected by the forensic scientist and may reveal fibres or particulate debris, but pubic hair may be recovered from the child's body.

Examination of unwashed clothing, bedding, carpets, chair covers, or objects used to assault the

Table 14.6 Forensic investigations (DHSS 1988, McLay 1990)

Specimen	Site	Test	Storage/labelling
1. *Semen* — plain sterile dampened cotton wool swab (cws)	• mouth (around teeth) • perigenitally • vaginal • perianally • anally • 'wet' areas • umbilicus	• microscopy for sperm	Freeze
2. *Seminal stain* — plain sterile dampened cotton wool swabs (cws)	• skin (abdomen, thighs) • clothing	• ABO system etc. • acid phosphatase • DNA profile	Freeze Cool room (clothing) Freeze

3. *Blood:* a. EDTA bottle
b. Sodium fluoride and potassium oxalate bottle
	5 ml	• blood groups
		• DNA profile
		• alcohol/drug assay
		• solvent/glue
			Refrigerate
			Freeze
			Freeze
			Freeze ⎫
			  ⎬ record time sample
			  ⎪ taken and date

4. *Urine* — sodium fluoride bottle		• drug assay	Refrigerate ⎭
5. *Saliva* — glass bottle, mouth swabs (cws)	• mouth • bite marks	• microscopy for sperm • acid phosphatase • ABO secretor status	Freeze
6. *Hair* — (head, pubic) loose or combing or matted *Not* usually indicated to comb or cut pubic hair	• mouth (oral sex) • body • pubic area • head hair (matted)	• ABO grouping	Refrigerate in polythene bag
7. Fingernail samples	Rarely useful		
8. Clothing, fibres, debris—may use clear adhesive tape	As appropriate – damaged/stained areas	• fibre identification • lubricant identification • blood/semen • pubic hair	Cool room (clothes) in paper bag for dry items, open polythene bag for wet Refrigerate
9. Lubricant CONTROL SAMPLES may take at time or later if indicated	as for semen • blood • saliva • head hair • pubic	• lubricant identification Interpretration of grouping reaction from stains of blood, saliva, etc.	

child is more likely to give evidence than examination of the child.

Materials such as textiles, head hair, paint or wood fragments are unlikely to be evidentially important when the abuser is known to the child and family.

Taking of samples:

- Use sampling materials and containers from a sexual assault pack (provided by police).
- Store samples as instructed, e.g. in a refrigerator or freezer (Table 14.6).
- Label each specimen with
  - — child's name
  - — date taken
  - — person taking sample
  - — type of sample.
- Attach a 'Criminal Justice Label' to container or outer wrapping.
  - — Complete the label with type of sample, sample number and signature of all who handle the sample until it gets to court.
  - — The sample number consists of the doctor's initials and the number of the sample, e.g. JMW/1 saliva sample, JMW/2 urine sample.
  - — Usually the numbering starts again with each examination; the only exception is if 2 or more children are examined as part of the same enquiry — label consecutively.
- *Seal* all samples with clear adhesive tape over the signed label, use freezer tape for specimens which are to be put in the refrigerator or freezer. Wind the tape completely around the top of bottles and turn the top of bags over twice and seal.

Samples to be taken are listed in Table 14.7.

The forensic investigation depends on the clinical situation. The complete examination which is appropriate for an adult woman who has been raped on waste ground differs in many respects from the more limited examination needed of a 4-year-old girl who has been indecently assaulted by her older brother at home. A 'sexual offences form' should be available with kits and is a useful aide-memoire and means of record.

Table 14.7   Forensic samples may include (after Jenkins & Lewington 1991)

Sample	Method	Example of indication
Debris collected	Undress on sheet of paper	Stranger rape
Clothing	Damage or stained, dry clothes if possible	Useful until washed
Mouth swabs	Around teeth, tooth cavities	12–14 hours
Saliva	Spit into bottle (difficult to obtain)	12–14 hours
Genital swabs (damp, plain, sterile swab)	Perigenitally External vaginal *before* internal Internal only if penetration possible	6 days (usually < 72 hrs)
Anal swab (damp, plain, sterile swab)	Perianally External and before internal	3 days
Penile swab (damp, plain, sterile swab)	Outside penis Urethral swab only for STD	
Skin swab (damp, plain, sterile swab)	Any stain, inner thighs, lower abdomen, chest, umbilicus, etc.	Lubricants, semen—until washed
Blood (sodium fluoride bottle)	Any stain Sample drawn	Assailant/child Drugs/alcohol
Urine (sodium fluoride bottle)	Sample	Drugs, alcohol
Hair: • head hair • pubic hair • loose pubic	Matted cut off (semen?) Collect	Assailant/child

The Metropolitan Police Laboratory no longer collects pubic hair by combing or cutting because improved DNA testing facilities make it unnecessary.
Note: Unless abuse has occurred recently, medical examination is less likely to yield useful evidence than bedding, carpets, sofa covering, etc.

The examination, which is part of a medico-legal investigation, should be described carefully. Points to remember include:

- Write legible notes, date and sign them, use professional address.
- Include the child's full name and address, date of birth and who accompanied him and gave consent; why, where and when the examination took place.
- Record a full history and detailed examination with diagrams if useful.
- Note if photographs are taken and by whom.
- Use a forensic check list to record specimens taken and where dispatched (sexual offences form).
- Use appropriate containers and swabs (in forensic kit supplied by police).
- Write a police statement as requested, keep a copy and usually complete a medical report for SSD, GP and child health.

The examination of the assailant is not described (McLay 1990).

DNA profiling

In the past, by using conventional blood grouping (ABO and Rhesus) techniques, it was possible only to exclude a man from paternity or show that his blood was not that found on a victim. By including secretor status and less common blood groupings, the ability to demonstrate the reverse increases, i.e. the likelihood of paternity increases with the number of matched additional systems. The specificity of testing has been greatly enhanced by DNA profiling.

DNA profiles may be obtained from blood, semen and hair roots, but there is little DNA in saliva. Likewise in blood stains there is little DNA as the DNA is found in the nuclei of white blood cells. Thus DNA profiling is a less sensitive technique when applied to blood stains than conventional grouping. Semen is rich in DNA: for semen stains or vaginal swabs DNA profiling is more sensitive than conventional grouping.

Calculations show that an individual has a 1 in 4 chance of having a band in a given position. DNA profiles yield about 11 bands and, if all match, the chance of obtaining that particular profile in the general population is 1 in 2 700 000; if there are 14 bands the chance occurrence is 1 in 155[10] If the specimen is small and the amount of DNA limited, fewer bands may be obtained; however, 4 bands reduce the chance occurrence to 1 in 200, better than conventional grouping methods. Conventional grouping methods continue to have uses in excluding suspects and testing blood stains and saliva specimens.

Police statement (See example, Fig. 14.5)

Police statements differ in their presentation from medical reports. The investigating police officer will request that a statement is written and doctors will often prefer to write their own statement rather than sign one written in the police officer's language. Statements are written on a form provided by the police; each sheet should be signed at the bottom and copies always kept. A fee is payable for the statement.

Criminal proceedings take place at the direction of the Crown Prosecution Service. For a guilty verdict the case must be 'proved beyond all reasonable doubt' and, given the difficulty for children to give evidence, even with videolinks, the percentage of successful prosecutions, especially of child sexual abuse, is low (less than 5% of all alleged CSA).

Police statements differ from medical reports in that the court will only hear factual information and not hearsay.

The format of a statement:

- Name, date of birth and address of child.
- Name, *professional* address, degrees and current post of examining doctor with short statement of relevant clinical experience.
- Why the medical was requested, e.g. 'following an allegation by the child that she had been sexually abused'.
- Where the child was seen, who brought her, who was present to give a history, present during the examination (what time of day and how long the examination took may be asked in court).
- Describe the child's demeanour during the examination and the details of the examination in full.

STATEMENT OF: ....

AGE/Date of Birth: JOHN L BROWN   OCCUPATION: ....

ADDRESS: Over 21 Paediatrician
            Belmont House, Belmont Grove,
            Leeds General Infirmary   POSTCODE: ....

This statement (consisiting of _____ pages signed by me) is true to the best of my knowledge and belief and I make it knowing that, if it is tendered in evidence, I shall be liable to prosecution if I have stated in it anything which I know to be false or do not believe to be true.

Dated the _____ day of _____ , 19 John Brown

STATEMENT OF WTINESS

(C.J. Act, 1967, s 9,
M.C. Act, 1980, s 102,
M.C. Rules, 1981, r 70)

re: TRACEY Y. d.o.b. 9.9.80   5, Green Sweet, Leeds 34.
I am Dr John L Brown, my degrees are Mb ChB MRCP. My current post is Consultant Community Paediatrician, at Leeds General Infirmary. I was appointed in 1984. I have an interest in Child Abuse, and have examined abused children over the last ten years.

I examined Tracey Y, aged 10 years, at 3.00 pm on 7.7.90 at the request of West Yorkshire Police. She was brought to Leeds General Infirmary by her mother, Mrs Y. and Policewoman Z.

I had been asked to examine Tracey following an allegation that she had been sexually abused.

ON EXAMINATION: Well, co-operative child. Ht 140 cm (75 pc). Wt 35 kg. (75 pc). Pre-pubertal. Became very anxious when genitalia examined.
Heart — normal
Lungs — normal
Abdomen —   soft. Genitalia. Minimal but uniform reddening of vulva.
            Hymenal opening gaping, 1.5 cm horizontally and 1.5 cm vertically, thin rim of hymen remaining with irregularities at 5 pm and 9 pm.
            No discharge, scarring or tears.
Anus — normal.
Investigations — Forensic swabs not taken, last alleged assault 3 weeks earlier.
            — Bacteriological swabs taken 7.7.90 and initial report negative 9.7.90.

Mrs Y told me that Tracey had told her Aunt Susan that her father had been putting his fingers into her tuppence. Tracey had complained that he had hurt her and it had started when she was 7 years old, on her birthday. It happened about once a week.

Policewoman Z had already taken a Statement from Tracey and confirmed this history.

OPINION: The physical examination is consistent with digital penetration of the hymen. The hymenal opening is wide for a pre-pubertal girl, only a thin rim persists, there are no definite tears but I note two irregularities which may represent healed tears.

I note the history of alleged painful digital penetration over a period of 3 years. The signs are consistent with this history.

The reddening of the vulva is a non-specific sign. The swab was negative, showing no evidence of bacterial infection.

Statement taken by:

Given a clear disclosure by the child, physical signs which are consistent with the child's description, the probability is that she has been sexually abused.

JOHN L BROWN — Paediatrician

Fig. 14.5 A sample police statement.

- Record simply any history given, and say by whom.
- Describe any relevant symptoms such as pain, vaginal bleeding.
- Record if photographs were taken and by whom.
- Record if blood tests, X-rays, microbiological investigations were performed, and results if available.
- Forensic tests:
  — record which tests were carried out
  — who the specimens were handed on to
  — label, date, sign and seal all samples (see details, p. 254).

Opinion

- Are the physical signs consistent with the history?
- Was the physical examination normal, as might be consistent with an allegation of oral sex?
- Is the probability of abuse very high, as for example would be the case if the child has gonorrhoea?
- Is it possible to give a time scale to the abuse (albeit roughly)?
- Are there signs to suggest recent or chronic abuse, or both?

Note: Always check a police statement with a senior doctor before dispatch.

Summary

1. Local guidelines, provided by the Area Child Protection Committee in line with Working Together 1991 and the Children Act 1991, should underpin all multi-agency practice.

2. Investigation of a case of possible child abuse should be logical and considered (Figs 14.1 and 14.2).

3. Doctors have a responsibility to recognise possible child abuse and to work together with other professionals in order to protect children.

4. Child protection teams based on each district general hospital enable doctors and other professionals to work together, share expertise, give support, teach, research and audit practice.

5. Child protection work spans community and hospital practice and should be well coordinated. Resources are needed to improve all aspects of practice.

6. Clinical management is often complex and should not be the sole responsibility of junior medical staff.

7. Allegations of abuse by professionals must be considered and procedures are needed to protect children and professionals.

8. The welfare of children usually over-rides issues of confidentiality where child abuse is concerned.

9. Consent is necessary before any medical examination.

10. Adequate training is needed for all doctors undertaking child protection work — paediatrically and forensically. Co-working with colleagues (police surgeons) is indicated where a paediatrician is not experienced in collection of forensic samples.

REFERENCES

American Academy of Pediatrics 1991 Guidelines for the evaluation of sexual abuse of children. Pediatrics 87 No 2 254–260

BAAF 1991 Consent to medical treatment for children. Practice Nov 23. BAAF, 11 Southwark Street, London SE1 1RQ

Butler-Sloss E 1988 Report of the Inquiry into Child Abuse in Cleveland 1987. HMSO, London

de la Haye Davis H 1987 Protocol for the forensic medical examination of a sexually abused child. The Police Surgeon 32

DHSS 1988 Sexually abused children—the sensitive medical examination and management. Royal Society of Medicine, pp 40–43

Diagnosis of Child Sexual Abuse: Guidance for Doctors 1988 HMSO

DoH 1991a An Introductory Guide for the NHS: the Children Act 1989

DoH 1991b Child abuse: a study of inquiry reports 1980–1989. HMSO

General Medical Council: Annual Report 1987, p. 15

Gillick v West Norfolk and Wisbech Health Authority 1986 AC 112

Hobbs C J, Wynne J M 1987 Management of sexual abuse. Archives of Diseases of Childhood 62: 1182–1187

Jenkins & Lewington 1991 In: Forensic evidence in physical signs of sexual abuse in children, ch. 9. Royal College of Physicians

Kolvin I (Chairman) 1988 Child sexual abuse: principles of good practice. British Journal of Hospital Medicine

39: 54–62

McLay W D S 1990 Rape. The New Police Surgeon. Association of Police Surgeons of Great Britain, pp 82–111

Protecting Children: Guidance for Social Workers 1988 DoH, HMSO

RCP 1991 Physical signs of sexual abuse in children

Working Together: a guide to the arrangements for interagency cooperation for the protection of children from abuse 1988 DHSS and Welsh Office. HMSO, London

Working Together under the Children Act 1989: a guide to the arrangements for interagency cooperation for the protection of children from abuse 1991 DHSS and Welsh Office. HMSO, London

FURTHER READING

McMurray J 1989 Case conferences Jones & McQuiston 1988

Bentovim et al 1988 Annual Report of Council (BMA) 1989–90 DNA Profiling. HOFSL

15. Psychological intervention and treatment

Children who have experienced abuse or maltreatment need help. During the last two decades much has been written about the way in which the cycle of abuse might be broken and how the psychological consequences can be understood and possibly treated.

Considerable advances have been made in the treatment area and these advances have been based on well-developed techniques, particularly of child treatments. This chapter will, after an overview of the needs of the children, provide a guide to the major therapies and the theories on which they are based, and then proceed to what has been learnt about how to treat children and their families.

Professionals working in the area of child abuse are not left in any doubt that abuse or maltreatment has consequences for the child in both the short and long term (Kempe & Kempe 1984, McFarlane & Waterman 1986, Bentovim et al 1988, Browne et al 1988, Sgroi 1988, Wyatt & Powell 1988, Cicchetti & Carlson 1989, Sgroi 1989).

The needs of the child

Depending on the maltreatment of the child, a number of psychological interventions can be used. The needs of any particular child will be influenced by the age and developmental stage of the child, the form of abuse, whether the abuse has occurred inside or outside the family, and in what way the maltreatment is recognised by those caring for the child and the authorities. All of these aspects should play a part in the decision process as to how to proceed in the selection of help offered and be considered in assessing the child's needs. The range of interventions is wide — while a considerable number of children, even when they have been maltreated in some form or other, will reach an acceptable level of personal development because of the growing up process itself, or because of help from friends, teachers, or non-maltreating parents, for a much larger number of children who have been maltreated the outlook is poor and their special circumstances need to be addressed (Hotaling et al 1988, Wyatt & Powell 1988).

Not all, but many of the maltreated children need help of a professional kind so that their distorted development does not remain forever stuck and does not impede their own emotional growth as well as that of the children they may have in the future. The children and their families will be the central point of discussion about what kind of help and therapy they may receive from different agencies.

What help and when

The question is always, 'how do we know when help is appropriate?'. Some children are evidently distressed — for others the memories of the abusive experience may be repressed, lie dormant and as if invisible to the outside world until something triggers the expression of the emotional turmoil. If a small child has not been too badly maltreated the disturbed behaviour may indicate some of the distress. For the children who have been badly abused the disturbed behaviour and emotional distress is apparent, not only by how the children are perceived by others but also by how difficult it is to care for them when they are in foster-care.

The trigger for the teenager may be a first close emotional relationship; for the adult it may be when they get married or have their first child. Here one may see the emergence of an intergenerational pattern with poor parenting skills being a main component for further abuse in the next generation. It is now better understood that the experiences of maltreatment in childhood — whether the abuse was physical, emotional, sexual abuse, failure to thrive or other forms of maltreatment — have consequences which present themselves at the time and re-emerge in the teenage years, in adulthood particularly during times of stress.

One common consequence is that the future parent may lack experience and understanding of how to care for the children in the next generation. For others the emotional consequences simply make it impossible for them to provide appropriate affectionate care.

The increasing numbers of adults who have come for therapy over the last decade indicate that much maltreatment can be ignored for a long time despite often severe symptoms and distress. Disturbances in behaviour, ill health or distress are being attributed to 'nerves', instead of acknowledging the antecedents of the childhood problems. It is well understood that the effects of abuse will re-emerge through the children's developmental stages, from childhood to old age.

Some discussion will centre on the voluntary services who can provide a crisis intervention service, or more long-term involvement for the family. It will also show how child care can be directed towards the child's needs when abuse has occurred and how carers and the child can be supported through community interventions once the child has been protected. Child abuse and its treatment can not be discussed without thinking about families, parents, siblings, foster-parents and care-takers in institutions. Nor should the stress that accompanies this kind of work for professionals go unmentioned.

As indicated in previous chapters, child maltreatment presents in a combination of abusive behaviours, and the jigsaw mentioned in Chapter 9 can give a clear picture of the interaction between various factors surrounding the abuse. The child, the circumstances, as well as the details of the maltreatment need to be assessed and recognised as a first step towards psychological treatment. For children who have been sexually or ritually abused this almost invariably includes the child being unable to disclose what has happened to him. Children who have been maltreated in other ways also need to have the opportunity to disclose but often the physical marks or neglect are sufficient and telling and make it easier for the child to say what has been happening.

The story of abuse, as already stated, unfolds like a jigsaw and the issue of treatment has its own corner in the jigsaw with a particularly intricate and complex pattern and fit. Putting this corner together can take a long time and often it looks as if a piece of information, memory or emotion does not fit. The story, like a difficult piece, has to be turned this way and that before it does make sense, both to the child, the carers and professionals.

Assessment

The chapters discussing specific forms of child abuse (physical, emotional, failure to thrive, etc.) have incorporated strategies for assessment and these can be usefully followed when making decisions about therapy. However there are aspects of the child and adult which need to be specifically attended to in choosing psychological treatment.

The severity of the abuse will need to be assessed separately and physical as well as psychological evidence is to be taken into account. Stratton & Hanks (1991) have proposed a model — broad questions which need consideration:

• How did the child or adult perceive the maltreatment?
• Do they feel to blame for the maltreatment?
• How anxious is the child/adult?
• Are they depressed, phobic?
• What are the behavioural difficulties?
• Are they underachieving or overachieving?

When a child has been sexually abused the impact of this abuse needs to be assessed:

• What sense did the child make of the abuse?
• What perception have they of themselves?
• Was the child coerced or forced?

- Did the child 'cooperate' or 'accommodate' (Summit 1983) so that the abuse could continue?
- When did the abuse start?
- How long did to go on for?
- Was it kept hidden from the outside world?
- Note the different forms of maltreatment.
- Note other important life events for the child (e.g. parents' illness, death, etc.).
- Any other trauma in the child's life.

Developmental issues

- Age when abuse began.
- The length of time abused.
- At what stage did the sexual abuse become intrusive?
- Was the abuse kept a secret?
- Was there a disclosure, if so to whom and what was the response?
- How was the child treated after disclosure?

Sgroi (1988, 1989) in her two volumes on child sexual abuse has described different forms of assessment in more detail. This section is aimed to help the reader think about the issues involved in making decisions and giving advice (treating the information as a guideline). Procedures, treatments and strategies for understanding abused children and adults are developing at a steady pace. Practitioners need to be mindful of the different laws, procedures in their agency as well of the developments in therapeutic techniques.

TYPES OF PSYCHOLOGICAL TREATMENT

We will now examine how the major therapies and treatments may help a child and his family when child abuse has occurred. A brief discussion about what therapy is in principle will be followed by a description of the four major theoretical frameworks which are most influential in underpinning psychological therapies practised all over the world. We then continue by describing a number of interventions and therapies which may follow the discovery that a child has been abused.

What is psychotherapy?

Principally it is a 'talking cure'. In the various psychotherapies both the client/patient and the therapist use conversation and language as a means of communicating with each other. Even in play therapy with very small children who have not acquired language in the fullest sense some words and sounds pass between the participants. Psychotherapies are distinct from physical treatments and should only be carried out by trained professionals. Many specific psychotherapies have been developed. Each of the therapies is based on a psychological theory and currently there are four major approaches to psychotherapy which form the basis for many subgroups and divisions which developed from one or other theoretical model.

Behaviour psychotherapy

This is based on learning theory and was developed from Pavlov's conditioning principles. This psychotherapy focuses on the maladaptive behaviour as such, and, broadly speaking, attempts to change such behaviours by using positive or negative reinforcers in order to extinguish or inhibit certain behaviours. So, for instance, when a child wets or soils the therapy concentrates on eliminating this behaviour. The reason why the behaviour may have occurred is not explored, the effort is spent on modifying the undesirable behaviour. Many specific treatment procedures exist under this umbrella, e.g. desensitisation techniques for reducing excessive emotional reactions such as fears, aversion therapy to reduce over-dependence on specific gratifications, token economy programmes, assertiveness training, etc. B F Skinner (1953) developed techniques on the principles of learning theory which are used to manipulate deviant or maladaptive behaviours towards a goal. Behaviour therapy may also be used to get a symptom under control so that other therapies can be used.

Cognitive psychotherapy

This is based on the individual's perceptions and thinking and was first developed around the issues of depression. The psychotherapist actively modifies the patient's way of thinking and attempts to change the negative outlook of the patient into a more positive one. Non-directive psychotherapies also developed from a cognitive model. Rational-emotive therapy is another cognitive therapy which centres on people's belief systems and the fact that the beliefs can be distorted in their thinking, causing them psychological difficulties. These difficulties, whether in terms of people's cognitions or behaviour, can be modified by this therapy.

More recently behavioural and cognitive psychotherapies have been used together; new specific ways of working within this framework have been developed under the umbrella of *cognitive-behavioural therapy*. This combination of therapies has been found to be effective in alleviating many problems of individuals.

Psychodynamic psychotherapy

This is based on theories of motivation and drive in human beings and the interaction between them. It relies on understanding the developmental history of the patient — what effects upbringing and relationships in early childhood have on psychological well-being and disturbances in the child and what the effects on later development may be. The therapist pays attention not only to the dynamics in the patient's outside world, particularly the family, but also to what happens inside the session. Much of what patients express in the session will make it possible to understand their functioning and malfunctioning. The story told by the patient — adult or child — will often represent the antecedents to the disturbance. The relationship between therapist and patient is one of the most important tools in this therapy. Brown & Pedder (1979) provide a clear introduction to the field.

Psychoanalysis belongs in a category of its own. Psychodynamic and analytic psychotherapy are both derived from psychoanalytic principles. Since psychoanalysis as such is rarely available in the National Health Service the reader is referred to Rycroft's *Critical Dictionary of Psychoanalysis* for a full definition.

Systemic therapy

This is one of the more recent forms of therapy, which was developed particularly for helping families. All behaviour, whether functional or not, is regarded as an attempt by the individual to cope with the systems in which they function. This approach avoids interpreting symptoms and other behaviours as caused by characteristics of the individual, but rather sees them as the outcome of the history of the person and of their attempts to cope with the situations to which they have been exposed. The systems in which interpersonal relationships play a major role are regarded as the most important. The systemic approach has a particular value in helping the therapist to understand the adjustments that an abused child and other family members will make in an attempt to survive physically and psychologically in an abusive environment (Stratton & Hanks 1991). It has also been found useful because other therapeutic approaches can be used and coordinated within a general systemic perspective. It therefore makes it easier for professionals with different training to find common ground and work together productively.

There are many different types of schools of psychotherapy (e.g. the Humanistic-Existential School, Gestalt therapy, Drama therapy) which will not be discussed here. However, the applicability of psychodrama and play therapy relevant to children will be explored subsequently. The choice of therapy depends not only on the age of the child and the form of the abuse but also on the stage of the process the child has reached. We will first consider the options soon after the abuse has been identified and then review the major forms of therapy which attempt to deal with long-term consequences.

Who should be included in the therapy?

The common model of treatment for an adult or child who is not well or is having difficulties is to treat this adult or child and then return him/her home. However, in the area of child abuse this model does not seem to work well. The child may have been admitted with injuries and treated satisfactorily in hospital but if no intervention and/or collaborative and supportive work with the parents and other professionals has taken place this child will be back, possibly in hospital, with further injuries and the cycle will simply have been repeated. So it is important to assess the situation with the care-takers, and possibly other siblings, in mind.

The range of people to be included in therapy when a child has been abused is indicated in Table 15.1.

There may be other combinations which make up the specific group receiving help; this table is not meant to give the impression that therapy can only be offered with a rigid framework in mind. It should also be emphasised that more than one type of therapy may be helpful at any one given time and this will be discussed further. As an example, the family may come for family therapy but one child may also be seen in individual therapy in order that specific emotional and behavioural aspects can be attended to. A parent who has been abused as a child may also need individual help.

At this point it will help to consider the different forms of child abuse in our thinking about therapies. It is important to fit the therapy to the needs of the individual child and family but so often this is not possible because the services may not be available in a given area. Careful planning and matching of needs and available services is essen-

Table 15.1 People who may be involved together in therapy when a child has been abused

the individual	the child alone
the dyad	mother and child
the triad	mother, father and child
the family	including all who live in the household, possibly also grandparents
the sibling group	particularly when the children of the family are together without their parent(s)
foster-parents	with the specific child or all the children in the family
foster-parents	support for foster-parents
therapeutic groups	for children and teenagers, mothers, fathers, perpetrators
groups for perpetrators	men, women, adolescents, boys and girls
marital couple	for mother and father
community programmes	as proposed by Henry Giaretto
educational programmes	as proposed by KIDSCAPE
for staff in institutions	consultations to children's homes
supervision for staff	one-to-one, or group supervision on case work, group work or family work
stress management and support for staff	

tial when assessing which treatment to recommend. Most small children would benefit from their parent(s) being involved in the therapeutic process if not actually present. However, there are instances when it is beneficial even for the very small child to be given time on their own. This is particularly so if the child is being hurt, neglected or sexually abused. An example would be if the care-takers of this child are in a frame of mind that would not allow them to acknowledge their behaviour towards the child. In such circumstances they would, simply by their presence, be most likely to intimidate the child and not allow him/her to voice what is causing distress. There may be many reasons for this, not least that the child needs to be keeping his/her 'secrets' and not telling on the abusing adult. The child left alone with a therapist might tell about his/her experiences but a careful assessment of this situation has to be made in advance. Not every child who tells can be thought of as being safe on return home after a disclosure. Summit (1983), with his concept of the accommodation syndrome, emphasises this point only too well.

CASE HISTORY 1
A mother and her two children had been coming for therapy because of what was termed 'difficult behaviour of the children'. In the fourth session one of the children made a spontaneous disclosure and the other child drew a picture saying 'this is what is happening to us both'. The children were describing sexual contact with an adult. When the mother asked them who this grown-up was, the children became anxious and only after some coaxing from the mother did they tell her that it was their father. This mother had considerable difficulties believing that her husband could harm her children. On the other hand she was convinced that if he knew what had been said he would become extremely angry with all of them. When she telephoned him to say that she would not come home today but had gone to stay with her parents he threatened her and the children with a 'good hiding' if they did not come home. It was only after the conversation with her husband that she could believe that the children needed protection, and maybe so did she.

Children often make unexpected, spontaneous disclosures if they have been abused because the therapeutic situation, whether in the medical or psychotherapeutic environment, invites exploration of causes of their illness or behaviour and provides an atmosphere in which the child and adult are offered trust. When an ordinary consultation or therapy session turns into a disclosure session this can bring about considerable problems, not least for the children. The professionals in such a situation need to be as clear as possible what the immediate future holds. They should have already acquainted themselves with the procedures and be aware of who to contact in the professional network if such a situation occurs.

Would an abused child benefit from therapy on his/her own, or would it be better if they were seen with some other family member? Table 15.2 was constructed to provide a simple indication of which groups it is usually appropriate to treat. In considering these various possibilities it became clear that most forms of abuse can be treated in most groupings, so that there will rarely be any need to assume that only one form of treatment is worth considering. However, another implication of the table is how important it is to construct an individual case profile and base decisions on that. This would take full account of the age of the child, his/her home circumstances, the willingness and motivation of all to participate and a professional judgement of what would most benefit the child.

As Table 15.2 indicates, therapy can be helpful in many different combinations with family members and carers. The immediate response once abuse has been identified will inevitably have implications for all family members and will usually be more effective if they are all actively involved (Bentovim et al 1988, Sgroi 1988).

Interventions designed to support the family when abuse has occurred

A child or teenager who has taken the courageous step to tell about his/her abuse or has been found to have been abused because of injuries or what they have 'inadvertently' said or done needs help to follow swiftly. The child or teenager is usually not in a position to cope with the disclosure situation alone.

Equally, when child abuse has been recognised and a diagnosis formulated by professionals, the next step is usually to think of help in the form of interventions and/or treatment. For the child who has been sexually or ritually abused and has made

Table 15.2 Would an abused child benefit from therapy on their own, with others and/or in groups

Therapy	Type of abuse				
	physical	*neglect*	*emotional*	*FTT*	*sexual*
individual	B	C	A	C	A
mother + child	A	B	B	A	A*
parents + child	A	C	C	B	A*
family	A	A	B	B	C*
siblings	C	C	C	D	C*
foster-parents	B	B	B	A	A*
marital couple	C	D	D	D	C
group	C	C	C	C	B

Key: A — Method of choice, likely to be essential
       B — often useful
       C — sometimes useful
       D — rarely useful
* = treatment with non-abusing adults

a disclosure to an adult, care-taker and/or professional, special and careful preparations should be made for the child to go to the next step. This next step may involve the police and social workers instigating a disclosure interview in accordance with their procedures (see Ch. 14). Following this, further assessment by professionals should lead to interventions appropriate for the child.

The help that follows can take many forms and some of these are discussed briefly below. While this help can be called therapeutic as such, it is not therapy in the sense that many children and families will need further, complimentary, help. Porter (1984) addressed the role of self-help groups and alternative support networks, emphasising that they play an important part in dealing with the problem of child sexual abuse. The same can be said for other forms of abuse too.

The list of therapies mentioned below includes community programmes as an attempt to counteract child abuse in society as a whole. In Britain such programmes have not taken off but in the USA Giaretto's (1977) model has been evaluated and shown to be effective. Bagley & King (1990) have also described their research which includes descriptions of how whole communities can be educated and given information about how to counteract child abuse in their neighbourhood.

Educational programmes for children have figured largely in the area of child sexual abuse and in Britain the lead has been taken by KIDSCAPE with Michelle Elliott in developing such programmes. Brassard et al (1983) have produced video material which can be used to help children understand about child sexual abuse.

Crisis intervention

This is applicable for many problems, in response to an acute crisis which has overwhelmed the person(s). The main aim is to give reassurance, support and guidance. In most cases the aims are set in terms of short-term work with the client. In cases of child abuse there may be an initial telephone line but most often there is face-to-face contact with those involved in the abusive situation. Generally, as well as in abuse cases, this form of intervention focuses on the acute, present situation. A drop-in centre could be the vehicle for crisis intervention, but most often it involves a professional intervening quickly, concerned with the child's safety as a priority.

Telephone lines

These have been found to be useful in the past, particularly when parents and care-takers reached the end of their tethers and felt they would hurt a child in their care. The NSPCC (National Society for the Prevention of Cruelty to Children) provides such a service in some areas. More recently, and with the acknowledgement that sexual abuse exists, such telephone helplines have also been made available for children. 'Childline' is probably the best known nationally, but there are many more local telephone lines which are set up by either the NSPCC or NCH (National Children's Homes). What is established is that these telephone lines are being used extensively; evaluation of such services is in progress (Browne & Saqi 1988).

Nurseries

A nursery is an invaluable resource when small children have been abused. It can provide care and safety for the child who has been abused on the one hand, and a break from the child for the carer, mother and/or father, on the other. Often nursery staff are trained to help parents gain vital skills such as how to care for the child, feed the child, play with the child, etc. They may provide a model of child care which has not been hitherto accessible for the parent(s) and for some parent(s) this contact can be sufficient to change the way they treat their children. The nurseries in the NSPCC are particularly geared to help parents learn different parenting skills and provide both education and therapy.

There are further support services available in various parts of the country and *family aides* are amongst them. They are usually women who are employed (by social services) from the community and neighbourhood, who may move into a family with difficulties including child abuse. They can participate with the parent(s) in tasks such as cooking, feeding the children, bathing the children, and playing with them, etc. *Family Service Units* provide nursery facilities and can make interventions which include therapy.

Most interventions, though, rely on the child and family receiving therapy in some form or other over a period of time. As indicated, voluntary help can be very useful but most of the time a trained counsellor or therapist is needed to help the child and family develop.

Therapies with longer-term objectives

Once the immediate crisis, usually after disclosure, has passed, the task of planning for longer-term therapeutic objectives arises. In most cases, a range of choices exists, and the information acquired during the first stages of intervention will help guide the choice. The purpose of this chapter is to provide a picture of what can be expected from the major therapeutic approaches and is there to help make decisions about how to proceed therapeutically. The basic choice is whether psychological treatment should be offered to the family (whole or part) to the child in a group setting or to the child individually. In some cases more than one form of therapy may be desirable and practicable, while in others it may be judged that one form of intervention should be tried and evaluated before others are considered.

The advantages and limitations of three groups of therapies are reviewed after they have been described, but a preliminary orientation is worthwhile. Family work will be chosen when it is clear that:

1. the future welfare of the child requires

changes in the attitudes and behaviours of other family members, and

2. the psychological problems that the abuse has created for the child will best be resolved within the matrix of the family relationships.

Treatment outside the family may be necessary if the child has to be removed (or in the case of older children when they remove themselves) from the family. It may also be useful, for instance in conjunction with family work, to give the child some space and distance from the pressures of the family in which they can make their own adjustment to what has happened. Group therapy has the advantage of reducing the sense of isolation so common in children and adults who have been abused. This work can be more cost effective but assessment for group work, as for other therapies, is essential because the motivation, psychological capacity to work in therapy, and the timing in terms of the state of mind of the person are important milestones to be considered. Individual work can be more focused on the needs of the individual child and may be important if the child is young, handicapped, or unable to work within any kind of group setting.

The position of the perpetrator is of course crucial. Research has so far indicated that family therapy with perpetrators is extremely difficult and in many cases simply not successful. Family work with non-abusing family members has a much greater potential to achieve positive and lasting changes.

Patterns of maltreating families

Crittenden & Ainsworth (1989) distinguished between families who physically abused, neglecting families, and families who both physically abused their children and neglected them. She found characteristics which differed between the parent groups and showed how important it is to recognise into which pattern the parents fit. This does not have to be done at the referral stage, but early on in the therapeutic work and during assessment. Furniss et al (1984), Bentovim et al (1988), and Hanks & Stratton (1988) have researched and written about how the pattern of family functioning can be understood when sexual abuse has occurred and what implications this has for therapy.

Crittenden & Ainsworth (1989) found that the prognosis for the *physically abusing families* once they entered therapy was very good. She found that most of the time the parents were motivated to change but that their coping strategies were poor. Their need to use power over others and dominate wherever possible was paramount. For instance the mothers in this group use punishment as the only means of discipline in order to control and teach their offspring.

The characteristics of the *neglecting families* differed significantly in that these parents' coping strategies relied on withdrawal from difficult situations rather than control. Disciplining the children seemed not to be an option. The mothers always felt that others knew better and rarely finished tasks they had begun. The parents had no plans or expectations for themselves, let alone their families, and their children were particularly passive in infancy. The treatment for these families has to be quite different from the above group because these mothers are not easily motivated and often have little understanding of why any change is needed in the way they care for their children.

The pattern for the *abusing and neglecting families* is different again. The research showed that when considering the issue of interventions for this group it became clear that only for some can change be predicted, and then only when long-term support was available. To break the cycle of abuse in these families proved much more difficult than in the other two groups. Members of such families feel that they have no control over their lives and that the possibility for change is beyond their reach. In these families parental coping strategies oscillate from sullen withdrawal to violent outbursts. The children are not treated consistently and all are inclined to feel both utter frustration and helplessness. The children are often out of control and resist control while the parents' expectations of them are either very high or they have no expectations of their children at all.

When Furniss et al (1984) investigated families where sexual abuse had occurred they found a pattern which showed that the emotional and sexual relationship between the parents was poor and tension laden, despite outward appearances to the contrary. The relationship between the mother and her abused children was distant. The child was brought up to act as both peer and partner to the father and became trapped in what Summit (1983) calls the 'accommodation syndrome' which includes secrecy and denial. Furniss et al (1984), Furniss (1991) and Bentovim et al (1988) indicated that the strength of this pattern varies between families and that they can, along a continuum, be grouped into either *conflict-avoiding families* or *conflict-regulating families* (Furniss 1985). The first type of family avoids looking at the issues and is afraid of being discovered. They are often described as moralistic and rigid. The second type of family shows a more disorganised and quarrelsome pattern of interaction. Here more actual disturbance can be visible, the boundaries between adult roles and those of the children are blurred or non-existent, and violence is used when frustration and confusion reach a peak.

Describing such family patterns, however briefly, illustrates the interactions that take place in the abusive families and it shows why treating one member of such a system is not likely to break the cycle of abuse. The next section describes some of the more widely used therapies available and indicates sources of research and practice.

FAMILY THERAPY

When a child is maltreated at least two people are directly involved, and if the maltreatment takes place within the family it is most often a parent who is doing something to the child. Once such a dyad exists within the family it usually affects the other members of the family too. They become disturbed or worried by what they see, or hear, and have to keep out of the way lest they get involved. In the case of another adult they may find it too painful to acknowledge and therefore have 'to look the other way'. Crittenden & Ainsworth's (1989) work shows the complex interactions that may occur within the different families.

Family therapy is often the most direct way to bring about change, though the individual child or parent may also need specific help. Psychoanalytic family therapy was practised and developed as a therapeutic tool and specifically concentrated on the fact that neuroses are intrafamilial disturbances. Subsequently other forms of family therapy were proposed, either as a development from analytic or deriving from other theoretical frameworks such as systems theory. After Jay Haley's (1963) paper called 'Whither Family Therapy', rapid development occurred to incorporate new ideas and particularly systems theory as a basis for these new ideas. Moving away from focusing on the individual to working with the system became an exciting and fruitful way of helping to achieve change. Over the last decade it has become a more accepted tool, and individual, group, and family therapy are seen to be more complementary than had originally been thought.

As most commonly practised, family therapy takes as its basis the assumption that what people do is largely determined by the contexts in which they find themselves. For most people, and particularly for children, the family contains the most important relationships in their lives. To bring about major change in a person's life, it will often be useful or even essential, to bring together their family, so that repeating patterns can be exposed, and relationships re-negotiated. This theoretical position has given rise to a body of practical techniques for bringing about change in families. Hoffman (1981) provides an excellent general overview of the work of the pioneers of family therapy; de Shazar (1986) offers a useful account of why family therapy practice takes the form it now does; Burnham (1986) is a sound and readable survey of the field; and Stratton et al (1990) have attempted to provide a highly practical manual which shows what family therapists do, and why. Bentovim et al (1982) explore the applicability of systemic family therapy to all kinds of family problems.

Family therapy is practised most often by a team working together, with a therapist in the room with the family and the rest of the team behind a one-way mirror to observe the family and give help to them from a perspective where they can quietly listen and form helpful interventions for the family. Because families and their interactions are very complex, a team helping the therapist to help the family has been proven to be of considerable value (Campbell & Draper 1985, Stratton et al 1990).

Developments in the field of child sexual abuse produced further, more specific, work with families:

Furniss (1983), Furniss et al (1984), Bentovim et al (1988), Glaser & Frosh (1988) and Hanks & Stratton (1988) all describe ways in which families can be conceptualised and worked with when sexual abuse has occurred.

Families where physical maltreatment to a child or children has occurred need to work together on change and the case described here illustrates several of the most important issues.

CASE HISTORY 2

John, aged 2½ was referred to the hospital because his mother had said that if John was not placed in hospital she could not guarantee that he would not be hurt again. John's mother had suffered from depression on and off since his birth, she had injured John previously and the social worker involved with the case was concerned not only for John but for his two older brothers, aged 6 and 9, as well as the mother and father. This was a well-off family, with father a professional in a large organisation. John was not a planned baby, unlike the other two. Mother had just started a career and felt that she could not continue, that it was her duty to look after him. Mother came with John for therapy and it became very clear that there were many problems which had developed. John had simply no language, and would only point. He continually tried to have physical contact with his mother but she could not bear it and pushed him away time and again. At the same time she was as deeply distressed as John. The house was immaculate, nothing was out of place. After some sessions of therapy together with his mother John began to play with some toys — an aeroplane, bricks, cars — and interact with the therapist. Mother moved away into the furthest corner and watched. Encouraged by the therapist John began to play, make noises, move the toys around, etc. Mother watched for many sessions as John progressed in his play and began to speak, naming the toys and even the colours. Mother said she knew that he could understand many things, but that he simply did not speak at home. By this time mother had moved her chair much closer and began to watch John's play with a little more interest. The other two children joined mother and John in the sessions and it became clear that they too were at times distressed and hit very hard or put into bath water that was far too hot. Mother had told them not to tell anyone but the children could not help but play out the upset they felt and what they had experienced. The therapist interpreted their play not only in terms of their psychological hurt but also by exploring the realities of the situation and what had happened. Through drawing, playing and talking, the children and mother began a conversation and at that point father, who had been very reluctant to become involved, attended the sessions as well. Over a considerable number of sessions the situation eased. Father took much more responsibility for the day-to-day care of his children. John went to nursery for 2 mornings a week at the age of 3 years and mother found some work which she could do during this time. This brought her into contact with other people and her social life improved.

Alongside therapy there occurred of course monitoring by social services, visits to the paediatrician and contact between the different systems. All of these processes should be regarded as part of the intervention.

Equally, in cases of failure to thrive a family therapy approach can be most helpful because children often fail to thrive because of emotional difficulties in, and between, members of the family. Some of the therapeutic interventions are described in Chapter 3. In cases of failure to thrive it has been found to be more productive to offer therapy for the mother and child or for the whole family. Food is one of the most emotionally laden aspects of family life and withholding or refusing food is an intensely powerful communication. The children can become barometers of how the rest of the family are coping by their weight gains or losses. This can include the child being frightened because of physical or emotional harm coming to them and not being able to eat, or a mother becoming depressed about the loss of a parent, the husband's health, or her own weight. It can of course also be because there is poor bonding between mother and child resulting from resentment. Winnicott (1964) described in detail his observations of mother and baby feeding at a very early stage in the child's life and how the relationship between family members can influence this.

Family therapy may be indicated when sexual abuse has occurred, particularly when the abuse has been perpetrated by someone outside the nuclear family:

- a stranger
- a friend of the family
- a relation of the family (aunt, uncle, cousin, etc.)
- a grandparent.

The primary issue here is that the child is, in principle at least, believed, and that the parent(s) are motivated and committed to protect their child(ren). Many families are devastated when one of their children has been sexually abused and have the greatest fears about the consequences for these children. They naturally worry about how to approach the subject with the child, whether the other siblings 'know', and also quite often feel that their child has been tainted with something immoral from which neither the child nor they themselves will ever properly recover. A considerable number of these children end up rejected and misunderstood, miserable and uncared for.

Equally, if the abuse has been within the family but the abusing family member has left the family and the non-abusing parent is committed to protect the child(ren), family therapy may be of considerable benefit, especially in dealing with the unexpressed guilt and resentment that are such a common aftermath to the disclosure of intrafamilial abuse.

When the sexual abuse is perpetrated within the nuclear family, family therapy can be appropriate with:

- the non-abusing parent and child(ren)
- the above group plus a social worker
- the above group plus grandparents
- the children plus foster-parent(s).

When children are not supported or believed by their parents but have for instance been taken into care, family therapy can be very helpful in doing important work with the siblings. One of the most important aspects is that it helps each of them to examine their perceptions of each other and themselves. Family therapy helps also to preserve a sense of the family, albeit as a sub-system, and can give tremendous support to the individual and the sibling group.

Family therapy can also be appropriate, though within considerable constraints and with legal back-up, when the abusing parent is joining the family after having been in prison or ending a period of probation. It is not possible to discuss this issue in this chapter and the reader is directed to Salter (1988) and Hotaling et al (1988).

Furniss (1991), Bentovim et al (1988) and Glaser & Frosh (1988) are some of the authors who have described in detail those interventions using family therapy which may contribute to change when sexual abuse has occurred.

GROUP THERAPY FOR CHILDREN AND ADULTS

It has long been understood that groups of people, at whatever age, working together in therapy can be most productive and bring about change in the individual. There are many forms of group therapy, broadly divided into behavioural, humanistic, analytic, psychodynamic, and cognitive schools of thought and theory. The theories guiding group therapies are in essence the same as those used in individual therapy but the main emphasis is on the problems between individuals rather than within the person alone. Group work in Great Britain developed during and after the Second World War, with Bion (1961) and Foulkes (1964) and later Yalom in the USA pioneering the work. Rogers (1961) and Yalom in the USA (1975) developed group therapies away from the analytic model.

Essential criteria for group therapy are:

- professional leadership
- consistent attendance
- that the experience is therapeutic.

The therapist's role is:

- to monitor the individuals' progress and needs
- to facilitate the group process
- to formulate appropriate interventions
- to avoid injury to members of the group.

Group therapy, for children and adults who have been abused or are abusing, has been found to be of immense value. The aim of this section is to describe different ways of selecting groups for specific patients and explain why it might be useful for individuals to experience sharing and examining problems in the presence of others. Here we will concentrate on the difficulties group members have when they attempt to relate to each other, rather than discussing the differences of technique and theory related to therapeutic groups.

For children, the groups are usually formed on a peer group basis while groups for adults can function with a considerable age span between members. Therapeutic groups generally do not have to be constructed of people who have the same or similar problems. It is thought that most often people learn from each other because of their differences not because of their sameness. However, in order to deal with a specific aspect of people's lives, it can be useful to form groups with adults or children who have the same basic complaint. Groups based on a common problem have a particular advantage in changing the belief that the individual is alone in their experience. Issues of child sexual abuse have particularly highlighted this aspect of therapeutic group work (Glaser & Frosh 1988, Hildebrand 1988, Sgroi 1988, 1989).

There are possibilities for mothers and fathers to come together into a group and learn about parenting their children, how to control their impulses and how to understand that their own background may have contributed largely to how they are behaving today in a family setting. They may recognise why they can not bear a demanding child. But most of all they may begin, in company and in the safety of a group led by a trained therapist, to change their behaviour. Talking with others about difficulties that these parents and children are experiencing is often the first opportunity group members have to discuss the details surrounding the maltreatment.

Groups for parents who have a child or children who have been abused usually have specific aims and a fixed number of sessions, with time and space being the same for every session. The frequency of meetings is set, and the group lasts for a specific time (usually 1½ hours). The group therapist and group members leave at the end of the therapeutic time. Groups are most often time-limited and meet on a weekly basis, but they can also be ongoing and open-ended. Whether the membership of the group can be added to (an open group) or whether the group is closed (a fixed number of people) will have been decided by the group leader(s) or therapist(s) in advance. The members of the group will be informed of all of these particulars and this information will be necessary to help them make choices. An assessment as to whether they would benefit from the group and the group from them is always carried out before they can be accepted.

Mothers are almost always at the centre of child abuse. The children are more often in her care than in the father's and even if it is not the mother who abused the child, she is the one who did not manage to protect. This is a difficult area and many mothers blame themselves terribly, while others feel helpless or deny that they could have been more aware and protecting. Mothers are also the ones who, unless they divorce themselves from what has happened to their child(ren), pick up the pieces and have to provide ongoing care. The mother's wellbeing is paramount and a group may provide a place and time where she can express her emotions, share her ideas and worries, and learn both from other members of the group and from the leadership and the interactions between all of them.

Many of the parents have experienced emotional deprivation in their own childhood and this may make them resentful and ambivalent about understanding their children's needs. Many such parents base their ideas of child-rearing on what their own needs are rather than the needs of the children. Cognitive change under such circumstances can prove difficult because there is often a direct contradiction to what the mother's/parents' own needs are. For example not hitting the child when s/he has done something the mother has said they should not do, despite the mother's feelings of frustration.

For these parents the experience in which the idea originated must somehow be revived enough to be recognised and understood, so that they can bring reason to bear. Otherwise they are apt to talk wisely in their groups about what to do with their children, but then at home, perhaps after a brief attempt to do what seems 'not really right', revert to their own practices, convinced that these are the only ones that work for their particular children. Kempe & Kempe (1978, p. 106)

Groups with mothers whose children are failing to thrive

Such groups may have specific topics which they aim to cover. For instance a group for mothers who have children who fail to thrive will discuss not only the children's behavioural patterns but also the role of food, feeding, and the preparation of food. Mothers' ideas about weight and dieting can be on the agenda, not only for the children but also for themselves. Sharing with other women the problem of having a child who is very thin and not developing can lessen the feelings of isolation and guilt. It can also help to end the denial about the failure to thrive and bring about an acceptance that something different needs to be done to help the child to grow.

The way in which interventions can be planned when children are failing to thrive is discussed in more detail in Chapter 3. Research (Hanks et al 1987) with this patient group has shown that mothers working with each other on some very practical things — like cooking, shopping, where to find information about resources available to them, how to fill in forms in order to get assistance, how to speak to officials as well as developing the courage to ask for things — were all issues that could usefully be shared once the mothers met in groups. These groups can be formed either on the basis of self-help groups or led by a health visitor or social worker, psychologist or psychiatrist. These groups will have very specific aims and the leader will have to make clear where her/his competence lies and what will be undertaken. However, it must also be stressed that mothers and fathers of children who fail to thrive often have psychological difficulties which contribute to the child's failure to grow. Kempe & Kempe (1978) described a mother who is typical of parents who abuse. They showed the difficulties many mothers have in helping their children to individuate — to see them as other than an extension of themselves. Kempe & Kempe (1978) quoted a mother as saying, "No, I am sure the baby doesn't need to be fed yet; I'm not hungry yet". She was quite unable to distinguish between her own body needs and his'.

Because of the abusing parent's own, often appalling experiences in childhood, they have few inner resources to care adequately for their children. A group may be of help, particularly when it can become cohesive and begin to acknowledge that there may be differences in how children are being cared for. Kempe & Kempe (1978, p. 106) pointed out that one characteristic of abusing parents relates to their distorted views about what to expect of their children; they 'often cling to those ideas tenaciously, in the face of all kinds of professional persuasions'. Discussing such issues with fellow mothers or fathers can make different ideas more acceptable and may make it possible for them to learn how to imagine themselves to be in the child's position, recognising the child's needs rather than their own. Seeing and experiencing in a group how other mothers/parents achieve such changes in their perceptions can make it more acceptable for the others.

Groups for mothers/parents of children who have been physically abused

Groups for mothers when the child has been physically abused by her or her husband/partner offer a particular opportunity to work with what has happened. Violence is a very tricky subject and many women would not be able to discuss the issues of their and their children's battering by their husbands in front of the husbands/partners. For this reason alone it is important to have clear assessment criteria. During the assessment and selection period for a group such issues can be addressed in advance by gaining a clear history of the group member's past and present. Only after it has been established what the mother and/or father experienced and how they have abused their children or have not been able to protect the children, can a decision be made about what would be most helpful. In many cases this leads squarely into the area of families and the interaction between family members. This is not to say that groups of parents meeting to work on their children's maltreatment can not be helpful. However, much is known through research about families and parenting in maltreating families (Browne et al 1988, Hotaling et al 1988, Cicchetti & Carlson 1989), and this knowledge can assist in the development of specific group work and in setting the goal and aims.

We have found that groups of mothers and toddlers coming for therapy have a strengthening effect on the relationship between the mother and her toddler, and that this sometimes generalises to other children and partners. These mother and toddler groups are focused on everyday problems which the mother can discuss and thereby learn about different ways of caring for her children. Such groups may also give the mother a chance to have a therapeutic experience which gives her confidence to mobilise her positive characteristics and competencies, first in the safe environment of the group and later outside the group. It may also become a stepping stone towards accepting that therapy for her is a way forward. Many men and women in abusive situations are quite frightened of therapy. Many professionals may join them in their fear, particularly when they have witnessed others becoming distressed during therapy. This is sometimes thought to be 'the fault' of the therapy rather than a reaction to the abuse that has been experienced. Therapy is a tool to help people come to terms with what they have experienced in their lives, and this includes taking responsibility for their own behaviours and reactions.

It seems that for other forms of abuse the family model of therapy can provide a useful framework for change, particularly when small and dependent children are involved. Though it is quite different in the area of child sexual abuse.

Groups for sexually abused children, adolescents and adults

Over the last ten years more research and practice has concentrated on groups for sexually abused children, adolescents and adults as well as for perpetrators of sexual abuse, both men and women.

Groups have been formed for:

- women who have been sexually abused in childhood
- men who have been sexually abused in childhood
- mixed groups of men and women sexually abused in childhood
- adolescent females who have been sexually abused
- adolescent males who have been sexually abused
- children of various age bands who have been sexually abused
- children under the age of 5 years who have been sexually abused
- men who have sexually abused children
- women who have sexually abused children
- adolescents who have sexually abused children (this work is more often with male offenders).

Groups with sexually abused children

During the last decade it has become particularly

clear that working in groups with sexually abused children shows benefits, and the pioneering work was carried out in the USA. Gottlieb & Dean (1981) and Giaretto (1981) were amongst the first to recognise the value of group work with children who had been sexually abused.

Glaser & Frosh (1988, p. 133) indicate that groups for sexually abused children should be for about 8–10 members and that the children are most helped if they are placed in groups which reflect their age and maturity. Age bands could be for 4–6-year-olds, 7–9-year-olds, 10–12-year-olds, 13–15-year-olds and 16–18-year-olds. The pros and cons of putting children into therapeutic groups are not only age-dependent but also relate to 'the nature of the children's respective relationship with the abuser and with each other'; Glaser & Frosh advise that it is important to include more than one child with a specific experience, so that none of the children should feel that their experience has been one which no-one else has gone through. This highlights one of the central issues for children and adults alike, namely the isolation that so many feel, an isolation which can become a crippling aspect of people's development. Hildebrand (1988) describes very clearly the work carried out at the Hospital for Sick Children, London, based on the work of Giaretto (1981) and Berliner & Stevens (1982).

Porter (1986) also reported on early treatment for young male victims of sexual assault and indicated that 'group and family therapy are the two most important modalities for treatment of young male victims of sexual abuse. The peer group is the preferred and most productive mode of group treatment. The preferred number of group members is 8, no less than 4, and no more than 10. Though developmental as well as chronological age must be considered, generally the younger the children, the narrower the age spacing'.

Berliner & Ernst (1984) described group work with young children who had been sexually abused. Nelki & Watters (1989) also described a group programme with girls aged between 4 and 8 years using Summit's (1983) accommodation syndrome as a basis for their focused work. They paid particular attention to issues like 'meeting strangers, safe touching, secrets, telling someone, anger and punishment, fault and responsibility and helping the children to understand that their body belonged to them'. Such work has been found to help the children develop more adequately, increase their confidence and help them to distinguish between abusive and non-abusive situations more clearly.

Furniss et al (1988) reported the work of a goal-directed group for adolescent girls, one of the first of such groups set up in Britain. This group work was undertaken to offer the girls help in their own right and was added to the family therapy sessions that they were already involved in with other members of their families. Furniss et al (1988) reported that: 'the therapists used a number of methods. Firstly, interpretation was used, centring on the processes both within the group and between the girls and the therapists (Bion 1961)'. Because it was anticipated that these children would show considerable disturbance during the treatment, including the group, the therapists 'were prepared to intervene actively, if required, even going so far as to restrain the girls physically in situations of extreme and potentially dangerous acting out'. This work is of particular importance because it describes the process of the group step by step and shows the tremendous emotional distress the children experience in their attempts to make sense of what has happened to them.

Groups for men and women who have been sexually abused as children

It is not possible to discuss the group work which is being carried out for adult victims of child sexual abuse in detail. Many of the women and men who have been abused benefit from individual and then group therapy. Sometimes it is important that the person speaks to a therapist on their own at first. In this one-to-one situation she may begin the work of reconstructing the events, distinguishing between what she thought happened and her recollection of what actually did happen. Many women and men realise that they had only been able to keep in their conscious thoughts some of the events. Some realise that they have entirely blocked the experiences of their childhood and need the one-to-one relationship in therapy to work out what happened and when. However, in many therapies it becomes clear that talking to other

people is a step many patients do not think they can ever take. Looking for help from close relatives or friends therefore remains a closed option. Working on such issues in a therapeutic group where people learn to speak out in the presence of more than one other is invaluable to most. Group work facilitates changes in the patient which are not as easily achieved in individual or family therapy.

These groups can be long-term in duration, but it has also been found useful to have groups with limited sessions and very specific aims which are shared between the therapists and patients. For instance working on relationship issues or difficulties surrounding child care. Barnett et al (1989), Furniss et al (1988) and Sgroi (1989) described in detail the work of a goal-oriented group for sexually abused adolescent girls and adults. They found that after follow-up considerable improvements had been achieved by these young people on a number of indicators in their present life.

The short-term aims relate to the difficulties these women and men experience in the present: the tensions in their relationships, the confusions in their struggle to communicate their needs in relationships. Many patients have become socially isolated and can be burdened with phobias or depression which limit their life style considerably. Their relationship with their children is only too often distorted and causes not only problems for the children but also for the women and men.

Long-term group work with people who have been abused as children can be very beneficial and is usually conducted on group therapy principles (Yalom 1975, Sgroi 1989). It has been found to help these patients, in some cases, to make profound changes in their adult lives.

The adult male sex offender and treatment.

Groups for men who have been sexually abusing children

Work with male perpetrators has been developing with some speed, particularly in the USA. Salter (1988) has given a clear practical guide to the treatment available. Group treatment is a valuable tool, but has also shown the enormity of the problem and the difficulties which emerge for the perpetrators and those who are attempting to help them change their sexually abusive behaviours towards children. This must be viewed in the context of the behaviours known to be part of the perpetrator's repertoire. Wolf (1988) described the patterns in which perpetrators 'groom' and prepare their child victims for abuse and how they keep control over their victims. Wolf (1988) and Bremer (1991) describe the denial by perpetrators of the abuse and point out that it persists way into treatment, whether this be in individual therapy or in groups. Wolf describes the Northwest Treatment Associates of Seattle programme for sex offenders and quotes from their work, saying that 'offenders will only tell 25% of the sexual abuse they have committed'. Salter (1988) describes the same programme and other treatments in detail. This includes the perpetrator's acknowledgement of the sexual abuse he has committed. It demands that all the sexual maltreatments are spoken of, and how sexual impulses and inappropriate behaviours in the present are coped with. These groups are very different from those conducted for children or adults who have been sexually abused, and behavioural cognitive theories are the underpinning to the work. Vizard (1990 personal communication) confirms the structure of groups with perpetrators of sexual abuse to be as described above, even if the group members are motivated to change.

Salter (1988) has provided an excellent and comprehensive overview of how to identify, assess and treat perpetrators of sexual abuse of children. She also describes how men come to sexually abuse children and distinguishes between the activities of paedophiles and those men who are not paedophiles but who sexually abuse children. Bremer (1991) writes about how adolescents and adults abuse sexually and 'groom' or prepare children for abusive activities. Wolf (1988) discussed the 'sex offender's search for a child' and described the pattern which sex offender's have reported they have adopted when offending against the child. Wolf, like Salter, believes that treatment can be effective for a number of such offenders. The programme developed by the Northwest Treatment Associates of Seattle, Washington, has been operating since 1977 and treats up to 200 offenders at any given time. Group therapy, covert sensitisation, behavioural therapy, social skills training, sex education and cognitive restructuring are all aspects of

the treatments allocated to the individual. Salter concludes that, 'The insight-oriented therapist who wishes to treat sex offenders must accept the fact that compulsive behaviours respond first and foremost to cognitive/behavioural techniques'. Vizard (1990) described the East London Sex Offenders Group's work with adult sex offenders which she and her colleagues are undertaking and confirms that, in a therapeutic group, confronting the denial and taking responsibility for the abuse are a first step towards change in the abusive behaviour.

Groups for women who have been sexually abusing children

There is considerable resistance to acknowledgement that women can and will sexually abuse their own and other children. However, the literature and research on this topic are increasing and a greater understanding is developing. Welldon (1988) gave a clear description of women who sexually abused their own children and those of others. Faller (1987) described her findings about women abusers and Mathews et al (1989) carried out a thorough study in an attempt to understand the psychological mechanisms of women who abuse children sexually. The outcome of the therapeutic intervention reported in the latter study shows that, unlike men, women do not seem to have the same 'criminal personality' characteristics and that treatment can be more effective. The women viewed as 'caring and nonjudgemental, showed that the direct treatment modality was most helpful in creating change'. In this study many of them did change, as measured by a number of criteria including their insight into the sexual abuse. Barnett et al (1989) described their group work with women who had been abusing children sexually and concluded that the distorted beliefs held by these women to justify their abuse of children were reduced by the majority. They acknowledged that outcome studies must rely on long-term follow-up before such group treatment can be shown to be effective.

Groups for adolescents who have been abusing younger children

Working with adolescents who have been abused

and become abusers in their turn poses specific difficulties. However, changes have been shown to be possible with this group. A number of treatment programmes exist in the USA and Bremer (1989) said 'The sexual assault cycle provides an understanding of how the youth gives himself permission to hurt others, how the victim is selected and identifies what must change to develop a non-abusive lifestyle. Denial is the sex offenders first line of defence', and this is no different for adolescents. Confronting this denial is a necessary process which must be undertaken continuously until change has taken place. The work carried out by Bremer and others in the Hennepin County Home School, Minnetonka, USA, includes working in groups. Bremer also outlined specific characteristics shown by juvenile sex offenders. They include:

1. a distorted understanding about the self in relation to others
2. irrational thinking
3. sexualisation of non-sexual needs
4. compulsivity
5. poor impulse control
6. mood disorders
7. dysfunctional patterns of family functioning.

Providing a safe and secure environment away from the victim of the abuse is one of the most important aspects of treatment with this group — only then can the denial, history and other specific characteristics be addressed.

Though it should be stressed that individual work, during or after the ending of the group, is in almost all cases an essential component of any offender's programme with adolescents, group work is an integral part of the treatment. It is not possible here to describe the treatments that are thought helpful for adolescent offenders, except to say that the work in the USA indicates that treatment with adolescent offenders has more longlasting effects than treatment for adults who have been in the habit of sexually abusing children for many years.

INDIVIDUAL THERAPY

As already discussed above, individual psychotherapy involves two people — a trained therapist and a patient — who together attempt to work through life experiences and, as in child abuse cases, through the traumatic events experienced. The aim of psychotherapy is to relieve troubling symptoms and achieve changes in personality in the child or adult (Bloch 1979, Brown & Pedder 1979). The reader is referred to these and other references for further information about what psychotherapy is. The complexities and the dynamics which are part of the therapeutic relationship will not be discussed here. There are many references already given in this chapter which will lead the reader to an explanation of therapy but Brown & Pedder (1979), Bloch (1979), Boston & Szur (1983) and Walker et al (1988) provide further answers, including case material. In this section the treatment for both the abused child and adolescent will be discussed. A description of 'play therapy' for the very young child will also be included.

Individual therapy is almost always concerned with the entire person: adult or child, their experiences in all areas of life need to be considered. This applies even when a very specific problem such as child abuse has been part of the person's history. Therapists using behaviour therapy as a means to bring about change prefer to concentrate on the symptoms and their manifestation, rather than on the history and dynamics of a person, adult or child. However, in cases of child abuse the history and origin as well as the relationships and context in which the abuse occurs need to be understood by the therapist and often by the patient before change can take place. Exploration of the abuse — who was involved, when and where it took place — can lead, at least in part, to the patient understanding the role of symptoms they might carry. What has most often been found in cases of child sexual abuse is that the children at times need behavioural treatments in order to change some of the behaviours, for instance very sexualised behaviours which have become habitual, as well as insight and psychodynamic understanding. It is no paradox that these children need to have established firm boundaries, be allowed to think in a clear and undenying manner and at the same time become flexible and more at ease. Their vulnerability and strength need to be understood. The flexibility of therapeutic interventions with these children can be taxing but also reward-ing (Boston & Szur 1983, Copley & Forryan 1987, Bentovim et al 1988, Glaser and Frosh 1988).

CASE HISTORY 3

A 16-year-old girl came to the clinic with epileptic fits for which the doctors could find no organic cause. All manner of tests had been carried out but nothing was found. She was on medication to alleviate the fits but was also referred for therapy because she had become very distressed. As therapy began she realised that the first fit occurred just after she had been hit hard on the head by one of her parents and she had fallen, hitting her head against a wall. The parent who had not hit her felt devastated and protective towards the daughter ever afterwards and would recall this event frequently. The patient then began to speak of the frequency of the fits and made the connection that they always occurred when she was in a potentially argumentative or aggressive situation. While talking about this she realised that the arguments usually stopped once she started a fit, whether it happened at school or at home. Once she fitted, people paid attention to her and cared for her instead of continuing their argument either with her or with a third party. She said she felt bad about that at times and that family and friends had told her that they dared not be cross with her because they knew this would always bring on a fit. After recognising these connections — arguments, being hit on the head, falling, being comforted, etc. — the fits disappeared but the patient became very sad and depressed. At that point the therapy began to address the maltreatment this young girl had experienced throughout her life, how she had developed and as a consequence learnt to behave towards others. In this case the girl having recognised some of the underlying reasons for her behaviour, namely the neglect and maltreatment she had experienced, had no difficulties in:

a. acknowledging her sadness and depression over this lack of care,
b. recognising her anger and her consequent bullying behaviour towards others,
c. seeing that the 'fits' were part of her attempt to be cared for rather than neglected, and
d. beginning to think of how to do things differently.

Not all therapy patients can unravel their diffi-culties in this way, let alone work out resolutions to their problems. The therapy can not be de-scribed in more detail here but it may be worth pointing out what Winnicott (1965) highlighted so clearly. He recognised that much antisocial or illness behaviour of children who have been neglected by parental figures and the environment is in fact a plea for help. Boston & Szur (1983), in their descriptions of children in psychotherapy,

come to the same conclusion and the reader is referred for detailed case studies to these authors.

As discussed in the section on groups, some-times it is relevant to focus only on the very specific issues of the abuse, but most often the person/child as a whole needs to be considered. Long-term analytic therapy has been shown to be bene-ficial in many cases. Anna Freud (1981) said about a child's sexual abuse that:

. . . he (child) is also experiencing a type of stimulation for which, developmentally, he is wholly unprepared. Nevertheless, he cannot avoid being physically aroused and this experience disastrously disrupts the normal sequence in his sex organisation. He is forced into premature phallic or genital development while his legitimate developmental needs and their accompanying mental expressions are by-passed and short-circuited. (p. 33–4).

For other patients more focused, goal-directed therapeutic work has also been found to be help-ful, particularly as the number of people who come forward speaking of their abuse in childhood is rising steadily and resources are scarce. It may be useful to consider once more the continuum along which the consequences of all child abuse can occur:

short-term ————————————— death
consequences

There has been evidence (Finkelhor 1986, Bagley & King 1990) that some people suffer con-siderably less than others in the long term when they have been abused as children. This depends largely on the parenting the children receive, and the environment they have grown up in. There are some children and adults who can become well adjusted, particularly if the abuse has not been denied and if they have been protected, believed and respected as individuals with rights to emo-tional wellbeing, rights to grow, rights to physical health and rights to develop sexually. If this is granted to the child in an appropriate way, then indeed development can progress largely unhin-dered. However, this is a difficult state to achieve when the abuse of a child has continued undetec-ted over many years or if those parenting the child were in collusion with the abuser, or denied it altogether (Kempe & Kempe 1978, 1984, Wolfe

1987; Walker et al 1988). The consequences in such cases are usually far more serious and can span the life of the individual and even affect future generations. The abuse can lead to scars and injuries never healed, permanent handicap, brain damage, learning difficulties, stunted growth and failure to thrive. Emotionally the consequences can range from difficult behaviours, nightmares, aggression and relationship problems, through to depression, apathy and self-mutilation, and to the child or adult becoming mute, showing psychosomatic illnesses like paralysis, or becoming schizoid and mentally ill. At the end of the continuum is death itself.

For many small children who have been abused therapeutic help is most appropriate when the non-abusing parents, a foster-parent or care-taker can partake in the process and learn along with the child to interact in a different way and understand each other so that the child can give up those behaviours that contribute to, or are a consequence of, the abuse. Wetting and soiling, nightmares, destructive behaviours, not eating, not being able to sleep, hurting themselves or others are just some of these behaviours. Not all adults are capable of that change and in such situations it is essential that an assessment of this capacity, motivation and willingness for change is carried out before the therapeutic process can begin. When children have been sexually abused by one or by both of their parents the picture changes. When both parents have been involved in their child's sexual maltreatment it will not be appropriate to involve them in therapy with the child. Also, when the non-abusing parent is denying the abuse the child may need space and the experience of an adult who can be more accepting of the child's experience and help the child to express this. Because of the almost addictive quality of behaviour in the adults when they have sexually abused the child, it will simply not be safe for the child to be in the abusive parent's presence until major changes have occurred in the abusing adult's life.

Individual therapy with the child means that an adult and child work together on forming a close therapeutic relationship which may last over a long time, sometimes years. It is necessary to match the therapy to the child in an age- and developmentally-appropriate fashion; this process should be carefully assessed. With some children it is important to realise that after some therapeutic work has been done the therapy may have to stop for a while and allow the child to grow. At a later stage, possibly around the age of 10–12 years or during adolescence, further therapeutic work may be undertaken in order to build on the child's earlier experience in therapy. In this way children may be helped to continue to grow, making sense of their lives and particularly helping them to form relationships. The work with the child focuses not only on the abuse itself but also on all the other experiences, good and bad, which the child had — what their relationships have been like and with whom, and what they feel about themselves. Many abused children feel they are to blame for whatever maltreatment they received. This has been particularly highlighted when therapists attempted to treat sexually abused children. Children who have been physically abused and neglected often need therapeutic help in their own right, and a plan for such therapy may develop out of the children's and families' needs rather than out of something that is dictated from the beginning, as the case below illustrates. At the assessment stage it was very clear that this family needed to be seen together and that they could not be separated abruptly without leaving them all feeling insecure and possibly anxious about what each was going to say about the other in their session. Parents quite naturally find it threatening when their children are taken into individual therapy where they might say things or describe the parents in a way that is unacceptable to the parents. Winnicott (1982) describes with superb clarity and detail the therapeutic work he undertook with children and how be negotiated the interactions between parents and child so that the therapy should strengthen their relationships rather than weaken them. Axline (1964), Copley & Forryan (1987) and Bolton & Szur (1983) provide excellent accounts with details of individual therapy with children who are disturbed, often as a consequence of their maltreatment by adults.

CASE HISTORY 4
Zoe, aged 7, and her brother Lee, aged 5, came for therapy with their mother because both children were failing to thrive and their mother had found no other

way of 'controlling the children' than by hitting them hard, sometimes with her hands, sometimes with objects. In the session the children would cower in a corner whenever the mother said anything to them, but once mother became engrossed in telling her story to the therapist the children became giggly and restless, breaking toys, drawing on the furniture and being generally difficult. Mother would then shout and the children would return to their cowering positions. At neither the cowering nor the excitable stage did they play constructively. It soon became clear that the children were in a constant state of alert, watching mother's every move. If mother left they would become quiet and cry but not attempt to follow her until she said they could. Neither of them would speak except in whispers to each other which frustrated the mother.

Their drawings consisted of scribbles and resembled drawings of children aged 3 rather than 5 and 7 years. How superbly children draw is of course not the issue, what is important is that their drawings are seen as a communication revealing some of their inner state. To acknowledge this communication in an appropriate way, neither too effusively pleased nor dismissive, is the job of the adult. This is a fine and important balance for the therapist, parental figures, or other professionals.

The children, in their attempt to anticipate mother's moves and protect each other from her behaviours, became locked in an almost symbiotic relationship. Therapeutic work on their individuation from each other was one important goal which led to them having therapy individually as well as with their mother. It was in the individual sessions that age-appropriate developmental tasks could be worked through; the children's fear for each other and themselves that mother would hurt them or leave them could also be tackled, and their anger and frustration dealt with. The children both became more relaxed and managed to concentrate on their play in a more developmentally-appropriate way. The change for Zoe was particularly visible. She began to work at school and after a couple of months was reading like the other children in her class. She had also stopped wetting, and was able to separate from her brother more securely.

Therapy with the sexually abused child

Jones (1986) pointed out that 'The child's experience has to be understood by the therapist in order to provide treatment. . . . In particular, the predicament of the sexually abused child, the impact of abuse upon thinking, attitude, self-view, sexuality and making relationships with other people, as well as the effects of sexual abuse on behaviour have proved useful bases for treatment'.

Jones found that children in individual therapy move through three specific phases of treatment. The starting phase is particularly concerned with the child getting a sense of the task ahead, the working through of his/her feelings and emotions and letting them become visible, so to speak. The middle phase can persist for a considerable time and consists of the main body of therapy. This phase includes the child and therapist becoming aware of the child's guilt about what has happened and this is also linked to the threats that may have been made to the child. Often angry and frightening feelings come to the surface during this phase and children can become aggressive, usually copying what has been done to them. The child may be most ambivalent about meeting the therapist at this stage. This is followed by a period where the child becomes acutely aware of the lack of care received from parental figures and of the lack of emotional warmth and security, leading to another stage of dissociation — dissociating oneself from physical and psychological pain. It is during this phase in particular that a secure home with co-operation from those who look after the child is of importance. The 'closing phase' is another powerful experience for the child, particularly when endings and separations have always been abrupt and without preparation. This phase of therapy often leads to the children reflecting on the difficult times in their lives and it leaves them wondering how the therapist will 'make goodbye happen'. The child will have become somewhat dependent on the therapist and is trusting him/her with very difficult feelings. Discussing the ending with the child well in advance, helping him/her express what s/he thinks might happen and what s/he would would like to happen can be explored in detail during this phase. Reviewing the path therapy has taken and what happened during this time, both inside and outside the sessions, can be used to help the child bring together parts of his/her life in a meaningful way. Other professionals involved with the child may also have to be communicated with specifically to let them know about the significance of this stage in therapy. Professionals and parental figures involved with the child need to be informed about the ending and understand how important the proper resolution of this phase is. Now more than ever is it important that the child actually gets to the sessions, and on time.

CASE HISTORY 5

5 year-old Katy's therapy had reached the 'closing phase' and five more sessions had been arranged for her. An extra session had been arranged where Katy and the therapist told her mother about the plan. Katy's mother had said she was pleased about that. The fourth session Katy was brought almost 20 minutes late; the mother was distraught and said she thought she would 'never manage to get to the hospital for the appointment'. She had thought that the therapist would have given up on her and the session was spent on working through the different anxieties that this incident had brought to a head. The following session Katy did not come at all and mother telephoned after the session saying that Katy had been at a birthday party enjoying herself and she did not want to spoil her fun; she also thought that Katy was so much better that it 'would not have mattered if she missed a session'. The therapist repeated that it was very important for mother to bring Katy for her sessions and on time. Two difficult sessions followed with Katy being very unsettled and angry, not only outside the session and with her mother but also inside the session and with the therapist. However the ending did come about as planned and Katy was able to leave her therapy as planned.

The reason for bringing this vignette to the reader's attention is to illustrate that therapy with adults and children is different from other interventions. A commitment to this work in children has also to be undertaken by the adults who support the child while in therapy. If this commitment is not present the therapy may cause the child more distress, bringing up feelings of disloyalty amongst other difficulties. MacFarlane & Waterman (1986) discuss therapy for very young children in detail and throw light on many of the difficulties that surround therapy for the sexually abused child.

Play therapy is a technique devised particularly for very young children who are not quite able to let the adult world know in words what they wish to communicate. They are usually well able to communicate in other forms and dolls, animals, doll's houses, doll's house furniture, sand, water, Plasticine and other play materials are used with the children to make it easier for them to tell their story to the adults. This technique is useful for all forms of child abuse. Doyle (1987) paid particular attention to showing how this form of therapy might be applied with children who have been sexually abused.

Individual therapy for the adolescent can be of particular help though as seen from the discussion in the section on group treatment the two types of therapy may be tailored to the child's needs and a third, family therapy, also considered. The older boy and girl who have been sexually abused over a number of years will have to address their many deeply disturbing feelings, including their sense of guilt, their feeling of it all having been their fault, their ambivalence, their feeling of worthlessness and their feelings of being rejected or of being worth rejecting. Sinason (1988) discussed some of the issues that children in individual therapy have to work through when they have been sexually abused and, though the child she describes was aged 5 years, the older child also experiences very similar feelings during therapy.

McCarthy (1988) examines the consequences for the child once s/he has disclosed. He brings to our attention that 'Incest victims frequently exhibit very strong and even overwhelming feelings of hate. For them, managing this hate is a major task.'

THE DISCLOSURE INTERVIEW FOR THE SEXUALLY ABUSED CHILD

When children have been sexually abused they are almost always interviewed or prepared to make a disclosure statement about their abuse. It is not possible to go into specific detail of how to conduct such interviews but Jones & McQuiston (1988) have concentrated on all the issues surrounding these specific interviews. Though disclosure work with children does not constitute therapy, all such interviews have to be therapeutic in essence and provide the child with understanding of their situation and support. The legal requirements need to be addressed when preparing for such interviews and the 1989 Children Act has to be adhered to. Jones & McQuiston point out that

Great care needs to be taken to remain open and honest throughout the interviewing process as in any constructive, supportive interaction with children. The style of this relationship may be quite different from the usual experience of the abused child with adults and can pave the way for future interviews. Although it is a natural tendency to attempt to protect children from pain and disappointment, it will harm them if they are told that 'everything will be okay don't worry'. The child will quickly see through this, and see no reason to trust another in a long line of disappointing adults. (p. 16)

THERAPY FOR CHILDREN AND ADULTS WITH LEARNING DIFFICULTIES WHEN THEY HAVE BEEN SEXUALLY ABUSED

More recently professionals have become alert to the many abused children and adults who have learning difficulties. Again it is not possible to enter into a discussion about the difficulties and complexities of this work, let alone consider the person who has learning difficulties.

Workers from the USA and Britain have made a concerted effort to bring to notice the plight of this group of people. Sinason (1990) described her therapeutic work with patients with learning difficulties and has highlighted some very important findings. The most outstanding finding seems to be that many people with learning difficulties have their condition made far worse by the abuse and present as more severely handicapped than their potential level. Sinason (1990) has carried out psychodynamic psychotherapy with such individuals and found a remarkable improvement following resolution of inner conflicts related to the abuse. Group therapy does not always benefit these children and adults. Because of their very individual difficulties they need the attention of a one-to-one relationship in order to come to an understanding about what has happened to them. Family therapy can be helpful as an additional form of therapy if the family are cooperative. It is during such family therapy sessions that family members, often for the first time, see their child as operating at a far higher level than they had up until then believed possible. Ordinary members of the family often take more convincing that the level of functioning of the person with learning difficulties could be heightened.

TRAINING AND SUPERVISION FOR PROFESSIONALS

One aspect of therapy and treatment for abused children is to consider the necessity of training and supervision for those working in this area. It is important to recognise that people from all walks of life are able to contribute in a positive way to alleviating some of the problems of child abuse. Training and supervision and support will be necessary almost at every level, from government departments making resources available, to parental figures and professionals making decisions about the children's daily lives when child abuse has taken place. Foster-parents for instance, who do a vital job, may need formal training but definitely need some introduction to the topic of child abuse and they will require far more support than they are at present allocated. The successful placement of a child depends on the strength the foster-parent(s) can continue to put into the job of caring for the child and understanding (training) and support will be a vital part of this. For judges, on the other hand, who have the immense responsibility of making decisions about the children's lives, training is more important than ongoing support.

Each person in this network will bring to the situation their own professional training but, because some of the issues in child abuse are so new to all, much sharing of facts and information about the subject and interprofessional training is essential. The emotional impact on those working in the area can at times feel overwhelming. Burn-out has increased amongst many professionals. The denial and scapegoating that can ensue has been shown to be a powerful aspect of many cases. Psychotherapists with a systemic and dynamic theoretical framework have had some insight into this because of their therapeutic work in general and are therefore well placed in supporting others in this area.

Child abuse demands a response which is imaginative, based on clear knowledge, and which sometimes demands courage in confronting our own or others' emotional reactions. This chapter has concentrated on the kinds of external help that might be provided for abused children and their families. Professionals too need outside help to provide them with a perspective on what is happening to them, and to help free them to take the action that is needed.

REFERENCES

Axline V 1964 Dibs: in search of self. Penguin Books, UK
Bagley C, King K 1990 Child sexual abuse. Tavistock/
Routledge, London
Barnett S, Corder F, Jehu D 1989 Group treatment for

women sex offenders. Practice 2: 118–159

Bentovim A, Gorrel Barnes G, Cooklin A (eds) 1982 Contents of family therapy, vol. 2. Grune & Stratton, London

Bentovim A, Elton A, Hildebrand J, Tranter M, Vizard E 1988 Child sexual abuse within the family. Wright, London

Berliner L, Ernst E 1984 Group work with preadolescent sexual assault victims. In: Stuart I R, Greer J G (eds) Victims of sexual aggression: Treatment of children, women and men. Van Nostrand Reinhold, New York

Berliner L, Stevens D L 1982 Clinical issues in child sexual abuse. In: Conte J R, Shope D (eds) Social work and child sexual abuse. Hawarth, New York

Bion W R 1961 Experiences in groups. London, Tavistock

Bloch S 1979 An introduction to the psychotherapies. Oxford University Press, Oxford

Boston M, Szur R 1983 Psychotherapy with severely deprived children. RKP, London

Brassard M R, Tyler A II, Kehle T J 1983 School programs to prevent intrafamilial child sexual abuse. Child Abuse and Neglect 7: 214–245

Bremer J 1989 Sex offender specific treatment with juveniles: critical components. Presented at a conference on Child Abuse and Neglect, Breaking the Cycle, Leeds University

Bremer J 1991 Intervention with the juvenile sex offender. Human Systems Journal of Systemic Consultation and Management 2 (3–4): 235–246

Brown D, Pedder J 1978 Introduction to psychotherapy. Tavistock Publications, London

Browne K, Saqi S 1988 Approaches to screening for child abuse and neglect. In: Browne K, Davies C, Stratton P (eds) Early prediction and prevention of child abuse. Wiley & Sons, Chichester

Browne K, Davies C, Stratton P (eds) Early prediction and prevention of child abuse. Wiley & Sons, Chichester

Burnham J B 1986 Family therapy. Tavistock Publications, London

Campbell D, Draper R (eds) 1985 Applications of systemic family therapy. Grune & Stratton, London

Cicchetti D, Carlson V 1989 Child maltreatment. Cambridge University Press, Cambridge

Copley B, Forryan B 1987 Therapeutic work with children and young people. Robert Royce, London

Crittenden P 1988 Family and dyadic patterns of functioning in maltreating families. In: Browne K, Davies Stratton P (eds) Early prediction and prevention of child abuse. Wiley & Sons, Chichester

Crittenden P, Ainsworth M D S 1989 Child maltreatment and attachment theory. In: Cicchetti D, Carlson V (eds) Child maltreatment. Cambridge University Press, Cambridge

De Shazar S 1986 Keys to solution in brief family therapy. W W Norton, London

Doyle C 1987 Sexual abuse: giving help to the children. Children and Society 3: 210–223

Faller K 1987 Women who sexually abuse children. Violence and Victims 2 (4): 263–276

Finkelhor D 1986 A sourcebook on child sexual abuse. Sage, Beverly Hills, California

Foulkes S J 1964 Therapeutic group analysis. Maresfield Reprint, London

Freud A 1981 A psychoanalyst's view of sexual abuse by parents. In: Mrazek P B, Kempe C H (eds) Sexually abused children and their families. Pergamon Press, Oxford

Furniss T 1983 Mutual influence and interlocking professional–family processes in the treatment of child sexual abuse and incest. Child Abuse and Neglect 7: 207–223

Furniss T 1985 Conflict-avoiding and conflict-regulating patterns in incest and child sexual abuse. Acta Paedopsichiatrica 50: 299–313

Furniss T 1991 The multi-professional handbook of child abuse. Routledge. London

Furniss T, Bingley-Miller L, Bentovim A 1984 Therapeutic approach to sexual abuse. Archives of Disease in Childhood 59 (9): 865–870

Furniss T, Bingley-Miller L, Van Elburg A 1988 Goal-oriented group treatment for sexually abused adolescent girls. British Journal of Psychiatry 152: 97–106

Giaretto H 1977 Humanistic treatment of father–daughter incest. Child Abuse and Neglect 1: 411–426

Giaretto H 1981 A comprehensive child sexual abuse treatment program. In: Mrazek P B, Kempe C H (eds) Sexually abused children and their families. Porgamon Press, Oxford

Glaser D, Frosh S 1988 Child sexual abuse. Macmillan, Education, London

Gottlieb B, Dean J 1981 The co-therapy relationship in group treatment of sexually mistreated adolescent girls. In: Mrazek P B, Kempe C H (eds) Sexually abused children and their families. Pergamon Press, Oxford

Haley J 1963 Strategies of psychotherapy. Grune & Stratton, New York

Hanks H, Stratton P 1988 Family perspectives of early sexual abuse. In: Browne K, Davies C, Stratton P (eds) Early prediction and prevention of child abuse. Wiley & Sons, Chichester

Hanks H, Hobbs C, Seymore D, Stratton P 1987 Infants who fail to thrive: an intervention for poor feeding practices. Journal of Reproductive and Infant Psychology 6 (2): 101–111

Hildebrand J 1988 Use of groupwork in treating child sexual abuse. In : Bentovin A, Elton A, Hildebrand J, Tranter M, Vizard E (eds) Child sexual abuse within the family.

Hoffman L 1981 Foundations of family therapy. Basic Books, New York

Hotaling G T, Finkelhor D, Kirkpatrick J T, Straus M A (eds) 1988 Family violence. Sage, London

Jones D 1986 Individual psychotherapy for the sexually abused child. Child Abuse and Neglect 10: 377–385

Jones D P H, McQuiston M G 1988 Interviewing the sexually abused child. Gaskell Royal College of Psychiatrists, London

Kempe R S, Kempe C H 1978 Child abuse. Fontana Books, London

Kempe R S Kempe C H 1984 The common secret: sexual abuse of children and adolescents. W H Freeman, New York

MacFarlane K, Waterman J 1986 Sexual abuse of young children. Holt, Rinehart & Winston, London

Mathews R, Matthews J K, Speltz K 1989 Female sexual offenders. The Safer Society Press Orwell, USA

McCarthy B 1988 Are incest victims hated? Psychoanalytic Psychotherapy 3 (2): 113–120

Mrazek P B, Kempe C H (eds) 1981 Sexually abused children and their families. Pergamon Press, Oxford

Nelki J S, Watters J 1989 A group for sexually abused young children: unravelling the web. Child Abuse and Neglect 13 (3): 369–378

Porter E 1986 Treating the young male victim of sexual abuse. Safer Society Press, Syracuse, New York

Porter R (ed) 1984 Child sexual abuse within the family. Ciba Foundation, Tavistock Publications, London

Rogers J 1961 A therapists view of psychotherapy. Constable, London

Rycroft C 1968 A critical dictionary of psychoanalysis. Penguin Books, Harmondsworth

Salter A C 1988 Treating child sex offenders and victims. Sage, Newbury Park, California

Sgroi S 1988 Vulnerable populations, Vol. 1. Lexington Books, Lexington

Sgroi S 1989 Vulnerable populations, Vol. 2. Lexington Books, Lexington

Sinason V 1988 Smiling, swallowing and stupefying: the effect of sexual abuse on the child. Psychoanalytic Psychotherapy 3 (2): 97–111

Sinason V 1990 Presentation at ACPP Conference, Research and Child Abuse, Cardiff

Skinner B F 1953 Science and human behaviour. Macmillan, New York

Stratton P, Hanks H 1991 Incorporating circularity in defining and classifying child maltreatment. Human Systems Journal of Systemic Consultation and Management 2 (3–4) 181–200

Stratton P, Preston-Shoot M, Hanks H 1990 Family therapy. Venture Press, Birmingham

Summit R C 1983 The child sexual abuse accommodation syndrome. Journal of Child Abuse and Neglect 7: 177–193

Vizard E 1990 Presentation at Child Abuse Practice in the 1990's (Conference) July

Walker C E, Bonner B L, Kaufman K L 1988 The psychologically and sexually abused child. Pergamon Press

Welldon E V 1988 Mother, madonna, whore. Free Association Books, London

Winnicott D W 1964 The child, the family and the outside world. Penguin Books, Harmondsworth

Winnicott R W 1965 The maturational process and facilitating environment. Hogarth Press, London

Winnicott D W 1982 Through paediatrics to psycho-analysis. Hogarth Press, London

Wolfe D A 1987 Child abuse; implications for child development and psychology. Sage, Newbury Park, California

Wolf S C 1988 The sex offender's search for the child. Presented at SRIP Conference on Child Abuse and Neglect, Breaking the Cycle, Leeds University

Wyatt G E, Powell G J (eds) 1988 Lasting effects of child sexual abuse. Sage, London

Yalom I D 1975 The theory and practice of group psychotherapy. Basic Books, New York

16. Children in care

Children who are, or who have been accommodated by (or in the care of) the local authority are a special group. All have in common the fact that at some time in their lives they have been cared for away from home by people who are expected to be experts on the emotional needs of children. Bamford & Wolkind (1988) have summarised the physical and mental health of children in care. As a group they have a higher risk for psychiatric ill health and social deviance than any other easily identifiable group in our society.

In recent times 4–5% of children in the UK have been taken into care, for a variety of reasons and variable amounts of time. Their experience in care and the outcome are equally varied, depending on the extent of disruption to their lives and the quality of care provided.

There has been a marked fall in the number of children in residential care, to a third of the number 10 years ago. These children are often the more troubled and troublesome children, yet are cared for in the main by unqualified residential case workers.

Most younger children are cared for by foster-parents and over the last 10 years it has been recognised that children with special needs may be fostered successfully rather than given placements within large institutions. Fostering of teenagers remains problematic and not always appropriate. There clearly is a continuing need for the resi-

dential sector to provide a good child care service, as review of placements shows an unacceptable large number of breakdowns in teenager foster placements (HMSO 1991).

The main types of placements are listed in Table 16.1 and the reported breakdown of placements in Table 16.2.

A recent review (Farmer & Parker 1991) showed that 1 child in 5 in care is unlikely to go home, and for 38% of children who went home there was a further breakdown. The outlook for children on second and third attempts to rehabilitate home was poor.

Although adoption in infancy has a generally good outcome with few breakdowns, the rate of breakdown again increases with the age of the child to 30–50% in adolescence. Adoption of children with special needs has been unexpectedly successful and perhaps reflects the adopters and also, importantly, the support they receive (O'Hara 1991, Triseliotis 1991a). Intercountry adoption works satisfactorily for many children, although there may be issues of identity as the child grows up (Triseliotis 1991b). More recently there has

Table 16.2 Breakdown in placement (Thorburn 1990, HMSO 1991)

Placement at home*	25–49%
Short-term fostering	20%
Professional fostering of adolescents	38–53%
Long-term fostering at 5 yrs	20–41%
Adoption in infancy	Few
Adoption 3 years +	20%
Adoption adolescents	30–50%
Residential care moves	21%
Children with special needs < 10 yrs	10%
> 10 yrs	15–20% } 25–40%
15 yrs	50%

* 1 in 4 'home on trial' neglected or reabused.

Table 16.1 Main types of placement (Rowe et al 1989)

Age — yrs	Foster-home	Adoptions	Residential
0–4	77%	8%	6%
5–10	65%	1%	25%
11 +	15%	0%	62%

been concern about the adequacy of screening procedures of prospective adoptors, of, for example, Romanian orphans.

Unmarried mothers are now much less likely to offer their baby for adoption than formerly. In 1968, 15/1000 babies born were adopted but only 2.9/1000 in 1984 (in the UK). In 1980, 2599 babies were adopted and in 1988 the number fell to 1235 (Thorburn 1990).

Only a small percentage (5% in 1985) of the children in care are there because of proven child abuse but many have had a difficult family life, possibly involving abuse, before care. The Children Act 1989 places a duty on local authorities to support families and children in need with the expectations that fewer children will live away from home. This may be effective for some small children but the plight of teenage runaways suggests that different strategies are needed for this group (Newman 1989).

The reasons necessitating the removal of a child from his home should be compelling. The problems of providing good alternative care, especially as the child grows older, are great but leaving a child at home who wants to leave has consequences too. Children taken into care are often unhappy and emotionally disturbed; they may have been abused. Does the foster-home have the strength and support to care for the child or will he be moved from foster-home to foster-home to children's home? Will he be abused in care? Will he run away?

A survey of the family background of children in care as opposed to the general population (OPCS General Household Survey 1985) showed that — of the children in care — 6 times as many had a single parent, 5 times as many come from families receiving income support, and 3 times as many from families living in rented housing. The classic picture is of poverty, single parents or unemployed fathers and large families. To prevent family breakdown which may lead to the child leaving home, either at the child or parents request, by the child running away or by statutory action by the Local Authority requires a major societal response.

The origins of poor parenting need to be addressed if the cycle of deprivation is to be altered. Prevention will involve education, real support of families in need and the alleviation of child poverty. Poverty is a major stress and a significant factor in the final break-up of already disadvantaged families. Child rearing patterns are changing in other ways with an increased divorce rate and numbers of reconstituted and one-parent families. As the shape of society changes it is children who are affected most by insecurity and disruption.

When children are received into care, it is generally the case that the younger the child the better the outcome, as long as subsequent care is good. Although it is now recognised that early emotional damage may have effects lasting for life, it is also evident that repeated reception into care and/or frequent change of foster-home is damaging. Being left in a poor home is no solution; children who leave care for continuing abuse or neglect at home also do badly. By the time a child is 8 years old the risk of a foster-care breakdown is 1 in 4, by 12 years 1 in 2, and of 15–16-year-old runaways 1 in 2–3 are running from care.

The consequences of a neglectful or abusive childhood are given in Table 16.3 and the problems arising for carers in Table 16.4. It is evident that foster-parents or residential case workers are often given an extraordinarily difficult task, caring for disturbed children who will only learn if given time, patience and skilled handling. Carers are not given adequate training, support and resources to do this and the spread of provision is poor.

The situation for carers has become even more difficult with the increased recognition of child

Table 16.3   Consequences of a neglectful or abusive childhood

1. Fail to grow — physically
                 — intellectually
                 — emotionally
2. Develop difficult behaviours
3. Persisting medical problems: deafness, squint, under-treated asthma, unimmunised
4. Present to carers — small thin child
                      — overweight adolescent (more girls)
                      — poor social habits e.g. blowing nose, use of WC
                      — wetting, soiling, feeding, sleep problems
                      — depressed, withdrawn, 'blank'
                      — angry, aggressive 'conduct disorders'
                      — wander, fail to recognise stranger v family or friend, over friendly, shallow relationship
                      — sexually precocious
                      — school failure

Table 16.4   Consequences for carer

Problem	Result or actions needed
1. *Emotional* — feeding (in 50–60%)	Each mealtime disrupted
— wetting, soiling, withdrawn	Endless patience and time needed — upset to rest of family
— anger, destructive	Time needed for child, other children upset, frightened, toys broken
— wander	Anxiety
2. *Poor social habits*	Patience and teaching — upset to other family members
3. *Learning*/school problems (occur	Attendance at clinic, e.g. speech therapy, educational psychology
in > 10%)	Involvement of carers in therapeutic programmes
4. *Medical* problems or psychological disorder	Attend clinics, become involved in therapy, family sessions
5. *Antisocial* behaviours — theft, lies,	Involvement with other agencies, e.g. police, school but disruption to family
smoking, running away	life too. Attend court, police stations, etc.
6. *Sexually* precocious behaviour or abusive	Education, support, therapy See (4)
or provocative behaviour (towards	Educate carers and their children
carers or children)	
Pregnancy/STD	Appropriate care/advice

sexual abuse; sexually abused children are often very disturbed and their sexualised behaviours difficult to tolerate. Children in care do not need (and deserve) 'good enough' care — they need better than average parenting to help heal the wounds and scars resulting from previous poor care and maltreatment. Much good, caring work is done and many children succeed but there is an unacceptable 'failure' rate. Too many children move from home to home, continue to fail and finally leave care with few skills and nowhere to go. The Children Act 1989 says, 'An order should only be made if the court is also satisfied that the order it is considering will positively contribute to the child's well being and be in his best interests'.

This puts a burden on all professionals and carers to ensure that the child is doing better in foster-care — otherwise why is he there? The situation for children and carers is made much more difficult by uncertainty and delay in making long-term plans. Contact with parents is essential for most but is destructive for some children. Children who do best in the care system are those who are adopted at a young age, although there is a breakdown rate here too. Children do not handle conflict well (as is also shown in studies of children of divorced parents) and security is essential for emotional wellbeing and growth.

It is evident that long-term planning is needed whether the child is accommodated voluntarily with parental responsibility continuing (the majority) or has been taken into care. The child must know as soon as possible what his future holds: where he will live, which school he is to attend, what arrangements will be made about seeing his friends, his pets and his 'family'. Children should understand their situation and be involved, as much as possible in an age-appropriate way, with decision-making concerning their own lives and futures.

Paediatricians, psychologists and psychiatrists have not met the challenge of children in care. There has been little research into the physical health of children in care in the UK, but their mental health has been examined in some detail and summarised in a recent review (Bamford & Wolkind 1988). Consequently little is known of the children's health; although their emotional needs have been evaluated they also have been met. Studies in the USA suggest that many foster-children have physical as well as emotional problems. Growth problems are common, but cardiovascular abnormality and poor dentition occur too (Hochstadt et al 1987).

Table 16.5 outlines tasks for paediatricians, whether working in the community or hospital.

The Boarding Out Regulations (New Regulations and Associated Guidance: Boarding-out of Children Regulations 1988; Fig. 16.1)

These were introduced in an attempt to repair the deficiencies in the medical support given to children in care. The local authority has thereby a responsibility to arrange examinations and obtain a written assessment of the state of health of the child, the need for medical and dental care and to review the welfare and progress of the child.

Table 16.5   Tasks for the community paediatrician

At home	In care (whatever reason — voluntary or on order)
1. Recognise abuse early	1. Recognise abuse in care
2. Recognise neglect	2. Monitor growth, development and 'emotional wellbeing'
3. Work with parents, child and primary care team	3. Assess any special needs (educationally)
— support use of local resources	4. Work with carers, social worker closely, especially on management problems
— facilitate services for e.g. squint, glue ear, immunisation	5. Arrange appropriate medical, psychological, psychiatric treatment
— ensure parents understand professional concern	6. Work with child's natural family if appropriate
— advise on behaviour problems	7. Be prepared to say if the placement is failing
4. Be prepared to give evidence in court	8. Advise SSD/adoption panel
5. Advise SSD	

Table 16.6   Boarding Out Regulations — requirements of medical examination

1. 'Baseline' assessment of growth, development and emotional state, diagnose any specific medical disorder
2. 'Provide' child's carers with relevant medical information, e.g. past illnesses, immunisation status, allergies, current health needs
3. Listen to child's and carers' worries
4. Complete 'My Health Passport' if provided (see text)
5. Refer for appropriate investigation or treatment (after discussion with GP)
6. Provide a written report to GP, SSD, Child Health Department to include: — review of child's health
   — physical, developmental, emotional growth
   — progress (i.e. at subsequent visits)

The Regulations are outlined in Table 16.6. Appropriate forms have been supplied by BAAF (British Agency for Adoption and Fostering) which allow necessary detail to be collected. BAAF have also produced 'My Health Passport' for children in care. It is designed for older children (8 years upwards) who, it is suggested, can complete sections themselves. The passport is intended to encourage awareness of health issues but also gives information to the child about his or her own medical history. It will also help, if kept up-to-date, when children move placement and there

is an inevitable time lag as GP records follow on behind. If the Boarding Out Regulations also work properly the social worker should have an up-to-date medical dossier in the social work file.

For the medical service to work in the children's best interest the doctors must be trained and ideally offer a continuity of service. The old 'army medical' approach is simplistic and unhelpful. Whilst the child will need to be weighed and measured the physical examination should be completed as appears appropriate. Older children should give consent and, in practice, listening to the child and hearing his concerns is likely to be more fruitful than regular physical check-ups. Emotional problems are common — if the doctor does show interest teenagers usually are ready to talk. It is also essential to give time to listen to the carers and take note of their worries and concerns, advising or referring on as necessary (Table 16.6).

There are considerable resource implications if this work is to be done well but it could be truly preventive medicine. The outlook for children in care has traditionally been poor and earlier recognition of problems may help in the long term. It is often alleged that 'care' itself causes all the problems but this is clearly simplistic. If 95% of children in care are there because their families cannot cope, 5% because of proven abuse or neglect, children obviously enter the system with pre-existing problems. The 'system' should thus be geared to the needs of infants through to teenagers.

Young children may do well in foster-care and then go home; whilst some families subsequently

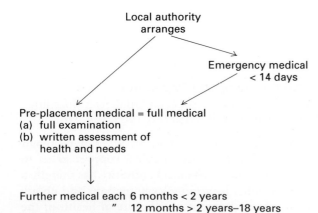

Fig. 16.1   Boarding Out Regulations 1988 (replacing 1955 regulations).

cope, others fail again. Children may continue to be damaged: of children returned home after care the percentage experiencing problems increases with age. Medical surveillance for these children who may now be 'out of care' or at home on various orders should continue (Tizard & Hodges 1989, 1990). The consequence of poor care in childhood, emotional retardation, leads to shallow relationships, and antisocial behaviour becomes conduct disorder (Bamford & Wolkind 1988). As a result young men who have been in care are over-represented in the prison population. This high percentage has a negative correlation with the time in care — the longer the boy was in care the fewer the convictions. Children who are adopted in the long term do better than those who are fostered, who do little better than those left at home. However, those in good foster-homes with continuity and consequent security do better than those teenagers brought up at home who are 'out of control' and then are inappropriately cared for in under-resourced, large children's homes or other institutions (HMSO 1991).

Girls who have received poor parenting and care tend to drift into pregnancy and transient relationships which fail. As teenage mothers their babies are often small, the mother–child interaction is poor and by the time the child goes to school he is likely to have behaviour problems. Thus the cycle of disadvantage repeats itself (Janus et al 1987, Bamford & Wolkind 1988).

The reasons why some children in care do better than others are not fully understood but there are clearly several factors involved. Some children just appear to be more resilient to life's adversities. Children of schizophrenic parents are over-represented in care. Children in care tend to be of lower birth weight — what are the effects of intrauterine growth retardation? Yet environmental factors are the most important when considering the reasons why children are in care. These children often come from large, poor, stressed families where problems and disharmony lead to eventual family breakdown and care. This pattern may alter with current changes in family structure. The care experience may then compound the poor start offered the child. The care system itself is not the sole reason for the poor outcome but the system has failed to meet children's needs.

Research shows again that adopted children have fewer long-term problems in ordinary living as well as a lower rate of psychiatric disorder. Foster-care, residential care and staying in poor, abusive homes will continue to offer children an impoverished lifestyle. 'Keeping them out of care' as an answer to the ills of the care system is not a solution. If superficially attractive to those with money to save. The high number of runaways demonstrates the failure of parenting and the care system of the 1980s which appears set to deteriorate further in the 1990s.

Recent work has highlighted the level of institutional abuse; American research shows 39 per 1000 children in care report abuse but only 1 in 5 incidents are officially reported (Westcott 1992). Frequently abuse in care is not adequately investigated even when reported, although authorities are now instituting more appropriate procedures (Working Together 1991). Paediatricians and child psychiatrists must be aware of abuse in residential settings, involving staff or peers, recognise warning signs and act on behalf of individual children. The abuse may be institutionalised and part of the 'treatment' of disturbed children as in 'pin-down' where the report documented 132 cases of solitary confinement in Staffordshire homes in 1983–89 (Westcott 1992).

However, unless residential staff are adequately trained, supervised and paid as skilled professionals the standard of care will remain inadequate for many emotionally disturbed children. Closing down all the children's homes is not an acceptable alternative to attempting to raise standards and meet children's needs. The rapidly rising numbers of teenagers running away from unhappy or abusive homes or inadequate local authority care (Abrahams & Mungall 1992) should point the way to more imaginative initiatives to meet the needs of this distressed and disadvantaged group.

RUNAWAYS — TEENAGE HOMELESSNESS

Most published research into teenage runaways is from the USA but there is an increasing body of information in the UK which is providing a similar and worrying picture, with an estimated 75 000–90 000 young people running away each year.

The Children's Society have researched young

runaway using the safe house in London, the first in the UK (Newman 1989). Of the one-third of the children who ran away because of problems at home, the usual complaint was of constant arguments and breakdown in communications. Many had been thrown out of the parental home or had left because of violence (Table 16.7).

Of the total sample of 532 young people, 98 said they had been sexually abused at some time, that is 18% of the group or 29% females and 6% males. 25% of those admitted to the house had run away from care. The paper notes the unhappiness of children placed in secure units — young people whose only 'crime' was running away. As others have written (Heany 1989), it is a lottery whether the often abused runaway is helped or punished.

Other were unhappy in children's homes, foster-home or assessment centre. Several had been bullied and physically abused in residential care. Many felt that in care they were not appropriately involved in the planning of their own future, and that their own opinion was not considered. This has been well expressed — 'When I was in care I felt that no-one had the time to talk to me as an individual to find out what I wanted and how I felt. I felt no-one cared for me so I got hurt and bitter and then I fought out and was labelled a problem and locked away' (Heany 1989).

The reality of running away and subsequent homelessness is described (Newman 1989) as a national problem which needs urgent attention by 'providing appropriate care and resources to which young runaways should have a right'. Homelessness exists in all our cities and a description of homeless adults looked at the origins and morbidity of the adults, which again reflects the urgent need to help the teenager (Lancet 1989). It de-

scribes 'a high morbidity for physical illness, psychiatric disorder and social disadvantage, both current and from the adverse circumstances of childhood'.

On the streets of our cities are children of 8–9 years upwards, absent from school and wanderers, who eventually go home but may be at considerable risk nonetheless. These children are often involved in shop-lifting, may drift into prostitution (boys and girls, especially if sexually abused previously), smoke or abuse solvents. Other older children run, and run repeatedly, away from home or care. These children need a lot of skilled support, not punishment or to be locked up.

The abuse of adolescents in the USA is well documented. In spite of a general view that child maltreatment is the major problem, family violence does not stop at the end of childhood and may increase (Powers & Eckenrode 1988). The association of maltreatment at home with runaway and homeless youth has been looked at in more detail (Powers et al 1990). The characteristics of runaways in the USA are summarised in Table 16.8. In general most runaways are in their mid-teens and give a long history of emotional conflict and abuse. Boys are more likely to be pushed out (thrown out) of home and so become homeless, whereas girls, especially sexually abused girls, run away. They are an unhappy group as a whole, at real risk of suicide, especially those who have been sexually abused. They have often failed at school, although before running only 15% have a history of delinquency. Once on the street, 70% of a sample (Powers et al 1990) were approached with offers of illegal activities. For the teenager on the streets there is a continuation of the spiral of abuse, neglect and exploitation (Powers et al 1990).

'Running away to sea' used to be considered a normal expression of adolescent behaviour and the separation process, but the picture has changed and these 'throwaway children' are a reflection of current familial and societal pathology (Powers et al 1990). These teenagers are unhappy; they run because of social and environmental determinates. The families are dysfunctional and emotionally abusive. The runners come from all sections of UK society. There may have been physical or sexual abuse. The children may have been pushed out and can not return.

Table 16.7 Reasons for leaving home and care (1985–87) This informations was available for 84% admitted in safe house (Newman 1989)

Reasons for leaving	%
Problems at home	33
Problems in care	25
General unhappiness	16
More specific problems	13
Problems at school	6
(non-runaways)	5
Total	98

Table 16.8   Characteristics of runaways (Kufeldt & Nimmo 1987, Lancet 1989, Abrahams & Mungall 1992)

Gender	More boys pushed out More girls run away Approximately equal numbers
Age	Peak 15–17 years Range 12–18 years (⅔ are 14–16 but 7% under 11 year)
Family	25% lived with both parents (cf 68% general population) > 33% single parent more from single, broken, divorced homes Afro-Caribbean and Asian children are over-represented
Care	33–50% (96% from residential homes)
Recurrence	Most run more than once 30% run 5 times or more
Mood	Depressed Poor self-image >50% Suicidal
School	Average 2 years behind peers, school problems 25%, learning problems 7%
Antisocial behaviour	Delinquency 15%, drug/alcohol abuse 20%
Maltreatment	30–70% — may be more than one type Physical abuse 20–40% (? = /) Sexual abuse 5–12% (> /) Neglect 20–42% (? = /) Emotional abuse ? 100%
Referral	< 10% had told welfare agencies of abuse
Where do they run?	98% of runaways stay within a few miles of home To friends, relatives and many return voluntarily
How long do they stay?	Most stay away a few day; 2% were away longer than 2 weeks
Why did they run?	Arguments with parents Abuse

The tragedy is that they are not running to anything which offers promise but away from an intolerable situation. The teenager sacrifices his adolescence, growth and development running to another hostile, stressful environment without real hope of a better future.

The challenge is an urgent one. 'Safe houses' offer emergency care to a small proportion of teenagers, but only if this large group are seen as victims rather than villains will realistic proposals be made. Given the lack of legitimate provisions — that is, housing, training, jobs — many will inevitably drift into criminal activity, prostitution, drug abuse or early parenthood. This will cost them years of their life (or life itself) and society will have to bear the cost of inappropriate imprisonment and the effects of another generation of deprived babies.

Summary

1.   Children who are cared for away from home have particular emotional needs; these needs may not be recognised or met.

2.   Children who have been or are in care have a higher risk of mental ill health and social deviance than any other easily identifiable group in our society.

3.   The numbers of children accommodated by the local authority have fallen markedly in recent years.

4.   Children may be abused in foster-homes, adoptive homes and institutions.

5.   In general, younger children who are adopted have the best long-term outlook.

6.   Adoption of children with special needs has proved successful in many instances.

7.   An increasing number of children run away from home and care each year. More local support for child, parents and carers is advocated (Abrahams & Mungall 1992).

8.   Doctors have an important task: to recognise the physical and emotional needs of children in care and to offer advice and support to carers whilst arranging appropriate treatment or therapy for children (Table 16.5).

9.   Specialist doctors also advise SSD and adoption panels.

REFERENCES

Abrahams C, Mungall R 1992 Runaways: exploding the myths. National Children's Home, 85 Highbury Park, London N5 1HO. £10
Bamford F, Wolkind S N 1988 The physical and mental health of children in care. Economic and Social Research Council

Farmer R, Parker R 1991 Trials and tribulations. HMSO
Heany A 1989 A number not a name. A voice for the child in care. VCC paper no 4, London
HMSO 1991 Patterns and outcomes in child placement.
Hochstadt N et al 1987 The medical and social needs of children entering foster care. Child Abuse and Neglect

11(1): 53

Janus M et al 1987 Adolescent runaways: causes and consequences. Lexingham Books, Lexingham M A

Kufeldt K, Nimmo M 1987 Youth on the street: abuse and neglect in the 80s. Child Abuse and Neglect 11: 531–543

Lancet 1989 Homelessness (leader). Lancet ii: 778

Newman C 1989 Young runaways . . . finds from Britain's first safe house. The Children's Society, Edward Rudolf House, Margery Street, London WC1X 0JL

New Regulations and Associated Guidance: Boarding-out of children (foster placement) — Regulations 1988 Accommodation of children (charge and control) Regulations 1988. Local Authority Circular LAC (89) 4. DoH

O'Hara G 1991 Placing children with special needs — outcomes and implications for practice. Adoption and Fostering 15(4): 46

Powers J L, Eckenrode B 1988 The maltreatment of adolescents. Child Abuse and Neglect 12: 189–199

Powers J L, Eckenrode B, Jaklitsch 1990 Maltreatment among runaway and homeless youth. Child Abuse and Neglect 14: 87–98

Rowe J, Hundleby M, Garnett L 1989 Child care now. BAAF Research Series 6

Thorburn J 1990 Inter-departmental review of adoption law. Background Paper no 2. Review of research relating to adoption. DoH

Tizard B, Hodges J 1989 IQ and behavioural adjustments of ex-institutional adolescents. Social and family relationships of ex-institutional adolescents. Journal of Child Psychology and Psychiatry 30: 53–75, 77–97

Tizard B, Hodges J 1990 Ex-institutional children: a follow-up study to age 16. Adoption and Fostering 14(1)

Triseliotis J 1991a Perceptions of permanence. Adoption and Fostering 15(4): 6

Triseliotis J 1991b Inter-country adoption: a brief overview of research. Adoption and Fostering 15(4): 46

Westcott H 1992 Institutional abuse of children — from research to policy. NSPCC, 67 Saffron Hill, London EC1N 8RS

Working Together under the Children Act 1989: a guide to the arrangements for interagency cooperation for the protection of children from abuse 1991 DHSS and Welsh Office. HMSO, London

Address

British Agency for Adoption and Fostering (BAAF) 11 Southwark Street, London SE1 1RQ

17. Legal aspects of child abuse work

COURTS

Which court?

Doctors who recognise child abuse will inevitably become involved in civil cases and care proceedings. Much less commonly will they be asked to give evidence in criminal proceedings (Table 17.1). This is because of the difficulties in collecting evidence, particularly when young children are involved. The Crown Prosecution Service (in England) makes the decision whether to bring a criminal case and only will do so if the crime is serious, if it is in the public interest, and if there is a real possibility of a successful prosecution. Prosecutions are mounted more often when the defendant has pleaded guilty and hence the child and professional witnesses are unlikely to be called to give evidence. The number of cases which are eventually heard in criminal proceedings is low and so successful prosecutions are few, and appear to be falling from around 10% in 1989 to less than 5% in 1991 (West Yorkshire Police Child Abuse Statistics 1992).

1. Giving evidence

Few doctors enjoy giving evidence in court. Doctors tend to be hesitant about appearing and when they do they expect the proceedings to be 'fair and the court to hear what they have to say'. In the event the court often feels more like a battle ground, with more concern for the law and the demolition of the witness than for the child. Professional witnesses become frustrated when they feel they are not able to share with the court their full knowledge of the child. The Rules of Evidence differ in criminal from civil courts and the professional witness needs to understand in particular about hearsay evidence. *Hearsay evidence* is information which the doctor has learned secondhand, for example, what the child said caused the injury rather than what the doctor can describe from his examination and so deduce, which is his opinion. In criminal courts the rules of evidence are adhered to strictly with no hearsay evidence allowed, which is at least straightforward. Also a defendant may only be convicted if the case has been 'proved beyond all reasonable doubt'.

Table 17.1 Which court?

Criminal Court (Magistrate, Crown)	Police statement is basis of evidence, given orally if not agreed Proof needed 'beyond all reasonable doubt' No hearsay evidence Videolink and screens may be used if witness under 14 years old. Public and Press present. Child's identity may not be disclosed[4]
'Family Proceedings Court' (Magistrate, County, High)[3]	Evidence may be oral, written or both if not agreed[1,2] Proof needed 'on balance of probability'. Hearsay evidence allowed Videoed evidence may be allowed Judge or Magistrate gives reason for decisions made No public present Press allowed but reporting restricted and child may not be identified[4]

Notes:
1. Medical report usually available to Magistrate and all involved parties.
2. Affidavits in High Court, oral evidence may be restricted to elucidation of points in affidavit only.
3. Divorce and other civil matters included as well as child abuse cases.
4. The Cleveland Inquiry commented on the need to protect children from identification by the media (Butler-Sloss 1988, p. 253)

In courts concerned with the welfare of children the position is different. The court wants to hear from the child and it may only be through third parties, for example the guardian ad litem, the parents, social worker or a doctor, that all the collected evidence may be put. In care proceedings, the laws of evidence have recently been changed and hearsay evidence is admissible. The case must be proved 'on the balance of probability', this being a lower burden of proof but still an exacting one.

Giving evidence clearly is a skill which doctors working with abused children must acquire but it does take considerable time to feel confident in court. Giving evidence is never easy.

When a paediatrician examines a child who has allegedly been physically abused he may be called as a professional witness to give evidence of fact, that is to describe his examination of the child. The court will expect the paediatrician to explain the child's injuries, in the light of the available history but also with a view to the child's development, and any medical disorder. Criminal courts may wish to hear of first hand evidence the paediatrician has of neglect whereas care courts will usually explore growth and development in a much more general way, allowing third party information too.

Other doctors may be called as professional witnesses to give evidence of, for example, physical assault. Unless the doctor is trained appropriately and can demonstrate he has the experience he should be careful to keep to his brief and not

Table 17.2   Giving evidence

Be well prepared — talk to lawyers pre-court.
Take all relevant notes, X-rays, reports and statements to court.
Be on time.
Give evidence clearly, slowly, avoid jargon.
Expect to justify your medical opinion.
Be impartial — the child's welfare is paramount.
Say if you do not understand a question.
Say if you do not know the answer.
Answer the question which is put.
Try to be succinct, only agree to 'yes' or 'no' if appropriate, but do not give unnecessary detail.
Only comment on topics on which you are informed.

include opinions on, for example, the child's development.

The paediatrician uses his contemporaneous notes (i.e. notes made during and immediately after the examination) diagrams, X-rays, photographs other laboratory results and increasingly may discuss the relevant literature, referring to published work. The paediatrician may give expert testimony and the distinction between a professional and expert witness is not clear-cut. An expert witness may be called who has not seen the child but who can interpret the case for the court using his specialised knowledge.

It is evident that a doctor should give his evidence in a way in which the court can use it most effectively (Tables 17.2 and 17.3). This means speaking clearly, not too fast, not too quietly, in layman's terms so that the evidence can be understood by all in the court — not just the judge, but the jury members, defendants and parents as well

Table 17.3   How to unsettle a doctor as a witness (a doctor's view; after Anderson 1990)

Question	Reply
How many cases have you seen like this, Dr?	Give direct reply.
Have you been trained in this work specifically, Dr?	Give direct reply.
What work in this field have you had published, Dr?	Give direct reply.
Why have you altered the date in the notes?	You may not remember — say so.
Why is the medical report dated differently in various copies?	Has the computer print-out done this automatically?
Why have you changed pen?	Demonstrate different pens in your possession.
Why have you written on the back of an investigation mount sheet, Dr?	Convenience.
Complex question with several subsidiary queries.	Ask to repeat question, and insist on answering each question separately.
Ask to discuss a hypothetical but unlikely scenario.	Comment logically and say it is unlikely, if it is.
Are you 100% certain, Dr?	Explain cannot be 100% certain but highly probable, or unlikely, etc.
Question each injury, even the most minor, in order to destroy the whole.	Explain the importance of pattern recognition — and acknowledge if there are accidental injuries.

as the lawyers. As in any clinical presentation the doctor should be able to justify all he says and avoid exaggeration or dogmatism. He will be much more credible as a witness if he is impartial.

To give evidence in a calm, collected way requires careful preparation including a pre-court conference with the lawyers. The lawyers may help by explaining the legal aspects of the case to the doctor who can in turn ensure his medical opinion is understood. However, lawyers may also attack the witness. Courts are more of a battlefield than a cricket-field. Table 17.4 is taken from a lawyer's guide to cross-examination.

2. Court procedure

Table 17.5 chronicles the sequence of court procedure and Figures 17.1 and 17.2 show the court layout.

The doctor will be initially sworn, or affirmed, by the court clerk. He will then be invited to sit or stand. In care proceedings, where attempts are being made to make the court less threatening, the chairman of the bench will often invite the witness to sit. In other courts where the witness is more comfortable sitting or has a lot of papers it may be more practicable to sit, with the judge's permission. The advocate may stand or set, and replies are directed to the judge or chairman of the bench, and not to the questioner. Forms of address are given in Table 17.6.

The witness will first be led through his evidence, in a straightforward way, by the advocate for the prosecution in criminal cases or the lawyers representing the local authority (or his instructing lawyer) in care cases; then he is cross-examined. It is usually during the cross-examination that the

Table 17.4 How to unsettle a doctor as a witness (a lawyer's guide)

1. Generally avoid frontal attack.
2. Conduct a positive cross-examination, at least initially.
3. Raise doubt about the expert in a subtle way:
   a. use leading questions,
   b. limit expert's opportunity to explain opinion,
   c. hide the ball.
4. Undermine the expert's assumption.
5. Raise the possibility of bias or partiality.
6. As a last resort use other ammunition – sexist, political, personal attack.

Table 17. 5   Court procedure

Know your way about the courtroom (see Figs 17.1 and 17.2).
Wait outside court — do not discuss evidence with other witnesses.
Stand and bow with the court as judge or magistrates enter or leave court.
If court already sitting, bow to judge or bench from witness box on arrival and departure.
The court clerk will administer the oath or affirmation.
Stand or sit to give evidence (see text).
Expert witnesses may sit by the lawyer to listen to all the evidence. Do not whisper or cause distraction.
At the end of your evidence the court will usually release you — your instructing lawyer will ask permission.

doctor will be tested most. There is usually a reasonable dialogue which often allows the doctor to make points missed in his evidence-in-chief. However, more time may be spent (or so it seems to the witness) in examining his curriculum vitae than his evidence. This is an increasing trend but if the doctor keeps calm the threatening lawyer will appear bullying rather than the doctor incompetent. If the doctor does become angry the lawyer has succeeded: an emotionally wrought witness gains little credibility and will be dismissed as emotionally involved in the case and therefore biased (Butler-Sloss 1988, pp. 202–252).

If a witness does feel threatened and is losing confidence it is as well to take a deep breath and avoid eye contact with the lawyer: avoidance of eye contact is achieved more easily when sitting and distances the lawyer.

Always remember, a children's doctor knows more about children than any lawyer (almost) and if he 'sticks to his last' his knowledge will become apparent. Do not assume a high level of understanding of child health issues in court or a sophisticated appreciation of children's needs. A

Table 17.6   Forms of address

Personal	Court	Address
Magistrate	Magistrates Court	Sir or Madam
Circuit Judge } Recorder	Crown or County Court	Your Honour
High Court Judge	High Court	My Lord or My Lady
Lords Justice	Court of Appeal	My Lord or My Lady
Lords of Appeal	House of Lords	My Lord or My Lady

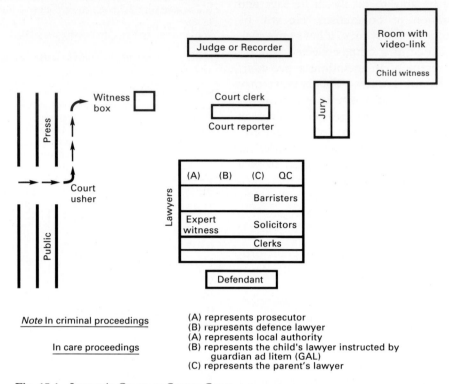

Wigs and Gowns are worn in Criminal Proceedings only

Note In criminal proceedings

In care proceedings

(A) represents prosecutor
(B) represents defence lawyer
(A) represents local authority
(B) represents the child's lawyer instructed by
     guardian ad litem (GAL)
(C) represents the parent's lawyer

Fig. 17.1   Layout in Crown or County Court.

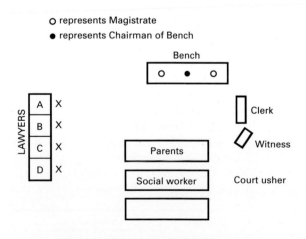

Note A represents lawyer for local authority (usually)
      B represents lawyer for child instructed by GAL
      C represents lawyer for father
      D represents lawyer for mother
      X represents expert witness (for A, B, C or D)

Fig. 17.2   Layout in Magistrates Court (care court).

paediatrician is an expert and can explain to the court the fundamentals of good child care.

However, a well-prepared witness must be aware of the legal system and its rules: 'The medical profession needs to appreciate the legal implications of and their responsibility for the evidential requirements of their work' (Butler-Sloss 1988, p. 252).

PLANNING A COURT APPEARANCE

Witness summons

The courts are aware that doctors may only give evidence at the expense of other work and are usually accommodating about the timing of a doctor's appearance to avoid inconveniencing patients, for example in an outpatient clinic. The instructing lawyer should plan a rough timetable with the other lawyers so that the doctor is able to set aside a half-day in which to give evidence. This is usually adequate in child abuse cases but inevitably timing is often inexact. Expert witnesses may choose to sit for days on end in court. Each individual doctor must consider where his priorities lie in court work.

When a doctor is called to give evidence he will usually accept this as part of his professional duty, hence a witness summons is unnecessary. Courts have powers to compel the attendance of a witness, and Magistrate's High Courts and County Courts may also order the doctor to produce relevant documents or notes. If the court feels the doctor has evidence which is relevant, for example in a criminal case, the witness really has no choice and may be arrested if he fails to attend. In other circumstances, such as the defendant pleading guilty or if medical reports are agreed, the doctor may not be called.

Lawyers often seem to come to decisions at the last minute, and the case is suddenly settled, when lawyers representing all parties meet in the courtroom. The attending doctor does his best to smile benignly, go away and put in a bill, if the case is settled in this way.

Children's evidence

1. Interviewing

The interviewing of children has been scrutinised and the Home Office are currently (1992) developing a code of practice which would be acceptable in criminal proceedings. Working Together (1991) has also given guidance as to good practice:

● Interviewers are to be of acknowledged competence.
● Interviews should be conducted under Area Child Protection Committee procedures.
● The number of investigative interviews should be kept to a minimum.
● Interviewers should retain an open mind.
● The interview should focus on the needs of the child, be at his pace and level and enable the child to talk.
● Recording of interviews should be accurate and differentiate fact, hearsay and opinion. Interviews may be audio- or video-taped. These tapes may be used in family proceedings where there is no restriction on hearsay and in certain circumstances in criminal proceedings (see later).

2. Children giving evidence

In December 1989 the Pigot Committee proposed radical changes to the rules governing the evidence of children in criminal proceedings (Advisory Group on Video Evidence (Pigot Report) 1989). An emasculated version of these proposals appeared in the Criminal Justice Act 1991 (Spencer 1991). However, Spencer acknowledges that there are important changes in the Act:

● At committal proceedings the defence no longer have the right to call the child to give live evidence and must make do with a written statement (hence the child is not cross-examined twice).
● The Director of Public Prosecutions may serve 'notice of transfer' in child abuse cases and bypass the committal stage altogether.
● Competency: children under the age of 14 years shall give unsworn evidence.

In effect, the judge may continue to rule a witness incompetent and advise the jury to ignore the child's evidence if he or she is incoherent or fails to communicate in a way that makes sense. It is currently unclear whether the court will also disqualify children who do not understand the duty to tell the truth, which was the hurdle felt by many to be inappropriate for young witnesses and hence the advice of Pigot that the competence requirement should be dispensed with.

The Children Act 1991 makes young children competent in civil cases.

Cross-examination of the child has altered in that an unrepresented defendant loses the right to cross-examine the child himself. But the trauma of a cross-examination of an abused child, up to 2 years after the initial interview, remains.

The Pigot Committee proposed a scheme where the child would first have been examined by a trained expert and the interview videotaped. The defence would see the tape and if the case was contested the defence would cross-examine the child before a judge in chambers at a pre-trial hearing and this too would be video-recorded. At trial the first tape would have replaced the child's live examination in chief, the second the child's cross-examination. The child would therefore have given his initial evidence in less formal circumstances and have dropped out of the trial at an early stage.

The Home Office's scheme has prevailed and although an initial videotape of an interview with a child becomes admissible, as a new exception to the hearsay rule, it is only on condition that the child attends court to be cross-examined at court (Spencer 1991).

In order to attempt to relieve some of the stress on the child early trial dates are to be sought and children may give evidence on 'live-link' video apparatus or be screened from the defendant in court (for children under 14 years).

The failure to implement Pigot's scheme means that few children will give evidence, and fewer still will give evidence successfully, breaking down under cross-examination, traumatised by the abuse and then by the legal process (Spencer et al 1990).

Children may be prepared by going to the court pre-trial and having a private place to wait, the judge and lawyers may remove their wigs, screens or a videolink may be used, but still many children will not be heard, as the low successful prosecution rate testifies. Parents and professionals also remain anxious about the short- and longer-term effects of giving evidence. Children show anxiety before going to court (and trials may be delayed as long as 2 years) and it is at least a further 12 months post-trial before their anxiety symptoms are comparable with abused children who did not give evidence. If the alleged abuser is convicted this may be therapeutic but if he is acquitted, for whatever reason, the child may feel he has been publicly shown to be a liar.

3. Other evidence

Pre-recorded videos have been used for several years already, particularly in wardship courts. This use has caused controversy, especially when child psychiatrists have videoed sessions as part of usual practice and the disclosure of abuse has been made during a therapeutic rather than investigative interview. This has led to criticism in courts of technique, particularly the use of leading and more complex hypothetical questions. Doubt has also been expressed as to the amount of pressure put on children during sessions. It has, though, to be acknowledged that some adults put a lot of pressure on children *not* to talk, with threats of violence, even death, and therapists may be con-

fronted with a silent 'frozen' child who will only be helped if she can unburden herself; in such a case simple questioning is not enough.

Protocols have been written and different techniques are used by those interviewing children as part of a routine child abuse investigation, for example a social worker and police officer, from the sophisticated interview of the frozen child disclosing abuse after years of silence, conducted by a child psychiatrist or psychologist with a particular interest in child abuse.

In the future it may be appropriate to have a video camera available in all rooms where possible abused children are interviewed and examined. Children not infrequently disclose during or after a physical examination and the spontaneity of such a disclosure makes it particularly valuable.

Techniques of interviewing are not described in detail here but authoritative works are those of Jones & McQuiston (1988) and the chapters on interviewing and assessment of sexually abused children in a description of the work of the Great Ormond Street Sexual Abuse Team (Bentovim et al 1988), and Furniss (1991) on the preparation for disclosure and the management of disclosure of CSA.

In the Recommendations of the Report into Child Abuse in Cleveland 1987 there is included the paragraph 'Children should not be subjected to repeated interviews nor to the probing and confrontational type of "disclosure" interview for the same purpose, for it in itself can be damaging and harmful to them' (Butler-Sloss 1988, p. 245).

This advice has been taken into account by investigators — there is a place for straightforward interviews of the type many social workers and police officers (from Child Abuse Units) do routinely. It is also clear from recent complex cases in the UK that more highly trained interviewers are also needed and workers skilled in more specialised techniques are required to undertake this work. Such interviewers are likely to be social workers, psychologists or psychiatrists who have developed a particular interest in this aspect of child abuse. Poorly conducted interviews will hinder rather than help child protection.

The Cleveland Report also states 'Children should not be subjected to repeated medical examinations, solely for evidential purposes' (Butler-

Sloss 1988, p. 245). This puts a burden on the initial medical examination to be thorough; clearly children do not like being physically examined, yet in order to protect them the examination should yield as much information as possible. Clearly written medical notes with a good description of physical signs, annotated diagrams, and clinical photographs should provide such a record and obviate the need for further examinations. A further medical opinion may be obtained from scrutinising the notes rather than the child. If interviews are taped children may also be spared repeated questioning.

CHILD ABUSE AND THE CRIMINAL INJURIES COMPENSATION SCHEME

A scheme for compensating victims of violent crime was first established in 1964. The Criminal Injuries Compensation Board considers claims where the applicant has sustained 'personal injury directly attributable to a crime of violence'. Physical assault and sexual abuse are both considered crimes of violence whether the CSA is indecent assault or rape, incest or buggery. The injury may also be psychological trauma due to the crime of violence.

There is a time limit for claiming of 3 years from the assault although the Board may waive this on behalf of children. The injury must also be one for which a civil court would award compensation of not less than £1000 (1992).

Usually a complaint has to have been made to the police but a conviction is not necessary in order to uphold an application. If the abuser is within the child's own household and a prosecution has not been brought, the Board will require a full explanation on the child's behalf. The Board will then decide if it is in the child's best interest to make an award but will also satisfy itself that the offender will not benefit from the compensation.

The claim is made on behalf of children up to the age of 18 years by the adults who have parental rights over them. This may be the child's parents or, if the child has been abused at home, the Director of Social Services, or, for a ward, the court. Enquiries are made by the Board of police, doctors and social workers to gain information on the full circumstances of the assault, the extent of

the injury and the prognosis. The payment is assessed on the same basis as damages in the civil courts and is usually awarded as a lump sum.

Application forms and further details are available from the Board. Although doctors are not in a position to claim for a child they may suggest to a parent or social worker that a claim is in order, as most children are still not compensated. Doctors will also be asked to fill in the inquiry forms, for a small fee.

THE LAW —THE CHILDREN ACT 1989

The Children Act 1989 is a comprehensive piece of legislation which integrates and simplifies the law regarding children. It was implemented in October 1991. In terms of child protection the Act seeks to strike a balance between family independence and the protection of children, recognising that the welfare of the child is paramount whilst ensuring fairness for parents and emphasising family upbringing (Shepherd 1991) (Table 17.7).

The impetus to change the law came from the recognition that the law was unnecessarily complex, parents felt they had inadequate rights when SSD thought their children were at risk, and SSD felt they had inadequate powers to intervene effectively when children were at risk (The Children Act 1989: An Introductory Guide for the NHS 1991).

The Children Act does not alter the adversarial

Table 17.7 Main points of the Children Act 1989 (child protection aspects)

1. The Act is comprehensive, and consolidates earlier law dealing with children.
2. It was implemented in October 1991.
3. It seeks to be 'user-friendly', i.e. comprehensible.
4. The upbringing of children is primarily the responsibility of parents.
5. A balance between child protection and undue interference in family life is sought.
6. Child protection is improved by the introduction of Child Assessment Orders and lower threshhold for Emergency Protection Orders.
7. Emergency Protection Order may be challenged in court after 72 hours by parents.
8. In courts 'the child's welfare is paramount'.
9. A court order should not be made unless it is better for the child than not making an order.
10. A timetable will be set by the court to avoid undue delay.

system in English courts which many child care professionals find destructive to the overall management of cases of child abuse often causing an unnecessary degree of polarisation of children, families and professionals.

Public and private law relating to children are brought together under the Children Act:

• Public law deals with those areas where society intervenes in the action of individuals (such as care proceedings).
• Private law addresses the behaviour of adults towards each other (such as with whom the children should live following divorce).

The main principles of the Children Act 1989 are (The Children Act 1989: An Introductory Guide for the NHS 1991):

• The welfare of the child is the paramount consideration in court proceedings.
• Wherever possible children should be brought up and cared for within their own family.
• Children should be safe and protected by effective intervention if they are in danger.
• When dealing with children, courts should ensure that delay is avoided, and may only make an order if to do so is better than making no order at all.
• Children should be kept informed about what happens to them, and should participate when decisions are made about their future.
• Parents continue to have parental responsibility about their children, even when their children are no longer living with them. They should be kept informed about their children and participate when decisions are made about their children's future.
• Parents with children in need should be helped to bring up their children themselves.
• This help should be provided as a service to the child and his family, and should:
   — be provided in partnership with the parents
   — meet each child's identified needs
   — be appropriate to the child's race, culture, religion and language
   — be open to effective, independent representations and complaints procedures
   — draw upon effective partnership between

the local authority and other agencies, including voluntary agencies.

Child protection and the Children Act

The Act contains a new framework for the care and protection of children. It introduces new orders for use when children are at risk of significant harm. Care and supervision orders remain, but the grounds have been rationalised. There are new provisions to enable local education authorities to take action where children are not receiving proper education.

Significant harm (Children Act 1989)

Under the Children Act, harm is defined as ill-treatment or impairment of health or development. Ill-treatment may be physical, sexual or emotional ill-treatment of the child. The Children Act requires the court to be satisfied as to the occurrence of significant harm, or the likelihood of it, and its causes before making a care or supervision order (Hobbs 1991). Courts will define over the next few years what is meant by significant harm (see later).

Fig. 17.3 on page 299 (White 1991) illustrates the criteria used in assessing harm. The court will then find if the 'threshold criteria' (of significant harm) have been met, but this does not mean that a care or supervision order will necessarily be made. Other orders, for example under section 8 of the Act may be made.

• Ill-treatment of the child is sufficient in itself to satisfy the criteria.
• It is not necessary to show that impairment of health or development follows the ill-treatment.
• The court may wish to identify who ill-treated the child — did the carer harm the child or fail to prevent harm?
• Impairment of development includes physical, intellectual, emotional or behavioural development.
• Significant harm is thought to mean considerable or important (case law will elucidate this further).
• Existence of past harm is not in itself sufficient to meet the criteria, although it may be relevant as to whether further harm is likely.

- Probability of further harm is not yet defined but means a risk greater than a possibility — that which on the balance of probability is likely (White 1991).
- The court also has to find that the harm is attributable to the care given, or likely to be given (by the carers).
- The care which the court expects parents to give is that standard which reasonable parents could be expected to provide (with appropriate support from community-wide services).
- The care expected may not be of a lower standard because the parents are unintelligent, alcoholic, drug abusers or otherwise disadvantaged.
- If the child has particular needs because of behaviour or handicap the court may require a higher standard of care than for an average child.

The paediatrician's assessment of significant harm (Lynch 1991)

The contribution of the paediatrician in an individual case will vary. The evidence of harm (Fig. 17.3) caused by:

- ill-treatment (physical, mental, sexual)
- impairment of health (physical or mental)
- impairment of development (physical, emotional, behavioural, intellectual or social)

may be assessed by a paediatrician with skills in the recognition of:

- child abuse (physical, sexual)
- manifestations of child neglect and emotional deprivation
- growth failure
- developmental disorders.

The law wants evidence that:

- the child is suffering or likely to suffer significant harm
- the harm is attributable to care given or likely to be given to the child
- the making of an order is better for the child than making no order).

A paediatrician should be in a position to give an overall view of the child, his abuse and his needs. The court wishes to obtain from the paediatrician:

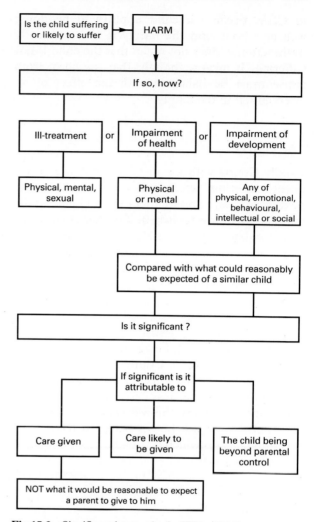

Fig 17.3 Significant harm criteria (White 1991)

- the assessment of the child's condition
- an opinion as to the reason or reasons for the child's condition
- advice on a management plan
- the likely prognosis.

Hobbs (1991) makes the important point that the severity of injury does not necessarily correlate with the seriousness of harm and it is the psychological component of a child's care which is the central issue. An abused child may not grow, develop intellectually or learn to love and an assessment of the child's past and current condition (growth charts, developmental progress, emotional/behavioural state) gives a multifaceted view. Harm and abuse may be well hidden, particularly in CSA; because a child appears to be doing well at school, and the family is not apparently dysfunctional, does not mean that the child is not suffering. It means, though, that the harm from abuse must be balanced with the effect of an intervention in the family.

The courts

Family Courts with a non-adversarial and an inquisitorial ethos, which many feel would be the next appropriate development in child and family matters, are not established. The Act creates 'the court' which includes the High Court, the County Court and the Magistrates Court. The High Court already has a Family Division and in the lower courts Family Proceedings Courts are also now established.

All applications for care and supervision orders will start at the Magistrates Court, and most will be heard there. If, however, there is reason to transfer the case to the County or High Court an order is made to that effect. Depending on their complexity or seriousness cases may move within 'the court'. Access to the wardship jurisdiction of the High Court will be restricted to those truly exceptional cases which cannot be accommodated in the lower courts.

The child

The main principle of the Act is that the child's welfare must be the paramount consideration of the court. The court must ensure that the child's wishes and feelings are known before coming to any decision. Consideration must also be given to the child's racial origin and cultural and linguistic background.

An order should not be made, even if the grounds are established in care proceedings, unless this is better for the child than not making an order. It is also acknowledged that delay in making decisions about a child's upbringing is likely to prejudice the child's welfare.

A 'Welfare check list' sets out the relevant factors to be taken into account by the court when considering care proceedings and contested family proceedings (Table 17.8). Children's lives will

Table 17.8 The court's welfare checklist

1. The wishes of the child.
2. His physical, emotional and educational needs.
3. The likely effect on him of any change in his circumstances.
4. His age, sex, background and any characteristic the court considers relevant.
5. Any harm he has suffered or is at risk of suffering.
6. How capable are his parents or any other potential carer.

be determined by four additional types of order available in family proceedings (Section 8 orders; Table 17.9) as well as case and supervision orders.

The parents

Parents are responsible for looking after their children, and local authorities have a duty to support them. The concept of parental responsibility is used instead of parental rights. Children are individuals and parents are expected to meet their child's needs whether moral, physical or emotional. Separated parents continue to share this responsibility, and unmarried fathers will find it easier to share parental responsibility under the Act.

The care which parents are expected to provide for their children is that of a 'reasonable parent'. The standard of care which is reasonable for a normal, healthy child may not be reasonable if the child has special needs, for example cystic fibrosis. That a parent is physically disabled or intellectually slow is not relevant as long as the child receives reasonable care. However, if a disabled parent by virtue of the disability cannot cope, whether they seek or accept help or not, this is unreasonable and grounds for an order.

When children are living away from home because their parents cannot care for them properly this is preferably a voluntary arrangement. The parents then retain responsibility and act as partners with the local authority. If a child is under a care order the local authority has parental

Table 17.9 Section 8 orders

1. Residence Order: where children will live.
2. Contact Order: who will have access.
3. Specific Steps Order: determining parental responsibility.
4. Prohibited Steps Order: steps not to be taken without the leave of the court.

responsibility and the power to prescribe the parents' responsibility but only as far as is necessary whilst safeguarding the child's welfare. The local authority shares parental responsibility with any parents or guardian as far as possible.

The local authority

The local authority has a duty to safeguard and promote the welfare of children 'in need' in its area and promote their upbringing by their families. The social services may ask for help from housing, health and education authorities, with the expectation that they will receive it.

Broadly, the SSD should identify children in need, maintain a register of disabled children and make sure its services are publicised. The support given by SSD should then reduce the need for care or criminal proceedings by 'preventing' child abuse and neglect. The range of support should include home-help, holidays, transport costs and counselling as well as day care for under-fives 'in need'.

Child protection (Fig. 17.4)

The Act aims to protect children from harm, which may be from failure or abuse within the family or the harm which can be caused by 'unwarranted intervention in family life'. Before a court will make an order it must be satisfied of certain preconditions:

1. that the child is suffering or is likely to suffer significant harm which is attributable to the care he is receiving from his parents, or
2. that the child is beyond parental control.

The definition of harm (Table 17.10) includes physical or sexual abuse as well as other forms of maltreatment which do not cause physical injury (see p. 299). However the court will also consider, in making an order, whether it will positively contribute to the child's wellbeing and be in his best interests.

The courts have discretion, subject to the above preconditions, to:

1. order the assessment of a child;
2. order the removal or retention of a child in an emergency;
3. order that a child be put under local authority care or supervision pending a full investigation and hearing of the proceedings;
4. order that the child be put under the longer-term supervision of a local authority;
5. make private law orders altering the arrangements about with whom the child lives, regulating his contact with other people, determining any particular matter relating to his upbringing and prohibiting any particular step being taken in respect of him.

Court orders which may be made:

Emergency Protection Orders. The precondition of an Emergency Protection Order is that there is reasonable cause to believe that the child is likely to suffer significant harm unless

1. he is removed from where he is to another place;
2. he is kept where he is;
3. the parents unreasonably withhold access to the child and there is reason to believe that access is required as a matter of urgency.

The order may last for 8 days, and can be extended once for a period of 7 days. It may be challenged at 72 hours by the parents if they were not present at the initial hearing. There is a presumption of reasonable parental access during this period and if the social worker becomes satisfied that the child would be safe the child should go home.

Any person may apply to the court for an Emergency Protection Order although it would usually be a social worker employed by the local authority.

Child Assessment Order. A Child Assessment Order is used when the parents are uncooperative and there is a need to decide whether significant harm is likely but there is not an emergency. Notice is given to all those involved and a full hearing takes place so that all sides can be represented.

Table 17.10 What is significant harm?

- Compare the child's health and development with a similar child.
- The care given by the parents should be what might reasonably be expected.
- Minor shortcomings in care or deficits in development may have a cumulative effect which results in significant harm.

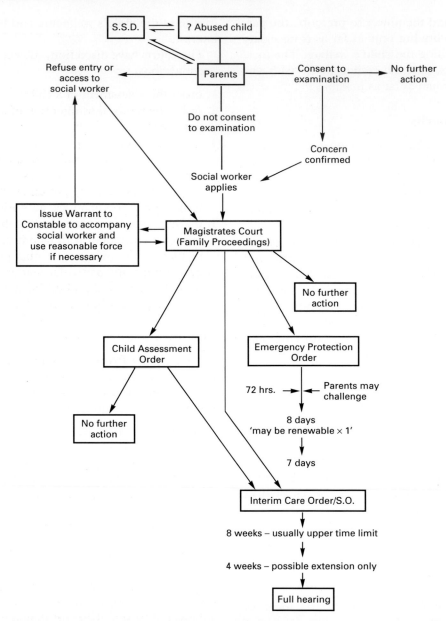

Fig. 17.4   The organisation and timing of child protection procedures.

If an order is made, it lasts 7 days; it does not give parental responsibility to the holder and the court directs what the assessment should be. It is acknowledged that 7 days may not be long enough to complete a full multidisciplinary assessment but after this period enough should be known to enable decisions to be made as to further action, if any.

An application may be made by a local authority or NSPCC social worker.

Interim Care and Supervision Order. The preconditions for making an Interim Care or Supervision Order are as for a Care Order, except that the court only has to conclude that there are reasonable grounds for believing the circumstances fulfill the conditions rather than being satisfied on the balance of probabilities that they do (see previously for the grounds).

A first Interim Care Order or Supervision order

may last for 8 weeks but subsequent orders may not last more than 4 weeks. The court may also, when making an Interim Care Order, make an order regarding contact or a medical examination. It is expected that the final hearing will be held within 12 weeks.

Care and Supervision Orders. The preconditions for these orders have been given previously. Supervision Orders last 12 months in the first instance but may be renewed for a period of up to 3 years in total.

Non-attendance at school is no longer in itself grounds for a Care Order — the usual grounds must exist. The local education authority may, however, apply for an Educational Supervision Order. The supervising education officer has powers to give directions to children and parents to ensure the child receives a proper education. Committing offences is no longer grounds for care but if the child is already subject to a Supervision Order the court may require him to live away from home for a period of 6 months.

Before a Care Order is made the court must consider the proposed arrangements for contact (access) and all the parties' views on these arrangements.

When young people leave care the local authorities have increased duties and powers to prepare, advise and assist them. The duty to advise and assist extends until the age of 21 years.

Guardians ad litem are appointed in almost all care and related proceedings but also in applications for Emergency Protection or Child Assessment Orders.

Evidence and procedural matters

The Children Act gave the Lord Chancellor power to provide by order for hearsay evidence to be admissible in civil proceedings relating to children. From March 1990 hearsay evidence was allowed in Juvenile Court or civil proceedings. The Act also enables the court to hear the unsworn evidence of a child in all civil proceedings if the child understands his duty to speak the truth and has sufficient understanding to justify his evidence being heard.

The rules of privacy have been altered under the Act in that a Magistrates Court may sit in private in the same way as the High and County Courts already do. It is an offence for television and radio as well as newspapers to publish material which will allow a child to be identified.

Implications of the Children Act for health authorities

Children's doctors will need to have knowledge of the Children Act whether they work with children with special needs, abused children or children in care, adoption of children or other children living away from home. An excellent summary of the Act has been published (An Introduction to the Children Act 1989), the full Act with interpretation (White et al 1990), and training advice (The Children Act 1989: Training Together 1990, The Children Act 1989; An Introductory Guide for the NHS 1991). The major issues are:

1. working together — interagency cooperation;
2. medical input — examination, assessment, treatment;
3. care of children by health authorities;
4. training (Butler-Sloss 1988, p. 252).

1. Working together

As has been discussed previously, all agencies involved in child protection must work together, but this is equally true for children with special needs and their families. This is emphasised in the Act.

2. Medical input

Medical and psychiatric examinations, assessment and treatment may be directed by the court from the earliest stage of the proceedings, that is if a child is subject to an Emergency Protection Order, an Interim Care Order or Child Assessment Order.

Consent (Table 17.11):

a. The situation for consent is clarified in that, once a child is the subject of a court order, parental responsibility and hence the right to give consent goes to the applicant (usually SSD).

b. Emergency treatment is much as previously — a carer who does not have parental responsibility may 'do what is reasonable in the circumstances

Table 17.11 Consent

- Who has the right to consent?
- Is the child subject to a court order?
- What are the directions of the court?
- Who has parental responsibility?
- Will the assessment be used in court proceedings?
- What are the views of the child? Has a guardian ad litem been appointed?
- Does the child have any difficulty in communicating for which special arrangements need to be made?

for the purpose of safeguarding or promoting the child's welfare'. The carer could be anyone caring for the child, and indeed in life-threatening circumstances a doctor would act immediately without consent.

c. If parents unreasonably refuse an examination, and the grounds are met, a Child Assessment Order may be made and the court directs the examination.

d. If parents — both having parental responsibility for the child and whether married, unmarried, separated or divorced — can not agree whether to consent to examination or treatment the court could make a Specific Issues Order to determine the matter.

e. The child's consent is necessary for psychiatric or medical examination, if he has sufficient understanding to make an informed decision. If a child refuses to give consent he may not be overruled by his parents or the court.

Court orders:

a. The courts have increased powers to authorise the medical or psychiatric examination of children either at the time the order is made or during the course of Emergency Protection Orders, Child Assessment Orders or Interim Care Orders. The court may also prohibit medical examination or assessment of the child. This should stop unnecessary examination once an adequate assessment has been carried out.

b. Many children will be examined with parental consent before an Emergency Protection Order is made but if this examination is likely to be controversial the applicant for the order may ask for court directions. Similarly, the initial examination may make it clear that a more detailed assessment

is needed and this may also be directed by the court when making the order.

c. The Child Assessment Order allows for 'a multi-disciplinary assessment in a non-emergency situation' over 7 days. This will allow information to be gathered to enable further decision-making to occur: are the concerns confirmed or refuted? Longer periods of assessment, including full psychiatric and family assessments, are likely to take place during Interim Care or Supervision Orders.

d. Treatment Orders can only be made by the court on the advice of a registered medical practitioner or psychiatrist registered under the Mental Health Act, and if the child consents and if satisfactory arrangements can be made. Any change in treatment plan should be referred back to the court.

Timing. The Act recognises that delays may be detrimental to the child, and courts will set timetables. See Figure 17.4. There are clear resource implications involved in the courts directing that medical and psychiatric assessments are to be completed. If priority is given to the orders even less preventative work will be done with children and families. Similarly, if professionals spend longer periods in court they will have less time with their other patients.

3. Care of children in hospital

The Act also seeks to protect the welfare of children who spend long periods in health or education authority or private homes or hospitals. The local authority must be informed of such children by the health authority or owner of private establishments. The local authority is then required to see not only that the child's welfare needs are met but to promote contact with his family and to rehabilitate home if appropriate.

4. Training

Training is needed not only by individual agencies but also by multidisciplinary groups to ensure that policy in each district develops along sound lines.

REFERENCES

Advisory Group on Video Evidence (Pigot Report) 1989. HMSO, London

Anderson L C 1990 Physician expert testimony. In: Wissow L S (ed) child advocacy for the clinician. Williams & Wilkins

An Introduction to the Children Act 1989. HMSO, London

Bentovim A, Elton A, Hildebrant J, Tranter M, Vizard E 1988 Child sexual abuse within the family: assessment and treatment. Wright, London

Butler-Sloss E 1988 Report of the Inquiry into Child Abuse in Cleveland 1987. HMSO, London

Furniss T 1991 The multiprofessional handbook on child sexual abuse. Routledge

Hobbs C J 1991 Significant harm. Paper in Conference Report no. 6. The Michael Sieff Foundation

Jones D P H, McQuiston M G 1988 Interviewing the sexually abused child. Gaskell, London

Lynch 1991 Significant harm: the paediatric consultation. In: Adcock et al (eds) Significant harm. Significant Publications, London

Shepherd S 1991 Aspects of the Children Act — a medical perspective. Health Trends 23(2)

Spencer J 1991a Reformers despair. New Law Journal June 7 1991: 787(b)

Spencer J 1991b Children's evidence and the Criminal Justice Act: a lost opportunity. The Magistrate Nov 1991: 181–182(a)

Spencer J, Nicholson G, Flin I R, Bull R 1990 Children's evidence in legal proceedings. Law Faculty, University of Cambridge

The Children Act 1989: An Introductory Guide for the NHS 1991 DoH

The Children Act 1989: Training Together 1990 The Family and Child Care Law Training Group, London

West Yorkshire Police Child Abuse Statistics 1992 Report 1989/1990/1991

White 1991 Significant harm: its management and outcome, Adcock et al, Significant Publications, London

White R, Carr P, Lowe N 1990 A guide to the Children Act 1989. Butterworths

Working Together under the Children Act 1989: a guide to the arrangements for interagency cooperation for the protection of children from abuse 1991 DHSS and Welsh Office. HMSO, London

Address

Criminal Injuries Compensation Board, Whittington House, 19 Alfred Place, London WC1E 7LG: Tel 071 636 9501. Blythswood House, 200 West Regent Street, Glasgow G2 4SW: Tel 041 221 0945.

18. Fatal child abuse

There is plenty of historical evidence that the practice of infanticide was a widespread form of disposal of unwanted children over the ages. Accounts of children being exposed on mountain tops, thrown into pools to see if they would float, or being actively killed are all well known. Illegitimate children who would bring disgrace upon the mother and handicapped children who might pass on their defects if allowed to live were especially vulnerable. It is also likely that many more children died from starvation and neglect as their parents did not have the means to support the numbers of children to which even a moderately healthy woman can give birth in her reproductive life.

In modern times death from child abuse and neglect remains a major cause of mortality. Controversy continues to surround this area and this is reflected in the debate over the epidemiology of fatal child abuse.

EPIDEMIOLOGY OF FATAL CHILD ABUSE

'An increasing number of people are being murdered by strangers. The most common method of murder is strangulation of women and stabbing of men, and the most vulnerable group to be murdered are babies under the age of one year' (Rose 1990). Murder of people of all ages has become more common in society, figures rising from around 250 deliberate killings per year in the 1950s to around 750 per year in England, Scotland and Wales at the present time. This is only a fraction of the annual total for the USA. There, child homicide accounts for about 5% of all child deaths (aged 1–17) and 1% of deaths in those aged 18 or over (Wissow 1990).

Home Office statistics show that babies under a year old have the highest risk of murder, with rates of 68 per million. Children aged 1–5 were the safest group with fewer than 12 per million murdered. However official figures are likely to underestimate the true scale of fatal child abuse because in cases where the findings are in any way doubtful the parents will be given the benefit of the doubt because of the tragic circumstances which accompany the death of a child.

There has been a long debate over the incidence of fatal child abuse. Jobling (1976) wrote 'estimates of children who die each year from their injuries range from 100–750. What the exact numbers might be has now become a controversial guessing game, some arguing that these figures are almost certainly an underestimate whereas others believe that the lower estimates are nearer the mark.' An analysis for 1974–1983 of the International Classification of Disease (ICD) codes

- E904 — hunger, thirst, exposure, neglect
- E960–969 — homicide and injury purposely inflicted by other persons (includes E967 child battering and other maltreatment)
- E980–989 — injury undetermined, whether accidentally or purposely inflicted,

revealed that on average over this period there were 138 deaths per year and an additional 50 deaths where violence played a part but death was recorded as from natural causes. Adjusting for the fact that 68% of deaths were caused by parents or care-givers (although in another 20% by someone well-known to the child), and allowing for 12 missed diagnoses, the figure of 156 deaths per year from child abuse or neglect at the hands of the parents was arrived at. The figure of 3 per week was adopted by the NSPCC in its publicity in the 1980s (Creighton 1984).

As in the USA, the rates for fatal abuse fall with age. In 1987 in the USA the rate was 6.15 per 100 000 under 1 year of age, 2.09 from 1–4 and 0.67 from 5–9. The rate was 1.24 from 10–14, and for 15–19 it rose dramatically to 8.32, reflecting the heightened vulnerability of teenagers (Wissow 1990).

RECOGNITION OF FATAL CHILD ABUSE

Clinical presentation of fatal child abuse

1. Severely battered infant or child
2. Unexpected death where occult injury found
3. Cot death presentation (death due to asphyxiation)
4. Neglect — child deliberately or passively left in dangerous situation e.g. drowning, house fire
5. Deliberate poisoning
6. Recurrent unexplained deaths
7. Child death associated with sexual assault.

The severely battered infant

The cause of such deaths is usually obvious and many of these cases have been the subject of public inquiries. In England, Maria Colwell, Kimberley Carlile, Jasmine Beckford and Tyra Henry are examples (Child Abuse 1991). This form of lethal abuse has perhaps been studied more than any other. The picture that has emerged has been of the violent besieged family often in touch with but avoiding professional intervention, which frequently was unable to address the dangerousness of the family situation for the child.

Study of these deaths indicates that many of the children were already known to child protection agencies and that the parents were young, poor and socially isolated (Greenland 1980). Warning signals and help-seeking behaviour had not been interpreted by child protection workers who lacked experience or appropriate training and whose practice could be characterised as showing an absence of assessment, goal-setting and effective communication with other professionals

(Greenland 1980). These deaths have in many ways fuelled changes in the law as well as in professional practice.

Unexpected death where occult injury is found

Christoffel et al (1985) from Chicago reviewed deaths at a paediatric teaching hospital over two years. They identified 43 'unexpected deaths' (defined as deaths occurring before arrival at the hospital or within 10 days of hospitalisation in children past the first month of life and unrelated to any previously known congenital anomaly or medical condition). 27 were due to natural causes but 9 were thought to be due to child abuse or neglect. In 3 of these cases injury was only discovered at autopsy. Deaths due to suspected child abuse and neglect were so categorised:

- if the child demonstrated inflicted or unexplained trauma,
- if there had been inadequate supervision,
- if there was probable delay in seeking care.

Two factors — 'dead on arrival' and '1 year of age or less' — had predictive value for child abuse.

The finding of an injury such as a fractured rib in an infant dying unexpectedly raises serious concerns if there is no obvious explanation for it.

Suffocation

Awareness of the reality of suffocation as a lethal form of child abuse has been sharpened by the use of covert video-recording of children being smothered in hospital by a parent (Southall et al 1987). A group of children who usually presented acutely to accident and emergency departments moribund or cyanosed, and who would recover with resuscitation or spontaneously, were called 'near miss cot deaths' or children with 'apparent life-threatening event' (ALTE). After admission to hospital such events would in some cases be observed on the ward, in others they might cease. It was with similar cases that video-recording demonstrated the smothering taking place.

CASE HISTORY 1
A 19-year-old mother became pregnant to a violent alcoholic boyfriend who had beaten her up. When her own family found out about the pregnancy they

abandoned her although later there was some reconciliation. The mother herself had a history of failing to thrive as a child, of sexual abuse by an uncle as a teenager, and she was admitted to a children's home with behaviour problems at the age of 13. During early pregnancy she suffered from serious depression and was admitted to hospital at 32 weeks with vaginal bleeding. There were difficulties with accommodation and several moves. At three weeks of age the baby was admitted to hospital with a history of 'going blue'. His mother said that he had become limp and floppy, and she needed to resuscitate him. During the admission the mother reported two further episodes but nothing untoward was noticed either on this or any subsequent occasion by the staff. The mother was described as anxious and found it difficult not to keep picking him up. She gave a history that her sister had recently had a cot death. She was discharged, but the baby was readmitted at eight weeks of age with further apnoeic attacks. Further investigation failed to reveal an adequate cause. The child was discharged; three days later he was admitted moribund and subsequently died. The infant had been monitored at home with an apnoea alarm, and this apparently had sounded as the mother entered the room. The history given was that the baby's face was blotchy and discoloured immediately the mother picked him up. The sequel to this tragic case was that the mother attempted suicide and required long-term psychiatric care. This case had a sense of inevitability about the outcome which staff looking after the mother and child expressed as a grave concern. In such cases there appears to be an open warning by the mother of impending disaster and the need is for support and acknowledgement of the risk.

There are links between this kind of abuse and Munchausen syndrome by proxy. Meadow (1990) reviewed 27 young children who, using strict criteria (confession, prosecution or video observation), were thought likely to have been suffocated. 18 children survived and 9 died. The important features included:

- sudden and unexpected deaths in previous siblings
- excess of boys in index and sibling groups
- 'near miss cot death' presentation
- petechiae on face or mouth, bruises to neck in a minority
- survival with handicap a possibility
- recurring attacks which failed to reveal a cause on extensive investigation
- pillow, pad of material or hand used
- many children outside the usual range for true SIDS cases i.e. > 6months.

The concern that some infants found dead in their cots might have died from abuse due to suffocation has been raised from time to time.

The establishment of the diagnostic category of 'sudden infant death syndrome' (SIDS) has done a great deal to absolve all sense of guilt from both parents and physicians alike, and has enabled bereavement care programmes to be established and funds to be obtained for research into the cause(s) of SIDS (Emery 1992). Emery also points out that SIDS as an entity does not exist and that there are many patterns of causes. Filicide is defined as child death caused by a parent and differs from infanticide which relates only to the mother and has a specific meaning in law. Emery (1985) estimated that filicide as the probable mechanism of death in unexplained, unexpected deaths could be as high as 1 in 10 or as low as 1 in 50 where the deaths were looked at on a more superficial level. This of course means that the majority of such deaths are not due to filicide.

Further evidence of an association between cot death and child abuse comes from the finding that the SIDS rate for siblings of children on the child abuse register in South Derbyshire was 15.6 per thousand births, whereas the national rate for SIDS was 2.0 and the local rate 3.1 (Newlands & Emery 1991). Detailed and long-term studies in another part of England of known abusive and neglectful families and kinships (Oliver 1983) revealed that, out of 147 families studied over 21 years, of 560 children, 41 had died (26 in the first year of life). In only 3 cases was there a criminal conviction and many cases would have fitted the SIDS category, had it then been in existence.

'Accidents' where neglect is a major factor

Childhood injury is now the major cause of mortality after infancy. Use of the term 'accident' has been criticised because it may imply 'an act of God' rather that an event which arises out of a set of circumstances which may be modifiable or preventable. 'An injury event' may be a better term — inviting analysis of the factors responsible for its occurrence.

A notable example of the link between neglect and child death is seen in children dying in fires, either at home or in cars. Many children who die in these situations have been left alone in the house, including those of pre-school age. Gill (1984) reported the deaths of 7 pre-school children left alone in conflagrations in 10 cars. 7 other children who were burned survived. Interestingly, in conclusion Gill suggests that parents should be advised against leaving pre-school children alone in cars as though this might otherwise be seen as reasonable child care practice. Up to one-third or more children who die or are injured in house fires have been left alone at the time.

The law is more specific with regard to leaving young children unattended in the home. In an earlier study in London which looked at 24 child deaths in house fires, 10 children had been left alone or with other children in the house at the time. Because many parents in such situations are seen as victims of their own inadequacy, limited intellectual ability, poverty or other seemingly unavoidable factors, such deaths will officially be reported as 'accidental' to spare the parents further suffering.

Safety neglect is defined as 'a situation where an injury occurs because of a gross lack of supervision' (Schmitt 1981). It can be difficult to diagnose as there may be other factors responsible for behaviour which on the face of it might seem seriously neglectful. Single mothers with several children may have little option but to leave them alone briefly, particularly if an unexpected situation arises. In neglect it is the establishment of a regular pattern of inadequate parenting which is characteristic. Repeated accidents should be a warning sign that the child is at risk and be acted upon.

Another way in which neglect may be a major factor in child death is through a failure to seek appropriate medical care for an ill child. A well-known situation is that of the Jehovah's Witness family who, believing that blood transfusion is against the laws of God, prevent that child from having a life-saving transfusion. A much more commonly encountered situation is where a common illness in a neglected and weakened child (e.g. failing to thrive) is not adequately attended to, becomes serious, treatment is delayed and the child is admitted in a moribund state perhaps too late to avert disaster.

CASE HISTORY 2
An 11-month-old child died at home from measles.

There had been longstanding concerns about this child and the other three older children because of failure to thrive, including delayed development thought to be the result of inadequate parenting. Various agencies were involved in helping the family. Shortly before the youngest child died, the family moved area without letting the professional agencies know and into accommodation which was cold and sparsely furnished, in the middle of winter. The child was discovered dead in bed. Post mortem showed advanced measles bronchopneumonia.

Poisoning

Non-accidental poisoning as a form of child abuse has been recognised for some time (Kempe et al 1962, Rogers et al 1976). In a review of the literature (Dine & McGovern 1982) of 48 children intentionally poisoned, 8 died (17%). These cases present in a variety of ways making diagnosis a challenge. The fatal cases included the use of such diverse substances as pepper, which induced apnoea, table salt, phenformin and barbiturates. Paracetamol poisoning may induce fatal acute liver necrosis; because of the delay in onset, by the time the child is admitted to hospital there may only be therapeutic serum levels of the drug present and differentiation from other possible causes of acute liver necrosis may be impossible. Links with Munchausen syndrome by proxy are also described.

Recurrent unexplained deaths

Families in which two or more cot deaths occurred were reviewed by Emery (1986). Out of 12 families with two or more cot deaths, in 2 the care was seriously at fault and could have contributed to death, and in 5 filicide was probable. The risk of a cot death in the population at large is about 1 in 500, whilst the risk of a second one is estimated at about 1 in 150. Recurrences appear to increase the likelihood that abuse has been responsible. In one well-known case in the USA over a period of 14 years two parents, Mary Beth and Joseph Tinning, buried their 9 children. Until the last child, the authorities never suspected or acted (Wallace 1986). Sometimes parents will fail to reveal details of these deaths at a later date. The lack of prosecution or conviction hampers the protection of future children.

CASE HISTORY 3

An infant of two months was dead on arrival at hospital. Intubation and ventilation was attempted but there was no response. The mother said that the child had fallen about 14 inches from a settee onto a linoleum-covered floor. Half an hour after this the baby stopped breathing. There was bruising to the back of the head and buttocks, and at necropsy a single but extensive skull fracture, four old healing rib fractures and a healing clavicular fracture were found. The cause of death was said to be the inhalation of vomit. Although some concern was expressed, 'the mother was given the benefit of the doubt' and no prosecution was taken. Two years later, the same mother was left to mind a friend's 4 year-old child while the child's mother went away for a weekend, causing anxiety to the social service worker who knew of the arrangement but was powerless to prevent it. On the mother's return, severe bruising to the child's face was found and reported to the police. During the course of interviewing the woman an admission was made that she had injured the child and also that she had violently thrown her baby, hitting his head on a hearth and thereby causing his death.

Child death associated with sexual assault

The association of battering and sexual abuse has been described (Reinhardt 1987, Hobbs & Wynne 1990). Violence is frequently a part of the sexual assault, in addition it can be used as a means to threaten or silence the child. If the abuser is threatened or frightened of exposure by the child, violence may escalate and ultimately the child's life may be at risk. Out of a total of 130 children identified where evidence of physical injury and sexual assault coincided, there were 4 deaths. The ages ranged from 0.4–13.8 years. Other cases have been provided by colleagues elsewhere. The following Case History 4 was supplied by Dr Arnon Bentovim.

CASE HISTORY 4

A 2-year-old boy died as a result of injuries thought to be non-accidental. There was fresh and old bruising to the forehead, retinal haemorrhages and deep bruising to the retroperitoneal tissues at the lower end of the aorta anterior to the lumbar spine. In addition there was fresh bruising around the penis with the appearances of a bite mark. Death was related to a large subdural haematoma. there were also bite marks on the cheek and the back of the thigh. The anus was normal.

CASE HISTORY 5

A 14-month-old infant was brought in dead to the Accident and Emergency Department. The step-father who accompanied the child said he had left her briefly in the bath and on returning found her face down in the water. Bruising was noted around the mouth and her hair was dry although he later told the police that he had given her mouth-to-mouth resuscitation and put her in front of the fire which had dried her hair. At post-mortem examination the lungs were dry; the cause of death was consistent with asphyxia but the following were noted: old healing midshaft fracture of femur, several fingertip bruises around both knees, a grossly gaping and dilated anus (noted on arrival at hospital) and weight below the third centile.

Two surviving siblings were removed into foster-care and a case conference was held at which further information became available:

- The dead child's weight had progressed reasonably well until the mother married the new step-father, when it had fallen significantly below the third centile.
- The fractured femur had allegedly occurred when the child had fallen over and as the child had not been too upset she was not taken to hospital.
- The bruises had allegedly occurred from crawling on a stone floor.
- Shortly after the step-father joined the family the 2-year-old sibling sustained a burn on the back of the hand from a clothes iron. The mother failed to take the child to hospital as advised by the GP and the Health Visitor no longer felt welcome at the house.
- Both siblings in foster-care began to disclose of oral and anal abuse by the step-father. There was no prosecution although care orders were made in the juvenile court on the surviving children.

The danger to older children who are being sexually abused also needs to be stressed. Hobbs & Wynne (1990) describe the case of a 13-year-old girl who was abused by her step-father. The abuse involved aggressive and sadistic acts. Attempts were made to protect the girl with apparent cooperation from the mother. The step-father became aware that the authorities were increasingly involved. The girl, who had been staying away with a friend, returned home where she was murdered along with her mother. The step-father committed suicide.

Abduction and murder of children by strangers frequently involves a sexual motive. Jones & Krugman (1986) describe the case of a 3-year-old child who was sexually and physically assaulted and left for dead but who survived and gave evidence.

INVESTIGATION OF SUSPICIOUS DEATH

- Necropsy should preferably be performed by a pathologist who has training in both forensic and paediatric pathology.
- Necropsy may be unrevealing in cases of suspected abuse in young children.
- Smothering and drowning cannot always be excluded.
- Medical and social history play a major role in the interpretation of the necropsy findings.
- Severe head trauma can occur without fractures.
- Previous deaths, injuries, abuse or admissions to care may be covered up by the parents.
- Current crises should be sought in the parents' personal lives.
- The need for toxicology or electrolyte samples to check for inappropriate drug or salt ingestion should be considered. Samples of vitreous humor, blood, urine, stomach contents and various tissues can be sent for analysis.
- Site of death examination may involve police, pathologist and forensic scientist.
- Post-mortem X-rays may reveal occult bony injury.
- A confidential professional inquiry to share information concerning a child's death may conclude that factors were present in the care of the child which contributed to the death of the child. Such information may assist professional agencies in providing care to the family if a further child is born.

Summary

1. Fatal child abuse is often not recognised and reported. Statistics can therefore be misleading.

2. The observation that death due to abuse is particularly high in the first year of life reflects the burden of unwanted pregnancies and the vulnerability of infancy.

3. Teenagers, especially if homeless or unsupported, are especially at risk both of abuse and of abusing their own infant.

4. Links with all forms of abuse are evident.

5. Patterns of unexplained infant and childhood deaths are recognised in abusive families and kinships.

6. Clinical recognition depends on confidential information-sharing, skilled pathology and an appreciation of the social issues for the family.

7. A link exists between a subgroup of 'cot deaths' and child abuse.

REFERENCES

Child Abuse 1991 A Study of Inquiry Reports 1980–1989. Department of Health. HMSO, London

Christoffel K K, Zeiserl E J, Chiaramonte J 1985 Should child abuse and neglect be considered when a child dies unexpectedly? American Journal of Diseases in Children 139: 876–880

Creighton S J 1984 Trends in child abuse. NSPCC, London

Dine M S, McGovern M E 1982 Intentional poisoning of children — an overlooked category of child abuse: report of seven cases and review of literature. Pediatrics 70: 32–35

Emery J L 1985 Infanticide, filicide and cot death. Archives of Disease in Childhood 60: 505–507

Emery J L 1986 Families in which two or more cot deaths have occurred. Lancet i: 313–315

Emery J L 1993 Cot death and child abuse. In: Hobbs C J, Wynne J M (eds) Bailliere's Clinical Paediatics, Bailliere Tindall, London

Gill D G 1984 Conflagration of children in cars. British Medical Journal 288: 973

Greenland C 1980 Lethal family situations: an international comparison of deaths from child abuse. In: Anthony E J, Chiland C C (eds). The child in his family, vol 6. John Wiley, New York, pp. 389–408

Hobbs C J, Wynne J M 1990 The sexually abused battered child. Archives of Disease in Childhood 65: 423–437

Jobling M 1976 The abused child. National Children's Bureau, London

Jones D P H, Krugman R 1986 Can a three-year-old child bear witness to her sexual assault and attempted murder? Child Abuse and Neglect 10: 253–258

Kempe C H, Silverman F N, Steele B F, Droegmueller W, Silver H K 1962 The battered child syndrome. Journal of American Medical Association 181: 17–24

Meadow R 1990 Suffocation, recurrent apnea, and sudden death. Journal of Pediatrics 117: 351–357

Newlands M, Emery J L 1991 Child abuse and cot deaths. Child Abuse and Neglect 15: 275–278

Oliver J E 1983 Dead children from problem families in NE Wiltshire. British Medical Journal 286: 115–117

Reinhardt M A 1987 Sexual abuse of battered young children. Pediatric Emergency Care 3: 36–38

Rogers D, Tripp J, Bentovim A, Robinson A, Berry D, Goulding R 1976 Non-accidental poisoning: an extended syndrome of child abuse. British Medical Journal 1: 793–796

Rose D 1990 Murder in Britain. The Guardian, 1 Jan 1990

Schmitt B D 1981 Child neglect. In: Ellerstein N S (ed) Child abuse and neglect. A medical reference. J Wiley, New York

Southall D P, Stebbens V A, Rees S V, Lang M H, Warner J O, Shinebourne E A 1978 Apnoeic episodes induced by smothering: two cases identified by covert video surveillance. British Medical Journal 294: 1637–1641

Wallace A 1986 After 9 deaths in 14 years, mother arrested. New York Times, 8 Feb 1986: 1

Wissow L S 1990 Fatal maltreatment. In: Child advocacy for the clinician. Williams & Wilkins, Baltimore, pp. 172–184

Index